THE PRINCETON REVIEW

Cracking the SAT & PSAT®

ADAM ROBINSON AND JOHN KATZMAN
WITH A FOREWORD BY DAVID OWEN

1999 EDITION

RANDOM HOUSE, INC.
NEW YORK 1998
www.randomhouse.com

Princeton Review Publishing, L.L.C.
2315 Broadway
New York, NY 10024
E-mail: info@review.com

The SAT questions listed below were selected from the following publications of the College Entrance Examination Board: *5 SATs, 1981; 6 SATs, 1982; 5 SATs, 1984; 10 SATs, 1983, 5 SATs, 1992.* These questions, as well as test directions throughout the book, are reprinted by permission of Educational Testing Service, the copyright owner of the sample questions. Permission to reprint the above material does not constitute review or endorsement by Educational Testing Service or the College Board of this publication as a whole or of any other sample questions or testing information it may contain.

SAT questions: p. 30, #25; p. 31, #1; p. 51, #15; p. 61, #1, #6, #9; p. 66, #9; p. 63, #6; pp. 92–93, #16–18, #20, #21; p. 100, #17; p. 165, #25; p. 166, #24; p. 169, #24; p. 207, #11; p. 208, #18; p. 210, #3, #17; p. 211, #17; p. 212, #25; p. 216, #20; p. 241, #10; p. 242, #13; p. 249, #25; p. 254, #24; p. 265, #13; p. 269, #11; pp. 369–370, Passage; p. 370, #25; pp. 383–384, Passage; p. 384, #34; pp. 395–396, Passage; p. 396, #3, p. 499, #8; p. 501, #13; p. 505, #7; p. 506, #11; p. 516, #24; p. 524, #1; p. 525, #16; p. 526, #23.

All other questions in the book were created by the authors.

The passage on p. 367 was reprinted from *Memoirs of an Anti-Semite* by Gregor von Rezzori with kind permission of Viking Penguin.

SAT is a registered trademark and PSAT is a trademark of the College Entrance Examination Board.

ISSN 1049-6238
ISBN 0-375-75158-0

Editor: Lesly Atlas
Designer: Illeny Maaza
Production Editor: Amy Bryant
Illustrations by: The Production Department of The Princeton Review

Manufactured in the United States of America on partially recycled paper.

9 8 7 6 5 4 3 2 1

1998 Edition

ACKNOWLEDGMENTS

An SAT course is much more than clever techniques and powerful computer score reports; the reason our results are great is that our teachers care so much about their kids. Many of them have gone out of their way to improve the course, often going so far as to write their own materials, some of which we have incorporated into our course manual as well as into this book. The list of these teachers could fill this page, but special thanks must be given to Lisa Edelstein, Thomas Glass, Len Galla, Rob Cohen, Fred Bernstein, and Jayme Koszyn.

For production and editing help, thanks to Lesly Atlas, John Bergdahl, Bruno Blumenfeld, Amy Bryant, Greta Englert, Doug French, Julian Ham, Effie Hadiioannou, Adam Hurwitz, Yahya Jeffries-El, Scott Karp, Meher Khambata, John (Chun) Pak, Illeny Maaza, Jefferson Nichols, Carrie Smith, Melanie Sponholz, Christopher Thomas, and Jeannie Yoon.

Special thanks go to Alex Freer Balko for sharing her expertise on this project. A talented writer with the ability to see the big picture and an amazing eye for detail, Alex's work is always top-notch.

The Princeton Review would never have been founded without the advice and support of Bob Scheller. Many of the questions on our diagnostic tests are the result of our joint effort. Bob's program, Pre-test Review, provides the best sort of competition; his fine results make us work all the harder.

Finally, we would like to thank the people who truly have taught us everything we know about the SAT: our students.

CONTENTS

Acknowledgments v
Foreword ix
Introduction xiii

PART I: ORIENTATION 1

1   How to Think About the SAT 9

2   Cracking the SAT: Basic Principles 15

3   Cracking the SAT: Advanced Principles 25

4   Intro to the PSAT 37

PART II: HOW TO CRACK THE VERBAL SAT 45

5   Joe Bloggs and the Verbal SAT 49

6   Sentence Completions 53

7   Analogies 69

8   Critical Reading 87

9   Writing Skills Component 117

PART III: HOW TO CRACK THE MATH SAT 151

10   Joe Bloggs and the Math SAT 161

11   The Calculator 171

12   Arithmetic 177

13   Algebra: Cracking the System 203

14   Geometry 227

15   Quantitative Comparisons: Cracking the System 259

16   Grid-Ins: Cracking the System 273

Part IV: Taking the PSAT/SAT 287

Part V: Vocabulary 295

Part VI: Answer Key to Drills 339

Part VII: The Princeton Review Diagnostic Test and
    Explanations I 351

17 **Diagnostic Test I** 355

18 **Explanations I** 407

Part VIII: The Princeton Review Diagnostic Test and
    Explanations II 495

19 **Diagnostic Test II** 497

20 **Explanations II** 543

Part IX: Writing Skills Component Sample Section 631

21 **Writing Skills Component Explanations** 647

Afterword 663

A Parting Shot from FairTest 667

About the Authors 669

Foreword

The publishers of the Scholastic Assessment Test don't want you to read this book. For nearly sixty years they have claimed that the SAT cannot be coached, but this book proves that it can be.

Cracking the SAT & PSAT contains information that could help you raise your SAT scores substantially and improve your chances of being admitted to the college of your choice. It also contains information that should make you think twice before boasting about a high SAT score or becoming depressed about a low one. The SAT, you will discover, is not the test that your teachers, guidance counselors, parents, and friends may have led you to believe. Despite its reputation as an "objective" examination, the SAT doesn't measure much more than your ability to take the SAT.

Unfortunately, though, your ability to take the SAT could have a significant impact on the course of your life. Virtually all the nation's most selective colleges—and a great many less selective ones—require their applicants to submit SAT scores. (Many other schools require scores from the SAT's chief competitor, the ACT, published by the American College Testing Program.) Most admissions officers won't understand how to interpret the scores they are sent, but this won't keep them from speculating freely about your intelligence and even your personality on the basis of how you do. Where you spend the next four years of your life may be determined in part by what they decide. The test's effect can even carry over into the years beyond college. More than a few employers require recent college graduates to submit their high school SAT scores when applying for jobs. This practice is illegal, but some companies do it anyway. For the time being, you're probably stuck with the SAT.

Since you are, you owe it to yourself to learn as much as you can about the test. If you're like most of the 1.3 million high school students who will take it this year, you probably don't have a very clear idea of what you're in for. You may have glanced at an SAT preparation book or even taken a coaching course. But most coaching materials don't have much to do with the real SAT. Partly because most available materials are so bad, many teachers and guidance counselors believe that it is impossible for students to improve their SAT scores through coaching. Another reason they believe this is that the test's publishers have always told them coaching doesn't work. The College Board, which sponsors the test, has claimed that score gains resulting from coaching "are always small regardless of the coaching method used or the differences in the students coached." The Educational Testing Service (ETS)—which has written and administered the SAT for the College Board since 1947—says the same thing: "The abilities measured by the SAT develop over a student's entire academic life, so coaching—vocabulary drill, memorizing facts, or the like—can do little or nothing to raise the student's scores." Despite all the official denial, though, the SAT can very definitely be coached.

Cracking the SAT & PSAT is different from other coaching guides because it contains strategies that really work on the SAT. These strategies are taught at The Princeton Review. The school is based in New York City and has branches in more than sixty cities and seven foreign countries. The strategies were developed by Adam Robinson, formerly a private SAT tutor, and John Katzman, the founder of the school. The Princeton Review has become legendary among many high school and college students. A guidance counselor at an exclusive private academy in New York once told me that most of her juniors were enrolled at The Princeton Review and that their SAT scores had risen so much that she was no longer certain how to advise them about where they ought to apply to college. At Harvard not long ago, a freshman was overheard saying, "Yeah, he got a 750 on the verbal, but it was only a Princeton Review 750."

If you read this book *carefully*, you will have a huge advantage when you actually take the SAT. In fact, students who take the test without knowing these strategies are, in effect, taking it blindfolded.

ETS often refers to the SAT as an "objective" test, meaning that the score you receive on it isn't just one person's judgment (the way a grade in a course is) but is arrived at "scientifically." Few people stop to think that the word *objective* in this case applies only to the mechanical grading process. Every question still has to be written—and its answer determined—by highly subjective human beings. The SAT isn't really an "objective" test. Banesh Hoffman, a critic of standardized testing, once suggested that a better term for it would be "child-gradable," because marking it doesn't require any knowledge or intelligence. The principal difference between the SAT and a test that can't be graded by a child is that the SAT leaves no room for more than one correct answer. It leaves no room, in other words, for people who don't see eye to eye with ETS.

In 1962, Banesh Hoffman wrote a wonderful book called *The Tyranny of Testing*. It begins with a letter reprinted from the *Times* of London:

Sir—Among the "odd one out" type of questions which my son had to answer for a school entrance examination was: "Which is the odd one out among cricket, football, billiards, and hockey?"

I said billiards because it is the only one played indoors. A colleague says football because it is the only one in which the ball is not struck by an implement. A neighbour says cricket because in all the other games the object is to put the ball into a net; and my son, with the confidence of nine summers, plumps for hockey, "because it is the only one that is a girl's game." Could any of your readers put me out of my misery by stating what is the correct answer?

Yours Faithfully,

T. C. Batty

Other answers were suggested in Hoffman's book: billiards, because it's the only one that's not a team sport; football, because it's the only one played with a hollow ball; billiards, because it's the only one in which the color of the ball matters; hockey, because it's the only one whose name ends in a vowel.

The "odd one out" problem is an "objective" question: A grading machine will mark it the same way every time, whatever the answer really is. But you won't be able to answer it correctly unless you know what the testers had in mind when they wrote it. If you aren't on the same wavelength they were on, you won't come up with the answer they wanted.

The same is true with the SAT. In order to do well, you need to understand how the test makers at ETS were thinking when they sat down to write the questions. This book will teach you how to do precisely that.

David Owen,
author of *None of the Above:
Behind the Myth of Scholastic
Aptitude*

Introduction

Welcome to the 1999 edition of *Cracking the SAT & PSAT*. The SAT has undergone significant changes in the past few years, and you are holding the most up-to-date book on the new test. In fact, most of you will probably never have seen the SAT in its old format. And that's a good thing. You need only concentrate on the techniques and strategies in this book to perform well on the SAT.

Back in the early 1980s, when we started preparing students for the SAT with our revolutionary methods, invariably they would say things like, "Wow! These techniques are amazing! But won't ETS change the SAT once everyone finds out about this?" We were a small company back then, so we reassured our students that ETS was highly unlikely to change the test just because a few hundred students each year showed seemingly miraculous score improvements.

By the mid-1980s, however, several hundred students had grown to several thousand. And in 1986, when we revealed our methods to the general public in the first edition of the book you're holding—a book that became a *New York Times* bestseller—our students threw up their hands. "Now you guys have done it. You've let the secrets out of the bag. For sure ETS is going to change the SAT now to stop your techniques."

Well, they have changed the test (several times), but we've changed with them. Not only do our techniques still work, they're better than ever.

Students in our SAT course improve their test scores a lot—an independent study by Roper Starch Worldwide showed an average improvement of 127 points combined math and verbal.

The Princeton Review spends almost two million dollars every year improving our materials. We send fifty teachers into each test administration to make sure nothing slips by us. *Cracking the SAT & PSAT* incorporates our observations, giving you the most up-to-date information possible.

Our approach involves more than great techniques. Classes are small (eight to twelve in a group), and they're grouped by shared ability, so each student receives personal attention. When students don't understand something in class, we work with them in even smaller groups, and then one-on-one in tutoring.

We realize, however, that many kids can't get to our courses. That's why we wrote *Cracking the SAT & PSAT*. Although the book is no substitute for small classes and great teaching, it can help you improve your score. Make sure you take your time and do the drills carefully. The techniques are too complex to try them out the week before the SAT, so give yourself four or five weeks to practice our suggestions. We recommend that you devote six to ten hours a week to studying our techniques.

Furthermore, this is *not* a textbook; anyone charging you for a course that uses this book is ripping you off. You're better off just buying the book in a bookstore.

So relax. Work hard and get the SAT scores that the colleges you care about will love. And if you need more intense work than a book can offer, give us a call at 1-800-2REVIEW. Whatever you do, we wish you good luck.

John Katzman
President and Co-founder

Adam Robinson
Co-founder

PART I

Orientation

WHAT IS THE SAT I REASONING TEST?

The SAT I—from now on, we'll refer to it simply as the SAT—is a three-hour multiple-choice test that is divided into seven sections:

1. two thirty-minute verbal sections
2. one fifteen-minute verbal section
3. two thirty-minute math sections
4. one fifteen-minute math section
5. one thirty-minute experimental section, either math or verbal

The fifteen-minute verbal section consists of one or two critical reading passages followed by thirteen questions. The fifteen-minute math section consists of ten multiple-choice math questions.

Only six of the seven sections on the SAT will count toward your scores. The experimental section on your SAT will look just like a thirty-minute verbal or math section, but it won't be scored; ETS uses it to try out new SAT questions and to determine whether the test you are taking is harder or easier than ones ETS has given in the past. (Unfortunately, it's *not possible* to figure out which section on your SAT is the experimental section.)

The verbal SAT contains three types of questions:

1. sentence completions
2. analogies
3. critical reading

The math SAT also contains three types of questions:

1. regular multiple-choice math (arithmetic, algebra, and geometry)
2. quantitative comparisons
3. grid-ins

Each of these question types will be dealt with in detail later in the book.

THE PSAT

All of the techniques discussed in this book also apply to the PSAT, the Preliminary Scholastic Assessment Test. The PSAT is a two-hour-ten-minute exam originally designed as a practice exam for the SAT. It is also the National Merit Scholarship Qualifying Test. It is typically administered in the eleventh grade.

Unfortunately, the PSAT has begun to take on greater significance in the past few years. Many high schools choose to include students' PSAT scores on the transcripts they send to colleges. As a result, more and more students have started to prepare for the PSAT, rather than use it as a practice exam.

Keep on Schedule

You'll take the PSAT in the fall of your junior year. Plan to take the SAT in either the spring of your junior year or fall of your senior year. Since you might be expected to take as many as three SAT II: Subject Tests, don't save everything for the last minute. Sit down with your SAT I and SAT II registration booklets and work out a schedule.

How much should you prepare for the PSAT? Well, that all depends. If you have a shot at National Merit, you should prepare a lot (see chapter 4 for more information on the PSAT and National Merit Scholarships). If not, you should still do some preparation so that you're not totally in the dark when you take the exam. Plus, if your PSAT scores are to be included on your high school transcript (in other words, colleges will see them), you don't want them to be an eyesore. Luckily, everything you learn about the Math and Verbal sections of the SAT applies to the PSAT Math and Verbal sections. In addition, the PSAT also has a section called the Writing Skills Component. Be sure to work through chapter 9 so you are prepared for this portion of the test.

Chapters 4 and 9 are geared exclusively to the PSAT. If you are preparing for the PSAT, these chapters, combined with the rest of the information in this book, will provide you with all the information you need to know to crack the PSAT. For simplicity's sake, we will typically refer to the SAT when we mean techniques that apply to both PSAT and SAT. To be as prepared as possible, be sure to take a practice PSAT (see chapter 353 for instructions).

WHERE DOES THE SAT COME FROM?

The SAT is published by the Educational Testing Service (ETS) under the sponsorship of the College Entrance Examination Board (the College Board). ETS and the College Board are both private companies. We'll tell you more about them in chapter 1.

HOW IS THE SAT SCORED?

Four to five weeks after you take the SAT, you'll receive a report from ETS containing a verbal score and a math score. Each score will be reported on a scale that runs from 200 to 800; the best score is 800, and the average student scores around 500. The third digit of an SAT score is always a zero, which means that scores can go up or down only ten points at a time. In other words, you might receive a 490, a 500, or a 510 on the verbal; you won't ever receive a 492, a 495, or a 507. Every question on the SAT is worth about ten points. (Easy questions are worth the same as hard ones.)

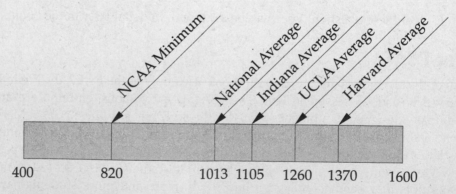

PSAT scores are reported on a scale that runs from 20 to 80. This is exactly like the SAT scale, except that the final zero has been removed. If you think this sounds needlessly complicated, you're right.

RAW SCORES AND PERCENTILES

You may hear about two other kinds of scores in connection with the SAT: raw scores and percentile scores. Here's what they mean:

Raw Scores

Your raw score is simply the number of questions you answered correctly, minus a fraction of the number of questions you answered incorrectly. It is used to calculate your final *scaled* score. We'll tell you more about raw scores in chapter 2.

Percentile Scores

A percentile score tells you how you did in relation to everyone else who took the test. If your score is in the 60th percentile, it means you did better on the test than 60 percent of the people who took it. People who are disappointed by their SAT scores can sometimes cheer themselves up by looking at their percentile scores.

HOW IMPORTANT ARE SAT SCORES?

The SAT is an important factor when you apply to colleges, but it is not the only one. A rule of thumb: The larger the college, the more important the SAT score. Small liberal arts colleges will give a good deal of weight to your extracurricular activities, your interview, your essays, and your recommendations. Large state universities often admit students based on formulas consisting of just two ingredients: SAT scores and grade point average.

Size Matters

Large schools process more applications, so they rely more heavily on SAT scores. Small schools have the time to read the rest of your application.

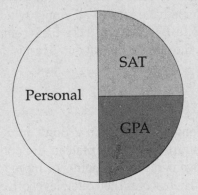

Small Liberal Arts Colleges

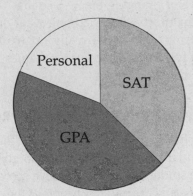

Large State Universities

Even at a small liberal arts college, though, SAT scores can be the deciding factor. If your scores fall below a school's usual range, admissions officers will look very critically at the other elements in your application folder. For most college applicants, an SAT score is the equivalent of a first impression. If your scores are good, an admissions officer will be more likely to give you the benefit of the doubt in other areas.

WHAT IS THE PRINCETON REVIEW?

The Princeton Review is the nation's fastest-growing test-preparation school. We have conducted courses in roughly 500 locations around the country, and we prepare more students for the SAT and PSAT than anyone else. We also prepare students for the ACT, GRE, GMAT, LSAT, MCAT, and other standardized tests.

The Princeton Review's techniques are unique and powerful. We developed them after scrutinizing dozens of real SATs, analyzing them with computers, and proving our theories with real students. Our methods have been widely imitated, but no one else achieves our score improvements.

This book is based on our extensive experience in the classroom. Our techniques for cracking the SAT will help you improve your SAT scores by teaching you to:

1. think like the test writers at ETS

2. take full advantage of the limited time allowed

3. find the answers to questions you don't understand by guessing intelligently

4. avoid the traps that ETS has laid for you (and use those traps to your advantage)

EVEN ETS KNOWS OUR TECHNIQUES WORK

ETS has spent a great deal of time and money over the years trying to persuade people that the SAT can't be cracked. At the same time, ETS has struggled to find ways of changing the SAT so that The Princeton Review won't be able to crack it—in effect acknowledging what our students have known all along, which is that our techniques really do work. Despite ETS's efforts, the SAT remains highly vulnerable to our techniques. In fact, the current format of the test is more coachable than ever.

A NOTE ABOUT SCORE IMPROVEMENTS

We have found in our courses that students' scores usually don't improve gradually. Instead, they tend to go up in spurts, from one plateau to another. Our students typically achieve score improvements of 100 points or more after mastering the initial concepts of the course. Their scores then often level off, only to take another jump a few weeks later when more course material has been assimilated.

If you work steadily through this book, you too will find yourself moving from plateau to plateau. But you will have to work. You won't have one of our teachers standing over you, reminding you to review what you have learned.

A Warning

Many of our techniques for beating the SAT may seen a bit unorthodox. That means using them will sometimes require a leap of faith. In order to get the full benefit from our techniques, you must trust them. The best way to develop this trust is to practice the techniques and convince yourself that they work.

But you have to practice them properly. If you try our techniques on the practice questions in most popular SAT-coaching books, you will probably decide that they don't work. Why?

The practice questions in those books aren't really like the questions on the actual SAT. There may be "analogies" and "quantitative comparisons" in those books, but if you compare them with the questions on real SATs, you will discover that they are different. In fact, studying the practice questions and techniques in some of those other books could actually hurt your SAT score. In contrast, the practice questions on the diagnostic tests in the back of this book are created with the same writing and testing processes that ETS uses. They are then tried out on students to ensure that they are as much like real SAT questions as they can possibly be.

We strongly recommend that you purchase *10 Real SATs*, which is published by the folks who write and administer the SAT (the College Board and ETS). *10 Real SATs* contains ten actual SATs that have been administered over the last few years. This book will give you the opportunity to practice with real SAT questions that were written by the same people at ETS who will write your SAT. By practicing our techniques on real SATs, you will be able to prove to yourself that the techniques really do work. This will increase your confidence when you actually take the test.

If you don't find *10 Real SATs* in your local bookstore, you can order it directly from the College Board (see page 289 for ordering information). You should also ask your guidance counselor for free copies of *Taking the SAT I: Reasoning Test*. This booklet is published by the College Board and contains a full-length practice test.

Are you ready? Let's get cracking!

1

How to Think About the SAT

ARE YOU A GENIUS OR AN IDIOT?

If you're like most high school students, you think of the SAT as a test of how smart you are. If you score 800 on the verbal, you'll probably think of yourself as a "genius"; if you score 200, you may think of yourself as an "idiot." You may even think of an SAT score as a permanent label, like your Social Security number. The Educational Testing Service (ETS), the company that publishes the test, encourages you to think this way by telling you that the test measures your ability to reason and by claiming that you cannot significantly improve your score through special preparation.

Nothing could be further from the truth.

THE SAT IS NOT A TEST OF REASONING

The SAT isn't a test of how well you reason, and it isn't a test of how smart you are. More than anything else, it is a test of how good you are at taking the SAT.

Can you learn to be better at taking the SAT? Of course you can. That's what this book is all about. You can improve your SAT score in exactly the same way you would improve your grade in chemistry: by learning the material you are going to be tested on.

Closed Loop
The SAT is a test of how well you take the SAT.

LEARN TO THINK LIKE ETS

If you got a D on a chemistry test, what would you do? You'd probably say to yourself, "I should have worked harder" or "I could have done better if I'd studied more." This is exactly the attitude you should have about the SAT. If you were disappointed by your score on the PSAT, you shouldn't say, "I'm stupid." Instead you should say, "I need to get better at taking this test."

You also need to get better at thinking like the people at ETS who write the questions. In your chemistry class, you know how your teacher thinks, and you know that he or she tends to ask certain kinds of questions. You also know what sorts of answers will win you points, and what sorts of answers won't.

You need to learn to think of the SAT in exactly the same terms. The test writers at ETS think in very predictable ways. You can improve your scores by learning to think the way they do and by learning to anticipate the kinds of answers that they think are correct.

WHAT IS ETS?

ETS is a big company. It sells not only the SAT, but also about 500 other tests, including ones for CIA agents, golf pros, travel agents, firefighters, and barbers. ETS is located outside Princeton, New Jersey, on a beautiful 400-acre estate that used to be a hunting club. The buildings where the SAT is written are surrounded by woods and hills. There is a swimming pool, a goose pond, a baseball diamond, lighted tennis courts, jogging trails, an expensive house for the company's president, a chauffeured motor pool, and a private hotel where single rooms cost more than $200 a night.

You may have been told that ETS is a government agency or that it's a part of Princeton University. It is neither. ETS is just a private company that makes a lot of money by selling tests. The company that hires ETS to write the SAT is called the College Entrance Examination Board, or the College Board.

THE SAT IS NOT WRITTEN BY GENIUSES

Many people believe the SAT questions are written by famous college professors or experts on secondary education. This is not true. Virtually all questions are written by ordinary company employees or by college students and others who are hired part time from outside ETS. Sometimes the questions are even written by teenagers. Frances Brodsky, the daughter of an ETS vice president, spent the summer after she graduated from high school writing questions for ETS tests.

Why are we telling you this? Because you should always remember that the test you are going to take was written by real people. The Wizard of Oz turned out not to be a wizard at all; he was just a little man behind a curtain. The same sort of thing is true of the SAT.

To remind you that your test was written by ordinary people, we will refer to the author of the verbal SAT as Pam and the author of the Math SAT as Jim throughout this book. Pam Cruise is a real person who has worked as the head of the Verbal Development Department at ETS, and Jim Braswell is a real person who has worked as Pam's equivalent in the Math Development Department at ETS. Therefore, the "correct" answer to a verbal question is merely Pam's answer, and the "correct" answer to a math question is merely Jim's answer. Seems a lot less frightening already, doesn't it?

FORGET ABOUT THE "BEST" ANSWER

The instructions for the SAT tell you to select the "best" answer to every question. What does "best" answer mean? It means the answer that ETS believes to be correct. Specifically, it means the answer that Pamela Cruise or James Braswell selected when the questions were written in the first place.

For that reason, we're not going to talk about "best" answers in this book. Instead, we're going to talk about "Pam's answer" and "Jim's answer." These are the only answers that will win you points. Your job on the verbal SAT is to find Pam's answer to every question; your job on the math SAT is to find Jim's answer.

HOW TO CRACK THE SYSTEM

In the following chapters we're going to teach you our method for cracking the SAT. Read each chapter carefully. Some of our ideas may seem strange at first. For example, when we tell you that it is sometimes easier to answer hard SAT questions without looking at the questions but only at the answer choices, you may say, "That's not the way I'm taught to think in school."

The SAT Isn't School

We're not going to teach you math. We're not going to teach you English. We're going to teach you the SAT.

Why do you need to know the SAT? Because knowledge of the SAT is what the SAT tests.

In the next chapter we're going to lay down a few basic principles. We're going to show you that it is possible to:

◆ Find a correct answer by eliminating incorrect ones, even if you don't know why your answer is correct.

◆ Take advantage of the SAT's "guessing reward."

◆ Earn credit for partial information.

2

Cracking the SAT: Basic Principles

THE JOY OF MULTIPLE CHOICE

What's the capital of Malawi? Give up?

Unless you spend your spare time studying an atlas, you may not even know that Malawi is a tiny country in Africa, much less what its capital is. If this question came up on a test, you'd have to skip it, wouldn't you? Well, maybe not. Let's turn this question into a multiple-choice question—the only kind of question you'll find on the verbal SAT, and virtually the only kind of question you'll find on the math SAT—and see if you can't figure out the answer anyway.

1. The capital of Malawi is

   (A) Washington, D.C.
   (B) Paris
   (C) Tokyo
   (D) London
   (E) Lilongwe

The question doesn't seem that hard anymore, does it? Of course, we made our example extremely easy. (By the way, there won't actually be any questions about geography on the SAT.) But you'd be surprised at how many people give up on SAT questions that aren't much more difficult than this one just because they don't know the correct answer right off the top of their heads. "Capital of Malawi? Oh no! I've never heard of Malawi!"

These students don't stop to think that they might be able to find the correct answer simply by eliminating all the answers they know are wrong.

YOU ALREADY KNOW ALMOST ALL OF THE ANSWERS

All but ten of the questions on the SAT are multiple-choice questions, and every multiple-choice question is followed by five (or, in a few cases, four) answer choices. On every single multiple-choice question, one of those choices, and only one, will be the correct answer to the question. You won't have to come up with that answer from scratch. You only have to identify it.

How will you do that?

LOOK FOR THE WRONG ANSWERS INSTEAD OF THE RIGHT ONES

Why? Because wrong answers are usually easier to find. Remember the question about Malawi? Even though you didn't know the answer off the top of your head, you figured it out easily by eliminating the four obviously incorrect choices. You looked for wrong answers first.

In other words, you used the process of elimination, which we'll call POE for short. This is an extremely important concept, one we'll come back to again and again. It's one of the keys to improving your SAT score. When you finish reading this book, you will be able to use POE to answer many questions that you don't understand.

A Moral Dilemma

What if someone approached you moments before the SAT began and offered to give you the answers to the test? You'd be shocked; SHOCKED! Right? But what if we told you that the person making the offer was the proctor running the test? The fact is that every student who takes the test gets to see virtually all of the answers ahead of time: They're printed in the test booklet, right underneath each question.

The great artist Michelangelo once said that when he looked at a block of marble, he could see a statue inside it. All he had to do to make a sculpture, he said, was to chip away everything that wasn't part of it. You should approach difficult SAT multiple-choice questions in the same way, by chipping away everything that's not correct. By first eliminating the most obviously incorrect choices on difficult questions, you will be able to focus your attention more effectively on the few choices that remain.

SAT ≠ School

If the SAT is not like the tests you take in high school, then why do colleges want you to take it? Good question.

THIS ISN'T THE WAY YOU'RE TAUGHT TO THINK IN SCHOOL

In school, your teachers expect you to work carefully and thoroughly, spending as long as it takes to understand whatever it is you're working on. They want you to prove not only that you know the answer to a question, but also that you know how to derive it. When your algebra teacher gives you a test in class, he or she wants you to work through every problem, step by logical step. You probably even have to show your work. If you don't know all the steps required to arrive at the solution, you may not receive full credit, even if you somehow manage to come up with the correct answer.

But the SAT is different. It isn't like school. You don't have to prove that you know why your answer is correct. The only thing ETS's scoring machine cares about is the answer you come up with. If you darken the right space on your answer sheet, you'll get credit, even if you didn't quite understand the question.

PROCESS OF ELIMINATION (POE)

There won't be many questions on the SAT in which incorrect choices will be as easy to eliminate as they were on the Malawi question. But if you read this book carefully, you'll learn how to eliminate at least one choice on virtually any SAT multiple-choice question, and two, three, or even four choices on many.

What good is it to eliminate just one or two choices on a four- or five-choice SAT question?

Plenty. In fact, for most students, it's an important key to earning higher scores.

Here's another example:

2. The capital of Qatar is

    (A) Paris
    (B) Dukhan
    (C) Tokyo
    (D) Doha
    (E) London

On this question you'll almost certainly be able to eliminate three of the five choices by using POE. That means you're still not sure of the answer. You know that the capital of Qatar has to be either Doha or Dukhan, but you don't know which.

Should you skip the question and go on? Or should you guess?

Close Your Eyes and Point

You've probably heard a lot of different advice about guessing on multiple-choice questions on the SAT. Some teachers and guidance counselors tell their students never to guess and to mark an answer only if they're absolutely certain that it's correct. Others tell their students not to guess unless they are able to eliminate two or three of the choices.

Both of these pieces of advice are incorrect.

Even ETS is misleading about guessing. Although it tells you that you *can* guess, it doesn't tell you that you *should*. In fact, if you can eliminate even one incorrect choice on an SAT multiple-choice question, guessing blindly from among the remaining choices will most likely improve your score. And if you can eliminate two or three choices, you'll be even more likely to improve your score by guessing.

Don't Pay Attention to ETS

ETS tries to discourage students from guessing on multiple-choice questions by telling them that there is a "guessing penalty" in the way the test is scored. But this is not true. There is no penalty for guessing on the SAT. Even if you can't eliminate any of the choices, random guessing isn't going to hurt your score in the long run.

There Is No Guessing Penalty on the SAT

Your raw score is the number of questions you got right, minus a fraction of the number you got wrong (except on the ten grid-ins, which are scored a little differently). Every time you answer an SAT question correctly, you get one raw point. Every time you leave an SAT question blank, you get zero raw points. Every time you answer an SAT question incorrectly, ETS subtracts one-fourth of a raw point if the question has five answer choices, one-third of a raw point if it has four answer choices, or nothing if it is a grid-in.

It is the subtracted fraction—one-fourth or one-third, depending on the type of question—that ETS refers to as the "guessing penalty." But it's nothing of the sort. An example should help you understand.

Raw scores are a little confusing, so let's think in terms of money instead. For every question you answer correctly on the SAT, ETS will give you a dollar. For every multiple-choice question you leave blank, ETS will give you nothing. For every multiple-choice question you get wrong, you will have to give twenty-five cents back to ETS. That's exactly the way raw scores work.

What happens to your score if you select the correct answer on one question and incorrect choices on four questions? Remember what we said about money: ETS gives you a dollar for the one answer you guessed correctly; you give ETS a quarter for each of the four questions you missed. Four quarters equal a dollar, so you end up exactly where you started, with nothing—which is the same thing that would have happened if you had left all five questions blank.

In Fact, There's a Guessing Reward

Now, what if you were able to eliminate one incorrect choice on each question? Random odds say you would get one question right—get a dollar—and miss the next three questions—give back 75 cents. You've just gained a quarter! In other words, there would be a guessing reward. All you would have to do to earn this reward is eliminate one choice, close your eyes, and take a shot.

Let's recap: If you eliminate nothing and guess, you break even (earn a dollar, give back four quarters.) If you eliminate one or more answer choices, you gain points. So why would anyone hesitate to guess?

One of the most common misconceptions about the SAT is that you're better off leaving a multiple-choice question blank than "taking a chance" on getting it wrong. Some students even believe that they could earn a perfect score on the test by answering just four or five questions correctly and leaving all the others blank. They think they won't lose any points unless they give an answer that is actually wrong.

Nothing could be further from the truth.

In order to earn an 800 on the SAT you have to mark an answer for nearly every question, and just about every question you mark has to be correct. If you leave just one question blank in a math section, for instance, the best math score you can hope for is 780 or 790; if you leave forty questions blank, then the best score you can get is 400.

Why This Is True

Let's use money again to illustrate why this is true. When you take the SAT, you start the test with the equivalent of $1,600 ($800 math, $800 verbal) in the bank. If you answer all the questions on each half correctly, you get to keep all $1,600.

For every question you answer incorrectly, though, you lose $10. Now, here's the important part: For every question you leave blank, you still lose $8.

Because of the way ETS calculates raw scores on the SAT, an incorrect answer is only a tiny bit worse than a blank. The one thing you can be certain of is that if you leave a question blank, you are definitely going to lose $8, whereas if you guess, you have the possibility of keeping $10. If you guess incorrectly, you'll lose just $2 more than you would have if you hadn't guessed at all. And if you guess correctly, you'll get to keep your money. That's not much of a gamble, is it?

Credit for Partial Information

Be Test Smart

Many students with good grades get below-average scores because they refuse to guess.

We hope we've been able to persuade you that guessing on multiple-choice questions isn't going to hurt you and that, if you learn to do it well, it will help you raise your score. If you're like most people, though, you probably still feel a little funny about it. Earning points for a guess probably seems a little bit like cheating or stealing: You get something you want, but you didn't do anything to earn it.

This is not a useful way to think on the SAT. It's also not true. Look at the following example:

3. The sun is a

   (A) main-sequence star
   (B) meteor
   (C) asteroid
   (D) white dwarf star
   (E) planet

If you've paid any attention at all in school for the past ten years or so, you probably know that the sun is a star. You can easily tell, therefore, that the answer to this question must be either A or D. You can tell this not only because it seems clear from the context that "white dwarf" and "main-sequence" are kinds of stars—as they are—but also because you know for a fact that the sun is not a planet, a meteor, or an asteroid. Still, you aren't sure which of the two possible choices is correct.

HEADS, YOU WIN A DOLLAR; TAILS, YOU LOSE A QUARTER

By using POE you've narrowed your choice down to two possibilities. If you guess randomly you'll have a fifty-fifty chance of being correct—like flipping a coin. Those are extremely good odds on the SAT: Heads you win a dollar, tails you lose a quarter. But let's say that, in spite of everything we've told you, you just can't bring yourself to guess. You decide to leave the question blank.

Now, let's say there is a guy sitting next to you who is, to put it politely, no rocket scientist. When it comes to this question, he has no idea what the sun is: planet, asteroid, meteor—he's clueless. So he leaves the question blank, too.

Even though you know more about the sun than this guy, you both earn exactly the same score: zero. According to the SAT, you don't know any more about the sun than he does. (The answer, by the way is A. And don't worry, there won't be any questions about astronomy on the SAT.)

If you were in class, this probably wouldn't happen. Your teacher might give you credit for knowing that the sun is some kind of star. In math class, your teacher probably gives you partial credit on a difficult problem if you set it up right, even if you make a silly mistake and get the wrong answer.

GUESSING INTELLIGENTLY WILL INCREASE YOUR SCORE

Guessing makes it possible to earn credit for partial information on the SAT. You won't know everything about every question on the test, but there will probably be a lot of questions about which you know something. Doesn't it seem fair that you should be able to earn some sort of credit for what you do know? Shouldn't your score be higher than the score of someone who doesn't know anything?

Of course, there are times you shouldn't guess. We will discuss these in the next chapter. However, if you spend any time working on a problem, you deserve to take a shot at the answer and possibly get credit. Guessing is only unfair if you don't do it—unfair to you, that is. Your SAT score won't be a fair indication of what you know unless you guess and earn some credit for partial information.

A Word Before We Begin

Write Now

Feel free to write all over this book, too. You need to get in the habit of making the SAT booklet your own. Start now by writing the names of the colleges you really want to attend in the margin above.

At school you probably aren't allowed to write in your textbooks, unless your school requires you to buy them. You probably even feel a little peculiar about writing in the books you own. Books are supposed to be read, you've been told, and you're not supposed to scrawl all over them.

Because you've been told this so many times, you may be reluctant to write in your test booklet when you take the SAT. Your proctor will tell you that you are supposed to write in it—the booklet is the only scratch paper you'll be allowed to use; it says so right in the instructions from ETS—but you may still feel bad about marking it up.

Don't Be Ridiculous!

Your test booklet is just going to be thrown away when you're finished with it. No one is going to read what you wrote in it and decide that you're stupid because you couldn't remember what 2 + 2 is without writing it down. Your SAT score won't be any higher if you don't make any marks in your booklet. In fact, if you don't take advantage of it, your score will probably be lower than it should be.

Own Your Test Booklet

You paid for your test booklet; act as though you own it. Scratch work is extremely important on the SAT. Don't be embarrassed about it. After all, writing in your test booklet will help you keep your mind on what you're doing.

- When you work on a geometry problem that provides a diagram, don't hesitate to write all over it. If there's no diagram? Draw one yourself—don't simply try to imagine it. Keep track of your work directly on the diagram to help you avoid making careless mistakes.

- On verbal questions, you will often need to come up with your own word or sentence to help you answer a question. Write it down! Trying to retain information in your head leads to confusion and errors. Your test booklet is your scratch paper—use it.

- When you use POE to eliminate a wrong answer choice, physically cross off the answer in your test booklet. Don't leave it there to confuse you. You may often need to consider carefully two remaining answer choices. You want to be clear which answer choices are left in the running.

- When you answer a question but don't feel entirely certain of your answer, circle the question or put a big question mark in the margin beside it. That way, if you have time later on, you can get back to it without having to search through the entire section.

You probably think of scratch paper as something that is useful only in arithmetic. But you'll need scratch paper on the verbal SAT, too. The verbal sections of your booklet should be just as marked up as the math ones.

TRANSFER YOUR ANSWERS AT THE END OF EACH GROUP

Scratch work isn't the only thing we want you to do in your test booklet. We also want you to mark your answers there. In the verbal sections, you should transfer your answers when you come to the end of each group of questions. (For example, when you answer a group of analogies, answer all the questions, then transfer your answers to the answer sheet.) You should transfer your answers a page at a time in the math sections.

Doing this will save you a great deal of time, because you won't have to look back and forth between your test booklet and your answer sheet every few seconds. You will also be less likely to make mistakes in marking your answers on the answer sheet.

The only exception to this is the grid-ins, the ten non-multiple-choice math questions. You will need to grid each answer as you find it. We'll tell you how to grid your answers later in the book.

BASIC PRINCIPLES SUMMARY

1. When you don't know the right answer to a multiple-choice question, look for wrong answers instead. They're usually easier to find.

2. When you find a wrong answer choice, eliminate it. In other words, use POE, the process of elimination.

3. ETS doesn't care if you understand the questions on the SAT. All it cares about is whether you darken the correct space on your answer sheet.

4. There is no guessing penalty on the SAT. In fact, there is a guessing reward. If you can eliminate just one incorrect choice on an SAT multiple-choice question, you will most likely improve your score by guessing from among the remaining choices.

5. Leaving a question blank costs you almost as many points as answering it incorrectly.

6. Intelligent guessing on multiple-choice questions enables you to earn credit for partial information.

7. Do not hesitate to use your test booklet for scratch paper.

8. Transfer your answers to your answer sheet all at once when you reach the end of each group of questions in the verbal sections and a page at a time in the math sections (except for the grid-ins).

3

Cracking the SAT:
Advanced Principles

Putting the Basic Principles to Work

In the preceding chapter, we reviewed some basic principles about the SAT. We showed you that it is possible to:

- find correct answers by using POE, the process of elimination, to get rid of incorrect ones

- take advantage of the SAT's "guessing reward"

- earn credit for partial information

But how will you know which answers to eliminate? And how will you know when to guess? In this chapter, we'll begin to show you. We will teach you how to:

- take advantage of the order in which questions are asked

- make better use of your time by scoring the easy points first

- use the Joe Bloggs principle to eliminate obviously incorrect choices on difficult questions

- find the traps that ETS has laid for you

- turn those traps into points

To show you how this is possible, we first have to tell you something about the way the SAT is arranged.

Order of Difficulty

If you've already taken the SAT once, you probably noticed that the questions got harder as you went along. You probably didn't think much of it at the time, but it's always true on the SAT. Every group of questions starts out easy and then gets hard.

For example, the thirty-minute verbal sections begin with a group of sentence completions. The first of these questions is so easy that you and virtually everyone else will answer it correctly. The second is a bit harder. The eighth is much, much harder, and the last is so hard that most of the people taking the test are unable to even answer it.

Is This Always True?

SAT questions are always arranged in increasing order of difficulty (PSAT takers—this is true of all the sections on the PSAT except the Writing Skills Component. See chapters 4 and 9 for details.) Think about it: If your gym teacher wanted to find out how high the people in your gym class could jump, she wouldn't start out by setting the high-jump bar at seven feet. She'd set it at a height that almost everyone could clear, and then she'd gradually raise it from there.

Questions on the SAT work the same way. If they were arranged differently, many students would become discouraged and give up before finding questions they were able to answer.

EASY, MEDIUM, DIFFICULT

Every group of questions on the SAT can be divided into three parts according to difficulty:

1. *The easy third*: Questions in the first third of each group are easy. ETS defines an easy question as one that most students answer correctly.

2. *The medium third*: Questions in the middle third are medium. ETS defines a medium question as one that about half of all students answer correctly.

3. *The difficult third*: Questions in the last third are difficult. ETS defines a difficult question as one that most students answer incorrectly.

For example, within a group of ten sentence completion questions, as mentioned, questions 1 through 3 are easy, questions 4 through 7 are medium, and questions 8 through 10 are difficult. Then, if the next group of questions is a set of eleven analogies, questions 11 through 14 are easy, questions 15 through 17 are medium, and questions 18 through 21 are difficult, and so on.

THE PRINCETON REVIEW DIFFICULTY METER

Before you attack any SAT question, it is important to check out how difficult the question is. To remind you to do this, we will precede each SAT question in this book with The Princeton Review Difficulty Meter.

The Difficulty Meter divides each group of questions into thirds to indicate which question numbers are easy, which are medium, and which are hard. Before you begin working on an example, check the question number against the Difficulty Meter to determine how hard the question is.

Here's how the difficulty meter for a set of ten sentence completions would look:

SENTENCE COMPLETIONS		
1 2 3	4 5 6 7	8 9 10
EASY	MEDIUM	HARD

KNOWING QUESTION DIFFICULTY CAN RAISE YOUR SCORE

Knowing that SAT questions are presented in order of difficulty can help you in several ways. First, it enables you to make the best use of your limited time. You should never waste time wrestling with the last (and therefore hardest) question in the sentence completion group if you still haven't answered the first (and therefore easiest) question in the analogies group, which follows it. Hard questions aren't worth more than easy ones. Why not do the easiest ones first? Smart test takers save hard questions for last, after they've scored all the easy points. Knowing how questions are arranged on the SAT can also help you find Jim's and Pam's answers on questions you don't understand. To show you why this is

Easy to Be Hard

Remember, the SAT isn't a huge intellectual challenge; it's just tricky. When we talk about difficult questions on the SAT, we mean ones that people most often get wrong. Get your hands on an old SAT and look at some of the difficult math questions. Do any of them test anything you didn't learn in high school? Probably not. But do they all resemble the kind of straightforward questions you're used to seeing on a regular test? Probably not. ETS specializes in confusing and misleading test takers.

true, we need to tell you something about how most people take the SAT and other standardized tests.

CHOOSING ANSWERS THAT "SEEM" RIGHT

When most people take the SAT, they don't have time to do every problem, let alone double check their work. They tend instead to work a problem as far as they can, then pick the answer that seems right based on the work they've done. For most people, this method works well at the beginning of a section. They feel confident about the answers they are choosing. However, as they get to the middle of the section, they have more and more trouble solving the problems completely, and feel less and less sure of their guesses. By the time they get to the hard questions, they are often choosing answers not because they know how to solve the questions, but because the answer "seems right."

SHOULD YOU CHOOSE ANSWERS THAT "SEEM" RIGHT?

That depends on where you are scoring and how hard the questions are.

◆ On easy multiple-choice questions, Jim's or Pam's answers seem right to virtually everyone: high scorers, average scorers, and low scorers.

◆ On medium questions, Jim's or Pam's answers seem wrong to low scorers, right to high scorers, and sometimes right and sometimes wrong to average scorers.

◆ On hard questions, Jim's or Pam's answers seem right to high scorers and wrong to everyone else.

What we've just said is true by definition. If the correct answer to a difficult question seemed correct to almost everyone, the question wouldn't really be difficult, would it? If the correct answer seemed right to everyone, everyone would pick it. That would make it an easy question. For the average student, an "easy" solution to a hard question will always be wrong.

MEET JOE BLOGGS

We're going to talk a lot about "the average student" from now on. For the sake of convenience, let's give him a name: Joe Bloggs. Joe Bloggs is just the average American high school student. He has average grades and average SAT scores. There's a little bit of him in everyone, and there's a little bit of everyone in him. He isn't brilliant. He isn't dumb. He's exactly average.

Rule #1

Answer easy questions first; save hard questions for last.

Rule #2

Easy questions tend to have easy answers; hard questions tend to have hard answers.

How Does Joe Bloggs Approach the SAT?

Joe Bloggs, the average student, approaches the SAT just like everybody else does. Whether the question is hard or easy, he always chooses the answer that seems to be correct.

Here's an example of a very hard question from a real SAT:

PROBLEM SOLVING

1 2 3 4 5 6 7 8	9 10 11 12 13 14 15 16 17	18 19 20 21 22 23 24 **25**
EASY	MEDIUM	HARD

25 A woman drove to work at an average speed of 40 miles per hour and returned along the same route at 30 miles per hour. If her total traveling time was 1 hour, what was the total number of miles in the round trip?

(A) 30

(B) $30\frac{1}{7}$

(C) $34\frac{2}{7}$

(D) 35

(E) 40

This was the last problem in a 25-problem math section. Therefore, according to the order of difficulty, it was the hardest problem in that section. Why was it hard? It was hard because most people answered it incorrectly. In fact, only about one student in ten got it right.

How Did Joe Bloggs Do on This Question?

Joe Bloggs—the average student—got this question wrong.

Why?

Because if the average student had gotten it right, it wouldn't have been a hard problem, would it?

Which Answer Did Joe Pick?

Joe picked choice D on this question; 35 just seemed like the right answer to him. Joe assumed that the problem required him to calculate the woman's average speed, and 35 is the average of 30 and 40.

But Joe didn't realize that he needed to account for the fact that the woman's trip didn't take the same amount of time in each direction. Her trip to work didn't last as long as her trip home. The answer would be 35 only if the woman had driven for a half-hour at 40 miles an hour and a half-hour at 30 miles an hour, and she did not.

Choice D was a trap: Jim Braswell included it among the answer choices because he knew that it would seem right to the average student. He put a trap among the choices because he wanted this problem to be a hard problem, not an easy one. (The answer, by the way, is C. The woman spent more time going 30 mph than she did going 40 mph, so the answer must be a little less than 35.)

COULD JIM HAVE MADE THIS QUESTION EASIER?

Yes, by writing different answer choices.

Here's the same question with choices we have substituted to make the correct answer obvious:

1. A woman drove to work at an average speed of 40 miles per hour and returned along the same route at 30 miles per hour. If her total traveling time was 1 hour, what was the total number of miles in the round trip?

    (A) 1 million

    (B) 1 billion

    (C) $34\frac{2}{7}$

    (D) 1 trillion

    (E) 1 zillion

When the problem is written this way, Joe Bloggs can easily see that Jim's answer has to be C. It seems right to Joe, because all the other answers seem obviously wrong.

Remember:

- An SAT question is easy if the correct answer seems correct to the average person—to Joe Bloggs.

- An SAT question is hard if the correct answer seems correct to almost no one.

THE JOE BLOGGS PRINCIPLE

When you take the SAT a few weeks or months from now, you'll have to take it on your own, of course. But suppose for a moment that ETS allowed you to take it with Joe Bloggs as your partner. Would Joe be any help to you on the SAT?

YOU PROBABLY DON'T THINK SO

After all, Joe is wrong as often as he is right. He knows the answers to the easy questions, but so do you. You'd like to do better than average on the SAT, and Joe earns only an average score (he's the average person, remember). All things considered, you'd probably prefer to have someone else for your partner.

But Joe might turn out to be a pretty helpful partner, after all. Since his hunches are always wrong on difficult multiple-choice questions, couldn't you

Take another look at question 25. Answer choice D was included to lure Joe Bloggs into a trap. But it isn't the only trap answer choice. Other tempting choices are A and E. Why? Because they are numbers included in the question itself, and Joe Bloggs is most comfortable with familiar numbers. When Jim selects wrong answers to hard questions, he looks for three things:

1. The answer you'd get doing the simplest possible math. In this case, that's D.

2. The answer you'd get after doing some, but not all, of the necessary math.

3. Numbers that are already in the question itself (choices A and E).

Jim doesn't use all of these every time, but there's at least one in every set of difficult answer choices.

improve your chances on those questions simply by finding out what Joe wanted to pick, and then picking something else?

If you could use the Joe Bloggs principle to eliminate one, two, or even three obviously incorrect choices on a hard problem, couldn't you improve your score by guessing among the remaining choices?

HOW TO NAVIGATE WITH A BROKEN COMPASS

If you were lost in the woods, would it do you any good to have a broken compass? You probably don't think so. But it would depend on how the compass was broken. Suppose you had a compass that always pointed south instead of north. Would you throw it away? Of course not. If you wanted to go north, you'd simply see which way the compass was pointing and then walk in the opposite direction.

JOE BLOGGS IS LIKE THAT BROKEN COMPASS

On difficult SAT questions, he always points in the wrong direction. If Joe Bloggs were your partner on the test, you could improve your chances dramatically just by looking to see where he was pointing, and then going a different way.

We're going to teach you how to make Joe Bloggs your partner on the SAT. When you come to difficult questions on the test, you're going to stop and ask yourself, "How would Joe Bloggs answer this question?" And when you see what he would do, you are going to do something else. Why? Because you know that on hard questions, Joe Bloggs is always wrong.

WHAT IF JOE BLOGGS IS RIGHT?

Remember what we said about Joe Bloggs at the beginning. He is the average person. He thinks the way most people do. If the right answer to a hard question seemed right to most people, the question wouldn't be hard, would it?

Joe Bloggs is right on some questions: the easy ones. But he's always wrong on the hard questions.

PUTTING JOE BLOGGS TO WORK FOR YOU

In the chapters that follow, we're going to teach you many specific problem-solving techniques based on the Joe Bloggs principle. The Joe Bloggs principle will help you:

- ◆ use POE to eliminate incorrect answer choices
- ◆ make up your mind when you have to guess
- ◆ avoid careless mistakes

The more you learn about Joe Bloggs, the more he'll help you on the test. If you make him your partner on the SAT, he'll help you find Pam's and Jim's answers on problems you never dreamed you'd be able to solve.

Joe's Hunches

Should you always just eliminate any answer that seems to be correct? No! Remember what we said about Joe Bloggs:

1. His hunches are correct on easy questions.
2. His hunches are sometimes correct and sometimes incorrect on medium questions.
3. His hunches are always wrong on difficult questions.

On easy multiple-choice questions, pick the choice that Joe Bloggs would pick. On hard questions, be sure to eliminate the choices that Joe Bloggs would pick.

BECAUSE THIS IS SO IMPORTANT, WE'RE GOING TO SAY IT AGAIN

Here's a summary of how Joe Bloggs thinks:

Question Type	Joe Bloggs Looks For	Joe Bloggs Selects	Time Joe Spends	How Joe Does
Easy	the answer	the one that seems right	very little	mostly right
Medium	the answer	the one that seems right	not much	so-so
Difficult	the answer	the one that seems right	too much	all wrong!

YOU SHOULD PROBABLY SKIP SOME QUESTIONS

There are some very difficult questions on the SAT that most test takers shouldn't even bother to read. On the difficult third of every group of questions, there are some questions that almost no one taking the test will understand. Rather than spending time beating your head against these questions, you should enter a guess quickly and focus your attention on questions that you have a chance of figuring out.

Since most test takers try to finish every section ("I had two seconds left over!"), almost every test taker hurts his or her score. The solution, for almost anyone scoring less than 700 on a section, is to slow down.

Most test takers could improve their scores significantly by attempting fewer questions and devoting more time to questions they have a chance of answering correctly. Slow down, score more.

YOU HAVE TO PACE YOURSELF

It's very important to set realistic goals. If you're aiming for a 500 on the verbal section, your approach to the SAT is going to be different from that of someone who is aiming for an 800. The following charts will give you some idea of what you realistically need to know in order to score at various levels on the SAT. Use the chart to gauge your progress as you work through the practice tests in *10 Real SATs*.

Now before you decide you must get a 700 in verbal no matter what, do a reality check: To date, what have you scored on the verbal SAT? The math? Whatever those numbers are, add 50–70 points to each to determine your goal score. Then get cracking! Work through this book, practice the techniques, and, after a time, take a practice test (timed). If you achieve your goal score on the practice test, great! Could you have worked a little more quickly yet maintained your level of accuracy? If so, increase your goal by another 50 points.

Rule #3

Any test taker shooting for a score below 700 on either the math section or the verbal section will hurt his or her score by attempting every question.

In other words, you must set an attainable goal in order to see any improvement. If you scored a 400 on the last math SAT you took (a 40 on the math PSAT), but immediately shoot for a 700, you will be working too quickly to be accurate, and won't see any increase in your score. However, if you instead use the "460–500" pacing guide, you may jump from a 400 to a 480! After that you can work to score over a 500, etc.

Come back to these pages after each practice test you take to re-assess your pacing strategy. Remember, accuracy is more important than speed. Finishing is not the goal; getting questions right is! Besides, all the hard problems are at the end. If you are missing easy questions due to your haste to get to the difficult questions, you are throwing points away.

VERBAL PACING CHART

Score	Right	Wrong	Blank
400	20	0	58
400	23	12	43
500	36	0	42
500	39	12	27
550	44	0	34
550	46	8	24
600	52	0	26
600	54	8	16
650	60	0	18
650	62	8	8
700	66	0	12
700	68	8	2

MATH PACING CHART

If, on your last practice exam, you scored between:	Your target score is: ◉	In the 25-question section, you should answer:	In the Quant Comp section, you should answer only:	In the Grid-in section you should answer:	In the 10-question section you should answer:
200–280	350	1–6	1–5	16–18	1–3
290–350	400	1–12	1–7	16–19	1–5
360–400	450	1–15	1–9	16–20	1–6
410–450	500	1–18	1–10	16–22	1–8
460–500	550	1–21	1–12	16–23	1–9
510–550	600	1–22	1–13	16–23	1–9
560–600	650	1–24	All	16–24	All
610–650	700	All	All	All	All
660–up	800	All	All	All	All

ADVANCED PRINCIPLES SUMMARY

1. The problems in almost every group of questions on the SAT start out easy and gradually get harder. The first question in a group is often so easy that virtually everyone can find Pam's or Jim's answer. The last question is so hard that almost no one can.

2. Because this is true, you should never waste time trying to figure out the answer to a hard question if there are still easy questions that you haven't tried. All questions are worth the same number of points. Why not do the easy ones first?

3. Most every group of questions on the SAT can be divided into thirds by difficulty, as follows:

   ◆ On the easy third of each group of questions, the average person gets all the answers right. The answers that seem right to the average person actually are right on these questions.

   ◆ On the medium third of each group, the average person's hunches are right only some of the time. Sometimes the answers that seem right to the average person really are right; sometimes they are wrong.

   ◆ Finally, on the difficult third, the average person's hunches are always wrong. The average person picks the correct answer on the hardest questions only by accident. The answers that seem right to the average person on these questions invariably turn out to be wrong.

4. Joe Bloggs is the average student. He earns an average score on the SAT. On easy SAT questions, the answers that seem correct to him are always correct. On medium questions, they're sometimes correct and sometimes not. On hard questions, they're always wrong.

5. On hard questions, Joe Bloggs is your partner. Decide what Joe would do, then *do something else*. Cross off Joe Bloggs answers to increase your guessing potential.

6. Most test takers could improve their scores significantly by attempting fewer questions and devoting more time to questions they have a chance of answering correctly.

7. It's very important to set realistic goals. If you're aiming for a 500 on the verbal, your approach to the SAT is going to be very different from that of someone who is aiming for an 800.

8. After each practice exam, go back to the pacing chart. You may need to answer more questions on the next exam to earn the score you want.

4

INTRO TO THE PSAT

IF YOU'RE PREPARING FOR THE **PSAT,** READ THIS CHAPTER NOW! OTHERWISE, SKIP TO CHAPTER FIVE.

THE PSAT

You've just spent several chapters learning how to think about the SAT. The good news is 99% of what you've learned so far can be directly applied to the PSAT as well. Like the SAT, the PSAT math and verbal sections are written in order of difficulty (Hello, Joe Bloggs!), test the same kinds of math and verbal problems, and respond to the same guessing strategies.

SO WHAT MAKES THE PSAT DIFFERENT?

There are four things that make the PSAT different from the SAT: test structure, scoring, pacing, and the Writing Skills Component. Let's look at each of these differences.

The Biggie: Writing Skills Component

The biggest difference between the SAT and the PSAT is that the PSAT contains an additional section called the "Writing Skills Component"—WSC for short. This section supposedly tests your writing ability. In actuality, it vaguely tests your ability to evaluate other people's writing, namely ETS test writers' writing. Chapter 9 will cover all the grammar you need for the WSC, plus provide you with tools and strategies to beat this section.

Test Structure

There are several structural differences between the SAT and the PSAT. First, the PSAT is shorter: five sections total two hours and ten minutes. Two of the sections are verbal (with a total of 52 questions), two are math (with a total of 40 questions, and one is the Writing Skills Component (with a total of 39 questions). You will be given 25 minutes for each of the verbal and math sections and 30 minutes for the WSC. Also, there is *no experimental section* on the PSAT!

More good news: unlike the SAT, the PSAT sections are always given in the same order: verbal, math, verbal, math, WSC. See the chart on the next page for details on the composition of each section.

Section 1–Verbal	# of Questions
Sentence Completions	6 or 7
Analogies	6 or 7
Critical Reading	10 or 15

Section 2–Math	# of Questions
Multiple-Choice	20

Section 3–Verbal	# of Questions
Sentence Completions	6 or 7
Analogies	6 or 7
Critical Reading	12 or 13

Section 4–Math	# of Questions
Quantitative Comparisons	12
Grid-Ins	8

Section 5–Writing Skills	# of Questions
Error ID	19
Improving Sentences	14
Improving Paragraphs	6

Scoring

The PSAT is scored on a 20–80 point scale, with separate scores for math, verbal, and WSC (prior to 1997 there were just two scores, math and verbal). Since the PSAT is intended to predict SAT scores, you can just add a zero to each score to find your predicted score on the SAT (for example, if you got a 51 on the math portion of the PSAT, you will supposedly score a 510 on the math portion of the SAT). The WSC allegedly predicts your performance on the SAT II: Writing Subject Test. All other aspects of scoring (raw score conversion, "guessing penalty," etc.) are the same on the PSAT as they are on the SAT.

Pacing

The PSAT gives only 25 minutes for each math and verbal section, and each of these sections contains a different number of questions from the SAT math and verbal sections. Therefore, your pacing will be slightly different from the SAT. Use the following charts to determine your pace per section on the PSAT. Remember accuracy, not speed, raises scores. Choose a goal score that is reasonable for you. If you achieve that score consistently, you may raise your goal and increase the number of questions you attempt. The numbers listed below indicate the number of problems you should do on *each section*:

VERBAL PACING CHART:

SAT score	Prior PSAT	Target PSAT	Analogies per section	Sentence Comps per section	Critical Reading per section
200–290	20–29	35	3	3	1 passage
300–390	30–39	45	4	4	1 passage
400–490	40–49	55	5	5	1 + 1/2 passages
500–590	50–59	65	6	6	1 + 3/4 passages
600–690	60–69	75	all	all	all
700–790	70–79	80	all	all	all

MATH PACING CHART:

SAT score	Prior PSAT	Target PSAT	20-Q Problem Solving	Quant Comps	Grid-Ins
200–280	20–28	35	9	4	2
290–350	29–35	40	10	5	3
360–400	36–40	45	12	6	4
410–450	41–45	50	14	7	5
460–500	46–50	55	16	9	6
510–550	51–55	60	18	10	6
560–600	56–60	65	19	11	7
610–650	61–65	70	all	all	all
650–800	65–80	80	all	all	all

WRITING SKILLS PACING CHART:

Prior WSC score	Target Score	# to do
20–30	35	10
31–35	40	15
36–40	45	20
41–45	50	25
46–50	55	28
51–55	60	32
56–60	65	37
61–65	70	39
66–70	75	39
71–80	80	39

What About Pacing on the WSC?

Unlike the other sections of the PSAT and SAT, the Writing Skills Component is not set up in order of difficulty. There are, of course, still a mix of easy, medium, and difficult questions, but due to the nature of the section, you will need to determine for yourself which problems are difficult and which are easy.

What makes a WSC question difficult? A question can be difficult because you don't know the grammar the question is testing, or because the question is very long and time-consuming. As you work through chapter 9, we'll give you more guidelines regarding when to skip a problem. Remember, however, if you can cross off even one answer choice, you should guess. Smart guessing will raise your score.

NATIONAL MERIT SCHOLARSHIP

We mentioned already that the PSAT is used as a qualifier for National Merit. In fact, many of you who are preparing for the PSAT are doing so in the hopes of qualifying as a National Merit Scholar. We'd like to take a few minutes to tell you more about the National Merit Scholarship Program so you have a good idea what to expect, and what *not* to expect, if you are competing for a scholarship.

Do you stand a chance?

While becoming a National Merit Scholar is a high honor, it is also one that is awarded to a very small percentage of high school students. The National Merit folks award about 6,700 scholarships a year to students who demonstrate academic excellence. Sounds great, until you realize that over a million students a year take the PSAT. That means you stand about a half-a-percent chance of receiving a scholarship.

Now don't give up yet. National Merit also awards "Letters of Commendation" to about 35,000 students each year—that's 3.5 percent of the pool. These Letters of Commendation look great on a college application, so if you stand a chance of getting one of these letters, it is definitely worth your time to go for it. The letters are typically awarded to students scoring above the 95th percentile on the PSAT. If you receive this honorable mention from National Merit, you should be proud. You should also know that you are out of the running for a scholarship.

About 15,000 students become semifinalists for National Merit Scholarships. These semifinalists are chosen according to their state's specific score cutoff, which is determined by the number of high school students taking the PSAT in that state. These students usually are the top half of the 99th percentile of their state.

To become *finalists*, these students must:

- be U.S. citizens or permanent residents who intend to become citizens

- be enrolled full-time in secondary school

- be fully endorsed and recommended for a Merit Scholarship by their high school principals

- have a record of consistently high academic performance and standing throughout grades 9–12

- complete the NMSC Scholarship Application

- achieve high scores on the SAT

But wait, there's more

About 14,000 of the 15,000 semifinalists become finalists. Do they get the money yet? Nope. There is a final screening—based on what we do not know. Six thousand seven hundred students are chosen as award recipients. What do these students get? Well, it depends.

Two thousand of these students receive a National Merit $2,000 Scholarship. These national awards are allocated to states based on the number of students that attend college from each state. In other words, if your state supplies 5 percent of the nation's incoming college freshmen, 5 percent of the national winners will be chosen from your state.

But what about the rest of them? The other 4,000-plus winners receive scholarships sponsored by specific corporations and colleges. These scholarships are based on various criteria, and their monetary awards vary in amount.

THE BOTTOM LINE ABOUT NATIONAL MERIT

It is an honor to be commended by the National Merit folks. However, the scholarship—if you manage to be one of the 2,000 students who actually get it—won't pay your meal ticket at college. If you think you stand a chance of being recognized by National Merit, go for it. If not, prepare for the PSAT because it is good practice for the SAT. If you would like more details about the National Merit Scholarship Program, consult your guidance counselor or write to:

National Merit Scholarship Corporation
1560 Sherman Avenue, Suite 200
Evanston, IL 60202-4897
(847) 866-5100

PART ◆ II

How to Crack the Verbal SAT

A Few Words About Words

The SAT contains seven sections. Three of these will be verbal, or "English," sections. There may be a fourth verbal section on your test, but it will be experimental, so it won't count toward your score. Don't worry about trying to identify the experimental section. Just work at your normal pace.

Each of the three scored verbal sections on the SAT contains the following three types of questions:

- sentence completions
- analogies
- critical reading

What Does the Verbal SAT Test?

ETS says that the verbal SAT tests "verbal reasoning abilities" or "higher order reasoning abilities." You may be wondering exactly what these statements mean, but don't sweat it—they're not true anyway. The verbal SAT is mostly a test of your vocabulary. Even critical-reading questions often test nothing more than your familiarity with certain words. If you have a big vocabulary, you'll probably do well on the exam. If you have a small vocabulary, you're going to be in trouble no matter how many techniques we teach you.

For this reason, it's absolutely essential that you get to work on your vocabulary now! The best way to improve your vocabulary is by reading. Any well-written book is better than television. Even certain periodicals—newspapers and some magazines—can improve your verbal performance if you read them regularly. Always keep a notebook and a dictionary by your side as you read. When you encounter words with meanings you don't know, write them down, look them up, and try to incorporate them into your life. The dinner table is a good place to throw around new words.

Building a vocabulary this way can be slow and painful. Most of us have to encounter new words many times before we develop a firm sense of what they mean. You can speed up this process a great deal by taking advantage of the vocabulary section (Part V) in the back of this book. It contains a short list of words that are highly likely to turn up on the SAT, a section on word roots, and some general guidelines about learning new words. If you work through it carefully between now and the time you take the test, you'll have a much easier time on the verbal SAT. The more SAT words you know, the more our techniques will help you.

Before you go on, turn to Part V on page 295 for a few minutes. Read through it quickly and sketch out a vocabulary-building program for yourself. You should follow this program every day, at the same time that you work through the other chapters of this book.

The techniques described in the three verbal chapters that follow are intended to help you take full advantage of your growing vocabulary by using partial information to attack hard questions. In a sense, we are going to teach you how to get the maximum possible mileage out of the words you know. Almost all students miss SAT questions that they could have answered correctly if they had used POE.

Read What You Like

Some folks think it's necessary to read nothing but crusty books on obscure subjects in order to build a better vocabulary. Not true. Identify something that interests you and find some books on that subject. You'll be spending time on something you enjoy, and hey, you just might learn something.

5

Joe Bloggs and the
Verbal SAT

JOE BLOGGS AND THE VERBAL SAT

Joe Bloggs will be a big help to you on the verbal SAT. By keeping him in mind as you take the test, you will substantially improve your score. Joe will help you identify and eliminate incorrect answer choices before you have a chance to be tempted by them, and he will help you zero in on Pam's answer.

JOE BLOGGS AND THE ORDER OF DIFFICULTY

The verbal sections of SAT contain three question types: sentence completions, analogies, and critical reading. The analogies and sentence completions are arranged in order of increasing difficulty. That is, in a group of ten sentence completions, the first three or four will be easy, the next three or four will be medium, and the last three or four will be hard. Critical-reading questions are not arranged in order of difficulty. They follow the structure of the passage to which they refer. (More on that later.)

How does Joe Bloggs do on verbal questions? As always on the SAT, he gets the easy ones right, does so-so on the medium ones, and crashes and burns on the hard ones. When you take the SAT, you must constantly be aware of where you are in each group of questions. Knowing where a question falls in the order of difficulty will tell you how much faith you can put in your hunches and it will help you avoid making careless mistakes. In addition, your knowledge of Joe's test-taking habits will enable you to eliminate incorrect choices on the hardest questions, thus greatly improving your odds of guessing Pam's answer.

A Reminder

On easy questions, the answers that seem right to Joe really are right; on hard questions, the answers that seem right to Joe are wrong.

HOW JOE THINKS

When Joe looks at a verbal SAT question, he is irresistibly attracted to choices containing easy words that remind him of the question. On easy questions, this tendency serves Joe very well. On hard questions, though, it gets him into trouble every time.

Here's an example. This is a very difficult analogy question. Don't worry if you don't know how to answer a question like this; we'll deal with the SAT analogies thoroughly in another chapter. For now, all you have to do is look at the words.

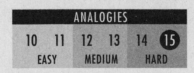

15 FLORID : SPEECH ::
   (A) harsh : voice
   (B) fluid : style
   (C) vivid : image
   (D) fertile : soil
   (E) ornate : design

Analysis

This is a very hard question from a real SAT. Only about 8 percent of test takers answered it correctly. More than twice as many of them would have answered it correctly if they had simply closed their eyes and picked one of the choices at random. Why did the vast majority of test takers—including, of course, Joe Bloggs—do so poorly on this question? Because they all fell into a trap. Like Joe, they didn't know what *florid* means, so they focused their attention on *speech*, an easy word. Then they looked for an answer choice containing something similar. Like Joe, they were immediately drawn to choice A. *Speech* and *voice* seem similar. Joe quickly marked A on his answer sheet.

Was Joe (along with several hundred thousand test takers) correct? No, of course not. Joe never picks the right answer on hard SAT questions.

WHAT DOES THAT MEAN FOR YOU?

It means that on hard questions like this one, you can simply eliminate any answer choice or choices that you know will be attractive to Joe. We'll tell you more about how to do this as we go along. (Incidentally, Pam's answer to this question is E. *Florid* means using flowery or heavily embellished *speech*, and *ornate* means having a fancy or heavily embellished *design*.)

PUTTING JOE TO WORK ON THE VERBAL SAT

Generally speaking, the Joe Bloggs principle teaches you to:

- trust your hunches on easy questions
- double-check your hunches on medium questions
- eliminate Joe Bloggs answers on difficult questions

The next few chapters will teach you how to use your knowledge of Joe Bloggs to add points to your SAT score.

6

Sentence Completions

MEMORIZE THE INSTRUCTIONS

Before we begin, take a moment to read the following set of instructions and answer the sample question that comes after it. Both appear here exactly as they do on the real SAT. Be certain that you know and understand these instructions before you take the SAT. If you learn them ahead of time, you won't have to waste valuable seconds reading them on the day you take the test.

> Each sentence below has one or two blanks, each blank indicating that something has been omitted. Beneath the sentence are five lettered words or sets of words labeled A through E. Choose the word or set of words that, when inserted in the sentence, <u>best</u> fits the meaning of the sentence as a whole.
>
> Example:
>
> Medieval kingdoms did not become constitutional republics overnight; on the contrary, the change was ----.
>
> (A) unpopular
> (B) unexpected
> (C) advantageous
> (D) sufficient
> (E) gradual   Ⓐ Ⓑ Ⓒ Ⓓ ●

Pam's answer to this sample question is E.

SAT SENTENCE COMPLETIONS: CRACKING THE SYSTEM

It's important to know the instructions printed before each group of sentence completions on the SAT, but it's vastly more important to understand what those instructions mean. ETS's instructions don't tell you everything you need to know about SAT sentence completions. The rest of this chapter will teach you what you need to know.

The two thirty-minute verbal sections of your test will contain one group of sentence completions each. One group will have ten sentence completions, the other nine. In each group, the questions will be arranged in order of increasing difficulty. That is, the first question in each group of sentence completions will be the easiest in the group; the last question in each group will be the hardest.

Because our techniques vary depending on the difficulty of the question, we have placed a Difficulty Meter before each example. Look at the meter to determine how hard the example is.

Level of Difficulty

Set of Nine
1–3 Easy
4–6 Medium
7–9 Difficult

Set of Ten
1–3 Easy
4–7 Medium
8–10 Difficult

GET A CLUE

Sentence completions are sentences from which one or two words have been removed. Your job is to find the missing word or words. How will you do this? By finding the clue(s) Pam has left for you in the sentence. Each sentence completion contains a clue that will tell you the word(s) that goes in the blank(s).

All you have to do is find the clue, and you've cracked the question.

Sound too good to be true? Try the following example. The answer choices have been removed so you can concentrate solely on the sentence. Read the sentence, look for the clue, and decide which word goes in the blank.

1 Historical buildings in many American cities, rather than being destroyed, are now being ----.

Analysis

What word did you come up with? Probably something like *fixed* or *restored*. How did you decide that was the word you needed? Because of the clue. The clue in this sentence is "rather than being destroyed." It tells us that the historical buildings are being *fixed* or *restored* instead of being destroyed.

Now that you have decided on the word that goes in the blank, look at the following answer choices. Cross off the answers that are not close to yours (ones that don't mean *fixed* or *restored*), and pick the best answer.

(A) condemned
(B) constructed
(C) described
(D) renovated
(E) designed

Answer choices (A), (C), and (E) are out right away. You may have gotten stuck between (B) and (D), but think about which one is closer to your word. Are the historical buildings being *constructed*? No—they wouldn't be historical if they were only now being constructed. The historical buildings are being *renovated*. Pam's answer is (D).

But Why?

You may be wondering why we didn't just plug each answer into the sentence to see which one sounded right. That's because all the answers are designed to *sound* right. Look back to the question we just did. The sentence would "sound" just fine if you plugged in any one of those answer choices. But only one of them is Pam's answer.

More importantly, plugging each word into the sentence is how Joe Bloggs would solve the question. Does Joe get all sentence-completion questions correct? No way. Joe doesn't know that Pam has given him a clue in the sentence that tells him exactly what the answer is. He just plugs in choices and takes a guess.

You, on the other hand, know the inside scoop. In each sentence, Pam must include a clue that reveals her answer. If she didn't, no one would agree on the right answer (there wouldn't *be* a right answer) and lots of people would sue her. However, she *can* make the answer choices as attractive as possible, so that the Joe Bloggses of the world get caught by trying to find an answer that sounds right. How can you avoid getting caught in the "sounds right" trap?

COVER UP

Cover the answer choices before you begin each sentence completion. Place your hand (or your answer sheet) over the five answer choices so that you are not tempted to look at them too soon. Then, read the sentence and find Pam's clue. Decide what you think the word in the blank should be, then use POE to get to Pam's answer.

Try another example:

4   The onset of the earthquake was gradual, the tremors occurring ---- at first, then with greater frequency.

Here's How to Crack It

What is the clue in this sentence? Two things give you the full picture: *gradual* and *then with greater frequency*. Since we know the earthquake came on gradually and that the tremors later came with greater frequency, we can assume that the tremors occurred "infrequently" or "gradually" at first.

Now that you have a clue, use POE to get to Pam's answer:

         (A) continuously
         (B) intensely
         (C) sporadically
         (D) unexpectedly
         (E) chronically

The only word that comes close to meaning "infrequently" or "gradually" is (C) sporadically. This is Pam's answer.

Sentence Completion Rule #1

Cover the answer choices until you know what the answer should be.

CLUELESS

The following two examples will further illustrate what we've been talking about. The first is a sentence completion that has no clue. The second is virtually the same sentence except with Pam's clue. Which one of the following is easier?

I. The woman told the man, "You're very ----."

    (A) rich
    (B) correct
    (C) preposterous
    (D) cloistered
    (E) sick

II. The doctor told the man, "You're very ----."

    (B) rich
    (C) correct
    (D) preposterous
    (E) cloistered
    (F) sick

As you can see, questions I and II are identical, with the exception of a single word. And yet that word makes all the difference in the world. In Question I, several of the choices are possible. In fact, this question cannot be answered (don't worry—you won't have one like this on the SAT.) But in Question II, the word *doctor* makes the answer (E). The key word *doctor* determines Pam's answer.

So that you always know what we are talking about, we will refer to Pam's clue as "the doctor." For each sentence completion, find the doctor. Once you do, use it to determine the missing word or words.

WHAT'S UP, DOC?

Try the following example. Before you begin, cover up the answer choices. Then read the sentence and underline the doctor. Fill in the blank with your own word, then use POE to get to Pam's answer.

4 Some developing nations have become remarkably ----, using aid from other countries to build successful industries.

    (A) populous
    (B) dry
    (C) warlike
    (D) prosperous
    (E) isolated

Here's How to Crack It

The doctor in this sentence is *build successful industries*. It indicates that some nations "have become remarkably *successful*."

Let's look at each answer choice:

(A) Does *populous* mean *successful*? No. Cross off this answer.

(B) Does *dry* mean *successful*? Not at all. Cross it off.

(C) Does *warlike* mean *successful*? Nope. Ditch it.

(D) Does *prosperous* mean *successful*? Sure does.

(E) Does *isolated* mean *successful*? Nope. Ditch it.

Pam's answer must be (D).

IS THERE A DOCTOR IN THE HOUSE?

If you are having trouble finding the doctor, ask yourself two simple questions about each sentence:

1. What is the blank talking about?

2. What *else* does the sentence say about this?

For example, look back to the problem we just did. What is the blank talking about? Some nations. What else does the sentence say about the nations? They were able to *build successful industries*. This must be the doctor of the sentence, because it refers to the same thing the blank refers to.

Find and underline the doctor in the following sentence. Then fill in the blank with your own word. If you have any trouble, ask:

1. What is the blank talking about?

2. What *else* does the sentence say about this?

> **1** Medwick was so outstanding a thinker that her colleagues were often so dazzled by her ---- that they failed to appreciate fully her other virtues.

Analysis

What is the blank talking about? Medwick. What else does the sentence say about Medwick? She was an outstanding thinker. Therefore, her colleagues were dazzled by her *thinking*.

PICK A WORD, ANY WORD

The word you select to fill the blank doesn't have to be an elegant word, or a hard word, or the perfect word. It doesn't even have to be a word; instead, it can be a phrase—even a clunky phrase—as long as it captures the correct meaning.

In an episode of *The Simpsons*, a lawyer couldn't think of the word *mistrial*, so he asked the judge to declare a "bad court thingie." *Bad court thingie* is an accurate enough substitute for *mistrial* on the SAT. With *bad court thingie* as your "word," POE will get you to *mistrial*.

RECYCLE THE DOCTOR

Instead of coming up with a different word for the blank, you can often just recycle the doctor. Remember, the doctor is the clue that Pam puts in the sentence which indicates what should go in the blank. If you can put the doctor itself in the blank, you can be sure that you've put your finger on Pam's answer.

Is the blank always the same as the doctor? Sometimes the blank is exactly the same, while other times it is exactly the opposite. You must use the rest of the sentence to determine if the blank and the doctor are the same or opposite. In other words, you must be on the lookout for "trigger words."

TRIGGER WORDS

Very often on sentence completions, the most important clue to Pam's answer is a trigger word: a single revealing word or expression that lets you know exactly where Pam is heading. About half of all SAT sentence completions contain trigger words. Combining trigger words with your doctor make filling in the blank a breeze.

Some trigger words are negative, and some are positive. The most important negative trigger words are *but, though,* and *although*. These are words that "change the direction" of a sentence. The most important positive trigger words are *and* and *because*. These are words that maintain the direction of a sentence.

Negative trigger words are more common on the SAT than positive trigger words. Both provide terrific clues that you can use to find Pam's answer. To see what we mean, take a look at the following incomplete sentences. For each one, fill in a few words that complete the thought in a plausible way. There's no single correct answer. Just fill in something that makes sense in the context of the entire sentence:

I really like you, *but*_____.

I really like you, *and*_____.

Here's how one of our students filled in the blanks:

I really like you, *but I'm going to kill you*.

I really like you, *and I'm going to hug you*.

Analysis

In the first sentence, the word *but* indicates that the second half of the sentence will contradict the first half. Because the first half of the sentence is positive, the second half must be negative. I like you, *but* I'm going to kill you. The sentence "changes direction" after the negative trigger word *but*.

In the second sentence, the word *and* indicates that the second half of the sentence will confirm or support the first half. Because the first half of the sentence is positive, the second half must be positive as well. I like you, *and* I'm going to hug you. In this case, the sentence continues in the same direction after the positive trigger word *and*.

DRILL 1

Circle the trigger word (if there is one) and underline the doctor in each of the following sentences. Then, write your own word in the blank. If you have trouble finding the doctor, ask yourself, "What is the blank talking about?" and "What else does the sentence say about this?" Don't worry if you can't think of a single, perfect word for the blank; use a phrase that catches Pam's meaning. Once you've finished these questions, go on to Drill 2 and use POE to find Pam's answer.

1. Although the critics agreed that the book was brilliant, so few copies were sold that the work brought the author little ---- reward.

6. Sadly, many tropical rain forests are so ---- by agricultural and industrial over-development that they may ---- by the end of the century.

9. My plea is not for drab and ---- technical writing about music but for pertinent information conveyed with as much ---- as possible.

DRILL 2

Here are the same questions, this time with the answer choices. Refer to your notes from Drill 1 and make a choice for each question. Remember to use POE. Pam's answers are on page 341.

1. Although the critics agreed that the book was brilliant, so few copies were sold that the work brought the author little ---- reward.
   (A) theoretical
   (B) thoughtful
   (C) financial
   (D) abstract
   (E) informative

6 Sadly, many tropical rain forests are so ---- by agricultural and industrial over-development that they may ---- by the end of the century.

(A) isolated. .separate
(B) threatened. .vanish
(C) consumed. .expand
(D) augmented. .diminish
(E) rejuvenated. .disappear

9 My plea is not for drab and ---- technical writing about music but for pertinent information conveyed with as much ---- as possible.

(A) repetitive. .redundancy
(B) obscure. .felicity
(C) inscrutable. .ambivalence
(D) euphonious. .harmony
(E) provocative. .exhilaration

AND THEN THERE WERE TWO

About half of all sentence completions contain two blanks. Many students fear these questions because they look long and intimidating. But two-blank sentence completions are no more difficult than single-blank sentence completions. The key is to take them one blank at a time.

To crack two-blank sentence completions, read the sentence, circling the trigger word(s) and underlining the doctor(s) (there may be a doctor for *each* blank). Then fill in whichever blank seems easier to you. Once you have filled in one of the blanks, go to the answer choices and check just the words for that blank, using POE to get rid of answers that are not close to yours. Then go back to the other blank, fill it in, and check the remaining choices. You do not need to check both words at one time. If one of the words doesn't work in a blank, then it doesn't matter what the other word is. One strike and the answer is out.

When eliminating answers, draw a line through the entire answer choice. That way you won't get confused and check it again when you are checking the other blank. Even if you do fill in both blanks the first time you read the sentence, only check one blank at a time. It is much easier to concentrate on one word than on a pair of words. Use POE to check one blank, then the other. Sometimes you'll be able to get rid of four choices by checking only one blank, and won't even need to check the other blank.

Here's an example of a two-blank sentence completion:

> **SENTENCE COMPLETIONS**
> 1 2 3 4 5 **6** 7 8 9 10
> EASY   MEDIUM   HARD

6 While the ---- student openly questioned the teacher's explanation, she was not so ---- as to suggest that the teacher was wrong.

(A) complacent . . suspicious
(B) inquisitive . . imprudent
(C) curious . . dispassionate
(D) provocative . . respectful
(E) ineffectual . . brazen

Here's How to Crack It

Let's start with the first blank. The doctor is *openly questioned*, and we can simply recycle the doctor and put *questioning* in the blank. Now let's take a look at the first-blank words in the answer choices and eliminate any words that are definitely not a good match for *questioning*. Eliminate choices A and E, because *complacent* and *ineffectual* have nothing to do with *questioning*. All we want to do at this point is eliminate any words that are way off base. Then we can move on to the second blank.

The doctor for the second blank is *suggest that the teacher was wrong*. How would you describe a student who accuses the teacher of being wrong? *Bold* or *rude*, maybe? Look at the remaining choices and get rid of any second words that don't mean something like *bold* or *rude*. (C) is out—*dispassionate* does not mean *bold* or *rude*. Also, (D) is out since this student is anything but *respectful*. Pam's answer must be (B).

Notice that we only had to eliminate one of the words in each answer choice in order to get rid of the entire choice. Attacking this question using POE also made it easier, because we could eliminate four answers without much trouble. If four answers are wrong, the one that's left must be Pam's answer.

THE TRICKY ONES

Every now and then, the doctor for one of the blanks in a two-blank sentence completion turns out to be the other blank. What? How can Pam get away with making the doctor a *blank*?

Don't worry—if Pam has decided to use one blank as the doctor for the other blank, you know she has inserted another way for you to find her answer. Let's look at an example:

> **SENTENCE COMPLETIONS**
> 1 2 3 4 5 6 **7** 8 9 10
> EASY   MEDIUM   HARD

7 Most of Rick's friends think his life is
unbelievably ---- , but in fact he spends most
of his time in ---- activities.

(A) fruitful . . productive
(B) wasteful . . useless
(C) scintillating . . mundane
(D) varied . . sportive
(E) callow . . simple

Here's How to Crack It

The trigger word in this sentence is *but*. We gather from the sentence that most
of Rick's friends think his life is one way, but in fact it is another. We cannot tell
if his friends think his life is great and busy while it's really lousy and slow, or
vice versa. However, we do know that our blanks are opposites: the first is
positive while the second is negative *or* the first is negative while the second is
positive.

Knowing this is enough to get us to Pam's answer. Let's look at each answer
choice, keeping in mind that we need a pair of words that are opposite:

(A) *Fruitful* is positive, *productive* is positive.
Eliminate this choice.
(B) *Wasteful* is negative, *useless* is negative.
Cross it off.
(C) *Scintillating* is positive, *mundane* is
negative. Keep it.
(D) *Varied* is positive, *sportive* is positive.
Cross it off.
(E) *Callow* is negative, *simple* is neutral. A
possibility, but not great.

Pam's answer is (C): Rick's life may look *scintillating*, but he spends most of
his time in *mundane* activities. If the doctor of one of the blanks is the other blank
in a two-blank sentence completion, look for the trigger and determine the
relationship between the blanks. Then use POE to find Pam's answer.

ARE YOU A GOOD WORD OR A BAD WORD?

Notice in the last example that we didn't use *words* to fill in the blanks. Instead,
we looked for positive and negative words. On difficult sentence completions,
you may find it hard to determine what the word in the blank is supposed to be.
However, you will usually have an idea if that word should be a good word
(something positive) or a bad word (something negative). Knowing whether a
blank is positive or negative can help you eliminate answer choices. If you are
unable to come up with your own word, use + or − to get rid of answers and
make smart guesses.

Here's an example:

SENTENCE COMPLETIONS

1 2 3 4 5 6 7 **8** 9 10
EASY   MEDIUM   HARD

8. Ruskin's vitriolic attack was the climax of the ---- heaped on paintings that today seem amazingly ----.

   (A) criticism. .unpopular
   (B) ridicule. .inoffensive
   (C) praise. .amateurish
   (D) indifference. .scandalous
   (E) acclaim. .creditable

Here's How to Crack It

A *vitriolic* attack is something bad (and so is a plain attack, if you don't know what vitriolic means). The climax of a vitriolic attack must also be bad, and therefore the first blank must be a bad word. Already we can eliminate choices C and E (and possibly choice D). We don't have to worry about the second word in these answer choices, because we already know that the first word is wrong.

Now look at the second blank. The first part of the sentence says that Ruskin thought the paintings were very bad; today, *amazingly*, they seem—what? Bad?

No! The word in the second blank has to be a good word. Choices C and E are already crossed out. We can now also eliminate choices A and D (without bothering to look at the first words again) because the second blank words are bad words. The only choice left is B—Pam's answer. You've earned 10 points for answering a very hard question simply by figuring out whether the words in Pam's answer were good or bad. Not bad!

The good-word/bad-word method is also helpful when you have anticipated Pam's answer but haven't found a similar word among the choices. Simply decide whether your anticipated answer is positive or negative, then determine whether each of the answer choices is positive or negative. Eliminate the choices that are different, and you'll find Pam's answer.

A Gentle Reminder

Your aim is to eliminate wrong answers. Get rid of as many incorrect choices as you can, guess from among the remaining choices, and then move on.

WHAT ABOUT JOE?

As you know, the last few questions in each group of sentence completions will be quite difficult. On these hard questions, you will find it useful to remember the Joe Bloggs principle and eliminate choices that you know would attract Joe. Here's an example:

9 The phenomenon is called viral ---- because the presence of one kind of virus seems to inhibit infection by any other.

   (A) proliferation
   (B) mutation
   (C) interference
   (D) epidemic
   (E) cooperation

Important!

Eliminating Joe Bloggs attractors should always be the first thing you do when considering answer choices on a hard sentence completion. If you don't eliminate them immediately, you run the risk of falling for them as you consider the various choices.

Here's How to Crack It

Joe Bloggs is attracted to choices containing words that remind him of the subject matter of the sentence. The words in the sentence that Joe notices are *virus* and *infection*—words related to biology or illness. Which answers attract him? Choices B and D. You can therefore eliminate both.

Where's the doctor in this sentence? It's the word *inhibit*. By recycling the doctor and putting *inhibit* in the blank, you can anticipate Pam's answer: "The phenomenon is called viral *inhibition* because the presence of one kind of virus seems to inhibit infection by any other." Which answer choice could mean something similar to inhibition? *Interference.* Pam's answer is C.

How Hard is It?

Let's assume you've tried everything: You've looked for the doctor and trigger, tried to anticipate Pam's answer, eliminated the Joe Bloggs answers, and used the good-word/bad-word technique. You still can't find Pam's answer. What should you do?

Remember order of difficulty: easy questions have easy answers and hard questions have hard answers. Joe Bloggs tends to avoid choices containing words whose meaning he doesn't understand. As a result, we can be fairly certain that on easy questions (which Joe gets right) Pam's answer will contain easy words. However, on hard questions (which Joe gets wrong) her answer will contain hard words, ones that Joe would never pick.

And an easy word will usually not be Pam's answer on a hard question.

When you come down to the wire and need to guess on the hardest couple of sentence completions, simply pick the hardest choice—the one with the weirdest, most difficult words. Eliminate any choice whose word or words you can define, and guess from among what's left. No problem!

Easy to Be Hard

How to exploit the order of difficulty on sentence completions:
1. On easy questions, be very suspicious of hard choices.
2. On hard questions, be very suspicious of easy choices.

Drill 3

The following two questions contain answer choices from sentence completions. These are both numbers eight out of nine—in other words, tough problems. Eliminate the easy answer choices, then guess the hardest, weirdest answer choices. See page 341 to check your answers.

SENTENCE COMPLETIONS

1	2	3	4	5	6	7	**8**	9
EASY			MEDIUM			HARD		

8   (A) adjusted
  (B) tainted
  (C) contained
  (D) ignored
  (E) decreased

8   (A) cogent . . perfunctory
  (B) provocative . . poignant
  (C) tactful . . amiable
  (D) predictable . . uninspired
  (E) mundane . . trenchant

SENTENCE COMPLETIONS SUMMARY

1. Cover the answer choices. Learn to anticipate Pam's answer by filling in each blank before you look at the answer choices. If you look at the answer choices first, you will often be misled.

2. Always look for the doctor—the key word or words that give you the clue you need to fill in the blank(s).

3. If you have trouble finding the doctor, ask yourself:

   1. What is the blank talking about?

   2. What else does the sentence say about this?

4. Look for trigger words—revealing words or expressions that give you important clues about the meanings of sentences. The most important negative trigger words are *but, though,* and *although*. These are words that "change the direction" of a sentence. The most important positive trigger words are *and* and *because*. These are words that maintain the direction of the sentence.

5. Fill in the blank with any word or phrase that will help you get to Pam's answer. Don't worry if you need to use a clunky or awkward phrase. If you can, recycle the doctor. If you can't come up with any words for the blank, use + or −. Use POE to get to Pam's answer.

6. Attack two-blank sentence completions by focusing on one blank at a time. Use the same techniques you would use on one-blank questions. If you can eliminate either word in an answer choice, you can cross out the entire choice. If the doctor for one of the blanks is the other blank, use the trigger word to determine the relationship between the blanks.

7. Never eliminate a choice unless you are sure of its meaning.

8. Eliminate Joe Bloggs answers. On difficult questions, Joe is attracted to answers containing easy words that remind him of the subject matter of the sentence. Learn to recognize these words and be extremely suspicious of the answer choices in which they appear.

9. Take advantage of the order of difficulty. Easy sentence completions have easy answers, hard ones have hard answers. If you can do nothing else on a hard sentence completion, simply pick the choice with the hardest or weirdest words.

7

Analogies

MEMORIZE THE INSTRUCTIONS

This chapter is about analogies, the second of the three types of verbal SAT questions. There will be at least two groups of analogy questions on the SAT you take, one in each of the two scored thirty-minute verbal sections (of course, if your experimental section is verbal, you'll have a third set of analogies).

Before we begin, take a moment to read the instructions and to answer the sample question that follows. Both appear here exactly as they do on the real SAT. Be certain that you know and understand these instructions before you take the SAT. If you learn them ahead of time, you won't have to waste valuable seconds reading them on the day you take the test.

> Each question below consists of a related pair of words or phrases, followed by five pairs of words or phrases labeled A through E. Select the pair that best expresses a relationship similar to that expressed in the original pair.
>
> Example:
> CRUMB : BREAD ::
>
> (A) ounce : unit
> (B) splinter : wood
> (C) water : bucket
> (D) twine : rope
> (E) cream : butter   Ⓐ ● Ⓒ Ⓓ Ⓔ

Pam's answer to this sample question is choice B. A CRUMB is a small piece of BREAD just as a *splinter* is a small piece of *wood*.

SAT ANALOGIES: CRACKING THE SYSTEM

It's important to know the instructions printed before each analogy group on the SAT, but it is vastly more important to understand what those instructions mean. ETS's instructions don't tell you everything you need to know about SAT analogies. The rest of this chapter will teach you what you need to know.

One of your two scored thirty-minute verbal sections will contain a group of six analogies; the other will contain a group of thirteen. Each group of analogies will be arranged in order of increasing difficulty, from very easy to very hard.

In each group of analogies:

1. The first third will be easy.

2. The middle third will be medium.

3. The final third will be difficult.

Because our techniques vary depending on the difficulty of the question, the examples we use in this chapter will always be preceded by a Difficulty Meter. Always pay attention to where you are on the test when answering SAT questions.

Level of Difficulty

Set of 6
10–11 Easy
12–13 Medium
14–15 Difficult

Set of 13
11–14 Easy
15–19 Medium
20–23 Difficult

WHAT IS AN ANALOGY?

Every analogy question on the SAT begins with a pair of capitalized words called stem words. Your task is to determine how these words are related to each other and then select another pair of words that are related to each other *in exactly the same way*.

As you can see, determining the relationship between the stem words is pretty important. To get analogy questions right, you need to have more than just a vague idea of how these words are related. How can you determine the relationship between the stem words?

MAKE A SENTENCE

Make a *defining* sentence that connects the stem words. The operative word here is *defining*. You cannot make a sentence about the weather that just happens to include the stem words if you plan to get any of these questions right.

A defining sentence is one that:

- ◆ Uses one of the words to define the other.

- ◆ Is short and simple.

- ◆ Starts with one word and ends with the other.

The Dictionary, please

Your sentence should read like a dictionary definition, defining one word in terms of the other. For example, "KENNEL : DOG." If you were to look up *kennel* in the dictionary, you would find something like, "A *kennel* is a place to keep *dogs*."

Write a defining sentence for the following pair of words:

APPLE : FRUIT

An apple _____ fruit.

What Did You Get?

If you wrote something like, "An apple is a type of fruit," you are on the right track. If you wrote something flowery or descriptive like, "An apple is the most beautiful of all fruits," you are making it too complicated. You want to write a short, simple sentence that clearly indicates the relationship between the two words, as if you were looking them up in the dictionary.

DRILL 1

Make It Clear

Your sentence should be short, sweet, and to the point. If you are using words like "could," "might," or "sometimes," you are not identifying the definitional relationship between the words.

Practice making good defining sentences for the following pairs of words. Be sure to start each sentence with one of the words and end it with the other. By the way, it doesn't matter which word you place first and which you place second. If you find it easier to make a good sentence by switching the order of the words, go right ahead. See page 342 to check your answers.

ARCHITECT : BUILDING :: _____

WARDEN : PRISON :: _____

EDUCATION : IGNORANCE :: _____

AQUATIC : WATER :: _____

LETTERS : ALPHABET :: _____

Pam's Favorite Relationships

Certain kinds of analogy relationships tend to crop up again and again on the SAT. Here are the four most common types.

Type of

These are relationships in which one of the words is a "type of" the other word. For these pairs, your ready-made sentence is, "_is a type of_."

> LOLLIPOP : CANDY
>
> JUICE : BEVERAGE
>
> MAPLE : TREE

Degree

These are relationships in which one of the words is an extreme degree of the other. For each pair, your sentence will be, "_means extremely_" or "_means very little_."

Here are some examples:

> POUR : DRIP
>
> BREEZE : GALE
>
> FAMISHED : HUNGRY

Pour is an extreme form of *drip*. A *gale* is an extremely strong *breeze*. *Famished* means extremely *hungry*.

Means Without

In these relationships, one word means a lack of the other. Your sentence is, "_means without_."

Here are three examples:

> SHALLOW : DEPTH
>
> JUVENILE : MATURITY
>
> RANDOM : PATTERN

Shallow means without *depth*. *Juvenile* means without *maturity*. *Random* means without *pattern*.

Used to

In these relationships, one word describes the use or the purpose of the other word. "_is used to ."

Here are three examples:

SCISSORS : CUT

JOKE : AMUSE

BUTTRESS : SUPPORT

Scissors are used to *cut*. The purpose of a *joke* is to *amuse*. A *buttress* is used to *support*.

DOES IT FIT?

Once you've made a sentence, you need to find an answer choice that fits in it. Plug each answer choice into your sentence. Eliminate the answers that don't fit.

Try the following example:

10 COMPANY : PRESIDENT ::
(A) team : athlete
(B) hospital : patient
(C) airline : passenger
(D) library : reader
(E) army : general

Here's How to Crack It

First make a defining sentence: "A president is the head of a company." Then plug in the answer choices:

(A) Is an *athlete* the head of a *team*? Well, an athlete is a part of a team, but the head of a team would be a captain. Eliminate.

(B) Is a *patient* the head of a *hospital*? No. Eliminate.

(C) Is a *passenger* the head of an *airline*? No. Eliminate.

(D) Is a *reader* the head of a *library*? No. A reader might use a library, but a librarian is the head of the library. Eliminate.

(E) Is a *general* the head of an *army*? Yes. That's exactly what a general is. This is Pam's answer.

Let's try another one.

ANALOGIES

10 **11** 12 13 14 15

EASY   MEDIUM   HARD

11 APPLE : FRUIT ::

(A) meal : restaurant
(B) macaroni : cheese
(C) dessert : vegetable
(D) beef : meat
(E) crust : pizza

Consider the Possibilities

Read every answer choice before deciding which is "best." On question 11, even though D looked good immediately, we still checked choice E. If you answer too quickly, you may end up with a choice that sounds all right to you but is not as good as a choice you haven't read yet.

Here's How to Crack It

"An apple is a kind of fruit." Which answer choice fits?

(A) Is a *meal* a kind of *restaurant*? No. A restaurant is a place that serves meals. Eliminate.
(B) Is *macaroni* a kind of *cheese*? No. Eliminate.
(C) Is *dessert* a kind of *vegetable*? No. Eliminate.
(D) Is *beef* a kind of *meat*? Yes. A possibility.
(E) Is *crust* a kind of *pizza*? No. Eliminate.

Pam's answer has to be choice D. It's the only one we weren't able to eliminate.

You can even use this process when you don't know one of the words in an answer choice. Try the following example:

ANALOGIES

11 12 13 14 15 **16** 17 18 19 20 21 22 23

EASY   MEDIUM   HARD

16. DEHYDRATE : WATER ::

(A) polish : gloss
(B) soak : liquid
(C) ???? : steel
(D) rise : ????
(E) ???? : color

Here's How to Crack It

"Dehydrate means to lose water." Now we will plug in each answer choice. For the choices in which you are missing a word, simply ask if there's a word that *could* mean what the sentence is looking for.

(A) Does *polish* mean to lose *gloss*? No. It might mean to gain it, but this is not our answer. Eliminate.

(B) Does *soak* mean to lose *liquid*? No, it means to place in liquid. Eliminate.

(C) Could *something* mean to lose *steel*? Can you actually lose steel? This sentence doesn't make sense, even though we don't know one of the words. Cross it off.

(D) Could *rise* mean to lose *something*? Rise could probably mean to gain something, but not to lose something. Cross it off.

(E) Could *something* mean to lose *color*? Sure—fade means to lose color. Besides, we eliminated everything else. (E) is Pam's answer.

As you can see, making a good sentence can get you to the answer even when you don't know all the words in the answer choices.

MAKE IT BETTER

Sometimes, after plugging the choices into your sentence, you may find yourself with two or more answers that seem possible. In such cases, you'll have to go back, make your sentence more specific, and try again.

Here's an example:

12 TIGER : ANIMAL ::

(A) pigeon : hawk
(B) dinosaur : fossil
(C) shark : fish
(D) colt : horse
(E) tulip : flower

Suppose that your first sentence is "A tiger is a kind of animal." Plug in the choices:

(A) Is a *pigeon* a kind of *hawk*? No. Eliminate.
(B) Is a *dinosaur* a kind of *fossil*? Not really, although some people might think so. We won't eliminate it yet, although it isn't a very good possibility.
(C) Is a *shark* a kind of *fish*? Yes, a possibility.
(D) Is a *colt* a kind of *horse*? Yes, in a way. Another possibility.
(E) Is a *tulip* a kind of *flower*? Yes. Yet another possibility.

As you can see, the initial sentence isn't specific enough.

Here's How to Crack It

Make your sentence more specific. How do we do that? By keeping in mind *precisely* what the words mean. The important fact about a tiger is not simply that it is a kind of animal, but that it is a ferocious one, or a dangerous one, or a meat-eating one. The only answer choice that fulfills this requirement is C.

THE TOUGHER STUFF

By now you're probably getting pretty good at making defining sentences with the stem words. But what happens when you don't know one of the stem words? You certainly can't make a good sentence with the words if you are not sure what one of them means.

Relax. You can still answer an analogy question correctly, even if you don't know one of the stem words. Sounds impossible? It's not. It's called Working Backwards.

WORKING BACKWARDS

Do I Know vs. Could I Know?

When working backward, don't get bogged down in trying to think of a word to stand in for the word you don't understand. The question is not "What is yeast a kind of?" The question is, "Is there something that yeast is a kind of?" Combine your common sense with the understanding that the English language consists of hundreds of thousands of words. If an idea makes sense (yeast must fall into some kind of category) then you can assume that there is an English word that describes this category.

If you cannot make a sentence with the stem words, go to the answer choices and try to make defining sentences with each choice. One of two things will happen: either you won't be able to make a good, defining sentence, in which case you can eliminate that answer choice, or you will be able to make a good sentence, which would allow you to plug in the stem word you do know to see if it fits.

Think of it this way:

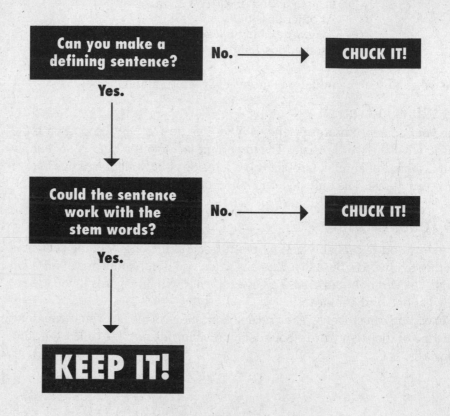

Try the following example:

ANALOGIES					
10	**11**	12	13	14	15
EASY		MEDIUM		HARD	

11   ???? : WIND DIRECTION::

  (A) thermometer : mercury
  (B) speedometer : pedal
  (C) hourglass : sand
  (D) barometer : heat
  (E) sundial : time

Here's How to Crack It

Since you don't know one of the stem words, you can't make a sentence. Instead, you need to Work Backwards. Let's look at each answer choice:

(A) Can you make a defining sentence with *thermometer* and *mercury*? Sure. "Mercury is in a thermometer." Can this sentence work with the stem word we know? Can *wind direction* be in something? No. This cannot be the answer. Eliminate.

(B) Can you make a defining sentence with *speedometer* and *pedal*? No. The speedometer and the pedal actually have nothing to do with each other. If you went to the dictionary and looked up either word, you would not find the other. Cross this answer off.

(C) Can you make a defining sentence with *hourglass* and *sand*? Sure. "Sand is in an hourglass." But this is the same sentence we made for answer choice (A). It doesn't work with the stem words. Cross it off.

(D) Can you make a sentence with *barometer* and *heat*? No. A barometer measures pressure; it has nothing to do with heat. Cross this answer off.

(E) Can you make a sentence with *sundial* and *time*? Sure. "A sundial shows the time." Could *something* show the *wind direction*? Yes. This is Pam's answer.

You've gotten the correct answer to a question in which you didn't even know one of the stem words. Pretty amazing, huh? Let's try another example:

???????? : MOTION ::

(A) numerology : progress
(B) navigation : ocean
(C) astronomy : weather
(D) criminology : perversion
(E) psychology : mind

Parts of Speech

When you are trying to make good sentences, it may help you to note the part of speech being used. All parts of speech are consistent throughout an analogy, so if the first word in a pair is a noun, all the first words will be nouns, etc. If you are having trouble making a sentence, check out the rest of the analogies to determine the part of speech being used.

Here's How to Crack It

Since you can't make a sentence of the stem words, go right to the answer choices and Work Backwards. Let's look at each answer choice:

(A) Can you make a sentence with *numerology* and *progress*? No. Numerology involves numbers, which doesn't have anything to do with progress (won't find these words together in the dictionary). Cross this answer off.

(B) Can you make a sentence with *navigation* and *ocean*? Sure. "Navigation is the science used to make one's way across the ocean." Now check the stem words: Is there *something* that means to make one's way across *motion*? No. This cannot be the answer. Eliminate it.

(C) Can you make a sentence with *astronomy* and *weather*? No. Don't confuse *astronomy* with *meteorology*. Cross off this answer.

(D) Can you make a sentence with *criminology* and *perversion*? No. These words don't really have anything to do with each other in a definitional sense (remember to avoid words like "sometimes" and "might.") Cross this off.

(E) Can you make a sentence with *psychology* and *mind*? Sure (not to mention, it's the only answer left). "*Psychology* is the study of the *mind*." Could *something* be the study of *motion*? Sure (it's called dynamics). This is Pam's answer.

Drill 2

Use the following drill to practice Working Backwards. For each pair of words, decide if they have a definitional relationship. If they do, write a defining sentence in the space provided. If not, write "No Relationship" in the blank.

If you aren't absolutely certain of the meaning of a word, look it up, add it to your word list, and make sure you know it before you take the SAT. Vocab plug: You can't write a defining sentence if you don't know what the words mean. We've answered the first three questions for you. Be sure to check your answers against the key on page 342.

1. acorn : nut   An *acorn* is a type of *nut*.

2. cardiologist : operations   No relationship

3. counselor : advice   A *counselor's* job is to give *advice*.

4. solar : sun _____

5. sticky : glue _____

6. purr : hunger _____

7. grateful : thanks _____

8. morsel : quantity _____

9. equine : horse _____

10. speculation : profit _____

11. preach : exhortation _____

12. dive : cliff _____

13. alias : identity _____

WHAT IF I DON'T KNOW EITHER WORD?

If you don't know either of the words in an *answer choice*, you obviously cannot make a sentence. However, don't simply cross it off! You cannot eliminate answers simply because you don't know the words. That would be very Joe Bloggs-like. Instead, leave the choice as a possibility. If you are working on a very hard question, the hardest answer choice may be your best guess (more on this later).

If you don't know either of the *stem words*, you can still Work Backwards. You won't be able to check your sentences again the stem words, but you will be able to eliminate the answer choices for which you could *not* make a good sentence.

Try the following example:

    12   __ : __
         (A) plentiful : resource
         (B) wealthy : money
         (C) voluntary : result
         (D) neutral : activity
         (E) humorous : movie

Here's How to Crack It

Since we have no idea what the given words are, ignore them and go right to the answer choices. Let's look at the choices one at a time:

> (A) Can we make a defining sentence with *plentiful* and *resource*? Not really. Plentiful means "lots of something" (not necessarily resources), and resources may or may not be plentiful. Cross this answer off.
>
> (B) Can we make a defining sentence with *wealthy* and *money*? Yes. "Wealthy means having lots of money." This is a possibility.

Take Five (Seconds)

If you can't find the relationship between two words after looking at them for five seconds (assuming you know the meanings of both words), then you should probably assume that there is no relationship. Pam isn't interested in how imaginative you are. You won't score any points with her for coming up with a brilliant justification for an incorrect answer. Pam thinks that the analogy section is fairly straightforward.

(C) Can we make a defining sentence with *voluntary* and *result*? Not at all. Eliminate it.

(D) Can we make a sentence with *neutral* and *activity*? No. Cross it off.

(E) Can we make a defining sentence with *humorous* and *movie*? Be careful—some movies are humorous, others are not. And, if you looked up "humorous" in the dictionary, you wouldn't find the word "movie." Eliminate this answer.

Pam's answer has to be (B). By Working Backwards, you were able to get this question right without having any idea what the stem words are. (FYI: The missing words are MASSIVE : SIZE.)

WILL IT ALWAYS WORK?

You may not always be able to eliminate the four wrong answer choices, but you will always be able to eliminate some answers on analogy questions, even when you don't know either stem word. In addition, Working Backwards can help you stretch your vocabulary. If, for example, you come to a pair of stem words that you *sort of* know (you've seen them before, you kind of know what they mean, but you don't feel entirely comfortable making a sentence), you can Work Backwards instead of trying to make a sentence with the stem words. Eliminate the answers that are not definitionally related. Make sentences with the answers that you can, and then test the stem words. Since you sort of know the meaning of the stem words, testing them in your Working Backwards sentences will be easy.

JOE BLOGGS AND SAT ANALOGIES

As is always true on the SAT, Joe Bloggs finds some answer choices much more appealing than others on analogy questions. Most of all, Joe is attracted to choices containing words that:

- ◆ remind him of one or both of the stem words
- ◆ "just seem to go with" the stem words
- ◆ are easy to understand

Cross It Out

When you eliminate an incorrect answer choice on any SAT question, draw a line through it in your test booklet. On harder questions, you may have to reread the answers several times before you settle on one. If you cross out choices you've eliminated, you won't waste time reconsidering wrong answers over and over again.

ELIMINATING JOE'S ANSWERS ON DIFFICULT QUESTIONS

The Joe Bloggs principle is most useful in helping you eliminate incorrect answer choices on the difficult third of the analogies. To do this, you need to know how to spot choices that seem right to Joe.

Here's an example:

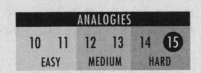

```
              ANALOGIES
    ⑩   11   12   13   14   15
       EASY   MEDIUM   HARD
```

10 SONG : VERSES ::

(A) moon : phases
(B) tree : roots
(C) battle : soldiers
(D) poem : stanzas
(E) newspaper : reporters

Here's How to Crack It

Which choice attracts Joe Bloggs on this question? Choice D. SONGS and VERSES just seem to go with *poems* and *stanzas*. Does that mean choice D is wrong? No! Look at the number of this question. It's a number 10, the easiest in its group. Joe Bloggs gets the easy ones right, and D is Pam's answer.

But Joe's impulse to pick answers that "just seem to go with" the words in capital letters will get him in trouble on hard questions. After all, if Joe knew the answer to a hard analogy, it wouldn't be hard, would it? On the hardest analogy questions, therefore, you can safely eliminate choices that you know would seem attractive to Joe Bloggs. Before you do anything else on a hard question, look for Joe's answers and cross them out.

Try this:

```
              ANALOGIES
    10   11   12   13   14   ⑮
       EASY   MEDIUM   HARD
```

15 INFINITESIMAL : SIZE ::

(A) trifling : significance
(B) distant : galaxy
(C) cacophonous : music
(D) lucid : behavior
(E) enormous : mountain

Here's How to Crack It

Which choices attract Joe on this question? Choice E definitely does, because *enormous* makes Joe think of SIZE. What does that mean? It means that E cannot possibly be Pam's answer, because this is a hard question and Joe doesn't get the hard questions right.

Joe may also be attracted to choice B: *Galaxies* are large, so in Joe's mind this choice "just seems to go with" the words in capital letters. That means you can also eliminate choice B. Even if you can't eliminate anything else, you've already got a once-in-three chance of guessing Pam's answer.

(Pam's answer is A. INFINITESIMAL means extremely small, or lacking in SIZE, and *trifling* means lacking in *significance*.)

A Gentle Reminder

Easy questions tend to have easy answers. Hard questions tend to have hard answers.

cacophonous (adj.) harsh-sounding, unpleasant sounding, discordant. The Greek root *phon* describes sound. A *telephone* transmits sound. A *megaphone* increases the loudness of a sound. A *phonograph* is a recording of sound.

Here's another example:

| 14 | DESTITUTION : MONEY ::

    (A) budget : options
    (B) sobriety : inebriation
    (C) opulence : wealth
    (D) deficit : finance
    (E) pollution : factory

Here's How to Crack It

This is the next-to-last question in its group, which means it's hard. Joe Bloggs will definitely get it wrong.

DESTITUTION is a very hard word. Most people, including Joe Bloggs, don't know what it means. MONEY, however, is an easy word. Joe looks through the choices for a word that seems to go with money. He finds three choices that attract him: *budget* in choice A, *wealth* in choice C, and *finance* in choice D. Joe will weigh these three choices and then pick one of them.

With choices A, C, and D out of the way, let's take a look at the remaining choices. Answer choice B has hard words, so it could definitely be the answer. Choice E, on the other hand, has easier words. So you can ask yourself: Can I make a defining sentence with *pollution* and *factory*? Pollution can come from a factory, but does it *have* to come from a factory? If you looked up *pollution* in the dictionary, would the definition be something that comes from a factory? Probably not (look it up and see). Would the definition of *factory* be something that produces pollution? No, that's not what a factory is by definition. If you can't make a defining sentence, it can't be the answer. Pam's answer must be (B).

By Working Backwards and using the Joe Bloggs principle, we were once again able to find Pam's answer without even knowing one of the stem words.

HARD QUESTIONS, HARD ANSWERS

Joe Bloggs doesn't like problems that look too hard, and he doesn't like complicated solutions. This means that he has a strong tendency to select choices containing words that he understands and is familiar with. When Joe takes a stab at a question, he picks something easy and familiar.

This can be a big help for you. Because Joe is so irresistibly drawn to easy choices, one of the best places to look for Pam's answer on a hard analogy question is among the hard choices—choices containing words that Joe doesn't understand. When you find yourself stumped on a hard analogy, simply eliminate what you can and then select the remaining choice that contains the hardest and weirdest words.

PICK THE WEIRD ONE

Easy analogies have easy answers; hard analogies have hard answers. If you've eliminated what you can and are guessing on a hard analogy, go with the hardest, *weirdest* answer choice.

Drill 3

In the following two examples, Work Backwards to eliminate what you can. Then guess the hardest, weirdest answer for each question. See page 342 to check your answers.

15 ???? : ???? ::

- (A) fabric : weaving
- (B) watercolor : painting
- (C) script : drama
- (D) embellishments : description
- (E) partner : dance

15 ???? : ???? ::

- (A) dither : choice
- (B) dawdle : excuse
- (C) chatter : speech
- (D) mope : laughter
- (E) bustle : arrival

ANALOGIES SUMMARY

We've now given you several effective techniques that you can use to find Pam's answer to analogy questions. To summarize our approach, we're going to show you which techniques to use and when to use them, depending on whether you can make a good sentence with the stem words. If you don't know the meaning of both stem words, then you'll probably have trouble making a sentence. But as you've seen, you can still attack the answer choices.

When you attack any analogy question, you will find yourself in one of the following three situations. Here's the definitive approach for each of them.

When You Can Make a Sentence with the Stem Words

1. Make a short, specific defining sentence with the stem words. By defining sentence, we mean a sentence that:
    ◆ Uses one word to define the other.
    ◆ Is short and simple.
    ◆ Starts with one word and ends with the other.

2. Plug each answer choice into your sentence. Be sure to check *every* answer choice. Cross out any answer choices that don't fit your sentence. Pam's answer will be the answer choice the fits your sentence best.

3. If you find that more than one answer choice works with your sentence, go back and make your sentence more specific. Then try your new sentence with the remaining answer choices.

When You Can't Make a Sentence, But You Know at Least One of the Stem Words

1. If you are working on a hard question, eliminate Joe Bloggs answers.

2. Work Backwards. Go to each answer choice and try to make a defining sentence. If you can make a sentence, plug in the stem word or words you know to see if they fit. If they do, keep that choice. If not, cross it off.

3. If you cannot make a defining sentence with an answer choice, cross it off.

4. If you are left with more than one possible answer choice after Working Backwards, take a guess (easy questions have easy answers; hard questions have hard answers).

When You Can't Make a Sentence and You Don't Know Either of the Words in Capital Letters

1. Eliminate any Joe Bloggs answers.

2. Work Backwards. Try to make a defining sentence with each answer choice. Cross off the answers that do not have a definitional relationship.

3. When all else fails, pick the choice with the hardest, weirdest words that Joe Bloggs would never want to pick.

8

Critical Reading

MEMORIZE THE INSTRUCTIONS

This chapter is about critical reading, the last of the three question types on the verbal SAT. Critical reading appears in all three verbal sections of the test, and accounts for half of all the points that can be scored on the verbal SAT, so this chapter is important.

Before we begin, take a moment to read the following set of instructions, which appears exactly as it does on the real SAT.

> Each passage below is followed by questions based on its content. Answer the questions following each passage on the basis of what is stated or implied in that passage and in any introductory material that may be provided.

Be sure that you know and understand these instructions before you take the SAT. If you learn them ahead of time, you won't have to waste valuable seconds reading them on the day you take the test.

SAT CRITICAL READING: CRACKING THE SYSTEM

It's important to know the instructions printed before each group of critical reading passages in the SAT, but it's vastly more important to understand what those instructions mean. ETS's instructions don't tell you everything you need to know about critical reading. The rest of this chapter will tell you what you need to know.

Our techniques will enable you to:

1. read for what you need,
2. eliminate answer choices that could not possibly be correct,
3. take advantage of outside knowledge,
4. take advantage of inside knowledge (about how Pam thinks),
5. make better use of your limited time by skipping a difficult passage.

JUST THE QUESTIONS, PLEASE

The least important part of Critical Reading is the passage. No, really. The name of the section implies you will be doing lots of reading, but it doesn't tell you that most of the reading you'll be doing is of the questions. Critical reading is *not* about learning something new and interesting—it's about scoring points by answering questions correctly.

Many students have difficulty with Critical Reading because they place too much emphasis on the passage and not enough on the questions. In actuality, you could probably answer many questions more effectively if you never read the passage at all.

Look at the following question. Without so much as a glance at a passage, use your common sense and knowledge of ETS to cross off impossible answers.

The Fact Bank

Somebody once asked notorious thief Willie Sutton why he robbed banks. "Because that's where the money is," he replied. While cracking Critical Reading is safer and slightly more productive than larceny, the same principle applies: Concentrate on the questions and answer choices, because that's where the points are. The passage is just a place for Pam to stash facts and details. You'll find them when you need to. What's the point of memorizing all sixty-seven pesky details about plankton if Pam only asks you about twelve?

Then take a guess at Pam's answer.

18 The author believes that federal judges can sometimes be criticized for

(A) failing to consider the meaning of the law
(B) ignoring the rights of defendants
(C) letting their personal opinions influence the outcomes of trials
(D) slowing the flow of court cases by caring too much about the requirements of justice
(E) forgetting that the Constitution is the foundation of the American legal system

Here's How to Crack It

The question wants to know what an *ETS author* might criticize a federal judge for. The answer, of course, is "not much." ETS is a very pro-American, pro-justice system organization. After all, they as a company are thriving on the American way. Therefore, ETS is very careful to be respectful of the right people.

Let's look at each answer choice to see if it is possible:

(A) Could ETS criticize federal judges for "failing to consider the meaning of the law"? A federal judge doesn't consider the law? Not likely. This answer is not possible because it would never happen. Even though you have no idea what this passage is about, you can cross off this answer choice.

(B) Could ETS criticize federal judges for "ignoring the rights of defendants"? Another unlikely practice of a federal judge. Even if *you* have a jaded opinion of our federal legal system, *ETS* doesn't. This answer is not possible—cross it off.

(C) Could ETS criticize federal judges for "letting their personal opinions influence the outcomes of trials"? Although this answer seems a little more plausible, it's still pretty unlikely. Federal judges represent the epitome of impartiality, at least according to ETS. Keep it for now, but it is unlikely.

(D) Could ETS criticize federal judges for "slowing the flow of court cases by caring too much about the requirements of justice"? What a laudable error, huh? ETS could criticize them for this honorable mistake. Lookin' good as a choice.

(E) Could ETS criticize federal judges for "forgetting that the Constitution is the foundation of the American legal system"? Would a federal judge simply *forget* about the Constitution? Not likely. Cross this off.

Of the two choices remaining, the most reasonable guess is (D). It is also Pam's answer.

GOOD ANSWER

You just answered a Critical Reading question correctly without ever seeing the passage it was associated with. What does that tell you about Critical Reading questions? It tells you that there's a lot more to answering a Critical Reading question than reading the passage. In fact, reading the passage is the least important part of answering CR questions.

Will you be answering lots of questions without reading the passage? No, for two reasons: 1) It takes longer to answer a question when you have no knowledge of the passage, and 2) Why should you answer the question this way when all the answers are right there in front of you?

OPEN BOOK TEST

Critical Reading is nothing more than an open book test. If your history teacher tells you that Friday's exam is going to be an open book test, what's your reaction? Okay, you can sit down now. Most people do the "this is gonna be easy" dance when they are told that all the info they need to know will be right in front of them.

Well, Critical Reading is exactly the same as an open book test. What's more, you only have to scan a few paragraphs to find your answers. For each CR passage, you will do the following:

1. **Read What You Need**. Do a topic search so that you have a clue about the passage's topic and organization.

2. **Translate the Question.** Reword each question so you know exactly what you are being asked.

3. **Put Your Finger On The Answer.** Go back to the passage and find the exact location of the answer you are looking for.

4. **Answer the Question in Your Own Words**. Answer the question in your own words before you read any of the answer choices.

5. **Use POE.** Get rid of answers that are not close to yours.

SAMPLE PASSAGE AND QUESTIONS

Here is an example of what a CR passage and questions look like. We will use this passage to illustrate CR techniques. You may want to stick a paper clip on this page to make it easier to flip back to it.

Questions 16–21 are based on the following passage.

The following passage is a summary of a sociological study concerning groups of Mexican-American women.

The subject of my study is women who are initiating social change in a small region in Texas. The women are Mexican-Americans who are, or
Line
(5) were, migrant agricultural workers. There is more than one kind of innovation at work in the region, of course, but I have chosen to focus on three related patterns of family behavior.

The pattern I lifestyle represents how migrant farm workers of all nationalities lived in the past
(10) and how many continue to live. I treat this pattern as a baseline with which to compare the changes represented by patterns II and III. Families in pattern I work on farms year round, migrating for as many as ten months each year. They work and
(15) travel in extended kin units, with the eldest male occupying the position of authority. Families are large—eight or nine children are not unusual—and all members are economic contributors in this strategy of family migration. The children receive
(20) little formal schooling.

Families in pattern II manifest some differences in behavior while still maintaining aspects of pattern I. They continue to migrate but on a reduced scale, often modifying their schedules of migration to
(25) allow children to finish the school year. Parents in this pattern often find temporary local jobs as checkers or clerks to offset lost farming income. Pattern II families usually have fewer children than do pattern I families, and the children make a far
(30) smaller contribution to the economic welfare of the family.

The greatest amount of change from pattern I, however, is found in pattern III families, who no longer migrate at all. Both parents work full time in
(35) the area, and they have an average of three children. The children attend school for the entire year. In pattern III, the women in particular create new roles for themselves for which no local models exist. They not only work full time but may, in
(40) addition, return to school. They also assume a greater responsibility in planning family activities, setting household budgets, and making other domestic decisions than do women in the other patterns. Although these women are in the minority
(45) among residents of the region, they serve as role

models for others, causing ripples of change to spread in their communities.

New opportunities have continued to be determined by pre-existing values. When federal
(50) jobs became available in the region, most involved working under the direction of female professionals such as teachers or nurses. Such positions were unacceptable to many men in the area because they were not accustomed to being
(55) subordinate to women. Women therefore took the jobs, at first, because the income was desperately needed. But some of the women decided to stay at their jobs after the family's distress was over. These women enjoyed their work, its responsibility, and
(60) the companionship of fellow women workers. The steady, relatively high income allowed their families to stop migrating. And, as the efficaciousness of these women became increasingly apparent, they and their families
(65) became even more willing to consider changes in their lives that they would not have considered before.

16 Which of the following titles best reflects the main focus of the passage?

(A) A Study of Three Mexican-American Families at Work in Texas
(B) Innovative Career Women: Effects on Family Unity
(C) Changes in the Lifestyles of Migrant Mexican-American Families
(D) Farming or Family: The Unavoidable Choice for Migrant Farm Workers
(E) Recent Changes in Methods of Farming in Texas

17 According to the passage, pattern I families are characterized by which of the following?

(A) Small numbers of children
(B) Brief periods of migrant labor
(C) Female figures of family authority
(D) Commercial as well as agricultural sources of income
(E) Parents and children working and traveling together

18 All of the following statements about pattern II children express differences between them and pattern I children EXCEPT:

(A) They migrate for part of each year.
(B) They have fewer siblings.
(C) They spend less time contributing to family income.
(D) They spend more months in school.
(E) Their parents sometimes work at jobs other than farming.

19 The word "domestic" in line 43 most nearly means

(A) crucial
(B) native
(C) unspoken
(D) imported
(E) household

20 According to the passage, which of the following is NOT true of women in pattern III families?

(A) They earn a reliable and comparatively high income.
(B) They continue to work solely to meet the urgent needs of their family.
(C) They are more involved in the deciding of family issues than they once were.
(D) They enjoy the fellowship involved in working with other women.
(E) They serve as models of behavior for others in the region.

21 The author's attitude toward the three patterns of behavior mentioned in the passage is best described as one of

(A) great admiration
(B) grudging respect
(C) unbiased objectivity
(D) dissatisfaction
(E) indifference

READ WHAT YOU NEED

Passage Types

Critical Reading passages come from four broad subject areas:

1. Science: discoveries, controversies, or other topics in physics, chemistry, astronomy, biology, medicine, botany, zoology, and the other sciences.

2. Humanities: excerpts from essays about art, literature, music, philosophy, or folklore; discussions of artists, novelists, or historical figures.

3. Social sciences: topics in politics, economics, sociology, or history.

4. Narrative: usually excerpts from novels, short stories, or humorous essays. (We have yet to see a poem on the SAT.)

Pam usually includes a passage involving a historically overlooked community or social group. This "ethnic" passage, as we call it, is usually either a social science or humanities passage.

What do you need to know about a CR passage before you head to the questions? Three things:

◆ The author's point

◆ The author's tone

◆ The passage layout

Virtually every SAT reading passage has the same basic structure: The author has a point. Her primary purpose is to develop or explain this point. She does this by stating her point and then supporting it with details, facts, examples, metaphors, and secondary ideas. The author also has an attitude toward her subject (she may be *for* something, *against* something, or neutral), which she conveys in her tone or style.

You also need to get the gist of how the passage is organized. Remember our open book test from history class? You may not go home and study for that open book test, but it would behoove you to organize your notes a bit so you can find answers in a timely fashion. The same holds true for CR passages. You want a sense of where the author put stuff so you can find answers easily.

To access the initial stuff you need from a passage quickly and easily, you're going to do a topic search. To do a topic search, read:

◆ **The blurb.** Most CR passages are introduced by a brief italicized paragraph that gives you some idea of what the passage is about. Read it carefully.

◆ **The first few sentences of paragraph one.** Get an idea of what the author is saying. Once you feel you have a clue, jot a note and move on.

◆ **The first sentence of the remaining paragraphs.** Jot a note next to each paragraph so you have a handle on the passage structure.

◆ **The last sentence.** Read the last sentence so you know how the passage winds up. Jot a note to yourself about the author's overall point and tone.

TOPIC SEARCH TEST DRIVE

Flip back to our sample passage on page 92 and try a topic search. Be sure to jot quick notes to yourself so you know what's going on. Then flip back here to see how you did.

Here's How to Crack It

First, read the blurb:

> *The following passage is a summary of a sociological*
> *study concerning groups of Mexican-American women.*

This sets you on the right track. Now read the first few sentences of the passage:

> "The subject of my study is women who are
> initiating social change in a small region in Texas.
> The women are Mexican-Americans who are, or
> were, migrant agricultural workers."

As you read, the following phrases ought to attract your attention: *women who are initiating social change; Mexican-American; migrant agricultural workers*. The author's point, or most of it, is right here. The main idea might be stated quickly, as "Mexican-American migrant women workers initiating social change," or something similar. Don't sweat the details. Move on.

The structure of this passage is so straightforward that you won't even need so much as the entire first sentence of any succeeding paragraph. By glancing at the first sentence of each paragraph you can figure out that the second paragraph is about *pattern I lifestyle*, the third paragraph is about *pattern II*, and the fourth paragraph is about *pattern III*.

Remember: You aren't looking for details right now. You're looking for the author's point, and you're getting a sense of how the passage is put together. The author is writing about lifestyles, and each of these paragraphs deals with a different one.

The last paragraph is full of details and sociological jargon. Don't get bogged down on big words. Focus on the final sentence. In the future, the women and their families will be "even more willing to consider changes." That's all you need to notice for now.

Jot a quick note to yourself on the author's point and tone:

- The author's point: Mexican-American women workers are initiating change.

- The author's tone: Neutral-positive.

Why Write It Down?

As you know, when you take a test under pressure, it's easy to forget stuff, lose your focus, and then feel rushed and out of control. The more you write in your test booklet, the less likely you are to do a mental drift, or lose information that "you know you saw *somewhere* in the passage." On Critical Reading it is imperative that you jot notes as you go along so you can easily find the info you need when you go back.

HEAD FOR THE QUESTIONS

Your initial search should only take a minute or two. Once you have a clue about the author's point and the layout of the passage, head for the questions.

Unlike the other sections of the SAT, CR questions are *not* arranged in order of difficulty. They are, however, arranged in chronological order. In other words, a question about the first paragraph will come before a question about the second paragraph, and so on. Most of the questions you'll encounter will ask for specific details from the passage. For the most part, you will answer CR questions in the order they are given.

TRANSLATING

In the Form of a Question

One way Pam confuses test takers is by replacing questions with incomplete sentences: "The primary purpose of the passage is..." instead of "What is the primary purpose of the passage?" Many students find it easier to understand what Pam is driving at if they rephrase her incomplete sentences as questions beginning with "What" or "Why." "What" questions ask for things (facts, ideas). "Why" questions ask for reasons.

The most important reading you will do on the CR section of the test is when you read the questions. Pam has gone out of her way to make CR questions hard to understand. Therefore, before you go searching for answers to any question, put the question in "English" so you know what you are being asked.

Take a look at the following question. What are you being asked?

1. According to the passage, the "language of bureaucracy" and the "language of liberation" are alike in that they take into account which one of the following?

Let's simplify this a bit. "According to the passage..." means look at the passage. Cross off this phrase since it is extra and simply adds confusion. "The 'language of bureaucracy' and the 'language of liberation' are alike..." How are these two languages similar?

The rest of the sentence is fluff ("in that they take into account") followed by a *see the answer choices* phrase ("which of the following"). Cross off the last part of the sentence. To answer this question, you need to know how the two languages mentioned are similar.

Flip back to our passage on page 92. Read each question and translate it. If there is anything about the question you find confusing, put it into "English." Cross off unnecessary phrases. Make sure you know exactly what you are being asked. When you finish, flip back here to see how you did.

What the Questions Really Ask

16. What's the best title for this passage?

17. What are characteristics of pattern I families?

18. Pattern II children are different from pattern I children in lots of ways. Four of the answer choices are differences. Pick out the answer that is *not* a difference.

19. Clear as written.

20. Four of the answer choices are truths about pattern III women. Which one is *not* true?

21. What's the author's attitude?

Now let's talk about how to answer each of these questions.

GIVE IT THE FINGER

Once you know what a question is asking, you can head back to the passage to find the answer. For the most part, the only way to answer CR questions correctly is to put your finger on the answer in the passage. Use the notes you jotted as you searched the passage to help you locate the answers you need. Once you find the part of the passage that contains your answer, translate it into "English." In other words, *answer the question in your own words* before you look at any answer choices.

Translate the following passage excerpt into "English" :

> The luminist school of American landscape
> painting drenched the monumental vistas of the
> American West in golden, surreal light,
> transforming already striking scenes into glimpses
> of Utopia.

In other words, "luminist school painters used lots of light to paint scenes of the West, making the scenes even more beautiful."

ANSWER THE QUESTION

Answering the questions in your own words before looking at any answer choices will keep you from getting trapped by Pam's distracter answers. You can bet that Joe Bloggs isn't answering the questions in his own words. In fact, Joe is reading the passage slowly and carefully, trying to memorize a bunch of facts he hardly understands, and then trying to answer a bunch a questions he hardly understands without going back to the passage. He's sunk from the start.

You, on the other hand, have already searched the passage, translated the question, and are now ready to find your answer. How can you do this?

Questions often contain clues that point to the answer in the passage. In addition to your notes, you can use these clues to zero in on the answers you are looking for.

Line References

The best clue that Pam gives you for finding her answer within a passage is a *line reference*. The majority of the questions in each critical reading section will refer to some line or lines in the passage. For example, Pam might ask you to determine what the passage says about "new research in the field of genetics" in lines 21–25.

Line reference questions will be phrased something like this:

> "According to paragraph 3 (lines 34–50),
> scientists studied the comet in order to"

> "In lines 56–75, the narrator is primarily
> concerned with"

> "The author uses the quote from Johnson's
> book (line 79) to demonstrate that"

They Don't Care What You Know

More than one million students take the SAT every year. They can't all have studied the same subjects, so Pam can't expect you to know anything she hasn't told you. This is important to remember on specific questions. All you have to do is find something the passage already states.

Pam will try to trip you up by asking questions that seem to have one answer but actually have another. Often the real answer will be hiding behind a trigger word. In writing her questions, Pam looks for places in the passage where meanings change. She thinks of each of these changes as a trap for a careless reader — for Joe Bloggs. If you pay attention to the trigger words, you will be able to avoid many of Pam's traps. See the Sentence Completion chapter for a review of trigger words.

"According to paragraph 2, the new species of penguins are an 'important find' (line 20) because they are"

These line references will be a big help when you go back to the passage to look for Pam's answer, because they tell you approximately where to look. We say approximately because, of course, Pam never makes your life that easy. If Pam refers to lines 33–36, the answer to her question will actually be in lines 31–32, or in lines 37–39.

Read at least five lines above and five lines below the lines mentioned in the question in order to be sure that you've found Pam's answer.

VOCABULARY IN CONTEXT

Pam also uses line reference questions to test vocabulary. For example, a question may ask you for the meaning of the word *stupefying* in line 12. Attack these questions aggressively, handling them in exactly the same way we've taught you to handle sentence completions. Even if you don't know the meaning of the word, the context should enable you to eliminate several incorrect choices using POE. Here's our step-by-step strategy:

1. Cover the answer choices so that you won't be influenced by them.

2. Go to the passage and read the sentence that contains the word being tested.

3. Draw a line through the word with your pencil. Read the sentence again and come up with your own word for the blank (just as you would on a sentence completion). If you don't come up with a word on your first try, read one sentence before and one sentence after. Using the context will give you clues.

4. Once you've settled on your own word, uncover the answer choices and use POE to eliminate those choices that are not like your word.

It is very important to use this method in answering these questions. If you simply plug in the choices—Joe Bloggs's favorite technique—you may fall into a trap. Pam's answer will often be a secondary meaning of the word she has asked you to define. If you go straight to the choices, you may be irresistibly attracted to one that might be correct in a different context, but is dead wrong in this one. Covering up the answer choices will eliminate temptation. Don't get careless.

Take another look at question 19 in our sample passage.

> **19** The word "domestic" in line 43 most nearly means
>
> (A) crucial
> (B) native
> (C) unspoken
> (D) imported
> (E) household

Here's How to Crack It

Cover up the answer choices. Then find the word in the passage and lightly draw a line through it. Now proceed as though trying to anticipate Pam's answer for a sentence completion problem.

Here's the sentence you are trying to complete:

"They also assume a greater responsibility in planning family activities, setting household budgets, and making other _____ decisions than do women in the other patterns."

The *decisions* in question are *other* decisions, meaning that making them is like *planning family activities* or *setting household budgets*. As a result, the word that belongs in the blank means something like *family* or *household*. Now look at the choices.

(A) Nothing like the word you anticipated. This may be a tempting choice for a test taker who doesn't have any idea what *domestic* means. Joe is drawn to this choice, because he figures that the women's new decisions must be important. Eliminate.

(B) Nothing like the word you anticipated. This is one meaning of *domestic*, but it is not Pam's answer. *Domestic* in the context of the passage does not mean *native* or *from one's own country* (as it might if the paragraph were discussing the difference between domestic and foreign cars).

(C) Nothing like the word you anticipated.

(D) Nothing like the word you anticipated. This is the opposite of a meaning of *domestic* that doesn't apply in this context.

(E) Here's one of the words you anticipated. This is Pam's answer.

Lead Words

Some specific questions in the critical reading section will not have line references. For these questions, Pam gives a different clue that tells you where to look for her answer. For example, if a question asked about the author's opinion of the "volcano theory," you would naturally go back to the passage and find the lines that mention the volcano theory. Every specific question that does not have a line reference has a word or phrase that you can use to find Pam's answer in the passage. We call these *lead words*. In our example, *volcano theory* would be the lead words for the question.

Lead word questions are phrased like this:

"The author suggests that science fiction writers have a tendency to"

"According to the passage, which of the following is a feature of architecture in the 1960s?"

"The author of the passage suggests that she was able to sell her first painting because"

"In the passage, the invention of the microchip was similar to"

In each of the questions above, there is a phrase—*science fiction writers, architecture in the 1960s, sell her first painting, invention of the microchip*—that you could use as lead words to find Pam's answer in the passage. And you won't have to search the whole passage to find where the lead words are mentioned. Since questions about a passage are in chronological order, you can use line reference questions that come before and after a lead word question to help you locate your answer.

As with line references, once you find the lead words in the passage, you must read at least five lines above and five lines below the line that contains the lead words. Keep reading until you can put your finger on Pam's answer. Answer the question in your own words, then eliminate answers that don't match yours.

Take another look at question 17 following our sample passage:

17 According to the passage, pattern I families are characterized by which of the following?

(A) Small numbers of children
(B) Brief periods of migrant labor
(C) Female figures of family authority
(D) Commercial as well as agricultural sources of income
(E) Parents and children working and traveling together

Here's How to Crack It

Our translated question asks, "What are characteristics of pattern I families?" This question doesn't have a line reference, but it does have some excellent lead words: *pattern I families*. Where did the author discuss pattern I families? Paragraph two. Go back and read what you need. Once you've gotten a handle on the characteristics of pattern I families (a.k.a. answered the question in your own words), go through each answer choice and use POE.

Let's look at each answer choice:

(A) Eliminate. The paragraph says pattern I families *are large—eight or nine children are not unusual.*

(B)   Eliminate. Pattern I families migrate *for as many as ten months each year*.

(C)   Eliminate. In pattern I families, *the eldest male* is the figure of family authority.

(D)   Eliminate. Pattern I families *work on farms year round*.

(E)   This is Pam's answer. The paragraph says that pattern I families *work and travel in extended kin units*. (Besides, we've eliminated everything else.)

THE AUTHOR'S POINT

There are some questions that ask general stuff about the passage. Usually, these questions want to know the author's main idea, tone, etc. Do you need to go back to the passage to answer these questions? No. You already know the author's point from your topic search. Simply use that information plus the information you gather from answering specific questions to answer any general questions you come across.

Let's look at number 16 from our sample passage.

Cross It Off

On CR questions, it is very likely you may need to read a few of the answer choices more than once. To avoid confusion, be sure you cross off each answer entirely when you eliminate something. That way, if you have two or three choices you are considering, you can easily tell which choices are left in the running and which you have eliminated.

16   Which of the following titles best reflects the main focus of the passage?

(A) A Study of Three Mexican-American Families at Work in Texas
(B) Innovative Career Women: Effects on Family Unity
(C) Changes in the Lifestyles of Migrant Mexican-American Families
(D) Farming or Family: The Unavoidable Choice for Migrant Farm Workers
(E) Recent Changes in Methods of Farming in Texas

Here's How to Crack It

Our translated question asks, "What the best title for this passage?" Answer the question in your own words before you read Pam's choices. We said the passage was about Mexican-American women workers initiating change, so our title should be something like, "Mexican-American Women Make Changes."

Let's look at each answer choice:

(A) This answer seems close, but it is actually the Joe Bloggs answer. It doesn't mention anything about changes. Be careful of Pam's attractive distracters.

(B) Again be careful. This answer mentions career women, not *Mexican-American* career women. Also, the passage doesn't focus on family unity. Eliminate this answer choice.

(C) Sounds good.

(D) This passage does not say the women must choose one or the other. Cross this off.

(E) This answer is plain wrong—the passage is not about farming.

Pam's answer is (C). Answering the question in your own words before looking at the answer choices saved you from picking the Joe Bloggs answer. Be sure to have a good idea of the answer to a question in your mind before you read any answer choices.

Try number 21 in our sample passage. When you have finished, come back here to check your work.

Here's How to Crack It

The question asks for the author's tone, which we said was neutral-positive. You can therefore immediately cross off any extreme or negative choices. This eliminates answers (B) and (D). What about (E)? Can an author be *indifferent*? If she doesn't care about a subject, she wouldn't write about it. *Indifferent* is never the author's tone. Cross off (E).

You are down to (A) and (C). "Great admiration" is very positive—in fact, too positive for our passage. Our author was essentially neutral. Pam's answer is (C).

THE TOUGH STUFF

As we mentioned, you will answer most critical reading questions in the order they appear. However, there are some CR questions that are harder and more time-consuming to answer than the others. These will be your "Later" questions.

Later questions ask you for a lot more than just some basic information from the passage. They may ask you to weaken or strengthen the author's point. They may ask you to identify an underlying assumption the author is making. If you read a question that sounds time-consuming, save it for later. Also, if you read a question and have no clue where to find the answer in the passage, save it for later. The information you learn from answering the other questions about a passage will often make these *later* questions a little easier to do.

There are a few types of *later* questions that come up frequently on a test. Let's take a look at them.

EXCEPT . . . NOT!

Pam's EXCEPT/LEAST/NOT questions are big time-wasters. Think about it: You're really answering four questions for the price of one. Most of these questions expect you to find four pieces of information in the passage, but only reward you with one measly point. Do them last, if at all.

Do It Later

Look at question #18 from our sample passage.

18 All of the following statements about pattern II children express differences between them and pattern I children EXCEPT:

(A) They migrate for part of each year.
(B) They have fewer siblings.
(C) They spend less time contributing to family income.
(D) They spend more months in school.
(E) Their parents sometimes work at jobs other than farming.

When we translated our question, we took into account what the word "EXCEPT" means in a question. "EXCEPT" in a question means that *four* of the choices you read will be true, while only *one* of the answer choices will be false. Your job is to identify the false answer choice. This takes a bit more work than a normal question.

To crack an "EXCEPT" question, first go back to the passage and put your finger on the answer to the question (disregarding the "EXCEPT" part). In question 18, we need to know the differences between pattern II children and pattern I children. Go back and read the third paragraph to familiarize yourself with the differences and similarities. Then come back here to answer the question.

Once you have a clue as to what the differences are, read each answer choice and mark it "T" for true if it is a difference between the two groups, or "F" for false if it is not. Don't hesitate to go back to paragraph three as often as you need to.

Here's How to Crack It

Let's look at each answer choice:

(A) False. According to paragraph three, both groups migrate for part of the year. This is not a difference between the groups.

(B) True. The parents often have fewer children in pattern II than the parents in pattern I.

(C) True. This is stated in paragraph three.

(D) True. This is also stated in paragraph three.

(E) True. It says so in the paragraph.

What is the answer to this question? Use the *Sesame Street* Method: One of these things in not like the other. Pam's answer is (A).

Notice that although getting the answer to this question was not difficult, it was more time-consuming. Leave these questions for later—do them after you have done the shorter, easier questions about a passage.

I, II, III Questions

Occasionally on the SAT, you will find a question like the following:

29 According to the author, which of the
following characteristics is (are) common to
both literature and biology?

   I. They are concerned with living creatures.
  II. They enrich human experience.
 III. They are guided by scientific principles.

(A) I only
(B) II only
(C) III only
(D) I and III
(E) I, II, and III

EXCEPT . . . NOT

There's another reason why you should answer EXCEPT/LEAST/NOT questions last. Once you've answered all the other questions, you have a good idea of what facts in the passage are important to Pam and where to find them. By answering other questions, you may also have gathered information that you can use to eliminate wrong answers on EXCEPT/LEAST/NOT questions. You're the one taking the test; make it work for *you*.

We call these "I, II, III questions." We could also call them "triple true/false questions," because you are really being asked to determine whether each of three separate statements is true or false. These questions are very time-consuming, and you will receive credit only if you answer all three parts of the question correctly. Therefore, you should save them for last. Still, these questions are excellent for educated guessing, because you can improve your odds dramatically by using POE.

As is usually true on the SAT, the key to success is taking one step at a time. Consider each of the numbered statements individually. If you discover that it's true, you can eliminate any choice that does not contain it. If you discover that it is false, you can eliminate any choice that does contain it.

For example, suppose you know from reading the passage that statement II is false. That means you can eliminate two choices, B and E. Since B and E both contain II, neither can be correct. (Similarly, if you know that one of the statements is correct, you can eliminate any answer choice that does not contain it.) Incidentally, Pam's answer in this case is C.

Continuing on

Now try question number 20 from our sample passage. When you have finished, return here to see how you did.

Here's How to Crack It

The fourth paragraph tells you all you need to know about pattern III women. Remember, the question wants to know what is "NOT" true of these women. Use the True/False method to find Pam's answer.

Let's look at each answer choice:

  (A) True. This is implied in the passage.

  (B) False. They do not work *solely* to meet the needs of the family.

  (C) True. See paragraph four.

  (D) ????. You may not be sure about this answer from reading paragraph four. It sounds possible, but you didn't see it. Leave it as a choice, and deal with it later.

  (E) True. It says so in paragraph four.

You are left with (B) as false, and (D) as unknown. Do you need to do more work? No. Pam's answer is (B). Since you know that (B) is false, (D) doesn't actually matter. If you were to read through the next paragraph, you would find that the women did enjoy the female company (mentioned in lines 59-60). However, you did enough work to make a smart guess without finding out about choice (D).

Common Sense

What made answer choice (B) on the last question so wrong? The word *solely* made the answer choice quite extreme—it said that the *only* thing these women were doing was trying to meet the needs of the family. Even if you weren't 100 percent sure if they were trying to meet the needs of the family, you knew that that wasn't the only thing they were doing. Common sense told you this had to be wrong.

Don't underestimate the power of common sense. When Pam and her team get together to write up questions and answer choices, it takes them quite a while to come up with the "perfect" Pam's answer. If they want to get their work done, they can't spend all day writing wrong answer choices. They just need to make sure the other four choices are clearly wrong. That's where your common sense comes into play.

Stupid Answers

The CR section of the SAT is filled with stupid answers—answers that can't possibly be Pam's answer. Don't assume that you are trying to find the "best" answer from a pool of five good answer choices. Rather, you are trying to find the "least wrong" answer from a pool of pretty bad answer choices. That's why you can sometimes answer a question without even reading the passage to which it refers.

Look at the following example:

16 According to the passage, all of the following are true of living organisms EXCEPT:

(A) They are able to reproduce themselves.
(B) They are past the point of further evolution.
(C) They are capable of growth.
(D) They respond to stimuli.
(E) They are characterized by a capacity for metabolism.

Here's How to Crack It

If you know even a little about biology, you will probably be able to answer this question without reading the passage. (Remember that on this question you are asked to look for a statement that is *not* true.) Now let's consider each choice in turn.

(A) The ability to reproduce is one of the obvious differences between living things and nonliving things. Rocks don't reproduce. Eliminate.

(B) Have living organisms stopped evolving? Of course not. This must be Pam's answer.

(C), (D), and (E)
These are all part of the standard biological definition of life. Eliminate.

Without even reading the passage, you could figure out which one of the answer choices had to be Pam's answer.

Buzzwords

Avoid answer choices that
contain the following words:
must
always
impossible
never
cannot
each
every
totally
all
solely
only

Don't Go to Extremes

Likewise, answers that use extreme language or express information that could be argued with are not going to be Pam's answer. If even one percent of the 1.5 million students who take the SAT each year were able to raise a plausible objection to Pam's answer to a question, Pam would have to spend all her time arguing with students. In order to keep this from happening, she tries to make her answers impossible to argue with.

How does she do that? Let's look at an example:

> Which of the following statements is impossible to argue with?
>
> (A) The population of the world is 4.734 billion people.
> (B) The population of the world is quite large.

Analysis

Statement A sounds precise and scientific; statement B sounds vague and general. Which is impossible to argue with?

Statement B, of course! Does anyone know exactly what the population of the world is? What if some experts say that the population of the world is 4.732 billion people? Doesn't the population of the world change from minute to minute? A number that is correct today will be wrong tomorrow. It's easy to think of dozens of reasons why statement A could be wrong.

Statement B, on the other hand, is so vague and general no one could argue with it. Anyone can see easily that it is true. If it were Pam's answer to an SAT critical reading question, no one would be able to quibble with her.

Pam and the other question writers at ETS understand that the more detailed and specific a statement is, the easier it is for someone to quibble with it or raise an objection to it. And they understand that the more general and vague a statement is, the harder it is for someone to quibble with it.

Let's look at an example. Assume that you've already eliminated some of the choices. You can answer this question now without even reading the passage.

> **27** With which of the following statements would the author of the passage probably agree?
>
> (A) No useful purpose is served by examining the achievements of the past.
> (B) A fuller understanding of the present can often be gained from the study of history.
> (C) [eliminated]
> (D) [eliminated]
> (E) Nothing new ever occurs.

Here's How to Crack It

Which of these statements are too extreme? Choices A and E. Choice A says that studying the past has *no* useful purpose. This statement is absolute. Once you find just one exception to the statement, you've proved the statement false. Therefore, the author of the passage probably wouldn't be any more likely to agree with it than we would.

Similarly, choice E says that nothing new ever occurs. This, too, is an extreme statement. Therefore, it's easy to raise objections to it. Nothing at all new ever occurs? Not even once in a while? Surely there must be an exception somewhere. This statement is easy to attack. If we find a single small exception, we have proven the statement wrong.

Choice B, however, is so general and vague that no one could argue with it. A single example would be enough to prove it correct. It must be Pam's answer.

Here's a silly example that makes the same point:

> **20** With which of the following statements would the weather forecaster probably agree?
>
> (A) It will begin raining tomorrow at 3:36.
> (B) Tuesday's low temperature will be 38 degrees.
> (C) Next year's snowfall will total 45 inches.
> (D) Tomorrow may be cooler than today.
> (E) Next month will be the wettest month of the year.

Here's How to Crack It

This question and the answer choices don't refer to an actual reading passage, of course. But even without seeing a passage (or knowing a weather forecaster), you ought to be able to tell that D is the only statement with which our imaginary weather forecaster, or anyone else, would probably agree. *Tomorrow may be cooler than today* is vague enough to be true no matter what. It may be cooler tomorrow, or it may not. All the bases are covered. The other four statements, by contrast, are so specific and absolute that no weather forecaster would make them. If a television weather forecaster said, *It will begin raining tomorrow at 3:36*, your reaction would be, "Oh, yeah? How do you know?"

If a statement says that something is always true, then you need to find only one exception in order to prove it wrong. If a statement says that each child ordered a hot dog, then you need to find only one child with a hamburger to prove it wrong. These words are highly specific, and therefore make the choices that contain them easier for you to attack and, very likely, to eliminate.

Choose Vague

The vague choice is usually correct. And the specific choice is usually incorrect. So when you are trying to decide between two choices, both of which seem good, the more specific choice will be much easier to poke holes in. And a choice that is easier to poke holes in will most likely be the wrong choice.

WEIRD PASSAGES

Narratives

Some passage you read will be more like stories than like passages. These passages are called Narratives. Why do you care? Because it is tough to do a topic search on a narrative. If you read the blurb of a passage and it sounds like it is going to be an excerpt from a story, use a "Trigger Search" to read what you need. In other words, go through the passage circling trigger words and reading the info that comes after each trigger. (See the sentence completion chapter for a review of trigger words). Then attack the questions as usual, looking for answers around the trigger words.

Dual Passages

Sometimes you will be given two passages for the price of one. You will be asked questions about the first passage, questions about the second passage, and questions about both. Do these passages one at a time. Read the blurb, then read what you need for Passage One. Then, answer the Passage One questions (they will come first).

After you finish the Passage One questions, go back and read what you need for Passage Two. Do the Passage Two questions. Finally, do the questions that involve both passages.

SKIP IT

Finally, critical reading takes longer than any other question type on the SAT. Depending on where you are scoring, it may be to your benefit to skip some or all of a passage. Remember, easy questions are worth just as many points as hard questions. Rushing through analogies to get to critical reading will hurt your accuracy and cost you points. See the verbal pacing chart on page 34 to determine if you should be skipping any critical reading.

THE TAIL END

Whether or not you are doing all the Critical Reading questions, you should definitely do them last of all the question types. In the thirty-minute verbal sections, Critical Reading questions will come after Sentence Completions and Analogies. Be sure to do all the Sentence Completions and Analogies you plan to do before you begin Critical Reading. If you run out of time on Critical Reading, no problem—all the easy stuff is already done.

The fifteen-minute verbal section consists solely of Critical Reading. Work this section smartly, not rushing to get through but rather working to answer questions correctly. You can do just as well on Critical Reading as you can on Analogies and Sentence Completions if you remember to:

- read what you need,
- translate the questions,
- put your finger on the answers,
- answer the questions in your own words,
- Use POE

DRILL 1

Use the following dual passage to *put it all together*. Review your strategy for attacking a dual passage before you begin, then crack this passage. Remember, the questions are more important than the passage. Focus on answering questions correctly by putting your finger on each answer in the passage and answering the questions in your own words before looking at any answer choices. Use your common sense and POE to avoid Pam's traps. When you have finished, see page 343 to check your work.

Critical Reading Takes Time

If you were offered a job that paid $10 an hour and another that paid $10 a minute, which one would you choose? Be good to yourself and do critical reading last.

Dual Passage Strategy

1. Read the Blurb
2. Passage One
   (A) Read What You Need
   (B) Attack the Passage One questions
3. Passage Two
   (A) Read What You Need
   (B) Attack the Passage Two questions
4. Attack the questions about both passages.

DUAL PASSAGES—ONE AT A TIME

- ◆ Search Passage 1
- ◆ Answer only those questions that deal with Passage 1
- ◆ Search Passage 2
- ◆ Answer only those questions that deal with Passage 2
- ◆ Only then should you proceed to questions that deal with both passages.

In 1959, the Hawaiian Islands were admitted into the United States as the forty-ninth state. Both of the following passages discuss the United States' annexation of Hawaii.

Passage I

On January 28, 1893, Americans read in their evening newspapers a bulletin from Honolulu, Hawaii. Two weeks earlier, said the news report, a group of American residents had overthrown a
(5) young native queen and formed a provisional government. Marines from the U.S.S. *Boston* had landed at the request of the American minister in order to protect lives and property. Violence had ended quickly. The rebels were in full control and
(10) were said to have enthusiastic support from the populace. Most noteworthy of all, they had announced the intention of asking the United States to annex the islands.

The proposal was not as startling as it might
(15) have seemed. Most of the large landowners in the islands were Americans or the children of Americans. So too were the men who grew, refined, and shipped the sugar that was Hawaii's principal export. In addition, many of the kingdom's
(20) Protestant clergymen, lawyers, bankers, factory owners, and other leading personages were also American citizens. Though numbering only two thousand of the island's total population of around ninety thousand, these Americans had
(25) already given Hawaii the appearance of a colony. This influence could be seen as far back as 1854 when they nearly persuaded a native monarch to request annexation by the United States. Subsequently, the American element helped secure
(30) tariff reciprocity from the United States while the island ceded a naval station to the United States. Such measures sparked enough concern by the United States to lead Presidents from Tyler on down to periodically warn European powers
(35) against meddling in Hawaiian affairs. Thus, by 1893, the new proposal might have been charac-
terized as simply a plan to annex a state already Americanized and virtually a protectorate.

Nonetheless, the proposition came unexpect-
(40) edly, and neither politicians nor journalists knew quite what to make of it. Editorials and comments from Capitol Hill were at first noncommittal. The molders of public opinion seemed intent on learning what mold the public wanted.
(45) San Francisco's leading Republican and Democratic dailies, the *Chronicle* and *Examiner*, declared that Hawaii should certainly be accepted as a state. On January 29, the *Chronicle* reported a poll of local businessmen demonstrating overwhelm-
(50) ing support for this view. Some businessmen focused on potential profits. Claus Spreckels, for example, who owned Hawaii's largest sugar plantation, hoped to obtain the two-cent-a-pound bounty paid by the United States government to
(55) domestic sugar producers. In addition, he anticipated increased freight for his Oceanic Steamship line as well as more plentiful and cheaper raw sugar for his California Sugar Refinery Company.

Businessmen elsewhere on the Pacific coast
(60) followed their lead. San Diego, for example, was virtually the property of the Spreckels family. Moreover, in Los Angeles, Fresno, and San Jose, the Spreckels were allied, to some extent, in the battle against the railroad with merchants,
(65) bankers, warehouse owners, real estate dealers, and contractors; and the Chambers of Commerce of Portland and Seattle had long cooperated with that of San Francisco in pressing for national policies advantageous to the West. It was not long before businessmen all along the coast were reported as favoring annexation.

1 In Passage 1, what event occurred "two weeks earlier" (line 3) than January 28, 1893?

(A) Hawaii became the fiftieth state of the United States.
(B) The United States annexed the Hawaiian islands.
(C) American rebels seized governmental control of the Hawaiian islands.
(D) Marines from the U.S.S. *Boston* arrived to protect the young native queen from rebels.
(E) Angry Hawaiian natives rebelled against American rule in Honolulu.

2 According to the second paragraph of Passage 1, Americans on the Hawaiian islands

(A) outnumbered native islanders by about 88,000
(B) were largely in opposition to the American proposal of an annexation of the islands
(C) already owned all the land, and thus rightly usurped the power of the monarchy
(D) had established themselves there in such a way that annexation seemed the next likely step
(E) were reluctant to establish a tariff reciprocity that would make it difficult to export sugar

3 The word "ceded," as used in line 31, most nearly means

(A) sowed with new plants
(B) took as tax
(C) paid as tax
(D) donated as charity
(E) gave over

4 In describing the response of the "molders of public opinion," (line 43) the author of Passage 1 suggests that they

(A) persuaded the United States government to annex the Hawaiian islands
(B) really had little to do with the public's opinion on annexation
(C) were unfamiliar with the politics of the Hawaiian islands
(D) wanted to learn about the events that took place on the islands
(E) never spoke out on the possible annexation of Hawaii

5 In Passage 1, the author mentions Claus Spreckels in order to

(A) present an example of how businessmen would profit from the annexation of Hawaii
(B) demonstrate that some people in the United States were opposed to annexation
(C) prove that Hawaiians were predominantly in favor of statehood
(D) further the argument concerning the ambiguity of public opinion
(E) show the role that Americans played in Hawaii

6 All of the following served as reasons that Claus Spreckels supported annexation EXCEPT:

(A) the two-cent-a-pound bounty
(B) more plentiful sugar for his refineries
(C) support for the railroads
(D) cheaper sugar for his refineries
(E) more cargo for his steamship line to carry

Passage II

President Cleveland was opposed to annexation throughout his term of office. He believed
taking the Islands was immoral, and without his
Line support annexationists had no hope. The Provi-
(5) sional Government, however, did not cease to
push its cause in Washington—in fact, the vocal
commissioner Lorrin Thurston pushed so hard
that he was declared *persona non grata*.

When the Cleveland administration rejected
(10) annexation, it requested that the Provisional
Government restore the monarchy. This request
created additional hard feelings in Hawaii, and
the new government flatly refused to comply. For
a time it appeared that American forces might be
(15) called upon to wrest power from the Provisional
Government, but the request was not unduly
pressed by the United States and tensions soon
eased. The Provisional Government now became
the Republic of Hawaii. A new constitution was
(20) written and the Islands settled down to await
more favorable times.

As a consequence of Cleveland's decision, a
battle of words raged across the U.S. in the
nation's newspapers. Many newspapers sup-
(25) ported the royalists while others hailed the
Republic. In San Francisco, the *Call* warned that
the annexation of Hawaii "will be the open door
through which the least desirable elements in

Japan will enter upon American citizenship." The
(30) *New York Journal and Advertiser* thought Hawaii
belonged to the United States: "The acquisition of
Hawaii is an imperative patriotic duty."

The most powerful opponent of annexation was
the sugar trust, which was comprised of the sugar
(35) refiners. The sugar trust was divided into Eastern
and Western camps, with Claus Spreckels con-
trolling the West. The refiners subsidized many of
the nation's sugar planters. The refiners, therefore, were able not only to name the price main-
(40) land farmers received for their crops, but also to
control the retail price of sugar as well. The
admission of Hawaii created many questions, and
the refiners feared a loss of their monopoly
control. Perhaps high-grade Hawaiian sugars
(45) would not need refining. Certainly all hopes of a
tariff barrier would be gone; and it was possible
that Hawaiian sugar could be produced at lower
costs. All of these things loomed as threats.

The sugar trust lobby in Washington was a
(50) powerful one, and its weight was felt in Con-
gress. The lobbyists also conducted a campaign
aimed at turning the American public against
acquisition of the Islands. One of their favorite
suggestions was that a popular vote on annex-
(55) ation be taken in Hawaii. This the Republic of
Hawaii wanted to avoid at all costs.

---

7 According to the first paragraph of Passage 2,
in order for Hawaii to be annexed, the
annexationists needed

(A) additional funding
(B) the support of the President
(C) to overthrow the Provisional
Government
(D) to eliminate the sugar monopoly
(E) to gain the backing of major United
States newspapers

8 Passage 2 suggests that the Provisional
Government of Hawaii

(A) often caved in to pressure from the
mainland
(B) was merely a puppet of American
economic interests
(C) received a large amount of support from
the American government
(D) persisted despite resistance from the
American government
(E) was completely representative of the
people of Hawaii

9 The third paragraph of Passage 2 implies that
public opinion as expressed in newspapers on
the issue of Hawaii's annexation was

(A) solidly in favor of annexation
(B) overwhelmingly opposed to annexation
(C) unvoiced, and therefore neither favored
nor opposed annexation
(D) split between support for and opposition
to annexation
(E) limited to only a few public elites

10 The discussion of Hawaiian sugars in lines
33-48 suggests that these products were

(A) clearly superior to domestic sugars
(B) faced with a high tariff upon entry to the
United States
(C) not controlled by the American sugar
trust
(D) more expensive than domestic products
(E) not required to undergo a refining
process similar to that undergone by
domestic sugars

11 The final paragraph of Passage 2 implies that a popular vote on annexation taken in Hawaii would

(A) have overwhelming success
(B) most likely fail to gain enough votes for annexation
(C) have been the political method of choice for the Republic of Hawaii
(D) not present a true representation of public sentiment
(E) result in the demise of the Republic of Hawaii

12 Which of the following does the author of Passage 2 cite as possible opposition to annexation that is not mentioned by the author of Passage 1?

(A) The exiled Hawaiian monarchy
(B) Marines from the U.S.S. *Boston*
(C) Politicians and journalists
(D) The *Chronicle* and *Examiner*
(E) The President of the United States

13 One major difference between the two passages is that

(A) while both authors analyze the same events, they appear to reach different conclusions concerning the possibility of Hawaii's annexation
(B) the author of the first passage fails to provide specific examples of public sentiment similar to those presented in Passage 2
(C) one passage focuses on support for annexation, while the other emphasizes resistance
(D) the authors disagree over how much Hawaii had already become Americanized
(E) the authors arrive at different conclusions concerning the importance of sugar as an import

CRITICAL READING SUMMARY

1. Critical reading accounts for half of all the points on the verbal SAT.

2. The passage is the least important part of every critical reading group.

3. Begin by reading what you need. Do a topic search (or a trigger search on Narratives) to determine:
   - The author's point,
   - The author's tone,
   - The passage layout.

4. On critical reading, the questions are *not* presented in order of difficulty.

5. Translate the questions into "English." You can't answer a question if you don't understand what you are being asked.

6. Put your finger on the answer. Go back to the passage and find the answer to each specific question.

7. Use line references and lead words to help you find Pam's answer in the passage. Always read five lines above and five lines below the line reference or the lead word.

8. Answer the questions in your own words before you read Pam's answers. You will avoid Joe Bloggs answer choices by knowing what the answer is before you read any of the choices.

9. Use POE to get rid of choices that don't match yours. Cross out incorrect choices as you go. You should have a definite sense of zeroing in on Pam's answer. If you don't cross out incorrect choices, you'll waste time and energy rereading wrong answer choices.

10. Eliminate answer choices that have extreme wording (*must*, etc.) or violate common sense.

11. Be careful on EXCEPT/LEAST/NOT questions. Pam's answer is the choice that is *not* true. Use the True/False technique. Do these questions last.

12. I, II, III questions are also very time-consuming and should therefore be saved for last. Still, eliminating choices is easy and straightforward.

13. Treat double passages as two separate passages. The majority of the questions won't require you to think of any connection whatsoever between the two passages.

14. To read what you need for a narrative passage, do a Trigger Search. Circle the trigger words and look for important information around the trigger words.

15. Save critical reading for last in each verbal section of the SAT. These problems take a great deal of time to answer correctly, but they don't earn you any more points than analogies or sentence completions.

16. It's okay to run out of time on critical reading. Most people do. If you are working at the proper pace, the questions you don't have time to tackle are questions you would have missed anyway.

WSC

The Writing Skills Component contains 39 questions, comprised of nineteen Error Identifications (Error ID), fourteen Improving Sentences (Better the Sentence), and six Improving Paragraphs (Fix the Paragraph). The Writing Skills Component (WSC for short) will be the last section of the PSAT. You will have thirty minutes to answer 39 questions. In other words, you have been allotted less than one minute per question.

How will you do well on the WSC?

1. By reviewing/learning PSAT grammar,
2. by knowing how to attack each type of question,
3. by knowing which questions to do and which to skip.

PSAT Grammar

The grammar Pam chooses to test on the PSAT is pretty basic. Of course, she does her best to trip you up with extraneous phrases and distracting words. Don't sweat it: this chapter will review all the grammar you need to see through Pam's tricks and traps. If, after working through this chapter, you feel particularly weak on any of the areas of grammar reviewed, pick up a copy of The Princeton Review's *Grammar Smart* for a more in-depth review.

Question Strategy

Every question type on the SAT and PSAT can be cracked, and WSC questions are no exception. While reviewing the basic grammar you need, you will also learn how to crack Error ID and Better the Sentence questions. After you solidify your approach to these question types, you'll learn how to crack Fix the Paragraph questions by employing the grammar and skills you've already mastered. Of course, you need to practice this stuff to really make it work. After working through the drills in this chapter, be sure to take a full-length PSAT (see page 353 for instructions).

To Do or Not To Do

Unlike the other sections of the PSAT, the WSC is not arranged in order of difficulty. Therefore, to do well on these questions, you need to determine when a problem is hard and should be skipped. What makes a question hard? It either contains grammar that you don't know, or it's long and time-consuming. As a general rule, you will approach the section in order: Do Error ID's first, since they're quick and POE works well; do Better the Sentence questions next, but plan to skip ones in which the entire sentence is underlined; do Fix the Paragraph questions last because you are dealing with an entire passage for only six questions.

9

Writing Skills Component

IF YOU ARE TAKING THE **PSAT**, READ THIS SECTION NOW. OTHERWISE, SKIP TO CHAPTER TEN.

SNEAK PREVIEW

Before we begin reviewing Pam's grammar, let's take a peek at the first two question types you'll see on the WSC.

> This is an example of an Error ID
> A   B
> question that has no error. No error
>   C   D   E

Error ID questions give you a sentence which has four words or phrases underlined each with a corresponding letter underneath. At the end of each sentence will be "No error"—choice E. There are some important things you need to know about Error ID's:

◆ There is never more than one error per sentence.

◆ If there is an error, it's always underlined.

◆ Approximately 20% of all Error ID questions are correct as written, so don't be afraid to pick choice (E).

◆ Error ID's are short, and you should usually be able to eliminate at least one answer choice, so guess on all Error ID questions.

◆ Do Error ID questions first.

IMPROVING SENTENCES — A.K.A. "BETTER THE SENTENCE"

> This is an example of an Improving Sentences question that does not contain an error.
>
> (A) that does not contain
> (B) that has not been containing
> (C) which has not been contain
> (D) which is not being with
> (E) about which there is nothing to indicate it being with

Improving Sentences questions give you a sentence, part or all of which is underlined. The underlined part may or may not contain a grammatical error. There are some important things you need to know about Improving Sentences questions:

◆ Answer choice (A) is a reprint of the underlined section. Therefore, if you decide that the sentence contains no error, choose answer choice (A).

◆ Approximately 20% of all Improving Sentences questions are correct as written, so don't be afraid to pick choice (A).

◆ If you decide the underlined portion of the sentence contains an error, eliminate choice (A). Also, eliminate any other choice that does not fix the error.

- If you are unsure whether the sentence contains an error, look to your answer choices for a clue (more on this later).

- KISS: Keep It Short and Sweet. Concise answers are preferable.

GRAMMAR? UGH!

To do well on the WSC, you need to remember some basic grammar rules. Now, don't get worked up about being tested on grammar. PSAT grammar is not difficult, nor is it extensive. In fact, the WSC really only tests five basic grammatical concepts:

1. Verbs

2. Nouns

3. Pronouns

4. Prepositions

5. Other Little Things

These are the five areas in which a sentence can "go wrong." They will function as a checklist for you—every time you read a sentence, you will look at these five areas to find the error. If you don't find one after checking these five things, then there probably isn't one.

NO ERROR?

As we've mentioned, 20 percent of Error ID questions and Better the Sentence questions contain No Error. If you've used your checklist and can't find a mistake, chances are there isn't one. Don't be afraid to pick No Error—(E) on Error ID and (A) on Better the Sentence questions.

We will use Error ID questions to illustrate the first four areas of grammar. Before we get going on the grammar stuff, let's learn how to crack an Error ID question.

CRACKING ERROR ID's

As we mentioned, an Error ID question is a short sentence that has four words or phrases underlined and lettered. Your job is to determine if any one of those four underlined segments contains an error. If so, you are to blacken the corresponding oval on your answer sheet. If not, you are to choose "(E) No error."

Let's look at an example of an Error ID to learn how to beat these questions:

The Halloween party was a <u>great</u> success:
                                A

the children <u>enjoyed</u> bobbing <u>for apples</u>,
               B   C

playing party games, and <u>to put</u> costumes
                            D

on. <u>No error</u>
      E

THE APPROACH

To solve an Error ID, you need to look at the sentence one piece at a time. As you read through the sentence, pause after each underlined segment and ask, "Is there anything wrong yet?" Run through the first four categories of your grammar check list. Verb problem? Noun problem? Pronoun problem? Preposition problem? If these four areas check out, cross off the segment (it's not your answer) and move on.

Look at the first segment of this sentence: "The Halloween party was a great success…" Is there a problem with the word *great*? No. Put a slash through answer choice (A). Next segment: "the children enjoyed…" Any problem with this verb? No—it's in the past tense, just like the "was" in the first line, so everything is fine. Cross it off.

Continuing on: "bobbing for apples…" No problem here—cross off (C). Keep going: "playing party games, and to put costumes on." Wait a minute—something doesn't sound right. "To put" is a verb. Notice in this example Pam gives you a series of activities (verbs): "bobbing," "playing," and "to put." When in a series, all the verbs need to have the same form. Therefore, "to put" should be "putting." The answer is (D).

By the way, you have just learned the first verb rule to watch: When a series of activities is described in a sentence, make sure all the verbs are expressed the same way—make sure they are *parallel*.

CUT THE CRAP

Often an Error ID will contain extraneous phrases that distract from the meat of the sentence and cause you to miss an error. How can you avoid getting waylaid by distracting phrases? "Cut the Crap." As you work through a sentence, cross off anything that is not essential to the sentence: prepositional phrases, phrases offset by commas, etc. Crossing out the distracting phrases puts the important parts of a sentence, the subject and verb for example, together and keeps you from making careless errors.

Let's look at another example.

Japan, since the early part of the 1980s,
      A
have been able to export the high quality
  B   C
technology demanded by consumers. No error
        D   E

Here's How to Crack It

First, Cut the Crap. What's the subject of the sentence? Japan. Cross off the stuff between the commas—it's there to distract you. What's the verb? Have been. "Japan have been?" Don't think so. Japan is singular, so it needs a singular verb. The answer is (B).

BE AGGRESSIVE

Error ID's are typically short and uncomplicated. Be aggressive as you go through these sentences. Read the sentence quickly once, keeping your checklist in mind. If you spot a problem, jump to it—you don't need to labor over the whole sentence if your eye is drawn to a problem right away.

DO I HAVE TO READ THE WHOLE THING?

Once you've found the error, do you need to read the rest of the sentence? Well, if you're sure of the error you've found, a quick read will be easy and reassuring. If you are not so sure, you will need to read the rest of the sentence to be sure you haven't missed anything. Since Error ID's are short and sweet, take a quick second to read them through.

GUESSING

There are three reasons why you should always guess on an Error ID question:

1. **You can always eliminate at least one answer choice**. If you read a sentence that sounds wrong, you can immediately eliminate answer choice (E), even if you are not sure which underlined segment is the culprit.

2. **The odds are with you**. Only one of the four underlined parts of the sentence is wrong, if at all. You're bound to be able to determine a few of the segments that are correct even if your grammar's not great.

3. **You don't have to fix the error in the sentence; you only have to identify it**. Therefore, guessing is easy. Once you've narrowed it down, take a guess and move on.

As we review the first four areas of grammar, you will work a bunch of Error ID questions. This will give you a feel for how they work and how easy it is to guess aggressively.

Now that you know how to approach Error ID's, let's work on reviewing Pam's grammar rules.

VERBS

A verb is an action word. It tells what the subject of the sentence is doing. You've already seen two ways in which a verb can "go wrong." There are a total of three things to check out about a verb:

(a) Does it **agree** with its subject?

(b) Is it **parallel** in structure to the other verbs in the sentence?

(c) Is it in the proper **tense**?

Do they agree?

The rule regarding subject-verb agreement is simple: singular with singular, plural with plural. If you are given a singular subject (he, she, it), then your verb must also be singular (is, has, was). (In case you don't remember, the subject of the sentence is the noun that the verb modifies—the person or thing that is *doing* the doing.)

Easy enough except, as you have already seen, Pam has a way of putting lots of stuff between the subject and the verb to make you forget whether your subject was singular or plural. Remember Japan from the last example? Look at another:

> The statistics <u>released by</u> the state
>   A
>
> department <u>makes</u> the economic situation
>   B
>
> look <u>bleaker than</u> it really <u>is</u>. <u>No error</u>
>   C   D   E

Here's How to Crack It

At first glance, this sentence may appear fine. But let's pull it apart. What is the sentence about? The statistics—a plural subject. If the subject is plural, then the verb must be plural too. "Makes" is the verb modifying "statistics," but it is a singular verb—no can do. The answer is (B).

Why did the sentence sound okay at first? Because of the stuff stuck between "statistics" and "makes." The phrase "released by the state department" places a singular noun right before the verb. Get rid of the extraneous stuff (i.e., Cut the Crap) and the error becomes obvious.

Knowing When It's Single

Sometimes you may not know if a noun is singular or plural, making it tough to determine whether its verb should be singular or plural. Of course you know nouns like "he" and "cat" are singular, but what about "family" or "everybody"? The following is a list of "tricky" nouns—technically called collective nouns. They are nouns that typically describe a group of people but are considered singular and thus need a singular verb:

The family *is*

The jury *is*

The group *is*

The audience *is*

The congregation *is*

The United States (or any other country) *is*

The following pronouns also take singular verbs:

Either *is*

Neither *is*

None *is*

Each *is*

Anyone *is*

No one *is*

Everyone *is*

"And" or "Or"

Subjects joined by "and" are plural: Bill and Pat *were* going to the show. However, nouns joined by "or" can be singular or plural—if the last noun given is singular, then it takes a singular verb; if the last noun given is plural, it takes a plural verb.

Pam Cruise and Jim Braswell,

neither of <u>whom</u> takes the bus to work, <u>is</u>
    A   B   C

secretly plotting <u>to take over</u> the world. <u>No error</u>
               D   E

Here's How to Crack It

Once again Pam is trying to trip you up by separating the subject from the verb. You know what to do—Cut the Crap! What's the subject? Pam Cruise *and* Jim Braswell. We know the subject is plural because of the "and." Cross off the stuff between commas and you have "Pam Cruise and Jim Braswell...is." Can we use the singular verb "is" with our plural subject? No way—the answer is (C).

ARE THEY PARALLEL?

The next thing you need to check out about a verb is whether it and the other verbs in the sentence are parallel. In the first example used in this chapter, the children at the Halloween party were "bobbing," "playing," and "to put." The last verb, "to put" is not written in the same form as the other verbs in the series. In other words, it's not parallel. The sentence should read, "the children were *bobbing* for apples, *playing* party games, and *putting* costumes on."

Try another example:

As a <u>competitor</u> in the Iron Man competi-
         A

tion, Scott <u>was</u> <u>required</u> to swim 2.4 miles, to
            B

bike 112 miles, and <u>running</u> the last 26 miles. <u>No error</u>
              C   D

Here's How to Crack It

If an Error ID contains an underlined verb that is part of a series of activities, isolate the verbs to see if they are parallel. In this sentence, Scott is required "to swim," "to bike," and "running." What's the problem? He should be required "to swim," "to bike," and "to run"—and then to collapse. The answer is (D).

ARE YOU TENSE?

As you know, verbs come in different tenses—for example, "is" is present tense, while "was" is past tense. You've probably heard of other tenses like "past past" and "past perfect." Well, first of all, don't worry about identifying the kind of tense used in a sentence—you will never be asked to identify verb tense, only to make sure tense is consistent throughout a sentence.

For the most part, verb tense should not change within a sentence. Look at the following example:

> $\underline{\text{Throughout}}$ the Middle Ages, women $\underline{\text{work}}$
> $\quad$A$\qquad\qquad\qquad\qquad\qquad\qquad$B
>
> $\underline{\text{beside men}}$, knowing that the effort of men and
> $\quad$C
>
> women alike was $\underline{\text{essential to}}$ survival. $\underline{\text{No error}}$
> $\qquad\qquad\qquad\qquad$D$\qquad\qquad\qquad$E

Just the Answer, Please

Remember, when solving Error ID questions, all you have to do is identify the error. Don't worry if you don't know exactly how to fix an error—Pam only cares if you can identify it.

Here's How to Crack It

Our subject? Women. Our verb? Work—which would be fine if the sentence hadn't started out with "Throughout the Middle Ages…" Is the sentence talking about women working beside men right now? No, it's talking about the Middle Ages. The verb should be "worked"—the answer is (B).

NOUNS

The only thing you really have to check for with nouns is agreement. Agreement is a big thing for most grammarians, Pam included. Verbs must agree with their subjects, nouns must agree with other nouns, and pronouns must agree with the nouns they represent. When you read an Error ID, if you come across an underlined noun, check to see if it refers to or is associated with any other nouns in the sentence. If so, make sure they match in number.

For example:

> $\underline{\text{As elections approach}}$, campaign managers
> $\qquad$A
>
> pay more $\underline{\text{attention to}}$ swing voters, $\underline{\text{who}}$
> $\qquad\qquad$B$\qquad\qquad\qquad\qquad$C
>
> often don't make their $\underline{\text{decision}}$ until the day
> $\qquad\qquad\qquad\qquad\qquad$D
>
> of the election. $\underline{\text{No error}}$
> $\qquad\qquad\qquad$E

Here's How to Crack It

Take it one piece at a time. "<u>As elections approach</u>…" has a subject and a verb, but they agree. No problem here. Cross off (A).

Continuing on, "…campaign managers pay more <u>attention </u>to…." No problem we can see. Cross it off. Going on, "…swing voters, <u>who</u>…" Hey, is this one of those who/whom things? Maybe you are not too sure about when to use "who" versus when to use "whom." If you aren't sure whether an underlined segment is right, leave it and check out the rest of the sentence. You may get rid of everything else, or you may find an error somewhere else.

Going on: "often don't make their <u>decision</u>…." Is it correct to say "their decision"? Who is being discussed, anyway? The swing voters, which is plural. Can all the swing voters make one and the same decision? Of course not. They make *decisions*. The answer is (D).

PRONOUNS

As with verbs, there are three things you need to check when you have pronouns:

  (a) Do they **agree**?

  (b) Are they **ambiguous**?

  (c) Do they use the right **case**?

I AGREE

As you know, a pronoun is a little word that is inserted to represent a noun (he, she, it, they, etc.) As with everything else, pronouns must agree with their nouns: the pronoun that replaces a singular noun must also be singular, and the pronoun that replaces a plural noun must be plural. If different pronouns are used to refer to the same subject or one pronoun is used to replace another, the pronouns must also agree.

This may seem obvious, but it is also the most commonly violated rule in ordinary speech. How often have you heard people say, "*Everyone* must hand in *their* application before leaving." Remember from our list of singular pronouns that "everyone" is singular? But "their" is plural. This sentence is incorrect.

To spot a pronoun agreement error, look for pronouns that show up later in a sentence. If you see a pronoun underlined, find the noun or pronoun it is replacing and make sure the two agree. Let's look at an example:

Everyone <u>on the softball</u> team <u>who came up</u> to bat
A   B
squinted <u>at the pitcher </u>in order to keep the sun's
C
glaring rays out of <u>their eyes</u>. <u>No error</u>
D   E

Here's How to Crack It

Is there an underlined pronoun late in this sentence? There sure is: "their eyes." Whose eyes are being referred to? Let's Cut the Crap to check this sentence:

> "Everyone...*squinted...to keep the sun's...rays...out of* their eyes." "Everyone" is singular, but "their" is plural, so it cannot replace "everyone."
>
> The answer is (D).

TO WHOM DO YOU REFER?

When a pronoun appears in a sentence, it should be infinitely clear which noun it replaces. For example:

> "*After looking over the color samples, Mary agreed with Martha that her porch should be painted green.*"

Whose porch is being painted green? Mary's or Martha's? This sentence would be unacceptable to Pam, because it is not perfectly clear who the "her" in the sentence is. This is pronoun ambiguity, and it is unacceptable on the PSAT.

If you see a pronoun late in a sentence, check to see if it clearly refers to its noun. Be especially wary if the early part of the sentence contains two singular or two plural nouns. Try the following example:

> The director <u>told</u> the star of the
>   A
>
> production that <u>he</u> was making far too
>   B
>
> much money <u>to tolerate</u> such nasty
>   C
>
> <u>treatment from</u> the producer. <u>No error</u>
>   D   E

Here's How to Crack It

Let's take it apart a piece at a time. "The director <u>told</u>..." Do a quick tense scan of the sentence. Is it past tense? Yes. Cross off (A) and go on.

Let's Cut the Crap to check the next answer choice:

> "*The director told the star...that* <u>*he*</u> *was making far too much money...*"

Who was making far too much money? It is not clear whether the pronoun "he" is referring to the director or the star. The answer is (B).

CASE? WHAT CASE?

Pronouns come in two "flavors" known as cases: subjective or objective. The subject, as you know, is the person or thing performing the action in the sentence. The object is the person or thing *receiving* the action. Think of it this way: an object just sits there. It doesn't *do* anything; rather, things are done to it. The subject, by contrast, does stuff.

When it comes to pronouns, subjects and objects are represented by different pronouns. For example, "I" is a subjective pronoun, as in "I did it," while "me" is an objective pronoun, as in "it happened to me." Most of the time, you will know if the wrong pronoun case (as it's called) is used because the sentence will sound funny. However, this is another area that is often butchered by our spoken language. When in doubt, Cut the Crap to figure out whether the pronoun is the subject (performing the action) or the object (receiving the action).

SUBJECT PRONOUNS

Singular	Plural
I	We
You	You
He	They
She	
It	
Who	Who

OBJECT PRONOUNS

Singular	Plural
Me	Us
You	You
Him	Them
Her	
It	
Whom	Whom

Try the following example:

The leading roles in the <u>widely acclaimed play</u>, a
                              A

modern <u>version of</u> an Irish folktale, were
         B

<u>performed by</u> Jessica and <u>him</u>. <u>No error</u>
     C   D   E

Here's How to Crack It

Read through the sentence, checking each underlined segment. "The leading roles in the <u>widely acclaimed play</u>...." No problem here—cross (A) off and move on. Next segment: "...a modern <u>version of</u>...." Again, it seems fine. Cross it out and keep going.

To check the next two, do a little Cutting: "The leading roles...were per-formed by Jessica and him." "Performed by" is fine. What about "him"? Get rid of Jessica to check: "The...roles...were performed by...him." "Him" is an objective pronoun and, in this sentence, is used correctly. "He performed" would need the subjective pronoun; "performed by him" is the correct use of the objective pronoun. The answer is (E) No Error.

I or Me?

Are you frequently being correctly on the "I" versus "me" thing? If so, you're not alone. In the example we just did, if you were to replace "him" with either "I" or "me," which would it be? You would use "me" since you need an objective pronoun. It is often difficult to tell which case to use when the pronoun is coupled with another noun or pronoun. If you are having trouble deciding which case to use, remember to Cut the Crap: in this case, remove the other person (Jessica in the example we just did).

Which One is Correct?

The book belongs to Jerry and I.

The book belongs to Jerry and me.

If you're not sure, take Jerry out of the picture:

The book belongs to _____.

Me, of course. It's much easier to tell which is correct if the extraneous stuff is removed. Here's a tricky one:

Clare is more creative than me.

Clare is more creative than I.

Be careful. This may look as though the pronoun is an object, but actually the sentence is written in an incomplete form. What you are really saying in this sentence is, "Clare is more creative than I am." The "am" is understood. When in doubt, say the sentence aloud, adding on the "am" to see if it is hiding at the end of the sentence.

DON'T BE PASSIVE

One final note about subjects and objects: ETS prefers sentences written in the active voice rather than the passive voice. If a sentence is written in the active voice, the subject of the sentence is doing something. If a sentence is written in the passive voice, the main player becomes an object and things happen to him.

Which of the following is written in the active voice?

She took the PSAT.

The PSAT was taken by her.

"She took the PSAT," is active because "she" is the subject of the sentence and she is doing something. "The PSAT was taken by her," is passive because "her" is now the object of "by," not the subject of the sentence. This will be important to know when attacking Better the Sentence questions.

PREPOSITIONS

Remember prepositions? "About, above, across, around, along..." You use prepositions all the time to add information to a sentence. Using different prepositions can change the meaning of a sentence. For example:

I am standing *by* you.

I am standing *for* you.

I am standing *near* you.

I am standing *under* you.

Drill 1

In the English language, certain words must be paired with certain prepositions. These pairs of words are called idioms. There are really no rules to idioms, so you need to just use your ear and memorize ones that are tricky. Here is a list of some common idioms you may come across. Fill in the blanks with the missing prepositions (some may have more than one possibility). See page 344 to check your answers.

1. I am *indebted* _____ you.

2. I am *resentful* _____ you.

3. I am *delighted* _____ you.

4. I am *jealous* _____ you.

5. I am *worried* _____ you.

6. I am *astounded* _____ you.

7. The women had a *dispute* ____ politics.

8. You have a *responsibility* ____ take care of your pet.

9. My friends are not so *different* ____ your friends.

Try an Error ID example:

<u>Despite</u> the <u>poor weather</u>, my sister <u>and I</u> were
    A   B   C

planning <u>on attending</u> the festival. <u>No error</u>
                 D   E

Here's How to Crack It

Let's pull it apart: "<u>Despite</u> the <u>poor weather</u>…" Both of these seem okay, so let's move on. Next phrase: "my sister <u>and I</u> were…" Is the "I" okay? It's the subject, so it's okay (if you can't tell, reword the sentence, leaving out "my sister"). How about the next part: "planning <u>on attending</u>…"? You may have heard people say this, but it's wrong. The preposition that should accompany "planning" is "to." The sentence should read, "…my sister and I were planning *to attend* the festival." The answer is (D).

ERROR ID AND YOUR GRAMMAR CHECKLIST

Let's do a quick review. On Error ID questions, have your Grammar Checklist ready (keep it in your head, or jot it on your test booklet). It should look like this:

1. Is there an underlined **verb**? If so,
   (a) Does it **agree** with its subject?
   (b) Is it **parallel** in structure to the other verbs in the sentence?
   (c) Is it in the proper **tense**?

2. Is there an underlined **noun**? If so,
   (a) Does it **agree** in number with any other noun to which it refers?

3. Is there an underlined **pronoun**? If so,
   (a) Does it **agree** with the noun/pronoun it represents?
   (b) Can you tell to which noun it refers or is it **ambiguous**?
   (c) Does it use the right **case** (subjective or objective)?

4. Is there an underlined **preposition**? If so,
   (a) Is it the **right one**?

When you approach Error ID questions, remember to :

- read them with your checklist in mind,
- cross off underlined stuff that is right,
- Cut the Crap,
- not be afraid to pick (E) No error,
- guess on all of them.

Drill 1

Use the following drill to solidify your Error ID strategy. See page 344 for the answers.

1. <u>Many</u> young adults find it extremely
   A
   difficult <u>to return</u> home from college
   B
   and <u>abide with</u> the rules <u>set down</u> by
   C   D
   their parents. <u>No error</u>
   E

2. I <u>recently</u> heard an <u>announcement where</u>
   A   B
   the Rangers <u>will be playing</u> a game at
   C
   home <u>this</u> weekend. <u>No error</u>
   D   E

3. Just <u>last month</u>, two weeks
   A
   after the announcement <u>of elections</u>
   B
   in Soviet Georgia, 92-year-old Fydor

   <u>has cast</u> his first vote <u>in 70 years</u>.
   C   D
   <u>No error</u>
   E

4. When the student council announced

   its intention <u>to elect</u> a minority
   A
   representative, neither the <u>principal</u>
   B
   <u>nor</u> the superintendent <u>were</u> willing to
   C   D
   comment on the issue. <u>No error</u>
   E

5. It is a <u>more difficult</u> task to learn to
   A
   type than <u>mastering</u> a <u>simple</u> word
   B   C
   processing <u>program</u>. <u>No error</u>
   D   E

6. Educators and parents <u>agree</u> that a
                          A

    daily reading time will not only

    enhance a child's education <u>but also</u>
                                 B

    <u>encouraging</u> the child to read
     C

    <u>independently</u>. <u>No error</u>
         D   E

BETTER THE SENTENCE

So far we have been concentrating on Error ID questions while reviewing grammar. The good news is Improving Sentence questions (from here on out we will refer to them as "Better the Sentence" questions) test a lot of the same grammar. Let's look at a sample question to see how to crack Better the Sentence questions.

> Although Tama Janowitz and Jay McInerney both have new books on the market, <u>only one of the two are successful</u>.
>
> (A) only one of the two are successful
> (B) only one of the two is successful
> (C) only one of the two books are successful
> (D) only one of the two books is successful
> (E) one only of the books has been successful

Here's How to Crack It

There are two ways to go about cracking a Better the Sentence question. The preferable way is for you to identify the error as you read the underlined part of the sentence. How will you do that, you ask? By using your handy-dandy grammar checklist, of course. Let's try it on this example. The underlined portion of the sentence says, "only one of the two are successful." Let's run through your list. Is there an underlined verb? Yes—"are." Does it agree with its subject? What is its subject? If we Cut the Crap—in this case, the prepositional phrase "of the two"—we can easily see the subject is "one." Is it correct to say "one are"? Of course not.

So you've identified the problem—great. However, Better the Sentence questions require you to go further than just identifying the error—they also require you to fix the error, thus "bettering" the sentence. To do this, you will use your old friend: Process Of Elimination. First, we know that answer choice (A) is simply a repeat of the underlined portion. Therefore, once you've identified an error, cross off answer choice (A).

Next, scan the rest of the answer choices and cross off any answer choices that don't fix the problem you've identified. In our example, we know the verb "are" is wrong. What answer choice can we get rid of? Answer choice (C).

So far, we have eliminated answer choices (A) and (C). Let's look at the remaining choices to see how they fix the error we found. Answer choice (B) changes "are" to "is," a singular verb. That works. Answer choice (D) does the same thing. Both of these choices are possible. Answer choice (E) changes the verb to "has been." A quick glance at the sentence tells us that this is in the wrong tense—we need present tense. Cross off answer choice (E).

Okay, down to two. The last thing to check is the difference between the two choices that fixed the original problem. Sometimes the underlined portion of the sentence contains a secondary error that also needs to be fixed. Other times, an answer may fix the original problem, but introduce a new error. In this example, the difference between (B) and (D) is that (B) uses the vague language "only one of the two is successful" while (D) clarifies "only one of the two books is successful." We know that Pam hates to be ambiguous, and (B) does not make it infinitely clear that the sentence is referring to one of the two books as opposed to one of the two authors. Therefore, our answer is (D).

Can You Say Time Consuming?

Wow—that took a while! As you can see, Better the Sentences are a bit more work than Error ID's. That's why you want to do all the Error ID questions before you attempt the Better the Sentences questions. Also, you may, on occasion, find it necessary to skip a Better the Sentence question, especially the ones that underline the entire sentence. As a general rule, if you can spot the error, you should do the question, since POE is on your side. If you can't spot the error immediately, try the back-up plan, but be ready to bag out if you are spending too much time on the question.

BACK-UP PLAN?

What's the back-up plan? Let's say you couldn't tell if there was an error in the example we just did. You thought it might be okay, but you weren't sure. How could you check? By scanning your answer choices. Your answer choices can tip you off to the error contained in a sentence by revealing what is being fixed in each choice. In the example we just did, a quick scan of the answer choices reveals that the verb is being altered:

    (A) ...are...
    (B) ...is...
    (C) ...are...
    (D) ...is...
    (E) ...has been...

Once you pick up on the error being tested, you can try to figure out which form is correct. Let's try another example, using our back-up plan to illustrate how it works:

Whenever people hear of a natural disaster, even in a distant part of the world, <u>you feel sympathy for the people affected</u>.

(A) you feel sympathy for the people affected
(B) people being affected causes sympathy
(C) they feel sympathetic for those people

(D) they feel sympathy for the people
affected
(E) you feel sympathetic for the people
affected

Here's How to Crack It

When you first read this sentence, you may feel that something is wrong, but may not be able to pinpoint what it is. No problem—let your answer choices do the work for you. A quick scan of the answer choices reveals a possible pronoun problem:

(A) you...
(B) people...
(C) they...
(D) they...
(E) you...

Now that you know what to check, let's Cut the Crap:

"Whenever people hear of a natural disaster...you..."

Is "you" the right pronoun to represent people? No. Cross off (A) and any other answer that doesn't fix the "you." That leaves us with (B), (C), and (D). If you have no idea how the rest of the sentence should read, you've still given yourself great odds of "guessing" this question correct. But let's forge ahead.

Answer choice (B) doesn't make any sense upon closer inspection. Cross it off. Now you're down to two. Which answer choice is more clear and less awkward? Answer choice (D):

"Whenever people hear of a natural
disaster...they feel sympathy for the people
affected."

OTHER LITTLE THINGS

We mentioned back at the beginning of this chapter that your grammar checklist should include a number 5: Other Little Things. In addition to testing the four main areas we've already reviewed, other little grammar things will be tested on the Better the Sentence questions. Let's look at some of these little grammar tidbits so you are ready for them when they turn up.

5. If everything else checks out, is the sentence
testing **other little things** like

(a) **faulty comparisons**?
(b) **misplaced modifiers**?
(c) **adjective/adverbs**?
(d) **diction**?

CAN YOU COMPARE?

There are several little things Pam tries to trip you up with when it comes to comparing. These things are not difficult, but are notoriously misused in spoken English, so you will need to make a note of them. First, when comparing two things, make sure what you are comparing can be compared. Sounds like double-talk? Look at the following sentence:

> Larry goes shopping at Foodtown because the prices are better than Shoprite.

Sound okay? Well, sorry—it's wrong. As written, this sentence says that the prices at Foodtown are better than Shoprite—the entire store. What Larry means is the prices at Foodtown are better than the *prices* at Shoprite. You can only compare like things (prices to prices, not prices to stores).

While we're on the subject of Foodtown, how many of you have seen this sign:

> Express Checkout: Ten items or less.

Unfortunately, supermarkets across America are making a blatant grammatical error when they post this sign. When items can be counted, you must use the word *fewer*. If something cannot be counted, you would use the word *less*. For example:

> If you eat *fewer* french fries, you can use *less* ketchup.

Other similar words include *many* (can be counted) versus *much* (cannot be counted):

> *Many* hands make *much* less work.

And *number* (can be counted) versus *amount* (cannot be counted):

> The same *number* of CDs played different *amounts* of music.

Two's Company; Three Or More Is . . .?

Finally, when comparing two things the English language uses different comparison words than when comparing more than two things. The following examples will jog your memory:

- **More** (for two things) vs. **Most** (for more than two)
  Given Alex and Dave as possible dates, Alex is the *more* appealing one.
  In fact, of all the guys I know, Alex is the *most* attractive.

- **Less** (for two things) vs. **Least** (for more than two)
  I am *less* likely to be chosen than you are.
  I am the *least* likely person to be chosen from the department.

- **Better** (for two things) vs. **Best** (for more than two)
  Taking a cab is *better* than hitch-hiking.
  My Princeton Review teacher is the *best* teacher I have ever had.

◆ **Between** (for two things)

> Just *between* you and me, I never liked her anyway.

> Jack was disappointed because his score on
> the test <u>was not as outstanding as Rob</u>.

> (A) was not as outstanding as Rob
> (B) did not stand out as much as Rob
> (C) was not as outstanding as Rob's score
> (D) did not surpass Rob
> (E) was not as outstanding than Rob's

Here's How To Crack It

What is being compared in this sentence? Jack is comparing his score with Rob. Can he do that? No! He really wants to compare his score with Rob's score.

Since you have identified an error, immediately cross off (A). Next, cross off any other answer choice that doesn't fix the error. That gets rid of (B) and (D). Now compare our remaining choices. While (E) technically fixes our problem by inserting the apostrophe (implying Rob's *score*), it makes a new error: "not as outstanding *than*." This is an incorrect idiom (remember those?). Pam's answer is (C).

MISPLACED MODIFIERS

A modifier is a descriptive word or phrase inserted in a sentence to add dimension to the thing it modifies. For example:

> *Because he could talk*, Mr. Ed was a unique horse.

"Because he could talk" is the modifying phrase in this sentence. It describes a characteristic of Mr. Ed. Generally speaking, a modifying phrase should be right next to the thing it modifies. If it's not, the meaning of the sentence may change. For example:

> Every time he goes to the bathroom outside, John praises his
> new puppy for being so good.

Who's going to the bathroom outside? In this sentence, it's John! There are laws against that! The descriptive phrase, "every time he goes to the bathroom outside" needs to be near the puppy in order for the sentence to say what it means.

When you are attacking Better the Sentence questions, watch out for sentences that begin with a descriptive phrase followed by a comma. If you see one, make sure the thing that comes after the comma is the person or thing being modified.

Try the following example:

> Perhaps the most beautiful natural vegetation in the world, the West of Ireland explodes each spring with a tremendous variety of wildflowers.
>
> (A) Perhaps the most beautiful natural vegetation in the world
> (B) In what may be the world's most beautiful natural vegetation
> (C) Home to what may be the most beautiful natural vegetation in the world
> (D) Its vegetation may be the world's most beautiful
> (E) More beautiful in its natural vegetation than anywhere else in the world

Here's How To Crack It

Is the West of Ireland vegetation? No, so cross off (A). We need an answer that will make the opening phrase modify the West of Ireland. Answer choice (B) is still modifying the vegetation, so cross it off. All three other choices fix the problem, but (C) does it the best. (D) makes the sentence a bit awkward, and (E) actually changes the meaning of the sentence by saying that the West of Ireland definitively has the most beautiful vegetation while the original sentence says "perhaps." Pam's answer is (C).

ADJECTIVES/ADVERBS

Misplaced modifiers aren't the only descriptive errors ETS will throw at you. Another way they try to trip you up is by using adjectives where they should use adverbs and vice versa. Remember that an *adjective* modifies a noun, while an *adverb* modifies verbs, adverbs, and adjectives. The adverb is the one that usually has an "- ly" on the end. In the following sentence, circle the adverbs and underline the adjectives:

> The stealthy thief, desperately hoping to evade the persistent police, ran quickly into the dank, dark alley after brazenly stealing the stunningly exquisite jewels.

First, let's list the adjectives along with the nouns they modify: *stealthy* thief, *persistent* police, *dank* alley, *dark* alley, *exquisite* jewels. Now for the adverbs with the words they modify: *desperately* hoping (verb), ran (verb) *quickly*, *brazenly* stealing (verb), *stunningly* exquisite (adjective).

Now try the following Better the Sentence example:

> Movie cameras are no longer particularly costly, but film, development, and editing equipment cause the monetary expense of making a film to add up tremendous.
>
> (A) cause the monetary expense of making a film to add up tremendous
> (B) add tremendously to the expense of making a film

(C) much increase the film-making expenses

(D) add to the tremendous expense of
    making a film

(E) tremendously add up to the expense of
    making a film

Here's How to Crack It

Hopefully you identified the error as soon as you read the sentence. What should the last word in the sentence be? Tremendous*ly*. Cross off (A), and also (D) since it doesn't fix the error (it also changes the meaning of the sentence). (C) is way out there, so cross it off too. In (E), the placement of the "tremendously" is awkward and slightly changes the meaning of the sentence. Pam's answer is (B).

DICTION

Finally, ETS may occasionally slip in a diction error just to keep you on your toes. Diction means choice of words. Diction errors are tough to spot because the incorrect word often looks a lot like the word that should have been used.

Drill 3

Here's a list of some potential diction traps. Indicate the difference between the words in each pair. See page 344 to check your work.

1. Imminent _____
   and Eminent _____?

2. Proscribe _____
   and Prescribe _____?

3. Intelligent _____
   and Intelligible _____?

4. Incredible _____
   and Incredulous _____?

5. Irritated _____
   and Aggravated _____?

6. Stationary _____
   and Stationery _____?

7. Illicit _____
   and Elicit _____?

GIVE IT A SHOT

Drill 4

Before we move on to Fix the Paragraph questions, try putting together what you've learned. Do the following Error ID and Better the Sentence questions using your Grammar Checklist. Remember to Cut the Crap and use POE. On Better the Sentences, do not hesitate to check out the answer choices for a clue to the error. You may wish to jot down your Grammar Checklist before you begin. (See page 344 for answers).

1. Eric's new CD <u>was destroyed</u> when Paula Ann,
    A
    running <u>quick</u> <u>through the office</u>, stepped on <u>it</u>.
    B   C   D
    <u>No error</u>
    E

2. <u>Because</u> <u>their class</u> was going on a field
    A   B
    trip that day, James and Alice <u>each</u> needed
    C
    <u>a lunch</u> to bring to school. <u>No error</u>
    D   E

3. None <u>of the students</u> on the review board
    A
    <u>is qualified</u> to ascertain <u>whether</u> the
    B   C
    money was <u>well spent</u>. <u>No error</u>
    D   E

4. Just <u>between</u> you and <u>I</u>, Wayne's World 2 was
    A   B
    the dumbest movie I <u>have</u> ever <u>seen</u>. <u>No error</u>
    C   D   E

5. If you <u>look</u> at the prices <u>close</u>, you'll see that the
    A   B
    "economy size" of detergent is <u>actually</u> more
    C
    expensive than the <u>smaller</u> trial sizes. <u>No error</u>
    D   E

6. The <u>new</u> course schedule worked out
              A

    <u>splendid</u> for all of <u>those students</u> who
         B   C

    <u>had been</u> concerned. <u>No error</u>
         D   E

7. Artists can offer startling representations of
    the world <u>but with their responsibility</u> to
    elevate humanity.

    (A) but with their responsibility
    (B) with the responsibility
    (C) having also the responsibility
    (D) but ought also
    (E) their responsibility being as well

8. When the bridge was built in the 1890s, <u>the
    intention was for two small towns that they
    once were to be connected, not the large cities
    that they have become.</u>

    (A) the intention was for two small towns
         that they once were to be connected, not
         the large cities that they have become
    (B) it was intended to connect the two small
         towns that existed at that time, rather
         than the large cities that the towns have
         become
    (C) there were not two large cities, like now,
         but rather two small towns that the
         bridge was intended to connect
    (D) it was intended to connect not the two
         large cities that they have become but
         rather the two small towns that then
         existed
    (E) the connection was rather between the
         two small towns then in existence than
         the two large cities that the two small
         towns have become

9. <u>In 1962 Jackie Robinson gained admission to the National Baseball Hall of Fame, he was the first Black baseball player in the major leagues.</u>

(A) In 1962 Jackie Robinson gained admission to the National Baseball Hall of Fame, he was the first Black baseball player in the major leagues

(B) In 1962 Jackie Robinson, the first Black major-league baseball player, gained admission to the National Baseball Hall of Fame

(C) In the National Baseball Hall of Fame in 1962, Jackie Robinson, the first Black baseball player in the major leagues, was admitted to it

(D) With admission to the National Baseball hall of fame in 1962, he was the first Black major-league player to do it, Jackie Robinson

(E) The first Black major-league player was when he was Jackie Robinson, admitted to the national Baseball Hall of Fame in 1962

10. A well-organized person can go through the day efficiently, <u>wasting little time or they waste none at all.</u>

(A) wasting little time or they waste none at all

(B) wasting little or no time

(C) wasting little time or wasting none at all

(D) wasting either little time or none

(E) either little or no time being wasted

11. When Michelle Shocked recorded her *Arkansas Traveler* album, <u>regional American folk songs were used as inspiration, but it was never copied exactly by her.</u>

(A) regional American folk songs were used as inspiration, but it was never copied exactly by her

(B) regional American folk songs were used as inspiration, but she never copied them exactly

(C) regional American folk songs were used as inspiration by her and not copied exactly

(D) she used regional American folk songs, but they were not exactly copied

(E) she used regional American folk songs as inspiration, but never copied them exactly

12. The patient began his difficult post-surgery <u>recovery, but he was</u> able to recover from the psychological effects of the injury.

(A) recovery, but he was
(B) recovery, where he was
(C) recovery only when he was
(D) recovery only when being
(E) recovery, also he was

IMPROVING PARAGRAPH A.K.A. FIX THE PARAGRAPH

After you do all of the Error ID and Better the Sentence questions, you'll be left with six Improving Paragraph questions (hence forth to be known as Fix the Paragraph questions). Luckily, these questions come last in the section. They are not particularly difficult, but they are more time-consuming than the other two question types.

The six Fix the Paragraph questions require you to make corrections to a replica "first draft" of a student's essay. You will be given a "rough draft" comprised of approximately three paragraphs. Each paragraph contains numbered sentences. Your job is to "edit" the rough draft to make it better.

Here is a sample passage:

(1) Conservation and ecology are the hot topics at our school. (2) Students used to just throw everything out in one big garbage pail. (3) Sure, it was easy. (4) It wasn't good for the environment.

(5) I volunteered to head up the conservation team. (6) My friends and I decided to map out our strategies. (7) First we needed to get students to become aware of the problem. (8) Educating was important. (9) A thing to do was implement a recycling program. (10) We checked with the local town government. (11) They would supply the recycling bins. (12) We had to supply the people who'd be willing to recycle. (13) The most important thing students had to learn to do was to separate their garbage. (14) Glass in one container. (15) Plastic in another.

(16) Our final step was to get the teachers and administrators involved. (17) Paper can be recycled too. (18) We ran a poster contest. (19) The winners are hanging in our halls. (20) Reuse, recycle, renew. (21) That's our school's new motto.

Now before you get out your red pencil and jump in, there are a few more things you need to know. Your passage may consist of 15–20 or more sentences, each potentially containing some kind of error. However, you will only be asked six questions. Don't spend time fixing errors for which there's no question.

THE QUESTIONS

There are three basic questions you will be asked:

- ◆ **Revision questions**: These questions ask you to revise sentences or parts of sentences much the way Better the Sentence questions do.

- ◆ **Combination questions**: These questions ask you to combine two or more sentences to improve the quality and/or flow of the paragraph.

- ◆ **Content Questions**: These questions ask you about passage content, typically by asking you to insert a sentence before or after a paragraph.

Go to the Questions, Go Directly to the Questions

Instead of wasting a lot of time reading the rough draft, go directly to the questions. There are far more errors in the passage than you'll ever be asked about—reading the passage first will simply waste your time and confuse you.

Also, for many of the questions the sentences you need to fix are reprinted right under the question, so you won't necessarily need to go back to the paragraph to answer a question. Let's talk about each type of question so you know how to approach it.

REVISION QUESTIONS

As we mentioned, these questions are very similar to Better the Sentence questions. Therefore, you can follow the same basic approach. One warning: There is normally no such thing as "No Error" on Fix the Paragraph questions. Do not assume that (A) is merely a repeat of the given sentence.

Even though the sentence you are revising is provided for you, you may still need to go back to the passage to gain some context when trying to fix a sentence. Before going back, however, use POE. If you have spotted an error in the given sentence, cross off answers that don't fix it. Also, cross off answer choices that contain obvious errors. After doing some POE, go back and read a few sentences before and after the given sentence. This should be enough context for you to determine the best edit.

Try the following Revision Question—refer back to the sample passage when needed.

> In context, what is the best way to revise sentence 9 (reproduced below)?
>
> *A thing to do was implement a recycling program.*
>
> (A) Next, we needed to implement a recycling program.
> (B) Implementing a recycling program was a thing to do.
> (C) A recycling program needed to be implemented.

(D) Implementing a program for recycling
was the step that would be next.
(E) A program would need to be
implemented next for recycling.

Here's How to Crack It

The correct revision will be concise and unambiguous. It will also flow well. We can get rid of choices (B), (D), and (E) before going back to the passage. Choice (B) is as clunky as the given sentence; choices (D) and (E) are awkwardly written.

After doing some elimination, go back and read, beginning with line (7). "First we needed to get students to become aware of the problem. Education was important. *Next...*" When you read this segment, the word next should be jumping into your brain. Sentence (9) seems out of place until you realize that it is a new thought, the next step. Pam's answer is (A).

COMBINATION QUESTIONS

Combination questions are revision questions with a twist: you are working with two sentences instead of one. The sentences are almost always reprinted for you under the question and usually you can answer these questions without going back to the passage at all. As with revision questions, do what you can first, then go back to the passage if necessary.

To combine sentences you will need to work with conjunctions. (Remember *School House Rock's* "Conjunction Junction"?) If the sentences are flowing in the same direction, look for an answer with words like "and," "since," "as well as," etc. If the sentences seem to be flowing in opposite directions, look for trigger words in the answer choices such as "however," "but," "on the contrary," etc.

Try the following without going back to the passage:

> Which of the following represents the most
> effective way to combine sentences 20 and 21
> (reproduced below)?
>
> *Reuse, recycle, renew. That's our school's new
> motto.*
>
> (A) Reuse, recycle, renew and you know our
> school's new motto.
> (B) The new motto of our school is that:
> Reuse, recycle, renew.
> (C) Reuse, recycle, renew are the new motto
> of our school now.
> (D) The new motto of our school is reusing,
> recycling, and renewing.
> (E) Reuse, recycle, renew is our school's new
> motto.

Here's How to Crack It

First, the sentences are moving in the same direction. Your job is to find a clear, concise way to combine them. (A) and (B) are out because they are poorly worded. (C) is a trap: "Reuse, recycle, and renew" *is* a motto. Don't be fooled into thinking you need a plural verb simply because of the "and." Choice (D) uses the passive voice (doesn't it just *sound* whimpy?) Pam's answer is (E).

Try another:

> Which of the following represents the best revision of the underlined portions of sentences 7 and 8 (reproduced below)?
>
> *First we needed to get students to become aware of the <u>problem. Educating was important.</u>*
>
> (A) problem for educating was important
> (B) problem of educating. It was important
> (C) problem to educate was important
> (D) problem: education was important
> (E) problem for education was important to us

Here's How to Crack It

Again we have a same direction combination going on. We need something that flows. (A) and (C) are using the wrong prepositions, which slightly change the meaning of the sentence. Cross them off. (B) is as awkward or more awkward than the original sentence. (E) uses the wrong preposition and adds extra awkward stuff. Pam's answer is (D). The colon is a nice, neat way to continue a thought without using two sentences.

CONTENT QUESTIONS

ETS will occasionally ask you a question regarding the content of the passage. These questions may ask:

1. Which sentence should immediately follow or precede the passage?

2. Which sentence should be inserted into a passage?

3. What is the best description of the passage as a whole?

If you are asked the third question, you will need to skim the whole passage. Ordinarily, however, you will more likely be asked one of the first two questions. To answer these, you will need to read the relevant paragraph.

Try this example using the sample passage from earlier in this section:

> Which of the following sentences, if added after sentence (4), would best serve to link the first paragraph to the second paragraph?
>
> (A) Unfortunately, the environment suffered.
> (B) Clearly, we had to make a change.
> (C) Easy things are often not good for the environment.
> (D) However, people can be very lazy.
> (E) The school was against any change.

Here's How to Crack It

To solve this question, you need to quickly read the first paragraph and the first sentence of the second paragraph. At the end of the first paragraph, something like "something had to be done" may have popped into your head. This is essentially what the connecting sentence needs to say.

(A), (C), and (D) are out because they focus on the "problems" theme from the first paragraph instead of making a transition to the second paragraph. (E) is not implied anywhere in the passage. Pam's answer is (B).

TIME IS OF THE ESSENCE

Now, keep in mind that this is the end of a 30-minute section at the end of a 2+ hour test. Chances are you won't have the time or the gumption to do all the Fix the Paragraph questions. Therefore, reorder the six Fix the Paragraph questions so you are doing the shorter, easier questions first. Then, if you have the time and the inclination, do the longer questions.

The shorter, easier questions are the Combination questions and the Revision questions that reprint the sentences you need to edit. Do anything that doesn't require you to go back to the passage. Then do questions that require you to go back to specific areas of the passage. Finally, do the ones that require some reading.

Drill 5

Try the following Fix the Paragraph drill to practice what you have learned. Check your answers on page 345.

(1) Censorship in the media is an extremely important issue throughout the twentieth century. (2) In the 1950s television programs and movies had to comply with codes that enforced strict standards of propriety. (3) Couples were shown sleeping in separate beds, and the concept of nudity or verbal profanity was unheard of. (4) In reaction to them, in the 1960s and 70s the media abandoned the codes in favor of more realistic representations of relationships and everyday life. (5) Filmmakers and songwriters were able to express themselves more honestly and freely. (6) The idea that in the early 60s the Rolling Stones had to change their lyrics from "let's spend the night together," to "let's spend some time together" seemed almost unlikely by the end of the decade.

(7) Yet in the mid-1980s a period of conservative reaction occurred, turning the cycle around. (8) Explicit song lyrics began to be censored. (9) Warning labels were added to the covers of albums. (10) The labels indicated that some of the language might be "offensive" to the consumer. (11) It is unfortunate that

people feel the need to blame the media for societal problems instead of realizing that the media only brings to *light the problems that already exist.*

(12) Hopefully, our reactions will ultimately break free of all previous patterns. (13) Yet until this happens we must remain content to know that the good parts of the past, as well as the bad, repeat themselves.

1. In context, what is the best version of the underlined portion of sentence 1 (reproduced below)?

   Censorship in the media <u>is an extremely</u> important issue throughout the twentieth century.

   (A) (As it is now)
   (B) was extremely
   (C) has been an extremely
   (D) has been extreme as an
   (E) will be an extremely

2. Which of the following would be the best subject for a paragraph immediately preceding this essay?

   (A) The types of movies most popular in the 1950s
   (B) The changing role of the media over the last ten years
   (C) The ways in which the economy affects society's political views
   (D) The role of the media in European countries
   (E) The roots of media censorship

3. The author wishes to divide the first paragraph into two shorter paragraphs. The most appropriate place to begin a new paragraph would be

   (A) between sentences 1 and 2
   (B) between sentences 2 and 3
   (C) between sentences 3 and 4
   (D) between sentences 4 and 5
   (E) between sentences 5 and 6

4. In sentence 4, the word "them" could best be replaced with which of the following?

   (A) couples
   (B) beds
   (C) nudity and profanity
   (D) relationships
   (E) the codes

5. What word could best replace "unlikely" in sentence 6?

   (A) strange
   (B) conventional
   (C) unpopular
   (D) inconceivable
   (E) unbearable

6. Which would be the best way to revise and combine the underlined portions of sentences 9 and 10 (reproduced below)?

   Warning labels were added to the covers of albums. The labels indicated that some of the language might be "offensive" to the consumer.

   (A) albums, indicating
   (B) albums, which indicated
   (C) albums, and they indicated
   (D) albums, the indication being
   (E) albums, being indicative

Final Words of Wisdom

As with all the sections of the PSAT, you are rewarded for answering the question. Don't be afraid to do some POE and guess. You will almost always be able to eliminate some answer choices, so allow your partial knowledge to earn you credit on the test.

PART ◆ III

How to Crack
the Math SAT

A Few Words About Numbers

Three of the six scored sections on the SAT are math sections. Two of the scored math sections will last thirty minutes each; the third will last fifteen minutes. There may be a fourth, thirty-minute math section on your test, but it won't count toward your score. Don't waste time trying to figure out which sections are the scored ones. Just work at your normal pace.

The math questions on your SAT will be drawn from the following three categories:

1. arithmetic
2. basic algebra
3. geometry

The math questions on your SAT will appear in three different formats:

1. regular multiple-choice questions
2. quantitative comparisons
3. grid-ins

Quantitative comparisons are questions in which you are asked to compare two values and determine whether one is greater than the other. Grid-ins are the only non-multiple-choice questions on the SAT; instead of selecting Jim's answer from among several choices, you will have to find Jim's answer independently and mark it in a grid. The quant comps and grid-ins on your test will be drawn from arithmetic, algebra, and geometry, just like regular SAT math questions. But these formats have special characteristics, so we will treat them separately.

What Does the Math SAT Measure?

ETS says that the math SAT measures "mathematical reasoning abilities" or "higher-order reasoning abilities." But this is not true. The math SAT is merely a brief test of arithmetic, first-year algebra, and a bit of geometry. By a "bit" we mean just that. The principles you'll need to know are few and simple. We'll show you which ones are important. Most of them are listed for you at the beginning of each math section.

Order of Difficulty

As was true on the verbal SAT, questions on the math SAT are arranged in order of difficulty. The first question in each math section will be the easiest in that section, and the last will be the hardest. In addition, the questions within the quantitative comparison and grid-in question groups will also be arranged in order of difficulty. The difficulty of a problem will help you determine how to attack it.

No Need to Know

Here are a few things that you won't need to know to answer SAT math questions: calculus, trigonometry, the quadratic formula. Essentially, the SAT tests the math you learned in junior high and your first two years of high school.

YOU DON'T HAVE TO FINISH

We've all been taught in school that when you take a test, you have to finish it. If you only answered two-thirds of the questions on a high school math test, you probably wouldn't get a very good grade. But as we've already seen, the SAT is not at all like the tests you take in school. Most students don't know about the difference, so they make the mistake of doing all the problems on each math section of the SAT.

Since they only have a limited amount of time to answer all the questions, most students are always in a rush to get to the end of the section. At first, this seems reasonable, but think about the order of difficulty for a minute. All the easy questions are at the beginning of a math section, and the hard questions are at the end. So when students rush through a math section, they're actually spending less time on the easier questions (which they have a good chance of getting right), just so they can spend more time on the harder questions (which they have very little chance of getting right). Does this make sense? Of course not.

Here's the secret. On the math SAT, you don't have to answer every question in each section. In fact, unless you're trying to score 600 or more, you shouldn't even look at the difficult last third of the math questions. The fact is, most students can raise their math scores by concentrating on getting all the easy and medium questions correct. In other words...

SLOW DOWN!

Most students do considerably better on the math SAT when they slow down and spend less time worrying about the hard questions (and more time working carefully on the easier ones). Haste causes careless errors (such as 6 × 8 = 42), and careless errors can ruin your score. In most cases, you can actually *raise* your scores by answering *fewer* questions. That doesn't sound like a bad idea, does it? If you're shooting for an 800, you'll have to answer every question correctly. But if your target is 550, you should ignore the hardest questions in each section and use your limited time wisely.

To make sure you're working at the right pace in each math section, refer to the math pacing chart on page 35. The chart will tell you how many questions you need to answer in each section in order to achieve your next score goal.

THE PRINCETON REVIEW APPROACH

We're going to give you the tools you need to handle the easier questions on the math SAT, along with several great techniques to help you crack some of the more difficult ones. But you must concentrate first on getting the easier questions correct. Don't worry about the difficult third of the math SAT until you've learned to work carefully and accurately on the easier questions.

Better Than Average

If you got 70% on a math test in school, you'd feel pretty lousy—that's a C minus, below average. But the SAT is not like school. Getting 42 out of 60 questions correct (70%) would give you a math score of about 600—100 points *above* the national average.

When it does come time to look at some of the harder questions, the Joe Bloggs principle will help you once again, this time to zero in on Jim's answer. You'll learn what kinds of answers appeal to Joe in math, and how to avoid those answers. Just as you did in the verbal section, you'll learn to use POE to find Jim's answer by getting rid of obviously incorrect answers.

Generally speaking, each chapter in the math section of this book begins with the basics and then gradually moves into more advanced principles and techniques. If you find yourself getting lost toward the end of the chapter, don't worry. Concentrate your efforts on principles you can understand but still need to master.

FUNDAMENTALS

Although we'll show you which mathematical concepts are most important to know for the SAT, this book cannot take the place of a basic foundation in math. For example, if you discover as you read this book that you have trouble working with fractions, you'll want to go back and review the fundamentals. Our drills and examples in this book will refresh your memory if you've gotten rusty, but if you have serious difficulty with the following chapters, you should consider getting extra help. For this purpose, we recommend our own *Math Smart*, which is designed to give you a thorough review of all the fundamental math concepts that you'll need to know on the SAT. Always keep in mind that the math tested on the SAT is different from the math taught in school. If you want to raise your score, don't waste time studying math that Jim never tests.

CALCULATORS

Students are permitted (but not required) to use calculators on the SAT. You should definitely bring a calculator to the test. It will be extremely helpful to you, as long as you know how and when to use it and don't get carried away. We'll tell you more about calculators as we go along.

BASIC INFORMATION

Before moving on, you should be certain that you are familiar with some basic terms and concepts that you'll need to know for the math SAT. This material isn't at all difficult, but you must know it cold. If you don't, you'll waste valuable time on the test and lose points that you easily could have earned.

INTEGERS

Integers are the numbers that most of us are accustomed to thinking of simply as "numbers." They can be either positive or negative. The positive integers are:

1, 2, 3, 4, 5, 6, 7, and so on

The negative integers are:

–1, –2, –3, –4, –5, –6, –7, and so on

Zero (0) is also an integer, but it is neither positive nor negative.

Note that positive integers get bigger as they move away from 0, while negative integers get smaller. In other words, 2 is bigger than 1, but –2 is smaller than –1. This number line should give you a clear idea of how negative numbers work.

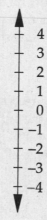

Negative Land

Think of integers as steps on a staircase leading up from the cellar (the negatives), through a doorway (zero), and above the ground (the positives). Five steps down (–5) is farther below ground than four steps down (–4) because you're one step farther away from the cellar door (0). Integers are like stairs because when climbing stairs, you can't use a fraction of a step.

You should also remember the types of numbers that are *not* integers. Here are some examples:

–2.7, .625, 15.898, –9.8

Basically, integers are numbers that have *no* fractions or decimals. So if you see a number with fractions or decimals, it's *not* an integer.

DISTINCT NUMBERS

You might see problems on the SAT that mention "distinct numbers." Don't let this throw you. All ETS means by distinct numbers is different numbers. For example, the set of numbers 2, 3, 4, and 5 are a set of distinct numbers, whereas 2, 2, 3, and 4 would not be a set of distinct numbers because 2 appears twice. Easy concept, tricky wording.

DIGITS

There are ten digits:

$$0, 1, 2, 3, 4, 5, 6, 7, 8, 9$$

All integers are made up of digits. In the integer 3,476, the digits are 3, 4, 7, and 6. Digits are to numbers as letters are to words.

The integer 645 is called a "three-digit number" for obvious reasons. Each of its digits has a different name depending on its place in the number:

5 is called the *units* digit

4 is called the *tens* digit

6 is called the *hundreds* digit

Thus the value of any number depends on which digits are in which places. The number 645 could be rewritten as follows:

$$6 \times 100 = 600$$
$$4 \times 10 = 40$$
$$+ 5 \times 1 = + 5$$
$$\overline{645}$$

POSITIVE AND NEGATIVE

There are three rules regarding the multiplication of positive and negative numbers:

1. pos × pos = pos
2. neg × neg = pos
3. pos × neg = neg

ODD AND EVEN

Even numbers are integers that can be divided evenly by 2. Here are some examples of even numbers:

$$-4, -2, 0, 2, 4, 6, 8, 10, \text{ and so on}$$

You can always tell at a glance whether a number is even: It is even if its final digit is even. Thus 999,999,999,992 is an even number because 2, the final digit, is an even number.

Odd numbers are integers that cannot be divided evenly by 2. Here are some examples of odd numbers:

$$-5, -3, -1, 1, 3, 5, 7, 9, \text{ and so on}$$

You can always tell at a glance whether a number is odd: It is odd if its final digit is odd. Thus, 222,222,222,229 is an odd number because 9, the final digit, is an odd number.

Several rules always hold true with odd and even numbers:

$$\text{even} + \text{even} = \text{even} \qquad \text{even} \times \text{even} = \text{even}$$

$$\text{odd} + \text{odd} = \text{even} \qquad \text{odd} \times \text{odd} = \text{odd}$$

$$\text{even} + \text{odd} = \text{odd} \qquad \text{even} \times \text{odd} = \text{even}$$

REMAINDERS

Leftovers

Don't try to figure remainders on your calculator. On your calculator, 25 divided by 3 is 8.3333333, but .3333333 is not the remainder. The remainder is 1.

If a number cannot be divided evenly by another number, the number left over at the end of the division is called the remainder. For example, 25 cannot be divided evenly by 3; 25 divided by 3 is 8 with 1 left over. The 1 is the remainder.

CONSECUTIVE INTEGERS

Consecutive integers are integers listed in increasing order of size without any integers missing in between. For example, –1, 0, 1, 2, 3, 4, and 5 are consecutive integers; 2, 4, 5, 7, and 8 are not. Nor are –1, –2, –3, and –4 consecutive integers, because they are decreasing in size.

PRIME NUMBERS

Prime Time

Here are a few important facts about prime numbers:

- 0 and 1 are not prime numbers.
- 2 is the smallest prime number.
- 2 is the only even prime number.
- Not all odd numbers are prime: 1, 9, 15, 21, and many others are *not* prime.

A prime number is a number that can be divided evenly only by itself and by 1. For example, the following are all the prime numbers less than 30: 2, 3, 5, 7, 11, 13, 17, 19, 23, 29. (Note: 1 is not prime.)

DIVISIBILITY RULES

You may be called upon to determine whether one number can be divided evenly by another. To do so, use your calculator. If the result is an integer, the number is evenly divisible. Is 4,569 divisible by 3? Simply punch up the numbers on your calculator. The result is 1,523, which is an integer, so you have determined that 4,569 is indeed divisible by 3. Is 2,789 divisible by 3? The result on your calculator is 596.33333, which is not an integer, so 2,789 is not divisible by 3. (Integers don't have decimal points with digits after them.)

STANDARD SYMBOLS

The following standard symbols are used frequently on the SAT:

SYMBOL	MEANING
$=$	is equal to
$\neq$	is not equal to
$<$	is less than
$>$	is greater than
$\leq$	is less than or equal to
$\geq$	is greater than or equal to

FINALLY, THE INSTRUCTIONS

Each of the three scored math sections on your SAT will begin with the same set of instructions. These instructions include a few formulas and other information that you may need to know in order to answer some of the questions. You must learn these instructions ahead of time. You should never have to waste valuable time by referring to them during the test.

Still, if you do suddenly blank out on one of the formulas while taking the test, you can always refresh your memory by glancing back at the instructions. Be sure to familiarize yourself with them thoroughly ahead of time, so you'll know which formulas are there.

The instructions as they will appear on your test are shown below. (Several abbreviations are used in the formulas: *A* means area, *r* means radius, *C* means circumference, and *V* means volume.)

The SAT Formula

Why would Jim give you all those geometric formulas on the test? Because the SAT is not really a geometry test. Jim doesn't care about geometric proofs, because ETS doesn't want to spend the money grading proofs. So, they dress up arithmetic and algebra with the occasional geometric figure. You need to know some rules of geometry, but not the way you do in a real geometry class.

Time—30 Minutes 25 Questions	In this section solve each problem, using any available space on the page for scratchwork. Then decide which is the best of the choices given and fill in the corresponding oval on the answer sheet.

Notes:

(1)   The use of a calculator is permitted. All numbers used are real numbers.

(2)   Figures that accompany problems in this test are intended to provide information useful in solving the problems. They are drawn as accurately as possible EXCEPT when it is stated in a specific problem that the figure is not drawn to scale. All figures lie in a plane unless otherwise indicated.

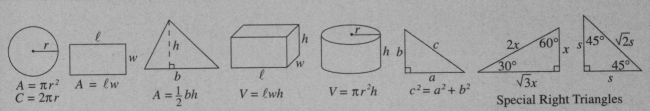

The number of degrees of arc in a circle is 360.
The measure in degrees of a straight angle is 180.
The sum of the measures in degrees of the angles of a triangle is 180.

10

Joe Bloggs and the Math SAT

Yo, Joe!

Joe Bloggs has already been a big help to you on the verbal SAT questions. By learning to anticipate which answer choices would attract Joe on difficult questions, you now know how to avoid careless mistakes and eliminate obviously incorrect answers.

You can do the same thing on the math SAT. In fact, Joe Bloggs answers are even easier to spot on math questions. Jim is quite predictable in the way he writes incorrect answer choices, and this predictability will make it possible for you to zero in on his answers to questions that might have seemed impossible to you before.

How Joe Thinks

As was true on the verbal SAT, Joe Bloggs gets the easy questions right and the hard questions wrong. In chapter 3, we introduced Joe by showing you how he approached a particular math problem. That problem, you may remember, involved the calculation of an average speed. Here it is again:

No Problem

Joe Bloggs is attracted to easy solutions arrived at through methods that he understands.

PROBLEM SOLVING		
1 2 3 4 5 6 7 8	9 10 11 12 13 14 15 16 17	18 19 20 21 22 23 24 ㉕
EASY	MEDIUM	HARD

25 A woman drove to work at an average speed of 40 miles per hour and returned along the same route at 30 miles per hour. If her total traveling time was 1 hour, what was the total number of miles in the round trip?

(A) 30

(B) $30\frac{1}{7}$

(C) $34\frac{2}{7}$

(D) 35

(E) 40

When we showed this problem the first time, you were just learning about Joe Bloggs. Now that you've made him your invisible partner on the SAT, you ought to know a great deal about how he thinks. Your next step is to put Joe to work for you on the math sections.

Here's How to Crack It

This problem was the last in a 25-question math section. Therefore, it was the hardest problem in that section. Naturally, Joe got it wrong.

The answer choice most attractive to Joe on this problem is D. The question obviously involves an average of some kind, and 35 is the average of 30 and 40, so Joe picked it. Choice D just seemed like the right answer to Joe. (Of course, it wasn't the right answer; Joe gets the hard ones wrong.)

Avoid Repeats

Joe Bloggs is attracted to answer choices that simply repeat numbers from the problem.

Because this is true, we know which answers we should avoid on hard questions: answers that seem obvious or that can be arrived at simply and quickly. If the answer really were obvious and if finding it really were simple, the question would be easy, not hard.

Joe Bloggs is also attracted to answer choices that simply repeat numbers from the problem.

This means, of course, that you should avoid such choices. In the problem about the woman traveling to work, you can also eliminate choices A and E, because 30 and 40 are numbers repeated directly from the problem. Therefore, they are extremely unlikely to be Jim's answer.

We've now eliminated three of the five answer choices. Even if you couldn't figure out anything else about this questions, you'd have a fifty-fifty chance of guessing correctly. Those are excellent odds, considering that we really didn't do any math. By eliminating answer choices that we knew were wrong, we were able to beat Jim at his own game. (Jim's answer to this question is C, by the way.)

PUTTING JOE TO WORK ON THE MATH SAT

Generally speaking, the Joe Bloggs principle teaches you to:

- ◆ trust your hunches on easy questions

- ◆ double-check your hunches on medium questions

- ◆ eliminate Joe Bloggs answers on difficult questions

The rest of this chapter is devoted to using Joe Bloggs to zero in on Jim's answers to difficult questions. Of course, your main concern is still to answer all easy and medium question correctly. But if you have some time left at the end of a math section, the Joe Bloggs principle can help you eliminate answers on a few difficult questions, so that you can venture some good guesses. And as we've already seen, smart guessing means more points. (In chapter 15, you'll learn how to use Joe Bloggs to answer quantitative comparison questions; in chapter 16, you'll learn how he can help you on grid-ins.)

BASIC TECHNIQUES

Hard Questions = Hard Answers

As we've just explained, hard questions on the SAT simply don't have correct answers that are obvious to the average person. Avoiding the "obvious" choices will take some discipline on your part, but you'll lose points if you don't. Even if you're a math whiz, the Joe Bloggs principle will keep you from making careless mistakes.

Here's an example:

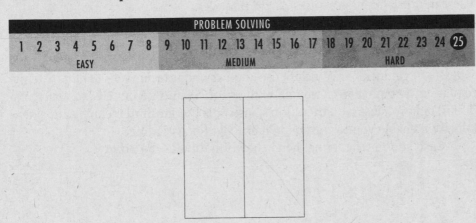

| PROBLEM SOLVING |
| 1 2 3 4 5 6 7 8   9 10 11 12 13 14 15 16 17   18 19 20 21 22 23 24 **㉕** |
| EASY   MEDIUM   HARD |

25. The figure above is a square divided into two nonoverlapping regions. What is the greatest number of nonoverlapping regions that can be obtained by drawing any two additional straight lines?

 (A) 4
 (B) 5
 (C) 6
 (D) 7
 (E) 8

Here's How to Crack It

This is the last question from a math section. Therefore, it's extremely difficult. One reason it's so difficult is that it is badly written. (Jim's strengths are mathematical, not verbal.) Here's a clearer way to think of it: The drawing is a pizza cut in half; what's the greatest number of pieces you could end up with if you make just two more cuts with a knife?

The most obvious way to cut the pizza would be to make cuts perpendicular to the center cut, dividing the pizza into six pieces, like this:

Joe Likes to Share

When it comes to the goofy "nonoverlapping region" questions, Joe's own good nature gets the best of him and he assumes that he must divide the figure evenly. That's why he likes to pick "(C) 6" on this problem. But, *nowhere does the question say the regions must be equal in size.* Read carefully.

There, that was fast and easy. So that means 6 is Jim's answer, right? Wrong. That was too easy, which means that 6 can't possibly be Jim's answer, and choice C can be eliminated. If finding Jim's answer were that simple, Joe Bloggs would have gotten this question right and it would have been an easy question, not a difficult one.

Will this fact help you eliminate any other choices? Yes. Because you know that if you can divide the pizza into at least six pieces, neither five nor four could be the greatest number of pieces into which it can be divided. Six is a greater number than either 5 or 4; if you can get six pieces you can also get five or four. You can thus eliminate choices A and B as well.

Discipline

When you actually take the SAT you may find that you are irresistibly attracted to an "obvious" choice on a hard SAT math question. You'll look at the problem and see no other possible solution. If this happens, you may say to yourself, "Aha! I've found an exception to the Joe Bloggs rule!" Don't be tempted. Eliminate obvious answers.

Now you've narrowed it down to two choices. Which will you pick? You shouldn't waste time trying to find the exact answer to a question like this. It isn't testing any mathematical principle, and you won't figure out the trick unless you get lucky. If you can't use another of our techniques to eliminate the remaining wrong answer, you should just guess and go on. Heads you win a dollar, tails you lose a quarter. (Jim's answer is D. Our third technique, incidentally, will enable you to zero in on it exactly. Keep reading.)

In case you're wondering, here's how Jim divides the pizza:

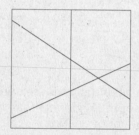

Here's another example:

PROBLEM SOLVING																								
1	2	3	4	5	6	7	8	9	10	11	12	13	14	15	16	17	18	19	20	21	22	23	**24**	25
		EASY									MEDIUM										HARD			

24 A 25-foot ladder is placed against a vertical wall of a building with the bottom of the ladder standing on concrete 7 feet from the base of the building. If the top of the ladder slips down 4 feet, then the bottom of the ladder will slide out how many feet?

(A) 4 ft
(B) 5 ft
(C) 6 ft
(D) 7 ft
(E) 8 ft

Here's How to Crack It

Which answer seems simple and obvious? Choice A, of course. If a ladder slips down 4 feet on one end, it seems obvious that it would slide out 4 feet on the other.

What does that mean? It means that we can eliminate choice A. If 4 feet were Jim's answer, Joe Bloggs would get this problem right and it would be an easy question, not one of the hardest in the section.

Choice A also repeats a number from the problem, which means we can be doubly certain that it's wrong. Which other choice repeats a number? Choice D. So we can eliminate that one, too.

If you don't know how to do this problem, working on it further probably won't get you anywhere. You've eliminated two choices; guess and move on. (Jim's answer is E. Use the Pythagorean theorem—see chapter 14.)

SIMPLE OPERATIONS = WRONG ANSWERS ON HARD QUESTIONS

Since Joe Bloggs doesn't usually think of difficult mathematical operations, he is attracted to solutions that use very simple arithmetic. Therefore, any answer choice that is the result of simple arithmetic should be eliminated on hard SAT math questions.

Here's an example:

PROBLEM SOLVING		
1 2 3 4 5 6 7 8	9 10 11 12 13 14 15 16 17	18 19 **20** 21 22 23 24 25
EASY	MEDIUM	HARD

20 A dress is selling for $100 after a 20 percent discount. What was the original selling price?

(A) $200
(B) $125
(C) $120
(D) $80
(E) $75

Here's How to Crack It

When Joe Bloggs looks at this problem he sees *20 percent less than $100* and is attracted to choice D. Therefore, you must eliminate it. If finding the answer were that easy, Joe Bloggs would be on his way to Harvard. Joe is also attracted to choice C, which is 20 percent more than $100. Again, eliminate.

With two Joe Bloggs answers out of the way, you ought to be able to solve this problem quickly. The dress is on sale, which means that its original price must have been more than its current price. That means that Jim's answer has to be greater than $100. Two of the remaining choices, A and B, fulfill this requirement. Now you can ask yourself:

(A) Is $100 20 percent less than $200? No. Eliminate.

(B) Is $100 20 percent less than $125? Could be. This must be Jim's answer. (It is.)

Temptation

With the Joe Bloggs attractors out of the way, you can often find Jim's answer quickly by using common sense to eliminate obviously incorrect choices. The temptations of Joe Bloggs answers often obscure more sensible answer choices.

LEAST/GREATEST

Hard SAT math problems will sometimes ask you to find the least or greatest number that fulfills certain conditions. On such problems, Joe Bloggs is attracted to the answer choice containing the least or greatest number. You can therefore eliminate such choices. (ETS sometimes uses similar words that mean the same thing: *most, maximum, fewest, minimum,* and so on. The same rules apply to problems containing all such terms.)

Look back at the square problem on page 165. The question asks you for the greatest number of regions into which the square can be divided. Which choice will therefore attract Joe Bloggs? Choice E. Eight is the greatest number among the choices offered, so it will seem right to Joe. Therefore, you can eliminate it.

Here's another example:

PROBLEM SOLVING																								
1	2	3	4	5	6	7	8	9	10	11	12	13	14	15	16	**17**	18	19	20	21	22	23	24	25
			EASY									MEDIUM										HARD		

17 If 3 parallel lines are cut by 3 nonparallel lines, what is the maximum number of intersections possible?

(A) 9
(B) 10
(C) 11
(D) 12
(E) 13

Here's How to Crack It

The problem asks you for the *maximum* or greatest number. What is the maximum number among the choices? It is 13; therefore, you can eliminate choice E. By the *simple = wrong* rule that we just discussed, you can also eliminate choice A. Joe's preference for simple arithmetic makes him think that the answer to this problem can be found by multiplying 3 times 3. The simple operation leads quickly to an answer of 9, which must therefore be wrong.

Jim's answer is D. Here's how he gets it:

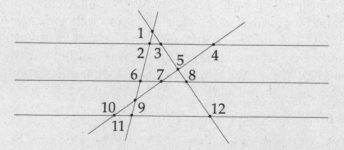

"IT CANNOT BE DETERMINED"

Occasionally on the math SAT, the fifth answer choice on a problem will be:

(E) It cannot be determined from the information given.

The Joe Bloggs principle makes these questions easy to crack. Why? Joe Bloggs can never determine the correct answer on difficult SAT problems. Therefore, when Joe sees this answer choice on a difficult problem, he is greatly attracted to it.

What Does This Mean?

It means that if "it cannot be determined" is offered as an answer choice on a difficult problem, it is usually wrong.

Here's an example:

PROBLEM SOLVING																								
1	2	3	4	5	6	7	8	9	10	11	12	13	14	15	16	17	18	19	20	21	22	23	**24**	25
		EASY									MEDIUM										HARD			

24 If the average of x, y, and 80 is 6 more than the average of y, z, and 80, what is the value of $x - z$?

(A) 2
(B) 3
(C) 6
(D) 18
(E) It cannot be determined from the information given.

Here's How to Crack It

This problem is the next-to-last question in a section. It looks absolutely impossible to Joe. Therefore, he assumes that the problem must be impossible to solve. Of course, he's wrong. Eliminate choice E. If E were Jim's answer, Joe would be correct and this would be an easy problem.

Choice C simply repeats a number from the problem, so you can eliminate that choice also. If you couldn't figure out anything else, you would have to guess. Since you already eliminated two answer choices the odds are in your favor. (Remember, tails you lose a quarter, but heads you win a dollar.)

Jim's answer is D. Don't worry about how to solve this problem right now. It's only important that you understand how to eliminate Joe Bloggs answers in order to get you that much closer to Jim's answer. If you have to guess, that's okay. Besides, that was a hard question; you should be concentrating on answering all the easy and medium questions correctly.

Easy/Medium

Don't automatically eliminate "it cannot be determined" on easy and medium problems. On medium problems, "it cannot be determined" has about one chance in two of being Jim's answer. So, if you are stuck on an easy or medium problem and "it cannot be determined" is one of the choices, pick it and move on. You will have one chance in two of being correct.

(E)

When Joe Bloggs picks "It cannot be determined from the information given" on a hard question, he's thinking, "If I can't get it, no one can."

JOE BLOGGS AND MATH SUMMARY

1. Joe Bloggs gets the easy math questions right and the hard ones wrong.

2. On difficult problems, Joe Bloggs is attracted to easy solutions arrived at through methods he understands. Therefore, you should eliminate obvious, simple answers on difficult questions.

3. On difficult problems, Joe Bloggs is also attracted to answer choices that simply repeat numbers from the problem. Therefore, you should eliminate any such choices.

4. On difficult problems that ask you to find the least (or greatest) number that fulfills certain conditions, you can eliminate the answer choice containing the least (or greatest) number.

5. On difficult problems, you can almost always eliminate any answer choice that says, "It cannot be determined from the information given."

11

The Calculator

The Calculator

You are allowed (but not required) to use a calculator when you take the SAT. You should definitely do so. A calculator can be enormously helpful on certain types of SAT math problems. This chapter will give you general information about how to use your calculator. Other math chapters will give you specific information about using your calculator in particular situations.

You'll need to bring your own calculator when you take the SAT. If you don't own one now, you can buy one for around twelve dollars, or you can ask your math teacher about borrowing one. If you do purchase one, buy it far enough ahead of time to practice with it before you take the test. We recommend the Sharp EL-509G Scientific Calculator, which has all the functions you need to answer SAT questions and which meets the guidelines prescribed by ETS for acceptable calculators. Even if you now use a calculator regularly in your math class at school, you should still read this chapter and the other math chapters carefully and practice the techniques we describe.

The only danger in using a calculator on the SAT is that you may be tempted to use it in situations in which it won't help you. Joe Bloggs thinks his calculator will solve all his difficulties with math. It won't. Occasionally, it may even cause him to miss a problem that he might have answered correctly on his own. But if you practice and use a little caution, you will find that your calculator will help you a great deal.

Gee, Jim Must Really Like Me

Why else would he let you use a calculator? Well, friend, a calculator can be a crutch and an obstacle. Jim hopes that many test takers will waste time using their machines to add 3 + 4. When it comes to simple calculations, your brain and pencil are faster than the fastest calculator.

What a Calculator Is Good At

Here is a complete list of what a calculator is good at on the SAT:

1. arithmetic
2. decimals
3. fractions
4. square roots
5. percentages
6. nothing else

We'll discuss the calculator's role in most of these areas in the next chapter, which is about SAT arithmetic, and in other chapters.

CALCULATOR ARITHMETIC

Adding, subtracting, multiplying, and dividing integers and decimals is easy on a calculator. You only need to be careful when you key in the numbers. A calculator will give you an incorrect answer to an arithmetic calculation only if you press the wrong keys. Here are two tips for avoiding mistakes on your calculator:

1. Check every number on the display as you key it in.

2. Press the *on/off* or *clear all* key after you finish each problem or after each separate step.

The main thing to remember about a calculator is that it can't help you find the answer to a question you don't understand. If you wouldn't know how to solve a particular problem using pencil and paper, you won't know how to solve it using a calculator either. Your calculator will help you, but it won't take the place of a solid understanding of basic SAT mathematics.

USE YOUR PAPER FIRST

Before you use your calculator, be sure to set up the problem or equation on paper. This will keep you from getting lost or confused. This is especially important when solving the problem involves a number of separate steps. The basic idea is to use the extra space in your test booklet to make a plan, and then use your calculator to execute it.

Working on scratch paper first will also give you a record of what you have done if you change your mind, run into trouble, or lose your place. If you suddenly find that you need to try a different approach to a problem, you may not have to go all the way back to the beginning. This will also make it easier for you to check your work, if you have time to do so.

Don't use the memory function on your calculator (if it has one). Because you can use your test booklet as scratch paper, you don't need to juggle numbers within the calculator itself. Instead of storing the result of a calculation in the calculator, write it on your scratch paper, clear your calculator, and move to the next step of the problem. A calculator's memory is fleeting; scratch paper is forever.

ORDER OF OPERATIONS

In the next chapter, we will discuss the proper order of operations when solving equations in which several operations must be performed. Be sure you understand this information, because it applies to calculators as much as it does to pencil and paper computations. (In the next chapter, we will teach you a mnemonic device that will enable you to remember this easily.) You must always perform calculations in the proper order.

CALCULATOR SUMMARY

1. You should definitely use a calculator on the SAT.

2. You need to bring your own calculator when you take the test. You don't need a fancy one.

3. Even if you already use a calculator regularly, you should still practice with it before the test.

4. Be careful when you key in numbers on your calculator. Check each number on the display as you key it in. Clear your work after you finish each problem or after each separate step.

5. A calculator can't help you find the answer to a question you don't understand. (It's only as smart as you are!) Be sure to use your calculator as a tool, not a crutch.

6. Set up the problem or equation on paper first. By doing so, you will eliminate the possibility of getting lost or confused.

7. Don't use the memory function on your calculator (if it has one). Scratch paper works better.

8. Whether you are using your calculator or paper and a pencil, you must always perform calculations in the proper order.

9. Make sure your calculator has a fresh battery at test time!

12

Arithmetic

THERE ARE ONLY SIX OPERATIONS

There are only six arithmetic operations that you will ever need to perform on the SAT:

1. addition (3 + 3)

2. subtraction (3 − 3)

3. multiplication (3 × 3 or 3 • 3)

4. division (3 ÷ 3)

5. raising to a power (3^3)

6. finding a square root ($\sqrt{3}$)

If you're like most students, you probably haven't paid much serious attention to these topics since junior high school. You'll need to learn about them again if you want to do well on the SAT. By the time you take the test, using them should be automatic. All the arithmetic concepts are fairly basic, but you'll have to know them cold. You'll also have to know when and how to use your calculator, which will be quite helpful.

In this chapter, we'll deal with each of these six topics.

What Do You Get?

You should know the following arithmetic terms:

1. The result of addition is a *sum* or *total*.

2. The result of subtraction is a *difference*.

3. The result of multiplication is a *product*.

4. The result of division is a *quotient*.

5. In the expression 5^2, the 2 is called an *exponent*.

The Six Operations Must Be Performed in the Proper Order

Very often, solving an equation on the SAT will require you to perform several different operations, one after another. These operations must be performed in the proper order. In general, the problems are written in such a way that you won't have trouble deciding what comes first. In cases in which you are uncertain, you only need to remember the following sentence:

Please **E**xcuse **M**y **D**ear **A**unt **S**ally, she limps from *left* to *right*

That's **PEMDAS**, for short. It stands for **P**arentheses, **E**xponents, **M**ultiplication, **D**ivision, **A**ddition, **S**ubtraction. First you clear the parentheses; then you take care of the exponents; then you perform all multiplication and division at the same time, from *left* to *right*, followed by addition and subtraction, from *left* to *right*.

The following drill will help you learn the order in which to perform the six operations. First set up the equations on paper. Then use your calculator for the arithmetic. Make sure you perform the operations in the correct order.

Do It Yourself

Some calculators automatically take order of operations into account, and some don't. Either way, you can very easily go wrong if you are in the habit of punching in long lines of arithmetic operations. The safe, smart way is to clear the calculator after every individual operation, performing PEMDAS yourself.

DRILL 1

Solve each of the following problems by performing the indicated operations in the proper order. Answers can be found on page 346.

1. $107 + (109 - 107) =$ _____

2. $(7 \times 5) + 3 =$ _____

3. $6 - 3(6 - 3) =$ _____

4. $2 \times [7 - (6 \div 3)] =$ _____

5. $10 - (9 - 8 - 6) =$ _____

Parentheses Can Help You Solve Equations

Using parentheses to regroup information in SAT arithmetic problems can be very helpful. In order to do this, you need to understand a basic law that you have probably forgotten since the days when you last took arithmetic—the distributive law. You don't need to remember the name of the law, but you do need to know how it works.

The Distributive Law

If you're multiplying the sum of two numbers by a third number, you can multiply each number in your sum individually. This comes in handy when you have to multiply the sum of two variables.

If a problem gives you information in "factored form"—$a\,(b + c)$—then you should distribute the first variable before you do anything else. If you are given information that has already been distributed—$ab + ac$—then you should factor out the common term, putting the information back in factored form. Very often on the SAT, simply doing this will enable you to spot Jim's answer.

For example:

Distributive: $6(53) + 6(47) = 6(53 + 47) = 6(100) = 600$

Multiplication first: $6(53) + 6(47) = 318 + 282 = 600$

You get the same answer each way, so why get involved with ugly arithmetic? If you use the distributive law, you don't even need to use your calculator.

The following drill illustrates the distributive law.

DRILL 2

Rewrite each problem by either distributing or factoring, whichever is called for. Questions 3, 4, and 5 have no numbers in them. Therefore, they can't be solved with a calculator. Answers can be found on page 346.

1. $(6 \times 57) + (6 \times 13) =$ _____

2. $51(48) + 51(50) + 51(52) =$ _____

3. $a(b + c - d) =$ _____

4. $xy - xz =$ _____

5. $abc + xyc =$ _____

FRACTIONS

A Fraction Is Just Another Way of Expressing Division

The expression $\dfrac{x}{y}$ is exactly the same thing as $x \div y$. The expression $\dfrac{1}{2}$ means

nothing more than $1 \div 2$. In the fraction $\dfrac{x}{y}$, x is known as the numerator

(hereafter referred to as "the top") and y is known as the denominator (hereafter

referred to as "the bottom").

Adding and Subtracting Fractions with the Same Bottom

To add two or more fractions that all have the same bottom, simply add up the tops and put the sum over the common bottom. For example:

$$\frac{1}{100} + \frac{4}{100} = \frac{1+4}{100} = \frac{5}{100}$$

Subtraction works exactly the same way:

$$\frac{4}{100} - \frac{1}{100} = \frac{4-1}{100} = \frac{3}{100}$$

Adding and Subtracting Fractions with Different Bottoms

In school you were taught to add and subtract fractions with different bottoms by finding a common bottom. To do this, you have to multiply each fraction by a number that makes all the bottoms the same. Most students find this process annoying.

Fortunately, we have an approach to adding and subtracting fractions with different bottoms that simplifies the entire process. Use the example below as a model. Just *multiply* in the direction of each arrow, and then either *add* or *subtract* across the top. Lastly, *multiply* across the bottom.

$$\frac{1}{3} + \frac{1}{2} =$$

$$\frac{1}{3} \nwarrow \nearrow \frac{1}{2}$$

$$\frac{2+3}{6} = \frac{5}{6}$$

That was easy, wasn't it? We call this procedure the *Bowtie* because the arrows make it look like a bowtie. Use the Bowtie to add or subtract any pair of fractions without thinking about the common bottom, just by following the steps above.

Multiplying All Fractions

Multiplying fractions is easy. Just multiply across the top, then multiply across the bottom.

Here's an example:

$$\frac{4}{5} \times \frac{5}{6} = \frac{20}{30}$$

When you multiply fractions, all you are really doing is performing one multiplication problem on top of another.

You should never multiply two fractions before looking to see if you can reduce either or both. If you reduce first, your final answer will be in the form that ETS is looking for.

$$\frac{63}{6} \times \frac{48}{7} = \frac{\overset{9}{\cancel{63}}}{6} \times \frac{48}{\cancel{7}} = \frac{\overset{9}{\cancel{63}}}{\cancel{6}} \times \frac{\overset{8}{\cancel{48}}}{\cancel{7}} =$$
$$\frac{9}{1} \times \frac{8}{1} =$$
$$\frac{72}{1} = 72$$

Reducing Fractions

When you add or multiply fractions, you will very often end up with a big fraction that is hard to work with. You can almost always reduce such a fraction into one that is easier to handle.

To reduce a fraction, divide both the top and the bottom by the largest number that is a factor of both. For example, to reduce $\frac{12}{60}$, divide both the top and the bottom by 12, which is the largest number that is a factor of both. Dividing 12 by 12 yields 1; dividing 60 by 12 yields 5. The reduced fraction is $\frac{1}{5}$.

Start Small

It is not easy to see that 26 and 286 have a common factor of 13, but it's pretty clear that they're both divisible by 2.

If you can't immediately find the largest number that is a factor of both, find any number that is a factor of both and divide both the top and bottom by that. Your calculations will take a little longer, but you'll end up in the same place. In the previous example, even if you don't see that 12 is a factor of both 12 and 60, you can no doubt see that 6 is a factor of both. Dividing top and bottom by 6 yields $\frac{2}{10}$. Now divide by 2. Doing so yields $\frac{1}{5}$. Once again, you have arrived at Jim's answer.

Dividing All Fractions

To divide one fraction by another, invert the second fraction and multiply. To invert a fraction, simply flip it over. Doing this is extremely easy, as long as you remember how it works. Here's an example:

$$\frac{2}{3} \div \frac{4}{3} =$$

$$\frac{2}{3} \times \frac{3}{4} = \frac{1}{2}$$

Be careful not to cancel or reduce until after you flip the second fraction. You can even do the same thing with fractions whose tops and/or bottoms are fractions. These problems look quite frightening but they're actually easy if you keep your cool.

Here's an example:

$$\frac{\frac{4}{4}}{3} =$$

$$\frac{4}{1} \div \frac{4}{3} =$$

$$\frac{4}{1} \times \frac{3}{4} =$$

$$\frac{\cancel{4}}{1} \times \frac{3}{\cancel{4}} =$$

$$\frac{3}{1} = 3$$

Just Do It

When dividing
(don't ask why)
Just flip the last
And multiply.

Just Don't Mix

For some reason, ETS thinks it's okay to give you mixed numbers as answer choices. On grid-ins, however, if you use a mixed number, Jim won't give you credit.

Converting Mixed Numbers to Fractions

A mixed number is a number like $2\frac{3}{4}$. It is the sum of an integer and a fraction. When you see mixed numbers on the SAT, you should usually convert them to ordinary fractions. Here's a quick and easy way to convert mixed numbers:

1. Multiply the integer by the bottom of the fraction.
2. Add this product to the top of the fraction.
3. Place this sum over the bottom of the fraction.

For example, let's convert $2\frac{3}{4}$ to a fraction. Multiply 2 (the integer part of the mixed number) times 4 (the bottom of the fraction). That gives us 8. Add that to the 3 (the top of the fraction) to give us 11. Place 11 over 4 to give us $\frac{11}{4}$.

The mixed number $2\frac{3}{4}$ is exactly the same as the fraction $\frac{11}{4}$. We converted the one to the other because fractions are easier to work with than mixed numbers.

DRILL 3

Try converting the following mixed numbers. See page 346 to check your answers.

1. $8\frac{1}{3}$

2. $2\frac{3}{7}$

3. $5\frac{4}{9}$

4. $2\frac{1}{2}$

5. $6\frac{2}{3}$

Comparing Fractions

The SAT sometimes contains problems that require you to compare one fraction with another and determine which is larger. There are two ways to compare fractions: convert them to decimals or use the bowtie.

Using the bowtie to compare fractions is quick and easy. Let's say you are given a problem in which you need to determine which is bigger, $\frac{9}{10}$ or $\frac{10}{11}$. As before, multiply in the direction of the arrows.

$$\frac{9}{10} \overset{99}{\underset{}{\times}} \frac{10}{11} \, 100$$

Notice that you don't need to multiply across the bottom when you are comparing fractions. Since 100 is bigger than 99, $\frac{10}{11}$ is bigger than $\frac{9}{10}$.

If you prefer, you can use your calculator to convert each fraction to a decimal. To do this, perform the division problem the fraction represents. Divide 9 by 10 on your calculator, which gives you 0.9. Then divide 10 by 11, which gives you 0.9090909. Which is bigger?

Fractions Behave in Peculiar Ways

Joe Bloggs has trouble with fractions because they don't always behave the way he thinks they ought to. For example, because 4 is obviously greater than 2, Joe Bloggs sometimes forgets that $\frac{1}{4}$ is less than $\frac{1}{2}$. He becomes especially confused when the top is some number other than 1. For example, $\frac{2}{6}$ is less than $\frac{2}{5}$.

Joe also has a hard time understanding that when you multiply one fraction by another, you will get a fraction that is smaller than either of the first two. For example:

$$\frac{1}{2} \times \frac{1}{4} = \frac{1}{8}$$

$$\frac{1}{8} < \frac{1}{2}$$

$$\frac{1}{8} < \frac{1}{4}$$

A Word About Fractions and Calculators

It's possible to key fractions into many scientific calculators. These calculators allow you to add, subtract, multiply, divide, and reduce fractions, and some also convert mixed numbers to fractions and back again. If you know how to work with fractions on your calculator, go ahead and use it. While you should still understand how to work with fractions the old-fashioned way, your calculator can be a tremendous help if you know how to use it properly. If you plan to use your calculator on fraction problems, make sure you practice with your calculator before the test.

DRILL 4

If you have trouble on any of these problems, go back and review the information just outlined. Answers can be found on page 347.

1. Reduce $\dfrac{18}{6}$. _____

2. Convert $6\dfrac{1}{5}$ to a fraction. _____

3. $2\dfrac{1}{3} - 3\dfrac{3}{5} =$ _____

4. $\dfrac{5}{18} \times \dfrac{6}{25} =$ _____

5. $\dfrac{3}{4} \div \dfrac{7}{8} =$ _____

6. $\dfrac{\frac{2}{5}}{5} =$ _____

7. $\dfrac{\frac{1}{3}}{\frac{3}{4}} =$ _____

DECIMALS

A Decimal Is Just Another Way of Expressing a Fraction

Fractions can be expressed as decimals. To find a fraction's decimal equivalent, simply divide the top by the bottom. (You can do this easily with your calculator.) For example:

$$\frac{3}{5} =$$
$$3 \div 5 = 0.6$$

Adding, Subtracting, Multiplying, and Dividing Decimals

Manipulating decimals is easy with a calculator. Simply punch in the numbers—being especially careful to get the decimal point in the right place every single time—and read the result from the display. A calculator makes these operations easy. In fact, working with decimals is one area on the SAT where your calculator will prevent you from making careless errors. You won't have to line up decimal points or remember what happens when you divide. The calculator will keep track of everything for you, as long as you punch in the correct numbers to begin with. Just be sure to practice carefully before you go to the test center.

DRILL 5

You can check your answers to the following drill on page 347.

1. $0.43 \times 0.87 = $ _____

2. $\dfrac{43 + 0.731}{0.03} = $ _____

3. $3.72 \div 0.02 = $ _____

4. $0.71 - 3.6 = $ _____

Comparing Decimals

Some SAT problems will ask you to determine whether one decimal is larger or smaller than another. Many students have trouble doing this. It isn't difficult, though, and you will do fine as long as you remember to line up the decimal points and fill in missing zeros.
Here's an example:

Problem: Which is larger, 0.0099 or 0.01?

Solution: Simply place one decimal over the other with the decimal points lined up, like this:

$$0.0099$$
$$0.01$$

To make the solution seem clearer, you can add two zeros to the right of 0.01. (You can always add zeros to the right of a decimal without changing its value.) Now you have this:

$$0.0099$$
$$0.0100$$

Which decimal is larger? Clearly, 0.0100 is, just as 100 is larger than 99. (Remember that $0.0099 = \dfrac{99}{10,000}$, while $0.0100 = \dfrac{100}{10,000}$. Now the answer seems obvious, doesn't it?)

Analysis

Joe Bloggs has a terrible time on this problem. Because 99 is obviously larger than 1, he tends to think that 0.0099 must be larger than 0.01. But it isn't. Don't get sloppy on problems like this! Jim loves to trip up Joe Bloggs with decimals. In fact, any time you encounter a problem involving the comparison of decimals, you should stop and ask yourself whether you are about to make a Joe Bloggs mistake.

Place Value

Compare decimals place by place, going from left to right.

RATIOS AND PROPORTIONS

A Ratio Is a Comparison

Many students get extremely nervous when they are asked to work with ratios. But there's no need to be nervous. A ratio is a comparison between the quantities of ingredients you have in a mixture, be it a class full of people or a bowl of fruit punch. Ratios can be written to look like fractions—don't get them confused.

The ratio of x to y can be expressed in the following three ways:

1. $\dfrac{x}{y}$

2. the ratio of x to y

3. x:y

Part, Part, Whole

Ratios vs. Fractions

Keep in mind that a ratio compares part of something to another part. A fraction compares part of something to the whole thing.

Ratios are a lot like fractions. In fact, anything you can do to a fraction (convert it to a decimal or percentage, reduce it, etc.), you can do to a ratio. The difference is that a fraction gives you a part (the top number) over a whole (the bottom number), while a ratio typically gives you two parts (boys to girls, CDs to cassettes, sugar to flour), and it is your job to come up with the whole. For example, if there is one cup of sugar for every two cups of flour in a recipe, that's three cups of stuff. The ratio of sugar to flour is 1:2.

Ratio to Real

If a class contains 3 students and the ratio of boys to girls in that class is 2:1, how many boys and how many girls are there in the class? Of course: There are 2 boys and 1 girl.

Now, suppose a class contains 24 students and the ratio of boys to girls is still 2:1. How many boys and how many girls are there in the class? This is a little harder, but the answer is easy to find if you think about it. There are 16 boys and 8 girls.

How did we get the answer? We added up the number of "parts" in the ratio (2 parts boys plus 1 part girls, or 3 parts altogether) and divided it into the total number of students. In other words, we divided 24 by 3. This told us that the class contained 3 equal parts of 8 students each. From the given ratio (2:1), we knew that two of these parts consisted of boys and one of them consisted of girls.

An easy way to keep track of all this is to use a tool we call the *Ratio Box*. Every time you have a ratio problem, set up a Ratio Box with the information provided in the problem and use it to find Jim's answer. Here's how it works.

Let's go back to our class containing 24 students, in which the ratio of boys to girls is 2:1. Quickly sketch a table that has columns and rows, like this:

	Boys	Girls	Whole
Ratio (parts)	2	1	3
Multiply By			
Actual Number			24

This is the information you have been given. The ratio is 2:1, so you have 2 parts boys and 1 part girls, for a total of 3 parts altogether. You also know that the actual number of students in the whole class is 24. You start by writing these numbers in proper spaces in your box.

Your goal is to fill in the two empty spaces in the bottom row. To do that, you will multiply each number in the *parts* row by the same number. To find that number, look in the last column. What number would you multiply by 3 to get 24? You should see easily that you would multiply by 8. Therefore, write an 8 in all three blanks in the *multiply by* row. (The spaces in this row will always contain the same number, although of course it won't always be an 8.) Here's what your ratio box should look like now:

	Boys	Girls	Whole
Ratio (parts)	2	1	3
Multiply By	8	8	8
Actual Number			24

The next step is to fill in the empty spaces in the bottom row. You do that the same way you did in the last column, by multiplying. First, multiply the numbers in the boys column ($2 \times 8 = 16$). Then multiply the numbers in the girls column ($1 \times 8 = 8$).

Here's what your box should look like now:

	Boys	Girls	Whole
Ratio (parts)	2	1	3
Multiply By	8	8	8
Actual Number	16	8	24

Now you have enough information to answer any question that ETS might ask you. For example:

- What is the ratio of boys to girls? You can see easily from the ratio (parts) row of the box that the ratio is 2:1.

- What is the ratio of girls to boys? You can see easily from the ratio (parts) row of the box that the ratio is 1:2.

- What is the total number of boys in the class? You can see easily from the bottom row of the box that it is 16.

- What is the total number of girls in the class? You can see easily from the bottom row of the box that it is 8.

- What fractional part of the class is boys? There are 16 boys in a class of 24, so the fraction representing the boys is $\frac{16}{24}$, which can be reduced to $\frac{2}{3}$.

What You Need

Always keep an eye on what you are being asked. You do not want to do more work than necessary. Example 18 never asks about green jelly beans, so leave that box empty.

As you can see, the Ratio Box is an easy way to find, organize, and keep track of information on ratio problems. And it works the same no matter what information you are given. Just remember that all the boxes in the *multiply by* row will always contain the same number.

Here's another example:

PROBLEM SOLVING																								
1	2	3	4	5	6	7	8	9	10	11	12	13	14	15	16	17	**18**	19	20	21	22	23	24	25
			EASY									MEDIUM									HARD			

18 In a jar of red and green jelly beans, the ratio of green jelly beans to red jelly beans is 5:3. If the jar contains a total of 160 jelly beans, how many of them are red?

(A) 30
(B) 53
(C) 60
(D) 100
(E) 160

Here's How to Crack It

First, sketch out a ratio box:

	Green	Red	Whole
Ratio (parts)	5	3	8
Multiply By			
Actual Number			160

Now find the multiplier. What do you multiply by 8 to get 160? You multiply 8 by 20. Now write 20 in each box on the *multiply by* row:

	Green	Red	Whole
Ratio (parts)	5	3	8
Multiply By	20	20	20
Actual Number			160

The problem asks you to find how many red jelly beans there are. Go to the red column and multiply 3 by 20. The answer is 60. Jim's answer is C. Notice that you would have set up the box in exactly the same way if the question had asked you to determine how many jelly beans were green. (How many are green? The answer is 5×20, which is 100.)

Proportions Are Equal Ratios

Some SAT math problems will contain two proportional, or equal, ratios from which one piece of information is missing.

Here's an example:

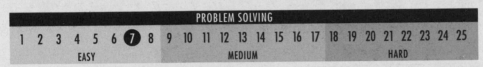

> **7** If 2 packages contain a total of 12 doughnuts, how many doughnuts are there in 5 packages?
>
> (A) 12
> (B) 24
> (C) 30
> (D) 36
> (E) 60

Here's How to Crack It

This problem simply describes two equal ratios, one of which is missing a single piece of information. Here's the given information represented as two equal ratios:

$$\frac{2 \text{ (packages)}}{12 \text{ (doughnuts)}} = \frac{5 \text{ (packages)}}{x \text{ (doughnuts)}}$$

Since ratios are fractions, we can treat them exactly like fractions. To find the answer all you have to do is figure out what you could plug in for x that would make $\frac{2}{12} = \frac{5}{x}$. One way to do this is to cross multiply:

$$\frac{2}{12} \diagdown \frac{5}{x}$$

so, $2x = 60$

$x = 30$

Jim's answer is C.

Careful

You can only cross multiply across an equal sign. You can't reduce across an equal sign.

PERCENTAGES

Percentages Are Fractions

There should be nothing frightening about a percentage. It's just a convenient way of expressing a fraction whose bottom is 100.

Percent means "per 100" or "out of 100." If there are 100 questions on your math test and you answer 50 of them, you will have answered 50 out of 100, or $\frac{50}{100}$, or 50 percent. To think of it another way:

$$\frac{\text{part}}{\text{whole}} = \frac{x}{100} = x \text{ percent.}$$

Memorize These Percentage-Decimal-Fraction Equivalents

$0.01 = \frac{1}{100} = 1 \text{ percent}$ $0.25 = \frac{1}{4} = 25 \text{ percent}$

$0.1 = \frac{1}{10} = 10 \text{ percent}$ $0.5 = \frac{1}{2} = 50 \text{ percent}$

$0.2 = \frac{1}{5} = 20 \text{ percent}$ $0.75 - \frac{3}{4} = 75 \text{ percent}$

Converting Percentages to Fractions

To convert a percentage to a fraction, simply put the percentage over 100 and reduce. For example:

$$80 \text{ percent} = \frac{80}{100} = \frac{8}{10} = \frac{4}{5}$$

Converting Fractions to Percentages

Another Way

You can also convert fractions to percentages by cross multiplying:

$$\frac{3}{4} = \frac{x}{100}$$

$$4x = 3(100)$$

$$x = \frac{3(100)}{4}$$

$$x = 75$$

Since a percentage is just another way to express a fraction, you shouldn't be surprised to see how easy it is to convert a fraction to a percentage. To do so, simply use your calculator to divide the top of the fraction by the bottom of the fraction, and then multiply the result by 100. Here's an example:

Problem: Express $\frac{3}{4}$ as a percentage.

Solution: $\frac{3}{4} = 0.75 \times 100 = 75 \text{ percent.}$

Converting fractions to percentages is easy with your calculator.

Converting Percentages to Decimals

To convert a percentage to a decimal, simply move the decimal point two places to the *left*. For example: 25 percent can be expressed as the decimal 0.25; 50 percent is the same as 0.50 or 0.5; 100 percent is the same as 1.00 or 1.

Converting Decimals to Percentages

To convert a decimal to a percentage, just do the opposite of what you did in the preceding section. All you have to do is move the decimal point two places to the right. Thus, 0.5 = 50 percent; 0.375 = 37.5 percent; 2 = 200 percent.

The following drill will give you practice working with fractions, decimals, and percentages.

DRILL 6

Fill in the missing information in the following table. Answers can be found on page 347.

	Fraction	Decimal	Percent
1.	$\frac{1}{2}$		
2.		3.0	
3.			0.5
4.	$\frac{1}{3}$		

What Percent of What?

Problem: What number is 10 percent greater than 20?

Solution: We know that 10 percent of 20 is 2. So the question really reads: What is 2 greater than 20? The answer is 22.

Analysis

Joe Bloggs gets confused on questions like this. You won't if you take them slowly and solve them one step at a time. The same holds true for problems that ask you what number is a certain percentage less than another number. What number is 10 percent less than 500? Well, 10 percent of 500 is 50. The number that is 10 percent less than 500, therefore, is 500 – 50, or 450. You will see the words *of*, *is*, *product*, *sum*, and *what* pop up a lot in the math sections of the SAT. Don't let these words fool you, because they all translate into simple math functions. Look to the "Translate" sidebar for The Princeton Review's translation of some terms and get to know them. It will save you time on the test and make your life with the SAT much nicer.

Translate

On a Math test like the SAT, we can convert (or translate) words into arithmetic symbols. Here are some of the most common:

Word	Symbol
is	=
of	× (multiply)
percent	/100
what	*n* (variable)

What Percent of What Percent of What?

On harder SAT questions, you may be asked to determine the effect of a series of percentage increases or decreases. The key point to remember on such problems is that each successive increase or decrease is performed on the result of the previous one.

Here's an example:

PROBLEM SOLVING

1 2 3 4 5 6 7 8 9 10 11 12 13 14 15 16 17 **18** 19 20 21 22 23 24 25

EASY   MEDIUM   HARD

18 A business paid $300 to rent a piece of office equipment for one year. The rent was then increased by 10 percent each year thereafter. How much will the company pay for the first three years it rents the equipment?

(A) $920
(B) $960
(C) $990
(D) $993
(E) $999

Here's How to Crack It

You are being asked to find a business's total rent for a piece of equipment for three years. The easiest way to keep from getting confused on a problem like this is to take it one step at a time. First, make an outline of exactly what you have to find out.

Year 1:

Year 2:

Year 3:

Write this down in the margin of your test booklet. There's one slot for each year's rent; Jim's answer will be the total.

You already know the number that goes in the first slot: 300, because that is what the problem says the business will pay for the first year.

What number goes in the second slot? 330, because 330 equals 300 plus 10 percent of 300.

Now, here's where you have to pay attention. What number goes in the third slot? Not 360! (Cross out choice C!) The rent goes up 10 percent each year. This increase is calculated from the previous year's rent. That means that the rent for the third year is $363, because 363 equals 330 plus 10 percent of 330.

Now you are ready to find Jim's answer:

Year 1:   300

Year 2:   330

Year 3:   <u>363</u>

           993

Jim's answer is thus choice D, $993.

What Percent of What Percent of Yikes!

Sometimes you may find successive percentage problems in which you aren't given actual numbers to work with. In such cases you need to plug in some numbers.

Here's an example.

								PROBLEM SOLVING											
1	2	3	4	5	6	7	8	9	10	11	12	13	14	15	16	17	18	19	20	**21**	22	23	24	25
			EASY									MEDIUM							HARD				

21 A number is increased by 25 percent and then decreased by 20 percent. The result is what percent of the original number?

(A) 80
(B) 100
(C) 105
(D) 120
(E) 125

Here's How to Crack It

Using the Joe Bloggs principle, you ought to be able to eliminate three choices right off the bat: A, D, and E. Joe loves easy answers. Choices A, D, and E are all equal to 100 plus or minus 20 or 25. All three choices seem right to Joe for different reasons. This is a difficult question, so answers that seem right to Joe must be eliminated. Get rid of them.

A somewhat more subtle Joe Bloggs attractor is choice C. Joe thinks that if you increase a number by 25 percent and then decrease by 20 percent, you end up with a net increase of 5 percent. He has forgotten that in a series of percentage changes (which is what we have here), each successive change is based on the result of the previous one.

We've now eliminated everything but choice B, which is Jim's answer.

Could we have found it without Joe's help? Yes. Here's how:

You aren't given a particular number to work with in this problem—just "a number." Rather than trying to deal with the problem in the abstract, you should immediately plug in a number to work with. What number would be easiest to work with in a percentage problem? Why, 100, of course:

1. 25 percent of 100 is 25, so 100 increased by 25 percent is 125.

2. Now you have to decrease 125 by 20 percent, 20 percent of 125 is 25, so 125 decreased by 20 percent is 100.

3. 100 (our result) is 100 percent of 100 (the number you plugged in), so Jim's answer, once again, is B.

Nevermind

Never try to solve a percentage problem by writing an equation if you can plug in numbers instead. Plugging in on percentage problems is faster, easier, and more accurate. Why work through long, arduous equations if you don't have to?

AVERAGES

What Is an Average?

On the SAT, the average (also called arithmetic mean) of a set of n numbers is simply the sum of all the numbers divided by n. In other words, if you want to find the average of three numbers, add them up and divide by 3. For example, the average of 3, 7, and 8 is $\frac{(3+7+8)}{3}$, which equals $\frac{18}{3}$, or 6.

That was an easy example, but Jim does not always write average questions with clear solutions. That is, he doesn't always give you the information for averages in a way that is easy to work with. For that reason, we have a visual aid, like the Ratio Box for ratios, that helps you organize the information on average questions and find Jim's answer.

We call it the *Average Pie*. Here's what it looks like:

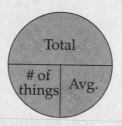

The *total* is the sum of all the numbers you're averaging, and the *number of things* is the number of elements you're averaging. Here's what the Average Pie looks like using the simple average example we just gave you.

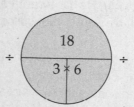

Here's how the Average Pie works mathematically. The line in the middle means *divide*. If you know the total and the number of things, just divide to get the average $(18 \div 3 = 6)$. If you know the total and the average, just divide to get the number of things $(18 \div 6 = 3)$. If you know the average and the number of things, simply multiply to get the total $(6 \times 3 = 18)$. The key to most average questions is finding the total.

Here's another simple example:

Problem: If the average of three test scores is 70, what is the total of all three test scores?

Solution: Just put the number of things (3 tests) and the average (70) in the pie. Then multiply to find the total, which is 210.

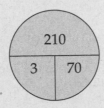

Here's another example:

Problem: What's the average of 10, 10, 10, and 50?

Solution: Simply add up the numbers to find the total, which is 80. The number of things is 4. Then just divide to find the average, which is 20.

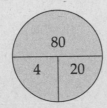

Averages: Advanced Principles

To solve most difficult average problems, all you have to do is fill out one or more Average Pies. Most of the time you will use them to find the total of the number being averaged. Here's an example:

Problem: Suppose a student has an average of 80 on four tests. If the student scores a 90 on the fifth test, what is her average on all five?

Solution: To find the average of all five tests, you need the total score. You need to start by finding the total of the first *four* tests. Draw an Average Pie and write in the average of the first four tests (80), and the number of things (4):

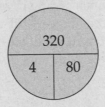

Then multiply to find the total, which is 320. Now, find the total of all five tests by adding the fifth score to the total of the first four: 320 + 90 = 410. Now draw another Average Pie to find the average of all five tests. Write in the total (410), and the number of things (5). Then divide to find the average: 82.

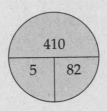

> **Total**
>
> When calculating averages and means, always find the total. It's the one piece of information that Jim loves to withhold.

Now let's try a difficult question:

20. If the average (arithmetic mean) of eight
    numbers is 20, and the average of five of these
    numbers is 14, what is the average of the
    other three numbers?
    (A) 14
    (B) 17
    (C) 20
    (D) 30
    (E 34

Here's How to Crack It

Start by drawing an Average Pie for all eight numbers; then multiply to find the total.

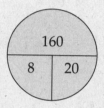

The total of the eight numbers is 160. Now draw another Average Pie for five of the numbers.

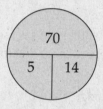

The total of those five numbers is 70. (Remember, those are five out of the original eight numbers.) To find the average of the other three numbers, you need the total of those three numbers. You have the total of all eight numbers, 160, and the total of five of those numbers, 70, so you can find the total of the other three by subtracting 70 from 160. That means the total of the three remaining numbers is 90. It's time to create one more Average Pie to find the average of those three numbers.

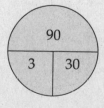

The average is 30, so Jim's answer is D.

On the SAT, you'll also need to know two other topics related to averages: *median and mode*.

What Is a *Median*?

The median of a group of numbers is the number that is exactly in the middle of the group when the group is arranged from smallest to largest, as on a number line. For example, in the group 3, 6, 6, 6, 6, 7, 8, 9, 10, 10, 11, the median is 7. Five numbers come before 7 in the group, and 5 come after.

What Is a *Mode*?

The mode of a group of numbers is the number in the group that appears most often. In the group 3, 4, 4, 5, 7, 7, 8, 8, 8, 9, 10, the mode is 8, because it appears three times while no other number in the group appears more than twice.

EXPONENTS AND SQUARE ROOTS

Exponents Are a Kind of Shorthand

Many numbers are the product of the same factor multiplied over and over again. For example, $32 = 2 \times 2 \times 2 \times 2 \times 2$. Another way to write this would be $32 = 2^5$, or "thirty-two equals two to the fifth power." The little number, or *exponent*, denotes the number of times that 2 is to be used as a factor. In the same way, $10^3 = 10 \times 10 \times 10$, or 1,000, or "ten to the third power," or "ten cubed." In this example, the 10 is called the *base* and the 3 is called the *exponent*. (You won't need to know these terms on the SAT, but you will need to know them to follow our explanations.)

Multiplying Numbers with Exponents

When you multiply two numbers with the same base, you simply add the exponents. For example, $2^3 \times 2^5 = 2^{3+5} = 2^8$.

Dividing Numbers with Exponents

When you divide two numbers with the same base, you simply subtract the exponents. For example, $\dfrac{2^5}{2^3} = 2^{5-3} = 2^2$.

Raising a Power to a Power

When you raise a power to a power, you multiply the exponents. For example, $(2^3)^4 = 2^{3 \times 4} = 2^{12}$.

Calculator Exponents

You can compute simple exponents on your calculator. Make sure you have a scientific calculator with a y^x key. To find 2^{10}, for example, simply use your y^x key, punching 2 in for the y value and 10 in for the x value. This may be especially useful if you are asked to compare exponents.

Median Median

To find the median of a set containing an even number of items, take the arithmetic mean of the two middle numbers.

Warning

The rules for multiplying and dividing exponents do not apply to addition or subtraction:
$2^2 + 2^3 = 12$
$(2 \times 2) + (2 \times 2 \times 2) = 12$
It does *not* equal 2^5 or 32.

Warning

Parentheses are very important with exponents, because you must remember to distribute powers to everything within them. For example, $(3x)^2 = 9x^2$, not $3x^2$.

Similarly, $\left(\dfrac{3}{2}\right)^2 = \dfrac{3^2}{2^2}$, not $\dfrac{9}{2}$.

The Peculiar Behavior of Exponents

Raising a number to a power can have quite peculiar and unexpected results, depending on what sort of number you start out with. Here are some examples:

1. If you square or cube a number greater than 1, it becomes larger. For example, $2^3 = 8$.

2. If you square or cube a positive fraction smaller than one, it becomes smaller.

   For example, $\left(\dfrac{1}{2}\right)^3 = \dfrac{1}{8}$.

3. A negative number raised to an even power becomes positive. For example, $(-2)^2 = 4$.

4. A negative number raised to an odd power remains negative. For example, $(-2)^3 = -8$.

You should also have a feel for relative sizes of exponential numbers without calculating them. For example, 2^{10} is much larger than 10^2. ($2^{10} = 1,024$; $10^2 = 100$.) To take another example, 2^5 is twice as large as 2^4, even though 5 seems only a bit larger than 4.

Square Roots

The sign $\sqrt{}$ indicates the positive square root of a number. For example, $\sqrt{25} = 5$.

The Only Rules You Need to Know

Here are the only rules regarding square roots that you need to know for the SAT:

1. $\sqrt{x}\sqrt{y} = \sqrt{xy}$. For example, $\sqrt{3}\sqrt{12} = \sqrt{36} = 6$.

2. $\sqrt{\dfrac{x}{y}} = \dfrac{\sqrt{x}}{\sqrt{y}}$. For example, $\sqrt{\dfrac{5}{4}} = \dfrac{\sqrt{5}}{\sqrt{4}} = \dfrac{\sqrt{5}}{2}$.

Note that rule 1 works in reverse: $\sqrt{50} = \sqrt{25} \times \sqrt{2} = 5\sqrt{2}$. This is really a kind of factoring. You are using rule 1 to factor a large, clumsy radical into numbers that are easier to work with.

Careless Errors

Don't make careless mistakes. Remember that the square root of a number between 0 and 1 is *larger* than the original number. For example, $\sqrt{\dfrac{1}{4}} = \dfrac{1}{2}$, and $\dfrac{1}{2} > \dfrac{1}{4}$.

ARITHMETIC SUMMARY

1. There are only six arithmetic operations tested on the SAT: addition, subtraction, multiplication, division, exponents, and square roots.

2. These operations must be performed in the proper order (PEMDAS), beginning with operations inside parentheses.

3. Apply the distributive law whenever possible. Very often, this is enough to find Jim's answer.

4. A fraction is just another way of expressing division.

5. You must know how to add, subtract, multiply, and divide fractions.

6. In any problems involving large or confusing fractions, try to reduce the fractions first. Before you multiply two fractions, for example, see if it's possible to reduce either or both of the fractions.

7. If you know how to work out fractions on your calculator, use it to help you with questions that involve fractions. If you intend to use your calculator for fractions, make sure you practice. You should also know how to work with fractions the old-fashioned way.

8. A decimal is just another way of expressing a fraction.

9. Use a calculator to add, subtract, multiply, and divide decimals.

10. A ratio can be expressed as a fraction.

11. Use a Ratio Box to solve ratio questions.

12. A percentage is just a convenient way of expressing a fraction whose bottom is 100.

13. To convert a percentage to a fraction, put the percentage over 100 and reduce.

14. To convert a fraction to a percentage, use your calculator to divide the top of the fraction by the bottom of the fraction. Then multiply the result by 100.

15. To convert a percentage to a decimal, move the decimal point two places to the left. To convert a decimal to a percentage, move the decimal point two places to the right.

16. In problems that require you to find a series of percentage increases or decreases, remember that each successive increase or decrease is performed on the result of the previous one.

17. To find the average (or arithmetic mean) of several values, add up the values and divide the total by the number of values.

18. Use the Average Pie to solve problems involving averages. The key to most average problems is finding the total.

19. The median of a group of numbers is the number that is exactly in the middle of the group when the group is arranged from smallest to largest, as on a number line.

20. The mode of a group of numbers is the number in the group that appears most often.

21. Exponents are a kind of shorthand for expressing numbers that are the product of the same factor multiplied over and over again.

22. To multiply two exponential expressions with the same base, add the exponents.

23. To divide two exponential expressions with the same base, subtract the exponents.

24. To raise one exponential expression to another power, multiply the exponents.

25. When you raise a positive number greater than 1 to a power greater than 1, the result is larger. When you raise a positive fraction less than 1 to an exponent greater than 1, the result is smaller. A negative number raised to an even power becomes positive. A negative number raised to an odd power remains negative.

26. When you're asked for the square root of any number ($\sqrt{x}$), you're being asked for the positive root only.

27. Here are the only rules regarding square roots that you need to know for the SAT:

   a. $\sqrt{x} \times \sqrt{y} = \sqrt{xy}$

   b. $\sqrt{\dfrac{x}{y}} = \dfrac{\sqrt{x}}{\sqrt{y}}$

13

Algebra:
Cracking the System

Princeton Review Algebra

About a third of the math problems on your SAT will involve algebra. Some students are terrified of algebra. Fortunately, we have several techniques that should enable you to solve the most frightening-looking algebra problems—even word problems.

This chapter is divided into three main sections:

1. Backsolving

2. Plugging In

3. Basic Princeton Review Algebra

Princeton Review Algebra is our name for the kind of algebra you need to know to do well on the SAT. It isn't the same as the algebra you were taught in math class. Why did we bother to create our own kind of algebra? Because math-class algebra takes too much time on the SAT. If you want big score improvements, you're going to have to forget about your algebra class and learn the techniques that work on the SAT.

Your biggest scoring gains will come from the next two sections: "Backsolving" and "Plugging In." These are two simple but extremely powerful techniques that work on multiple-choice questions. You won't need to know much algebra in order to use them, but you'll have to stay on your toes.

The third section of this chapter is a summary of basic Princeton Review Algebra. It's a bit dull by comparison with the rest of the chapter, but you should read it carefully, even if you already feel comfortable with algebra. You should think of our summary as a sort of guide to the handful of algebraic concepts you'll need to answer problems that can't be solved by Backsolving or Plugging In.

BACKSOLVING

Algebra uses letters to stand for numbers, but no one else does. You don't go to the grocery store to buy x eggs or y gallons of milk. Most people think in terms of numbers, not letters that stand for numbers.

You should think in terms of numbers on the SAT as much as possible. On many SAT algebra problems, even very difficult ones, you will be able to find Jim's answer without using any algebra at all. You will do this by working backward from the answer choices instead of trying to solve the problem using math-class algebra.

Backsolving is a technique for solving word problems whose answer choices are all numbers. Many so-called algebra problems on the SAT can be solved simply and quickly by using this powerful technique.

In algebra class at school, you solve word problems by using equations. Then, if you're careful, you check your solution by plugging in your answer to see if it works. Why not skip the equations entirely by simply checking the five solutions ETS offers on the multiple-choice questions? One of these has to be correct. You don't have to do *any* algebra, you will seldom have to try more than two choices, and you will never have to try all five.

Here's an example:

PROBLEM SOLVING																								
1	2	3	4	5	6	7	8	9	⑩	11	12	13	14	15	16	17	18	19	20	21	22	23	24	25
			EASY									MEDIUM									HARD			

10 The units digit of a 2-digit number is 3 times the tens digit. If the digits are reversed, the resulting number is 36 more than the original number. What is the original number?

(A) 26
(B) 31
(C) 36
(D) 62
(E) 93

Here's How to Crack It

Don't waste time fumbling around all the possible digit combinations. (There are only three, but it can take awhile to figure that out.) ETS has limited your decision to five choices—they've already done almost all the work.

What you want to do is look at each answer choice to see if it fulfills the conditions stated in the problem. If it doesn't, you can use POE to get rid of it.

Backsolving this problem is a piece of cake. You simply take the stated conditions one at a time and try them out against the answer choices.

The first condition stated in the problem is that the units (or ones) digit of the number you are looking for is three times the tens digit. Now you look at the choices:

(A) Is 6 three times 2? Yes. A possibility.

(B) Is 1 three times 3? No. Eliminate.

(C) Is 6 three times 3? No. Eliminate.

(D) Is 2 three times 6? No. Eliminate.

(E) Is 3 three times 9? No. Eliminate.

Jim's answer is A. You found it without even testing the other conditions stated in the problem. Mark your answer and move on.

When you Backsolve a question, don't select an answer until you've either tested all the conditions or eliminated all but one of the choices. In this problem, if there had been another choice whose units digit was three times its tens digit, you would have had to move on to the next condition.

Here's another example:

PROBLEM SOLVING																								
1	2	3	4	5	6	7	8	9	10	**11**	12	13	14	15	16	17	18	19	20	21	22	23	24	25
EASY								MEDIUM									HARD							

11 A woman made 5 payments on a loan with each payment being twice the amount of the preceding one. If the total of all 5 payments was $465, how much was the first payment?

(A) $5
(B) $15
(C) $31
(D) $93
(E) $155

Here's How to Crack It

To solve this problem in math class, you'd have to set up and solve an equation like this:

$$p + 2p + 4p + 8p + 16p = 465$$

Forget it! That's too much work, plus there's a lot of room for error. Why not just try out the answers?

Numeric answer choices on the SAT are always given in order of size. Thus, when you are Backsolving on a problem like this, you should always start out with the number in the middle—choice C. If that number turns out to be too big, you can try a lower number next; if it's too small, you can try a higher one. That way you'll save time.

Let's look at what happens when you try choice C: If the payments double each month, the woman will pay 31 + 62 + 124 + 248 + 496—you can stop right there. You don't have to add up these numbers to see clearly that the total is going to be much more than 465; the fifth number alone is more than that. You need to eliminate this choice, along with choices D and E. Try again with A or B.

Which one should you try? Why not A, the smaller of the two? It will be easier and faster to work with. If it works, you'll pick it; if it doesn't, you'll eliminate it and pick B.

Which Way?

Sometimes, it's hard to tell which way to go after eliminating C—higher or lower? Don't fret, just move. Find a choice with an easy-to-manipulate number. It may turn out to be wrong, but it won't take long to find out. It may also tell whether to go higher or lower.

Here's what you get when you try choice A: 5 + 10 + 20 + 40 + 80. You don't have to add up these numbers to see clearly that they aren't going to come anywhere near 465. Jim's answer must be B. (It is.)

BACKSOLVING: ADVANCED PRINCIPLES

Backsolving is the same on difficult problems as it is on easy and medium ones. You just have to watch your step and make certain you don't make any careless mistakes or fall for Joe Bloggs answers.

Here's one of our examples:

PROBLEM SOLVING																								
1	2	3	4	5	6	7	8	9	10	11	12	13	14	15	16	17	⑱	19	20	21	22	23	24	25
			EASY									MEDIUM									HARD			

18 Out of a total of 154 games played, a ball team won 54 more games than it lost. If there were no ties, how many games did the team win?

(A) 94
(B) 98
(C) 100
(D) 102
(E) 104

Here's How to Crack It

What's the Joe Bloggs answer here? It is choice C. Be careful!

To solve the problem all you have to do is Backsolve. You've eliminated choice C already, so start with D. If the team won 102 games, how many games did it lose? It lost 52 (154 – 102 = 52). Is 102 (wins) 54 greater than 52 (losses)? No. 102 – 52 = 50. You need more wins to make the problem come out right. That means that Jim's answer must be E. (It is.)

Here's another example we created:

PROBLEM SOLVING																								
1	2	3	4	5	6	7	8	9	10	11	12	13	14	15	16	17	18	19	20	21	㉒	23	24	25
			EASY									MEDIUM									HARD			

22 Committee A has 18 members and Committee B has 3 members. How many members from Committee A must switch to Committee B so that Committee A will have twice as many members as Committee B?

(A) 4
(B) 6
(C) 7
(D) 9
(E) 14

Here's How to Crack It

This problem represents one of the most difficult principles tested in the SAT math section. Only a small percentage of students get it right. But if you Backsolve, you won't have any trouble.

This problem is about two committees, so the first thing you should do is quickly draw a picture in your test booklet to keep from getting confused:

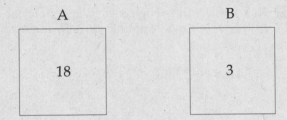

Now work backward, starting with answer choice C. If you move 7 members out of Committee A, there will be 11 members left in A and 10 members in B. Is 11 twice as many as 10? No, eliminate.

As you work through the choices, keep track of them, like this:

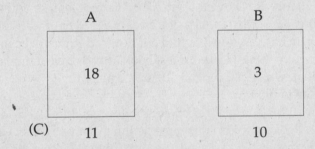

Choice C didn't work. To make the question work out right, you need more members in Committee A and fewer in Committee B. In other words, you need to try a smaller number. Try the smallest one, choice A. Moving 4 members from Committee A will leave 14 in A and 7 in B. Is 14 twice as many as 7? Yes, of course. This is Jim's answer.

PLUGGING IN

Working backward enables you to find Jim's answer on problems whose answer choices are all numbers. What about problems whose answer choices contain letters? On these problems, you will usually be able to find Jim's answer by Plugging In. Plugging In is similar to Backsolving. And, like Backsolving, it has very little to do with the algebra you learned in math class.

Plugging In is easy. It has three steps:

1. Pick numbers for the letters in the problem.

2. Using your numbers, find an answer to the problem.

3. Plug your numbers from step 1 into the answer choices to see which choice equals the answer you found in step 2.

Basic Plugging In

Plugging In is simple to understand. Here's an example:

PROBLEM SOLVING																								
1	2	**3**	4	5	6	7	8	9	10	11	12	13	14	15	16	17	18	19	20	21	22	23	24	25
	EASY									MEDIUM									HARD					

3   Kim was *k* years of age 2 years ago. In terms of *k*, how old will Kim be 2 years from now?

(A) $k + 4$

(B) $k + 2$

(C) $2k$

(D) k

(E) $\dfrac{k}{2}$

When to Plug In

- Phrases like "in terms of k" in the question
- Variable in the answers
- Unspecified values and fractions

Here's How to Crack It

First, pick a number for *k*. Pick something easy to work with, like 10. In your test booklet, write 10 directly above the letter *k* in the problem, so you won't forget.

If $k = 10$, then Kim was 10 years old 2 years ago. That means she's 12 right now. The problem has asked you to find out how old Kim will be in 2 years. She will be 14. Write a nice big 14 in your test booklet and circle it. Jim's answer will be the choice that, when you plug in 10 for *k*, equals 14.

Now it's time to plug in.

Plugging in 10 for *k* in answer choice A, you get 10 + 4, or 14. This is the number you are looking for, so this must be Jim's answer. (It is.) Go ahead and try the other choices just to make sure you're right and to practice plugging in.

Here's another example:

PROBLEM SOLVING																								
1	2	3	4	5	6	7	8	9	10	11	12	13	14	15	16	**17**	18	19	20	21	22	23	24	25
	EASY									MEDIUM									HARD					

17   The sum of two positive consecutive integers is *x*. In terms of *x*, what is the value of the smaller of these two integers?

(A) $\dfrac{x}{2} - 1$

(B) $\dfrac{x - 1}{2}$

(C) $\dfrac{x}{2}$

(D) $\dfrac{x + 1}{2}$

(E) $\dfrac{x}{2} + 1$

Plugging In Works

Don't try to solve problems like this by writing equations and "solving for *x*" or "solving for *y*." Plugging in is faster, easier, and less likely to produce errors.

Here's How to Crack It

If we pick 2 and 3 for our two positive consecutive integers, then $x = 5$. Write 2, 3, and $x = 5$ in your test booklet.

The smaller of our two integers is 2. Circle it; we are looking for the choice that equals 2 when we plug in 5. Let's try each choice:

(A) Plugging in 5 gives us $\frac{5}{2} - 1$. This won't even be an integer, and 2 is an integer. Eliminate.

(B) Plugging in 5 gives us $\frac{4}{2}$, or 2. This is Jim's answer.

Check all of your choices just to be sure.

WHICH NUMBERS?

Although you can plug in any number, you can make your life much easier by plugging in "good" numbers—numbers that are simple to work with or that make the problem easier to manipulate. Picking a small number, such as 2, will usually make finding the answer easier. If the problem asks for a percentage, plug in 10 or 100. If the problem has to do with minutes, try 60. If you plug in wisely, you can sometimes eliminate computation altogether.

Except in special cases, you should avoid plugging in 0 and 1; these numbers have weird properties. Using them may allow you to eliminate only one or two choices at a time. You should also avoid plugging in any number that appears in the question or in any of the answer choices.

Many times you'll find that there is an advantage to picking a particular number, even a very large one, because it makes solving the problem easier.

Here's an example:

PROBLEM SOLVING			
1 2 3 4 5 6 7 8	9 10 11 12 13 14 15 16 **17** 18	19 20 21 22 23 24 25	
EASY	MEDIUM	HARD	

17 If 100 equally priced tickets cost a total of d dollars, 5 of these tickets cost how many dollars?

(A) $\dfrac{d}{20}$

(B) $\dfrac{d}{5}$

(C) $5d$

(D) $\dfrac{5}{d}$

(E) $\dfrac{20}{d}$

Be Good

"Good" numbers make a problem less confusing by simplifying the arithmetic. This is your chance to make the SAT easier.

Here's How to Crack It

Should you plug in 2 for d? You could, but plugging in 200 would make the problem easier. After all, if 100 tickets cost a total of $200, then each ticket costs $2. Write $d = 200$ in your test booklet.

If each ticket costs $2, then 5 tickets cost $10. Write a 10 in your test booklet and circle it. You are looking for the answer choice that works out to 10 when you plug in 200 for d. Let's try each choice:

(A) $\dfrac{200}{20} = 10$

That was easy. A quick eyeball of the other choices confirms Jim's answer is (A).

Here's another example:

PROBLEM SOLVING
1 2 3 4 5 6 7 8 9 10 11 12 13 14 15 16 17 18 19 20 21 22 23 24 **25**
EASY   MEDIUM   HARD

25 A watch loses x minutes every y hours. At this rate, how many hours will the watch lose in one week?

(A) $7xy$

(B) $\dfrac{7y}{x}$

(C) $\dfrac{x}{7y}$

(D) $\dfrac{14y}{5x}$

(E) $\dfrac{14x}{5y}$

Here's How to Crack It

This is an extremely difficult problem for students who try to solve it the math-class way. You'll be able to find the answer easily, though, if you plug in carefully.

What should you plug in? As always, you can plug in anything, but if you select numbers wisely you'll make things easier on yourself. There are three units of time in this problem: minutes, hours, and weeks. If we plug in 60 for x, we can get it down to two, because 60 minutes equal an hour. Write $x = 60$ in your test booklet.

We can also make things easier for ourselves by plugging in 24 for y. There are 24 hours in a day. What we are saying so far is that the watch loses 60 minutes every 24 hours. In other words, it loses an hour a day. Write $y = 24$ in your test booklet.

At this rate, how many hours will the watch lose in a week? It will lose 7, obviously, because there are 7 days in a week. Write 7 in your test booklet and circle it. We are looking for the answer choice that equals 7 when we plug in 60 for x and 24 for y.

Now let's check each choice:

(A) $7xy = (7)(60)(24)$. Common sense, not computation, tells us that this is way too big. Eliminate.

(B) $7\dfrac{y}{x} = \dfrac{(7)(24)}{(60)} = \dfrac{168}{60} = 2.8$. Eliminate.

(C) $\dfrac{x}{7y} = \dfrac{(60)}{(7)(24)} = \dfrac{60}{168} = 0.35714$. Eliminate.

(D) $\dfrac{14y}{5x} = \dfrac{(14)(24)}{(5)(60)} = \dfrac{336}{300} = 1.12$. Eliminate.

(E) $\dfrac{14x}{5y} = \dfrac{(14)(60)}{(5)(24)} = \dfrac{840}{120} = 7$. This is Jim's answer.

INEQUALITIES

Plugging In works on problems containing inequalities, but you will have to follow some different rules. Plugging in one number is often not enough; to find Jim's answer you may have to plug in several numbers, including weird numbers like: $-1, 0, 1, \dfrac{1}{2}$, and $-\dfrac{1}{2}$.

The five numbers just mentioned all have special properties. Negatives, fractions, 0, and 1 all behave in peculiar ways when, for example, they are squared. Don't forget about them!

Sometimes you can avoid plugging in altogether by simplifying. Here's an example:

PROBLEM SOLVING																								
1	2	3	4	5	6	7	8	9	**10**	11	12	13	14	15	16	17	18	19	20	21	22	23	24	25
		EASY									MEDIUM								HARD					

10 If $-3x + 6 \geq 18$, which of the following must be true?

(A) $x \leq -4$
(B) $x \leq 6$
(C) $x \geq -4$
(D) $x \geq -6$
(E) $x = 2$

Here's How to Crack It

The inequality in the problem can be simplified quite a bit:

$$-3x + 6 \geq 18$$
$$-3x \geq 12$$
$$-x \geq 4$$

Weird Numbers

As you may have noticed, some numbers have uncommon properties. Because of this, we plug them in only under certain circumstances, usually when solving:

- Inequalities
- MUST BE problems
- Quantitative comparisons

What Are the Weird Numbers?

- fractions
- negatives
- big numbers
- 1 and 0

Gator!

Think of the inequality sign as the mouth of a hungry alligator. The alligator eats the bigger number.

We're close to one of the answer choices, but not quite there yet. Multiply both sides by –1 to make x positive. Remember to change the direction of the inequality sign! (If you are rusty on inequalities, see page 219 for a quick review.)

$$x \le -4$$

So choice A is Jim's answer.

OTHER SPECIAL CASES

Sometimes SAT algebra problems will require you to determine certain characteristics of a number or numbers. Is x odd or even? Is it small or large? Is it positive or negative?

On questions like this, you will probably have to plug in more than one number and/or plug in weird numbers, just as you do on problems containing inequalities and "it cannot be determined." Sometimes ETS's wording will tip you off. If the problem states only that $x > 0$, you know for certain that x is positive but you don't know that x is an integer. See what happens when you plug in a fraction.

Here are some other tip-offs you should be aware of:

If the problem asked for this	and you plugged in this	also try this, just to be sure
an integer	3	1, 0, or –1
a fraction	$\frac{1}{4}$	$-\frac{1}{4}$
two even numbers	2, 4	2, –2
a number	an integer	a fraction
a number	an even number	an odd number
a number	a small number	a huge number
a multiple of 7	7	7,000 or –7
consecutive numbers	1, 2, 3	–1, 0, 1
$x^2 = 4$	2	–2
$xy > 0$	(2, 4)	(–2, –4)
$x = 2y$	(4, 2)	(–4, –2) or (0, 0)

MUST BE TRUE

Try the following problem:

PROBLEM SOLVING

1 2 3 4 5 6 7 8	9 10 11 12 13 14 15 16 17	18 19 20 21 **22** 23 24 25
EASY	MEDIUM	HARD

22 If $x - y$ is a multiple of 3, then which of the following must also be a multiple of 3?

(A) $y - x$

(B) $\dfrac{y - x}{2}$

(C) $\dfrac{x + y}{2}$

(D) $x + y$

(E) xy

Here's How to Crack It

Since there are variables in the answer choices, we will plug in. First plug in easy numbers that make the given statement ($x - y$ is a multiple of 3) true. Let's make $x = 6$ and $y = 3$. The question asks which of the following must also be a multiple of 3. Let's plug in our numbers, and cross off any answer choices that are not multiples of 3.

(A) $3 - 6 = -3$ is a multiple of 3, so keep it.

(B) $3 - 6 /2$ is not a multiple of 3. Cross it off.

(C) $6 + 3 /2$ is not a multiple of 3. Cross it off.

(D) $6 + 3 = 9$. Keep it.

(E) $(6)(3) = 18$. Keep it.

Since this question asks for something that *must* be true and we are left with three answer choices, we must plug in again. The question asks us for a multiple of 3. The first time we plugged in, we used two other multiples of three ($x = 6$ and $y = 3$) to satisfy the first condition. Let's now use two numbers that make the initial statement true but are *not* multiples of 3. Plug in 5 for x and 2 for y. Now check the answers we didn't eliminate the first time:

(A) $2 - 5 = -3$. It still works, so keep it.

(D) $5 + 2 = 7$. Cross it off.

(E) $(5)(2) = 10$. Cross it off.

Jim's answer is (A)

PLUGGING IN: ADVANCED PRINCIPLES

As you have just learned, you should Plug In whenever you don't know what a number is. But you can also Plug In when you have numbers that are too big, too ugly, or too inconvenient to work with. On such problems you can often find Jim's answer simply by using numbers that aren't as ugly as the ones ETS has given you.

A Little Terminology

Here are some words that you will need to know to follow the rest of this chapter. The words themselves won't show up on the SAT, so after you finish the chapter you can forget about them.

Term: An equation is like a sentence, and a term is the equivalent of a word. For example, $9x^2$ is a term in the equation $9x^2 + 3x = 5y$.

Expression: If an equation is like a sentence, then an expression is like a phrase or a clause. An expression is a combination of terms and mathmatical operations with no equal or inequality sign. For example, $9x^2 + 3x$ is an expression.

Polynomial: A polynomial is any expression containing two or more terms. Binomials and trinomials are both known as polynomials.

Here's an example:

20 On the last day of a one-week sale, customers numbered 149 through 201 were waited on. How many customers were waited on that day?

(A) 51
(B) 52
(C) 53
(D) 152
(E) 153

Here's How to Crack It

This is a number 20—a difficult question. Finding Jim's answer has to be harder than simply subtracting 149 from 201 to get 52, which means that choice B has to be wrong. Cross it out. (You can also immediately eliminate D and E, which are much, much too big.)

One way to find the answer would be to count this out by hand. But to count from 149 to 201 is an awful lot of counting. You can achieve the same result by using simpler numbers instead.

It doesn't matter which numbers you use. How about 7 and 11? The difference between 7 and 11 is 4. But if you count out the numbers on your hand—7, 8, 9, 10, 11—you see that there are 5 numbers. In other words, if the store had served customers 7 through 11, the number of customers would have been 1 greater than the difference of 7 and 11. Jim's answer, therefore, will be 1 greater than the difference of 149 and 201. Jim's answer, in other words, is C.

Here's another example:

22 $2^{23} - 2^{22} =$

(A) 2^1

(B) $2^{\frac{23}{22}}$

(C) 2^{22}

(D) 2^{23}

(E) 2^{45}

Factoring with Exponents

We can also solve question 22 by factoring 2^{22} out of the parentheses, giving us a new expression: $2^{22}(2^1 - 1) = 2^{22}(2 - 1) = 2^{22}(1) = 2^{22}$.

Here's How to Crack It

These are big, ugly, inconvenient exponents. No wonder this question is a number 22. But you'll be able to solve it if you plug in easier numbers.

Instead of 2^{23}, let's use 2^4. And instead of 2^{22}, let's use 2^3. Now we can rewrite the problem: $2^4 - 2^3 = 16 - 8 = 8 = 2^3$.

Our answer is the second of the two numbers we started with. Jim's answer, therefore, must be the second number he started with, or 2^{22}, which is choice C.

(If you don't believe this always works, try it with 2^3 and 2^2, and with 2^5 and 2^4, or any other similar pair of numbers. By the way, choices A and B are Joe Bloggs answers.)

Basic Princeton Review Algebra

Backsolving and Plugging In will be of enormous help to you on the math SAT. But they won't be enough to answer every algebra problem. On some problems, you'll have to know the few basic principles of Princeton Review Algebra.

Simplifying Expressions

If a problem contains an expression that can be factored, you should factor it immediately. For example, if you come upon a problem containing the expression $2x + 2y$, you should factor it immediately to produce the expression $2(x + y)$.

If a problem contains an expression that is already factored, you should multiply it out according to the distributive law to return it to its original unfactored state. For example, if you come upon a problem containing the expression $2(x + y)$, you should unfactor it by multiplying through to produce the expression $2x + 2y$.

Here are five worked examples:

Something to Hide

Because factoring or unfactoring is usually the key to finding Jim's answer on such problems, learn to recognize expressions that could be either factored or unfactored. This will earn you more points. Jim likes to hide the answers in factors.

1. $4x + 24 = 4(x) + 4(6) = 4(x + 6)$

2. $\dfrac{10x - 60}{2} = \dfrac{10(x) - 10(6)}{2} = \dfrac{10(x - 6)}{2} = 5(x - 6) = 5x - 30$

3. $\dfrac{x + y}{y} = \dfrac{x}{y} + \dfrac{y}{y} = \dfrac{x}{y} + 1$

4. $2(x + y) + 3(x + y) = (2 + 3)(x + y) = 5(x + y)$

5. $p(r + s) + q(r + s) = (p + q)(r + s)$

Multiplying Polynomials

Multiplying polynomials is easy. Just be sure to use FOIL (First, Outer, Inner, Last):

$$(x + 2)(x + 4) = (x + 2)(x + 4)$$

$$= (x \times x) + (x \times 4) + (2 \times x) + (2 \times 4)$$

$$\text{FIRST} \quad \text{OUTER} \quad \text{INNER} \quad \text{LAST}$$

$$= x^2 + 4x + 2x + 8$$

$$= x^2 + 6x + 8$$

COMBINE SIMILAR TERMS FIRST

In manipulating long, complicated algebraic expressions, combine all similar terms before doing anything else. In other words, if one of the terms is $5x$ and another is $-3x$, simply combine them into $2x$. Then you won't have as many terms to work with. Here's an example:

$$(3x^2 + 3x + 4) + (2 - x) - (6 + 2x) =$$

$$3x^2 + 3x + 4 + 2 - x - 6 - 2x =$$

$$3x^2 + (3x - x - 2x) + (4 + 2 - 6) =$$

$$3x^2$$

EVALUATING EXPRESSIONS

Sometimes ETS will give you the value of one of the letters in an algebraic expression and ask you to find the value of the entire expression. All you have to do is plug in the given value and see what you come up with.

Here is an example:

Problem:

$$\text{If } 2x = -1, \text{ then } (2x - 3)^2 = ?$$

Solution:

Don't solve for x; simply plug in -1 for $2x$, like this:

$$(2x - 3)^2 = (-1 - 3)^2$$

$$= (-4)^2$$

$$= 16$$

SOLVING EQUATIONS

Learn Them, Love Them

Don't get bogged down looking for a direct solution. Always ask yourself if there is a simple way to find the answer. If you train yourself to think in terms of shortcuts, you won't waste a lot of time. However, if you don't see a quick solution, get to work. Something may come to you as you labor away.

In algebra class you learned to solve equations by "solving for x" or "solving for y." To do this, you isolate x or y on one side of the equal sign and put everything else on the other side. This is a long, laborious process with many steps and many opportunities for mistakes.

On the SAT, you usually won't need to solve equations this way. You've already learned how to Backsolve and Plug In. On the few problems where these techniques don't apply, you should be able to find direct solutions. To demonstrate what we mean, we'll show you the same problem solved two different ways.

Problem:

$$\text{If } 2x = 5 \text{ and } 3y = 6, \text{ then } 6xy = ?$$

Math-class solution:

Your teacher would tell you to:

1. find x
2. find y

3.   multiply 6 times x times y

Using this procedure, you find that $x = \dfrac{5}{2}$ and $y = 2$. Therefore, $6xy = (6)\dfrac{5}{2}(2)$, or 30.

The Princeton Review solution:

You notice that $6xy$ equals $(2x)(3y)$. Therefore, $6xy$ equals 5×6, or 30.

Analysis

Finding direct solutions will save you time. ETS expects you to perform long, complicated calculations on the SAT. You should always stop and think for a moment before beginning such a process. Look for a trick—a shortcut to the answer.

Here's another example:

> If a, b, c, and d are integers and $ab = 12$,
> $bc = 20$, $cd = 30$, and $ad = 18$, then $abcd = ?$

Here's How to Crack It

If you try to solve this the math-class way, you'll end up fiddling forever with the equations, trying to find individual values for a, b, c, and d. Once again, you may get the correct answer, but you'll spend an eternity doing it.

This problem is much simpler if you look for a direct solution. The first thing to notice is that you have been given a lot of information you don't need. For example, the problem would have been much simpler to answer if you had been given only two equations: $ab = 12$ and $cd = 30$. You should know that $(ab)(cd) = abcd$, which means that $abcd = (12)(30)$, which means that the answer is 360.

SOLVING INEQUALITIES

In an equation, one side equals the other. In an inequality, one side does not equal the other. The following symbols are used in inequalities:

$\neq$	is not equal to
$>$	is greater than
$<$	is less than
$\geq$	is greater than or equal to
$\leq$	is less than or equal to

Warning

When you multiply or divide inequality by a negative number, you must reverse the inequality sign.

Solving inequalities is pretty much like solving equations. You can collect similar terms, and you can simplify by doing the same thing to both sides. All you have to remember is that if you multiply or divide both sides of an inequality by a negative number, the direction of the inequality symbol changes. For example, here's a simple inequality:

$$x > y$$

Now, just as you can with an equation, you can multiply both sides of this inequality by the same number. But if the number you multiply by is negative, you have to change the direction of the symbol in the result. For example, if we multiply both sides of the inequality above by −2, we end up with the following:

$$-2x < -2y$$

Stack 'Em

Don't solve simultaneous equations on the SAT the way you would in school (by multiplying one equation by one number, and then adding or subtracting). We have rarely seen an SAT on which simultaneous equations had to be solved this way. Just stack 'em, and add 'em, or subtract 'em.

SOLVING SIMULTANEOUS EQUATIONS

Sometimes on the SAT you will be asked to find the value of an expression based on two given equations. To find Jim's answer on such problems, simply add or subtract the two equations.

Here's an example:

If $4x + y = 14$ and $3x + 2y = 13$, then $x - y = ?$

Here's How to Crack It

You've been given two equations here. But instead of being asked to solve for a variable (x or y), you've been asked to solve for an expression ($x - y$). Why? Because there must be a direct solution.

In math class, you're taught to multiply one equation by one number and then subtract equations to find the second variable. Or you're taught to solve one equation for one variable in terms of the other and to substitute that value into the second equation to solve for the other variable, and, having found the other variable, to plug it back into the equation to find the value of the first variable.

Forget it. There's a better way. Just add or subtract the two equations; either addition or subtraction will produce an easy answer. Adding the two equations gives you this:

$$\begin{array}{r} 4x + y = 14 \\ + 3x + 2y = 13 \\ \hline 7x + 3y = 27 \end{array}$$

This doesn't get us anywhere. So try subtracting:

$$\begin{array}{r} 4x + y = 14 \\ - 3x + 2y = 13 \\ \hline x - y = 1 \end{array}$$

The value of ($x - y$) is precisely what you are looking for, so this must be Jim's answer.

SOLVING QUADRATIC EQUATIONS

To solve quadratic equations, remember everything you've learned so far: Look for direct solutions and either factor or unfactor when possible. Here's an example:

If $(x + 3)^2 = (x - 2)^2$, then $x = ?$

Here's How to Crack It

Since both sides of the equation have been factored, you should unfactor them by multiplying them out:

Left: $(x + 3)(x + 3) = x^2 + 6x + 9$

Right: $(x - 2)(x - 2) = x^2 - 4x + 4$

Therefore: $x^2 + 6x + 9 = x^2 - 4x + 4$

Now you can simplify. Eliminate the x^2's since they are on both sides of the equal sign. Move the x's to the left, and the numbers to the right to give you:

$$10x = -5$$

$$x = -\frac{1}{2}$$

Here's another example:

If $x^2 - 4 = (18)(14)$, then what could x be?

Here's How to Crack It

$x^2 - 4$ is actually a common quadratic expression: $x^2 - y^2$. Since $x^2 - y^2 = (x + y)(x - y)$, that means $x^2 - 4$ can be factored in the same way:

$$x^2 - 4 = (x + 2)(x - 2)$$

Therefore: $(x + 2)(x - 2) = (18)(14)$

Notice that each side of the equation consists of two terms multiplied by each other. Set the corresponding parts equal to each other and see what you get.

$$(x + 2) = 18$$

$$(x - 2) = 14$$

Both equations work if x is 16 or –16.

SOLVING QUADRATIC EQUATIONS SET TO ZERO

If $ab = 0$, what do you know about a and b? You know that at least one of them has to equal 0. You can use this fact in solving some quadratic equations. Here's an example:

What are all the values of x for which
$x(x - 3) = 0$?

Here's How to Crack It

Because the product of x and $(x - 3)$ is 0, you know that x or $(x - 3)$—or both of them—has to equal 0. To solve the problem, simply ask yourself what x would have to be to make either expression equal 0. The answer is obvious: x could be either 0 or 3.

Predictable Functions

There are usually two or three function problems on every SAT. The last one will be extremely difficult. If you're not trying to score in the 700s, you should probably skip it. On the others, work very, very carefully.

FUNCTIONS

When you learned about functions in algebra class, you probably talked about "f of x," or $f(x)$.

The SAT is different. It tests functions, but in a peculiar way. Instead of using $f(x)$, it uses funny symbols to stand for operations. If you understand functions, just remember them when you see the funny symbols. If you don't understand functions, just follow what we tell you.

In a function problem, an arithmetic operation is defined and then you are asked to perform it on a number, a pair of numbers, or an ordered pair of numbers. All you have to do is keep your wits about you, use your booklet as scratch paper, and do as you are told. A function is like a set of instructions: follow it and you'll find Jim's answer.

Here's an example:

PROBLEM SOLVING		
1 2 3 4 5 6 7 8	9 10 11 12 13 14 15 16 17 **18**	19 20 21 22 23 24 25
EASY	MEDIUM	HARD

18 If $x \mathbin{\#} y = \dfrac{1}{x-y}$, what is the value $\dfrac{1}{2} \mathbin{\#} \dfrac{1}{3}$?

(A) 6

(B) $\dfrac{6}{5}$

(C) $\dfrac{1}{6}$

(D) -1

(E) -6

Here's How to Crack It

Finding Jim's answers is just a matter of simple substitution. Just substitute $\dfrac{1}{2}$ and $\dfrac{1}{3}$ for x and y in the function.

$$\frac{1}{2} \mathbin{\#} \frac{1}{3} = \frac{1}{\dfrac{1}{2}-\dfrac{1}{3}}$$

$$= \frac{1}{\dfrac{3}{6}-\dfrac{2}{6}}$$

$$= \frac{1}{\dfrac{1}{6}}$$

$$= 6$$

Jim's answer, therefore, is choice A.

Let's try a pair of functions:

Questions 16–17 refer to the following definition:

> For all integers x, let $\odot\, x = x^2$ if x is negative, and let $\odot\, x$ $= 2x$ if x is positive.

16 $\odot(-5) - \odot 5 =$
(A) −10
(B) −5
(C) 0
(D) 10
(E) 15

17 What is the value of $\odot(-(\odot x)) - \odot(\odot x)$ when x is equal to −3?

(A) −18
(B) −12
(C) 0
(D) 18
(E) 63

Here's How to Crack Them

If you are given two function problems that refer to the same definition, the second one will be significantly harder than the first. You should feel free to skip the second one if you are having trouble with functions. Let's look at number 16 first.

If x is negative, we are to square it. In this case, our first term is − 5. − 5 squared equals 25. If x is positive, multiply it by 2. Our second term is 5 so multiply it times 2 to get 10. We now have 25 − 10 or 15. Jim's answer is (E).

Number 17 is a bit messier. Just pull it apart one piece at a time. Remember PEMDAS? Do your parentheses first, from the inside out. In this problem we are told that x equals − 3. Fill − 3 in for x:

$$\odot(-(\odot - 3)) - \odot(\odot - 3)$$

In the first term, square − 3 to get 9. Get rid of the parentheses and you have − 9. Square that and you have 81.

In the second term, square − 3 to get 9. Multiply 9 times 2 (since 9 is positive) and you have 18. 81 minus 18 equals 63. Jim's answer is (E).

WORD PROBLEMS I

Most word problems can be solved quickly by Backsolving or Plugging In. But there will be a few algebra word problems on your SAT that will be more complicated. You'll still be able to answer them, but you should save them for last.

In solving a word problem that can't be done by Backsolving or Plugging In, you should simply translate the problem into an equation. As we said earlier, equations are a kind of shorthand. You will be able to set up equations easily if you train yourself to notice words that are longhand versions of arithmetic symbols. Here are some words and their equivalent symbols:

WORD	SYMBOL
is	=
of, times, product	×
what (or any unknown value)	any letter (x, k, b)
more, sum	+
less, difference	−
ratio, quotient	÷

Here are two examples:

Words: 14 is 5 more than some number

Equation: $14 = 5+x$

Words: If one-eighth of a number is 3, what is one-half of the same number?

Equation: $\frac{1}{8} n = 3, \frac{1}{2}n = ?$

ALGEBRA SUMMARY

1. Ordinary algebra takes too much time on the SAT. Do it our way instead. It's the last thing Jim expects you to do.

2. When Backsolving an SAT algebra problem, plug the numbers in the answer choices into the problem until you find one that works.

3. Plugging In is *the* technique for multiple-choice problems whose answer choices contain variables. It has three steps:
    1. Pick numbers for the variables in the problem.
    2. Using your numbers, find an answer to the problem.
    3. Plug your numbers from step 1 into the answer choices to see which choice equals the answer you found in step 2.

4. When you Plug In, use "good" numbers—ones that are simple to work with and that make the problem easier to manipulate.

5. Plugging in works on problems containing inequalities, but you will have to be careful and follow some different rules. Plugging in one number is often not enough; to find Jim's answer you may have to plug in several numbers.

6. You can also Plug In when you have numbers that are too big, too ugly, or too inconvenient to work with.

7. If a problem contains an expression that can be factored, factor it. If it contains an expression that already has been factored, unfactor it.

8. Don't "solve for x" or "solve for y" unless you absolutely have to. (Don't worry; your math teacher won't find out.) Instead, look for direct solutions to SAT problems. ETS never uses problems that *necessarily* require time-consuming computations or endless fiddling with big numbers. There's almost always a trick—if you can spot it.

9. To solve simultaneous equations, simply add or subtract the equations.

10. Learn to recognize SAT function problems. They're the ones with the funny symbols. Solve them like playing "Simon Says"—do what you are told.

11. If you come across a word problem you can't beat by Backsolving or Plugging In, simply translate the problem into an equation and solve it.

14

Geometry

SAT Geometry Problems: Cracking the System

About a third of the math problems on your SAT will involve geometry. Fortunately, you won't need much specific knowledge of geometry to solve them. You won't have to prove any theorems and you won't need to know many terms. You'll have to use a few formulas, but they will be printed on the first page of each math section in your test booklet.

In this chapter we will teach you:

- the fundamental facts you must know to solve SAT geometry problems,

- how to find Jim's answers and avoid careless mistakes by guesstimating,

- how to find Jim's answers by Plugging In,

- the advanced principles that will help you on harder problems.

Basic Principles: Fundamentals of SAT Geometry

The SAT doesn't test any really difficult geometry, but you will need a thorough knowledge of several fundamental rules. You will use these fundamentals in applying the techniques that we will teach you later in the chapter. You don't need to linger over these rules if you have already mastered them. But be sure you understand them completely before you move on. Some of these rules will be provided in the instructions on your SAT, but you should know them before you go to the test center. Consulting the instructions as you work is a waste of time. (On the other hand, if the Pythagorean theorem suddenly vaporizes from your brain while you are taking the test, don't hesitate to peek back at the instructions.)

We divide SAT geometry into four basic topics:

1. degrees and angles

2. triangles

3. circles

4. rectangles and squares

DEGREES AND ANGLES

1. A circle contains 360 degrees.

Every circle contains 360 degrees. Each degree is $\frac{1}{360}$ of the total distance around the outside of the circle. It doesn't matter whether the circle is large or small; it still has exactly 360 degrees.

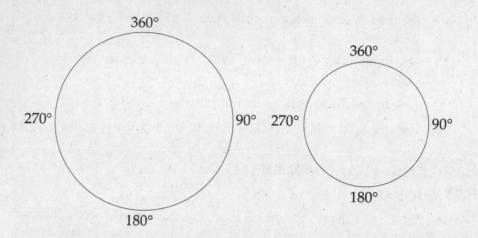

2. When you think about angles, remember circles.

An angle is formed when two line segments extend from a common point. If you think of the point as the center of a circle, the measure of the angle is the number of degrees enclosed by the lines when they pass through the edge of the circle. Once again, the size of the circle doesn't matter; neither does the length of the lines.

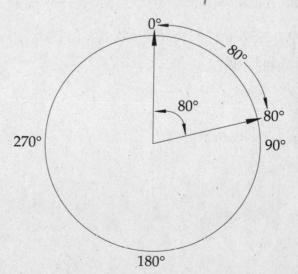

3. A line is a 180-degree angle.

You probably don't think of a line as an angle, but it is one. Think of it as a flat angle. The following drawings should help:

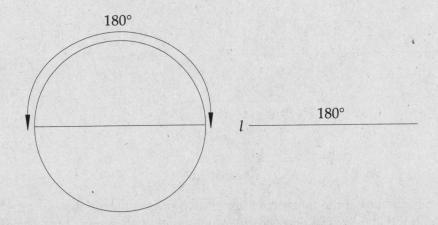

4. When two lines intersect, four angles are formed.

The following diagram should make this clear. The four angles are indicated by letters.

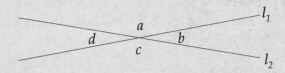

The measures of these four angles add up to 360 degrees. (Remember the circle.)

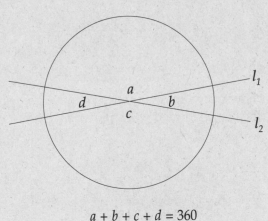

$$a + b + c + d = 360$$

If two lines are perpendicular to each other, each of the four angles formed is 90 degrees. A 90-degree angle is called a right angle.

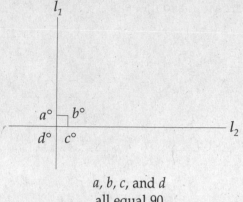

a, b, c, and d
all equal 90

The little box at the intersection of the two lines is the symbol for a right angle. If the lines are not perpendicular to each other, then none of the angles will be right angles.

5. **When two lines intersect, the angles opposite each other will have the same measures.**

Such angles are called vertical angles. In the following diagram, angles a and c are equal; so are angles b and d. The total of all four angles is still 360 degrees.

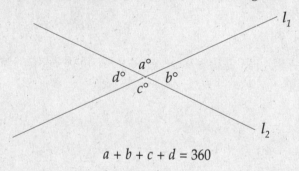

$$a + b + c + d = 360$$

It doesn't matter how many lines you intersect through a single point. The total measure of all the angles formed will still be 360 degrees.

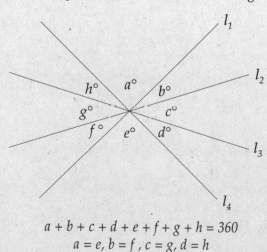

$$a + b + c + d + e + f + g + h = 360$$
$$a = e, b = f, c = g, d = h$$

6. **When two parallel lines are cut by a third line, the small angles are equal, the big angles are equal, and the sum of a big angle and a small angle is 180 degrees.**

At The Princeton Review, we call this concept Fred's Theorem. Parallel lines are two lines that never intersect, and the rules about parallel lines are usually taught in school with lots of big words. But we like to avoid big words whenever possible. Simply put, when a line cuts through two parallel lines, two kinds of angles are created: big angles and small angles. You can tell which angles are big and which are small just by looking at them. All the big angles look equal, and they are. The same is true of the small angles. Lastly, any big angle plus any small angle always equals 180 degrees. (Jim likes rules about angles that add up to 180 or 360 degrees.)

In any geometry problem, never assume that two lines are parallel unless the question or diagram specifically tells you so. In the following diagram, angle a is a big angle, and it has the same measure as angles c, e, and g, which are also big angles. Angle b is a small angle, and it has the same measure as angles d, f, and h, which are also small angles.

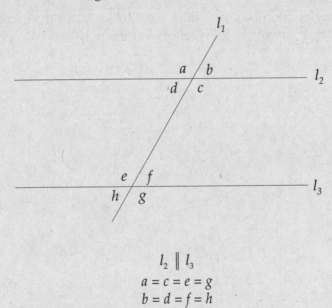

$$l_2 \parallel l_3$$
$$a = c = e = g$$
$$b = d = f = h$$

You should be able to see that the degree measure of angles a, b, c, and d add up to 360 degrees. So do angles e, f, g, and h. If you have trouble seeing it, draw a circle around the angles. What is the degree measure of a circle? The sum of any small angle (such as d) and any big angle (such as g) is 180°.

TRIANGLES

1. Every triangle contains 180 degrees.

The word *triangle* means "three angles," and every triangle contains three interior angles. The measures of these three angles always add up to exactly 180 degrees. You don't need to know why this is true or how to prove it. You just need to know it. And we mean know it.

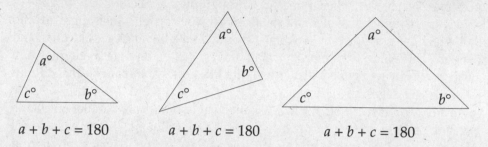

$$a + b + c = 180 \qquad a + b + c = 180 \qquad a + b + c = 180$$

Your Friend the Triangle

If ever you are stumped by a geometry problem that deals with a quadrilateral, hexagon, or circle, look for the triangles that you can form by drawing lines through the figure.

2. An equilateral triangle is one in which all three sides are equal in length.

Because the angles opposite equal sides are also equal, all three angles in an equilateral triangle are equal, too. (Their measures are always 60 degrees each.)

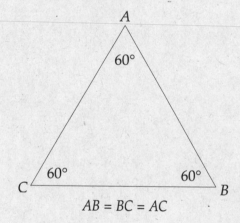

$$AB = BC = AC$$

3. **An isosceles triangle is one in which two of the sides are
   equal in length.**

The angles opposite those equal sides are also equal in length, because, as we just mentioned, angles opposite equal sides are also equal.

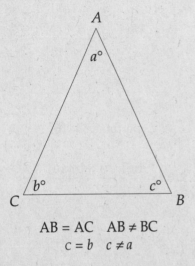

$$AB = AC \quad AB \neq BC$$
$$c = b \quad c \neq a$$

4. **A right triangle is a triangle in which one of the angles is a
   right angle (90 degrees).**

The longest side of a right triangle is called the *hypotenuse*.

Some right triangles are also isosceles.

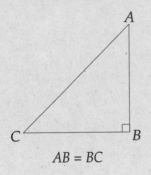

$$AB = BC$$

5. The perimeter of a triangle is the sum of the lengths of its
    sides.

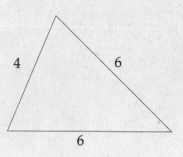

    perimeter = 16

6. The area of a triangle is $\dfrac{\text{height} \times \text{base}}{2}$.

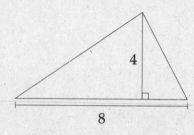 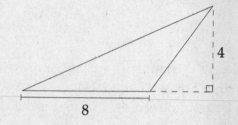

$$\text{area} = \frac{4 \times 8}{2} = 16 \qquad\qquad \text{area} = \frac{4 \times 8}{2} = 16$$

CIRCLES

1. **The circumference of a circle is $2\pi r$ or πd, where r is the radius of the circle and d is the diameter.**

You'll be given this information in your test booklet, so don't stress over memorizing these formulas. You will always be able to refer to your test booklet if you forget them.

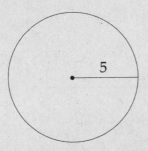 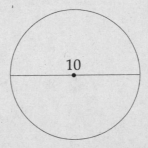

circumference = $2 \times \pi \times 5 = 10\pi$ circumference = 10π

In math class you probably learned that $\pi = 3.14$ (or even 3.14159). On the SAT, $\pi = 3^+$ (a little more than 3) is a good enough approximation. Even with a calculator, using $\pi = 3$ will give you all the information you need to solve difficult SAT multiple-choice geometry questions.

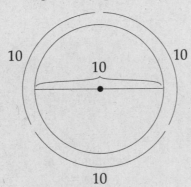

circumference = about 30

2. **The area of a circle is πr^2, where r is the radius of the circle.**

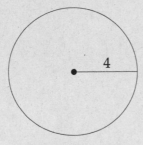

area = $\pi 4^2 = 16\pi$

RECTANGLES AND SQUARES

Little Boxes

Here's a progression of quadrilaterals from least specific to most specific:

quadrilateral = 4 sided figure
↓
parallelogram = a quadrilateral in which opposite sides are parallel
↓
rectangle = a parallelogram in which all angles = 90°
↓
square = a rectangle in which all sides are equal

1. The perimeter of a rectangle is the sum of the lengths of its sides.

Just add them up.

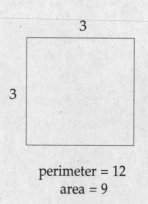

10

4   4

10

perimeter = 10 + 4 + 10 + 4 = 28

2. The area of a rectangle is length × width.

The area of the preceding rectangle, therefore, is 10 x 4, or 40.

3. A square is a rectangle whose four sides are all equal in length.

The perimeter of a square, therefore, is four times the length of any side. The area is the length of any side squared.

3

3

perimeter = 12
area = 9

4. In rectangles and squares all angles are 90° angles.

It can't be a square or a rectangle unless all angles are 90°.

Basic Principles: Guesstimating

On many SAT geometry problems, you will be presented with a drawing in which some information is given and you will be asked to find some of the information that is missing. In most such problems, Jim expects you to apply some formula or perform some calculation, often an algebraic one. But you'll almost always be better off if you look at the drawing and make a rough estimate of Jim's answer (based on the given information) before you try to work it out. We call this *guesstimating*.

Guesstimating is extremely useful on SAT geometry problems. At the very least, it will enable you to avoid careless mistakes by immediately eliminating answers that could not possibly be Jim's answer. In many problems, however, guesstimating will allow you to find Jim's answer without even working out the problem at all.

The Basic Guesstimating Tools

The basic principles just outlined (such as the number of degrees in a triangle and the fact that $\pi \cong 3$) will be enormously helpful to you in guesstimating on the SAT. You should also know the approximate values of several common square roots. Be sure to memorize them before moving on. Knowing them cold will help you solve problems and save time even if your calculator has a square root function.

Square Roots
$$\sqrt{1} = 1$$
$$\sqrt{2} \approx 1.4$$
$$\sqrt{3} \approx 1.7$$
$$\sqrt{4} = 2$$

You will also find it very helpful if you have a good sense of how large certain common angles are. Study the following examples.

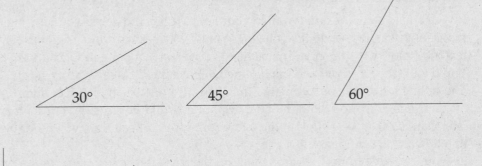

Pictures

Unless otherwise stated, the diagram Jim supplies you with is drawn to scale. This is not true of quant comp diagrams and diagrams labeled "<u>Note</u>: Figure not drawn to scale."

Rocket Science?

The SAT is a goofy college admissions test, not an exercise in precision. Because 50 of its 60 math questions are multiple choice, you can afford to approximate numbers like π, $\sqrt{2}$, $\sqrt{3}$, (3+, 1.4, and 1.7, respectively).

A Picture's Worth at Least Ten Points

If an SAT geometry problem has a drawing in it, you must never, never, ever leave it blank.

To get a little practice using the material you've memorized to help you guesstimate, do the following drill.

DRILL 1

Guesstimate the following values. Use simple values for $\sqrt{2}$, $\sqrt{3}$, and π (rather than using your calculator) to figure out each value. Check your answers on page 348.

1. $\sqrt{2} - 1 =$ _____

2. $3\sqrt{\pi} =$ _____

3. $2\sqrt{2} =$ _____

4. $\sqrt{\dfrac{3}{4}} =$ _____

5. $\sqrt{18} =$ _____

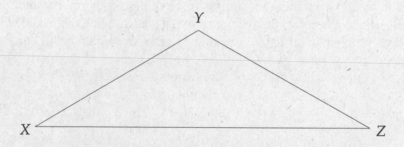

6. In the figure above, given $XY = 16$, estimate all the angles and the lengths of the other sides.

HOW HIGH IS THE CEILING?

If your friend stood next to a wall in your living room and asked you how high the ceiling was, what would you do? Would you get out your trigonometry textbook and try to triangulate using the shadow cast by your pal? Of course not. You'd look at your friend and think something like this: "Dave's about 6 feet tall. The ceiling's a couple of feet higher than he is. It must be about 8 feet high."

Your guesstimation wouldn't be exact, but it would be close. If your mother later claimed that the ceiling in the living room was 15 feet high, you'd be able to tell her with confidence that she was mistaken.

You'll be able to do the same thing on the SAT. Every geometry figure on your test will be drawn exactly to scale unless there is a note in that problem telling you otherwise. That means you can trust the proportions in the drawing. If line segment A has a length of 2 and line segment B is exactly half as long, then the length of line segment B is 1. All such problems are ideal for guesstimating.

Look at the following example:

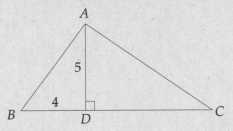

10 If the area of △ABC in the figure above is 30, then the length of DC is

(A) 2
(B) 4
(C) 6
(D) 8
(E) 12

Here's How to Crack It

In guesstimation problems like this, it's usually a good idea to start at the edges and work your way in. When an SAT problem has numeric choices, as this one does, they are always given in increasing or decreasing order of size. Choices at either extreme will be the easiest to dispute and hence the easiest to eliminate if they are wrong. Here's what we mean.

Look at the drawing. Line DC is obviously a good bit longer than line BD. Since BD = 4, we know for certain that DC has to be greater than 4. That means we can eliminate choices A and B. Just cross them out so you won't waste time thinking about them again. They couldn't possibly be correct.

Now look at DC again. Is it 3 times as long as BD? No way. That means choice E can be eliminated as well.

We've narrowed it down to choice C or D. Does DC look like it's twice as long as BD, or like it's one and a half times as long? That's all you have to decide.

(Jim's answer is D. Notice that you found it without having to use the area of the triangle, which was given in the problem.)

Think Back

You can also Backsolve this problem using the area formula for a triangle.

Here's another example:

PROBLEM SOLVING

1 2 3 4 5 6 7 8 9 10 11 12 **13** 14 15 16 17 18 19 20 21 22 23 24 25

EASY   MEDIUM   HARD

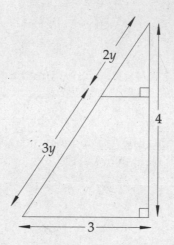

13 In the figure above, $y =$

(A) 1
(B) 2
(C) 3
(D) 4
(E) 5

Another Way

The hypotenuse of this triangle has to be shorter than the sum of the two sides (this is true of all triangles). So, $5y < 7$. Backsolve! Only A works.

Here's How to Crack It

You can use a number of guesstimating approaches to solve this problem. Here's one of them:

The hypotenuse of the little triangle is $2y$. That means that y equals half the length of the hypotenuse. Is half the length of the small hypotenuse larger or smaller than 3 (the base of the triangle)? Smaller, obviously. Therefore, you can eliminate choices C, D, and E, all of which are too large

You now know that y has to be either 1 or 2. If y is 2, then the hypotenuse of the small triangle would equal 4, but that's impossible because we just figured out that it must be less than 3. Therefore, Jim's answer must be A.

When You Can't Eyeball, Measure

Sometimes you won't be able to tell just by looking whether one line is longer than another. In these cases you should actually measure what you need to know. How will you do this? By using the ruler that ETS provides with every answer sheet.

You don't believe that ETS will give you a ruler with your answer sheet? Any piece of paper can be a ruler, if you mark off distances on it. You can use the top or bottom edge of your answer sheet (or your finger or your pencil) to measure distances and solve problems.

Here's how to make a Princeton Review ruler with your answer sheet. Take a look at the first example, problem number 10, on page 241. Take any piece of paper and make a dot on the bottom edge. Now put the dot on point *B*, lay the edge of the strip along *BD*, and mark another dot on the edge of the paper beside point *D*. Here's what it should look like:

Take a look at the first example, problem number 10, on page 241.

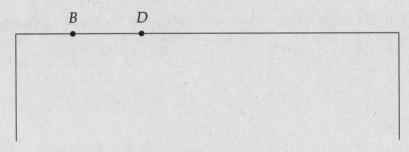

What's the length of the space between the dots? It's exactly 4, of course—the same as the length of *BD* in the diagram. You now have a ruler. You can use it to measure the length of *DC*, which is what the problem asks you for.

You can make your ruler as precise as you need to. By placing the ruler against side *AD* and noting the difference between its length and the length of *BD*, you'll be able to mark off your ruler in units of 1.

You can even use your Princeton Review ruler to measure the circumference of a circle or the length of a curved line. Just carefully turn the paper around the curved distance you want to measure, mark off the distance on your ruler with your pencil, and then compare the ruler with some known distance in the problem.

Ruler Rule

When making a ruler out of your answer sheet, never mark up the sides. That's where the computer reads your responses, and a stray mark could really foul up your score. Mark the top or bottom, mark lightly, and erase your marks after completing the problem.

Important Note

You'll have to make a new ruler for each problem on which you need to measure something. ETS figures are drawn to scale (unless they're labeled otherwise), but they aren't all drawn to the *same* scale. A ruler that measures 4 on one diagram won't measure 4 on another.

YOU CAN ALSO MEASURE ANGLES

ETS is also kind enough to give you a protractor. Where? On any of the square corners of your answer sheet. The square corner of a sheet of paper is a perfect 90-degree angle, like this:

If you fold the paper on the diagonal, taking care not to leave a crease, you end up with a perfect 45-degree angle, like this:

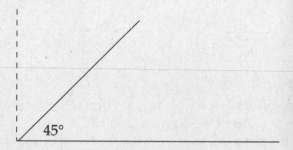

With a tool like this, you'll be able to measure almost any angle with a fair degree of accuracy. Actually, if you practice eyeballing angles, you may never need to consult the corner of your answer sheet. If you spend an hour or so teaching yourself to guesstimate the size of angles just by looking at them, you'll improve your SAT score. In fact, you should be able to answer at least one question on your SAT without doing anything except eyeballing or measuring.

Here's an example:

PROBLEM SOLVING

| 1 | 2 | 3 | 4 | 5 | 6 | 7 | 8 | 9 | 10 | 11 | 12 | 13 | 14 | 15 | 16 | 17 | 18 | 19 | 20 | 21 | 22 | 23 | 24 | 25 |

EASY   MEDIUM   HARD

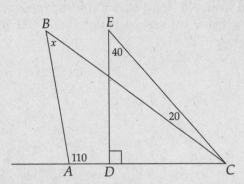

6   In the figure above, $x =$

(A) 15
(B) 20
(C) 30
(D) 40
(E) 50

Here's How to Crack It

By using your page-corner protractor you should be able to see that x is a little bit less than 45. (You should also be able to tell this just by eyeballing.) Therefore, you can definitely eliminate answer choices A, B, and E. Your best choice is D. (It is also Jim's answer.)

Redraw

Redrawing a figure to exaggerate differences is a great way to crack quant comp problems. See chapter 15.

WHAT IF A DIAGRAM IS NOT DRAWN TO SCALE?

Sometimes Jim uses a nonscale drawing because his answer would be obvious even to Joe Bloggs in a scale drawing. In many cases you will simply be able to redraw the diagram in your test booklet and then measure it.

Let's look at an example. Imagine a problem in which you are given a drawing like the one below and asked to determine which is bigger, line segment *AB* or line segment *BC*.

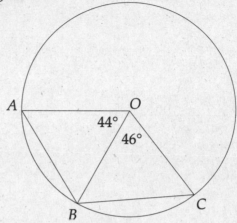

Note: Figure not drawn to scale.

Here's How to Crack It

This figure is not drawn to scale, so simply measuring the segments won't help. In addition, Jim has drawn the figure so that the segments seem to be the same length. What should you do? Redraw the figure in your test booklet, exaggerating the difference in the given information. In this case, you are given the measures of two angles. One angle is a little larger than the other, but both seem to be about the same size in the drawing. All you have to do is redraw the figure exaggerating this difference. Since one angle is bigger than the other, you should make it much bigger. Your drawing might look something like this:

Deception

Why would Jim suddenly choose to draw an inaccurate picture? To mislead you, of course! Any figure not drawn to scale is deliberately misleading. Redraw it.

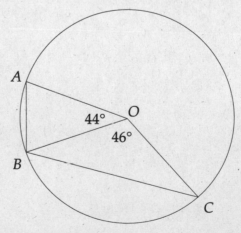

Now you shouldn't have any trouble seeing that line segment *BC* has to be bigger than line segment *AB*. Jim used a nonscale drawing because his answer would have been obvious if he had not.

When You Can't Measure, Sketch and Guesstimate

You will sometimes encounter geometry problems that have no diagrams, or that have diagrams containing only partial information. In these cases, you should use the given information to sketch a complete diagram and then use your drawing as a basis for guesstimating. Don't hesitate to fill your test booklet with sketches and scratch work: This is precisely what you are supposed to do. Finding Jim's answer will be much harder, if not impossible, if you don't take full advantage of the information ETS gives you.

Here's an example:

PROBLEM SOLVING		
1 2 3 4 5 6 7 8	9 10 11 12 13 14 15 16 17 **18** 19 20 21 22 23 24 25	
EASY	MEDIUM	HARD

18 All faces of a cube with a 4-meter edge are covered with striped paper. If the cube is then cut into cubes with 1-meter edges, how many of the 1-meter cubes have striped paper on exactly one face?

(A) 24
(B) 36
(C) 48
(D) 60
(E) 72

Here's How to Crack It

This problem doesn't have a diagram. It would be much easier to solve if it did. What should you do? Draw a diagram, of course! Just sketch the cube quickly in your test booklet and mark it off into 1-meter cubes as described. Your sketch might look like this:

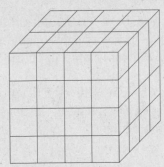

You should be able to see that there are four cubes on each side of the big cube that will have striped paper on only one face (the four center cubes—all the other cubes have at least two exterior sides). Since a cube has six sides, this means that Jim's answer is choice A.

Basic Principles: Plugging In

As you learned in chapter 13, Plugging In is one of the most powerful techniques for solving SAT algebra problems. It is also very useful on geometry problems. On some problems, you will be able to plug in guesstimated values for missing information and then use the results either to find Jim's answer directly or to eliminate answers that could not possibly be correct.

Here's an example:

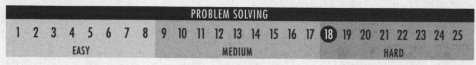

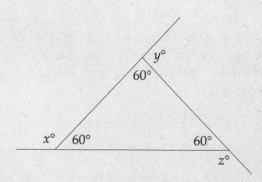

18 In the figure above, $x + y + z =$

(A) 90
(B) 180
(C) 270
(D) 360
(E) 450

Here's How to Crack It

We don't know the measures of the interior angles of the triangle in the drawing, but we do know that the three interior angles of any triangle add up to 180, and 180 divided by 3 is 60. Now, simply plug in 60 for the value of each interior angle.

This doesn't give you Jim's answer directly; the problem does not ask you for the sum of the interior angles. But plugging in does enable you to find Jim's answer. Look at the redrawn figure:

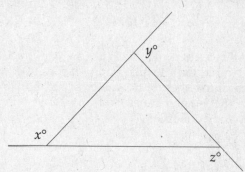

If the marked interior angle is 60, what must x be? Remember that every line is a 180-degree angle. That means that the measure of x must be $180 - 60$, or 120. You can now do the same thing for the other two angles. Using this method you find that x, y, and z each equal 120. That means that $x + y + z = 360$. Jim's answer, therefore, is choice D.

Guesstimating like this won't always give you Jim's answer exactly, but it will usually enable you to eliminate at least three of the four incorrect choices. Other kinds of geometry problems also lend themselves to Plugging In.

Here's another example:

PROBLEM SOLVING																								
1	2	3	4	5	6	7	8	9	10	11	12	13	14	15	16	17	18	19	20	21	22	23	24	**25**
			EASY								MEDIUM									HARD				

25 The length of rectangle S is 20 percent longer than the length of rectangle R, and the width of rectangle S is 20 percent shorter than the width of rectangle R. The area of rectangle S is

(A) 20% greater than the area of rectangle R
(B) 4% greater than the area of rectangle R
(C) equal to the area of rectangle R
(D) 4% less than the area of rectangle R
(E) 20% less than the area of rectangle R

Here's How to Crack It

This is a hard problem. You should recognize first of all that choices A, C, and E are Joe Bloggs answers and should be eliminated. Even if you don't see this, though, you'll be able to find Jim's answer by sketching and Plugging In.

When Plugging In, always use numbers that are easy to work with. Let's say that the length of rectangle R is 10; that means that the length of rectangle S, which is 20 percent longer, must be 12. You can use 10 again in figuring widths. If the width of rectangle R is 10, then the width of rectangle S, which is 20 percent shorter, must be 8. You should come up with two sketches that look like this:

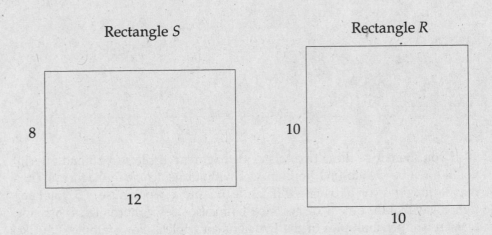

Rectangle S

Rectangle R

R turns out to be a square, but that's all right; squares are rectangles, too. The area of rectangle *R* is 100; the area of *S* is 96. The area of *S*, which is what the problem asks for, is thus a little bit less than the area of *R*. In fact, it is 4 percent less. Jim's answer is choice D.

ADVANCED PRINCIPLES: BEYOND THE FUNDAMENTALS

The Pythagorean Theorem

The Pythagorean Theorem states that in a right triangle (a triangle with one interior angle that is exactly 90 degrees), the square of the hypotenuse equals the sum of the squares of the other two sides. As we told you earlier, the hypotenuse is the longest side of a right triangle; it's the side opposite the right angle. The square of the hypotenuse is its length squared. Applying the Pythagorean Theorem to the following drawing, we find that $c^2 = a^2 + b^2$.

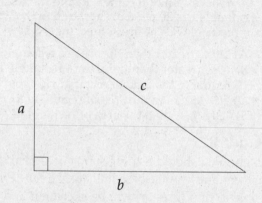

If you forget the Pythagorean Theorem, you can always look it up in the box at the beginning of the math section. Very often, however, you won't need to use the Pythagorean Theorem to find Jim's answer, because Jim writes very predictable geometry questions involving right triangles. Jim has two favorites:

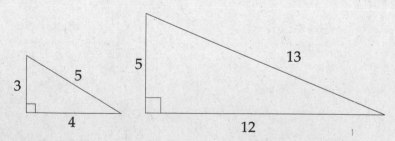

If you memorize these two sets of Pythagorean triplets (3:4:5 and 5:12:13), you'll often be able to find Jim's answer without using the Pythagorean Theorem. If Jim gives you a triangle with a side of 3 and a hypotenuse of 5, you know right away that the other side has to be 4. Jim also uses right triangles with sides that are simply multiples of the Pythagorean triplets. For example, Jim likes right triangles with sides of 6, 8, and 10. These sides are simply the sides of a 3:4:5 triangle multiplied by 2.

Polygons

Polygons are two-dimensional figures with three or more straight sides. Triangles and rectangles are both polygons. So are figures with five, six, seven, eight, or any greater number of sides. The most important fact to know about polygons is that any one of them can be divided into triangles. This means that you can always determine the sum of the measures of the interior angles of any polygon.

For example, the sum of the interior angles of any four-sided polygon (called a "quadrilateral") is 360 degrees. Why? Because any quadrilateral can be divided into two triangles, and a triangle contains 180 degrees. Look at the following example:

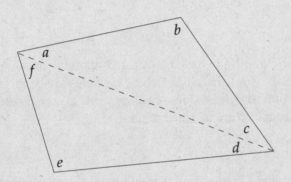

In this polygon, $a + b + c = 180°$; so does $d + e + f$. That means that the sum of the interior angles of the quadrilateral must be 360° $(a + b + c + d + e + f)$.

A *parallelogram* is a quadrilateral whose opposite sides are parallel. In the following parallelogram, side AB is parallel to side DC, and AD is parallel to BC. Because a parallelogram is made of two sets of parallel lines that intersect each other, Fred's Theorem applies to it as well: The two big angles are equal, the two small angles are equal, and a big angle plus a small angle equals 180 degrees. In the figure below, big angles A and C are equal, and small angles B and D are equal. Also, since A is a big angle and D is a small angle, $A + D = 180°$.

Angle-Side Relationships in Triangles

The longest side of any triangle is opposite the largest interior angle; the shortest side is opposite the smallest angle. In the following triangle, side A is longer than side B, which is longer than side C, because 80 > 60 > 40.

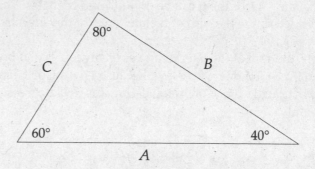

The same rule applies to isosceles and equilateral triangles. An isosceles triangle, remember, is one in which two of the sides are equal in length; therefore, the angles opposite those sides are also equal. In an equilateral triangle, all three sides are equal; so are all three angles.

VOLUME

Jim will occasionally ask a question that will require you to calculate the volume of a rectangular solid (a box or a cube) on the SAT. The formula for the volume of a rectangular solid is length × width × height. Since length, width, and height are equal in a cube, the volume of a cube can be calculated simply by cubing (where do you think they get the name?) the length of any edge of the cube.

Volume = $8 \times 4 \times 3 = 96$

$w = 4$

$h = 3$

$l = 8$

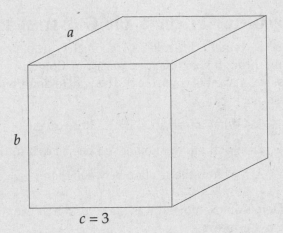

$\text{Volume} = 3^3 = 27$

GRIDS

If you've ever looked for a particular city on a map in an atlas, you're probably familiar with the idea behind grids. You look up Philadelphia in the atlas's index and discover that it is located at D5 on the map of Pennsylvania. On the map itself you find letters of the alphabet running along the top of the page and numbers running down one side. You move your finger straight down from the D at the top of the page until it is at the level of the 5 along the side, and there you are: in Philadelphia.

Grids work the same way. The standard grid is shaped like a cross. The horizontal line is called the *x-axis*; the vertical line is the *y-axis*. The four areas formed by the intersection of the axes are called quadrants. The location of any quadrant can be described with a pair of numbers (x, y), just the way you would on a map: $(0, 0)$ are the coordinates of the intersection of the two axes (also called the *origin*); $(1, 2)$ are the coordinates of the point one space to the right and two spaces up; $(-1, 5)$ are the coordinates of the point one space to the left and five spaces up; $(-4, -2)$ are the coordinates of the point four spaces to the left and two spaces down. All these points are located on the following diagram:

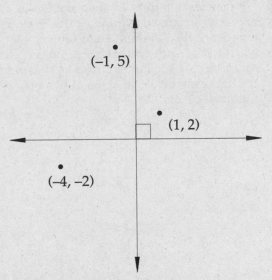

Zones

A grid has four distinct zones, called *quadrants*:

Quadrant I is the upper right-hand corner, where x and y are both positive.

Quadrant II is the upper left-hand corner, where x is negative and y is positive.

Quadrant III is the lower left-hand corner, where x is negative and y is negative.

Quadrant IV is the lower right-hand corner, where x is positive and y is negative.

Sometimes, pinning down a coordinate's quadrant is all you need to do to find Jim's answer.

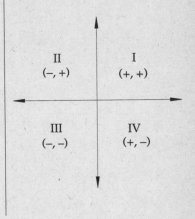

ADVANCED SKETCHING AND GUESSTIMATION

Some extremely difficult SAT geometry problems can be solved quickly and easily through sketching and guesstimation, but you will have to stay on your toes if you want to crack them. The way to do this is always to ask yourself three questions:

1. What information have I been given?

2. What information have I been asked to find?

3. What is the relation between them?

Here's an example. It was the second hardest problem on the SAT section in which it appeared:

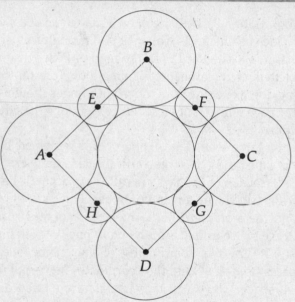

24 Four circles of radius 2 with centers *A*, *B*, *C*, and *D* are arranged symmetrically around another circle of radius 2, and four smaller equal circles with centers *E*, *F*, *G*, and *H* each touch three of the larger circles as shown in the figure above. What is the radius of one of the small circles?

(A) $\sqrt{2} - 2$

(B) $\sqrt{2} - 1$

(C) $2\sqrt{2} - 2$

(D) 1

(E) $3\sqrt{2} - 1$

Here's How to Crack It

First answer the three questions we mentioned before:

1. I have been given the radius of 5 large identical circles.

2. I have been asked for the radius of a small circle.

3. Both are distances, so both can be measured.

What at first appeared to be an extremely difficult geometry problem turns out to be a simple matter of measurement. Mark off the distance of one large-circle radius along the edge of your answer sheet. This equals 2. Now align your ruler on a small-circle radius. The small-circle radius is smaller, obviously. How much smaller? You can probably see that it is a little bit less than half as long. That means that the answer to the question is "a little bit less than 1."

Now turn to the answer choices and solve them one at a time:

(A) $\sqrt{2}$, as you know, equals 1.4, so $\sqrt{2} - 2 = -0.6$. A distance cannot be negative. Eliminate.

(B) $\sqrt{2} - 1 = 0.4$ This is less than 1, but a lot less. Not a great possibility.

(C) $2\sqrt{2} - 2 = 0.8$. This is a little bit less than 1. An excellent possibility.

(D) $1 = 1$. One can't be less than 1. Eliminate.

(E) $3\sqrt{2} - 1 = 3.2$. Eliminate.

Jim's answer is C.

GEOMETRY SUMMARY

1. Degrees and angles:

    a. A circle contains 360 degrees.

    b. When you think about angles, remember circles.

    c. A line is a 180-degree angle.

    d. When two lines intersect, four angles are formed; the sum of their measures is 360 degrees.

    e. Fred's Theorem: When two parallel lines are cut by a third line, the small angles are equal, the big angles are equal, and the sum of a big angle and a small angle is 180 degrees.

2. Triangles:

    a. Every triangle contains 180 degrees.

    b. An equilateral triangle is one in which all three sides are equal in length, and all three angles are equal in measure (60 degrees).

    c. An isosceles triangle is one in which two of the sides are equal in length, and the two angles opposite the equal sides are equal in measure.

    d. A right triangle is one in which one of the angles is a right angle (90 degrees).

    e. The perimeter of a triangle is the sum of the lengths of its sides.

    f. The area of a triangle is: $\dfrac{\text{height} \times \text{base}}{2}$.

3. Circles:

    a. The circumference of a circle is $2\pi r$ or πd, where r is the radius of the circle and d is the diameter.

    b. The area of a circle is πr^2, where r is the radius of the circle.

4. Rectangles and squares:

    a. The perimeter of a rectangle is the sum of the lengths of its sides.

    b. The area of a rectangle is length $\times$ width.

    c. A square is a rectangle whose four sides are all equal in length.

5. When you encounter a geometry problem on the SAT, guesstimate the answer before trying to work it out.

6. You must never skip an SAT problem that has a drawing with it.

7. You must know the following values:
$$\pi \approx 3$$
$$\sqrt{2} \approx 1.4$$
$$\sqrt{3} \approx 1.7$$

8. You must also be familiar with the size of certain common angles.

9. Most SAT geometry diagrams are drawn to scale. Use your eyes before you use your pencil. Try to eliminate impossible answers.

10. When your eyes aren't enough, use the edge and corner of your answer sheet as a ruler and a protractor.

11. When a diagram is not drawn to scale, redraw it.

12. When no diagram is provided, make your own; when a provided diagram is incomplete, complete it.

13. When information is missing from a diagram, guesstimate and plug in.

14. The Pythagorean Theorem states that in a right triangle, the square of the hypotenuse equals the sum of the squares of the other two sides. Remember Jim's favorite Pythagorean triplets (3:4:5 and 5:12:13).

15. Any polygon can be divided into triangles.

16. The longest side of any triangle is opposite the largest interior angle; the shortest side is opposite the smallest angle.

17. The volume of a rectangular solid is length × width × height. The formulas to compute the volume of other three-dimensional figures are supplied in the instructions at the front of every math section.

18. You must know how to locate points on a grid.

19. Some extremely difficult SAT geometry problems can be solved quickly and easily through sketching and guesstimation, but you will have to stay on your toes. The way to do this is always to ask yourself three questions:

    a. What information have I been given?

    b. What information have I been asked to find?

    c. What is the relationship between them?

15

Quantitative Comparisons: Cracking the System

WHAT IS A QUANTITATIVE COMPARISON?

One scored math section on your SAT will contain a group of fifteen quantitative comparison questions (or quant comps, as we call them). These quant comps will be arranged in an order of difficulty, just like in the other math sections. The first five will be easy, the next five medium, and the last five difficult.

Let's take a look at the instructions for the quant comps as they appear on the SAT:

Order of Difficulty: Quant Comps

1–5 Easy
6–10 Medium
11–15 Difficult

Directions for Quantitative Comparison Questions

Questions 1–15 each consist of two quantities in boxes, one in Column A and one in Column B. You are to compare the two quantities and on the answer sheet fill in oval

A if the quantity in Column A is greater;
B if the quantity in Column B is greater;
C if the two quantities are equal;
D if the relationship cannot be determined from the information given.

AN E RESPONSE WILL NOT BE SCORED.

Notes:

1. In some questions, information is given about one or both of the quantities to be compared. In such cases, the given information is centered above the two columns and is not boxed.
2. In a given question, a symbol that appears in both columns represents the same thing in Column A as it does in Column B.
3. Letters such as x, n, and k stand for real numbers.

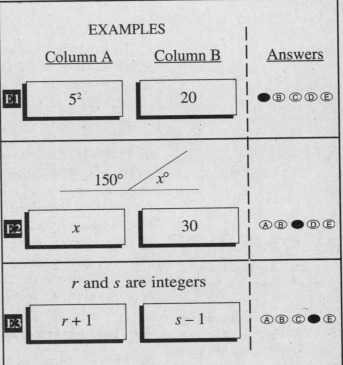

EXAMPLES

	Column A	Column B	Answers
E1	5^2	20	●Ⓑ©ⒹⒺ
E2	x	30	ⒶⒷ●ⒹⒺ
E3	$r + 1$	$s - 1$	Ⓐ Ⓑ © ● Ⓔ

(150° / x°)

r and s are integers

Make sure that you know these instructions cold before you take the SAT. If you have to consult them each time you answer a question, you waste time and rob yourself of points. In every quant comp question, Jim will give you quantities in two columns, A and B. Unlike the regular multiple-choice questions, quant comps have only four answer choices: A, B, C, and D. Here's what each answer choice means:

Choose A if the quantity in Column A is *always* greater.

Choose B if the quantity in Column B is *always* greater.

Choose C if the quantities in Column A and Column B are *always* equal.

Choose D if you can't figure out the relationship between the two quantities.

The meaning of each choice is best illustrated with some simple examples:

Do Not Mark E

There are only four answer choices (A, B, C, and D) on quant comp problems, but your SAT answer sheet has five bubbles (A, B, C, D, and E). If you mark circle E on a quant comp, your answer will be omitted. Check your answer sheet after finishing quant comps. If you marked E, chances are you meant to mark D. Change your answer sheet accordingly.

Let's start with a simple quant comp example:

Column A	Column B
2 + 2	2 × 2

Your task is to determine the relationship between the quantity in Column A and the quantity in Column B. The quantity in Column A is 4; so is the quantity in Column B. Will this *always* be true? Yes, 2 + 2 will always equal 4, and so will 2 × 2. Therefore, the correct answer is C, "the two quantities are equal."

Suppose we rewrite the problem as follows:

$$3 + 2 \qquad\qquad 2 \times 2$$

The quantity in Column A now equals 5, while the quantity in Column B still equals 4. Because 3 + 2 will always equal 5, and 5 will always be greater than 4, the correct answer now is A, "the quantity in Column A is greater."

Let's rewrite the problem one more time:

$$x + 2 \qquad\qquad 2 - x$$

What's the answer now? Suppose that x equals 5. In that case, the quantity in Column A would be greater than the quantity in Column B. But x can be any number; suppose it's 0. In that case, the two quantities would be equal. Now suppose that x equals –2. In that case the quantity in Column B would be greater than the quantity in Column A.

In other words, depending on which numbers we plug in for x, we can make choice A, B, or C seem to be the correct answer. That means that none of these answers is always correct. Jim's answer has to be D, "the relationship cannot be determined from the information given."

THE INFORMATION GIVEN

Many quant comps contain given information that you are supposed to use in solving the problem. This information is placed between the two columns. Here's an example:

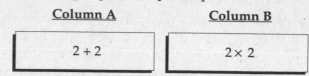

Column A	Column B
During a 100-day period last year, it rained on exactly 40 days.	
1 Percent of days when it did not rain	40%

Here's How to Crack It

You shouldn't have any trouble with this one. Since it rained on 40 percent of the days, 60 percent must have been dry. The quantity in Column A is thus always greater than the quantity in Column B, and Jim's answer is A.

QUANT COMPS ARE QUICK BUT TRICKY

Most students are able to answer quant comps very quickly. Answering quant comps usually takes much less time than answering regular math questions or grid-ins. Because of this, many students breathe a sigh of relief when they come to the quant comp section.

Don't be deceived. Quant comps go quickly because certain answers tend to seem correct immediately. Because of this, Joe Bloggs loves quant comps. When he looks at a question, he doesn't have to think very long before an "obvious" answer choice jumps off the page.

Predictable

Because of the way ETS designs their answer sheets, the quant comp/grid-in section will always be the third or fourth section of the SAT. So, if it isn't section 3, you know that it's just around the corner.

BAD NEWS FOR JOE, GOOD NEWS FOR YOU

Since certain answer choices on quant comps always seem correct to Joe Bloggs, he quickly finds himself in the same predicament as on the rest of the SAT:

1. On easy questions the answers that seem right to him really are right, so he earns points.

2. On medium questions his hunches are sometimes right and sometimes wrong, so he just about breaks even.

3. On difficult questions the answers that seem right to him are always wrong, so he loses points.

This is unlucky for Joe, but very lucky for you. Quant comps are the easiest math questions to crack because the Joe Bloggs answers are easy to spot—if you know what to look for and if you are careful. You can use POE, the process of elimination, to eliminate obviously incorrect choices, improve your guessing odds, and zero in on Jim's answer.

Write It Down

As you read through a quant comp question, jot down "A B C D" next to the problem. ETS doesn't supply you with answer choices to cross out, so do it yourself.

MATHEMATICAL CONTENT

In terms of mathematical content, most quant comps will seem familiar to you. You'll find arithmetic problems, algebra problems, and geometry problems. You will be able to solve most of these problems by using the techniques we have already taught you.

SOLVING QUANT COMPS: BASIC PRINCIPLES

Quant comps are a unique problem type, and there are a number of special rules and techniques that apply only to them.

Even on quant comps that can be solved simply by using techniques you already know, there are still some unique features that you need to be familiar with. For instance, some regular techniques must be modified slightly for quant comps. We'll start with some basic principles and then move on to some more advanced ones.

NUMBERS ONLY

If a quant comp problem contains nothing but numbers, choice D cannot be Jim's answer.

In a quant comp that has no variables, it will always be possible to obtain a definite solution. For example, the quantity 2 + 2 can only have one value: 4. The quantity 2 + x, on the other hand, can have an infinite number of values, depending on what you plug in for x.

Here's an example:

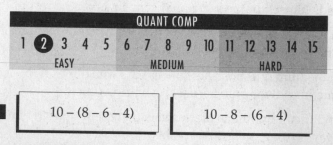

Here's How to Crack It

This problem contains nothing but numbers. Therefore, it must have a solution, and choice D can be eliminated.

(Jim's answer is A. Because you know you should perform any operations enclosed in parentheses first, you can see that the quantity in Column A equals 12, while the quantity in Column B equals 0.)

EQUATIONS

In the same way that you add or subtract on both sides of an equation, you can add or subtract on both sides of a quant comp. (Just don't multiply or divide on both sides.)

Here's an example:

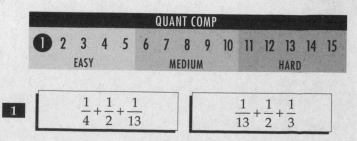

Here's How to Crack It

Before doing anything else, you should notice that this quant comp contains nothing but numbers, so choice D cannot possibly be Jim's answer.

Your next impulse may be to find a common denominator for all those fractions. Don't you dare! You can solve this problem in a second by eliminating common terms from both sides.

The quantities in Column A and Column B both include $\frac{1}{2}$ and $\frac{1}{13}$. That means you can subtract both fractions from both sides. Doing so leaves you with the following:

$$\frac{1}{4} \qquad\qquad\qquad \frac{1}{3}$$

It should be obvious to you now that Jim's answer has to be B, because $\frac{1}{3}$ is bigger than $\frac{1}{4}$. (Don't make the common careless error of thinking that $\frac{1}{4}$ is bigger than $\frac{1}{3}$ because 4 is bigger than 3!)

SOLVING QUANT COMPS: MEDIUM AND DIFFICULT QUESTIONS

Beware!

On medium and difficult quant comps, you should beware of your first impulse. Joe Bloggs' first impulse begins to let him down after the easy questions. By the time he reaches the difficult questions, his first impulse is invariably leading him to incorrect choices.

What does this mean for you? It means that on medium and difficult questions, be extremely suspicious of choices that *seem* right. For example, if you're looking at number 14 quant comp (a hard question) and Column A *looks* bigger than Column B, then A cannot possibly be the answer. Joe Bloggs picks A because it *looks* right to him. But if Joe Bloggs could answer a hard question correctly just by looking at it, it wouldn't be hard, would it? Never choose an answer to a medium or hard quant comp question just because it *looks* right.

QUANT COMP
1 2 3 4 5 6 7 8 9 10 11 12 **13** 14 15
EASY MEDIUM HARD

$$x > 0$$

13 | $x^2 + 1$ | | $x^3 - 1$

Here's How to Crack It

It is easy to think of a value for x that would make the quantity in Column B greater than the quantity in Column A. How about 4? You know that $4^3 - 1$ equals 63, and $4^2 + 1$ equals 17. Because 63 is greater than 17, the correct answer could be B.

Always

Before you choose answer A, B, or C on quant comps, ask yourself: "Is this always the case?" If not, mark D.

But would Column B always have to be greater than Column A? This is what you have to find out. (Before you do, notice that you have already eliminated choices A and C as possibilities: C is out because if one quantity is even sometimes greater than the other, the two quantities cannot always be equal; A is out because if Column B is even sometimes greater than Column A, then Column A cannot always be greater than Column B.)

The easiest number greater than 0 to plug in is 1. Doing so produces a value of 2 for Column A and a value of 0 for Column B. In other words, when you plug in 1, the value in Column A is greater—just the opposite of what happened when you plugged in 4. Since you have now found a case in which Column A could be greater than Column B, you can also eliminate choice B as a possibility. The only choice left is D—Jim's answer.

PLUGGING IN

When you plug in on quant comps, remember the numbers with special properties: negatives, fractions, 0, and 1.

In ordinary algebra problems on the SAT, you don't have to be very careful about which numbers you plug in. Since you're only looking for numbers that make the equations work, you can just pick numbers that are easy to work with.

Quant comps, though, are a little different. On these questions you are looking for answers that *always* work. A single exception, therefore, is enough to make an answer choice wrong. The key to finding Jim's answer on hard questions is being certain that you've taken into account all possible exceptions. This is why Joe Bloggs has trouble on medium and difficult quant comps.

This is a hard fact for many students to keep in mind. When plugging in on quant comps, they are attracted naturally to the numbers we use most often: positive whole numbers. But there are many other numbers, and Jim loves to write quant comp problems that depend on the special qualities of these numbers. In fact, many difficult quant comps are difficult only because these numbers must be considered in finding a solution, and Joe Bloggs forgets to consider them.

Because this is true, you should always ask yourself the following question on quant comp plug-ins:

Would my answer be different if I plugged in a negative number, a fraction, 0, or 1?

To find out whether you can get more than one result for a quant comp question, try plugging in these special numbers after you've plugged in an easy, positive integer that Joe would think of. In fact, to be sure you've found Jim's answer, you should *always* plug in at least twice.

Here's an example:

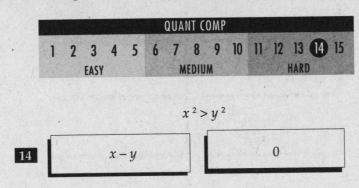

$$x^2 > y^2$$

| 14 | $x - y$ | | 0 |

Here's How to Crack It

When Joe Bloggs solves this problem, he plugs in easy positive integers—say, 3 for x and 2 for y. Because $3 - 2 = 1$, and 1 is greater than 0, he selects A as his answer. What happens? He loses points.

This is a number 14—a very hard question. If finding the answer were as easy as plugging in 3 and 2, Joe Bloggs would get this question right and it would be in the easy third. There must be something Joe has forgotten.

Indeed there is. Joe has forgotten the special cases. If you want to find Jim's answer, you're going to have to remember these special cases.

First, try plugging in negative numbers instead of positive ones: -3 for x and -2 for y. $(-3)^2$ is 9; $(-2)^2$ is 4. Because 9 is greater than 4, you've fulfilled the requirement in the given information. (Important! You *must* plug in numbers that conform to the given information.)

Now look at Column A. What is $x - y$ now? It is -1. Is -1 greater than 0? No, it's less than 0.

Before plugging in negatives, you had already proved that Jim's answer couldn't be B or C. (Do you see why?) Now you've proved that it also can't be A. This means that it must be D. (It is.)

Drill 1

Do the following quant comp plug-ins. As with most of the examples in this book, the question number indicates the level of difficulty of the problem. Remember, the harder the question, the more work you will need to do. See page 348 to check your answers.

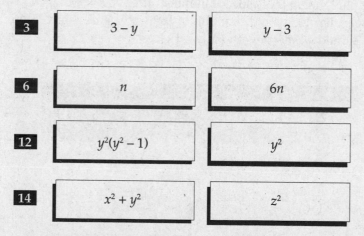

SKETCHING AND GUESSTIMATING

You must also be very careful about sketching and guesstimating on medium and difficult quant comp geometry problems.

Ordinary guesstimating can occasionally be misleading on these problems for the same reason that ordinary plugging in can be misleading on quant comp algebra. Because a single exception is enough to disqualify an answer choice, you must be certain that you have considered all the possibilities. Approximate answers are usually good enough on ordinary geometry problems, but they are very often wrong on geometry quant comps.

Here's an example:

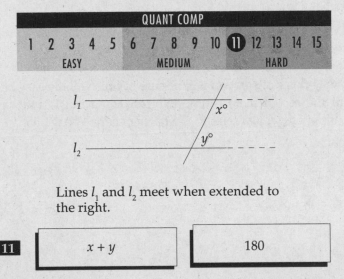

Lines l_1 and l_2 meet when extended to the right.

11	$x + y$		180

Here's How to Crack It

By simply eyeballing and guesstimating (or using your Princeton Review protractor) you would decide that $x + y$ equals about 180 degrees. Is Jim's answer therefore C?

No! You know from the information given that the two lines are not parallel, even though they look as though they are. So $x + y$ can only be a little bit less than 180. Jim's answer, therefore, must be B. (It is.)

On problems like this, it will help you to redraw the figure in exaggerated form. The information given says that the two lines meet somewhere to the right. Redraw the figure so that they meet immediately, something like this:

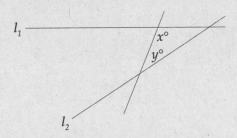

Now you can clearly see why Jim's answer is B. Since x and y are measures of two angles in a triangle, $x + y$ must be less than 180.

Ugly Pictures

Never trust a picture on medium or difficult quant comps. It may look drawn to scale, but it isn't necessarily perfect. Draw your own version of it to see if you can make it look different.

Order, Order!

Always note the order of difficulty on quant comps. On medium and difficult questions, you should be extremely suspicious of answer choices that seem obvious, or that have misleading diagrams, or that you arrive at quickly without much thought (unless you arrive at them by using our techniques!).

PACING AND DIFFICULTY

Quant comps and grid-ins will be in the same section of your SAT. (We'll tell you all you need to know about grid-ins in the next chapter.) Because the hardest quant comps are much harder than the easiest grid-ins, you should not waste time on the hardest quant comps until you have answered the easiest grid-ins. Here's what you should do:

1. Do the first ten quant comps (there are fifteen altogether).

2. Do the first few grid-ins (there are ten altogether).

3. If you have time left, do the remaining quant comps, then the remaining grid-ins.

4. When you can answer no more, check or double-check your work.

By following this strategy you will be sure to finish all the easy and medium questions in the section before time expires. For a quick and easy way to remember this strategy, just refer to the pacing chart on page 35.

QUANTITATIVE COMPARISONS SUMMARY

1. Quant comps, unlike all other SAT questions, offer only four answer choices: A, B, C, and D. These four choices are always the same. On every quant comp, you will be given two quantities or values and asked to select:

    Choice A if the quantity in Column A is *always* greater.

    Choice B if the quantity in Column B is *always* greater.

    Choice C if the two quantities are *always* equal.

    Choice D if it cannot be determined whether one quantity will always be greater than or equal to the other.

2. Since the answer choices are not given, write out A, B, C, D next to each problem to help you employ POE.

3. Many quant comps provide information that you are supposed to use in solving the problem. This information is placed between the two columns.

4. Quant comps are ideal for POE because the Joe Bloggs attractors are easy to spot—if you know what to look for and if you are careful.

5. Many quant comps can be solved using the techniques that you have already learned.

6. Many quant comps can be solved without any sort of computation.

7. If a problem contains nothing but numbers, choice D cannot be Jim's answer.

8. You can add and subtract from both Column A and Column B as if they were two sides of an equation.

9. On medium and difficult quant comps, attack your hunches.

10. When you plug in on quant comps, remember the numbers with special properties: negatives, fractions, 0, and 1.

11. You must also be very careful about sketching and guesstimating on medium and difficult quant comp geometry problems.

16

Grid-Ins:
Cracking the System

What Is a Grid-In?

One of the math sections on your SAT will contain a group of 10 problems without multiple-choice answers. Jim calls these problems Student Produced Responses. We call then *grid-ins*, because you have to mark your answers on a grid printed on your answer sheet. The grid looks like this:

Despite their format, grid-ins are just like other math questions on the SAT, and many of the techniques that you've learned so far still apply. You can still use Plugging In and other great techniques, such as the Ratio Box and the Average Pie. You can still use the order of difficulty and your knowledge of Joe Bloggs to avoid making obvious mistakes on hard questions. Your calculator will still help you out on many problems as well. So grid-ins are nothing to be scared of. In fact, many grid-in questions are simply regular SAT multiple-choice math problems with the answer choices lopped off. The only difference is that you have to arrive at your answer from scratch, rather than choose it from among four or five possibilities.

You will need to be extra careful when answering grid-in questions, however, because the grid format increases the likelihood of careless errors. It is vitally important that you understand the way the grid-in format works before you take the test. In particular, you'll need to memorize Jim's rules about which kinds of answers count, and which don't. The instructions may look complicated, but we've boiled them down to a few rules for you to memorize and practice.

Take a look at the grid again. Because of the way it's arranged, Jim can only use certain types of problems for grid-ins. For example, you'll never see variables (letters) in your answer (although there can be variables in the question), because the grid can only accommodate numbers. This is good for you, because no matter how good you are at algebra, you're better at arithmetic.

Also, this means that your calculator will be useful on several questions. As always, be careful to set up the problem on paper before you carefully punch the numbers into your calculator. Since you have to write in the answer yourself on the grid, you have to be more careful than ever to avoid careless mistakes.

Grid-ins are scored somewhat differently from multiple-choice questions on the SAT. On multiple-choice questions, you lose a fraction of a raw-score point for every incorrect answer. This deducted fraction is commonly referred to as a "guessing penalty." We explained earlier in the book why there is really no guessing penalty on SAT multiple-choice questions. For different reasons, there is no guessing penalty for grid-ins, either. Why? Because nothing is deducted for an incorrect answer on a grid-in. An incorrect answer on one of these questions is no worse for your score than a question left blank. And, by the same token, a blank is just as costly as an error. Therefore you should be very aggressive in answering these questions. Don't leave a question blank just because you're worried that the answer you've found may not be correct. ETS's scoring computers treat incorrect answers and blanks exactly the same. If you have arrived at an answer, you have a shot at earning points, and if you have a shot at earning points, you should take it.

That doesn't mean you should guess blindly. Your chance of helping your score with a blind guess on a grid-in is very, very small. You would be better off spending your time either working on problems that you know you can answer or checking your work on problems you have already finished.

THE INSTRUCTIONS

Here are the instructions for grid-in questions as they will appear on your SAT:

Directions for Student-Produced Response Questions

Each of the remaining 10 questions (16–25) requires you to solve the problem and enter your answer by marking the ovals in the special grid, as shown in the examples below.

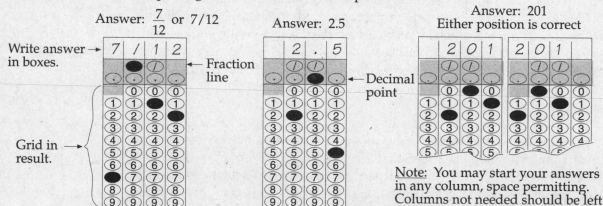

Note: You may start your answers in any column, space permitting. Columns not needed should be left blank.

- Mark no more than one oval in any column.
- Because the answer sheet will be machine-scored, **you will receive credit only if the ovals are filled in correctly.**
- Although not required, it is suggested that you write your answer in the boxes at the top of the columns to help you fill in the ovals accurately.
- Some problems may have more than one correct answer. In such cases, grid only one answer.
- No question has a negative answer.
- **Mixed numbers** such as $2\frac{1}{2}$ must be gridded as 2.5 or 5/2. (If $\boxed{2\ 1\ /\ 2}$ is gridded, it will be interpreted as $\frac{21}{2}$, not $2\frac{1}{2}$.)

- **Decimal Accuracy:** If you obtain a decimal answer, **enter the most accurate value the grid will accommodate.** For example, if you obtain an answer such as 0.6666 . . . , you should record the result as .666 or .667. **Less accurate values such as .66 or .67 are not acceptable.**

Acceptable ways to grid $\frac{2}{3}$ = .6666 . . .

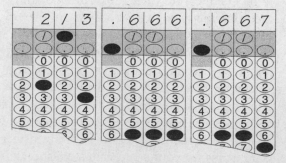

What the Instructions Mean

Of all the instructions on the SAT, these are the most important to understand thoroughly before you take the test. Pity the unprepared student who takes the SAT cold and spends ten minutes of potential point-scoring time reading and puzzling over Jim's confusing instructions. We've translated these unnecessarily complicated instructions into a few important rules. Make sure you know them all well.

Fill In the Boxes

Always write your answer in the boxes at the top of the grid before you darken the ovals below. Your written answers won't affect the scoring of your test; if you write the correct answer in the boxes and grid in the wrong ovals, you won't get credit for your answer (and you won't be able to appeal to ETS). However, writing in the answers first makes you less likely to make an error when you grid in, and it also makes it easier to check your work.

Fill In the Ovals Correctly

As we just pointed out, you receive no credit for writing in the answer at the top of the grid. ETS's computer only cares whether the ovals are filled in correctly. For every number you write into the grid, make sure that you fill in the corresponding oval.

Stay to the Left

Although you'll receive credit no matter where you put your answer on the grid, you should always begin writing in your answer in the far left column of the grid. This ensures that you have enough space for longer answers when necessary. You'll also cut down on careless errors if you always grid in your answers the same way.

Fractions or Decimals: Your Choice

You can grid in an answer in either fraction or decimal form. For example, if your answer to a question is $\frac{1}{2}$, you can either grid in $\frac{1}{2}$ or .5. It doesn't matter to Jim, because $\frac{1}{2}$ equals .5; the computer will credit either form of the answer. That means you actually have a choice. If you like fractions, grid in your answers in fraction form. If you like decimals, you can grid in the decimal. If you have a fraction that doesn't fit in the grid, you can simply convert it to a decimal on your calculator and grid in the decimal.

Here's the bottom line: When gridding in fractions or decimals, use whichever form is easier and least likely to cause careless mistakes.

Decimal Places and Rounding

When you have a decimal answer less than 1, such as .45 or .678, many teachers ask you to write a zero before the decimal point (for example, 0.45 or 0.678). On grid-in questions, however, Jim doesn't want you to worry about the zero. In fact, there is no 0 in the first column of the grid. If your answer is a decimal, just

Keep Left

No matter how many digits in your answer, always start gridding in the left-most column. That way, you'll avoid omitting digits and losing points.

write the decimal point in the first column of the grid and then continue from there.

You should also notice that if you put the decimal point in the first column of the grid, you only have three places left to write in numbers. But what if your decimal is longer than three places, such as .87689? In these cases, Jim will give you credit if you round off the decimal so that it fits in the grid. He'll *also* give you credit, however, if you just enter as much of the decimal as will fit.

For example, if you had to grid in .87689, you could just write .876 (which is all that will fit) and then stop. Remember, you only need to grid in whatever is necessary to receive credit for your answer. Don't bother with extra unnecessary steps. You don't have to round off decimals, so don't bother.

If you have a long or repeating decimal, however, be sure to fill up all the spaces in the grid. If your decimal is .666666, you *must* grid in .666. If you just grid in .6, that's not good enough.

REDUCING FRACTIONS

Lop

Why do extra work for ETS? After all, they won't give you extra points. If your decimal doesn't fit in the grid, lop off the extra digits and grid in what does fit.

If you decide to grid in a fraction, Jim doesn't care if you reduce the fraction or not. For example, if your answer to a problem is $\frac{4}{6}$, Jim will give you credit if you grid in $\frac{4}{6}$ or reduce it to $\frac{2}{3}$. So if you have to grid in a fraction, and the fraction fits in the grid, don't bother reducing it. Why give yourself more work (and another chance to make a careless error)?

The only time you might have to reduce a fraction is if it doesn't fit in the grid. If your answer to a question is $\frac{15}{25}$, it won't fit in the grid. You have two options: Either reduce the fraction to $\frac{3}{5}$ and grid that in, or use your calculator to convert the fraction to .6. Choose whichever process makes you the most comfortable.

Relax

If your answer is a fraction and it fits in the grid (fraction bar included), don't reduce it. What's the point? ETS won't give you an extra point. However, if your fraction doesn't fit, reduce it or turn it into a decimal on your calculator.

MIXED NUMBERS

Don't Mix

Never grid in a mixed number. Change it into a top-heavy fraction.

ETS's scoring machine does not recognize mixed numbers. If you try to grid in $2\frac{1}{2}$ by writing "2 1/2", the computer will read this number as $\frac{21}{2}$. You have to convert mixed numbers to fractions or decimals before you grid them in. To grid in $2\frac{1}{2}$, either convert it to $\frac{5}{2}$ or convert it to its decimal equivalent, which is 2.5. If you have to convert a mixed number in order to grid it in, be very careful not to change its value accidentally.

DON'T WORRY

The vast majority of grid-in answers will not be hard or tricky to enter in the grid. Jim won't try to trick you by purposely writing questions that are confusing to grid in. Just pay attention to these guidelines and watch out for careless errors.

GRIDDING IN: A TEST DRIVE

To get a feel for this format, let's work through two examples. As you will see, grid-in problems are just regular SAT math problems.

17 If $a + 2 = 6$ and $b + 3 = 21$, what is the value of $\dfrac{b}{a}$?

Here's How to Crack It

You need to solve the first equation for a and the second equation for b. Start with the first equation, and solve for a. By subtracting 2 from both sides of the equation, you should see that $a = 4$.

Now move to the second equation, and solve for b. By subtracting 3 from both sides of the second equation you should see that $b = 18$.

The question asked you to find the value of $\dfrac{b}{a}$. That's easy. The value of b is 18, and the value of a is 4. Therefore, the value of $\dfrac{b}{a}$ is $\dfrac{18}{4}$.

That's an ugly looking fraction. How in the world do you grid it in? Ask yourself: "Does $\dfrac{18}{4}$ fit?" Yes! Grid in $\dfrac{18}{4}$. Your math teacher wouldn't like it, but Jim's computer will. You shouldn't waste time reducing $\dfrac{18}{4}$ to a prettier fraction or converting it to a decimal. Spend that time on another problem instead. The fewer steps you take, the less likely you will be to make a careless mistake.

Here's another example. This one is quite a bit harder.

GRID-INS

16 17 18 | 19 20 21 22 **23** 24 25
EASY | MEDIUM | HARD

23 Forty percent of the members of the sixth-grade class wore white socks. Twenty percent wore black socks. If 25% of the remaining students wore gray socks, what percentage of the sixth-grade class wore socks that were not white, black, or gray? (Disregard the % when gridding your answer.)

Here's How to Crack It

The problem doesn't tell you how many students are in the class, so you can plug in any number you like. This is a percentage problem, so the easiest number to plug in is 100. Forty percent of 100 is 40; that means 40 students wore white socks. Twenty percent of 100 is 20. That means that 20 students wore black socks.

Your next piece of information says that 25 percent of the remaining students wore gray socks. How many students remain? Forty, because 60 students wore either white or black socks, and 100 − 60 = 40. Therefore, 25 percent of these 40—10 students—wore gray socks.

How many students are left? Thirty. Therefore, the percentage of students who aren't wearing white, black, or gray socks is 30 out of 100, or 30 percent. Grid it in, and remember to forget about the percent sign:

Say No to Joe

If it takes you four seconds to answer any grid question from 23 to 25, you've probably goofed. Check your work. Hard questions have hard answers.

ORDER OF DIFFICULTY

Like all other questions on the math SAT, grid-in problems are arranged in order of increasing difficulty. In each group of ten, the first third are easy, the second third are medium, and the final third are difficult. As always, the order of difficulty will be your guide to how much faith you can place in your hunches.

Guessing is highly unlikely to help you on grid-in questions. For that reason, you must not waste time on questions that are too hard for you to solve. Only students shooting for 700 or above should consider attempting all ten grid questions.

Guessing on hard grid-ins is unlikely to get you anywhere, while intelligent guessing on hard quant comps may earn you unexpected points.

Keep in mind, of course, that many of the math techniques that you've learned are still very effective on grid-in questions. Plugging In worked very well on question number 23 on the previous page.

Here's another difficult grid-in question that you can answer effectively by using a technique you've learned before:

GRID-INS

16	17	18	19	20	21	22	23	**24**	25
	EASY			MEDIUM				HARD	

24 Grow-Up potting soil is made from only peat moss and compost in a ratio of 3 pounds of peat moss to 5 pounds of compost. If a bag of Grow-Up potting soil contains 12 pounds of potting soil, how many pounds of peat moss does it contain?

Here's How to Crack It

To solve this problem, set up a Ratio Box (the Ratio Box is explained in detail on page 189).

	Peat Moss	Compost	Whole
Ratio (parts)	3	5	8
Multiply By			
Actual Number			12 (lbs)

What do you multiply by 8 to get 12? If you don't know, divide 12 by 8 on your calculator. The answer is 1.5. Write 1.5 in each of the boxes on the multiply-by row of your ratio box, like this:

	Peat Moss	Compost	Whole
Ratio (parts)	3	5	8
Multiply By	1.5	1.5	1.5
Actual Number			12 (lbs)

The problem asks you how many pounds of peat moss are in a bag. To find out, multiply the numbers in the peat moss column. That is, multiply 3×1.5, and you get 4.5. Jim's answer is 4.5.

	Peat Moss	Compost	Whole
Ratio (parts)	3	5	8
Multiply By	1.5	1.5	1.5
Actual Number	4.5 (lbs)	7.5 (lbs)	12 (lbs)

Grid it in like this:

JOE BLOGGS AND GRID-IN QUESTIONS

On grid-in questions, you obviously can't use the Joe Bloggs principle to eliminate tempting but incorrect answer choices, since there aren't any choices to choose from. But you can—and must—use your knowledge of Joe Bloggs to double-check your work and keep yourself from making careless mistakes or falling into traps.

The basic idea still holds true: Easy questions have easy answers, and hard questions have hard answers. On hard questions, you must be extremely suspicious of answers that come to you easily or through simple calculations.

Unfortunately, your knowledge of Joe Bloggs alone will never lead you all the way to Jim's answers, the way it sometimes does on multiple-choice questions. In order to earn points on grid-in questions, you're going to have to find the real answers, and you're going to have to be extremely careful when you enter your answers on your answer sheet. But Joe Bloggs may help you find the correct path to Jim's answer. On a hard problem, you may be torn between two different approaches, one easy and one hard. Which should you pursue? The harder one. Joe will take the easy path and, as always on hard questions, it will lead him to the wrong answer.

RANGE OF ANSWERS

Some grid-in problems will have many possible correct answers. It won't matter which correct answer you choose, as long as the one you choose really is correct.

Here's an example:

More Than One

Some grid-in questions have several possible correct answers. None is more correct than any other, so grid in the first one you find and move on.

GRID-INS
16 17 18 19 **20** 21 22 23 24 25
EASY   MEDIUM   HARD

20 What is one possible value for x such that

$\frac{1}{4} < x < \frac{1}{3}$?

Here's How to Crack It

Joe Bloggs has trouble imagining how anything could squeeze between $\frac{1}{4}$ and $\frac{1}{3}$, but you know there are lots and lots of numbers in there. Any one of them will satisfy Jim.

The numbers in this problem are both fractions, but your answer doesn't have to be. The easiest approach is to forget about math-class solutions and head straight for your calculator (or your mental calculator). Convert $\frac{1}{4}$ to a decimal by dividing 1 by 4, which gives you .25. Now convert $\frac{1}{3}$ to a decimal by dividing 1 by 3, which gives you .33333. All you need to answer the question is any number that falls between those two decimals. How about .26? Or .3? Or .331? Your answer merely has to be bigger than .25 and smaller than .33333. Pick one, grid it in, and move on.

DRILL 1

Don't lose points to carelessness. Practice by gridding the following numbers in the sample grids below. Answers can be found on page 349.

1. 1.5

2. 5.60

3. 81

4. $\dfrac{1}{3}$

5. $\dfrac{8}{11}$

6. 0.33333

7. $4\dfrac{2}{5}$

8. x, such that $6 < x < 7$

Ungriddable

Some things just won't go in the grid:
- variables
- pi (π)
- negative numbers
- square roots

If they show up in your answer, you've goofed. Redo the problem, or skip it.

GRID-INS SUMMARY

1. One of the math sections on your SAT will contain a group of ten problems without multiple-choice answers. ETS calls these problems Student-Produced Responses. We call then *grid-ins*, because you have to mark your answers on a grid printed on your answer sheet.

2. Despite their format, grid-ins are really just like other math questions on the SAT, and many of the same techniques that you have learned still apply.

3. The grid format increases the likelihood of careless errors. Know the instructions and check your work carefully.

4. There is no guessing penalty for grid-ins, so you should always grid in your answer, even if you're not sure that it's correct. Blind guessing, however, is very unlikely to improve your score.

5. Always write the numbers in the boxes at the top of grid before you fill in (carefully) the corresponding ovals.

6. Grid in your answer as far to the left as possible.

7. If the answer to a grid-in question contains a fraction or a decimal, you can grid in the answer in either form. When gridding in fractions or decimals, use whichever form is easier and least likely to cause careless mistakes.

8. There's no need to round decimals, even though it is permitted.

9. If you have a long or repeating decimal, be sure to fill up all the spaces in the grid.

10. If a fraction fits in the grid, you don't have to reduce the fraction before gridding it in.

11. ETS's scoring machine does not recognize mixed numbers. Convert mixed numbers to fractions or decimals before gridding them in.

12. The vast majority of grid-in answers will not be difficult or tricky to enter in the grid.

13. Some grid-in questions will have more than one correct answer. It doesn't matter which answer you grid in, as long as it's one of the possible answers.

14. Like all other questions on the math SAT, grid problems are arranged in order of increasing difficulty. In each group of ten, the first third are easy, the second third are medium, and the final third are difficult.

15. On grid-ins, as on all other SAT questions, easy questions have easy answers, and hard questions have hard answers. On hard grid-ins, you must be extremely suspicious of answers that come to you easily or through simple calculations.

PART ◆ IV

Taking the PSAT/SAT

The PSAT/SAT Is a Week Away.
What Should You Do?

First of all, you should practice the techniques we've taught you on real PSATs or SATs. If you don't own any real SATs, go buy a copy of *10 Real SATs* at your local bookstore. This book is published by the College Board and contains ten actual SATs that have been administered over the last few years. You can also use the full-length practice test in *Taking the SAT I: Reasoning Test*. You can get a free copy of this booklet from either your guidance counselor or ETS.

Take and score the two diagnostic tests at the back of this book. The more full-length SATs you practice, the better. If you are taking the PSAT, see page 353 to learn how to convert one of the SATs in this book to a PSAT.

If you have more than a week, you can order any publications directly from the College Board. Here's the toll-free phone number: 1-800-537-3160.

To order either *10 Real SATs* or copies of recent PSATs by phone, you'll need a credit card. If you prefer, *Taking the SAT I: Reasoning Test* also has a form you can use to order *10 Real SATs* by mail. Here's the address:

College Board SAT Program
Department E52
P.O. Box 6212
Princeton, NJ 08541-6212

If you want to order by mail, but you don't have a copy of the form, be sure to call the toll-free number to find out how to order.

If you're online, here's how to contact the College Board using the World Wide Web or E-mail:

World Wide Web: www.collegeboard.org
E-mail: sat@ets.org

More Real SATs

If you want to get your hands on more real SATs, in addition to the tests published in *10 Real SATs*, you can obtain copies of the most recent tests that have been released through ETS's Question and Answer Service. You can order copies of these tests directly from the College Board. Here's the address and phone number of the College Board's headquarters:

The College Board
45 Columbus Avenue
New York, NY 10023
(212) 713-8000

GETTING PSYCHED

The SAT is a big deal, but you don't want to let it scare you. Sometimes students get so nervous about doing well that they freeze up on the test and murder their scores. The best thing to do is to think of the SAT as a game. It's a game you can get good at, and beating the test can be fun. When you go into the test center, just think about all those poor slobs who don't know how to eyeball geometry diagrams.

The best way to keep from getting nervous is to build confidence in yourself and in your ability to remember and use our techniques. When you take practice tests, time yourself exactly as you will be timed on the real SAT. Develop a sense of how long 30 minutes is and how much time you can afford to spend on cracking difficult problems. If you know ahead of time what to expect, you won't be as nervous.

Of course, taking a real SAT is much more nerve-racking than taking a practice test. Prepare yourself ahead of time for the fact that 30 minutes will seem to go by a lot faster on a real SAT than it did on your practice tests.

It's all right to be nervous; the point of being prepared is to keep from panicking.

SHOULD YOU SLEEP FOR THIRTY-SIX HOURS?

Some guidance counselors tell their students to get a lot of sleep the night before the SAT. This probably isn't a good idea. If you aren't used to sleeping twelve hours a night, doing so will just make you groggy for the test. The same goes for going out and drinking a lot of beer: People with hangovers are not good test takers.

A much better idea is to get up early each morning for the entire week before the test and do your homework before school. This will get your brain accustomed to functioning at that hour of the morning. You want to be sharp at test time.

Before you go to sleep the night before the test, spend an hour or so reviewing the Hit Parade. This will make the list fresh in your mind in the morning. You might also practice estimating some angles and looking for direct solutions on a few real SAT math problems. You don't want to exhaust yourself, but it will help to brush up.

FURTHERMORE

Here are a few pointers for test day and beyond:

1. You must bring acceptable identification to the test center on the day of the test. According to ETS, acceptable identification must include: "(1) a photograph or a written physical description, (2) your name, and (3) your signature." Acceptable forms of ID include: your driver's license, a school ID with a photo, or a valid passport. If you don't have an official piece of ID with your signature and your photo, you can have your school make an ID for you. Just have your guidance counselor type up a physical description of you on school stationery, which both you and your guidance counselor then have to sign. Complete instructions for making such an ID are contained in ETS's *Registration Bulletin*. According to ETS, the following forms of ID are *unacceptable*: a birth certificate, a credit card, and a Social Security card.

   Make sure you read all of the rules in the *Registration Bulletin*, because conflicts with ETS are just not worth the headache. Your only concern on the day of the test should be beating the SAT. To avoid hassles and unnecessary stress, make *absolutely certain* that you take your admissions ticket and your ID with you on the day of the test.

2. The only outside materials you are allowed to use on the test are No. 2 pencils (take a dozen, all sharp), a wristwatch (an absolute necessity), and a calculator. Digital watches are best, but if it has a beeper, make sure you turn it off. Proctors will confiscate pocket dictionaries, word lists, portable computers, and the like. Proctors have occasionally also confiscated stopwatches and travel clocks. Technically, you should be permitted to use these, but you can never tell with some proctors. Take a watch and avoid the hassles.

3. Some proctors allow students to bring food into the test room; others don't. Take some fruit (especially bananas) with you and see what happens. If you don't flaunt them, they probably won't be confiscated. Save them until you're about halfway through the test or eat them at the break. Remember that it takes about ten minutes for sugar to work its way to your tired brain. If the proctor yells at you, surrender them cheerfully and continue with the test. Eat quietly—don't annoy the other students.

#1: Bring ID
A driver's license, a passport, or a school ID.

#2: Bring Equipment
#2 Pencils (at least 12), a watch, a calculator.

#3: Bring Good Fruit or Other Energy Food
Grapes or oranges can give you an energy boost if you need it.

#4: Your Desk . . .
should be comfortable and suited to your needs.

4. You are going to be sitting in the same place for more than three hours, so make sure your desk isn't broken or unusually uncomfortable. If you are left-handed, ask for a left-handed desk. (The center may not have one, but it won't hurt to ask.) If the sun is in your eyes, ask to move. If the room is too dark, ask someone to turn on the lights. Don't hesitate to speak up. Some proctors just don't know what they're doing.

#5: Your Test . . .
should be printed legibly in your booklet.

5. Make sure your booklet is complete. Booklets sometimes contain printing errors that make some pages impossible to read. One year more than ten thousand students had to retake the SAT because of a printing error in their booklets. Also, check your answer sheet to make sure it isn't flawed.

#6: Breaks
You're entitled to two — one after section 2 and another after section 4.

6. You should get a five-minute break after the first hour of the test. Ask for it if your proctor doesn't give it to you. You should be allowed to go to the bathroom at this time. You should also be allowed to take a one-minute break at your desk at the end of the second hour. The breaks are a very good idea. Be sure to get up, move around, and clear your head.

#7: Cancel with Care
Don't cancel your scores just because you feel icky. Think it over carefully, and NEVER cancel on the same day as the test.

7. ETS allows you to cancel your SAT scores. Unfortunately, you can't cancel only your math or your verbal score—it's all or nothing. You can cancel scores at the test center by asking your proctor for a "Request to Cancel Test Scores" form. You must complete this form and hand it in before you leave the test center. If you decide to cancel your scores after you leave, you can do so by contacting ETS by cable, overnight delivery, or E-mail (sat@ets.org). The addresses are available in the *Registration Bulletin*, or you can call ETS at (609) 771-7600 to find out where to send your score cancellation request.

We recommend that you not cancel your scores unless you know you made so many errors or left out so many questions that your score will be unacceptably low. Don't cancel your scores on Test Day because you have a bad feeling—even the best test takers feel a little shaky after the SAT. You've got five days to think it over.

#8: Bubble with Care
A stray mark can hurt your score.

8. Make sure you darken all your responses before the test is over. At the same time, erase any extraneous marks on the answer sheet. **A stray mark in the margin of your answer sheet can result in correct responses being marked wrong.**

9. Don't assume that your test was scored correctly. Send away for ETS's Question and Answer Service. It costs money, but it's worth it. You'll get back copies of your answer sheet, a test booklet, and an answer key. Check your answers against the key and complain if you think you've been misscored. (Don't throw away the test booklet you receive from the Question and Answer Service. If you're planning to take the SAT again, save it for practice. If you're not, give it to your guidance counselor or school library.)

10. You deserve to take your SAT under good conditions. If you feel that your test was not administered properly (the high school band was practicing outside the window, your proctor hovered over your shoulder during the test) call us immediately at 800-333-0369 and we'll tell you what you can do about it.

#9: Keep Tabs on ETS

Get a copy of your SAT, your answer sheet, and an answer key. Make sure your score is accurate.

#10: We're Here for You

The Princeton Review is proud to advise students who have been mistreated by ETS.

PART **V**

Vocabulary

WORDS, WORDS, WORDS

The verbal SAT is in large part a vocabulary test. The more words you know on the test, the easier it will be. It's as simple as that.

For this reason, it's important that you get to work on your vocabulary *immediately*.

THE HIT PARADE

What's a Hit Parade list? It consists of those words that show up most often on the SAT. Each word on the list is accompanied by the definition, a pronunciation guide, and a sentence within which the word is used. Your vocabulary-building program should start with these words.

LEARN THE WORDS IN GROUPS

The Hit Parade has been arranged by groups of related words. Learning groups of related words can help you better remember each word's meaning. Even when you don't remember the exact meaning of a word, you may remember what group it is from. This will give you an idea of the word's meaning, which can help you use POE to get to an answer.

Make each group of words a part of your life. Rip out one of the group lists, carry it around with you, and use the words throughout your day. For example, on Monday you may feel like using words of *disdain* (see the "If you can't say something nice" list), but on Friday you may wish to be more *affable* (see the "Friendly" list).

DON'T MEMORIZE THE DICTIONARY

Only a tiny percentage of all the words in the English language are ever used on the SAT. Generally speaking, the SAT tests the kinds of words that an educated adult—your English teacher, for example—would know without having to look them up. It tests the sort of words that you encounter in your daily reading, from a novel in English class to the newspaper.

HOW TO MEMORIZE NEW WORDS

Here are three effective methods for learning new words.

- **Flash Cards:** You can make your own flash cards out of 3 by 5 index cards. Write a word on one side and the definition on the other. Then quiz yourself on the words, or practice with a friend. You can carry a few cards around with you every day and work on them in spare moments, like when you're riding on the bus.

- **The Image Approach:** The image approach involves letting each new word suggest a wild image to you, then using that image to help you remember the word. For example, the word *enfranchise* means, "to give the right to vote."

Women did not become *enfranchised* in the United States until 1920, when the Nineteenth Amendment to the Constitution guaranteed them the right to vote in state and federal elections.

Franchise might suggest to you a McDonald's franchise: you could remember the new word by imagining people lined up to vote at a McDonald's. The weirder the image, the better you'll remember the word.

- **Mnemonics:** Speaking of "the weirder, the better," another way to learn words is to use mnemonics. This is the place to let your creativity loose! The funnier or the stranger you make your mnemonic, the more likely you are to remember it. Write down your mnemonics (your flash cards are a great place for these). Although you may not always be able to think of a mnemonic for *every* Hit Parade word, sometimes you'll end up learning the word just by thinking about the definition long enough.

LOOK IT UP

Well-written general publications—like *The New York Times* and *Sports Illustrated*—are good sources of SAT words. You should read them on a regular basis. When you come across a new word, write it down, look it up, and remember it. You can make flashcards for these words as well.

Before you can memorize the definition of a word you come across in your reading, you have to find out what it means. You'll need a real dictionary for that. Pam uses two dictionaries in writing the SAT: the American Heritage Dictionary and the Webster's New Collegiate Dictionary. You should own a copy of one or the other. (You'll use it in college, too—it's a good investment.)

Keep in mind that most words have more than one definition. The dictionary will list these in order of frequency, from the most common to the most obscure. ETS will trip you up by testing the second, third, or even the fourth definition of a familiar-sounding word. For example, the word *pedestrian* shows up repeatedly on the SAT. When ETS uses it, though, it never means a person on foot—the definition of pedestrian you're probably most familiar with. ETS uses it to mean common, ordinary, banal—a *secondary* definition.

Very often, when you see easy words on hard SAT questions, ETS is testing a second, third, or fourth definition that you may not be familiar with.

WAYS TO SPEAK

clarity · CLAIR uh tee

clearness in thought or expression

In a moment of blinding clarity, Carol realized that to burn down the school would be unwise.

cogent · KOE jent

convincing; reasonable

Since Claire was able to speak cogently on the topic, everyone agreed with her plan.

cohesive · koe HEE siv

condition of sticking together

The graduates were close; they were a very cohesive class.

compelling · kum PELL ing

forceful; urgently demanding attention

By ignoring the problems in his district, he didn't give people a very compelling reason to vote for him.

convoluted · kahn vuh LOO tid

intricate; complex

The boring teacher's lecture was so convoluted that nobody understood it.

didactic · die DAK tik

intended to instruct

The tapes were entertaining as well as didactic because they amused as well as instructed children.

dogmatic · dog MAT ik

characterized by a stubborn adherence to insufficiently proved beliefs

The principal was dogmatic about his belief that there should be no talking in school.

effusive · i FEW siv

describing unrestrained emotional expression; gushy

In her acceptance speech after winning the Oscar, Emma was effusive in her thanks to the Academy.

emphatic · em FAT ik

expressed with emphasis

The mayor issued an emphatic denial when he was asked if he had misused the city's money.

florid · FLOR id

describing flowery or elaborate speech

The speech of the man addressing the graduating class was so florid that it confused half of the class and bored the other half.

fluid FLOO id

easily flowing

The two old friends' conversation was fluid; each of them was able to respond quickly and easily to what the other had to say.

hackneyed HACK need

overfamiliar through overuse; trite

All my Mom could offer in the way of advice were these hackneyed old phrases that I'd heard a hundred times before.

rapport ruh PORE

a relationship of mutual trust or affinity

My cousin and I had a good rapport; we trusted each other and worked together well.

adage AD ij

a wise old saying

According to the old adage, "It is far better to give than to receive."

poignant POIN yunt

profoundly moving; touching

The end of that old movie was very poignant when the old man finally made up with his son.

THIS IS HARD! I DON'T GET IT!

abstruse   ab STROOS
hard to understand
Many students of philosophy find the subject abstruse.

arduous   AR dyoo us
difficult; painstaking
Mountain climbing is a very arduous task.

futile   FEW tul
having no useful purpose
It is futile to try to explain the difference between right and wrong to
your pet.

heinous   HAY nus
hatefully evil; abominable
To murder someone in cold blood is a heinous crime.

impede   im PEED
to slow the progress of
People should never do anything to impede the flow of progress.

impenetrable   im PEN uh truh bul
incapable of being understood
Since her explanation contains lots of technical lingo, many people
found it impenetrable.

DON'T HAVE MUCH

dilatory   DIL uh tor ee
describing one who habitually delays or is tardy
> Always waiting until the last moment to do his homework, Stephen was a dilatory student.

enervate   EN er vait
to weaken the strength or vitality of
> Paulette felt enervated after spending three sleepless nights finishing her term paper.

indolent   IN duh lunt
lazy
> Mr. Dithers accused his students of being indolent because none of them had done their homework.

listless   LIST less
lacking energy; lazy
> Since he is accustomed to an active lifestyle, Marty feels listless when he has nothing to do.

sedentary   SEH dun teh ree
not migratory; settled
> Galatea and her husband led a sedentary existence; they never even left their home unless they had to.

soporific   sah puh RIF ik
causing sleep or sleepiness
> The book had a soporific effect on everyone that read it; people can't even read three pages before falling asleep.

stupor   STOO per
a state of reduced or suspended sensibility
> After eating the enormous meal, the family was in a food-induced stupor.

torpor   TOR per
laziness; inactivity; dullness
> The hot and humid day filled everyone with an activity-halting torpor.

paucity   PAW si tee
fewness; an extreme lack of
> I was unable to pay my bills due to the paucity of funds in my bank account.

OVERBOARD

ebullience   ih BOOL yuns

intense enthusiasm

> A sense of ebullience swept over the crowd when the home team won the game.

farce   FARS

an absurdly ridiculous situation

> Although the meeting was supposed to provide a chance for people to share their ideas, it quickly turned into a farce when nobody would listen to what anyone else had to say.

frenetic   freh NEH tik

wildly excited or active

> The pace at the busy office was frenetic.

garrulous   GARE uh lus

given to excessive, rambling talk

> The fisherman was a garrulous old man who bored everyone with his endless stories about "the one that got away."

gratuitous   gruh TOO ih tus

given freely; unearned; unwarranted

> To say that just because Mr. Carnes is strict, he must also be mean is a gratuitous assumption.

insipid   in SIP id

uninteresting; unchallenging

> That insipid movie was so boring and predictable that I almost walked out.

ponderous   PAHN duh rus

having a great weight; massive

> That 700-page book on the meaning of life was so ponderous that I could not read more than one paragraph at a time.

sonorous   SAHN uh rus

having or producing sound

> The actors in the Shakespearean play had sonorous voices that could be heard clearly throughout the theater.

squalor   SKWAH ler

a filthy condition or quality

> They never cleaned their filthy home and they rarely had enough money to feed themselves; they lived in a state of squalor.

superfluous   soo PER floo us

extra; unnecessary

> Adding both honey and sugar to your tea is being superfluous.

BE CAREFUL WHAT YOU SAY!

specious SPEE shus

having the ring of truth or plausibility but actually false

> The advertisement made the new soda sound good, but it was a specious claim because it really tasted awful.

slander SLAN der

false charges and malicious oral statements or reports about someone

> After the politician stated that the movie star was a space alien, she sued him for slander.

ruse ROOZ

a crafty trick

> The offer of a free vacation to the Bahamas was merely a ruse to get people to listen to their sales pitch.

egregious uh GREE jus

conspicuously bad or offensive

> Forgetting to sterilize surgical tools before an operation would be an egregious error.

facetious fuh SEE shus

playfully humorous

> Although they pretended to be insulting each other, they were just being facetious.

pander PAN der

to cater to the lower tastes and desires of others or exploit their weaknesses

> By complimenting the man on his good looks, the door-to-door salesman was merely pandering.

propriety pruh PRY uh tee

appropriateness of behavior

> Anyone who gets up from the dinner table without saying "Excuse me" has no sense of propriety.

HA-HA

wry   RYE
> *dryly humorous, often with a touch of irony*
>> His sense of humor was very wry; in fact, sometimes you couldn't tell if he was kidding or not.

lampoon (n) or (v)   lam POON
> *a broad satirical piece; or to broadly satire*
>> *Saturday Night Live* is famous for the way it lampoons people in the news.

parody   PAIR uh dee
> *an artistic work that imitates the style of another work for comic effect*
>> *Saturday Night Live* is also famous for its parodies of popular movies.

THINGS ABOUT KINGS

abdicate   AB duh kait
> *to formally give up power*
>> He abdicated the throne when it was clear that he could no longer rule effectively.

annihilate   uh NYE uh late
> *to destroy completely*
>> He annihilated his enemies, destroying any chance they might have had to attack back.

benevolent   buh NEV uh lunt
> *kind; generous*
>> She was a kind and benevolent queen who was concerned about her subjects' well-being.

despotic   des POT ik
> *characterized by exercising absolute power tyrannically*
>> He was a despotic ruler whose every law was enforced with threats of violence or death to those who disobeyed.

dictatorial   dik tuh TOR ee ul
> *domineering; oppressively overbearing*
>> The king had a dictatorial manner and expected people to do whatever he demanded.

haughty   HAW tee
> *condescendingly proud*
>> He behaved in a really haughty manner and you could tell that he thought that he was better than everyone else.

imperious   im PEER ee us
> *arrogantly domineering or overbearing*
>> She had a very imperious way about her; she was really bossy and treated everyone like they were beneath her.

omnipotent   om NIP uh tent
> *all-powerful*
>> He liked to think that he was an omnipotent manager but he really had very little control over anything.

patronizing   PAY truh nye zing
> *treating in a condescending manner*
>> Patrick had such a patronizing attitude that he treated everyone around him like a bunch of little kids.

usurp   yoo SERP
> *to take power by force*
>> After a bloody battle, the rebels usurped the power of the evil dictator.

HARD WORKING

adamant   AD uh ment
> *extremely stubborn*
>> She was adamant about ordering sushi for lunch and would listen to no other options.

assiduous   uh SID yoo us
> *hard-working*
>> Spending hours in the hot sun digging out every tiny weed, Esther tended her garden with assiduous attention.

conscientious   kahn shee EN shus
> *careful and principled*
>> As a conscientious student, Clarence was sure that all of his homework was completed on schedule.

diligent   DIL uh jent
> *marked by painstaking effort; hard-working*
>> With a lot of diligent effort, they were able to finish the model airplane in record time.

dogged   DOG id
> *stubbornly persevering*
>> Her first few attempts resulted in failure, but her dogged efforts ultimately ended in success.

exemplary   egz EM pluh ree
> *commendable*
>> His behavior was exemplary; he never spoke out of turn or did anything to embarrass himself or his parents.

fastidious   fas TID ee us
> *possessing careful attention to detail*
>> You could eat dinner off of her bedroom floor because she was very fastidious about cleanliness.

intrepid   in TREH pud
> *courageous; fearless*
>> The intrepid young soldier scaled the wall and attacked the enemy forces despite being outnumbered two to one.

meticulous   muh TIK yoo lus
> *extremely careful and precise*
>> With meticulous attention to detail, Lawrence went over every word in the thousand-page document and circled every mistake he found.

obstinate   OB stin ut
> *stubbornly adhering to an opinion or a course of action*
>> Her parents said, "No," but she was obstinate in her desire to go to the candy store.

tenacity   ten ASS uh tee
   persistent adherence to a belief or a point of view
>   With his overwhelming tenacity, Clark was finally able to interview
>   Brad Pitt for the school newspaper.

milk   MILK
   to draw or extract profit or advantage from
>   Fran would chew a stick of gum for six hours straight; she milked
>   everything she could out of it.

zealous   ZEL us
   passionate; extremely interested in pursuing something
>   Studying non-stop, twenty-four hours a day, seven days a week for her
>   SAT, Melinda may have been a little over-zealous.

punctilious   punk TIL ee us
   strictly attentive to minute details; picky
>   Charlotte was so punctilious when it came to rules of grammar that she
>   was constantly correcting everybody's speech.

MAKE THINGS BETTER

alleviate   uh LEEV ee ayt
> *to ease a pain or a burden*
>> John took aspirin to alleviate the pain from the headache he got after taking the SAT.

asylum   uh SYE lum
> *a place of retreat or security*
>> The soldiers sought asylum from the cannons and bullets in the underground shelter.

auspicious   ah SPISH us
> *attended by favorable circumstances*
>> The trip began very auspiciously when the rain stopped, the clouds cleared and the sun started shining just as we started the car.

benign   buh NINE
> *kind and gentle*
>> Grandfather smiled benignly as his grandchild told him about his day.

emollient   uh MAHL yunt
> *softening and soothing*
>> His kind words served as an emollient to the pain she had suffered.

mitigate   MIT uh gait
> *to make less severe or painful*
>> The peace agreement helped to mitigate the tension between the two parties.

mollify   MAHL uh fye
> *to calm or soothe*
>> After listening to her son cry for two straight hours, Denise finally gave him a lollipop in an effort to mollify him.

sanction (v)   SANK shun
> *to give official authorization or approval to*
>> The students were happy when the principal agreed to sanction the use of calculators in math classes.

substantiated   sub STAN shee ayt id
> *supported with proof or evidence; verified*
>> The discovery of fingerprints substantiated the detective's claim that the suspect had been at the scene of the crime.

exculpate   EKS kul payt
> *to free from guilt or blame*
>> Keeping a level head during the discussion, Tori exculpated herself from the charge that she had a quick temper.

GOING AGAINST THE GRAIN

debunk   dih BUNK
> *to expose the falseness of*
>> Many years ago, Galileo helped to debunk the myth that the world was round.

deleterious   del uh TEER ee us
> *having a harmful effect; injurious*
>> Although it seems unlikely, taking too many vitamins can actually have a deleterious effect on your health.

disingenuous   dis in JEN yoo us
> *not straightforward; crafty*
>> Gelman was rather disingenuous; although he seemed to be simply asking about your health, he was really trying to figure out how many days you'd been absent.

disparate   DIS puh rut
> *fundamentally distinct or different*
>> All of the many disparate members of the alliance were unable to agree on many things.

fabricated   FAB ruh kait id
> *made; concocted in order to deceive*
>> Lars fabricated the story to make it seem as though he was honest and upright when, in fact, nothing could be further from the truth.

recalcitrant   ruh KAL sih trunt
> *defiant of authority; stubborn; not easily managed*
>> Kent was a recalcitrant student who wouldn't do anything his teachers told him to do.

spurious   SPER ee us
> *not genuine; false*
>> The ad for White-O toothpaste made a spurious claim when it said it could whiten your teeth, clean your oven, and wash your car at the same time.

capricious   kuh PREE shus
> *impulsive and unpredictable*
>> My capricious purchase of the lime-green dress turned out to be a big mistake; I hated it upon closer inspection.

IF YOU CAN'T SAY ANYTHING NICE

disdain (v)   dis DAIN
to regard or treat with contempt; to look down on
> The bully disdained the weaker boy in front of his sister.

glower   GLOW er
to look or stare angrily or sullenly
> Instead of yelling at each other or hitting each other, the two bitter enemies just stood there and glowered at each other.

pejorative   puh JOR uh tiv
describing words or phrases that belittle or speak negatively of someone
> Policemen should refrain from using such pejorative terms as "dummy" and "stupid" when dealing with people they should be helping.

plagiarism   PLAY juh riz um
the act of passing off as one's own the ideas or writings of another
> The author was accused of plagiarism when an older manuscript was discovered which contained passages that she had used, word for word, in her own original novel.

trite   TRITE
unoriginal; overused; stale
> "That's the way the ball bounces" is such a trite expression.

vacuous   VAK yoo us
devoid of matter; empty
> Larry's vacuous term paper said nothing new and offered no insight.

vilify   VIL uh fye
to make vicious statements about
> In order to get elected to the student council, Chad issued a series of pamphlets that did nothing but vilify his opponent.

disparage   dis PAIR uj
to speak of in a slighting way or negatively; to belittle
> Glen disparaged Wanda by calling her a cheat and a liar.

ODDITIES

aberration   ab uh RAY shun
   a deviation from the way things normally happen or are done
>   Since he usually gets A's on his tests, the D he got on his last test was an
>   aberration.

dubious   DOO bee us
   doubtful; of unlikely authenticity
>   Jerry's claim that he could "fly like Superman" seemed dubious.

ostentatious   ahs ten TAY shus
   describing a showy or pretentious display
>   Whenever the millionaire gave a party, the elaborate decorations and
>   enormous amounts of food were always part of his ostentatious display
>   of wealth.

quandary   KWAHN duh ree
   a state of uncertainty or perplexity
>   The incredibly difficult math problem left everyone in a quandary.

stymied   STYE meed
   thwarted; stumped; blocked
>   The question "Who built Stonehenge?" has left researchers stymied for
>   centuries.

wily   WYE lee
   cunning
>   The detective's wily counterpart was able to predict his every move and
>   proceed accordingly.

THAT'S PRETTY

aesthetic   as THET ik
having to do with the appreciation of beauty
> The arrangement of paintings in the museum had to do primarily with aesthetic considerations; as long as paintings looked good together, it didn't matter who painted them or when they were painted.

decorous   DEK er us
proper; marked by good taste
> The class was well-behaved and the substitute was grateful for their decorous conduct.

embellish   em BELL ish
to make beautiful by ornamenting; to decorate
> We embellished the account of our vacation by including descriptions of the many colorful people and places we visited.

idyllic   id IL ik
simple and carefree
> Since they have no responsibilities, house pets enjoy an idyllic life.

medley   MED lee
an assortment or a mixture, especially of musical pieces
> At the wedding, the band played a medley of all the songs the bride and groom enjoyed.

mural   MYUR ul
a big painting applied directly to a wall
> The mural on the wall of the library featured portraits of every librarian that had worked there.

opulent   AHP yuh lunt
exhibiting a display of great wealth
> Dances given at the king's palace are always very opulent affairs.

ornate   or NAYT
elaborately ornamented
> The carved wood was so ornate that you could examine it several times and still notice things you had not seen before.

pristine   pris TEEN
not spoiled; pure
> The Model T was in pristine condition; it looked as though it had just come off the line yesterday.

serene   suh REEN
calm
> The seaside resort provided a much-needed vacation in a serene locale.

lucid   LOO sid
easily understood
> We love our teacher because he provides lucid explanations of difficult concepts.

FRIENDLY

affable   AF uh bul

easy-going; friendly

We enjoyed spending time with Uncle Joe because he was such an affable man.

amenable   uh MEEN uh bul

responsive; agreeable

Since we had been working hard all day, the group seemed amenable to my suggestion that we all go home early.

amiable   AY mee uh bul

good-natured and likable

As an amiable collaborator, she seldom argued or made it difficult to work with her.

camaraderie   kahm RAH duh ree

good will between friends

There was great camaraderie between the various members of the team and this helped them to attain their common goals.

cordial   KOHR jul

warm and sincere; friendly

Upon my arrival at the camp, I received a warm and cordial greeting from the counselors.

gregarious   gruh GAIR ee us

enjoying the company of others; sociable

The Swensons are gregarious hosts; they are always anxious to talk to everyone they've invited to their parties.

salutary   SAL yoo tair ee

promoting good health

Although I had been angry for the past week, the recent pleasant weather had a salutary effect on my mood.

sanguine   SANG gwin

cheerfully confident; optimistic

She was so sanguine about her chances of winning the race that she had already decided how she was going to spend the prize money.

innocuous   in AHK yoo us

having no bad effect; harmless

Although a casual observer may have found Lance's comments offensive, those who knew him realized that they were really fairly innocuous.

NASTY

brusque   BRUSK
describing a rudely abrupt manner
Mr. Weir frightened his physics students with his brusque manner.

cantankerous   kan TANK uh rus
grumpy; disagreeable
Grumpy old men are often described as cantankerous.

caustic   KAW stik
bitingly sarcastic or witty
He had a very caustic wit and he seldom told a joke without offending
someone.

contemptuous   kun TEMP choo us
feeling hatred; scornful
She was so contemptuous of people who wore vintage clothing that she
made sure that everything she wore was up to date.

feral   FEER ul
savage, fierce, or untamed
Normally mild-mannered, Nick became feral when he turned into a
werewolf.

fractious   FRAK shus
quarrelsome; unruly
Leonard was a fractious child who disagreed with everything and refused to listen.

incorrigible   in KOR ij uh bul
unable to be reformed
She is absolutely incorrigible; no matter how many times you punish
her, she goes right ahead and misbehaves.

ingrate   IN grayt
an ungrateful person
It is a true ingrate who can accept favor after favor and never offer
anything in return.

insolent   IN suh lunt
insulting in manner or speech
It was extremely insolent of him to yell rude things at his father.

malevolent   muh LEV uh lunt
having or exhibiting ill will; wishing harm to others; hateful
The evil Darth Vader was a malevolent villain who wanted to destroy
the rebel alliance.

notorious   noh TOR ee us
known widely and usually unfavorably; infamous
Al Capone was a notorious gangster in 1930s Chicago.

obdurate   AHB dyur ut
> *stubborn; inflexible*
>> Leanna was so obdurate that she was unable to change her way of thinking on even the most minor issues.

repugnant   ree PUG nent
> *causing disgust or hatred*
>> I find it repugnant that some cultures consider chocolate covered bugs a delicacy.

unpalatable   un PAL ut uh bul
> *not pleasing to the taste*
>> Once he poured gasoline on my french fries, I found them unpalatable.

parsimonious   par sih MOH nee us
> *excessively cheap*
>> Ebeneezer Scrooge was a parsimonious old man with no spirit of generosity.

ON THE ROAD

itinerant   eye TIN uh runt
> *traveling from place to place*
>> Circus performers lead an itinerant life, performing in a different town every night.

remote   ruh MOAT
> *located far away*
>> Farmer Brown lived in a remote village that lacked running water, telephones, and even electricity.

transitory   TRAN zih toh ree
> *short-lived or temporary*
>> The sadness she felt was only transitory; tomorrow, she was certain, her mood would improve.

unfettered   un FET erd
> *set free from restrictions or bonds*
>> Having completed the last of her work for the semester, Carol was unfettered by scholastic responsibilities.

WHO KNOWS WHAT'LL HAPPEN?

harbinger   HAHR bin jer
> *one that indicates what is to come; a forerunner*
>> Ancient peoples believed that solar eclipses were harbingers of bad times to come.

ominous   AH min us
> *menacing; threatening*
>> *The Twilight Zone* had an ominous theme song that everyone associates with scary or unexplainable phenomena.

portend   por TEND
> *to serve as an omen or a warning of*
>> When a black cat crosses your path it portends bad luck in the future.

prophetic   pruh FET ik
> *foretelling or predicting future events*
>> Although written forty years ago, her book turned out to be prophetic because it accurately predicted such things as the fall of communism and the widespread use of computers.

impromptu   im PROMPT oo
> *not planned in advance; spur of the moment*
>> Our elaborately planned picnic in the park turned into an impromptu indoor lunch when it unexpectedly started raining.

SITTIN' ON THE FENCE

ambiguous   am BIG yoo us
> *open to more than one interpretation*
>> His eyes were an ambiguous color: some thought they were brown and some thought they were green.

ambivalent   am BIV uh lunt
> *simultaneously feeling opposing feelings, such as love and hate*
>> She had ambivalent feelings about her dance class: on the one hand, she enjoyed the exercise she was getting, but on the other hand, she thought the choice of dances it taught her could be more interesting.

arbiter   AHR buh ter
> *a judge who decides a disputed issue*
>> To settle the Major League Baseball strike, an arbiter was hired to decide whether the owners or the players had a more convincing argument.

inconsequential   in kahn suh KWEN shul
> *unimportant*
>> As it happened, the cost of the car was inconsequential to Mr. Fortas because he had more money than he knew what to do with.

FULL TO OVERFLOWING

ample   AMP ul
> *describing a large amount of something*
>> Since the day was cloudy, there was ample room on the beach to spread out our blanket.

burgeoning   BER jun ing
> *expanding or growing rapidly*
>> The republic was in trouble due to a burgeoning discontent among the citizens.

capacious   kuh PAY shus
> *roomy; spacious*
>> They were thrilled with all the room they had in their capacious new home.

copious   KOH pee us
> *plentiful; having a large quantity*
>> Since she didn't understand physics very well at all, she was sure to take copious notes during class.

permeated   PER mee ayt id
> *spread or flowing throughout*
>> After the Citrus Fest, the scent of fresh oranges permeated the air.

prodigious   pruh DIJ us
> *enormous*
>> The shattered vase required a prodigious amount of glue to repair.

replete   ruh PLEET
> *abundantly supplied; filled*
>> After an evening of "Trick or Treating," Charlie's bag was replete with candy bars, jelly beans, and chewing gum.

GET TO THE POINT

candor KAN der
sincerity; openness
> The productive conversation between the former enemies was marked by honesty and candor.

frank FRANK
open and sincere in expression; straightforward
> When speaking to the school board, the principal was very frank about her school's need for greater funding.

pragmatic prag MAT ik
practical
> Never one for wild and unrealistic schemes, the scientist took a very pragmatic approach to solving her problem.

purist PYER ist
one who is particularly concerned with maintaining traditional practices
> As a purist, Leslie criticized the recent film version of *Romeo and Juliet* for taking place in modern-day Los Angeles.

terse TERS
brief and to the point; concise
> Robert's description of the Grand Canyon was terse: "It's big."

insightful in SIGHT ful
perceptive
> Gloria's insightful review of the film eloquently described its theme in terms no one had considered before.

curtailed ker TAYLD
cut short; abbreviated
> After gaining 40 pounds in one week, Humbert curtailed his consumption of peanut butter cups.

EARTH, WIND, AND FIRE

arid   AIR id

describing a dry, rainless climate

Since there are no surrounding bodies of water, deserts are known for their arid climates.

conflagration   kahn fluh GRAY shun

a widespread fire

The firefighters required vast amounts of water to extinguish the conflagration.

nocturnal   nok TER nul

of or occurring in the night

Owls are nocturnal animals because they sleep during the day and fly around at night.

temperate   TEMP uh rut

moderate; mild

The climate in some Southern states is temperate: it's rarely too hot or too cold.

REVOLUTION'S IN THE AIR

clandestine   klan DES tin
  secretive, especially in regard to concealing an illicit purpose
      The spies planned a clandestine maneuver to take over the castle.

coup   KOO
  a brilliant and sudden overthrow of a government
      The peasants planned a coup in order to end the reign of the cruel
      dictator.

enmity   EN muh tee
  mutual hatred or ill-will
      There was great enmity between the opposing generals and each one
      wanted utterly to destroy the other.

heresy   HAIR uh see
  an opinion that disagrees with established, dearly-held beliefs
      The leaders of the church accused of heresy anyone who did not sub-
      scribe to their beliefs.

implacable   im PLAK uh bul
  impossible to appease
      Although in most areas he was pretty easy-going, when it came to some
      things he was absolutely implacable.

maverick   MAV uh rik
  one who is independent and resists adherence to a group
      Jeremy was a maverick; he often felt that the way to get things done was
      to go against the grain and follow his own heart.

mercurial   mer KYER ee ul
  quick and changeable in mood
      Joan's mercurial temper usually got her into trouble because one minute
      she'd be happy and the next minute she'd be screaming her head off.

pugnacious   pug NAY shus
  combative; belligerent
      Lorenzo was a pugnacious child who tended to settle his differences
      with people by fighting with them.

rancorous   RANK er us
  hateful; marked by deep-seated ill will
      They had such a rancorous relationship that no one could imagine if
      they had ever gotten along.

stratagem   STRAT uh jem
  a clever trick used to deceive or outwit
      It was a brilliant stratagem that would outwit even the most clever of
      opponents.

wary   WAIR ee

    on guard; watchful

        After being fooled time and time again by the Road Runner, the Coyote
        became very wary of him.

thwart   THWART

    to prevent the occurrence of

        Even though I had spent hours getting ready for the event, all it took
        was one little phone call to thwart my plans.

reclamation   rek luh MAY shun

    a restoration or rehabilitation to productivity or usefulness

        Thanks to the reclamation project, the once unusable land became a
        beautiful, productive farm.

furtive   FER tiv

    characterized by stealth; sneaky

        The escaping convict moved furtively through the halls in hopes that he
        would not be caught.

impetuous   im PET yoo us

    characterized by sudden energy or emotion

        It is much better to plan things out carefully than to be impetuous and
        act without thinking.

PUT YOUR AFFAIRS IN ORDER

catalog (v)   KAT uh log
> *to make an itemized list of*
>> His baseball card collection became so large that he thought it might be best to catalog it.

equanimity   ek wuh NIM uh tee
> *the quality of being calm and even-tempered; composure*
>> She showed great equanimity, even in the face of catastrophe.

feasible   FEE zuh bul
> *capable of being accomplished; possible*
>> After spending so much money on a new computer, it was no longer feasible to buy a new car as well.

apt   APT
> *suitable; appropriate*
>> "Big piece of junk" was a very apt description of the car because it was constantly in need of repair.

solvent   SAHL vunt
> *able to pay one's debts*
>> After spending years in debt, Flo's parents were finally solvent.

facile   FAS ul
> *done or achieved with little effort; easy*
>> Last night's math homework was such a facile task that I was done in less than ten minutes.

liquid   LIK wid
> *flowing readily*
>> The poem flowed out of his mouth in a liquid manner because he had memorized it very well.

plausible   PLAWZ uh bul
> *seemingly valid or acceptable; credible*
>> To say that the reason you missed school yesterday was that you were captured by space aliens is not a very plausible excuse.

I'LL BE THE JUDGE OF THAT

biased   BYE usd
> *prejudiced*
>> A judge should not be biased, but rather she should weigh the evidence before making up her mind on any aspect of the case.

incontrovertible   in kahn truh VERT uh bul
> *indisputable; not open to question*
>> The videotape of the shoplifting provided incontrovertible evidence of the guilt of the accused.

jurisprudence   jer is PROO duns
> *the philosophy or science of law*
>> Judges and lawyers are long-time students of jurisprudence and they know their fields well.

vindicated   VIN duh kayt id
> *freed from blame*
>> Mrs. Layton was finally vindicated after her husband admitted to the crime.

penitent   PEN uh tunt
> *expressing remorse for one's misdeeds*
>> His desire to make amends to the people he had wronged indicates that he was truly penitent and felt bad about his misdeeds.

FEELING AT HOME

incumbent (adj) in KUM bunt
imposed as a duty; obligatory
Since you are the host, it is incumbent upon you to see that everyone is having a good time.

indigenous in DIJ uh nus
originating and living in a particular area
Penguins are indigenous to the arctic regions.

innate in AYT
possessed at birth; inborn
Cats have an innate ability to see well in the dark.

inveterate in VET uh rut
long established; deep-rooted; habitual
Stan has always had trouble telling the truth; in fact, he's an inveterate liar.

parochial puh ROE kee ul
narrow in scope
The club had a parochial admission policy; every member had to come from the same neighborhood.

pervasive per VAY siv
having the quality or tendency to be everywhere at the same time
Whenever Thanksgiving dinner is being prepared, there is a pervasive smell of turkey throughout the house.

UNDER THE WEATHER

impinge   im PINJ
> *to encroach in a way that violates the rights of another*
>> By not allowing the students to publish a newspaper, the school was impinging on their right to free speech.

laconic   luh KAHN ik
> *using few words*
>> Although Kukla and Fran were very talkative, Ollie was a laconic individual who only spoke when he had to.

lament   luh MENT
> *to express grief for; mourn*
>> Thirsty after a long run, the joggers lamented the fact that no beverages were available.

obsolete   ahb suh LEET
> *no longer in use; old-fashioned*
>> Once, everybody wanted to own one, but now 8-Track tape players are obsolete.

reticent   RET uh sent
> *reluctant to speak*
>> Although June shares her opinions about everything, her sister is reticent.

sanction (n)   SANK shun
> *an economic or military measure put in place to punish another country*
>> The president felt that if he prohibited importation of the country's goods, the sanction would get that country to stop hurting its citizens.

suppressed   suh PRESD
> *subdued; kept from being circulated*
>> The author's new book was suppressed because the dictator thought it was too critical of his regime.

surreptitious   ser ep TISH us
> *done by secretive means*
>> The secret agent had to be surreptitious when he planted the listening devices at enemy headquarters.

truncated   TRUNK ay tid
> *shortened; cut off*
>> Since the class had only a week left in the semester, the teacher assigned a truncated version of the longer lesson she had planned.

wane   WAYN
> *to decrease gradually in intensity; decline*
>> Even though we used to be very excited about water skiing, our interest in that activity has waned.

EVER SO SLIGHTLY

ephemeral   ih FEM uh rul

lasting for a markedly brief time

The joy he felt at finishing his first draft was ephemeral; once he realized how much work was left to do he adopted a much more sober attitude.

obscure (adj or v)   ub SKYER

relatively unknown; or to conceal or make indistinct

The man in front of me was so tall that his head obscured my view of the movie.

tacit   TAS it

implied but not actually expressed

By not saying that we couldn't go to the concert, our parents gave us tacit approval to go.

tenuous   TEN yoo us

having little substance or strength; shaky; flimsy

Her grasp on reality is tenuous at best; she's not even sure about what year it is.

timorous   TIM uh rus

shy; timid

The normally obnoxious bully became timorous in the presence of Mr. Boyle.

trepidation   trep uh DAY shun

uncertainty; apprehension

We approached Mrs. Fielding with trepidation because we didn't know how she would react to our request for a field trip.

SO STATUS QUO

immutable   ih MYOOT uh bul
>   *not able to be changed*
>   The rules governing the club were immutable; everyone had to obey
>   them and there was no room for change.

mundane   mun DAYN
>   *commonplace; ordinary*
>   We hated going to school every day because it was so mundane; every
>   day seemed the same and nothing different ever happened.

prosaic   pro ZAY ik
>   *unimaginative; dull*
>   The organization had a very prosaic way of carrying out its business;
>   everything was done by the book and there was no room for creativity.

prudent   PROO dunt
>   *exercising good judgment or common sense*
>   It wouldn't be prudent to act until you've considered every possible
>   outcome.

tenet   TEN et
>   *a principle held as being true by a person or an organization*
>   One of the tenets of our society is that every citizen has the right to vote.

stoic   STOE ik
>   *indifferent to pleasure or pain; impassive*
>   Not one to complain, Jason stoically accepted the horrible-tasting meal.

austere   ah STEER
>   *somber, stern*
>   The grey walls and lack of furniture provided a very austere setting.

genre   ZHAHN ruh
>   *describing a category of artistic endeavor*
>   Bret only enjoyed science fiction movies; in fact, he never went to see
>   anything that was not in that genre.

staid   STAYD
>   *characterized by a strait-laced sense of propriety; serious*
>   Mr. Carver had such a staid demeanor that he allowed no behavior that
>   might seem frivolous: no dancing, no singing, and no laughing.

archaic   ar KAY ik
>   *characteristic of an earlier, more primitive period; old-fashioned*
>   "How dost thou?" is an archaic way of saying "How are you?"

I'M NEW AT THIS

emulate   EM yuh layt

to try to equal or excel, especially through imitation
> Since everything she said reminded us of her brother, it seemed that she would go to any length to emulate him.

naïve   nah YEEV

lacking sophistication
> It was naïve of him to think that he could write a novel in one afternoon.

nascent   NAY sunt

coming into existence; emerging
> When a caterpillar goes into its cocoon it is in the nascent stage of being a butterfly.

novice   NAH vus

a beginner
> Having only played chess a couple of times, Barry was a novice compared to the contestants who had been playing all their lives.

THINGS THAT SUCK

toxic   TAHK sik

poisonous
> Since many chemicals are toxic, it's a good idea not to drink from random flasks in the chemistry lab.

brittle   BRIT ul

easily broken when subjected to pressure
> You have to be careful when handling that thin sheet of ice because it is so brittle it might break at any moment.

malice   MAL is

extreme ill will or spite
> It was clear that he was acting with malice when he disconnected the brakes in his business partner's car.

malfeasance   mal FEEZ uns

misconduct or wrongdoing, especially by a public official
> The mayor was accused of malfeasance because of his questionable spending habits.

ISN'T THAT SPECIAL

dilettante   dih luh TAHNT
> *a dabbler in or one who superficially understands an art or a field of knowledge*
>> You can take Betsy's opinion with a grain of salt because she's just a dilettante who really doesn't understand the subtleties of the painting.

eclectic   uh KLEK tik
> *made up of a variety of sources or styles*
>> Lou's taste in music could be described as eclectic because he listens to everything from rap to polka.

intuitive   in TOO uh tiv
> *knowing or perceiving quickly and readily*
>> She's a good person to have on your side because she's so intuitive; her instincts are seldom wrong.

laudatory   LAW duh tor ee
> *expressing great praise*
>> It is very laudatory that he spends so much time and money to help feed the homeless.

novel   NAH vul
> *strikingly new, unusual, or different*
>> Sharon intrigued the scientific community with her novel approach to solving the problem.

paramount   PAIR uh mount
> *of chief concern or importance*
>> The workers had a series of minor complaints, but the paramount reason for their unhappiness was the low pay they received.

urbane   er BAYN
> *notably polite and elegant in manner; suave*
>> At the dinner party, the most popular guests were those urbane and witty guests who kept others entertained with their amusing stories.

epiphany   uh PIF uh nee
> *a sudden burst of understanding or discovery*
>> After weeks of confusion, the scientist suddenly realized the answer to her question in a moment of epiphany.

trenchant   TREN chunt
> *keen; incisive*
>> The professor kept his class on its toes with his trenchant remarks about the current crisis.

whimsical   WHIM zuh kul
> *subject to erratic behavior; unpredictable*
>> Egbert rarely behaved as expected; indeed, he was a whimsical soul whose every decision was anybody's guess.

OTHER WORDS

As important as Hit Parade words are, they aren't the only words on the SAT. As you go about learning the Hit Parade, you should also try to incorporate other new words into your vocabulary. The Hit Parade will help you determine what kinds of words you should be learning—good solid words that are fairly difficult but not impossible.

One very good source of SAT words is your local paper. Get it, read it, write down the words you don't know, and look them up. (You just may learn something about the world as well.) No one ever got dumber by reading.

ROOTS

Many of the words in the English language were borrowed from other languages at some point in our history. Words that you use every day contain bits and pieces of ancient Greek and Latin words that meant something similar. These bits and pieces are called "roots." The dictionary describes each word's roots by giving its etymology—a minihistory of where it came from. For example, the *American Heritage Dictionary* gives the following etymology for *apathy*, a word on the Hit Parade: "Greek *apatheia*, for *apathés*, without feeling: A-(without) + pathos, feeling." Similar-sounding words, like *pathos, pathetic, sympathy*, and *empathy*, are all related and all have to do with feeling.

Many people say the best way to prepare for the SAT is simply to learn a lot of roots. Students who know a lot of roots, they say, will be able to "translate" any unfamiliar words they encounter on the test. There is some truth in this; the more you know about etymology, the easier it will be to build your vocabulary. But roots can also mislead you. The hardest words on the SAT are often words that seem to contain a familiar root, but actually do not. For example, *audacity*, a hard word sometimes tested on the SAT, means "boldness or daring." It has nothing to do with sound, even though it seems to contain the root *aud-* from a Latin word meaning "to hear"—as in audio, audiovisual, or auditorium. *Audacity* really comes from the Latin word *audax*, courageous.

Still, learning about roots can be helpful—if you do it properly. You should think of roots not as a code that will enable you to decipher unknown words on the SAT, but as a tool for learning new words and making associations between them. For example, *eloquent, colloquial*, and *circumlocution* all contain the Latin root *loqu/loc*, which means to "speak." Knowing the root and recognizing it in these words will make it easier for you to memorize all of them. You should think of roots as a tool for helping you organize your thoughts as you build your vocabulary.

The worst thing you can do is try to memorize roots all by themselves, apart from words they appear in. In the first place, it can't be done. In the second place, it won't help.

HIT PARADE OF ROOTS

Just as the Hit Parade is a list of the most frequently tested words on the SAT, the Hit Parade of Roots is a list of the roots that show up most often in SAT vocabulary words. You may find it useful in helping you organize your vocabulary study. When approaching the Hit Parade of Roots, focus on the words, using the roots simply as reminders to help you learn or remember the meanings. When you take the SAT, you may be able to prod your memory about the meaning of a particular word by thinking of the related words that you associate with it.

The roots on the Hit Parade of Roots are presented in order of their importance on the SAT. The roots at the top of the list appear more often than the roots at the bottom. Each root is followed by a number of real SAT words that contain it. (What should you do every time you don't know the meaning of a word on the Hit Parade of Roots? Look it up!) Note that roots often have several different forms. Be on the lookout for all of them.

CAP/CIP/CEIPT/CEPT/CEIV/CEIT (take)

capture	exceptionable
intercept	susceptible
receptive	deception
recipient	conception
incipient	receive
perceptive	conceit
percipient	accept
anticipate	emancipate
except	precept
exceptional	

GEN (birth, race, kind)

generous	homogeneous
generate	heterogeneous
degenerate	genealogy
regenerate	indigenous
genuine	congenital
congenial	gender
ingenious	engender
ingenuous	genre
ingenue	progeny

DIC/DICT/DIT (tell, say, word)

predicament	malediction
condition	benediction
dictate	extradite
dictator	verdict
abdicate	indict
predict	diction
contradict	dictum
addict	

SPEC/SPIC/SPIT (look, see)

perspective	spectrum
aspect	specimen
spectator	introspection
spectacle	respite
suspect	conspicuous
speculation	circumspect
suspicious	perspicacious

SUPER/SUR (above)

surpass	supercilious
superficial	superstition
summit	superimpose
superlative	supersede
supernova	superfluous

TENT/TENS/TEND/TENU (stretch, thin)

tension

extend

tendency

tendon

tent

tentative

contend

contention

distend

tenuous

attenuate

portent

tendentious

TRANS (across)

transfer

transaction

transparent

transgress

transport

transform

transition

transitory

transient

transmutation

transcendent

intransigent

traduce

DOC/DUC/DAC (teach, lead)

conduct

reduce

seduce

conducive

inductee

doctrine

document

docile

didactic

indoctrinate

traduce

induce

CO/CON/COM (with, together)

company

collaborate

conjugal

congeal

congenial

convivial

coalesce

contrition

commensurate

conclave

conciliate

comply

congruent

VERS/VERT (turn)

controversy

convert

revert

subvert

inversions

divert

diverse

aversion

extrovert

introvert

inadvertent

versatile

adversity

LOC/LOG/LOQU (word, speech)

eloquent

logic

apology

circumlocution

monologue

neologism

philology

colloquial

eulogy

loquacious

dialogue

prologue

epilogue

SEN (feel, sense)

sensitive

sensation

sentiment

sensory

sensual

resent

consent

dissent

assent

consensus

sentry

sentinel

DE (away, down, off)

denounce

debility

defraud

decry

deplete

defame

delineate

deface

devoid

defile

desecrate

derogatory

NOM/NOUN/NOWN/NAM/NYM (name, order, rule)

name

anonymous

antonym

nominate

economy

astronomy

ignominy

renown

misnomer

nomenclature

CLA/CLO/CLU (shut, close)

closet

claustrophobia

enclose

disclose

include

conclude

exclusive

preclude

recluse

seclude

cloister

VO/VOC/VOK/VOW (call)

voice

vocal

provocative

advocate

equivocate

vocation

convoke

vociferous

irrevocable

evocative

revoke

MAL (bad)

malicious

malady

dismal

malfunction

malign

malcontent

malodorous

malefactor

malevolent

malediction

maladroit

FRA/FRAC/FRAG (break)

fracture

fraction

fragment

fragmentary

fragile

frail

refraction

refractory

infraction

infringe

fractious

OB (against)

objective

obsolete

oblique

obscure

obstruct

obstinate

obliterate

oblivious

obsequious

obfuscate

SUB (under)

submissive

subsidiary

subjugation

subliminal

subdue

subordinate

sublime

subtle

subversion

subterfuge

AB (from, away)

abandon	abstain
abhor	absolve
abnormal	abstemious
abstract	abstruse
abdicate	abrogate

GRESS/GRAD (step)

progress	degrade
regress	downgrade
retrogress	aggressor
retrograde	digress
gradual	transgress

SEC/SEQU (follow)

second	execute
sequel	subsequent
sequence	prosecute
consequence	obsequious
inconsequential	

PRO (much, for, a lot)

prolific	prodigal
profuse	protracted
propitious	proclivity
prodigious	propensity
profligate	prodigy

QUE/QUIS (ask, seek)

inquire	querulous
question	acquire
request	acquisitive
quest	acquisition
query	exquisite

SACR/SANCT/SECR (sacred)

sacred	sacrosanct
sacrifice	consecrate
sanctuary	desecrate
sanctify	execrable
sanction	sacrament

SCRIB/SCRIP (write)

scribble	proscribe
describe	ascribe
script	inscribe
postscript	circumscribe
prescribe	

PATHY/PAS/PAT (feeling)

apathy	compassion
sympathy	compatible
empathy	dispassionate
antipathy	impassive
passionate	

DIS/DIF (not)

dissonance	dispassionate
discrepancy	disparate
disdain	diffident
dissuade	disparage
dismay	

CIRCU (around)

circumference	circuitous
circulation	circumscribe
circumstance	circumvent
circumnavigate	circumlocutory

PART ◆ VI

Answer Key
to Drills

CHAPTER 6

DRILLS 1&2

1. Pam's answer is C.

   The trigger word *although* indicates a change is coming. "Although . . . the book was brilliant . . ." The doctor in the sentence is *so few copies were sold*. Therefore, the author got little *monetary* reward. The best match for monetary is answer choice (C), financial.

6. Pam's answer is B.

   Do this question one blank at a time. The trigger word *sadly* tells you that the tone of the sentence is negative. The doctor is *over-development*. If there is a lot of over-development, what will happen to the rain forests? They will *disappear*. This word fits perfectly in the second blank. Cross off answers (A) and (C) since the second word in each does not mean disappear. Answer choice (D) is weak, but keep it for now.

   In the first blank, we need a word that means something like hurt. Look at the remaining answer choices. The first words in both (D) and (E) do not mean hurt, so cross them off. The answer is (B).

9. Pam's answer is B.

   Do this question one blank at a time. In the first blank, the trigger word *and* tells you the blank means the same as *drab*. Go through the answer choices and cross off anything that doesn't mean *drab* or *boring*. If you don't know the meaning of a word, you cannot cross it off. Get rid of (E) (and (C) and (D) if you know what they mean).

   The trigger word *but* tells us the second blank means the opposite of drab and boring. Look for a second word that means *excitement* or *energy* from among the remaining choices. Redundancy does not mean excitement, so get rid of (A). Even if you didn't know the first words in (C) and (D), neither of their second words means excitement. The answer is (B).

DRILL 3

8. B

8. A

   Good second guesses: E, B.

CHAPTER 7

DRILL 1

An ARCHITECT designs a BUILDING.
A WARDEN is in charge of a PRISON.
IGNORANCE means without EDUCATION.
AQUATIC means pertaining to WATER.
LETTERS comprise the ALPHABET.

DRILL 2

4. *Solar* means pertaining to the *sun*.

5. *Glue* is a substance that is *sticky*.

6. No relationship.

7. *Grateful* means giving *thanks*.

8. A *morsel* is a small *quantity*.

9. *Equine* means pertaining to *horses*.

10. No relationship.

11. To *preach* is to engage in *exhortation*.

12. No relationship.

13. An *alias* is a false *identity*.

DRILL 3

15. D

15. A

CHAPTER 8

DRILL 1

1. C
2. D
3. E
4. B
5. A
6. C
7. B
8. D
9. D
10. C
11. B
12. E
13. C

CHAPTER 9

DRILL 1

1. to
2. of, for
3. by, for
4. of
5. about, for, by
6. by
7. about
8. to
9. from

DRILL 2

1. C
2. B
3. C
4. D
5. B
6. C

DRILL 3

1. About to happen *versus* prominent or distinguished
2. Forbid, condemn *versus* set down, order (as in medication)
3. Smart *versus* able to be understood
4. Unbelievable *versus* skeptical
5. Annoyed *versus* made worse
6. Fixed, not moving *versus* letter paper
7. Unlawful *versus* draw out

DRILL 4

1. B
2. E
3. E
4. B
5. B
6. B
7. D
8. B
9. B
10. B
11. E
12. C

DRILL 5

1. C
2. E
3. C
4. E
5. D
6. A

CHAPTER 12

DRILL 1

1. 109
2. 38
3. −3
4. 10
5. 15

DRILL 2

1. $6(57+13) = 6 \times 70 = 420$
2. $51(48+50+52) = 51(150) = 7{,}650$
3. $ab + ac - ad$
4. $x(y - z)$
5. $c(ab + xy)$

DRILL 3

1. $\dfrac{25}{3}$
2. $\dfrac{17}{7}$
3. $\dfrac{49}{9}$
4. $\dfrac{5}{2}$
5. $\dfrac{20}{3}$

Drill 4

1. 3

2. $\dfrac{31}{5}$

3. $-1\dfrac{4}{15}$ or $-\dfrac{19}{15}$

4. $\dfrac{1}{15}$

5. $\dfrac{6}{7}$

6. $\dfrac{2}{25}$

7. $\dfrac{4}{9}$

Drill 5

1. .3741

2. 1,457.7

3. 186

4. −2.89

Drill 6

	Fraction	Decimal	Percent
1.	$\dfrac{1}{2}$	0.5	50
2.	$\dfrac{3}{1}$	3.0	300
3.	$\dfrac{1}{200}$	0.005	0.5
4.	$\dfrac{1}{3}$	$0.333\overline{3}$	$33\dfrac{1}{3}$

CHAPTER 14

DRILL 1

1. 0.4
2. a little bit more than 5
3. 2.8
4. a little bit less than 1
5. a little bit more than 4
6. x = about 30°

   y = about 120°

   z = about 30°

   YZ is about 16

   XZ is about 30 (a little less than 32!)

(None of these angle measurements is exact, but remember, you don't have to be exact when you guesstimate. Even a very rough guesstimation will enable you to eliminate one or two answer choices.)

CHAPTER 15

3. A
6. D
12. D
14. D

CHAPTER 16

DRILL 1

(page 252)

PART ◆ VII

The Princeton Review Diagnostic Test and Explanations I

The best way to learn our techniques for cracking the SAT is to practice them. The following diagnostic tests will give you a chance to do that.

These diagnostic tests were designed to be as much like a real SAT as possible. They contain three verbal sections, three math sections, and an experimental section (two of the sections last for only 15 minutes). Our questions test the same concepts that are tested on real SATs. If you are preparing for the PSAT, use the instructions below to convert Diagnostic Test II to a PSAT (also, see page 289 to find out how to order some recent PSATs from ETS).

Since one of the sections in this test is experimental, none of the questions in it counts toward your final score. The actual SAT will have an experimental section—verbal or math—that ETS now euphemistically terms an "equating section."

When you take a diagnostic test, you should try to take it under conditions that are as much like real testing conditions as possible. Take it in a room where you won't be disturbed, and have someone else time you. (It's too easy if you time yourself.) You can give yourself a brief break halfway through, but don't stop for longer than five minutes or so. To put yourself in the proper frame of mind, you might take it on a weekend morning.

Keep Working

It is difficult for most people to tell if a section is experimental, so you should treat all of the sections as real sections.

After taking our tests, you'll have a very good idea of what taking the real SAT will be like. In fact, we've found that students' scores on The Princeton Review's diagnostic tests correspond very closely to the scores they earn on real SATs.

The answers to the questions and a scoring guide can be found beginning on page 403. The answer sheet is at the back of the book.

If you have any questions about the diagnostic test, the SAT, ETS, or The Princeton Review, give us a call, toll-free, at 1-800-2REVIEW.

The following sample tests were written by the authors and are not actual SATs. The directions and format were used by permission of Educational Testing Service. This permission does not constitute review or endorsement by Educational Testing Service or the College Board of this publication as a whole or of any sample questions or testing information it may contain.

Converting an SAT into a PSAT

As you know, the PSAT is structured slightly differently from the SAT. In order for you to get a real sense of what the PSAT is like, you need to take a timed PSAT by converting an SAT into a PSAT.

Use the following chart to convert Diagnostic Test II (chapter 19) into a PSAT. You can also use this chart as a guideline for converting any SAT from *10 Real SATs* into a PSAT. (Note: If you are converting tests in *10 Real SATs*, you will be able to check your answers, but you will not be able to convert your results into a score based on their scoring charts.) Remember that the PSAT is always given in the same order (Verbal, Math, Verbal, Math, WSC). Also, notice on the chart that specific question numbers have been omitted from each section. This is intentional. You cannot simply eliminate the last four sentence completions if you only need to take five sentence completions. Why? Order of

Difficulty, of course. Specific question numbers have been omitted to maintain the appropriate order of difficulty.

Before you begin, go through and cross out all the problems you are to omit. If you plan to practice this test using a bubble sheet, take it out and cross off the same numbers on the bubble sheet. Then, take the test like a real PSAT. Use the PSAT scoring chart at the end of chapter 20 to score your test when you have finished.

Give yourself	To take	Leave out
25 minutes	Verbal Section 2 of Diag. Test II	1, 4, 8, 9, and 30.
25 minutes	Math Section 1 of Diag. Test II	5, 10, 15, 20 and 25.
25 minutes	Verbal Section 5 of Diag. Test II	1, 10, 11, 14, 15, 19, 22 and 23.
25 minutes	Math Section 3 of Diag. Test II	5, 10, 15, 16 and 25.
30 minutes	Writing Skills Component, chapter 9	

17

Diagnostic Test I

Time—30 Minutes 25 Questions	In this section solve each problem, using any available space on the page for scratchwork. Then decide which is the best of the choices given and fill in the corresponding oval on the answer sheet.

Notes:

1.   The use of a calculator is permitted. All numbers used are real numbers.

2.   Figures that accompany problems in this test are intended to provide information useful in solving the problems. They are drawn as accurately as possible EXCEPT when it is stated in a specific problem that the figure is not drawn to scale. All figures lie in a plane unless otherwise indicated.

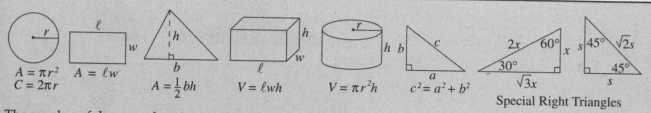

$A = \pi r^2$ $A = \ell w$ $A = \frac{1}{2}bh$ $V = \ell wh$ $V = \pi r^2 h$ $c^2 = a^2 + b^2$

$C = 2\pi r$

Special Right Triangles

The number of degrees of arc in a circle is 360.
The measure in degrees of a straight angle is 180.
The sum of the measures in degrees of the angles of a triangle is 180.

---

1 If $9b = 81$, then $3 \times 3b =$

(A)   9
(B)   27
(C)   81
(D) 243
(E) 729

2 In the figure above, what is the sum of $a + b + c$?

(A) 180
(B) 240
(C) 270
(D) 360
(E) It cannot be determined from the information given.

GO ON TO THE NEXT PAGE

3 $\dfrac{0.5 + 0.5 + 0.5 + 0.5}{4} =$

(A) 0.05
(B) 0.125
(C) 0.5
(D) 1
(E) 2.0

6 If 3 more than x is 2 more than y, what is x in terms of y?

(A) $y - 5$
(B) $y - 1$
(C) $y + 1$
(D) $y + 5$
(E) $y + 6$

4 Steve ran a 12-mile race at an average speed of 8 miles per hour. If Adam ran the same race at an average speed of 6 miles per hour, how many minutes longer than Steve did Adam take to complete the race?

(A) 9
(B) 12
(C) 16
(D) 24
(E) 30

7 $\dfrac{4^2}{2^3} + \dfrac{2^3}{4^2} =$

(A) $\dfrac{5}{2}$

(B) 2

(C) 1

(D) $\dfrac{1}{2}$

(E) $\dfrac{1}{4}$

Note: Figure not drawn to scale.

5 If $AB > CD$, which of the following must be true?

    I. $AB > BC$
   II. $AC > BD$
  III. $AC > CD$

(A) I only
(B) II only
(C) III only
(D) II and III only
(E) I, II, and III

GO ON TO THE NEXT PAGE

8 If 8 and 12 each divide *K* without a remainder, what is the value of *K*?

(A) 16
(B) 24
(C) 48
(D) 96
(E) It cannot be determined from the information given.

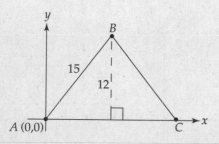

9 In the figure above, side *AB* of triangle *ABC* contains which of the following points?

(A) (3, 2)
(B) (3, 5)
(C) (4, 6)
(D) (4, 10)
(E) (6, 8)

10 What is the diameter of a circle with circumference 5?

(A) $\dfrac{5}{\pi}$

(B) $\dfrac{10}{\pi}$

(C) 5

(D) 5π

(E) 10π

11 Carol subscribed to four publications that cost $12.90, $16.00, $18.00, and $21.90 per year, respectively. If she made an initial down payment of one half of the total amount, and paid the rest in 4 equal monthly payments, how much was each of the 4 monthly payments?

(A) $8.60
(B) $9.20
(C) $9.45
(D) $17.20
(E) $34.40

GO ON TO THE NEXT PAGE

MERCHANDISE SALES		
Type	Amount of Sales	Percent of Total Sales
Shoes	$12,000	15%
Coats	$20,000	25%
Shirts	$x	40%
Pants	$y	20%

12 According to the table above, what were the sales, in dollars, of shirts and pants combined?

(A) $32,000
(B) $48,000
(C) $60,000
(D) $68,000
(E) $80,000

13 For all integers $n \neq 1$, let $< n > = \dfrac{n+1}{n-1}$. Which of the following has the greatest value?

(A) $< 0 >$
(B) $< 2 >$
(C) $< 3 >$
(D) $< 4 >$
(E) $< 5 >$

14 If the product of $(1 + 2)$, $(2 + 3)$, and $(3 + 4)$ is equal to one half the sum of 20 and x, then $x =$

(A)   10
(B)   85
(C)   105
(D)   190
(E)   1,210

15 If $\dfrac{2+x}{5+x} = \dfrac{2}{5} + \dfrac{2}{5}$, then $x =$

(A) $\dfrac{2}{5}$

(B)   1

(C)   2

(D)   5

(E)   10

GO ON TO THE NEXT PAGE

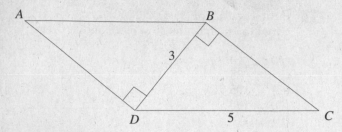

16 In parallelogram *ABCD* above, *BD* = 3 and *CD* = 5. What is the area of *ABCD*?

(A) 12
(B) 15
(C) 18
(D) 20
(E) It cannot be determined from the information given.

17 A survey of Town X found a mean of 3.2 persons per household and a mean of 1.2 televisions per household. If 48,000 people live in Town X, how many televisions are in Town X?

(A) 15,000
(B) 16,000
(C) 18,000
(D) 40,000
(E) 57,600

18 How many numbers from 1 to 200 inclusive are equal to the cube of an integer?

(A) one
(B) two
(C) three
(D) four
(E) five

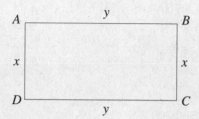

Note: Figure not drawn to scale.

19 If the perimeter of rectangle *ABCD* is equal to *p*, and $x = \frac{2}{3}y$, what is the value of *y* in terms of *p*?

(A) $\dfrac{p}{10}$

(B) $\dfrac{3p}{10}$

(C) $\dfrac{p}{3}$

(D) $\dfrac{2p}{5}$

(E) $\dfrac{3p}{5}$

GO ON TO THE NEXT PAGE

20 A basketball team had a ratio of wins to losses of 3:1. After winning six games in a row, the team's ratio of wins to losses was 5:1. How many games had the team won <u>before</u> it won the six games?

(A) 3
(B) 6
(C) 9
(D) 15
(E) 24

21 A college student bought 11 books for Fall classes. If the cost of his anatomy textbook was three times the mean cost of the other 10 books, then the cost of the anatomy textbook was what fraction of the total amount he paid for the 11 books?

(A) $\frac{2}{13}$

(B) $\frac{3}{13}$

(C) $\frac{3}{11}$

(D) $\frac{3}{10}$

(E) $\frac{3}{4}$

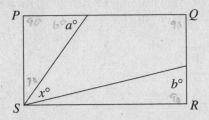

22 In rectangle $PQRS$ above, what is the sum of $a + b$ in terms of x?

(A) $90 + x$
(B) $180 - x$
(C) $180 + x$
(D) $270 - x$
(E) $360 - x$

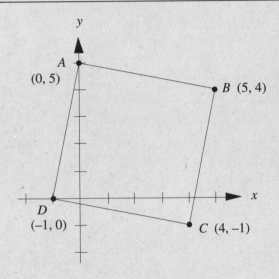

23 What is the area of square $ABCD$?

(A) 25
(B) $18\sqrt{2}$
(C) 26
(D) $25 + \sqrt{2}$
(E) 36

GO ON TO THE NEXT PAGE

24 If 0.1% of m is equal to 10% of n, then m is what percent of $10n$?

(A) $\dfrac{1}{1000}\%$

(B) 10%

(C) 100%

(D) 1,000%

(E) 10,000%

25 If $n \neq 0$, which of the following could be true?

    I. $2n < n^2$
    II. $2n < n$
    III. $n^2 < -n$

(A) None
(B) I only
(C) I and II only
(D) I and III only
(E) I, II, and III

IF YOU FINISH BEFORE TIME IS CALLED, YOU MAY CHECK YOUR WORK ON THIS SECTION ONLY. DO NOT TURN TO ANY OTHER SECTION IN THE TEST. **STOP**

NO TEST MATERIAL ON THIS PAGE.

Time—30 Minutes
30 Questions

For each question in this section, select the best answer from among the choices given and fill in the corresponding oval on the answer sheet.

Each sentence below has one or two blanks, each blank indicating that something has been omitted. Beneath the sentence are five words or sets of words labeled A through E. Choose the word or set of words that, when inserted in the sentence, <u>best</u> fits the meaning of the sentence as a whole.

Example:

Medieval kingdoms did not become constitutional republics overnight; on the contrary, the change was ----.

(A) unpopular
(B) unexpected
(C) advantageous
(D) sufficient
(E) gradual

Ⓐ Ⓑ Ⓒ Ⓓ ●

1 Since the island soil has been barren for so many years, the natives must now ---- much of their food.

(A) deliver
(B) import
(C) produce
(D) develop
(E) utilize

2 Because Jenkins neither ---- nor defends either management or the striking workers, both sides admire his journalistic ----.

(A) criticizes. .acumen
(B) attacks. .neutrality
(C) confronts. .aptitude
(D) dismisses. .flair
(E) promotes. .integrity

3 Some anthropologists claim that a few apes have been taught a rudimentary sign language, but skeptics argue that the apes are only ---- their trainers.

(A) imitating
(B) condoning
(C) instructing
(D) acknowledging
(E) belaboring

4 It is ironic that the ---- insights of the great thinkers are voiced so often that they have become mere ----.

(A) original. .clichés
(B) banal. .beliefs
(C) dubious. .habits
(D) philosophical. .questions
(E) abstract. .ideas

5 The most frustrating periods of any diet are the inevitable ----, when weight loss ---- if not stops.

(A) moods. .accelerates
(B) feasts. .halts
(C) holidays. .contracts
(D) plateaus. .slows
(E) meals. .ceases

6 Since the author's unflattering references to her friends were so ----, she was surprised that her ---- were recognized.

(A) laudatory. .styles
(B) obvious. .anecdotes
(C) oblique. .allusions
(D) critical. .eulogies
(E) apparent. .motives

7 Mark was intent on maintaining his status as first in his class; because even the smallest mistakes infuriated him, he reviewed all his papers ---- before submitting them to his teacher.

(A) explicitly   (B) perfunctorily   (C) honestly
   (D) mechanically   (E) assiduously

8 Since many disadvantaged individuals view their situations as ---- as well as intolerable, their attitudes are best described as ----.

(A) squalid. .obscure
(B) unpleasant. .bellicose
(C) acute. . sanguine
(D) immutable. .resigned
(E) political. .perplexed

9 The subtleties of this novel are evident not so much in the character ---- as they are in its profoundly ---- plot structure.

(A) assessment. .eclectic
(B) development. .trite
(C) portrayal. .aesthetic
(D) delineation. .intricate
(E) illustration. .superficial

GO ON TO THE NEXT PAGE

Each question below consists of a related pair of words or phrases, followed by five pairs of words or phrases labeled A through E. Select the pair that <u>best</u> expresses a relationship similar to that expressed in the original pair.

Example:

CRUMB : BREAD ::

(A) ounce : unit
(B) splinter : wood
(C) water : bucket
(D) twine : rope
(E) cream : butter

Ⓐ ● Ⓒ Ⓓ Ⓔ

10 SHIP : OCEAN ::

(A) fish : gill
(B) plane : air
(C) child : bath
(D) camel : water
(E) car : passengers

11 BOTANY : PLANTS ::

(A) agriculture : herbs
(B) astronomy : stars
(C) philosophy : books
(D) anthropology : religion
(E) forestry : evergreens

12 CENSUS : POPULATION ::

(A) catalog : pictures
(B) inventory : supplies
(C) detonation : explosion
(D) dictionary : words
(E) election : tally

13 CONSTELLATION : STARS ::

(A) earth : moon
(B) center : circle
(C) archipelago : islands
(D) rain : water
(E) maverick : herd

14 REFINE : OIL ::

(A) winnow : wheat
(B) harness : energy
(C) mine : coal
(D) mold : plastic
(E) conserve : resource

15 PERSPICACIOUS : INSIGHT ::

(A) zealous : mobility
(B) audacious : hearing
(C) delicious : taste
(D) avaricious : generosity
(E) amiable : friendliness

GO ON TO THE NEXT PAGE →

The passage below is followed by questions based on its content. Answer the questions on the basis of what is <u>stated</u> or <u>implied</u> in the passage and in any introductory material that may be provided.

Questions 16–21 are based on the following passage.

The following passage is an excerpt from a book by novelist Gregor von Rezzori.

Skushno is a Russian word that is difficult to translate. It means more than dreary boredom: a spiritual void that sucks you in like a vague but
Line intensely urgent longing. When I was thirteen, at a
(5) phase that educators used to call the awkward age, my parents were at their wits' end. We lived in the Bukovina, today an almost astronomically remote province in southeastern Europe. The story I am telling seems as distant—not only in space but also
(10) in time—as if I'd merely dreamed it. Yet it begins as a very ordinary story.

I had been expelled by a *consilium abeundi*—an advisory board with authority to expel unworthy students—from the schools of the then Kingdom of
(15) Rumania, whose subjects we had become upon the collapse of the Austro-Hungarian Empire after the first great war. An attempt to harmonize the imbalances in my character by means of strict discipline at a boarding school in Styria (my people
(20) still regarded Austria as our cultural homeland) nearly led to the same ignominious end, and only my pseudo-voluntary departure from the institution in the nick of time prevented my final ostracism from the privileged ranks of those for
(25) whom the path to higher education was open. Again in the jargon of those assigned the responsible task of raising children to become "useful members of society," I was a "virtually hopeless case." My parents, blind to how the
(30) contradictions within me had grown out of the highly charged difference between their own natures, agreed with the schoolmasters; the mix of neurotic sensitivity and a tendency to violence, alert perception and inability to learn, tender need for
(35) support and lack of adjustability, would only develop into something criminal.

One of the trivial aphorisms my generation owes to Wilhelm Busch's *Pious Helene* is the homily "Once your reputation's done / You can live a life of fun."
(40) But this optimistic notion results more from wishful thinking than from practical experience. In my case, had anyone asked me about my state of mind, I would have sighed and answered, "*Skushno!*" Even

though rebellious thoughts occasionally surged
(45) within me, I dragged myself, or rather I let myself be dragged, listlessly through my bleak existence in the snail's pace of days. Nor was I ever free of a sense of guilt, for my feeling guilty was not entirely foisted upon me by others; there were deep reasons
(50) I could not explain to myself; had I been able to do so, my life would have been much easier.

16 It can be inferred from the passage that the author's parents were

(A) frustrated by the author's inability to do well in school
(B) oblivious to the author's poor academic performance
(C) wealthy, making them insensitive to the needs of the poor
(D) schoolmasters who believed in the strict disciplining of youth
(E) living in Russia while their son lived in Bukovina

17 Lines 17–25 are used by the author to demonstrate that

(A) the author was an unstable and dangerous person
(B) the schools that the author attended were too difficult
(C) the tactics being used to make the author a more stable person were failing
(D) the author was not accepted well by his classmates
(E) the author's academic career was nearing an end

18 The word "ignominious" in line 21 means

(A) dangerous
(B) pitiless
(C) unappreciated
(D) disgraceful
(E) honorable

GO ON TO THE NEXT PAGE ⟹

19 In line 24, the word "ostracism" most likely means

(A) praise
(B) abuse
(C) appreciation
(D) departure
(E) banishment

20 The passage as a whole suggests that the author felt

(A) happy because he was separated from his parents
(B) upset because he was unable to maintain good friends
(C) melancholy and unsettled in his environment
(D) suicidal and desperate because of his living in Russia
(E) hopeful because he'd soon be out of school

21 The passage indicates that the author regarded the aphorism mentioned in the last paragraph with

(A) relief because it showed him that he would eventually feel better
(B) disdain because the author found it unrealistic
(C) contempt because he saw it working for others
(D) bemusement because of his immunity from it
(E) sorrow because his faith in it nearly killed him

GO ON TO THE NEXT PAGE ➡

The passage below is followed by questions based on its content. Answer the questions on the basis of what is <u>stated</u> or <u>implied</u> in the passage and in any introductory material that may be provided.

Questions 22–30 are based on the following passage.

Fear of communism swept through the United States in the years following the Russian Revolution of 1917. Several states passed espionage acts that restricted political discussion, and radicals of all descriptions were rounded up in so-called Red Raids conducted by the attorney general's office. Some were convicted and imprisoned; others were deported. This was the background of a trial in Chicago involving twenty men charged under Illinois's espionage statute with advocating the violent overthrow of the government. The charge rested on the fact that all the defendants were members of the newly formed Communist Labor party.

The accused in the case were represented by Clarence Darrow, one of the foremost defense attorneys in the country. Throughout his career, Darrow had defended the poor and the despised against exploitation and prejudice. He defended the rights of labor unions, for example, at a time when many sought to outlaw the strike, and he was resolute in defending constitutional freedoms. The following are excerpts from Darrow's summation to the jury.

Members of the Jury . . . If you want to convict these twenty men, then do it. I ask no consideration on behalf of any one of them. They are no better
Line than any other twenty men or women; they are no
(5) better than the millions down through the ages who have been prosecuted and convicted in cases like this. And if it is necessary for my clients to show that America is like all the rest, if it is necessary that my clients shall go to prison to show it, then let
(10) them go. They can afford it if you members of the jury can; make no mistake about that . . .

The State says my clients "dare to criticize the Constitution." Yet this police officer (who the State says is a fine, right-living person) twice violated the
(15) federal Constitution while a prosecuting attorney was standing by. They entered Mr. Owen's home without a search warrant. They overhauled his papers. They found a flag, a red one, which he had the same right to have in his house that you have to
(20) keep a green one, or a yellow one, or any other color, and the officer impudently rolled it up and put another flag on the wall, nailed it there. By what right was that done? What about this kind of patriotism that violates the Constitution? Has it

(25) come to pass in this country that officers of the law can trample on constitutional rights and then excuse it in a court of justice? . . .

Most of what has been presented to this jury to stir up feeling in your souls has not the slightest
(30) bearing on proving conspiracy in this case. Take Mr. Lloyd's speech in Milwaukee. It had nothing to do with conspiracy.

Whether that speech was a joke or was serious, I will not attempt to discuss. But I will say that if it
(35) was serious it was as mild as a summer's shower compared with many of the statements of those who are responsible for working conditions in this country. We have heard from people in high places that those individuals who express sympathy with
(40) labor should be stood up against a wall and shot. We have heard people of position declare that individuals who criticize the actions of those who are getting rich should be put in a cement ship with leaden sails and sent out to sea. Every violent
(45) appeal that could be conceived by the brain has been used by the powerful and the strong. I repeat, Mr. Lloyd's speech was gentle in comparison . . . .

My clients are condemned because they say in their platform that, while they vote, they believe the
(50) ballot is secondary to education and organization. Counsel suggests that those who get something they did not vote for are sinners, but I suspect you the jury know full well that my clients are right. Most of you have an eight-hour day. Did you get it
(55) by any vote you ever cast? No. It came about because workers laid down their tools and said we will no longer work until we get an eight-hour day. That is how they got the twelve-hour day, the ten-hour day, and the eight-hour day—not by voting
(60) but by laying down their tools. Then when it was over and the victory won . . . then the politicians, in order to get the labor vote, passed legislation creating an eight-hour day. That is how things changed; victory preceded law. . . .

(65) You have been told that if you acquit these defendants you will be despised because you will endorse everything they believe. But I am not here to defend my clients' opinions. I am here to defend

GO ON TO THE NEXT PAGE

their right to express their opinions. I ask you, then,
(70) to decide this case upon the facts as you have heard
them, in light of the law as you understand it, in
light of the history of our country, whose
institutions you and I are bound to protect.

22 Clarence Darrow's statement that "They can
afford it if you members of the jury can" is
most probably meant to imply that

(A) the defendants will not be harmed if
convicted
(B) if the jurors convict the defendants, they
will be harshly criticized
(C) the defendants do not care whether they
are convicted
(D) everyone involved in the trial will be
affected financially by whatever the
jury decides
(E) if the defendants are found guilty,
everyone's rights will be threatened

23 Lines 13–29 suggest that the case against
Owen would have been dismissed if the judge
had interpreted the Constitution in which of
the following ways?

(A) Defendants must have their rights read to
them when they are arrested.
(B) Giving false testimony in court is a crime.
(C) Evidence gained by illegal means is not
admissible in court.
(D) No one can be tried twice for the same
crime.
(E) Defendants cannot be forced to give
incriminating evidence against
themselves.

24 Darrow's defense in lines 28–47 relies mainly
on persuading the jury that

(A) the prosecution is using a double
standard
(B) the evidence used by the prosecution is
unreliable
(C) the defendants' views are similar to those
of the jury
(D) labor unions are guaranteed the right to
hold a strike
(E) a federal court is a more appropriate
place to try the defendants than is a
state court

25 Lines 28–47 indicate that the prosecution
attempted to characterize Mr. Lloyd's speech
as

(A) bitter sarcasm
(B) deceptive propaganda
(C) valid criticism
(D) a frightening threat
(E) a bad joke

26 What does Clarence Darrow accuse "people
in high places" (line 38) of doing?

(A) Trying to kill Communist Party members
(B) Advocating violence against labor
sympathizers
(C) Lying to the jury
(D) Encouraging the use of harsh
punishment against criminals
(E) Making foolish and insulting suggestions

27 The word "counsel" in line 51 refers to

(A) expert psychologists
(B) the prosecution
(C) an assembly
(D) a recommendation
(E) an expert

28 Lines 66–68 imply that the prosecution had
told the jury that finding for the innocence of
the defendants would be similar to

(A) denying the validity of the Constitution
(B) permitting workers to go on strike
(C) promoting passive resistance
(D) limiting freedom of expression
(E) promoting communism

GO ON TO THE NEXT PAGE ➡

29   In line 73, the word "bound" most nearly means

(A) intellectually committed
(B) personally determined
(C) morally compelled
(D) violently coerced
(E) inevitably destined

30   Darrow's defense hinges on the ability of the jurors to

(A) understand complicated legal terms and procedures
(B) sympathize with union organizers
(C) comprehend the beliefs of the Communist Labor party
(D) separate the defendants' rights from their views
(E) act in the interest of the national economy

IF YOU FINISH BEFORE TIME IS CALLED, YOU MAY CHECK YOUR WORK ON THIS SECTION ONLY. DO NOT TURN TO ANY OTHER SECTION IN THE TEST.   **STOP**

NO TEST MATERIAL ON THIS PAGE.

Time—30 Minutes	In this section solve each problem, using any available space
25 Questions	on the page for scratchwork. Then decide which is the best
	of the choices given and fill in the corresponding oval on the
	answer sheet.

Notes:

1.   The use of a calculator is permitted. All numbers used are real numbers.

2.   Figures that accompany problems in this test are intended to provide information useful in solving the problems. They are drawn as accurately as possible EXCEPT when it is stated in a specific problem that the figure is not drawn to scale. All figures lie in a plane unless otherwise indicated.

Reference Information

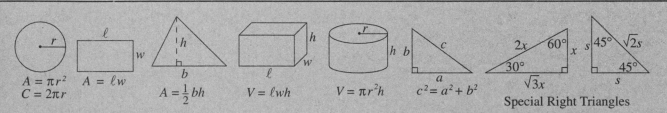

$A = \pi r^2$
$C = 2\pi r$ $A = \ell w$ $A = \frac{1}{2} bh$ $V = \ell wh$ $V = \pi r^2 h$ $c^2 = a^2 + b^2$ Special Right Triangles

The number of degrees of arc in a circle is 360.
The measure in degrees of a straight angle is 180.
The sum of the measures in degrees of the angles of a triangle is 180.

Directions for Quantitative Comparison Questions

Questions 1–15 each consist of two quantities in boxes, one in Column A and one in Column B. You are to compare the two quantities and on the answer sheet fill in oval

A if the quantity in Column A is greater;
B if the quantity in Column B is greater;
C if the two quantities are equal;
D if the relationship cannot be determined from the information given.

AN E RESPONSE WILL NOT BE SCORED.

Notes:

1. In some questions, information is given about one or both of the quantities to be compared. In such cases, the given information is centered above the two columns and is not boxed.
2. In a given question, a symbol that appears in both columns represents the same thing in Column A as it does in Column B.
3. Letters such as x, n, and k stand for real numbers.

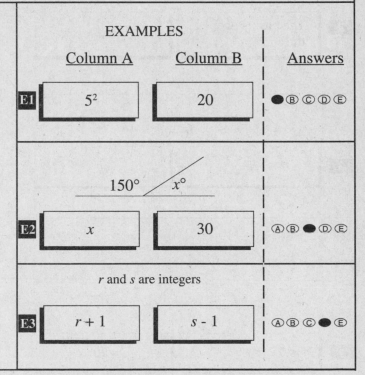

EXAMPLES

Column A	Column B	Answers
E1 5^2	20	●ⒷⒸⒹⒺ

150° $x°$

| E2 x | 30 | ⒶⒷ●ⒹⒺ |

r and s are integers

| E3 $r + 1$ | $s - 1$ | ⒶⒷⒸ●Ⓔ |

SUMMARY DIRECTIONS FOR QUANTITATIVE COMPARISON QUESTIONS

Answer: A if the quantity in Column A is greater;
         B if the quantity in Column B is greater;
         C if the two quantities are equal;
         D if the relationship cannot be determined from the information given.

AN E RESPONSE WILL NOT BE SCORED.

Column A	Column B

1 $\dfrac{3}{7}$ $\dfrac{1}{2}$

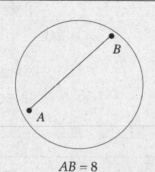

$AB = 8$

2 The radius of the circle   4

$7a > 4b$

3 a b

4 $x + y$ 90

Column A	Column B

The novelty clock above has hands that move at the correct speed, but counter-clockwise. The clock tells the correct time every 6 hours (at 6:00 and 12:00).

5 3 hours, 15 minutes   Amount of time that has passed since 12:00

$9^n - 8^n = 1^n$

6 1 n

A rectangle of area 4 has two sides of length r and s, where r and s are integers.

7 $\dfrac{r}{2}$ $2s$

GO ON TO THE NEXT PAGE →

SUMMARY DIRECTIONS FOR QUANTITATIVE COMPARISON QUESTIONS

<u>Answer:</u> A if the quantity in Column A is greater;
B if the quantity in Column B is greater;
C if the two quantities are equal;
D if the relationship cannot be determined from the information given.

AN E RESPONSE WILL NOT BE SCORED.

<u>Column A</u>	<u>Column B</u>

In a group of 28 children, there are 6 more girls than boys.

8
Two times the number of girls	Three times the number of boys

9
$\dfrac{\frac{3}{2}}{\left(\frac{3}{2}\right)^2}$	$\dfrac{2}{3}$

The area of the square is 25. Points A, B, C, and D are on the square. $ABCD$ is not a square.

10
Perimeter of the rectangle $ABCD$	20

<u>Column A</u>	<u>Column B</u>

x, y, and z are positive.
$x + y + z = 10$ and $x = y$

11
x	5

12
$\sqrt{3} + \sqrt{4}$	$\sqrt{3} \times \sqrt{4}$

13
The number of distinct prime factors of 30	The number of distinct prime factors of 60

14
x^2	$(x + 1)^2$

15
The percent increase from 99 to 100	The percent decrease from 100 to 99

GO ON TO THE NEXT PAGE

Directions for Student-Produced Response Questions

Each of the remaining 10 questions (16–25) requires you to solve the problem and enter your answer by marking the ovals in the special grid, as shown in the examples below.

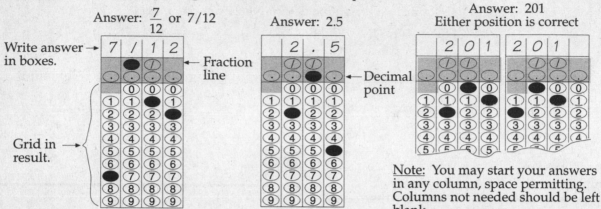

Answer: $\frac{7}{12}$ or 7/12

Answer: 2.5

Answer: 201
Either position is correct

Write answer → in boxes.

← Fraction line

← Decimal point

Grid in → result.

<u>Note:</u> You may start your answers in any column, space permitting. Columns not needed should be left blank.

- Mark no more than one oval in any column.

- Because the answer sheet will be machine-scored, **you will receive credit only if the ovals are filled in correctly.**

- Although not required, it is suggested that you write your answer in the boxes at the top of the columns to help you fill in the ovals accurately.

- Some problems may have more than one correct answer. In such cases, grid only one answer.

- No question has a negative answer.

- **Mixed numbers** such as $2\frac{1}{2}$ must be gridded as 2.5 or 5/2. (If ⌗2 1 / 2⌗ is gridded, it will be interpreted as $\frac{21}{2}$, not $2\frac{1}{2}$.)

- **Decimal Accuracy:** If you obtain a decimal answer, **enter the most accurate value the grid will accommodate.** For example, if you obtain an answer such as 0.6666 . . . , you should record the result as .666 or .667. **Less accurate values such as .66 or .67 are not acceptable.**

Acceptable ways to grid $\frac{2}{3}$ = .6666 . . .

16 If $\dfrac{x + 2x + 3x}{2} = 6$, then $x =$

17 There are 24 fish in an aquarium. If $\frac{1}{8}$ of them are tetras and $\frac{2}{3}$ of the remaining fish are guppies, how many guppies are in the aquarium?

GO ON TO THE NEXT PAGE

18 If l_1 is parallel to l_2 in the figure above, what is the value of y?

19 The daily newspaper always follows a particular format. Each even-numbered page contains 6 articles and each odd-numbered page contains 7 articles. If today's paper has 36 pages, how many articles does it contain?

20 When n is divided by 5, the remainder is 4. When n is divided by 4, the remainder is 3. If $0 < n < 100$, what is one possible value of n?

21 If $x^2 = 16$ and $y^2 = 4$, what is the greatest possible value of $(x - y)^2$?

22 Segment AB is perpendicular to segment BD. Segment AB and segment CD bisect each other at point x. If $AB = 8$ and $CD = 10$, what is the length of BD?

GO ON TO THE NEXT PAGE

23 At a music store, the price of a CD is three times the price of a cassette tape. If 40 CDs were sold for a total of $480, and the combined sales of CDs and cassette tapes totaled $600, how many cassette tapes were sold?

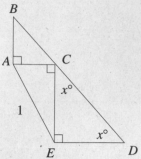

25 In the figure above, if $AE = 1$, what is the sum of the area of $\triangle ABC$ and the area of $\triangle CDE$?

24 At a certain high school, 30 students study French, 40 study Spanish, and 25 study neither. If there are 80 students in the school, how many study both French and Spanish?

IF YOU FINISH BEFORE TIME IS CALLED, YOU MAY CHECK YOUR WORK ON THIS SECTION ONLY. DO NOT TURN TO ANY OTHER SECTION IN THE TEST.　**STOP**

Time—30 Minutes
35 Questions

For each question in this section, select the best answer from among the choices given and fill in the corresponding oval on the answer sheet.

Each sentence below has one or two blanks, each blank indicating that something has been omitted. Beneath the sentence are five words or sets of words labeled A through E. Choose the word or set of words that, when inserted in the sentence, best fits the meaning of the sentence as a whole.

Example:

Medieval kingdoms did not become constitutional republics overnight; on the contrary, the change was ----.

(A) unpopular
(B) unexpected
(C) advantageous
(D) sufficient
(E) gradual

1 If it is true that morality cannot exist without religion, then does not the erosion of religion herald the ---- of morality?

(A) regulation
(B) basis
(C) belief
(D) collapse
(E) value

2 Certain animal behaviors, such as mating rituals, seem to be ----, and therefore ---- external factors such as climate changes, food supply, or the presence of other animals of the same species.

(A) learned. .immune to
(B) innate. .unaffected by
(C) intricate. .belong to
(D) specific. .confused with
(E) memorized. .controlled by

3 Shaken by two decades of virtual anarchy, the majority of people were ready to buy ---- at any price.

(A) order
(B) emancipation
(C) hope
(D) liberty
(E) enfranchisement

4 As a person who combines care with ----, Marisa completed her duties with ---- as well as zeal.

(A) levity. .resignation
(B) geniality. .ardor
(C) vitality. .willingness
(D) empathy. .rigor
(E) enthusiasm. .meticulousness

5 Her shrewd campaign managers were responsible for the fact that her political slogans were actually forgotten clichés revived and ---- with new meaning.

(A) fathomed
(B) instilled
(C) foreclosed
(D) instigated
(E) foreshadowed

6 The stoic former general led his civilian life as he had his military life, with simplicity and ---- dignity.

(A) benevolent
(B) informal
(C) austere
(D) aggressive
(E) succinct

GO ON TO THE NEXT PAGE

7 Although bound to impose the law, a judge is free to use his discretion to ---- the anachronistic barbarity of some criminal penalties.

(A) mitigate
(B) understand
(C) condone
(D) provoke
(E) enforce

8 Henry viewed Melissa to be ----; she seemed to be against any position regardless of its merits.

(A) heretical
(B) disobedient
(C) contrary
(D) inattentive
(E) harried

9 Dr. Schwartz's lecture on art, while detailed and scholarly, focused ---- on the premodern; some students may have appreciated his specialized knowledge, but those with more ---- interests may have been disappointed.

(A) literally. .medieval
(B) completely. .pedantic
(C) expansively. .technical
(D) voluminously. .creative
(E) exclusively. .comprehensive

10 Only when one actually visits the ancient ruins of marvelous bygone civilizations does one truly appreciate the sad ---- of human greatness.

(A) perspicacity
(B) magnitude
(C) artistry
(D) transience
(E) quiescence

GO ON TO THE NEXT PAGE

Each question below consists of a related pair of words or phrases, followed by five pairs of words or phrases labeled A through E. Select the pair that best expresses a relationship similar to that expressed in the original pair.

Example:

CRUMB : BREAD ::

(A) ounce : unit
(B) splinter : wood
(C) water : bucket
(D) twine : rope
(E) cream : butter

11 CAKE : DESSERT ::

(A) coach : football
(B) lawyer : jury
(C) poet : writing
(D) actor : troupe
(E) pediatrician : doctor

12 WEIGHTLIFTER : STRENGTH ::

(A) goalie : skill
(B) dancer : speed
(C) marathoner : endurance
(D) hiker : agility
(E) fisherman : luck

13 BREEZE : HURRICANE ::

(A) water : pebble
(B) gulf : coast
(C) eye : cyclone
(D) sun : cloud
(E) hill : mountain

14 IMMORTAL : DEATH ::

(A) anonymous : fame
(B) hopeless : situation
(C) vital : life
(D) indisputable : agreement
(E) daily : year

15 TAPESTRY : THREAD ::

(A) pizza : pie
(B) mosaic : tiles
(C) ruler : divisions
(D) computer : switch
(E) car : engine

16 LUBRICANT : FRICTION ::

(A) motor : electricity
(B) speed : drag
(C) insulation : heat
(D) adhesive : connection
(E) muffler : noise

17 PARODY : IMITATION ::

(A) stanza : verse
(B) limerick : poem
(C) novel : book
(D) portrait : painting
(E) riddle : puzzle

18 COMET : TAIL ::

(A) traffic : lane
(B) missile : trajectory
(C) vessel : wake
(D) engine : fuel
(E) wave : crest

GO ON TO THE NEXT PAGE

19 NEOLOGISM : LANGUAGE ::

(A) rhetoric : oratory
(B) syllogism : grammar
(C) innovation : technology
(D) iconography : art
(E) epistemology : philosophy

20 ADDENDUM : BOOK ::

(A) signature : letter
(B) vote : constitution
(C) codicil : will
(D) heading : folder
(E) stipulation : contract

21 PENCHANT : INCLINED ::

(A) loathing : contemptuous
(B) abhorrence : delighted
(C) burgeoning : barren
(D) loss : incessant
(E) decision : predictable

22 VAGRANT : DOMICILE ::

(A) pagan : morals
(B) despot : leadership
(C) arsonist : fire
(D) exile : country
(E) telephone : ear

23 MERITORIOUS : PRAISE ::

(A) captious : criticism
(B) kind : admiration
(C) questionable : response
(D) reprehensible : censure
(E) incredible : ecstasy

GO ON TO THE NEXT PAGE

The passages below is followed by questions based on its content. Answer the questions on the basis of what is <u>stated</u> or <u>implied</u> in the passage and in any introductory material that may be provided.

Questions 24–35 are based on the following passage.

The following passage is from a book written by a zoologist and published in 1986.

The domestic cat is a contradiction. No other
animal has developed such an intimate relationship
with humanity, while at the same time demanding
Line and getting such independent movement and action.
(5)   The cat manages to remain a tame animal because
of the sequence of its upbringing. By living both
with other cats (its mother and littermates) and with
humans (the family that has adopted it) during its
infancy and kittenhood, it becomes attached to and
(10) considers that it belongs to both species. It is like a
child that grows up in a foreign country and as a
consequence becomes bilingual. The young cat
becomes bimental. It may be a cat physically but
mentally it is both feline and human. Once it is fully
(15) adult, however, most of its responses are feline ones,
and it has only one major reaction to its human
owners. It treats them as pseudoparents. The reason
is that they took over from the real mother at a
sensitive stage of the kitten's development and went
(20) on giving it milk, solid food, and comfort as it grew
up.
     This is rather different from the kind of bond that
develops between human and dog. The dog sees its
human owners as pseudoparents, as does the cat.
(25) On that score the process of attachment is similar.
But the dog has an additional link. Canine society is
group-organized; feline society is not. Dogs live in
packs with tightly controlled status relationships
among the individuals. There are top dogs, middle
(30) dogs, and bottom dogs and under natural
circumstances they move around together, keeping
tabs on one another the whole time. So the adult pet
dog sees its human family both as pseudoparents
and as the dominant members of the pack, hence its
(35) renowned reputation for obedience and its
celebrated capacity for loyalty. Cats do have a
complex social organization, but they never hunt in
packs. In the wild, most of their day is spent in
solitary stalking. Going for a walk with a human,
(40) therefore, has no appeal for them. And as for
"coming to heel" and learning to "sit" and "stay,"
they are simply not interested. Such maneuvers have
no meaning for them.

     So the moment a cat manages to persuade a
(45) human being to open a door (that most hated of
human inventions), it is off and away without a
backward glance. As it crosses the threshold, the cat
becomes transformed. The kitten-of-human brain is
switched off and the wildcat brain is clicked on. The
(50) dog, in such a situation, may look back to see if its
human packmate is following to join in the fun of
exploring, but not the cat. The cat's mind has floated
off into another, totally feline world, where strange
bipedal* primates have no place.
(55)   Because of this difference between domestic cats
and domestic dogs, cat-lovers tend to be rather
different from dog-lovers. As a rule cat-lovers have a
stronger personality bias toward working alone,
independent of the larger group. Artists like cats;
(60) soldiers like dogs. The much-lauded "group loyalty"
phenomenon is alien to both cats and cat-lovers. If
you are a company person, a member of the gang, or
a person picked for the squad, the chances are that at
home there is no cat curled up in front of the fire.
(65) The ambitious Yuppie, the aspiring politician, the
professional athlete, these are not typical cat-owners.
It is hard to picture football players with cats in their
laps—much easier to envisage them taking their
dogs for walks.
(70)   Those who have studied cat-owners and dog-
owners as two distinct groups report that there is
also a gender bias. The majority of cat-lovers are
female. This bias is not surprising in view of the
division of labor evident in the development of
(75) human societies. Prehistoric males became
specialized as group-hunters, while the females
concentrated on food-gathering and childbearing.
This difference contributed to a human male "pack
mentality" that is far less marked in females.
(80) Wolves, the wild ancestors of domestic dogs, also
became pack-hunters, so the modern dog has much
more in common with the human male than with
the human female.
     The argument will always go on—feline self-
(85) sufficiency and individualism versus canine
camaraderie and good-fellowship. But it is
important to stress that in making a valid point I
have caricatured the two positions. In reality there

bipedal: having two feet

GO ON TO THE NEXT PAGE →

are many people who enjoy equally the company of
(90) both cats and dogs. And all of us, or nearly all of us,
have both feline and canine elements in our
personalities. We have moods when we want to be
alone and thoughtful, and other times when we
wish to be in the center of a crowded, noisy room.

24 The primary purpose of the passage is to

(A) show the enmity that exists between cats
and dogs

(B) advocate dogs as making better pets than
cats

(C) distinguish the different characteristics of
dogs and cats

(D) show the inferiority of dogs because of
their dependent nature

(E) emphasize the role that human society
plays in the personalities of domestic
pets

25 According to the passage, the domestic cat
can be described as

(A) a biped because it possesses the
characteristics of animals with two feet

(B) a pseudopet because it can't really be
tamed and will always retain its wild
habits

(C) a contradiction because although it lives
comfortably with humans, it refuses to
be dominated by them

(D) a soldier because it is militant about
preserving its independence

(E) a ruler because although it plays the part
of a pet, it really dominates humans

26 In line 17 the word "pseudoparents" means

(A) part-time parents that are only partially
involved with their young

(B) individuals who act as parents of adults

(C) parents that neglect their young

(D) parents that have both the characteristics
of humans and their pets

(E) adoptive parents who aren't related to
their young

27 The author suggests that an important
difference between dogs and cats is that,
unlike dogs, cats

(A) do not regard their owners as the leader
of their social group

(B) obey mainly because of their obedient
nature

(C) have a more creative nature

(D) do not have complex social organizations

(E) are not skilled hunters

28 It can be inferred from the passage that the
social structure of dogs is

(A) flexible

(B) abstract

(C) hierarchical

(D) male dominated

(E) somewhat exclusive

29 Lines 39–43 are used to stress

(A) the laziness of cats that keeps them from
being pack animals

(B) the ignorance of dogs, which makes them
more obedient pets

(C) the antipathy that cats feel for humans

(D) a difference between cats and dogs that
emphasizes the independent nature of
cats

(E) the stubborn and complacent disposition
of cats

30 In line 60, "much-lauded" means

(A) vehemently argued

(B) overly discussed

(C) unnecessarily complicated

(D) typically controversial

(E) commonly praised

31 The "ambitious Yuppie" mentioned in line 65
is an example of a person

(A) who is power hungry

(B) who craves virtue

(C) who is a stereotypical pet-owner

(D) who has a weak personality

(E) who seeks group-oriented status

GO ON TO THE NEXT PAGE ⟶

32 Paragraph 6 indicates that human females

(A) are more like dogs than cats
(B) developed independent roles that didn't require group behavior
(C) had to gather food because they were not strong enough to hunt
(D) are not good owners for the modern dog
(E) were negatively affected by the division of labor of human societies

33 The author uses lines 84–88 to

(A) show that the argument stated in the passage is ultimately futile
(B) disclaim glaring contradictions that are stated in the passage
(C) qualify the generalizations used to make the author's point
(D) ensure that the reader doesn't underestimate the crux of the passage
(E) highlight a difference between individualism and dependency

34 The last four sentences in the passage (lines 86–94) provide

(A) an example of the argument that has been made earlier
(B) a summary of the points made earlier
(C) a reason for the statements made earlier
(D) a modification of the position taken earlier
(E) a rebuttal to opposing views referred to earlier

35 The passage as a whole does all of the following EXCEPT

(A) use a statistic
(B) make parenthetic statements
(C) use a simile
(D) restate an argument
(E) make a generalization

NO TEST MATERIAL ON THIS PAGE.

Time—30 Minutes
25 Questions

In this section solve each problem, using any available space on the page for scratchwork. Then decide which is the best of the choices given and fill in the corresponding oval on the answer sheet.

Notes:

1.　The use of a calculator is permitted. All numbers used are real numbers.

2.　Figures that accompany problems in this test are intended to provide information useful in solving the problems. They are drawn as accurately as possible EXCEPT when it is stated in a specific problem that the figure is not drawn to scale. All figures lie in a plane unless otherwise indicated.

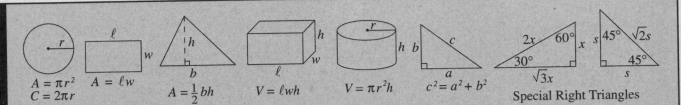

$$A = \pi r^2 \qquad A = \ell w \qquad A = \frac{1}{2}bh \qquad V = \ell w h \qquad V = \pi r^2 h \qquad c^2 = a^2 + b^2$$
$$C = 2\pi r$$

Special Right Triangles

The number of degrees of arc in a circle is 360.
The measure in degrees of a straight angle is 180.
The sum of the measures in degrees of the angles of a triangle is 180.

1　If $2 + a = 2 - a$, then $a =$

(A)　−1
(B)　0
(C)　1
(D)　2
(E)　4

2　In which of the following patterns is the number of horizontal lines three times the number of vertical lines?

(A) 　(B) 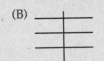　(C)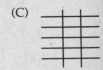

(D) 　(E)

GO ON TO THE NEXT PAGE

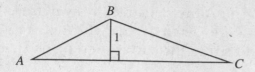

3 If $AC = 4$, what is the area of $\triangle ABC$ above?

(A) $\dfrac{1}{2}$

(B) 2

(C) $\sqrt{7}$

(D) 4

(E) 8

4 If $\dfrac{4}{5}$ of $\dfrac{3}{4} = \dfrac{2}{5}$ of $\dfrac{x}{4}$, then $x =$

(A) 12

(B) 6

(C) 3

(D) $\dfrac{3}{2}$

(E) 1

5 If $x + y = z$ and $x = y$, then all of the following are true EXCEPT

(A) $2x + 2y = 2z$

(B) $x - y = 0$

(C) $x - z = y - z$

(D) $x = \dfrac{z}{2}$

(E) $z - y = 2x$

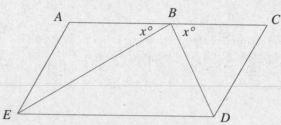

Note: Figure not drawn to scale.

6 In the figure above, $AC \parallel ED$. If the length of $BD = 3$, what is the length of BE?

(A) 3
(B) 4
(C) 5
(D) $3\sqrt{3}$
(E) It cannot be determined from the information given.

GO ON TO THE NEXT PAGE

7 $\frac{900}{10} + \frac{90}{100} + \frac{9}{1000} =$

(A) 90.09
(B) 90.099
(C) 90.909
(D) 99.09
(E) 999

8 Fifteen percent of the coins in a piggy bank are nickels and 5% are dimes. If there are 220 coins in the bank, how many are <u>not</u> nickels or dimes?

(A)   80
(B) 176
(C) 180
(D) 187
(E) 200

9 In the figure above, the perimeter of square A is $\frac{2}{3}$ the perimeter of square B, and the perimeter of square B is $\frac{2}{3}$ the perimeter of square C. If the area of square A is 16, what is the area of square C?

(A) 24
(B) 36
(C) 64
(D) 72
(E) 81

10 A bakery uses a special flour mixture that contains corn, wheat, and rye in the ratio of 3:5:2. If a bag of the mixture contains 5 pounds of rye, how many pounds of wheat does it contain?

(A)   2
(B)   5
(C)   7.5
(D) 10
(E) 12.5

GO ON TO THE NEXT PAGE

11 If $a^2b = 12^2$, and b is an odd integer, then a could be divisible by all of the following EXCEPT

(A)   3
(B)   4
(C)   6
(D)   9
(E)   12

12 A coin was flipped 20 times and came up heads 10 times and tails 10 times. If the first and last flips were both heads, what is the greatest number of consecutive heads that could have occurred?

(A)   1
(B)   2
(C)   8
(D)   9
(E)   10

13 If l_1 is parallel to l_2 in the figure above, what is the value of x?

(A)   20
(B)   50
(C)   70
(D)   80
(E)   90

14 Which of the following must be true?

   I.   The sum of two consecutive integers is odd.
  II.   The sum of three consecutive integers is even.
 III.   The sum of three consecutive integers is a multiple of 3.

(A)   I only
(B)   II only
(C)   I and II only
(D)   I and III only
(E)   I, II, and III

GO ON TO THE NEXT PAGE

15   Which of the following is equal to .064?

(A) $\left(\dfrac{1}{80}\right)^2$

(B) $\left(\dfrac{8}{100}\right)^2$

(C) $\left(\dfrac{1}{8}\right)^2$

(D) $\left(\dfrac{2}{5}\right)^3$

(E) $\left(\dfrac{8}{10}\right)^3$

16   If the average (arithmetic mean) of four distinct positive integers is 11, what is the greatest possible value of any one of the integers?

(A)   35
(B)   38
(C)   40
(D)   41
(E)   44

For $x = 0$, $x = 1$, and $x = 2$,
Set A = $\{x, \ x + 3, \ 3x, \ x^2\}$.

17   What is the mode of Set A?

(A)   0
(B)   1
(C)   2
(D)   2.5
(E)   3

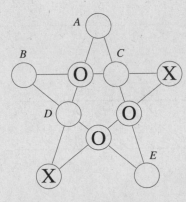

18   If the figure above is filled in so that each row of four circles contains two circles marked with an X and two circles marked with an O, which circle must be marked with an X?

(A) A
(B) B
(C) C
(D) D
(E) E

GO ON TO THE NEXT PAGE

19 If c is positive, what percent of $3c$ is 9?

(A) $\dfrac{c}{100}\%$

(B) $\dfrac{c}{3}\%$

(C) $\dfrac{9}{c}\%$

(D) 3%

(E) $\dfrac{300}{c}\%$

21 S is the set of all positive numbers n such that $n < 100$ and $\sqrt{n}$ is an integer. What is the median value of the members of set S?

(A) 5
(B) 5.5
(C) 25
(D) 50
(E) 99

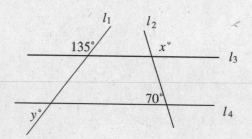

Note: Figure not drawn to scale.

20 If four lines intersect as shown in the figure above, $x + y =$

(A) 65
(B) 110
(C) 155
(D) 205
(E) It cannot be determined from the information given.

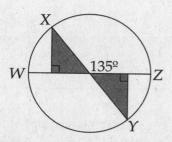

22 If segment WZ and segment XY are diameters with lengths of 12, what is the area of the shaded region?

(A) 36
(B) 30
(C) 18
(D) 12
(E) 9

GO ON TO THE NEXT PAGE

23 At the beginning of 1992, the population of Rockville was 204,000 and the population of Springfield was 216,000. If the population of each city increased by exactly 20% in 1992, how many more people lived in Springfield than in Rockville at the end of 1992?

(A)   9,600
(B) 10,000
(C) 12,000
(D) 14,400
(E) 20,000

24 Line A has a slope of $-\dfrac{3}{2}$. If points $(-2, 6)$ and $(m, -9)$ are on line A, then $m =$

(A)   3
(B)   4
(C)   6
(D)   8
(E) 12

25 A researcher found that a certain student's score on each of a series of tests could be predicted using the formula

$$P = \frac{310T + (LT)^2}{100}$$

where P is the number of points scored on the test, T is the number of hours spent studying, L is the number of hours of sleep the night before the test, and where $P \leq 100$. If, before a particular test, this student spent no more than 10 hours studying, what is the least number of hours of sleep she should get if she wants to score at least 80 points?

(A)   6
(B)   7
(C) $\sqrt{56}$
(D)   8
(E) $\sqrt{69}$

IF YOU FINISH BEFORE TIME IS CALLED, YOU MAY CHECK YOUR WORK ON THIS SECTION ONLY. DO NOT TURN TO ANY OTHER SECTION IN THE TEST.

STOP

NO TEST MATERIAL ON THIS PAGE.

Time—15 Minutes
13 Questions

For each question in this section, select the best answer from among the choices given and fill in the corresponding oval on the answer sheet.

The two passages below are followed by questions based on their content and on the relationship between the two passages. Answer the questions on the basis of what is <u>stated</u> or <u>implied</u> in the passage and in any introductory material that may be provided.

Questions 1–13 are based on the following passages.

In passage 1, the author presents his view of the early years of the silent film industry. In passage 2, the author draws on her experiences as a mime to generalize about her art. (A mime is a performer who, without speaking, entertains through gesture, facial expression, and movement.)

Passage 1

Talk to those people who first saw films when they were silent, and they will tell you the experience was magic. The silent film had
Line extraordinary powers to draw members of an
(5) audience into the story, and an equally potent capacity to make their imaginations work. It required the audience to become engaged—to supply voices and sound effects. The audience was the final, creative contributor to the process of
(10) making a film.

The finest films of the silent era depended on two elements that we can seldom provide today—a large and receptive audience and a well-orchestrated score. For the audience, the fusion of
(15) picture and live music added up to more than the sum of the respective parts.

The one word that sums up the attitude of the silent filmmakers is *enthusiasm*, conveyed most strongly before formulas took shape and when
(20) there was more room for experimentation. This enthusiastic uncertainty often resulted in such accidental discoveries as new camera or editing techniques. Some films experimented with players; the 1915 film *Regeneration*, for example, by using
(25) real gangsters and streetwalkers, provided startling local color. Other films, particularly those of Thomas Ince, provided tragic endings as often as films by other companies supplied happy ones.

Unfortunately, the vast majority of silent films
(30) survive today in inferior prints that no longer reflect the care that the original technicians put into them. The modern versions of silent films may appear jerky and flickery, but the vast picture palaces did not attract four to six thousand people a night by
(35) giving them eyestrain. A silent film depended on its visuals; as soon as you degrade those, you lose elements that go far beyond the image on the surface. The acting in silents was often very subtle, very restrained, despite legends to the contrary.

Passage 2

(40) Mime opens up a new world to the beholder, but it does so insidiously, not by purposely injecting points of interest in the manner of a tour guide. Audiences are not unlike visitors to a foreign land who discover that the modes, manners, and
(45) thoughts of its inhabitants are not meaningless oddities, but are sensible in context.

I remember once when an audience seemed perplexed at what I was doing. At first, I tried to gain a more immediate response by using slight
(50) exaggerations. I soon realized that these actions had nothing to do with the audience's understanding of the character. What I had believed to be a failure of the audience to respond in the manner I expected was, in fact, only their concentration on what I was
(55) doing; they were enjoying a gradual awakening—a slow transference of their understanding from their own time and place to one that appeared so unexpectedly before their eyes. This was evidenced by their growing response to succeeding numbers.
(60) Mime is an elusive art, as its expression is entirely dependent on the ability of the performer to imagine a character and to re-create that character for each performance. As a mime, I am a physical medium, the instrument upon which the figures of
(65) my imagination play their dance of life. The individuals in my audience also have responsibilities—they must be alert collaborators.

GO ON TO THE NEXT PAGE

They cannot sit back, mindlessly complacent, and wait to have their emotions titillated by mesmeric (70) musical sounds or visual rhythms or acrobatic feats, or by words that tell them what to think. Mime is an art that, paradoxically, appeals both to those who respond instinctively to entertainment and to those whose appreciation is more analytical and complex. (75) Between these extremes lie those audiences conditioned to resist any collaboration with what is played before them; and these the mime must seduce despite themselves. There is only one way to attack those reluctant minds—take them unaware! (80) They will be delighted at an unexpected pleasure.

1   Lines 14–16 of passage 1 indicate that

(A) music was the most important element of silent films

(B) silent films rely on a combination of music and image in affecting an audience

(C) the importance of music in silent film has been overestimated

(D) live music compensated for the poor quality of silent film images

(E) no film can succeed without a receptive audience

2   The "formulas" mentioned in line 19 of the passage most probably refer to

(A) movie theaters

(B) use of real characters

(C) standardized film techniques

(D) the fusion of disparate elements

(E) contemporary events

3   The author uses the phrase "enthusiastic uncertainty" in line 21 to suggest that the filmmakers were

(A) excited to be experimenting in an undefined area

(B) delighted at the opportunity to study new acting formulas

(C) optimistic in spite of the obstacles that faced them

(D) eager to challenge existing conventions

(E) eager to please but unsure of what the public wanted

4   The author uses the phrase "but the . . . eyestrain" (lines 33–35) in order to

(A) indicate his disgust with the incompetence of early film technicians

(B) suggest that audiences today perceive silent films incorrectly

(C) convey his regret about the decline of the old picture palaces

(D) highlight the pitfalls of the silent movie era

(E) argue for the superiority of modern film technology over that of silent movies

5   The word "legends" in line 39 most nearly means

(A) arguments

(B) symbolism

(C) propaganda

(D) movie stars

(E) misconceptions

6   The last sentence of passage 1 implies that

(A) the stars of silent movies have been criticized for overacting

(B) many silent film actors became legends in their own time

(C) silent film techniques should be studied by filmmakers today

(D) visual effects defined the silent film

(E) many silent films that exist today are of poor quality

7   The word "restrained" (line 39) most nearly means

(A) sincere

(B) dramatic

(C) understated

(D) inexpressive

(E) consistent

GO ON TO THE NEXT PAGE →

8 The author mentions the incident in lines 47–59 in order to imply that

(A) the audience's lack of response was a positive sign and reflected their captivated interest in the performance

(B) she was forced to resort to stereotypes in order to reach an audience that was otherwise unattainable

(C) exaggeration is an essential part of mime because it allows the forums used to be fully expressed

(D) her audience, though not initially appearing knowledgeable, had a good understanding of the subtlety of mime

(E) although vocalization is not necessary in mime, it is sometimes helpful for slower audiences

9 Lines 47–59 indicate that the author of passage 2 and the silent filmmakers of passage 1 were similar because

(A) neither used many props

(B) both conveyed universal truths by using sophisticated technology

(C) for both, trial and error was a part of the learning process

(D) both used visual effects and dialogue

(E) both had a loyal following

10 The sentence "As a . . . life" (lines 63–65) suggests that the author of passage 2 feels mimes

(A) cannot control the way audiences interpret their characters

(B) must suspend their own identities in order to successfully portray their characters

(C) have to resist outside attempts to define their acting style

(D) should focus on important events in the lives of specific characters

(E) know the limitations of performances that do not incorporate either music or speech

11 Which of the following pieces of information makes mime and silent film seem less similar?

(A) Vaudeville and theatrical presentations were also popular forms of entertainment during the silent film era.

(B) Silent films presented both fictional drama and factual information.

(C) Silent film sometimes relied on captions to convey dialogue to the audience.

(D) Musicians working in movie theaters were usually employed for long periods of time.

(E) Many of the characters in silent films gained wide popularity among moviegoers.

12 Passages 1 and 2 are similar in that both are mainly concerned with

(A) the use of special effects

(B) differences among dramatic styles

(C) the visual aspects of performance

(D) the suspension of disbelief in audiences

(E) nostalgia for a bygone era

13 Which of the following is an element that figures in the success of the dramatic arts described in both passages?

(A) A successful combination of different dramatic styles

(B) The exaggeration of certain aspects of a character

(C) The incorporation of current events in the narrative

(D) High audience attendance

(E) The active participation of the audience

IF YOU FINISH BEFORE TIME IS CALLED, YOU MAY CHECK YOUR WORK ON THIS SECTION ONLY. DO NOT TURN TO ANY OTHER SECTION IN THE TEST. **STOP**

NO TEST MATERIAL ON THIS PAGE.

Time—15 Minutes
10 Questions

In this section solve each problem, using any available space on the page for scratchwork. Then decide which is the best of the choices given and fill in the corresponding oval on the answer sheet.

Notes:

1. The use of a calculator is permitted. All numbers used are real numbers.

2. Figures that accompany problems in this test are intended to provide information useful in solving the problems. They are drawn as accurately as possible EXCEPT when it is stated in a specific problem that the figure is not drawn to scale. All figures lie in a plane unless otherwise indicated.

Reference Information

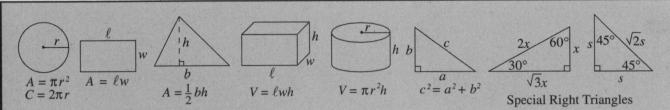

$A = \pi r^2$
$C = 2\pi r$
$A = \ell w$
$A = \frac{1}{2}bh$
$V = \ell wh$
$V = \pi r^2 h$
$c^2 = a^2 + b^2$
Special Right Triangles

The number of degrees of arc in a circle is 360.
The measure in degrees of a straight angle is 180.
The sum of the measures in degrees of the angles of a triangle is 180.

Price of Buttons in Store X	
Color	**Price**
Black	$2 per 5 buttons
Blue	$2 per 6 buttons
Brown	$3 per 8 buttons
Orange	$4 per 12 buttons
Red	$4 per 7 buttons

1   In Store X, which color button costs the most per individual unit?

(A) Black
(B) Blue
(C) Brown
(D) Orange
(E) Red

2   Which of the following numbers can be written in the form $6K + 1$, where K is a positive integer?

(A) 70
(B) 71
(C) 72
(D) 73
(E) 74

GO ON TO THE NEXT PAGE

3　$\left(\dfrac{4}{5} \times 3\right)\left(\dfrac{3}{4} \times 5\right)\left(\dfrac{5}{3} \times 4\right) =$

(A)　1
(B)　3
(C)　6
(D)　20
(E)　60

4　For which of the following values of x is $\dfrac{x^2}{x^3}$ the LEAST?

(A)　1
(B)　−1
(C)　−2
(D)　−3
(E)　−4

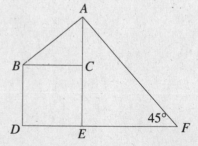

5　If the area of square $BCED = 25$, and the area of $\triangle ABC = 10$, what is the length of EF?

(A)　7
(B)　8
(C)　9
(D)　10
(E)　14

6　The Wilsons drove 450 miles in each direction to Grandmother's house and back again. If their car gets 25 miles per gallon and their cost for gasoline was $1.25 per gallon for the trip to Grandmother's but $1.50 per gallon for the return trip, how much <u>more</u> money did they spend for gasoline returning from Grandmother's than they spent going to Grandmother's?

(A)　$2.25
(B)　$4.50
(C)　$6.25
(D)　$9.00
(E)　$27.00

7　If the average measure of two angles in a parallelogram is $y°$, what is the average degree measure of the other two angles?

(A)　$180 - y$

(B)　$180 - \dfrac{y}{2}$

(C)　$360 - 2y$

(D)　$360 - y$

(E)　y

GO ON TO THE NEXT PAGE

8   A swimming pool with a capacity of 36,000 gallons originally contained 9,000 gallons of water. At 10:00 A.M. water begins to flow in at a constant rate. If the pool is exactly three-fourths full at 1:00 P.M. on the same day and the water continues to flow in at the same rate, what is the earliest time the pool will be completely full?

(A) 1:40 P.M.
(B) 2:00 P.M.
(C) 2:30 P.M.
(D) 3:00 P.M.
(E) 3:30 P.M.

9   On a map, 1 centimeter represents 6 kilometers. A square on the map with a perimeter of 16 centimeters represents a region with what <u>area</u>?

(A)   64 km²
(B)   96 km²
(C)   256 km²
(D)   576 km²
(E)   8,216 km²

10   If $4 < a < 7 < b < 9$, then which of the following best defines $\frac{a}{b}$?

(A) $\frac{4}{9} < \frac{a}{b} < 1$

(B) $\frac{4}{9} < \frac{a}{b} < \frac{7}{9}$

(C) $\frac{4}{7} < \frac{a}{b} < \frac{7}{9}$

(D) $\frac{4}{7} < \frac{a}{b} < 1$

(E) $\frac{4}{7} < \frac{a}{b} < \frac{9}{7}$

IF YOU FINISH BEFORE TIME IS CALLED, YOU MAY CHECK YOUR WORK ON THIS SECTION ONLY. DO NOT TURN TO ANY OTHER SECTION IN THE TEST.   **STOP**

NO TEST MATERIAL ON THIS PAGE.

DIAGNOSTIC I TEST ANSWERS

Section 1	Section 2	Section 3	Section 4	Section 5	Section 6	Section 7
1. C	1. B	1. B	1. D	1. B	1. B	1. E
2. C	2. B	2. A	2. B	2. D	2. C	2. D
3. C	3. A	3. D	3. A	3. B	3. A	3. E
4. E	4. A	4. C	4. E	4. B	4. B	4. B
5. D	5. D	5. B	5. B	5. E	5. E	5. C
6. B	6. C	6. C	6. C	6. A	6. A	6. B
7. A	7. E	7. D	7. A	7. C	7. C	7. A
8. E	8. D	8. A	8. C	8. B	8. A	8. C
9. E	9. D	9. C	9. E	9. E	9. C	9. D
10. A	10. B	10. B	10. D	10. E	10. B	10. A
11. A	11. B	11. B	11. E	11. D	11. C	
12. B	12. B	12. A	12. C	12. D	12. C	
13. B	13. C	13. C	13. E	13. C	13. E	
14. D	14. A	14. D	14. A	14. D		
15. E	15. E	15. A	15. B	15. D		
16. A	16. A	16. 2	16. E	16. B		
17. C	17. C	17. 14	17. B	17. A		
18. E	18. D	18. 145	18. C	18. E		
19. B	19. E	19. 234	19. C	19. D		
20. C	20. C	20. 19, 39,	20. C	20. C		
21. B	21. B	59, 79,	21. A	21. C		
22. A	22. E	or 99	22. D	22. C		
23. C	23. C	21. 36	23. D	23. D		
24. D	24. A	22. 3	24. C	24. D		
25. E	25. D	23. 30	25. C	25. B		
	26. B	24. 15	26. E			
	27. B	25. 1/2 or	27. A			
	28. E	.5	28. C			
	29. C		29. D			
	30. D		30. E			
			31. E			
			32. B			
			33. C			
			34. D			
			35. C			

You will find a detailed explanation for each question beginning on page 407.

HOW TO SCORE YOUR DIAGNOSTIC TEST

VERBAL

After you have checked your answers to the diagnostic test against the key, you can calculate your score. For the three verbal sections (sections 2, 4, and 6), tally up the number of correct answers and the number of incorrect answers. Enter these numbers on the worksheet on the opposite page. Multiply the number of incorrect answers by $\frac{1}{4}$ and subtract the result from the number of correct answers. Put this number in box A. Then round the numbers to the nearest whole number and place it in box B.

MATHEMATICS

Figuring your math score is a little trickier, because some of the questions have five answer choices, some have four, and some have none. In sections 1 and 7, count the number of correct answers and incorrect answers. Enter these numbers on the worksheet. Multiply the number of incorrect answers by $\frac{1}{4}$ and subtract this from the number of correct answers. Put the result in box C.

Count the number of correct and incorrect answers in section 3, questions 1–15. (Choice E counts as a blank.) Enter these on the worksheet. Multiply the number of incorrect answers by $\frac{1}{3}$ and subtract this from the number of correct answers in section 3. Put the result in box D.

Count up the number of correct answers in section 3, questions 16–25. Put the result in box E. There is no penalty for incorrect Grid-In questions.

Note: Section 5 is experimental and should not be scored.

Add up the numbers in boxes C, D, and E, and write the result in box F.

Round F to the nearest whole number, and place the result in box G.

WORKSHEET FOR CALCULATING YOUR SCORE

VERBAL

	Correct	Incorrect	
A. Sections 2, 4, and 6	_____	– (1/4 × _____) =	[___] A
B. Total rounded verbal raw score			[___] B

MATHEMATICS

	Correct	Incorrect	
C. Sections 1 and 7	_____	– (1/4 × _____) =	[___] C
D. Section 3 (Questions 1–15)	_____	– (1/3 × _____) =	[___] D
E. Section 3 (Questions 16–25)	_____	=	[___] E
F. Total unrounded math raw score (C + D + E)			[___] F
G. Total rounded math raw score			[___] G

Use the table on the next page to convert your raw score to scaled scores. For example, a raw score verbal score of 39 corresponds to verbal scaled score of 530; a math raw score of 24 corresponds to a math scaled score of 470.

Scores on the SAT range from 200 to 800.

Note: Since Section 5 is the experimental section it does not count toward your score.

SCORE CONVERSION TABLE

Raw Score	Verbal Scaled Score	Math Scaled Score	Raw Score	Verbal Scaled Scored	Math Scaled Score
78	800		36	510	560
77	800		35	510	550
76	800		34	500	540
75	800		33	490	530
74	780		32	480	520
73	760		31	480	520
72	750		30	470	510
71	740		29	460	500
70	740		28	460	490
69	730		27	450	480
68	720		26	450	480
67	710		25	440	480
66	700		24	430	470
65	690		23	430	460
64	680		22	420	450
63	670		21	410	440
62	670		20	400	430
61	660		19	390	430
60	660	800	18	380	430
59	650	790	17	380	420
58	640	770	16	370	410
57	640	760	15	360	400
56	630	740	14	350	390
55	620	730	13	350	390
54	620	720	12	340	380
53	610	700	11	330	370
52	600	690	10	310	350
51	600	680	9	300	340
50	600	660	8	290	340
49	590	650	7	270	330
48	590	650	6	270	310
47	580	640	5	230	300
46	570	630	4	230	300
45	570	620	3	230	280
44	560	610	2	230	260
43	560	600	1	230	250
42	550	600	0	230	240
41	550	590	−1	230	220
40	540	580	−2	230	220
39	530	570	−3	230	200
38	530	560	−4	230	200
37	520	560	−5 and below	230	200

18

Explanations I

What follows is a detailed explanation for each question in our diagnostic test I. Although you will naturally be more curious about the questions you got wrong, don't forget to read the explanations for the questions you left blank. In fact, you should even read the explanations for the questions you got right! Our explanations present the safest, most direct solution to each question. Even though you may have gotten a question right, that does not mean you solved it in the most efficient way.

SECTION 1

QUESTIONS	EXPLANATIONS

1 If $9b = 81$, then $3 \times 3b =$

(A) 9
(B) 27
(C) 81
(D) 243
(E) 729

1. Jim's answer is C.
    This question actually has a one-step solution. It isn't necessary to solve for b first, because the question is actually asking for the value of $3 \times 3b$, which equals $9b$. The question has already told you that $9b = 81$.

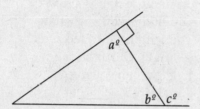

2 In the figure above, what is the sum of $a + b + c$?

(A) 180
(B) 240
(C) 270
(D) 360
(E) It cannot be determined from the information given.

2. Jim's answer is C.
    The number of degrees in a line is 180. Therefore, $b + c = 180$. And since $a + 90 = 180$, $a = 90$. So $a + b + c = 270$.

SECTION 1

3 $\dfrac{0.5 + 0.5 + 0.5 + 0.5}{4} =$

(A) 0.05
(B) 0.125
(C) 0.5
(D) 1
(E) 2.0

3. Jim's answer is C.

Here again, as with question 1, the "slow" way to solve the question would be to do the arithmetic on your calculator. The sum of the numerator is 2, divided by 4, which equals $\dfrac{1}{2}$ or 0.5. The point of the question was to see if you noticed that four equivalent decimals on top divided by 4 equals the decimal itself. Therefore, $\dfrac{4(0.5)}{4} = 0.5$.

4 Steve ran a 12-mile race at an average speed of 8 miles per hour. If Adam ran the same race at an average speed of 6 miles per hour, how many minutes longer than Steve did Adam take to complete the race?

(A)   9
(B) 12
(C) 16
(D) 24
(E) 30

4. Jim's answer is E.

Use the formula for distance: *distance = rate × time*. Steve runs 12 miles at 8 miles per hour, which means that he runs for $1\dfrac{1}{2}$ hours. (Or 1.5 hours, if you're using your calculator). Adam runs the same 12 miles at 6 miles per hour, which means that he runs for 2 hours. Adam takes half an hour longer to complete the race, and half an hour is 30 minutes.

SECTION 1

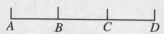

Note: Figure not drawn to scale.

5 If $AB > CD$, which of the following must be true?

   I. $AB > BC$
   II. $AC > BD$
   III. $AC > CD$

   (A) I only
   (B) II only
   (C) III only
   (D) II and III only
   (E) I, II, and III

5. Jim's answer is D.

You should have noticed several things about this question. First, that the figure was not drawn to scale. So a good first step would be to redraw the figure to comply with the condition ($AB > CD$). Second, the question asks for which of the following *must* be true. *Must* is an important word—which of the following *could* be true would change your analysis completely. So, redrawing the figure, you'd get something like this:

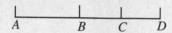

In this figure, AB is clearly larger than CD. Since plugging in numbers makes the distance more concrete, you might have made $AB = 3$, for example, and $CD = 2$. Since you don't know the length of BD, however, you'd have to leave it alone. Now, let's check the conditions. Option I: Well, this could be true, but it doesn't have to be. So Option I is out. This allows us to eliminate choices A and E. Option II: Since we let $AB = 3$ and $CD = 2$, then $AC = 3 + BC$ while $BD = BC + 2$. No matter what BC is, $AC > BD$. Option II is true. This allows us to eliminate choice C, which does not include Option II. We still need to check Option III. Option III: Since $AB > CD$, and $AC > AB$, then $AC > CD$. Option III is true; therefore, D is the answer.

SECTION 1

QUESTIONS	EXPLANATIONS

6 If 3 more than x is 2 more than y, what is x in terms of y?

(A) $y - 5$
(B) $y - 1$
(C) $y + 1$
(D) $y + 5$
(E) $y + 6$

6. Jim's answer is B.
Whenever you see variables in the answer choices, you must Plug In. Let's start by plugging in a number for x. If $x = 10$, then 3 more than 10 is 13. Now you know that 13 is 2 more than y, so $y = 11$. This is your target answer. When you plug 10 in for x in all the answer choices, choice B is the only one that works.

7 $\dfrac{4^2}{2^3} + \dfrac{2^3}{4^2} =$

(A) $\dfrac{5}{2}$

(B) 2

(C) 1

(D) $\dfrac{1}{2}$

(E) $\dfrac{1}{4}$

7. Jim's answer is A.
$$\frac{4^2}{2^3} + \frac{2^3}{4^2} = \frac{16}{8} + \frac{8}{16} = \frac{2}{1} + \frac{1}{2} = 2\frac{1}{2}, \text{ or } \frac{5}{2}$$

QUESTIONS	EXPLANATIONS

8 If 8 and 12 each divide *K* without a remainder, what is the value of *K*?

(A) 16
(B) 24
(C) 48
(D) 96
(E) It cannot be determined from the information given.

8. Jim's answer is E.
The best way to solve questions like this is to try choices rather than to reason it out algebraically. Now, trying our choices, B works, but so do C and D. If you chose A, you should review remainders. If you chose B, C, or D, you jumped at an answer too quickly. Remember, this question is already edging into medium territory, so you have to be on your toes.

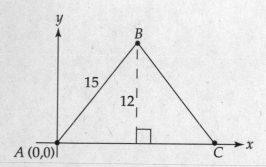

9 In the figure above, side *AB* of triangle *ABC* contains which of the following points?

(A) (3, 2)
(B) (3, 5)
(C) (4, 6)
(D) (4, 10)
(E) (6, 8)

9. Jim's answer is E.

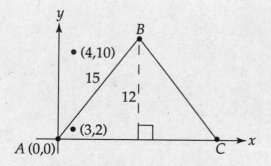

To solve this problem, you need to figure out the ratio between the *x* and *y* values on line segment *AB*. If you look at the figure, *AB* is the hypotenuse of a right triangle with a side of 12. Without even using the Pythagorean Theorem, you can tell that this triangle is one of Jim's favorite right triangles: a 3:4:5. So this has to be a 9:12:15 triangle, and the coordinates of point *B* are (9,12). All the points on line segment *AB* are in a ratio of 9 to 12 (which is the same as 3 to 4). The only answer with that ratio is E (6,8).

SECTION 1

QUESTIONS	EXPLANATIONS

10 What is the diameter of a circle with circumference 5?

(A) $\dfrac{5}{\pi}$

(B) $\dfrac{10}{\pi}$

(C) 5

(D) 5π

(E) 10π

10. Jim's answer is A.

The formula for the circumference of a circle is $C = \pi d$. (If you forget the formula, you can look it up at the beginning of the section.) The circumference of the circle is 5, so $5 = \pi d$.

Now, just solve for d, which equals $\dfrac{5}{\pi}$. If you picked choice D, you might have thought the question was asking for the circumference instead of the diameter.

11 Carol subscribed to four publications that cost $12.90, $16.00, $18.00, and $21.90 per year, respectively. If she made an initial down payment of one half of the total amount, and paid the rest in 4 equal monthly payments, how much was each of the 4 monthly payments?

(A) $8.60
(B) $9.20
(C) $9.45
(D) $17.20
(E) $34.40

11. Jim's answer is A.

The first step is to use your calculator to compute the sum of the subscriptions: $68.80. The down payment was half that amount, leaving $34.40 to be paid in 4 installments of $8.60 each. If you answered choices D or E, you misread the question.

MERCHANDISE SALES		
Type	Amount of Sales	Percent of Total Sales
Shoes	$12,000	15%
Coats	$20,000	25%
Shirts	$x	40%
Pants	$y	20%

12 According to the table above, what were the sales, in dollars, of shirts and pants combined?

(A) $32,000
(B) $48,000
(C) $60,000
(D) $68,000
(E) $80,000

12. Jim's answer is B.

We're solving for shirts and pants, which constitute 60% of total sales. Since shoes ($12,000) account for 15%, shirts and pants would be four times that amount, or $48,000. The more basic way to solve this is to find out the total value of sales and find 60% of that. If $20,000 represents 25% (or $\frac{1}{4}$) of sales, then the total must be $80,000. Using translation, you'll find that $\frac{60}{100} \times 80,000 = \$48,000$.

SECTION 1

QUESTIONS	EXPLANATIONS

13 For all integers $n \neq 1$, let $<n> = \dfrac{n+1}{n-1}$. Which of the following has the greatest value?

(A) $<0>$
(B) $<2>$
(C) $<3>$
(D) $<4>$
(E) $<5>$

13. Jim's answer is B.
You can tell by the question number that you have to be careful on this question. If you selected choice E, you grabbed impulsively at the Joe Bloggs answer. On this question, the safest way—as usual—is to try choices rather than to reason algebraically. Plugging in the choices for n, we get the following results:

(A) $\qquad <0> = \dfrac{0+1}{0-1} = \dfrac{1}{-1} = -1$

(B) $\qquad <2> = \dfrac{2+1}{2-1} = \dfrac{3}{1} = 3$

(C) $\qquad <3> = \dfrac{3+1}{3-1} = \dfrac{4}{2} = 2$

(D) $\qquad <4> = \dfrac{4+1}{4-1} = \dfrac{5}{3} = 1\dfrac{2}{3}$

(E) $\qquad <5> = \dfrac{5+1}{5-1} = \dfrac{6}{4} = \dfrac{3}{2} = 1\dfrac{1}{2}$

Choice (B) has the greatest value, so that must be Jim's answer.

14 If the product of $(1 + 2)$, $(2 + 3)$, and $(3 + 4)$ is equal to one half the sum of 20 and x, then $x =$

(A) 10
(B) 85
(C) 105
(D) 190
(E) 1,210

14. Jim's answer is D.
If you got this question wrong, you either misread it or forgot the correct order of operations. Remember to do parentheses first. Translating the information to an equation, we'd get the following:

$(1 + 2)(2 + 3)(3 + 4) = \dfrac{1}{2}(20 + x)$

$(3)(5)(7) = \dfrac{1}{2}(20 + x)$

$105 = \dfrac{1}{2}(20 + x)$

$210 = 20 + x$

$190 = x$

SECTION 1

QUESTIONS	EXPLANATIONS

15 If $\dfrac{2+x}{5+x} = \dfrac{2}{5} + \dfrac{2}{5}$, then $x =$

(A) $\dfrac{2}{5}$

(B) 1

(C) 2

(D) 5

(E) 10

15. Jim's answer is E.
If you selected choice A, you fell for a Joe Bloggs trap. This question is well into medium territory—check out the difficulty meter. Simplifying the equation, we get the following:

$$\frac{2+x}{5+x} = \frac{2}{5} + \frac{2}{5}$$

$$\frac{2+x}{5+x} = \frac{4}{5}$$

At this point, the fastest solution is to Backsolve by checking each of the choices until you found the answer. Using answer choice E,

$$\frac{2+x}{5+x} = \frac{4}{5}$$

$$\frac{2+(10)}{5+(10)} = \frac{4}{5}$$

$$\frac{12}{15} = \frac{4}{5}$$

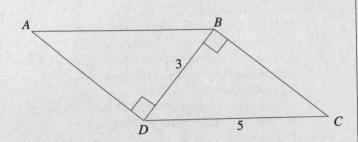

16 In parallelogram *ABCD* above, *BD* = 3 and *CD* = 5. What is the area of *ABCD*?

(A) 12
(B) 15
(C) 18
(D) 20
(E) It cannot be determined from the information given.

16. Jim's answer is A.

The trick to this question is to notice that this parallelogram is actually made up of two equal triangles. By finding the area of the triangles, you can find the area of the parallelogram. The triangles are both right triangles, and the two sides given to you in the figure follow the 3:4:5 pattern. If you look at triangle *DBC* from a different angle, the base is 3 and the height is 4. Now you can use the formula for the area of triangle:

$$A = \frac{1}{2} bh$$

$$A = \frac{1}{2}(3)(4)$$

$$A = 6$$

Since the parallelogram consists of two triangles, its area is 2 × 6, or 12. (By the way, if you had estimated the area of the parallelogram, the base is 5 and the height is less than 3.) The area must be less than 15, and only one answer choice is less than 15: A!

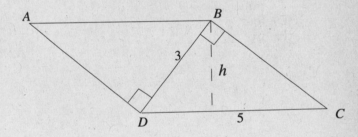

SECTION 1

QUESTIONS	EXPLANATIONS

17 A survey of Town X found an average of 3.2 persons per household and an average of 1.2 televisions per household. If 48,000 people live in Town X, how many televisions are in Town X?

(A) 15,000
(B) 16,000
(C) 18,000
(D) 40,000
(E) 57,600

17. Jim's answer is C.
This is an excellent time to turn on your calculator. Since 48,000 people live in Town X, and each household has 3.2 people, we can determine the number of households:

$$48,000 \div 3.2 = 15,000$$

And since each household has 1.2 televisions, we can now determine the number of televisions:

$$15,000 \times 1.2 = 18,000$$

18 How many numbers from 1 to 200 inclusive are equal to the cube of an integer?

(A) one
(B) two
(C) three
(D) four
(E) five

18. Jim's answer is E.
Once again, the way *not* to solve an SAT question is to reason algebraically when you can check each of the choices.
Instead, use your calculator to start cubing integers and stop just before you exceed 200.

Integer	Cube
1	1
2	8
3	27
4	64
5	125
6	216

5 integers

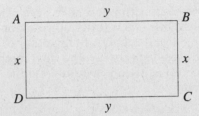

Note: Figure not drawn to scale.

19 If the perimeter of rectangle *ABCD* is equal to *p*, and $x = \frac{2}{3}y$, what is the value of *y* in terms of *p*?

(A) $\dfrac{p}{10}$

(B) $\dfrac{3p}{10}$

(C) $\dfrac{p}{3}$

(D) $\dfrac{2p}{5}$

(E) $\dfrac{3p}{5}$

19. Jim's answer is B.
A Princeton Review student, noticing the algebraic answer choices, would immediately plug in numbers to solve the problem. Since the values we choose for *x* and *y* must satisfy the equation, let's let *x* equal 2 and *y* equal 3. The perimeter *p* would then equal 2 + 2 + 3 + 3, or 10. Plugging 10 into *p* in each of the choices, we'd get B as the answer. Remember, the target is *y*, which is equal to 3.

Although some of you might have answered this question right by using algebra, doing so might have caused you to make a mistake without realizing it. Trust us. Plugging In is always the safer method for this type of problem. The Joe Bloggs choice, by the way, was C.

SECTION 1

20 A basketball team had a ratio of wins to losses of 3:1. After winning six games in a row, the team's ratio of wins to losses was 5:1. How many games had the team won <u>before</u> it won the six games?

(A) 3
(B) 6
(C) 9
(D) 15
(E) 24

20. Jim's answer is C.
And yet again, the slow way to solve a word problem like this is to set up equations. Letting w and l represent the number of wins and losses respectively, the slow method of setting up equations would yield the following:

$$\frac{w}{l} = \frac{3}{1}$$
$$\frac{w+6}{l} = \frac{5}{1}$$

Let's see how Princeton Review students approach this question. Using Backsolving, we start in the middle—choice C—and see if it works:

	Before		After	
	Wins	Losses	Wins	Losses
(A)	3			
(B)	6			
(C)	9	3 (3:1)	15	3 (5:1)
(D)	15			
(E)	24			

Bingo! We found the answer on the first try! If C didn't work, we'd move up or down depending on whether the result was too small or too big.

SECTION 1

21 A college student bought 11 books for fall classes. If the cost of his anatomy textbook was three times the average cost of the other 10 books, then the cost of the anatomy textbook was what fraction of the total amount he paid for the 11 books?

(A) $\dfrac{2}{13}$

(B) $\dfrac{3}{13}$

(C) $\dfrac{3}{11}$

(D) $\dfrac{3}{10}$

(E) $\dfrac{3}{4}$

21. Jim's answer is B.

Since we aren't given the cost of any book, we can plug in our own values. Let's say that the average cost of the textbooks, excluding the anatomy textbook, is $10. We can make all the books cost $10 to make the problem easier. The anatomy textbook, then, would cost $30. The total cost of our textbooks would then be $130 (one $30 textbook plus ten $10 textbooks). The anatomy textbook contributes $\dfrac{\$30}{\$130}$, or $\dfrac{3}{13}$ of this amount.

SECTION 1

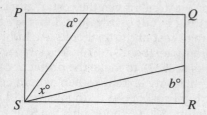

22 In rectangle *PQRS* above, what is the sum of *a* + *b* in terms of *x*?

(A) 90 + *x*
(B) 180 − *x*
(C) 180 + *x*
(D) 270 − *x*
(E) 360 − *x*

22. Jim's answer is A.
For those students who noticed the variables in the answer choices, this question was easily solved by Plugging In. It was easiest to plug in for *a* and *b* first, and then to solve for *x*. Let *a* = 50 and *b* = 70. Now, the two triangles are right triangles since they are formed from the corners of rectangle *PQRS*, so you can determine the measure of the third angle in each triangle.

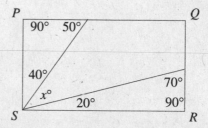

Since ∠ S = 90° = 40° + 20° + *x*°

$x° = 30$!

Having computed the value of *x*, you can now move to the answer choices. *a* + *b* = 50 + 70 = 120, so you are looking for the answer choice that equals 120°. Choice A is 90 + *x* = 90 + 30 = 120.

SECTION 1

QUESTIONS	EXPLANATIONS

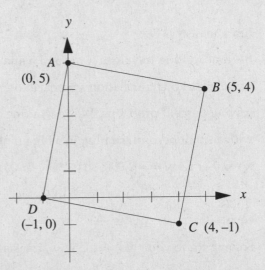

23 What is the area of square *ABCD*?

(A) 25

(B) $18\sqrt{2}$

(C) 26

(D) $25 + \sqrt{2}$

(E) 36

23. Jim's answer is C.
First a little error avoidance: Since 5 is one of the numbers we see, 5^2, or 25 is not going to be the answer. So, eliminate A. Next, let's estimate the area before we try to solve directly. The length of the square's side is a little more than 5, so the area is going to be a little more than 5^2 or 25. Choice E is too large, so before solving the problem, we've eliminated choices A and E. If we couldn't calculate the area exactly, we could guess from among the remaining choices. To determine the area, let's begin by assigning the variable *s* to indicate the length of the square's side. The area is given by the formula:

$A = s^2$

Now, using the Pythagorean Theorem, we can determine s^2 directly:

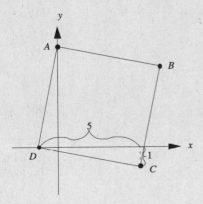

$s^2 = 5^2 + 1^2$
$s^2 = 25 + 1$
$s^2 = 26$

SECTION 1

24 If 0.1% percent of m is equal to 10% of n, then m is what percent of $10n$?

(A) $\dfrac{1}{1000}\%$

(B) 10%

(C) 100%

(D) 1,000%

(E) 10,000%

24. Jim's answer is D.

It's time to Plug In values for m and n and make use of our translation approach to solving percent problems. We're working with a small percent, so plug in a big number for m. Let's say $m = 2,000$, so 0.1% of 2,000 = $\dfrac{0.1}{100} \times \dfrac{2,000}{1} = 2$. Therefore, 10% of n equals 2; rewrite this as $\dfrac{10}{100} \times n = 2$. Solving for n, you get $n = 20$. Now, translate the rest of the problem: "m is what percent of $10n$" can be written as $2,000 = \dfrac{x}{100} \times 200$. Now just solve for x, which equals 1,000. The answer is 1,000%.

SECTION 1

QUESTIONS	EXPLANATIONS

25 If $n \neq 0$, which of the following could be true?

 I. $2n < n^2$
 II. $2n < n$
 III. $n^2 < -n$

(A) None
(B) I only
(C) I and II only
(D) I and III only
(E) I, II, and III

25. Jim's answer is E.

Plugging In is going to be your best approach. This is a COULD question, so you will want to try several different numbers to attempt to make I, II, and III true.

The exponents might have tipped you off that a negative fraction would be a good choice.

Plugging In $-\frac{1}{2}$ for n we find:

 I. $2n = 2(-\frac{1}{2}) = -1 < n^2 = (-\frac{1}{2})^2 = \frac{1}{4}$. TRUE

 II. $2n = 2(-\frac{1}{2}) = -1 < n = -\frac{1}{2}$. TRUE

 III. $n^2 = (-\frac{1}{2})^2 = \frac{1}{4} < -n = -(-\frac{1}{2}) = \frac{1}{2}$. TRUE

Thus, I, II, and III COULD be true, and E is the answer.

SECTION 2

QUESTIONS	EXPLANATIONS

1 Since the island soil has been barren for so many years, the natives must now ---- much of their food.

(A) deliver
(B) import
(C) produce
(D) develop
(E) utilize

1. Pam's answer is B.
The doctor in this sentence is the phrase *barren for so many years*, which provides answer B. If not from the soil, the natives must be getting their food from someplace else.

2 Because Jenkins neither ---- nor defends either management or the striking workers, both sides admire his journalistic ----.

(A) criticizes. .acumen
(B) attacks. .neutrality
(C) confronts. .aptitude
(D) dismisses. .flair
(E) promotes. .integrity

2. Pam's answer is B.
The doctor for the first blank is *defends* and the trigger word is *nor*, which means that the first blank is the opposite of *defends*. Since you need a negative word for the first blank, you can get rid of choice E. Now look at the second blank. According to the first part of the sentence, Jenkins doesn't do anything positive or negative, which means he must be somewhere in the middle. The word in the answer choices that means *somewhere in the middle* is *neutral*.

3 Some anthropologists claim that a few apes have been taught a rudimentary sign language, but skeptics argue that the apes are only ---- their trainers.

(A) imitating
(B) condoning
(C) instructing
(D) acknowledging
(E) belaboring

3. Pam's answer is A.
The doctor is *been taught*, which skeptics doubt. So the skeptics must be arguing that the apes have *not* been taught, or are *fooling* their trainers. Choice A works perfectly. Again, if you chose B, *condoning* is too difficult an answer for such an easy question.

4 It is ironic that the ---- insights of the great thinkers are voiced so often that they have become mere ----.

(A) original. .clichés
(B) banal. .beliefs
(C) dubious. .habits
(D) philosophical. .questions
(E) abstract. .ideas

4. Pam's answer is A.
Great thinkers must have *deep* insights; at any rate, the first blank is a positive word. The doctor here is *voiced so often*. Things that are voiced often can be called *repetitions*, or some related negative word. The only choice that has a positive word followed by a negative word is A. Once again, choice B would be too difficult in medium territory.

SECTION 2

5 The most frustrating periods of any diet are the inevitable ----, when weight loss ---- if not stops.

(A) moods. .accelerates
(B) feasts. .halts
(C) holidays. .contracts
(D) plateaus. .slows
(E) meals. .ceases

5. Pam's answer is D.
Let's start with the second blank. The doctor is *if not stops*, so the word in the blank must be something just short of stopping, such as *slowing down*. Which word in the second blank means *slowing down*? *Slow*, of course. The first word for D makes sense because a *plateau* is flat, so that means no weight is being gained or lost. Be careful not to choose B or E. The word in the second blank means something just short of stop. It doesn't actually mean *stop*.

6 Since the author's unflattering references to her friends were so ----, she was surprised that her ---- were recognized.

(A) laudatory. .styles
(B) obvious. .anecdotes
(C) oblique. .allusions
(D) critical. .eulogies
(E) apparent. .motives

6. Pam's answer is C.
The doctors for the sentence are *surprised* and *recognize*. If she's surprised that something was recognized, it must not have been obvious. So you can put *not obvious* in the first blank. That definitely gets rid of B and E. For the second blank, we also need something that means *not obvious*. The best matches for both blanks are in C. Both *oblique* and *allusion* have the sense of *not obvious*.

7 Mark was intent on maintaining his status as first in his class; because even the smallest mistakes infuriated him, he reviewed all his papers ---- before submitting them to his teacher.

(A) explicitly
(B) perfunctorily
(C) honestly
(D) mechanically
(E) assiduously

7. Pam's answer is E.
Because Mark hates mistakes, he will review his papers *carefully*. We can eliminate choices C and D immediately. If you weren't sure what A, B, or E mean, you had to guess. Give yourself a pat on the back if you guessed A or B rather than leaving the question blank. Even though you got the question wrong, you did the right thing. And in the long run, that's how your score goes up.

SECTION 2

8 Since many disadvantaged individuals view their situations as ---- as well as intolerable, their attitudes are best described as ----.

(A) squalid. .obscure
(B) unpleasant. .bellicose
(C) acute. .sanguine
(D) immutable. .resigned
(E) political. .perplexed

8. Pam's answer is D.
The first and second blanks are negative, possibly neutral, words. What's more, you should notice that they are saying similar things. Choice E is the only bad guess; choices A, B, and C are all good guesses. Again, guessing one of these choices would have been better than leaving the question blank.

9 The subtleties of this novel are evident not so much in the character ---- as they are in its profoundly ---- plot structure.

(A) assessment. .eclectic
(B) development. .trite
(C) portrayal. .aesthetic
(D) delineation. .intricate
(E) illustration. .superficial

9. Pam's answer is D.
The doctor for this sentence is *subtleties*. You can easily recycle the doctor in the second blank and say that the plot structure was profoundly *subtle*. The only word in the second that has a meaning in the same ballpark as *subtle* is *intricate*. Again, at the very least, you would have been better off guessing one of the hard words rather than leaving this question blank. If there were any words that you didn't know in this question, look them up!

10 SHIP : OCEAN ::

(A) fish : gill
(B) plane : air
(C) child : bath
(D) camel : water
(E) car : passengers

10. Pam's answer is B.
A SHIP travels in the OCEAN just as a *plane* travels in the *air*.

11 BOTANY : PLANTS ::

(A) agriculture : herbs
(B) astronomy : stars
(C) philosophy : books
(D) anthropology : religion
(E) forestry : evergreens

11. Pam's answer is B.
BOTANY is the study of PLANTS; *astronomy* is the study of *stars*.

12 CENSUS : POPULATION ::

(A) catalog : pictures
(B) inventory : supplies
(C) detonation : explosion
(D) dictionary : words
(E) election : tally

12. Pam's answer is B.
A CENSUS counts the POPULATION; an *inventory* counts the *supplies*. Choice E was close, but it doesn't quite work.

SECTION 2

QUESTIONS	EXPLANATIONS

13 CONSTELLATION : STARS ::

   (A) earth : moon
   (B) center : circle
   (C) archipelago : islands
   (D) rain : water
   (E) maverick : herd

13. Pam's answer is C.
A CONSTELLATION is a group of STARS. You could quickly eliminate A, B, and D. Now, let's say you didn't know what an archipelago is. Could it mean a group of islands? Sure, Hawaii is a group of islands; maybe that's what an *archipelago* is.
Looking at E, if you weren't sure what a *maverick* is, could it mean a group or herd? E is a good guess on a hard question like this, so we're proud of you if you guessed it rather than leave the question blank.

14 REFINE : OIL ::

   (A) winnow : wheat
   (B) harness : energy
   (C) mine : coal
   (D) mold : plastic
   (E) conserve : resource

14. Pam's answer is A.
If you weren't sure how to make a sentence with REFINE and OIL we hope you noticed that choices B, C, and E were Joe Bloggs traps, and that D was too easy. To refine oil is to purify it, just as to *winnow* wheat is to *purify* it.

15 PERSPICACIOUS : INSIGHT ::

   (A) zealous : mobility
   (B) audacious : hearing
   (C) delicious : taste
   (D) avaricious : generosity
   (E) amiable : friendliness

15. Pam's answer is E.
If you had trouble making a sentence, you should have eliminated answer choices with unrelated words and then worked backwards. You can eliminate C right away because the words are much too easy for a hard question. If you know what *zealous* and *audacious* mean, you know that the words in choice A and B are unrelated. If you were able to get rid of even one answer choice, then you should have guessed. (PERSPICACIOUS means having a lot of INSIGHT and *amiable* means having a lot of *friendliness*.)

SECTION 2

The passage below is followed by questions based on its content. Answer the questions on the basis of what is stated or implied in the passage and in any introductory material that may be provided.

Questions 16–21 are based on the following passage.

The following passage is an excerpt from a book by novelist Gregor von Rezzori.

Skushno is a Russian word that is difficult to translate. It means more than dreary boredom: a spiritual void that sucks you in like a vague but
(5) intensely urgent longing. When I was thirteen, at a phase that educators used to call the awkward age, my parents were at their wits' end. We lived in the Bukovina, today an almost astronomically remote province in southeastern Europe. The story I am
(10) telling seems as distant—not only in space but also in time—as if I'd merely dreamed it. Yet it begins as a very ordinary story.

I had been expelled by a *consilium abeundi*—an advisory board with authority to expel unworthy students—from the schools of the then Kingdom of
(15) Rumania, whose subjects we had become upon the collapse of the Austro-Hungarian Empire after the first great war. An attempt to harmonize the imbalances in my character by means of strict discipline at a boarding school in Styria (my people
(20) still regarded Austria as our cultural homeland) nearly led to the same ignominious end, and only my pseudo-voluntary departure from the institution in the nick of time prevented my final ostracism from the privileged ranks of those for
(25) whom the path to higher education was open. Again in the jargon of those assigned the responsible task of raising children to become "useful members of society," I was a "virtually hopeless case." My parents, blind to how the
(30) contradictions within me had grown out of the highly charged difference between their own natures, agreed with the schoolmasters; the mix of neurotic sensitivity and a tendency to violence, alert

(35) perception and inability to learn, tender need for support and lack of adjustability, would only develop into something criminal.

One of the trivial aphorisms my generation owes to Wilhelm Busch's *Pious Helene* is the homily "Once your reputation's done / You can live a life of fun."
(40) But this optimistic notion results more from wishful thinking than from practical experience. In my case, had anyone asked me about my state of mind, I would have sighed and answered, "*Skushno!*" Even though rebellious thoughts occasionally surged
(45) within me, I dragged myself, or rather I let myself be dragged, listlessly through my bleak existence in the snail's pace of days. Nor was I ever free of a sense of guilt, for my feeling guilty was not entirely foisted upon me by others; there were deep reasons
(50) I could not explain to myself; had I been able to do so, my life would have been much easier.

SECTION 2

QUESTIONS	EXPLANATIONS

16 It can be inferred from the passage that the author's parents were

(A) frustrated by the author's inability to do well in school

(B) oblivious to the author's poor academic performance

(C) wealthy, making them insensitive to the needs of the poor

(D) schoolmasters who believed in the strict disciplining of youth

(E) living in Russia while their son lived in Bukovina

---

16. **Pam's answer is A.**

The lead words in this question are *the author's parents*. You learn about the author's parents in line 6: *my parents were at their wit's end*. The author mentions his parents again in lines 29–32: *My parents… agreed with the schoolmasters*, who thought the author was a *virtually hopeless case*. Answer choice A paraphrases the answer well (*frustrated*).

Answer choice B is wrong because the author's parents clearly know that he's got a problem. How could they be oblivious to the fact that he was expelled from several schools?

Answer choice C has nothing to do with the passage. You might be able to infer that the author's parents were wealthy because they sent him to a boarding school, but their attitude toward the poor has nothing to do with the main idea of the passage.

Answer choice D confuses several unconnected ideas mentioned in the passage. There is nothing in the passage to suggest that the author's parents were schoolmasters or strict disciplinarians.

Answer choice E contradicts the passage. The first paragraph states that the author's family lived together in Bukovina.

SECTION 2

QUESTIONS	EXPLANATIONS

17 Lines 17–25 are used by the author to demonstrate that

(A) the author was an unstable and dangerous person

(B) the schools that the author attended were too difficult

(C) the tactics being used to make the author a more stable person were failing

(D) the author was not accepted well by his classmates

(E) the author's academic career was nearing an end

17. Pam's answer is C.
According to lines 17–21, *An attempt to harmonize the imbalances in my character by means of strict discipline at a boarding school… nearly led to the same ignominious end.*

Even if you don't know what ignominious means, it should still be clear that the attempt to straighten the author out had same result as it did the before—it didn't work. This idea is paraphrased in choice C, which says that the *tactics* were *failing.*

Answer choice A is too extreme. Perhaps the author was a bit *unstable*, but there is nothing in the passage that suggests the author was *dangerous*. And Pam doesn't like dangerous people. Remember, if an answer choice is half bad, it's all bad.

Answer choice B is one of Pam's traps. Maybe the author did poorly in school partly because the schools were too difficult. Or maybe not. The passage tells us nothing about the difficulty of the schools. All we know is that the author was having a really hard time.

Answer choice D is another trap. We have no way of knowing from the passage how well the author got along with his peers.

In answer choice E, Pam is trying to get you to anticipate what will happen to the author in the future. We know that his academic career is in bad shape, but does that mean he'll never finish school?

SECTION 2

QUESTIONS	EXPLANATIONS

18 The word "ignominious" in line 21 means

(A) dangerous
(B) pitiless
(C) unappreciated
(D) disgraceful
(E) honorable

18. Pam's answer is D.
Go back to the passage, find the word *ignominious*, and cross it out. Then read the sentence and come up with your own word. According to lines 24–25, the author just barely escaped a *final ostracism from the privileged ranks*. If he was about to get thrown out of the privileged ranks, the word that best describes that situation is *disgraceful*.

Answer choice E is wrong, because we definitely need a negative word. The other answer choices are wrong because they don't accurately describe the author's situation as it is described in the passage.

19 In line 24, the word "ostracism" most likely means

(A) praise
(B) abuse
(C) appreciation
(D) departure
(E) banishment

19. Pam's answer is E.
Go back to the passage, find the word *ostracism*, and cross it out. Then read the sentence and come up with your own word. Fortunately, we just worked on this sentence for the previous question. The sentence describes how the author got thrown out of the privileged ranks. The word in the answer choice that best matches *thrown out* is *banishment*.

Choice D is close, but it isn't sufficiently negative. The other answer choices are wrong because they are not negative words.

SECTION 2

QUESTIONS	EXPLANATIONS

20 The passage as a whole suggests that the author felt

  (A) happy because he was separated from his parents
  (B) upset because he was unable to maintain good friends
  (C) melancholy and unsettled in his environment
  (D) suicidal and desperate because of his living in Russia
  (E) hopeful because he'd soon be out of school

20. Pam's answer is C.
This is a general question, so you only need to know the main idea of the passage. You know that the author was not happy in the passage, because he says he felt *Skushno*, a word that means *more than dreary boredom*.

You can get rid of answer choices A and E because they're positive.

Answer choice D is too extreme. Pam would never suggest that someone was suicidal. She'd be in big trouble if she did.

Answer choice B is wrong because the passage never says that the author had trouble with his friends.

21 The passage indicates that the author regarded the aphorism mentioned in the last paragraph with

  (A) relief because it showed him that he would eventually feel better
  (B) disdain because the author found it unrealistic
  (C) contempt because he saw it working for others
  (D) bemusement because of his immunity from it
  (E) sorrow because his faith in it nearly killed him

21. Pam's answer is B.
Your first clue to the author's attitude toward the aphorism is that he calls it *trivial*. After he quotes the aphorism, the author says, *this optimistic notion results more from wishful thinking than from practical experience*. The author clearly has a very negative opinion of it. Answer choice B gives a perfect paraphrase of *wishful thinking* by saying that the author found the aphorism *unrealistic*.

You can get rid of answer choices A and D because they are positive, and you can eliminate choice E because it refers to his *faith in it*; the author clearly has no faith in the aphorism.

Answer choice C is wrong because the author doesn't say anything about the aphorism working for others.

SECTION 2

Questions 22–30 are based on the following passage.

Fear of communism swept through the United States in the years following the Russian Revolution of 1917. Several states passed espionage acts that restricted political discussion, and radicals of all descriptions were rounded up in so-called Red Raids conducted by the attorney general's office. Some were convicted and imprisoned; others were deported. This was the background of a trial in Chicago involving twenty men charged under Illinois's espionage statute with advocating the violent overthrow of the government. The charge rested on the fact that all the defendants were members of the newly formed Communist Labor party.

The accused in the case were represented by Clarence Darrow, one of the foremost defense attorneys in the country. Throughout his career, Darrow had defended the poor and the despised against exploitation and prejudice. He defended the rights of labor unions, for example, at a time when many sought to outlaw the strike, and he was resolute in defending constitutional freedoms. The following are excerpts from Darrow's summation to the jury.

Members of the Jury . . . If you want to convict these twenty men, then do it. I ask no consideration on behalf of any one of them. They are no better
Line than any other twenty men or women; they are no
(5) better than the millions down through the ages who have been prosecuted and convicted in cases like this. And if it is necessary for my clients to show that America is like all the rest, if it is necessary that my clients shall go to prison to show it, then let
(10) them go. They can afford it if you members of the jury can; make no mistake about that . . .

The State says my clients "dare to criticize the Constitution." Yet this police officer (who the State says is a fine, right-living person) twice violated the
(15) federal Constitution while a prosecuting attorney was standing by. They entered Mr. Owen's home without a search warrant. They overhauled his papers. They found a flag, a red one, which he had the same right to have in his house that you have to
(20) keep a green one, or a yellow one, or any other color, and the officer impudently rolled it up and put another flag on the wall, nailed it there. By what right was that done? What about this kind of patriotism that violates the Constitution? Has it

(25) come to pass in this country that officers of the law can trample on constitutional rights and then excuse it in a court of justice? . . .

Most of what has been presented to this jury to stir up feeling in your souls has not the slightest
(30) bearing on proving conspiracy in this case. Take Mr. Lloyd's speech in Milwaukee. It had nothing to do with conspiracy.

Whether that speech was a joke or was serious, I will not attempt to discuss. But I will say that if it
(35) was serious it was as mild as a summer's shower compared with many of the statements of those who are responsible for working conditions in this country. We have heard from people in high places that those individuals who express sympathy with
(40) labor should be stood up against a wall and shot. We have heard people of position declare that individuals who criticize the actions of those who are getting rich should be put in a cement ship with leaden sails and sent out to sea. Every violent
(45) appeal that could be conceived by the brain has been used by the powerful and the strong. I repeat, Mr. Lloyd's speech was gentle in comparison. . . .

My clients are condemned because they say in their platform that, while they vote, they believe the
(50) ballot is secondary to education and organization. Counsel suggests that those who get something they did not vote for are sinners, but I suspect you the jury know full well that my clients are right. Most of you have an eight-hour day. Did you get it
(55) by any vote you ever cast? No. It came about because workers laid down their tools and said we will no longer work until we get an eight-hour day. That is how they got the twelve-hour day, the ten-hour day, and the eight-hour day—not by voting
(60) but by laying down their tools. Then when it was over and the victory won . . . then the politicians, in order to get the labor vote, passed legislation creating an eight-hour day. That is how things changed; victory preceded law. . . .

(65) You have been told that if you acquit these defendants you will be despised because you will endorse everything they believe. But I am not here to defend my clients' opinions. I am here to defend their right to express their opinions. I ask you, then,
(70) to decide this case upon the facts as you have heard them, in light of the law as you understand it, in light of the history of our country, whose institutions you and I are bound to protect.

SECTION 2

22 Clarence Darrow's statement that "They can afford it if you members of the jury can" is most probably meant to imply that

(A) the defendants will not be harmed if convicted

(B) if the jurors convict the defendants, they will be harshly criticized

(C) the defendants do not care whether they are convicted

(D) everyone involved in the trial will be affected financially by whatever the jury decides

(E) if the defendants are found guilty, everyone's rights will be threatened

22. Pam's answer is E.

After the quoted statement, Darrow goes on to talk about the abuse of constitutional and personal liberty by people in authority. Keeping in mind that Pam loves America, you can see that choice E is the most patriotic answer. If the jury finds the defendants guilty, it will be saying, in effect, that abuses of constitutional rights are okay. This will threaten everybody's freedom. Pam is concerned about constitutional rights in America. Choice E is also most consistent with the main idea of the passage.

Answer choice A is way off base. Whether the defendants will be harmed if convicted is not the issue.

Answer choice B is wrong; there's nothing in the passage to suggest that the jurors would be criticized if they were to convict the defendants. (In fact, the opposite would probably be true.) Remember, the passage is about constitutional rights and abuses of those rights, not the reputation of the jurors.

Answer choice C doesn't make any sense. Of course the defendants care whether they are convicted!

Answer choice D is way off the mark because the passage is not at all about money. Don't forget the main idea.

23 Lines 13–29 suggest that the case against Owen would have been dismissed if the judge had interpreted the Constitution in which of the following ways?

(A) Defendants must have their rights read to them when they are arrested.

(B) Giving false testimony in court is a crime.

(C) Evidence gained by illegal means is not admissible in court.

(D) No one can be tried twice for the same crime.

(E) Defendants cannot be forced to give incriminating evidence against themselves.

23. Pam's answer is C.

In lines 13–29, Darrow stresses an inconsistency or contradiction on the part of the prosecution—that it's okay to disregard constitutional rights in order to prosecute someone for violating the Constitution. Answer choice C is Pam's answer because Darrow asserts that the evidence against Owen was obtained by violating his constitutional rights. Therefore, if the judge had interpreted the Constitution as answer choice C suggests, Owen's trial would have been dismissed.

All the other answer choices refer to things that could get a trial dismissed, but none of them are mentioned anywhere in the passage.

SECTION 2

24 Darrow's defense in lines 28–47 relies mainly on persuading the jury that

(A) the prosecution is using a double standard.

(B) the evidence used by the prosecution is unreliable.

(C) the defendants' views are similar to those of the jury.

(D) labor unions are guaranteed the right to hold a strike.

(E) a federal court is a more appropriate place to try the defendants than is a state court.

24. Pam's answer is A.

You can use the information you gained from answering the previous question to answer this one. Answer choice A is correct here because Darrow believes that the prosecution is using a double standard. Lines 28–47 cite more examples of how Darrow shows that the prosecution is guilty of doing exactly what it has accused the defendants of doing. In this case, the accused are said to have used violent words, and Darrow is giving examples of violent threats that have been aimed at the defendants.

Answer choice B is close, but the evidence is not *unreliable*. Darrow's point is that the evidence was *obtained* by unconstitutional means.

Answer choice C is way off base. There is nothing in the passage to suggest that the jury holds the same view as the defendants. They wouldn't be an impartial jury if they did, would they?

Answer choice D is wrong because the lines cited in the question are about *people in high places*, not about the labor unions. Read the lines again.

Answer choice E comes out of left field. The passage doesn't say anything about state courts versus federal courts.

25 Lines 28–47 indicate that the prosecution attempted to characterize Mr. Lloyd's speech as

(A) bitter sarcasm
(B) deceptive propaganda
(C) valid criticism
(D) a frightening threat
(E) a bad joke

25. Pam's answer is D.

Line 32 indicates that Lloyd's speech was accused of being a *conspiracy*, and line 47 says that it was *gentle in comparison* to the violent epithets of anti-Communists. But we're not concerned with what Darrow said about the speech. We want to know what the prosecution said about it. Therefore, answer choice D is correct. The violent part of the speech makes it *frightening*, and the conspiratorial nature of the speech makes it a *threat*.

Answer choice C is wrong because the prosecution would never say anything positive about the defendant's speech.

Answer choice E is silly, and answer choice A is not extreme enough.

Answer choice B might be tempting, but the passage never suggests that the speech was in any way *deceptive*.

SECTION 2

26 What does Clarence Darrow accuse "people in high places" (line 38) of doing?

(A) Trying to kill Communist party members
(B) Advocating violence against labor sympathizers
(C) Lying to the jury
(D) Encouraging the use of harsh punishment against criminals
(E) Making foolish and insulting suggestions

26. Pam's answer is B.
According to lines 37–40, *We have heard from people in high places that those individuals who express sympathy with labor should be stood up against a wall and shot.* The idea that the people in high places want to shoot people who express sympathy with labor is paraphrased in choice B.

Answer choice A is one of Pam's traps. According to Darrow, people in high places have suggested that labor sympathizers be shot, but that doesn't mean the people in high places have actually killed anyone.

Answer choice C is not mentioned in the passage. The *people in high places* to whom Darrow refers are not testifying in the trial.

Answer choice D is another trap. The people in high places have advocated violence against labor sympathizers, but the labor sympathizers are not necessarily criminals.

Answer choice E doesn't make sense. To suggest that labor sympathizers be stood up against a wall and shot is more than just a *foolish and insulting suggestion.*

27 The word "counsel" in line 51 refers to

(A) expert psychologists
(B) the prosecution
(C) an assembly
(D) a recommendation
(E) an expert

27. Pam's answer is B.
Throughout the passage, Darrow has been commenting on the prosecution's double standards, so when he talks about what *counsel suggests*, he is again making a point about what the prosecution has said. So *counsel* refers to *the prosecution.*

Answer choices A and E are wrong because there are no expert psychologists or experts of any other sort mentioned in the passage.

Answer choice C doesn't make sense. There may be an assembly in the court room, but Darrow is not talking about the spectators.

Answer choice D doesn't make sense in context. A recommendation itself doesn't suggest anything; rather, the person making the recommendation does the suggesting.

SECTION 2

QUESTIONS	EXPLANATIONS

28 Lines 66–68 imply that the prosecution had told the jury that finding for the innocence of the defendants would be similar to

(A) denying the validity of the Constitution
(B) permitting workers to go on strike
(C) promoting passive resistance
(D) limiting freedom of expression
(E) promoting communism

28. Pam's answer is E.
According to lines 65–67, the jury had been told that if the defendants were to be acquitted, the jury members would be despised for agreeing with the defendants. Since Darrow objects to what the jurors were told, they must have been told this by the prosecution. The idea that people will think that the jury agrees with the defendants' beliefs is paraphrased in choice E as *promoting communism*. Remember, the answer to most specific questions will be an exact *paraphrase* of what the passage says.

The other answer choices are wrong because the question is asking about what the *prosecution* told the jury, and the prosecution is only concerned with one thing—communism.

29 In line 73, the word "bound" most nearly means

(A) intellectually committed
(B) personally determined
(C) morally compelled
(D) violently coerced
(E) inevitably destined

29. Pam's answer is C.
In line 73 *bound* means morally compelled. By reading the last paragraph, you see that Darrow's argument is hinged on the jury's commitment to uphold the law despite how they feel personally about communism. Therefore, *bound* must mean something very compelling, something beyond an intellectual commitment and stopping short of inevitability. *Bound* means tied to something, and in this case Darrow is saying that the jury is tied to upholding the law by a moral obligation.

SECTION 2

30 Darrow's defense hinges on the ability of the jurors to

(A) understand complicated legal terms and procedures
(B) sympathize with union organizers
(C) comprehend the beliefs of the Communist Labor party
(D) separate the defendants' rights from their views
(E) act in the interest of the national economy

30. Pam's answer is D.

This is the only real general question in the bunch. It asks you to determine what Darrow is trying to get the jury to do through implication and examples. You know from your Blurb-2-1-1-F reading of the passage that the accused are said to be a threat to the Constitution (line 12) and the country. Darrow's summation also points to an inconsistency in the prosecution (paragraph 2) to highlight constitutionality as the issue, not communism. All of Darrow's testimony, which you can get a good feel for in Blurb-2-1-1-F, relies on getting away from what the defendants believe and focuses on their right under the Constitution to have this belief.

SECTION 3

QUESTIONS	EXPLANATIONS

SUMMARY DIRECTIONS FOR QUANTITATIVE COMPARISON QUESTIONS

<u>Answer:</u> A if the quantity in Column A is greater;
B if the quantity in Column B is greater;
C if the two quantities are equal;
D if the relationship cannot be determined from the information given.

AN E RESPONSE WILL NOT BE SCORED.

<u>Column A</u> <u>Column B</u>

1
$$\frac{3}{7}$$ $$\frac{1}{2}$$

1. Jim's answer is B.
Here's a perfect chance to use the Bowtie:

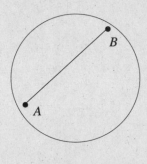

Since 7 > 6, you know that $\frac{1}{2}$ is greater, so

Column B is bigger.

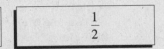

$AB = 8$

2 The radius of the circle | 4

2. Jim's answer is A.
Since AB is 8, the diameter of the circle must be more than 8. If the diameter is more than 8, the radius must be more than 4.

$7a > 4b$

3 a | b

3. Jim's answer is D.
Try Plugging In numbers for a and b. Since $7(1) > 4(1)$, you can set $a = 1$ and $b = 1$. Therefore, the columns could be equal. Eliminate choices A and B. You can also say that $a = 2$ and $b = 1$. So Column A could be bigger, and you can get more than one result.

SECTION 3

| QUESTIONS | EXPLANATIONS |

<u>Column A</u>   <u>Column B</u>

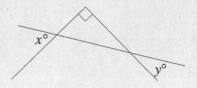

4 | $x + y$ | 90

4. Jim's answer is C.
   Although we don't know what x and y are, we can use their vertical angles within the triangle:

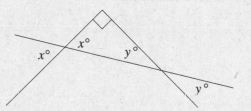

Since $x + y + 90 = 180$, $x + y = 90$.

The novelty clock above has hands that move at the correct speed, but counterclockwise. The clock tells the correct time every 6 hours (at 6:00 and 12:00).

5 | 3 hours, 15 minutes | Amount of time that has passed since 12:00

5. Jim's answer is B.
   This is a little confusing, but not that difficult if we're careful. Moving backward from 12:00, 11:00 would be 1 hour, 10:00 would be 2 hours, 9:00 would be 3 hours, and 8:00 would be 4 hours. 8:15 is 3 hours and 45 minutes.

SECTION 3

$$9^n - 8^n = 1^n$$

| 1 | n |

6. Jim's answer is C.
Don't be frightened if this looks like some complex equation. The first thing to notice is that the number 1 raised to any power remains 1:
$$9^n - 8^n = 1^n$$
$$9^1 - 8^1 = 1$$
The only value of n that satisfies this equation is 1.

A rectangle of area 4 has two sides of length r and s, where r and s are integers.

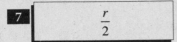

| $\dfrac{r}{2}$ | $2s$ |

7. Jim's answer is D.
The Joe Bloggs response to this question is B, so the answer should be A, C, or D. Joe Bloggs thinks $2s$ must be greater than $\dfrac{r}{2}$. Now, let's use the formula for the area of a rectangle:
$$A = rs$$
$$4 = rs$$
Let's make $r = 1$ and $s = 4$. Now, compare the quantities:

$$\dfrac{r}{2} \qquad 2s$$

$$\dfrac{1}{2} \qquad 2(4)$$

So the answer can't be A or C. If you let $r = 4$ and $s = 1$, the two quantities could be equal. You can get more than one result, so Jim's answer must be D.

In a group of 28 children, there are 6 more girls than boys.

| Two times the number of girls | Three times the number of boys |

8. Jim's answer is A.
If you subtract the 6 girls from the 28 children, there are now 22 children. Half of these kids must be boys, so there must be 11 boys and 11 girls. Now add the 6 girls back, and you have 11 boys and 17 girls. Two times the number of girls (34) is greater than three times the number of boys (33).

SECTION 3

QUESTIONS	EXPLANATIONS

<u>Column A</u>   <u>Column B</u>

9

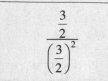
$$\frac{\frac{3}{2}}{\left(\frac{3}{2}\right)^2}$$

$$\frac{2}{3}$$

9. Jim's answer is C.
First, cross out D because the problem contains only numbers. Then work out Column A:

$$\frac{\frac{3}{2}}{\left(\frac{3}{2}\right)^2} = \frac{\frac{3}{2}}{\frac{9}{4}} = \frac{3}{2} \times \frac{4}{9} = \frac{12}{18} = \frac{2}{3}.$$

The quantities are equal.

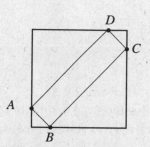

The area of the square is 25. Points A, B, C, and D are on the square.

10 | Perimeter of the rectangle $ABCD$

20

10. Jim's answer is B.
If the area of the square is 25, the length of each side is 5. The perimeter of the square, then, is 20. If the perimeter of the square is 20, the perimeter of the inscribed rectangle must be less than 20.

x, y, and z are positive.
$x + y + z = 10$ and $x = y$

11 | x

5

11. Jim's answer is B.
First, plug in some numbers. Let's say $x = 4$. Since $x = y$, that means $y = 4$ also. You know that $x + y + z = 10$, so $z = 2$. That works out, so Column B can be greater. Now, find out if the columns can be equal. If $x = 5$, then $y = 5$ and $z = 0$; that's no good, z has to be positive. Could Column A be greater? If $x = 6$, then $y = 6$ and $z = -2$. That doesn't work either. Column B has to be greater.

SECTION 3

QUESTIONS	EXPLANATIONS

Column A **Column B**

12. $\sqrt{3} + \sqrt{4}$ $\sqrt{3} \times \sqrt{4}$

12. Jim's answer is A.
The Joe Bloggs response here is B. This problem should give you little trouble on your calculator. Again, D should have been eliminated because there are only numbers.

13. The number of distinct prime factors of 30   The number of distinct prime factors of 60

13. Jim's answer is C.
The Joe Bloggs response here, of course, is B. Let's determine the prime factors of 30 and 60:

$$30 = 2 \times 15 \qquad\qquad 60 = 2 \times 30$$
$$ = 2 \times 3 \times 5 \qquad\qquad = 2 \times 2 \times 15$$
$$ = 2 \times 2 \times 3 \times 5$$

Now, 30 has three distinct prime factors (2, 3, 5) and so does 60! Remember, *distinct* just means *different*.

14. x^2 $(x + 1)^2$

14. Jim's answer is D.
The classic Joe Bloggs response here, of course, is B. The answer must be A, C, or D. Now, if we let x equal, say, 2, we get the following quantities:

x^2	$(x + 1)^2$
2^2	$(2 + 1)^2$
4	9

Since Column B is greater, the answer cannot be A or C. Only one choice remains: D. (If you had to prove this to yourself, try negative numbers.)

15. The percent increase from 99 to 100   The percent decrease from 100 to 99

15. Jim's answer is A.
The classic Joe Bloggs answer here is C. The increase from 99 to 100 and the decrease from 100 to 99 is 1 in both cases, but the *percent* increase and decrease are different. The percent increase from 99 to 100 is:

$$\frac{1}{99} \times 100 = 1.01\%.$$

The percent decrease from 100 to 99 is:

$$\frac{1}{100} \times 100 = 1\%.$$

SECTION 3

16 If $\dfrac{x + 2x + 3x}{2} = 6$, then $x =$

16. Jim's answer is 2.

$$\frac{x + 2x + 3x}{2} = 6$$

$$\frac{6x}{2} = 6$$

$$6x = 12$$

$$x = 2$$

Grid it like this:

Remember that the first grid–in question returns the difficulty meter to easy.

17 There are 24 fish in an aquarium. If $\dfrac{1}{8}$ of them are tetras and $\dfrac{2}{3}$ of the remaining fish are guppies, how many guppies are in the aquarium?

17. Jim's answer is 14.

Of the 24 fish, 3 are tetras. Of the remaining 21 fish, $\dfrac{2}{3}$ are guppies.

Two thirds of 21 is 14.

Grid it like this:

SECTION 3

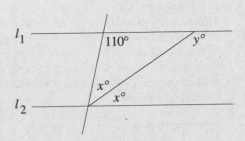

18 If l_1 is parallel to l_2 in the figure above, what is the value of y?

18. Jim's answer is 145.

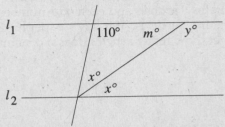

Since the two lines are parallel, $110 + 2x = 180$. Solving this equation for x, we get $x = 35$. Looking at the triangle, the missing angle (m) can be found by solving the equation $110 + x + m = 180$. Since $x = 35$, $m = 35$. Since $m + y = 180$ and $m = 35$, $y = 145$. Grid it like this:

SECTION 3

19 The daily newspaper always follows a particular format. Each even-numbered page contains 6 articles and each odd-numbered page contains 7 articles. If today's paper has 36 pages, how many articles does it contain?

19. Jim's answer is 234.
Since every even-numbered page has 6 articles and every odd-numbered page has 7, there are 13 articles for every two pages. A 36-page paper, then, would contain 18 such paired pages, or $18 \times 13 = 234$ articles. Grid it like this:

20 When n is divided by 5, the remainder is 4.
When n is divided by 4, the remainder is 3.
If $0 < n < 100$, what is one possible value of n?

20. Jim's answer is 19, 39, 59, 79, or 99.
The simplest way to solve this question would be to find values of n that satisfy the first condition, and then to check which of those also satisfy the second condition. So, let's find some numbers that leave a remainder of 4 when divided by 5:

9, 14, 19, 24, 29, . . .

That should be enough. Now, let's check which of these leaves a remainder of 3 when divided by 4.

$9 \div 4 = 2 \text{ R } 1$
$14 \div 4 = 3 \text{ R } 2$
$19 \div 4 = 4 \text{ R } 3$

Bingo. 19 is one acceptable response. Grid it like this:

SECTION 3

21. If $x^2 = 16$ and $y^2 = 4$, what is the greatest possible value of $(x - y)^2$?

21. Jim's answer is 36.

If $x^2 = 16$, then $x = \pm 4$. If $y^2 = 4$, then $y = \pm 2$. To maximize $(x - y)^2$, we need to maximize the difference:

$(4 - 2)^2 = 2^2 = 4$

$[4 - (-2)]^2 = 6^2 = 36$

$[(-4) - 2]^2 = (-6)^2 = 36$

$[(-4) - (-2)]^2 = (-2)^2 = 4$

Thus, the maximum value of the expression is 36. Grid it like this:

QUESTIONS	EXPLANATIONS

22 Segment *AB* is perpendicular to segment *BD*. Segment *AB* and segment *CD* bisect each other at point *x*. If *AB* = 8 and *CD* = 10, what is the length of *BD*?

22. Jim's answer is 3.
The first step is to draw a diagram, which requires some thought:

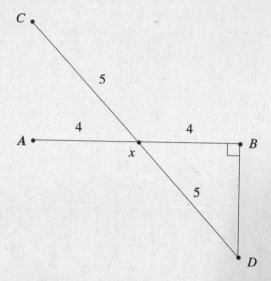

You should notice that *BD* is part of one of Jim's favorite right triangles: a 3:4:5 triangle. So *BD* = 3.

Grid it like this:

SECTION 3

23   At a music store, the price of a CD is three times the price of a cassette tape. If 40 CDs were sold for a total of $480, and the combined sales of CDs and cassette tapes totaled $600, how many cassette tapes were sold?

23.   Jim's answer is 30.

Let's proceed step by step, starting with the easiest equations to solve. If 40 CDs equal $480, each one equals $12. Since this is three times the cost of a cassette tape, each cassette tape costs $4. Since $600 equals the CDs ($480) and the cassette tapes, the total cassette tape sales were $120. At $4 a cassette tape, 30 cassette tapes were sold.

Grid it like this:

SECTION 3

QUESTIONS	EXPLANATIONS

24 At a certain high school, 30 students study French, 40 study Spanish, and 25 study neither. If there are 80 students in the school, how many study both French and Spanish?

24. Jim's answer is 15.
We call these group questions, and we have an easy formula for solving them:

Total = Group 1 + Group 2 − Both + Neither.

In this question the Total is 80 students, Group 1 is the 30 French students, and Group 2 is the 40 Spanish students. You also know that 25 students study Neither. Now plug those values into the formula:

$$80 = 30 + 40 - b + 25.$$

Then solve for *b*, which equals 15. Grid it like this.

SECTION 3

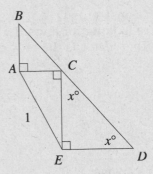

25 In the figure above, if $AE = 1$, what is the sum of the area of $\triangle ABC$ and the area of $\triangle CDE$?

25. Jim's answer is .5.

First, let's set up equations for the areas of the two triangles:

$(\frac{1}{2})(AC)(AB) + (\frac{1}{2})(CE)(ED)$

Since both triangles are isosceles, $AC = AB$ and $CE = ED$. Thus, the previous equation becomes

$(\frac{1}{2})(AC)^2 + \frac{1}{2}(CE)^2$

$\frac{1}{2}[(AC)^2 + (CE)^2]$

Now, using the Pythagorean Theorem, we know that

$(AC)^2 + (CE)^2 = 1$

So, the sum of the required areas is $\frac{1}{2}(1)$ or $\frac{1}{2}$.

Grid it like this:

SECTION 4

1   If it is true that morality cannot exist without religion, then does not the erosion of religion herald the ---- of morality?

(A) regulation
(B) basis
(C) belief
(D) collapse
(E) value

1. Pam's answer is D.
   We're looking for a word along the lines of *erosion*; *collapse* is the only choice that fits.

2   Certain animal behaviors, such as mating rituals, seem to be ----, and therefore ---- external factors such as climate changes, food supply, or the presence of other animals of the same species.

(A) learned. .immune to
(B) innate. .unaffected by
(C) intricate. .belong to
(D) specific. .confused with
(E) memorized. .controlled by

2. Pam's answer is B.
   The doctor here is *external factors*. If animal behaviors are *innate*, they would be relatively *unaffected by* external factors.

3   Shaken by two decades of virtual anarchy, the majority of people were ready to buy ---- at any price.

(A) order
(B) emancipation
(C) hope
(D) liberty
(E) enfranchisement

3. Pam's answer is A.
   The doctor in this sentence is *anarchy*, which means lack of order. If people have been *shaken* by the lack of order, they must be ready to buy *order* at any price. Pam's answer is, in fact, *order*.

4   As a person who combines care with ----, Marisa completed her duties with ---- as well as zeal.

(A) levity. .resignation
(B) geniality. .ardor
(C) vitality. .willingness
(D) empathy. .rigor
(E) enthusiasm. .meticulousness

4. Pam's answer is E.
   The doctor here is *care* and *zeal*. Even if you don't know what *zeal* means, the second blank must reflect Marisa's being careful. D and E are the only choices that indicate her careful completion of duties. *Zeal* means enthusiasm, which locks in E as the answer. If you chose A or B, remember that this is not yet a difficult question that calls for a difficult answer.

SECTION 4

5 Her shrewd campaign managers were responsible for the fact that her political slogans were actually forgotten clichés revived and ---- with new meaning.

    (A) fathomed
    (B) instilled
    (C) foreclosed
    (D) instigated
    (E) foreshadowed

5. Pam's answer is B.
We know that her slogans were *forgotten clichés*. Now, even if you aren't sure what a cliché is, you know that it has been *revived*. The blank must be a positive word and something along the lines of *given*. Choice C is negative; choice E misses the doctor. Choice D makes absolutely no sense, and for a medium question is probably too difficult to be the answer anyway. Choice A is way off base.

6 The stoic former general led his civilian life as he had his military life, with simplicity and ---- dignity.

    (A) benevolent
    (B) informal
    (C) austere
    (D) aggressive
    (E) succinct

6. Pam's answer is C.
We know the general's civilian life is simple, dignified, and *stoic*. The only blank that fits is C. Choices B and D miss the doctor. Choices A and E, if you weren't sure what they mean, are good guesses but wrong.

7 Although bound to impose the law, a judge is free to use his discretion to ---- the anachronistic barbarity of some criminal penalties.

    (A) mitigate
    (B) understand
    (C) condone
    (D) provoke
    (E) enforce

7. Pam's answer is A.
The doctor is *barbarity of some criminal penalties*. We're looking for a word that means avoid or lessen. Choices B and D miss the point completely. If you know what *condone* means, it also misses the point; if not, it's not a bad guess. Choice E is a Joe Bloggs trap that contradicts the doctor.

8 Henry viewed Melissa to be ----; she seemed to be against any position regardless of its merits.

    (A) heretical
    (B) disobedient
    (C) contrary
    (D) inattentive
    (E) harried

8. Pam's answer is C.
The doctor in this sentence is *against any position*. If Melissa is against everything, then she must not be very agreeable. The opposite of *agreeable* is *contrary*. Choice B may seem close, but the sentence says nothing about whether Melissa does what she is supposed to do.

SECTION 4

QUESTIONS	EXPLANATIONS

9 Dr. Schwartz's lecture on art, while detailed and scholarly, focused ---- on the premodern; some students may have appreciated his specialized knowledge, but those with more ---- interests may have been disappointed.

(A) literally. .medieval
(B) completely. .pedantic
(C) expansively. .technical
(D) voluminously. .creative
(E) exclusively. .comprehensive

9. Pam's answer is E.
The doctor for the second blank is *appreciated his specialized knowledge*, and the trigger word is *but*, which tells you that the second part of the sentence must mean the opposite of the doctor. If some students didn't appreciate the specialized knowledge, then the *disappointed* students had *non*-specialized interests. The only word in the answer choices that means *non-specialized* is *comprehensive*. The other word in choice E also makes sense, because it fits the doctor. We know that the professor has *specialized knowledge*, so if his lecture focused *exclusively* on something, then it was very specialized.

10 Only when one actually visits the ancient ruins of marvelous bygone civilizations does one truly appreciate the sad ---- of human greatness.

(A) perspicacity
(B) magnitude
(C) artistry
(D) transience
(E) quiescence

10. Pam's answer is D.
The doctors in this sentence are *ancient ruins of marvelous bygone civilizations* and *sad*. What is sad about looking at the ruins of ancient civilizations? Seeing that *human greatness* doesn't last. Therefore, you can put *doesn't last* in the blank, and the best match is *transience*.

11 CAKE : DESSERT ::

(A) coach : football
(B) lawyer : jury
(C) poet : writing
(D) actor : troupe
(E) pediatrician : doctor

11. Pam's answer is E.
A CAKE is a kind of DESSERT just as a *pediatrician* is a kind of *doctor*.

12 WEIGHTLIFTER : STRENGTH ::

(A) goalie : skill
(B) dancer : speed
(C) marathoner : endurance
(D) hiker : agility
(E) fisherman : luck

12. Pam's answer is C.
A good WEIGHTLIFTER needs STRENGTH just as a good *marathoner* needs *endurance*. A goalie may need skill, but strength and endurance are more specific.

13 BREEZE : HURRICANE ::

(A) water : pebble
(B) gulf : coast
(C) eye : cyclone
(D) sun : cloud
(E) hill : mountain

13. Pam's answer is E.
A HURRICANE is a larger version of a BREEZE just as a *mountain* is a larger version of a *hill*.

SECTION 4

QUESTIONS	EXPLANATIONS

14 IMMORTAL : DEATH ::

(A) anonymous : fame
(B) hopeless : situation
(C) vital : life
(D) indisputable : agreement
(E) daily : year

14. Pam's answer is A.
IMMORTAL means without DEATH, just as *anonymous* means without *fame*.

15 TAPESTRY : THREAD ::

(A) pizza : pie
(B) mosaic : tiles
(C) ruler : divisions
(D) computer : switch
(E) car : engine

15. Pam's answer is B.
A TAPESTRY is made of THREAD. A *mosaic* is made of *tiles*. If you had trouble making a sentence, you should have eliminated answer choices with unrelated words and then worked backward. The words in choice D do not have a clear and necessary relationship. *Pizza* comes in the shape of a *pie*. Does a TAPESTRY come in the shape of a THREAD? That doesn't make any sense. A *ruler* is separated into *divisions*. Is a TAPESTRY separated into THREADs? That doesn't makes sense either. A *car* is powered by an *engine*. Is a TAPESTRY powered by a THREAD? That's ridiculous. Choices A, C, and E can each be eliminated by working backward, leaving choice B, which is Pam's answer.

16 LUBRICANT : FRICTION ::

(A) motor : electricity
(B) speed : drag
(C) insulation : heat
(D) adhesive : connection
(E) muffler : noise

16. Pam's answer is E.
A LUBRICANT reduces FRICTION, and a *muffler* reduces *noise*. If you had trouble making a sentence, try using POE. A *motor* can be powered by *electricity*, but nothing can be powered by FRICTION. Eliminate A. *Speed* and *drag* have no relationship. Eliminate B. *Insulation* keeps in *heat*. Could something keep in FRICTION? Not likely. Eliminate C. You could say that an *adhesive* makes a *connection*, but that's a weak relationship, which means E is a better choice.

17 PARODY : IMITATION ::

(A) stanza : verse
(B) limerick : poem
(C) novel : book
(D) portrait : painting
(E) riddle : puzzle

17. Pam's answer is B.
A PARODY is a humorous IMITATION just as a *limerick* is a humorous *poem*. If you chose C, D, or E, your sentence may not have been specific enough.

SECTION 4

18 COMET : TAIL ::

(A) traffic : lane
(B) missile : trajectory
(C) vessel : wake
(D) engine : fuel
(E) wave : crest

18. Pam's answer is C.
A COMET is followed by a TAIL, and a *vessel* is followed by a *wake*. Did you use POE? A *lane* is for a single line of *traffic*. A TAIL is not for a single line of COMET. Eliminate A. A *trajectory* is the path that a *missile* travels along. A TAIL is not the path a COMET travels along. Eliminate B. An *engine* runs on *fuel*. A COMET doesn't run on TAIL. The *crest* is the top of a *wave*. The TAIL is not the top of a COMET.

19 NEOLOGISM : LANGUAGE ::

(A) rhetoric : oratory
(B) syllogism : grammar
(C) innovation : technology
(D) iconography : art
(E) epistemology : philosophy

19. Pam's answer is C.
First of all, choice B is a Joe Bloggs trap because *grammar* makes Joe think of LANGUAGE. Unless you know what a NEOLOGISM is, you're better off Working Backward to answer this question. You can come up with a sentence for choice C: An *innovation* is a new development in *technology*. Could a NEOLOGISM be a new development in LANGUAGE? Sure. Choice C is your best guess, even if you didn't know some of the words in the other answer choices.

20 ADDENDUM : BOOK ::

(A) signature : letter
(B) vote : constitution
(C) codicil : will
(D) heading : folder
(E) stipulation : contract

20. Pam's answer is C.
This is a hard question, so you can eliminate choices A and D because *letter* and *folder* make Joe think of BOOK. You can eliminate choice B because *vote* and *constitution* do not have a clear and necessary relationship. If you simply guessed the hardest word, *codicil*, you would have found Pam's answer, although E would not have been a bad guess. (An ADDENDUM is an addition to a BOOK and *codicil* is an addition to a *will*.)

SECTION 4

QUESTIONS	EXPLANATIONS

21 PENCHANT : INCLINED ::
- (A) loathing : contemptuous
- (B) abhorrence : delighted
- (C) burgeoning : barren
- (D) loss : incessant
- (E) decision : predictable

21. Pam's answer is A.
The words in choices D and E have no relationship, so those choices can be eliminated. Here's a way to decide among the remaining choices: The words in choices B and C have opposite meanings (one word is positive and the other word is negative), while the words in choice A have similar meanings (both words are negative). Choice A is the odd one out, which would make it the best guess. (Having a PENCHANT means being very INCLINED. *Loathing* means being very *contemptuous*.)

22 VAGRANT : DOMICILE ::
- (A) pagan : morals
- (B) despot : leadership
- (C) arsonist : fire
- (D) exile : country
- (E) telephone : ear

22. Pam's answer is D.
The words in E are too easy for a hard question, so you can eliminate them. If you know what a *pagan* is, you know it has no relationship with *morals*, so you can eliminate A. An *arsonist* starts a *fire*. Does a VAGRANT start a DOMICILE? No. Eliminate C. An *exile* is a person without a *country*. Is a VAGRANT a person without a DOMICILE? Yup.

23 MERITORIOUS : PRAISE ::
- (A) captious : criticism
- (B) kind : admiration
- (C) questionable : response
- (D) reprehensible : censure
- (E) incredible : ecstasy

23. Pam's answer is D.
Joe Bloggs picks B, so eliminate that right away. The words in choices C and E have no relationship, so eliminate them. Now you're down to a 50-50 guess. Not bad. *Reprehensible* means deserving *censure* and MERITORIOUS means deserving PRAISE.

SECTION 4

The passages below is followed by questions based on its content. Answer the questions on the basis of what is <u>stated</u> or <u>implied</u> in the passage and in any introductory material that may be provided.

Questions 24–35 are based on the following passage.

The following passage is from a book written by a zoologist and published in 1986.

The domestic cat is a contradiction. No other animal has developed such an intimate relationship with humanity, while at the same time demanding
Line and getting such independent movement and action.
(5) The cat manages to remain a tame animal because of the sequence of its upbringing. By living both with other cats (its mother and littermates) and with humans (the family that has adopted it) during its infancy and kittenhood, it becomes attached to and
(10) considers that it belongs to both species. It is like a child that grows up in a foreign country and as a consequence becomes bilingual. The young cat becomes bimental. It may be a cat physically but mentally it is both feline and human. Once it is fully
(15) adult, however, most of its responses are feline ones, and it has only one major reaction to its human owners. It treats them as pseudoparents. The reason is that they took over from the real mother at a sensitive stage of the kitten's development and went
(20) on giving it milk, solid food, and comfort as it grew up.

This is rather different from the kind of bond that develops between human and dog. The dog sees its human owners as pseudoparents, as does the cat.
(25) On that score the process of attachment is similar. But the dog has an additional link. Canine society is group-organized; feline society is not. Dogs live in packs with tightly controlled status relationships among the individuals. There are top dogs, middle
(30) dogs, and bottom dogs and under natural circumstances they move around together, keeping tabs on one another the whole time. So the adult pet dog sees its human family both as pseudoparents and as the dominant members of the pack, hence its
(35) renowned reputation for obedience and its celebrated capacity for loyalty. Cats do have a complex social organization, but they never hunt in packs. In the wild, most of their day is spent in solitary stalking. Going for a walk with a human,
(40) therefore, has no appeal for them. And as for "coming to heel" and learning to "sit" and "stay," they are simply not interested. Such maneuvers have no meaning for them.

So the moment a cat manages to persuade a
(45) human being to open a door (that most hated of human inventions), it is off and away without a backward glance. As it crosses the threshold, the cat becomes transformed. The kitten-of-human brain is switched off and the wildcat brain is clicked on. The
(50) dog, in such a situation, may look back to see if its human packmate is following to join in the fun of exploring, but not the cat. The cat's mind has floated off into another, totally feline world, where strange bipedal* primates have no place.
(55) Because of this difference between domestic cats and domestic dogs, cat-lovers tend to be rather different from dog-lovers. As a rule cat-lovers have a stronger personality bias toward working alone, independent of the larger group. Artists like cats;
(60) soldiers like dogs. The much-lauded "group loyalty" phenomenon is alien to both cats and cat-lovers. If you are a company person, a member of the gang, or a person picked for the squad, the chances are that at home there is no cat curled up in front of the fire.
(65) The ambitious Yuppie, the aspiring politician, the professional athlete, these are not typical cat-owners. It is hard to picture football players with cats in their laps—much easier to envisage them taking their dogs for walks.
(70) Those who have studied cat-owners and dog-owners as two distinct groups report that there is also a gender bias. The majority of cat-lovers are female. This bias is not surprising in view of the division of labor evident in the development of
(75) human societies. Prehistoric males became specialized as group-hunters, while the females concentrated on food-gathering and childbearing. This difference contributed to a human male "pack mentality" that is far less marked in females.
(80) Wolves, the wild ancestors of domestic dogs, also became pack-hunters, so the modern dog has much more in common with the human male than with the human female.

The argument will always go on—feline self-
(85) sufficiency and individualism versus canine camaraderie and good-fellowship. But it is important to stress that in making a valid point I have caricatured the two positions. In reality there are many people who enjoy equally the company of
(90) both cats and dogs. And all of us, or nearly all of us, have both feline and canine elements in our personalities. We have moods when we want to be alone and thoughtful, and other times when we wish to be in the center of a crowded, noisy room.

bipedal: having two feet

SECTION 4

24 The primary purpose of the passage is to

(A) show the enmity that exists between cats and dogs

(B) advocate dogs as making better pets than cats

(C) distinguish the different characteristics of dogs and cats

(D) show the inferiority of dogs because of their dependent nature

(E) emphasize the role that human society plays in the personalities of domestic pets

24. Pam's answer is C.

This is a general question, so you only need to know the main idea of the passage. In simple terms, the passage talks about the difference between cats and dogs. This is exactly what choice C says.

Notice that the author presents both sides of the issue and doesn't advocate one animal over the other. That's why answer choices B and D are wrong.

Answer choice A is way too extreme. If you don't know what *enmity* means, look it up and you'll see.

Answer choice E is too specific and only covers one section of the passage, not the primary purpose of the passage as a whole.

25 According to the passage, the domestic cat can be described as

(A) a biped because it possesses the characteristics of animals with two feet

(B) a pseudopet because it can't really be tamed and will always retain its wild habits

(C) a contradiction because although it lives comfortably with humans, it refuses to be dominated by them

(D) a soldier because it is militant about preserving its independence

(E) a ruler because although it plays the part of a pet, it really dominates humans

25. Pam's answer is C.

The lead words in this question are *the domestic cat*, which should lead you to the second paragraph. According to lines 12–14, *The young cat becomes bimental. It may be a cat physically, but mentally it is both feline and human.* To be both feline and human is definitely a *contradiction*.

Common sense kills answer choice A, because cats don't have two feet.

Answer choice B is wrong because domestic cats are tame by definition. Otherwise, they would be wild.

Answer choice D is wrong because cats aren't soldiers.

Answer choice E doesn't make any sense. Do cats dominate humans? No way!

SECTION 4

QUESTIONS	EXPLANATIONS

26 In line 17 the word "pseudoparents" means

(A) part-time parents that are only partially involved with their young
(B) individuals who act as parents of adults
(C) parents that neglect their young
(D) parents that have both the characteristics of humans and their pets
(E) adoptive parents who aren't related to their young

26. Pam's answer is E.
According to the passage, the cat treats its human owners as *pseudoparents* because *they took over from the real mother at a sensitive stage of the kitten's development.* That means the human owners are obviously not the kitten's real parents, but rather like adoptive parents that took over from the kitten's real mother. Choice E says exactly that.

Answer choice A is wrong because *pseudo-* doesn't mean *part-time*. Human owners can be full-time parents to a cat, but that doesn't make them the cat's *real* parents.

Answer choice B misses the mark because the passage is talking about the parents of cats, not the parents of adults.

Answer choice C is wrong because the passage doesn't say anything about *neglect*.

Answer choice D makes no sense. How can someone have the characteristics of both humans and cats?

27 The author suggests that an important difference between dogs and cats is that, unlike dogs, cats

(A) do not regard their owners as the leader of their social group
(B) obey mainly because of their obedient nature
(C) have a more creative nature
(D) do not have complex social organizations
(E) are not skilled hunters

27. Pam's answer is A.
The lead words in this question are *difference between dogs and cats*, which should lead you right to the beginning of the third paragraph. According to lines 32–38, *the adult pet dog sees its human family as both pseudoparents and dominant members of the pack.*

On the other hand, cats *never hunt in packs*, and *most of their day is spend in solitary stalking*. So while dogs see their owners as leaders of the pack, cats do not because they're solitary. This is paraphrased in choice A.

Answer choice B has it backward. Dogs are obedient, not cats.

Answer choice C comes out of nowhere. Where does it say that cats are creative?

Answer choice D directly contradicts the passage. According to lines 36–37, *Cats do have a complex social organization.* Read carefully.

Answer choice E also contradicts the passage. According to line 38, cats spend most of their time *in solitary stalking*, which means they must be good hunters.

SECTION 4

28 It can be inferred from the passage that the social structure of dogs is

   (A) flexible
   (B) abstract
   (C) hierarchical
   (D) male dominated
   (E) somewhat exclusive

28. Pam's answer is C.
According to the lines 27–30, *Dogs live in packs with tightly controlled status relationships among the individuals. There are top dogs, middle dogs, and bottom dogs.* This describes a social structure that is *hierarchical*. (If you don't know what hierarchical means, look it up!)

   The other answer choices are wrong because none of them accurately describes the social structure in the lines quoted above. There is nothing *abstract* or *flexible* about *tightly controlled status relationships*, nor is there any mention of male domination in the passage. And *exclusivity* is certainly not the issue.

29 Lines 39–43 are used to stress

   (A) the laziness of cats that keeps them from being pack animals
   (B) the ignorance of dogs, which makes them more obedient pets
   (C) the antipathy that cats feel for humans
   (D) a difference between cats and dogs that emphasizes the independent nature of cats
   (E) the stubborn and complacent disposition of cats

29. Pam's answer is D.
The third paragraph is all about the difference between cats and dogs. Lines 39–43 emphasize the solitary nature of cats, which differs from group-oriented nature of dogs. This is exactly what choice D says.

   Answer choice A comes out of left field. Where does it say that cats are lazy? According to the passage, cats don't hunt in packs because they are *solitary* creatures, not because they are lazy.

   Answer choice B is rude. To say that dogs are ignorant is insulting to dog owners, and Pam never insults anybody. Can you imagine all the angry phone calls she would get if this choice were Pam's answer?

   Answer choice C is way too extreme. *Antipathy* is a very strong word. (If you don't know what it means, look it up and you'll see.) Cat owners would certainly be angry if this choice were Pam's answer.

   Answer choice E is also rude to cat owners. Remember, Pam doesn't like to upset people.

SECTION 4

|

30 In line 60, "much-lauded" means

(A) vehemently argued
(B) overly discussed
(C) unnecessarily complicated
(D) typically controversial
(E) commonly praised

30. Pam's answer is E.
Go back to the passage, find *much-lauded*, and cross it out. Then read the sentence and come up with your own word. *Much-lauded* is describing the "group loyalty" phenomenon. From the context, there is no reason to believe that the "group loyalty" phenomenon is *overly discussed, complicated,* or *controversial,* so you can get rid of B, C, and D. Choice A is too extreme, which only leaves E.

31 The "ambitious Yuppie" mentioned in line 65 is an example of a person

(A) who is power hungry
(B) who craves virtue
(C) who is a stereotypical pet owner
(D) who has a weak personality
(E) who seeks group-oriented status

31. Pam's answer is E.
According to the passage, an *ambitious Yuppie* is an example of someone who is not a typical cat owner. Since cat-owners are solitary people, that means the *ambitious Yuppie* must be a group-oriented person. Accordingly, choice E is Pam's answer.
　　Answer choices A and D are insulting to Yuppies, and Pam wants to avoid controversy.
　　Answer choice B doesn't make any sense, and there is no mention of virtue anywhere in the passage.
　　Answer choice C might be tempting, but Pam likes to avoid *stereotypes* because they can get her in trouble.

32 Paragraph 6 indicates that human females

(A) are more like dogs than cats
(B) developed independent roles that didn't require group behavior
(C) had to gather food because they were not strong enough to hunt
(D) are not good owners for the modern dog
(E) were negatively affected by the division of labor of human societies

32. Pam's answer is B.
You can immediately eliminate choices A, C, D, and E because Pam would never say anything negative about women. According to the sixth paragraph, the differences between the roles of prehistoric men and women *contributed to a human male "pack mentality" that is far less marked in females.* This idea is paraphrased in choice B.

SECTION 4

QUESTIONS	EXPLANATIONS

33 The author uses lines 84–88 to

(A) show that the argument stated in the passage is ultimately futile
(B) disclaim glaring contradictions that are stated in the passage
(C) qualify the generalizations used to make the author's point
(D) ensure that the reader doesn't underestimate the crux of the passage
(E) highlight a difference between individualism and dependency

33. Pam's answer is C.
To answer this question, you have to know what *caricatured* means. A caricature is an exaggerated drawing, so the author is saying that he exaggerated in the passage. He is thus qualifying some of the generalizations he has made in the passage.

Answer choice A is too extreme. Pam would never suggest that the author of one of her passages made a *futile* argument.

Answer choice B is also too extreme. Pam doesn't deal with *glaring contradictions*.

Answer choice D goes in the wrong direction. In the lines cited in the question, the author admits that he exaggerated in order to make his point, so he's trying to ensure that readers don't overestimate what he said in the passage.

Answer choice E sounds like psychobabble, and it also has nothing to do with what the author is saying at the end of the passage.

34 The last four sentences in the passage (lines 86–94) provide

(A) an example of the argument that has been made earlier
(B) a summary of the points made earlier
(C) a modification of the position taken earlier
(E) a rebuttal to opposing views referred to earlier

34. Pam's answer is D.
You can use the answer to question 33 to help you answer this question. Since the author is qualifying some of the generalizations he made, he's modifying the position he took earlier.

There are no *examples* or *summaries* in the last four sentences of the passage, so kill answer choices A and B.

Answer choice C is wrong because there are no *reasons* in lines 86–94, and answer choice E is wrong because there are no *rebuttals* or *opposing views* anywhere in the passage.

35 The passage as a whole does all of the following EXCEPT

(A) use a statistic
(B) make parenthetic statements
(C) use a simile
(D) restate an argument
(E) make a generalization

35. Pam's answer is C.
This is a general question, but it is also an EXCEPT question, so do it last. The only way to answer this question is to search through the passage for each of the answer choices. Remember, you're looking for the answer choice that is *not* there. The passage uses a *statistic* in line 70–73, makes a *parenthetic statement* in lines 45–46, restates an *argument* in lines 84–86, and makes *generalizations* throughout the passage. Answer C is the only one left.

SECTION 5

| QUESTIONS | EXPLANATIONS |

1 If $2 + a = 2 - a$, then $a =$

    (A) −1
    (B)   0
    (C)   1
    (D)   2
    (E)   4

1. Jim's answer is B.
   This simple equation should present us with little difficulty, although beware: It is on precisely such questions that our guard comes down and we become careless!
   Backsolving is safest.
   Only B works:

   $$2 + (0) = 2 - (0)$$
   $$2 = 2$$

2 In which of the following patterns is the number of horizontal lines three times the number of vertical lines?

(A)   (B)   (C)

(D) 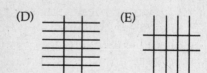   (E)

2. Jim's answer is D.
   If you missed this question, you either misread the question or miscounted the lines. Choice D has 6 horizontal lines and 2 vertical ones. Remember, horizontal means side to side, and vertical means up and down.

SECTION 5

QUESTIONS	EXPLANATIONS

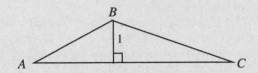

3 If $AC = 4$, what is the area of $\triangle ABC$ above?

(A) $\dfrac{1}{2}$

(B) 2

(C) $\sqrt{7}$

(D) 4

(E) 8

3. Jim's answer is B.

As the instructions to every math section remind us, the area of a triangle is given by the formula:

$A = \dfrac{1}{2}bh$

Since the base is 4 and the height is 1, the area is 2.

$A = \dfrac{1}{2}(4)(1)$

4 If $\dfrac{4}{5}$ of $\dfrac{3}{4} = \dfrac{2}{5}$ of $\dfrac{x}{4}$, then $x =$

(A) 12

(B) 6

(C) 3

(D) $\dfrac{3}{2}$

(E) 1

4. Jim's answer is B.

Translating the word *of* as *times*, we get the following equation:

$\left(\dfrac{4}{5}\right)\left(\dfrac{3}{4}\right) = \left(\dfrac{2}{5}\right)\left(\dfrac{x}{4}\right)$

$\dfrac{3}{5} = \dfrac{2x}{20}$

$\dfrac{3}{5} = \dfrac{x}{10}$

$5x = 30$

$x = 6$

QUESTIONS	EXPLANATIONS

5 If $x + y = z$ and $x = y$, then all of the following are true EXCEPT

(A) $2x + 2y = 2z$

(B) $x - y = 0$

(C) $x - z = y - z$

(D) $x = \dfrac{z}{2}$

(E) $z - y = 2x$

5. Jim's answer is E.
With algebraic answer choices, we should plug in numbers. Let's let $x = y = 2$, which makes $z = 4$. Plugging these values into the choices, we'd get the following:

[Yes] (A) $2(2) + 2(2) = 2(4)$

[Yes] (B) $2 - 2 = 0$

[Yes] (C) $2 - 4 = 2 - 4$

[Yes] (D) $2 = \dfrac{4}{2}$

[No] (E) $4 - 2 = 2(2)$

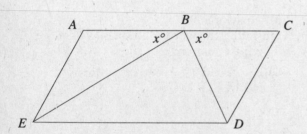

Note: Figure not drawn to scale.

6 In the figure above, $AC // ED$. If the length of $BD = 3$, what is the length of BE?

(A) 3
(B) 4
(C) 5
(D) $3\sqrt{3}$
(E) It cannot be determined from the information given.

6. Jim's answer is A.
Keep in mind that this figure is not drawn to scale. Since $AC \parallel ED$, we know that the following angles are equal:

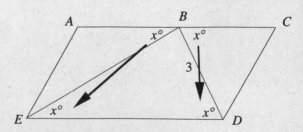

Since $\triangle EBD$ has two equal angles, the opposing sides are also equal. Therefore, $BE = BD = 3$.

SECTION 5

QUESTIONS	EXPLANATIONS

7 $\dfrac{900}{10} + \dfrac{90}{100} + \dfrac{9}{1000} =$

(A) 90.09
(B) 90.099
(C) 90.909
(D) 99.09
(E) 999

7. Jim's answer is C.
If you missed this question, you should review decimal place values:

$\dfrac{900}{10} = 90$

$\dfrac{90}{100} = 0.9$

$\dfrac{9}{1000} = 0.009$

$\begin{array}{r} 90 \\ 0.9 \\ +\ 0.009 \\ \hline 90.909 \end{array}$

Remember, you can use your calculator to help you solve this problem.

8 Fifteen percent of the coins in a piggy bank are nickels and 5% are dimes. If there are 220 coins in the bank, how many are <u>not</u> nickels or dimes?

(A) 80
(B) 176
(C) 180
(D) 187
(E) 200

8. Jim's answer is B.
Twenty percent of the coins are either nickels or dimes, so 80% are neither. Eighty percent of 220 equals 176. Use your calculator!

| QUESTIONS | EXPLANATIONS |

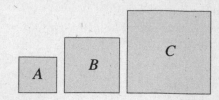

9 In the figure above, the perimeter of square A is $\frac{2}{3}$ the perimeter of square B, and the perimeter of square B is $\frac{2}{3}$ the perimeter of square C. If the area of square A is 16, what is the area of square C?

(A) 24
(B) 36
(C) 64
(D) 72
(E) 81

9. Jim's answer is E.
If the area of square A is 16, the length of each side is 4 and the perimeter is 16. We are told that this is two-thirds of B's perimeter, which we can calculate:

$$16 = \frac{2}{3}B$$

$$\left(\frac{3}{2}\right)16 = B$$

$$24 = B$$

Now that we know the perimeter of B, we can calculate the perimeter of C:

$$24 = \frac{2}{3}C$$

$$\left(\frac{3}{2}\right)(24) = C$$

$$36 = C$$

If the perimeter of C is 36, each side is 9 and the area of C is 9^2, or 81. If you chose B, you need to read the question more carefully.

SECTION 5

10 A bakery uses a special flour mixture that contains corn, wheat, and rye in the ratio of 3:5:2. If a bag of the mixture contains 5 pounds of rye, how many pounds of wheat does it contain?

(A) 2
(B) 5
(C) 7.5
(D) 10
(E) 12.5

10. Jim's answer is E.
First, by estimation, we know that the mixture contains more wheat than rye; so wheat must be more than 5. So let's eliminate choices A and B.
Use the Ratio Box.

Corn	Wheat	Rye	Total
3	5	2	10
	2.5	2.5	
	12.5	5	

11 If $a^2b = 12^2$, and b is an odd integer, then a could be divisible by all of the following EXCEPT

(A) 3
(B) 4
(C) 6
(D) 9
(E) 12

11. Jim's answer is D.
Note first that this is an EXCEPT question. Now, since $a^2b = 12^2$, and b is an odd integer, let's see what we can come up with. The first value for b that occurs to us is 1, so we get the following:
$a^2b = 12^2$
$(a^2)(1) = 12^2$
$a^2 = 12^2$
$a = 12$
If a equals 12, it is divisible by 1, 2, 3, 4, 6, and 12. So the only choice that remains is D.

SECTION 5

QUESTIONS	EXPLANATIONS

12 A coin was flipped 20 times and came up heads 10 times and tails 10 times. If the first and last flips were both heads, what is the greatest number of consecutive heads that could have occurred?

(A) 1
(B) 2
(C) 8
(D) 9
(E) 10

12. Jim's answer is D.
If the first and last flips were heads, we could have 9 consecutive heads, followed by 10 consecutive tails and the final head.

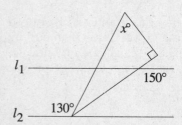

13 If l_1 is parallel to l_2 in the figure above, what is the value of x?

(A) 20
(B) 50
(C) 70
(D) 80
(E) 90

13. Jim's answer is C.
Estimating first, x is less than 90 and more than 20. So we can eliminate choices A and E. Now let's examine the figure:
Since $l_1 \parallel l_2$, 130 plus the other angle in the triangle is 150. So the other angle in the triangle must be 20, which means that x is 70.

SECTION 5

14 Which of the following must be true?

> I. The sum of two consecutive integers is odd.
> II. The sum of three consecutive integers is even.
> III. The sum of three consecutive integers is a multiple of 3.

(A) I only
(B) II only
(C) I and II only
(D) I and III only
(E) I, II, and III

14. Jim's answer is D.
Note before we begin that the question asks for what *must* be true. Let's start with the first option:

> I. $2 + 3 = 5$
> $3 + 4 = 7$

Option I must be true. Eliminate choice B.

> II. $2 + 3 + 4 = 9$

Option II is false. Eliminate choices C and E. We still need to check the third option:

> III. $2 + 3 + 4 = 9$
> $3 + 4 + 5 = 12$
> $4 + 5 + 6 = 15$

It's a safe bet III must be true.

15 Which of the following is equal to .064?

(A) $\left(\dfrac{1}{80}\right)^2$

(B) $\left(\dfrac{8}{100}\right)^2$

(C) $\left(\dfrac{1}{8}\right)^2$

(D) $\left(\dfrac{2}{5}\right)^3$

(E) $\left(\dfrac{8}{10}\right)^3$

15. Jim's answer is D.
If you use your calculator, this problem should not give you any trouble. You can convert each of the fractions to decimals with your calculator and then apply the exponent. In choice D:

$$\left(\frac{2}{5}\right)^3 = (.4)^3 = .064.$$

QUESTIONS	EXPLANATIONS

16 If the average (arithmetic mean) of four distinct positive integers is 11, what is the greatest possible value of any one of the integers?

(A) 35
(B) 38
(C) 40
(D) 41
(E) 44

16. Jim's answer is B.
Use an Average Pie to solve this one. Write in the number of things, which is 4, and the average, which is 11.

Multiply to find the total, which is 44. Now you have to be careful with the vocabulary in the question. We know that the four *distinct positive integers* add up to 44. To find the greatest possible value of one of them, you need to figure out the smallest possible value of the other three. Since distinct means different, the other three numbers have to be the smallest positive integers: 1, 2, and 3. Those add up to 6, so the fourth number must be 44–6, or 38.

For $x = 0$, $x = 1$, and $x = 2$,
Set A = $\{x,\ x + 3,\ 3x,\ x^2\}$.

17 What is the mode of Set A?

(A) 0
(B) 1
(C) 2
(D) 2.5
(E) 3

17. Jim's answer is A.
Plugging In was the appropriate first step.
When $x = 0$, A = $\{0,3,0,0\}$;
when $x = 1$, A = $\{1,4,3,1\}$;
when $x = 2$, A = $\{2,5,6,4\}$.
Thus, set A has 12 elements—3 of which equal 0. Choice A is the mode of the set. (The *mode* is the number in a group that appears most often.)

SECTION 5

QUESTIONS	EXPLANATIONS

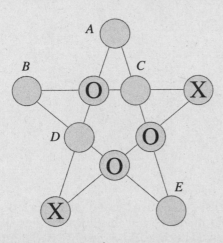

18 If the figure above is filled in so that each row of four circles contains two circles marked with an X and two circles marked with an O, which circle must be marked with an X?

(A) *A*
(B) *B*
(C) *C*
(D) *D*
(E) *E*

19 If *c* is positive, what percent of 3*c* is 9?

(A) $\dfrac{c}{100}$ %

(B) $\dfrac{c}{3}$ %

(C) $\dfrac{9}{c}$ %

(D) 3%

(E) $\dfrac{300}{c}$ %

18. Jim's answer is E.
This problem is probably best approached by the brute force method of trial and error. (On the SAT, with the clock ticking away, you'll often find that you don't have the time to be logical.) Eventually, you'd discover that circle *E* is the answer. If you were logical, you'd notice that rows *BE* and *AE* are identical. That being the case, circle *A* equals circle *B*, and circle *D* equals circle *C*. The odd man out is circle *E*.

19. Jim's answer is E.
Plug In 3 for *c*. The question is now asking what percent of 9 is 9. The answer would be 100. Whichever choice gives you 100 when 3 is plugged in for *c* is the answer. Therefore *E* is the answer. Remember, Plugging In good numbers will make your life much easier!

SECTION 5

QUESTIONS	EXPLANATIONS

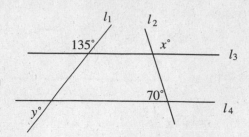

Note: Figure not drawn to scale.

20 If four lines intersect as shown in the figure above, $x + y =$

   (A)   65
   (B) 110
   (C) 155
   (D) 205
   (E) It cannot be determined from the information given.

20.   Jim's answer is C.
We trust you noticed that choice D is too simple an answer for this question since it can be arrived at by adding the only two numbers we are given. Likewise, choice E is another Joe Bloggs choice. Looking at the figure, we should not assume that the lines are parallel. (Did you?) Instead, we must use vertical angles to compute the following values:

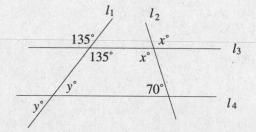

Since the sum of a quadrilateral's interior angles is 360°, we get the following equation:
$135 + x + 70 + y = 360$
$205 + x + y = 360$
$x + y = 155$

SECTION 5

21 S is the set of all positive numbers n such that $n < 100$ and $\sqrt{n}$ is an integer. What is the median value of the members of set S?

(A) 5

(B) 5.5

(C) 25

(D) 50

(E) 99

21. Jim's answer is C.
First, we need to compute all possible values of n:

$\sqrt{n}$	n
1	1
2	4
3	9
4	16
5	25
6	36
7	49
8	64
9	81

Now, careful! The median value for $\sqrt{n}$ is 5, but the median value for n is 25.

22 If segment WZ and segment XY are diameters with lengths of 12, what is the area of the shaded region?

(A) 36
(B) 30
(C) 18
(D) 12
(E)   9

22. Jim's answer is C.
You can find Jim's answer to this question by using the side of your answer sheet as a ruler and guesstimating. Since $XY = 12$, the hypotenuse of each triangle is 6. Now mark off the length of 6 with your home-made ruler and compare that to a side of one of the triangles. You can guesstimate that the side is about 4. Using that approximation, calculate that since the base and height of both triangles is 4, the area of each triangle is $\frac{1}{2}(4)(4)$, or 8. The area of both triangles together is 16, which is closest to 18, in choice C. Remember, Jim wants you to do complicated geometry, but all you care about is finding the answer.

SECTION 5

23 At the beginning of 1992, the population of Rockville was 204,000 and the population of Springfield was 216,000. If the population of each city increased by exactly 20% in 1992, how many more people lived in Springfield than in Rockville at the end of 1992?

(A) 9,600
(B) 10,000
(C) 12,000
(D) 14,400
(E) 20,000

23. Jim's answer is D.
Take out your calculator:
216,000 + 20% of 216,000 = 259,200
204,000 + 20% of 204,000 = 244,800
                                      14,400
Another route to the answer is to take the difference immediately (216,000 − 204,000 = 12,000) and then to increase that by 20%. On a calculator, either solution is equally effective.

24 Line A has a slope of $-\dfrac{3}{2}$. If points $(-2, 6)$ and $(m, -9)$ are on line A, then $m =$

(A) 3
(B) 4
(C) 6
(D) 8
(E) 12

24. Jim's answer is D.

The formula for slope is $\dfrac{y_2 - y_1}{x_2 - x_1}$. Plugging In our given points, we can solve for m.

$$\frac{6 - (-9)}{-2 - m} = \frac{-3}{2}$$

$$\frac{15}{(-2 - m)} = \frac{-3}{2}$$

$$30 = (-3)(-2 - m)$$
$$-10 = -2 - m$$
$$-8 = -m$$
$$8 = m.$$

SECTION 5

25 A researcher found that a certain student's score on each of a series of tests could be predicted using the formula

$$P = \frac{310T + (LT)^2}{100}$$

where P is the number of points scored on the test, T is the number of hours spent studying, L is the number of hours of sleep the night before the test, and where $P \le 100$. If, before a particular test, this student spent no more than 10 hours studying, what is the least number of hours of sleep she should get if she wants to score at least 80 points?

(A) 6
(B) 7
(C) $\sqrt{56}$
(D) 8
(E) $\sqrt{69}$

25. Jim's answer is B.
Substituting 10 for T and 80 for P, we get the following equation to solve:

$$80 = \frac{(3100) + (10L)^2}{100}$$

$$8000 = 3100 + (10L)^2$$
$$4900 = 100L^2$$
$$49 = L^2$$
$$7 = L$$

SECTION 6

The two passages below are followed by questions based on their content and on the relationship between the two passages. Answer the questions on the basis of what is <u>stated</u> or <u>implied</u> in the passage and in any introductory material that may be provided.

Questions 1–13 are based on the following passages.

In Passage 1, the author presents his view of the early years of the silent film industry. In Passage 2, the author draws on her experiences as a mime to generalize about her art. (A mime is a performer who, without speaking, entertains through gesture, facial expression, and movement.)

Passage 1

Talk to those people who first saw films when they were silent, and they will tell you the experience was magic. The silent film had
Line extraordinary powers to draw members of an
(5) audience into the story, and an equally potent capacity to make their imaginations work. It required the audience to become engaged—to supply voices and sound effects. The audience was the final, creative contributor to the process of
(10) making a film.

The finest films of the silent era depended on two elements that we can seldom provide today—a large and receptive audience and a well-orchestrated score. For the audience, the fusion of
(15) picture and live music added up to more than the sum of the respective parts.

The one word that sums up the attitude of the silent filmmakers is *enthusiasm*, conveyed most strongly before formulas took shape and when
(20) there was more room for experimentation. This enthusiastic uncertainty often resulted in such accidental discoveries as new camera or editing techniques. Some films experimented with players; the 1915 film *Regeneration*, for example, by using
(25) real gangsters and streetwalkers, provided startling local color. Other films, particularly those of Thomas Ince, provided tragic endings as often as films by other companies supplied happy ones.

Unfortunately, the vast majority of silent films
(30) survive today in inferior prints that no longer reflect the care that the original technicians put into them. The modern versions of silent films may appear jerky and flickery, but the vast picture palaces did not attract four to six thousand people a night by
(35) giving them eyestrain. A silent film depended on its visuals; as soon as you degrade those, you lose elements that go far beyond the image on the surface. The acting in silents was often very subtle, very restrained, despite legends to the contrary.

Passage 2

(40) Mime opens up a new world to the beholder, but it does so insidiously, not by purposely injecting points of interest in the manner of a tour guide. Audiences are not unlike visitors to a foreign land who discover that the modes, manners, and
(45) thoughts of its inhabitants are not meaningless oddities, but are sensible in context.

I remember once when an audience seemed perplexed at what I was doing. At first, I tried to gain a more immediate response by using slight
(50) exaggerations. I soon realized that these actions had nothing to do with the audience's understanding of the character. What I had believed to be a failure of the audience to respond in the manner I expected was, in fact, only their concentration on what I was
(55) doing; they were enjoying a gradual awakening—a slow transference of their understanding from their own time and place to one that appeared so unexpectedly before their eyes. This was evidenced by their growing response to succeeding numbers.

(60) Mime is an elusive art, as its expression is entirely dependent on the ability of the performer to imagine a character and to re-create that character for each performance. As a mime, I am a physical medium, the instrument upon which the figures of
(65) my imagination play their dance of life. The individuals in my audience also have responsibilities—they must be alert collaborators. They cannot sit back, mindlessly complacent, and wait to have their emotions titillated by mesmeric
(70) musical sounds or visual rhythms or acrobatic feats, or by words that tell them what to think. Mime is an art that, paradoxically, appeals both to those who respond instinctively to entertainment and to those whose appreciation is more analytical and complex.
(75) Between these extremes lie those audiences conditioned to resist any collaboration with what is played before them; and these the mime must seduce despite themselves. There is only one way to attack those reluctant minds—take them unaware! They will be delighted at an unexpected pleasure.

SECTION 6

QUESTIONS	EXPLANATIONS

1 Lines 14–16 of passage 1 indicate that

(A) music was the most important element of silent films

(B) silent films rely on a combination of music and image in affecting an audience

(C) the importance of music in silent film has been overestimated

(D) live music compensated for the poor quality of silent film images

(E) no film can succeed without a receptive audience

1. Pam's answer is B.
According to lines 14–16, the combination of live music and pictures add up to something truly spectacular and affecting. The phrase in the passage, *the fusion of picture and live music* is paraphrased in choice B as *a combination of music and image.*

Answer choice A is wrong because there's nothing in the passage to indicate that the author believes music is the most important element in silent films. In fact, this answer choice directly contradicts the lines cited in the questions, which tell us that there was a *fusion* of picture and music.

Answer choices C and D are wrong for the same reason. According to the passage, music and pictures in silent film are of equal importance, and one is not better or worse than the other.

Answer choice E is way off. The lines cited in the question are about *music* and *pictures.*

2 The "formulas" mentioned in line 19 of the passage most probably refer to

(A) movie theaters
(B) use of real characters
(C) standardized film techniques
(D) the fusion of disparate elements
(E) contemporary events

2. Pam's answer is C.
According to lines 17–20, the enthusiasm of the filmmakers was more evident *before formulas took shape and when there was more room for experimentation.* So *formulas* must have been followed after the period of experimentation, which means that *formulas* are the opposite of *experimentation.* In choice C, *standardized film techniques* are the opposite of experimentation.

Answer choices A and E don't make any sense. How can *events* or *theaters* be *formulas?* Use common sense.

Answer choice B is an example of *experimentation*, not a *formula.*

Answer choice D is not mentioned anywhere in the third paragraph.

SECTION 6

<table>
<tr><td>QUESTIONS</td><td>EXPLANATIONS</td></tr>
</table>

3 The author uses the phrase "enthusiastic uncertainty" in line 21 to suggest that the filmmakers were

(A) excited to be experimenting in an undefined area
(B) delighted at the opportunity to study new acting formulas
(C) optimistic in spite of the obstacles that faced them
(D) eager to challenge existing conventions
(E) eager to please but unsure of what the public wanted

3.   Pam's answer is A.
According to lines 20–23, the *enthusiastic uncertainty* led to *such accidental discoveries as new camera or editing techniques*. Thus, the filmmakers were excited to be trying new things.
   Answer choice B confuses several ideas. The *enthusiastic uncertainty* existed *before* formulas took shape.
   Answer choice C is wrong because there are no *obstacles* mentioned in the third paragraph.
   Answer choice D is wrong for the same reason that choice B is wrong. The passage is talking about the time *before* formulas and conventions, back when filmmakers still experimented.
   Answer choice E is way off base. The passage says nothing about filmmakers being *eager to please* or *unsure what the public wanted*. Go back to the passage and read more carefully.

4 The author uses the phrase "but the . . . eyestrain" (lines 33–35) in order to

(A) indicate his disgust with the incompetence of early film technicians
(B) suggest that audiences today perceive silent films incorrectly
(C) convey his regret about the decline of the old picture palaces
(D) highlight the pitfalls of the silent movie era
(E) argue for the superiority of modern film technology over that of silent movies

4.   Pam's answer is B.
According to lines 29–35, the prints of silent films that exist today are of poor quality, but the prints they used in the movie houses originally must have been of high quality in order to attract so many people. So the poor prints we have today don't show us what the films really looked like back them. This idea is best paraphrased in answer choice B.
   Answer choice A is much too extreme. Pam's authors are never *disgusted*.
   Answer choice C also expresses an emotion that Pam doesn't like. *Regret* is too negative.
   Answer choice D is wrong because the passage never mentions any *pitfalls*.
   Answer choice E completely contradicts the main idea of the passage. The author is clearly a big fan of silent films.

SECTION 6

5 The word "legends" in line 39 most nearly means

(A) arguments
(B) symbolism
(C) propaganda
(D) movie stars
(E) misconceptions

5. Pam's answer is E.
Go back to the passage, find *legends*, and cross it out. Then read the sentence and come up with your own word. The doctor, in effect, is *to the contrary*, so you can put *contradiction* in the blank. The best match in the answer choices is *misconceptions*.

Answer choices B, C, D make no sense whatsoever in context. Would you say, *despite movie stars to the contrary*? Of course not.

Answer choice A might be tempting, but it doesn't match the doctor in the passage.

6 The last sentence of passage 1 implies that

(A) the stars of silent movies have been criticized for overacting
(B) many silent film actors became legends in their own time
(C) silent film techniques should be studied by filmmakers today
(D) visual effects defined the silent film
(E) many silent films that exist today are of poor quality

6. Pam's answer is A.
You can use the last question to help you answer this question. The last sentence says that the acting in silent movies was very subtle and restrained, although people now have precisely the opposite view of it. The opposite of subtle and restrained acting is *overacting*, which is exactly what choice A is about.

Answer choice B mixes up the ideas in the last sentence. The *legends* were about the acting of silent film actors, not about the actors themselves.

Answer choice C is very wrong. The last sentence says nothing about what today's filmmakers should do.

Answer choice D is wrong because the last sentence says nothing about *visual effects*.

Answer choice E is mentioned earlier in the paragraph, but this is not what the last sentence says.

SECTION 6

QUESTIONS	EXPLANATIONS

7 The word "restrained" (line 39) most nearly means
(A) sincere
(B) dramatic
(C) understated
(D) inexpressive
(E) consistent

7. Pam's answer is C.
Again, you can use the previous question to answer this question. The last sentence says that the acting in silent movies was actually very *subtle* and *restrained*, and in the last question we said that this was the opposite of *overacting*. So *restrained* acting must be, in some sense, *underacting*. Therefore, the best match is *understated*.

  Answer choice A and B miss by a long shot because *restrained* doesn't mean *sincere* or *dramatic* in any context.

  Answer choice D is close, but something can be *expressive* even if it's *subtle* and *restrained*.

  Answer choice E doesn't fit in the context of the passage at all.

8 The author mentions the incident in lines 47–59 in order to imply that
(A) the audience's lack of response was a positive sign and reflected their captivated interest in the performance
(B) she was forced to resort to stereotypes in order to reach an audience that was otherwise unattainable
(C) exaggeration is an essential part of mime because it allows the forums used to be fully expressed
(D) her audience, though not initially appearing knowledgeable, had a good understanding of the subtlety of mime
(E) although vocalization is not necessary in mime, it is sometimes helpful for slower audiences

8. Pam's answer is A.
In lines 52–58, the author says, *What I believed to be a failure of the audience to respond in the manner I expected was, in fact, only their concentration on what I was doing.* So, although the author originally thought that she wasn't getting through to the audience, it turned out that they were actually paying very close attention to what she was doing. The best paraphrase for this idea is in choice A.

  Answer choice B is wrong because Pam's authors never *resort to stereotypes*.

  The author never says that exaggeration is an *essential* part of mime, so you can cross off C.

  Answer choice D is close, but the author is talking about the how well the audience responded to mime, not how much they knew about it.

  Answer choice E is ridiculous. The whole point of mime is that the actor remains completely silent!

SECTION 6

QUESTIONS	EXPLANATIONS

9 Lines 47–59 indicate that the author of passage 2 and the silent filmmakers of passage 1 were similar because

(A) neither used many props
(B) both conveyed universal truths by using sophisticated technology
(C) for both, trial and error was a part of the learning process
(D) both used visual effects and dialogue
(E) both had a loyal following

9. Pam's answer is C.
You can use what you learned from the last question to help you answer this question. The author of the second passage originally thought she was failing with her audience, but it turned out she had actually succeeded. The previous passage mentions experimentation and accidental discovery (look back at question 3). So the filmmakers in passage 1 and the author of passage 2 both used trial and error to make new discoveries. If you look at the other answer choices, they all apply to only one of the two passages.

Answer choice is A is wrong because props are not mentioned in either passage. If it's not mentioned in the passage, it's not Pam's answer.

Answer choice B makes no sense. Does a mime use sophisticated technology? Certainly not. Don't forget to use common sense.

Answer choice D completely contradicts the main idea of both passages. Both silent film and mime are *silent*. That means there's no *dialogue*!

Answer choice E is wrong because the lines cited in the question make no mention of *loyal followings*.

10 The sentence "As a . . . life" (lines 63–65) suggests that the author of passage 2 feels mimes

(A) cannot control the way audiences interpret their characters
(B) must suspend their own identities in order to successfully portray their characters
(C) have to resist outside attempts to define their acting style
(D) should focus on important events in the lives of specific characters
(E) know the limitations of performances that do not incorporate either music or speech

10. Pam's answer is B.
The sentence in question refers to mime as a *physical medium*. In this case, a medium is the material that an artist uses to create art. For example, a painter uses paint and a canvas as a medium. But for a mime, her own body is the physical medium through which *the figures of my imagination play their dance of life*. So she allows her characters (figuratively) to take over her body. The best paraphrase of this idea is in choice B.

Answer choice A is wrong because Pam would never suggest that artists have no control.

Answer choices C and D are not mentioned anywhere in the passage.

Answer choice E contradicts the main idea of the passage. The author is a mime, which means she doesn't use speech or music. So why would she suggest that such performances have limitations?

SECTION 6

QUESTIONS	EXPLANATIONS

11 Which of the following pieces of information makes mime and silent film seem less similar?

(A) Vaudeville and theatrical presentations were also popular forms of entertainment during the silent film era.

(B) Silent films presented both fictional drama and factual information.

(C) Silent film sometimes relied on captions to convey dialogue to the audience.

(D) Musicians working in movie theaters were usually employed for long periods of time.

(E) Many of the characters in silent films gained wide popularity among movie-goers.

11. Pam's answer is C
The connection between the topics of the two passages is that both mimes and silent films communicate without words. But if it were true that silent films actually used words, then the two arts would not be as similar as they seem. Choice C introduces this fact and, therefore, makes mime and silent film seem less similar.

Answer choice A gets completely off the topic. What do vaudeville and theater have to do with the similarity between mime and silent film?

Answer choice B doesn't lessen the similarity. Can't mime also present fictional drama and factual information?

Answer choice D is ridiculous. What could this possibly have to do the comparison between silent film and mime? Just because Pam wrote the answer choice doesn't mean you have to take it seriously.

Answer choice E also misses the mark. What does popularity of silent film have to do with its relationship to mime? Not much.

12 Passages 1 and 2 are similar in that both are mainly concerned with

(A) the use of special effects
(B) differences among dramatic styles
(C) the visual aspects of performance
(D) the suspension of disbelief in audiences
(E) nostalgia for a bygone era

12. Pam's answer is C.
As you know from the previous question, the similarity between silent film and mime is that they are both *silent*. If you're not using your ears to enjoy silent film and mime, then you must be using your *eyes*. So the similarity lies in the *visual* aspect, which leads you to answer choice C.

Answer choice A is silly. Do mimes use special effects? Of course not.

Answer choice B might be tempting, but the passages are not about *differences* in dramatic styles.

Answer choice D is not mentioned anywhere in either passage. Remember, this is a main idea question. How can something that is never mentioned be the main idea?

Answer choice E is wrong because there is no *nostalgia* in passage 2.

SECTION 6

13 Which of the following is an element that figures in the success of the dramatic arts described in both passages?

(A) A successful combination of different dramatic styles

(B) The exaggeration of certain aspects of a character

(C) The incorporation of current events in the narrative

(D) High audience attendance

(E) The active participation of the audience

13. Pam's answer is E.

According to lines 12–13 in passage 1, silent films depended on a *large and receptive audience*. The author of passage 2 says, *The individuals in my audience also have responsibilities—they must be collaborators* (lines 65–67). So the common element is audience participation.

Answer choice A is wrong because there is no mention of *different dramatic styles* in either passage. If it's not in the passage, then it's not Pam's answer.

Passage 1 never mentions any *exaggeration*, so cross off answer choice B.

Answer choices C and D are wrong because passage 2 never mentions *current events* or *high audience attendance.*

SECTION 7

QUESTIONS	EXPLANATIONS

Price of Buttons in Store X

Black	$2 per 5 buttons
Blue	$2 per 6 buttons
Brown	$3 per 8 buttons
Orange	$4 per 12 buttons
Red	$4 per 7 buttons

1 In Store X, which color button costs the most per individual unit?

(A) Black
(B) Blue
(C) Brown
(D) Orange
(E) Red

1. Jim's answer is E.
   This is an excellent calculator question.
   Here are the costs per unit for each color:

   Black = $\frac{2}{5}$ = .40 per button

   Blue = $\frac{2}{6}$ = .33 per button

   Brown = $\frac{3}{8}$ = .375 per button

   Orange = $\frac{4}{12}$ = .33 per button

   Red = $\frac{4}{7}$ = .57 per button

2 Which of the following numbers can be written in the form $6k + 1$, where k is a positive integer?

(A) 70
(B) 71
(C) 72
(D) 73
(E) 74

2. Jim's answer is D.
   To answer this just start plugging in values of k until you get into the 70–74 range:
   $6(12) + 1 = 73$

SECTION 7

|

3 $\left(\dfrac{4}{5}\times 3\right)\left(\dfrac{3}{4}\times 5\right)\left(\dfrac{5}{3}\times 4\right) =$

(A) 1
(B) 3
(C) 6
(D) 20
(E) 60

3. Jim's answer is E.
    A calculator might actually slow you down on this question. Instead, simply reduce the expression before calculation

$$= \left(\dfrac{4}{5}\times 3\right)\left(\dfrac{3}{4}\times 5\right)\left(\dfrac{5}{3}\times 4\right)$$

$$= \dfrac{4\cdot 3\cdot \cancel{3}\cdot \cancel{5}\cdot 5\cdot \cancel{4}}{\cancel{3}\cdot \cancel{5}\cdot \cancel{4}}$$

$$= 60$$

4 For which of the following values of x is $\dfrac{x^2}{x^3}$ the LEAST?

(A) 1
(B) −1
(C) −2
(D) −3
(E) −4

4. Jim's answer is B.
    Again, before you reach for your calculator, reduce the expression:

$$\dfrac{x^2}{x^3} = \dfrac{\cancel{x}\cdot \cancel{x}}{\cancel{x}\cdot \cancel{x}\cdot x} = \dfrac{1}{x}$$

then simply try each choice; $\dfrac{1}{-1}$ is the least value. If you selected E, you didn't work out each choice.

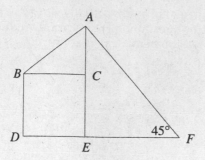

5 If the area of square *BCED* = 25, and the area of △*ABC* = 10, what is the length of *EF*?

(A) 7
(B) 8
(C) 9
(D) 10
(E) 14

5. Jim's answer is C.
First, we can estimate. Since square *BCED* has an area of 25, *DE* equals 5 and *EF* looks to be less than twice *DE*, or in the 7–9 range. Thus, we can eliminate D and E.
   Now, we're looking for the length of *EF*. Since angle *AEF* is a right angle, angle *EAF* must be 45°. So we know that *AE* = *EF*.
   We know that the area of triangle *ABC* is 10, and that its base (*BC*) is 5. Using the formula for area, we can calculate *AC*:

$$A = \frac{1}{2}bh$$

$$10 = (\frac{1}{2})\,(5)\,(h)$$

$$4 = h$$

So *AE* = *EF* = (5 + 4) = 9.

6 The Wilsons drove 450 miles in each direction to Grandmother's house and back again. If their car gets 25 miles per gallon and their cost for gasoline was $1.25 per gallon for the trip to Grandmother's but $1.50 per gallon for the return trip, how much <u>more</u> money did they spend for gasoline returning from Grandmother's than they spent going to Grandmother's?

(A) $2.25
(B) $4.50
(C) $6.25
(D) $9.00
(E) $27.00

6. Jim's answer is B.
First, let's calculate how many gallons are consumed in each direction:

$$\frac{450}{25} = 18$$

Now each of the 18 gallons cost us $0.25 more returning than going.
(18) (0.25) = $4.50

SECTION 7

QUESTIONS	EXPLANATIONS

7 If the average measure of two angles in a parallelogram is $y°$, what is the average degree measure of the other two angles?

(A) $180 - y$

(B) $180 - \dfrac{y}{2}$

(C) $360 - 2y$

(D) $360 - y$

(E) y

7. Jim's answer is A.
Let's begin by drawing a parallelogram and plugging in a number for y, say 50:

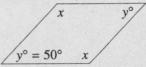

Since there are 360° in a quadrilateral, we know that $2x + 100° = 360°$, which means $x = 130°$. So, we're looking for the choice that gives us 130 when $y = 50°$. We simply plug 50 into the answer choices until we find our answer.

8 A swimming pool with a capacity of 36,000 gallons originally contained 9,000 gallons of water. At 10:00 A.M. water begins to flow in at a constant rate. If the pool is exactly three-fourths full at 1:00 P.M. on the same day and the water continues to flow in at the same rate, what is the earliest time when the pool will be completely full?

(A) 1:40 P.M.
(B) 2:00 P.M.
(C) 2:30 P.M.
(D) 3:00 P.M.
(E) 3:30 P.M.

8. Jim's answer is C.
Let's start by drawing a picture of the situation.

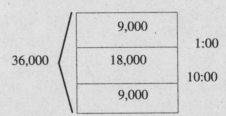

We know that by 1:00 the pool is three-fourths full. Three-fourths of 36,000 is 27,000. Since we started with 9,000 gallons, we added 18,000 gallons in 3 hours, or 6,000 gallons per hour. To fill the remaining 9,000 gallons at this rate will take 1.5 hours (9,000 ÷ 6,000). One and a half hours later would be 2:30.

SECTION 7

9 On a map, 1 centimeter represents 6 kilometers. A square on the map with a perimeter of 16 centimeters represents a region with what <u>area</u>?

(A)   64 km²
(B)   96 km²
(C)   256 km²
(D)   576 km²
(E)   8,216 km²

9.   Jim's answer is D.
     This is a tricky question.
     Let's draw a picture:

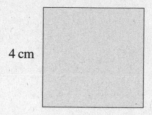

Since 1 centimeter equals 6 kilometers, 4 centimeters equals 24 kilometers:

The area of this region is 24² or 576.

---

10 If $4 < a < 7 < b < 9$, then which of the following best defines $\frac{a}{b}$?

(A) $\frac{4}{9} < \frac{a}{b} < 1$

(B) $\frac{4}{9} < \frac{a}{b} < \frac{7}{9}$

(C) $\frac{4}{7} < \frac{a}{b} < \frac{7}{9}$

(D) $\frac{4}{7} < \frac{a}{b} < 1$

(E) $\frac{4}{7} < \frac{a}{b} < \frac{9}{7}$

10.   Jim's answer is A.

We're looking for the range of the fraction $\frac{a}{b}$, from its minimum to its maximum value. The maximum value $\frac{a}{b}$ would be when a is as large as possible and b is as small as possible. Thus, $\frac{a}{b}$ must be less than $\frac{7}{7}$. Eliminate choices B, C, and E. At the other extreme, $\frac{a}{b}$ achieves its maximum value when a is as small as possible and b is as large as possible. Thus, $\frac{a}{b}$ must be greater than $\frac{4}{9}$.

PART VIII

The Princeton Review Diagnostic Test and Explanations II

19

Diagnostic Test II

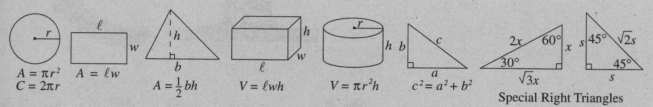

Time—30 Minutes
25 Questions

In this section solve each problem, using any available space on the page for scratchwork. Then decide which is the best of the choices given and fill in the corresponding oval on the answer sheet.

Notes:

1. The use of a calculator is permitted. All numbers used are real numbers.

2. Figures that accompany problems in this test are intended to provide information useful in solving the problems. They are drawn as accurately as possible EXCEPT when it is stated in a specific problem that the figure is not drawn to scale. All figures lie in a plane unless otherwise indicated.

Reference Information

$A = \pi r^2$ $A = \ell w$ $A = \frac{1}{2}bh$ $V = \ell wh$ $V = \pi r^2 h$ $c^2 = a^2 + b^2$ Special Right Triangles
$C = 2\pi r$

The number of degrees of arc in a circle is 360.
The measure in degrees of a straight angle is 180.
The sum of the measures in degrees of the angles of a triangle is 180.

---

1 If $\dfrac{12}{4} = x$, then $4x + 2 =$

(A) 2
(B) 3
(C) 4
(D) 12
(E) 14

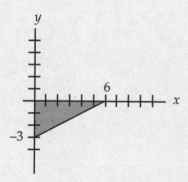

2 In the figure above, which of the following points lies within the shaded region?

(A) $(-1, 1)$
(B) $(1, -2)$
(C) $(4, 3)$
(D) $(5, -4)$
(E) $(7, 0)$

GO ON TO THE NEXT PAGE ⇒

3 If n is an even integer, which of the following must be an odd integer?

(A) $3n - 2$

(B) $3(n + 1)$

(C) $n - 2$

(D) $\dfrac{n}{3}$

(E) n^2

6 If Circle O has a diameter of 9, then what is the area of Circle O ?

(A) 81π

(B) $\dfrac{9}{2}\pi$

(C) $\dfrac{81}{4}\pi$

(D) 18π

(E) 9π

4 $x\sqrt{4} - x\sqrt{9} =$

(A) $-5x$
(B) $-x\sqrt{5}$
(C) $-x$
(D) x
(E) $3x$

7 Cindy has a collection of 80 records. If 40 percent of her records are jazz records, and the rest are blues records, how many blues records does she have?

(A) 32
(B) 40
(C) 42
(D) 48
(E) 50

5 Six cups of flour are required to make a batch of cookies. How many cups of flour are needed to make enough cookies to fill 12 cookie jars, if each cookie jar holds 1.5 batches?

(A) 108
(B) 90
(C) 81
(D) 78
(E) 72

8 How many even integers are there between 2 and 100, not including 2 and 100?

(A) 98
(B) 97
(C) 50
(D) 49
(E) 48

GO ON TO THE NEXT PAGE

9 If b equals 40 percent of a, then, in terms of b, 40 percent of $4a$ is equal to

(A) $\dfrac{b}{40}$

(B) $\dfrac{b}{4}$

(C) b

(D) $4b$

(E) $16b$

11 In the triangle ABC above, if AC is equal to 8, then BC is equal to

(A) $8\sqrt{2}$
(B) 8
(C) 6
(D) $4\sqrt{2}$
(E) $3\sqrt{2}$

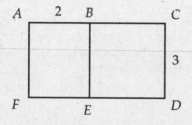

10 In the figure above, the perimeter of square $BCDE$ is how much smaller than the perimeter of rectangle $ACDF$?

(A)   2
(B)   3
(C)   4
(D)   7
(E)   16

	Number Sold	Average Weight per parrot (in pounds)
Red Parrot	5	2
Blue Parrots	4	3

12 The chart above shows the number of red and blue parrots Toby sold in May and the average weight of each type of bird sold. If Toby sold no other parrots, what was the average (arithmetic mean) weight of a parrot in pounds that Toby sold in May?

(A) 2

(B) $2\dfrac{4}{9}$

(C) $2\dfrac{1}{2}$

(D) 5

(E) 9

GO ON TO THE NEXT PAGE

13 If $999 \times 111 = 3 \times 3 \times n^2$, then which of the following could equal n?

(A)   9
(B)   37
(C) 111
(D) 222
(E) 333

14 If $x + 6 > 0$ and $1 - 2x > -1$, then x could equal each of the following EXCEPT

(A) −6

(B) −4

(C) −2

(D)   0

(E) $\dfrac{1}{2}$

15 In 1985, Andrei had a collection of 48 baseball caps. Since then he has given away 13 caps, purchased 17 new caps and traded 6 of his caps to Pierre for 8 of Pierre's caps. Since 1985, what has been the net percent increase in Andrei's collection?

(A)   6%

(B) $12\dfrac{1}{2}\%$

(C) $16\dfrac{2}{3}\%$

(D)   25%

(E) $28\dfrac{1}{2}\%$

Questions 16–17 refer to the following definition: For all real numbers x, let $\otimes x$ be defined as $2x^2 + 4$.

16 What is the value of $\otimes 4$?

(A) 16
(B) 18
(C) 20
(D) 36
(E) 72

17 What is the value of $\otimes 3 + \otimes 5$?

(A) $\otimes 4$
(B) $\otimes 6$
(C) $\otimes 8$
(D) $\otimes 10$
(E) $\otimes 15$

18 What is the greatest number of regions into which an equilateral triangle can be divided using exactly three straight lines?

(A) 4
(B) 6
(C) 7
(D) 8
(E) 9

GO ON TO THE NEXT PAGE

19 Elsa has a pitcher containing x ounces of root beer. If she pours y ounces of root beer into each of z glasses, how much root beer will remain in the pitcher?

(A) $\dfrac{x}{y} + z$

(B) $xy - z$

(C) $\dfrac{x}{yz}$

(D) $x - yz$

(E) $\dfrac{x}{y} - z$

20 A bag contains 4 red hammers, 10 blue hammers, and 6 yellow hammers. If three hammers are removed at random and no hammer is returned to the bag after removal, what is the probability that all three hammers will be blue?

(A) $\dfrac{1}{2}$

(B) $\dfrac{1}{8}$

(C) $\dfrac{3}{20}$

(D) $\dfrac{2}{19}$

(E) $\dfrac{3}{8}$

21 There are k gallons of gasoline available to fill a tank. After d gallons have been pumped, then in terms of k and d, what percent of the gasoline has been pumped?

(A) $\dfrac{100d}{k}\%$

(B) $\dfrac{k}{100d}\%$

(C) $\dfrac{100k}{d}\%$

(D) $\dfrac{k}{100(k-d)}\%$

(E) $\dfrac{100(k-d)}{k}\%$

22 If $a = 4b + 26$, and b is a positive integer, then a could be divisible by all of the following EXCEPT

(A) 2
(B) 4
(C) 5
(D) 6
(E) 7

GO ON TO THE NEXT PAGE

23 Ray and Jane live 150 miles apart. They each drive toward the other's house along a straight road connecting the two, Ray at a constant rate of 30 miles per hour and Jane at a constant rate of 50 miles per hour. If Ray and Jane leave their houses at the same time, how many miles are they from Ray's house when they meet?

(A) 40

(B) $51\frac{1}{2}$

(C) $56\frac{1}{4}$

(D) 75

(E) $93\frac{1}{4}$

24 If $x = y + 1$ and $y \geq 1$, then which of the following must be equal to $x^2 - y^2$?

(A) $(x - y)^2$
(B) $x^2 - y - 1$
(C) $x + y$
(D) $x^2 - 1$
(E) $y^2 + 1$

25 If x is an integer, which of the following could be x^3?

(A) 2.7×10^{11}
(B) 2.7×10^{12}
(C) 2.7×10^{13}
(D) 2.7×10^{14}
(E) 2.7×10^{15}

IF YOU FINISH BEFORE TIME IS CALLED, YOU MAY CHECK YOUR WORK ON THIS SECTION ONLY. DO NOT TURN TO ANY OTHER SECTION IN THE TEST. **STOP**

NO TEST MATERIAL ON THIS PAGE.

**Time—30 Minutes
30 Questions**

For each question in this section, select the best answer from among the choices given and fill in the corresponding oval on the answer sheet.

Each sentence below has one or two blanks, each blank indicating that something has been omitted. Beneath the sentence are five words or sets of words labeled A through E. Choose the word or set of words that, when inserted in the sentence, best fits the meaning of the sentence as a whole.

Example:

Medieval kingdoms did not become constitutional republics overnight; on the contrary, the change was ----.

(A) unpopular
(B) unexpected
(C) advantageous
(D) sufficient
(E) gradual

Ⓐ Ⓑ Ⓒ Ⓓ ●

1 Nuclear power plants are some of the largest producers of ---- wastes, with each plant producing barrels of radioactive material that must be stored in special protective containers.

(A) biodegradable   (B) artificial
   (C) reasonable   (D) durable   (E) hazardous

2 The scientific community was ---- when a living specimen of the coelacanth, long thought to be ----, was discovered by deep-sea fishermen.

(A) perplexed. .common
(B) overjoyed. .dangerous
(C) unconcerned. .local
(D) astounded. .extinct
(E) dismayed. .alive

3 After the governor's third trip overseas, voters complained that he was paying too little attention to ---- affairs.

(A) intellectual   (B) foreign   (C) professional
   (D) aesthetic   (E) domestic

4 The Roman Emperor Claudius was viewed with ---- by generations of historians until newly discovered evidence showed him to be a ---- administrator.

(A) suspicion. .clever
(B) reluctance. .inept
(C) antagonism. .eager
(D) indignation. .incompetent
(E) disdain. .capable

5 Communities in primitive areas where natural ---- is scarce must be resourceful in order to secure adequate nutrition.

(A) education   (B) competition   (C) sustenance
   (D) agriculture   (E) assistance

6 Anthony's ---- expression masked an essentially cheerful nature.

(A) jubilant   (B) inevitable   (C) dour
   (D) pert   (E) serene

7 Morgan's interest was focused on ---- the division between theory and empiricism; she was convinced that a ---- of philosophy and applied science was possible and necessary.

(A) eliminating. .synthesis
(B) maintaining. .restoration
(C) crossing. .stabilization
(D) ignoring. .duplicity
(E) denying. .delineation

GO ON TO THE NEXT PAGE

8 The professor highlighted the importance of ---- the experiences of many different ethnic groups when he warned against ---- policies that fail to consider the wide variety of cultural standards.

(A) portraying. .discriminatory
(B) considering. .myopic
(C) remembering. .alluring
(D) delineating. .captivating
(E) disparaging. .pedantic

9 Although at times Nikolai could be disagreeable and even ----, more often than not he was the most ---- person you could hope to meet.

(A) contentious. .complaisant
(B) disgruntled. .befuddled
(C) contradictory. .disconcerted
(D) misguided. .solicitous
(E) curmudgeonly. .didactic

Each question below consists of a related pair of words or phrases, followed by five pairs of words or phrases labeled A through E. Select the pair that best expresses a relationship similar to that expressed in the original pair.

Example:

CRUMB : BREAD ::

(A) ounce : unit
(B) splinter : wood
(C) water : bucket
(D) twine : rope
(E) cream : butter

 Ⓐ ● Ⓒ Ⓓ Ⓔ

10 SHEPHERD : SHEEP ::

(A) sociologist : statistics
(B) driver : conveyances
(C) gardener : plants
(D) critic : reviews
(E) artist : murals

11 VANDAL : DAMAGE ::

(A) victim : crime
(B) pest : annoyance
(C) temper : shouting
(D) addiction : weakness
(E) arbitrator : dispute

12 SNARE : ANIMAL ::

(A) nest : bird
(B) pouch : kangaroo
(C) net : fish
(D) kennel : dog
(E) forest : raccoon

13 CACOPHONOUS : EAR ::

(A) outrageous : order
(B) objectionable : commotion
(C) erroneous : mind
(D) noisome : mouth
(E) rank : nose

14 BELLIGERENCE : AGGRESSOR ::

(A) insensitivity : boor
(B) confidence : prelate
(C) irascibility : pacifist
(D) truculence : ingrate
(E) affectation : shrew

15 INCORRIGIBLE : REFORM ::

(A) immutable : speak
(B) intractable : manage
(C) impartial : decide
(D) intolerable : criticize
(E) intangible : understand

GO ON TO THE NEXT PAGE

Each passage below is followed by questions based on its content. Answer the questions following each passage on the basis of what is <u>stated</u> or <u>implied</u> in that passage and in any introductory material that may be provided.

Questions 16–22 are based on the following passage.

A parable is a symbolic story that, like a fable, teaches a moral lesson. The parable below was written by the Czech author Franz Kafka and was published in 1935.

Poseidon sat at his desk, doing figures. The administration of all the waters gave him endless work. He could have had assistants, as many as he
Line wanted—and he did have very many—but since he
(5) took his job very seriously, he would in the end go over all the figures and calculations himself, and thus his assistants were of little help to him. It cannot be said that he enjoyed his work; he did it only because it had been assigned to him; in fact, he
(10) had already filed petitions for—as he put it—more cheerful work, but every time the offer of something different was made to him it would turn out that nothing suited him quite as well as his present position. And anyhow, it was quite difficult to find
(15) something different for him. After all, it was impossible to assign him to a particular sea; aside from the fact that even then the work with figures would not become less but only pettier, the great Poseidon could in any case only occupy an
(20) executive position. And when a job away from the water was offered to him he would get sick at the very prospect, his divine breathing would become troubled and his brazen chest would begin to tremble. Besides, his complaints were not really
(25) taken seriously; when one of the mighty is vexatious the appearance of an effort must be made to placate him, even when the case is most hopeless. In actuality, a shift of posts was unthinkable for Poseidon—he had been appointed God of the Sea in
(30) the beginning, and that he had to remain.
What irritated him most—and it was this that was chiefly responsible for his dissatisfaction with his job—was to hear of the conceptions formed about him: how he was always riding about through the
(35) tides with his trident. When all the while he sat here in the depths of the world-ocean, doing figures uninterruptedly, with now and then a trip to Jupiter as the only break in the monotony—a trip, moreover, from which he usually returned in a
(40) rage. Thus he had hardly seen the sea—had seen it fleetingly in the course of hurried ascents to Olympus, and he had never actually traveled around it. He was in the habit of saying that what he was waiting for was the fall of the world; then,
(45) probably, a quiet moment would yet be granted in which, just before the end and after having checked the last row of figures, he would be able to make a quick little tour.
Poseidon became bored with the sea. He let fall
(50) his trident. Silently he sat on the rocky coast and a gull, dazed by his presence, described wavering circles around his head.

16 Lines 9–10 suggest that Poseidon regarded his work with

(A) resignation
(B) enthusiasm
(C) indifference
(D) intimidation
(E) destructiveness

17 In line 26, the word "vexatious" most nearly means

(A) pleased
(B) cursed
(C) doomed
(D) troubled
(E) indisposed

18 The word "conceptions" as used in line 33 most nearly means

(A) origins
(B) opinions
(C) discussions
(D) plans
(E) explanations

GO ON TO THE NEXT PAGE

19 It can be inferred from the author's description of Poseidon's routine (lines 40–43) that

(A) Poseidon prefers performing his duties to visiting Jupiter
(B) Poseidon is too busy to familiarize himself with his kingdom
(C) Poseidon requires silence for the performance of his duties
(D) if the world falls, Poseidon will no longer be able to travel
(E) Poseidon's dissatisfaction with his job detracts from his efficiency

20 According to the passage, Poseidon's dissatisfaction with his job primarily stems from

(A) the constant travel that is required of him
(B) the lack of seriousness with which his complaints are received
(C) the constantly changing nature of his duties
(D) others' mistaken notions of his routine
(E) his assistant's inability to perform simple bookkeeping tasks

21 The author of the passage portrays the god Poseidon as

(A) a dissatisfied bureaucrat
(B) a powerful deity
(C) a disgruntled vagabond
(D) a capable accountant
(E) a ruthless tyrant

22 Poseidon is unable to change occupations for all of the following reasons EXCEPT

(A) his appointment as God of the Sea is inherently unchangeable
(B) he has fallen into disfavor with the gods on Mount Olympus
(C) he cannot imagine a life away from the water
(D) nothing else suits him as well as his present position
(E) his job must be appropriate to his elevated status

GO ON TO THE NEXT PAGE

Questions 23–30 are based on the following passage.

The following passage was excerpted from a book called The Extraordinary Origins of Everyday Things, *which was published in 1987.*

Because early man viewed illness as divine punishment and healing as purification, medicine and religion were inextricably linked for centuries. This
Line notion is apparent in the origin of our word
(5) "pharmacy," which comes from the Greek *pharmakon*, meaning "purification through purging."

By 3500 B.C., the Sumerians in the Tigris-Euphrates valley had developed virtually all of our modern methods of administering drugs. They used gargles,
(10) inhalations, pills, lotions, ointments, and plasters. The first drug catalog, or pharmacopoeia, was written at that time by an unknown Sumerian physician. Preserved in cuneiform script on a single clay tablet are the names of dozens of drugs to treat ailments that
(15) still afflict us today.

The Egyptians added to the ancient medicine chest. The Ebers Papyrus, a scroll dating from 1900 B.C. and named after the German Egyptologist George Ebers, reveals the trial-and-error know-how
(20) acquired by early Egyptian physicians. To relieve indigestion, a chew of peppermint leaves and carbonates (known today as antacids) was prescribed, and to numb the pain of tooth extraction, Egyptian doctors temporarily stupefied a patient with ethyl
(25) alcohol.

The scroll also provides a rare glimpse into the hierarchy of ancient drug preparation. The "chief of the preparers of drugs" was the equivalent of a head pharmacist, who supervised the "collectors of drugs,"
(30) field workers, who gathered essential minerals and herbs. The "preparers' aides" (technicians) dried and pulverized ingredients, which were blended according to certain formulas by the "preparers." And the "conservator of drugs" oversaw the
(35) storehouse where local and imported mineral, herb, and animal-organ ingredients were kept.

By the seventh century B.C., the Greeks had adopted a sophisticated mind-body view of medicine. They believed that a physician must pursue the diagnosis
(40) and treatment of the physical (body) causes of disease within a scientific framework, as well as cure the supernatural (mind) components involved. Thus, the early Greek physician emphasized something of a holistic approach to health, even if the suspected
(45) "mental" causes of disease were not recognized as stress and depression but interpreted as curses from displeased deities.

The modern era of pharmacology began in the sixteenth century, ushered in by the first major
(50) discoveries in chemistry. The understanding of how chemicals interact to produce certain effects within the body would eventually remove much of the guesswork and magic from medicine.

Drugs had been launched on a scientific course, but
(55) centuries would pass before superstition was displaced by scientific fact. One major reason was that physicians, unaware of the existence of disease-causing pathogens such as bacteria and viruses, continued to dream up imaginary causative evils.
(60) And though new chemical compounds emerged, their effectiveness in treating disease was still based largely on trial and error.

Many standard, common drugs in the medicine chest developed in this trial-and-error environment.
(65) Such is the complexity of disease and human biochemistry that even today, despite enormous strides in medical science, many of the latest sophisticated additions to our medicine chest shelves were accidental finds.

(70)

23 The author cites the literal definition of the Greek word *pharmakon* in line 6 in order to

(A) show that ancient civilizations had an advanced form of medical science
(B) point out that many of the beliefs of ancient civilizations are still held today
(C) illustrate that early man thought recovery from illness was linked to internal cleansing
(D) stress the mental and physical causes of disease
(E) emphasize the primitive nature of Greek medical science

24 It was possible to identify a number of early Sumerian drugs because

(A) traces of these drugs were discovered during archaeological excavations
(B) the ancient Egyptians later adopted the same medications
(C) Sumerian religious texts explained many drug-making techniques
(D) a pharmacopoeia in Europe contained detailed recipes for ancient drugs
(E) a list of drugs and preparations was compiled by an ancient Sumerian

GO ON TO THE NEXT PAGE ➡

25 The passage suggests that which of the following is a similarity between ancient Sumerian drugs and modern drugs?

(A) Ancient Sumerian drugs were made of the same chemicals as modern drugs.

(B) Like modern drugs, ancient Sumerian drugs were used for both mental and physical disorders.

(C) The delivery of ancient Sumerian drugs is similar to that of modern drugs.

(D) Both ancient Sumerian drugs and modern drugs are products of sophisticated laboratory research.

(E) Hierarchically organized groups of laborers are responsible for the preparation of both ancient Sumerian and modern drugs.

26 The "hierarchy" referred to in line 27 is an example of

(A) a superstitious practice

(B) the relative severity of ancient diseases

(C) the role of physicians in Egyptian society

(D) a complex division of labor

(E) a recipe for ancient drugs

27 According to the passage, the seventh-century Greeks' view of medicine differed from that of the Sumerians in that the Greeks

(A) discovered more advanced chemical applications of drugs

(B) acknowledged both the mental and physical roots of illness

(C) attributed disease to psychological, rather than physical, causes

(D) established a rigid hierarchy for the preparation of drugs

(E) developed most of the precursors of modern drugs

28 In line 44, the word "holistic" most nearly means

(A) psychological

(B) modern

(C) physiological

(D) integrated

(E) religious

29 The passage indicates that advances in medical science during the modern era of pharmacology may have been delayed by

(A) a lack of understanding of the origins of disease

(B) primitive surgical methods

(C) a shortage of chemical treatments for disease

(D) an inaccuracy in pharmaceutical preparation

(E) an over-emphasis on the psychological causes of disease

30 In the final paragraph, the author makes which of the following observations about scientific discovery?

(A) Human biochemistry is such a complex science that important discoveries are uncommon.

(B) Chance events have led to the discovery of many modern drugs.

(C) Many cures for common diseases have yet to be discovered.

(D) Trial and error is the best avenue to scientific discovery.

(E) Most of the important discoveries made in the scientific community have been inadvertent.

IF YOU FINISH BEFORE TIME IS CALLED, YOU MAY CHECK YOUR WORK ON THIS SECTION ONLY. DO NOT TURN TO ANY OTHER SECTION IN THE TEST. **STOP**

Time—30 Minutes 25 Questions	In this section solve each problem, using any available space on the page for scratchwork. Then decide which is the best of the choices given and fill in the corresponding oval on the answer sheet.

Notes:

1.　The use of a calculator is permitted. All numbers used are real numbers.

2.　Figures that accompany problems in this test are intended to provide information useful in solving the problems. They are drawn as accurately as possible EXCEPT when it is stated in a specific problem that the figure is not drawn to scale. All figures lie in a plane unless otherwise indicated.

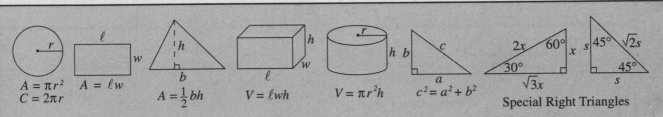

$A = \pi r^2$　$A = \ell w$　$A = \frac{1}{2}bh$　$V = \ell wh$　$V = \pi r^2 h$　$c^2 = a^2 + b^2$　Special Right Triangles
$C = 2\pi r$

The number of degrees of arc in a circle is 360.
The measure in degrees of a straight angle is 180.
The sum of the measures in degrees of the angles of a triangle is 180.

Directions for Quantitative Comparison Questions

Questions 1–15 each consist of two quantities in boxes, one in Column A and one in Column B. You are to compare the two quantities and on the answer sheet fill in oval

A if the quantity in Column A is greater;
B if the quantity in Column B is greater;
C if the two quantities are equal;
D if the relationship cannot be determined from the information given.

AN E RESPONSE WILL NOT BE SCORED.

Notes:

1. In some questions, information is given about one or both of the quantities to be compared. In such cases, the given information is centered above the two columns and is not boxed.
2. In a given question, a symbol that appears in both columns represents the same thing in Column A as it does in Column B.
3. Letters such as x, n, and k stand for real numbers.

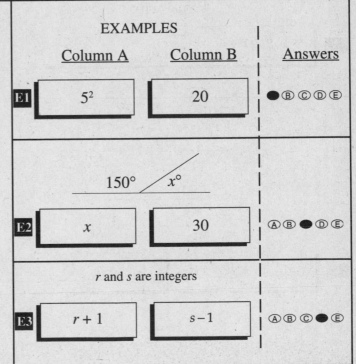

EXAMPLES

	Column A	Column B	Answers
E1	5^2	20	● Ⓑ Ⓒ Ⓓ Ⓔ

150° $x°$

| E2 | x | 30 | Ⓐ Ⓑ ● Ⓓ Ⓔ |

r and s are integers

| E3 | $r + 1$ | $s - 1$ | Ⓐ Ⓑ Ⓒ ● Ⓔ |

SUMMARY DIRECTIONS FOR QUANTITATIVE COMPARISON QUESTIONS

Answer:　A if the quantity in Column A is greater;
　　　　　B if the quantity in Column B is greater;
　　　　　C if the two quantities are equal;
　　　　　D if the relationship cannot be determined from the information given.

AN E RESPONSE WILL NOT BE SCORED.

Column A	**Column B**	**Column A**	**Column B**

$x = 3$

1

$\dfrac{x}{10}$	$\dfrac{x}{100}$

$3 > p > 1$

5

$\dfrac{p}{2}$	$\dfrac{p+2}{4}$

2

The average (arithmetic mean) of 1, 199, and 700	The average (arithmetic mean) of 10, 90, and 800

$-3 < z < 0$

3

$3 - z$	$z - 3$

R, 4, 11, Q, 12, S triangle

6

area of triangle QRS	perimeter of triangle QRS

$110°$ / $a°$

$111°$

$b°$

4

a	b

B, C, A, D square with diagonal AC

ABCD is a square

7

$\dfrac{the \ length \ of \ AC}{the \ length \ of \ AD}$	2

GO ON TO THE NEXT PAGE →

SUMMARY DIRECTIONS FOR QUANTITATIVE COMPARISON QUESTIONS

Answer: A if the quantity in Column A is greater;
B if the quantity in Column B is greater;
C if the two quantities are equal;
D if the relationship cannot be determined from the information given.

AN E RESPONSE WILL NOT BE SCORED.

Column A	Column B

Line segments FG and JK intersect at point X such that $FX = \frac{1}{2}GX$

8

| JX | $\frac{1}{2}KX$ |

1,000 milliliters = 1 liter

9

| The number of 1.9 milliliter portions that can be poured from a bottle containing 0.8 liters of fluid | 400 |

A is the average (arithmetic mean) of 2 consecutive positive even integers.

10

| The remainder when A is divided by 2 | 1 |

Column A	Column B

Questions 11 and 12 refer to the following definition:

For all numbers n, let $\{n\}$ be defined as $n^3 + 2n^2 - n$

11

| $\{-2\}$ | $\{-1\}$ |

12

| $\{x\}$ | $\{x + 1\}$ |

13

| The ratio of nickels to dimes in Jar A, where there are 4 more nickels than dimes | The ratio of nickels to dimes in Jar B, where there are 4 more dimes than nickels |

14

| The area of a parallelogram with base 8 and perimeter 36 | The area of a parallelogram with base 16 and perimeter 36 |

$$a + b = c$$
$$a - c = 5$$
$$b - c = 3$$

15

| c | 0 |

Directions for Student-Produced Response Questions

Each of the remaining 10 questions (16–25) requires you to solve the problem and enter your answer by marking the ovals in the special grid, as shown in the examples below.

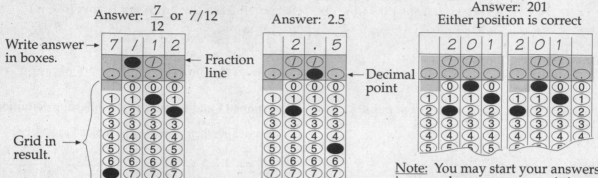

Write answer in boxes.

Answer: $\frac{7}{12}$ or 7/12 ← Fraction line

Answer: 2.5 ← Decimal point

Answer: 201 Either position is correct

Grid in result.

Note: You may start your answers in any column, space permitting. Columns not needed should be left blank.

- Mark no more than one oval in any column.

- Because the answer sheet will be machine-scored, **you will receive credit only if the ovals are filled in correctly.**

- Although not required, it is suggested that you write your answer in the boxes at the top of the columns to help you fill in the ovals accurately.

- Some problems may have more than one correct answer. In such cases, grid only one answer.

- No question has a negative answer.

- **Mixed numbers** such as $2\frac{1}{2}$ must be gridded as 2.5 or 5/2. (If $\boxed{2\;1\,/\,2}$ is gridded, it will be interpreted as $\frac{21}{2}$, not $2\frac{1}{2}$.)

- **Decimal Accuracy:** If you obtain a decimal answer, **enter the most accurate value the grid will accommodate.** For example, if you obtain an answer such as 0.6666 . . . , you should record the result as .666 or .667. **Less accurate values such as .66 or .67 are not acceptable.**

Acceptable ways to grid $\frac{2}{3}$ = .6666 . . .

---

16 If $3x = 12$, then $8 \div x =$

17 In the figure above, $a + b + c =$

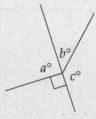

GO ON TO THE NEXT PAGE →

18 Twenty bottles contain a total of 8 liters of apple juice. If each bottle contains the same amount of apple juice, how much juice (in liters) is in each bottle?

19 If $4x + 2y = 24$, and $\dfrac{7y}{2x} = 7$, then $x =$

20 What is the sum of the positive even factors of 12?

21 Y is a point on segment XZ such that $XY = \dfrac{1}{2}XZ$. If the length of YZ is $4a + 6$, and the length of XZ is 68, then $a =$

22 One-fifth of the cars in a parking lot are blue and $\dfrac{1}{2}$ of the blue cars are convertibles. If $\dfrac{1}{4}$ of the convertibles in the parking lot are blue, then what percent of the cars in the lot are neither blue nor convertibles?

GO ON TO THE NEXT PAGE

23 Three numbers are considered a "prime set" if their sum is a prime number. If 31, −8, and n are a prime set, what is the least possible positive value for n ?

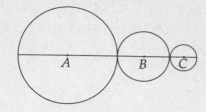

25 In the figure above, the radius of the circle with center A is twice the radius of the circle with center B and four times the radius of the circle with center C. If the sum of the areas of the three circles is 84π, what is the length of AC?

24 A ball bounces up $\dfrac{3}{4}$ of the distance it falls when dropped, and on each bounce thereafter, it bounces $\dfrac{3}{4}$ of the previous height. If it is dropped from a height of 64 feet, how many feet will it have traveled when it hits the ground the fourth time?

IF YOU FINISH BEFORE TIME IS CALLED, YOU MAY CHECK YOUR WORK ON THIS SECTION ONLY. DO NOT TURN TO ANY OTHER SECTION IN THE TEST. **STOP**

NO TEST MATERIAL ON THIS PAGE.

Time—30 Minutes
25 Questions

This section contains two types of questions. You have 30 minutes to complete both types. You may use any available space for scratchwork.

Notes:

(1)   The use of a calculator is permitted. All numbers used are real numbers.

(2)   Figures that accompany problems in this test are intended to provide information useful in solving the problems. They are drawn as accurately as possible EXCEPT when it is stated in a specific problem that the figure is not drawn to scale. All figures lie in a plane unless otherwise indicated.

Reference Information

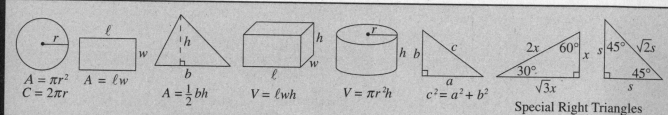

$A = \pi r^2$
$C = 2\pi r$

$A = \ell w$

$A = \frac{1}{2}bh$

$V = \ell wh$

$V = \pi r^2 h$

$c^2 = a^2 + b^2$

Special Right Triangles

The number of degrees of arc in a circle is 360.
The measure in degrees of a straight angle is 180.
The sum of the measures in degrees of the angles of a triangle is 180.

Directions for Quantitative Comparison Questions

Questions 1–15 each consist of two quantities in boxes, one in Column A and one in Column B. You are to compare the two quantities and on the answer sheet fill in oval

   A   if the quantity in Column A is greater;
   B   if the quantity in Column B is greater;
   C   if the two quantities are equal;
   D   if the relationship cannot be determined
       from the information given.

   AN E RESPONSE WILL NOT BE SCORED.

Notes:

1. In some questions, information is given about one or both of the quantities to be compared. In such cases, the given information is centered above the two columns and is not boxed.
2. In a given question, a symbol that appears in both columns represents the same thing in Column A as it does in Column B.
3. Letters such as x, n, and k stand for real numbers.

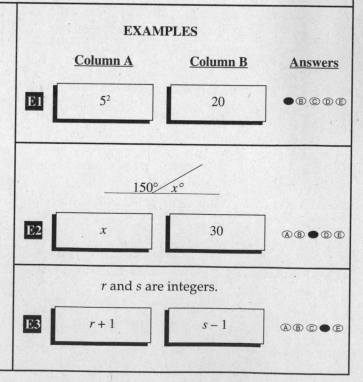

EXAMPLES

Column A	Column B	Answers

E1 5^2 20   ●Ⓑ©ⒹⒺ

$150° \quad x°$

E2 x 30   ⒶⒷ●ⒹⒺ

r and s are integers.

E3 $r + 1$ $s - 1$ Ⓐ Ⓑ © ● Ⓔ

GO ON TO THE NEXT PAGE →

SUMMARY DIRECTIONS FOR COMPARISON QUESTIONS

Answer: A   if the quantity in Column A is greater;
             B   if the quantity in Column B is greater;
             C   if the two quantities are equal;
             D   if the relationship cannot be determined from the information given.

Column A	Column B

$$3x + 5 = 20$$

1 | $6x$ | 40 |

The average of positive integers p and q is 3.

2 | p | q |

10% of x is 20% of 100

3 | x | 50 |

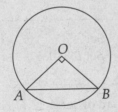

O is the center of a circle

4 | The measure of $\angle OAB$ | The measure of $\angle OBA$ |

Column A	Column B

On Sunday, 200 customers visited a gas station. Every 20th customer received a free fill-up. Every 30th customer received a discount tune-up.

5 | The number of customers who received both a free fill-up and a discount tune-up | 4 |

$$x^2 > 17$$

6 | $x + 4$ | 8 |

In squares A, B, and C above, the number of points that lie in exactly two squares

7 | In squares A, B, and C above, the number of points that lie in exactly two squares | 6 |

GO ON TO THE NEXT PAGE ⟹

<u>Column A</u>	<u>Column B</u>

$x \geq 1$

8
$x^{(x+2)}$ $(x+2)^x$

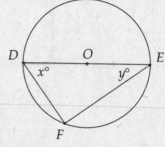

<u>Note:</u> Figure not drawn to scale.

O is the center of a circle with $DF = EF$.
Segment DE passes through point O.

9
x 60

10
The area of a triangle with base $3x$ and height $2x$ The area of a circle with radius x

x

$$\frac{1}{3} \quad\quad\quad\quad \frac{1}{2}$$

On the number line above, the marks are equally spaced

11
x $\dfrac{17}{37}$

<u>Column A</u>	<u>Column B</u>

12
The number of distinct 3-player teams that can be drawn from a pool of 5 players 12

PN and OM are line segments

13
$g + h$ $i + j$

Set A: $\{2, -1, 7, -4, 11, 3\}$
Set B: $\{10, 5, -3, 4, 7, -8\}$

14
The median of Set A The average of Set B

$ax \neq 0$

15
$(x - a)^2$ $-2ax$

GO ON TO THE NEXT PAGE ➡

Directions for Student-Produced Response Questions

Each of the remaining 10 questions (16–25) requires you to solve the problem and enter your answer by marking the ovals in the special grid, as shown in the examples below.

Answer: $\frac{7}{12}$ or 7/12

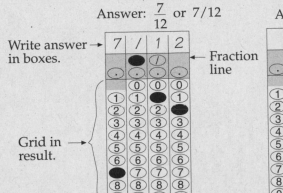

Write answer in boxes. ← Fraction line

Grid in → result.

Answer: 2.5

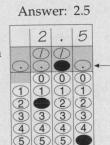

← Decimal point

Answer: 201
Either position is correct

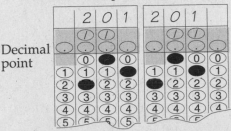

Note: You may start your answers in any column, space permitting. Columns not needed should be left blank.

- Mark no more than one oval in any column.

- Because the answer sheet will be machine-scored, **you will receive credit only if the ovals are filled in correctly.**

- Although not required, it is suggested that you write your answer in the boxes at the top of the columns to help you fill in the ovals accurately.

- Some problems may have more than one correct answer. In such cases, grid only one answer.

- No question has a negative answer.

- **Mixed numbers** such as $2\frac{1}{2}$ must be gridded as 2.5 or 5/2. (If $2\ 1\ /\ 2$ is gridded, it will be interpreted as $\frac{21}{2}$, not $2\frac{1}{2}$.)

- **Decimal Accuracy:** If you obtain a decimal answer, **enter the most accurate value the grid will accommodate.** For example, if you obtain an answer such as 0.6666 . . . , you should record the result as .666 or .667. **Less accurate values such as .66 or .67 are not acceptable.**

Acceptable ways to grid $\frac{2}{3}$ = .6666 . . .

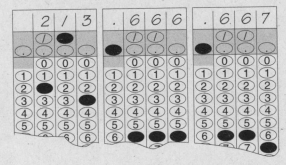

16 A certain clothing store sells only T-shirts, sweatshirts, and turtlenecks. On Wednesday, the store sells T-shirts, sweatshirts, and turtlenecks in a ratio of 2 to 3 to 5. If the store sells 30 sweatshirts on that day, what is the total number of garments that the store sells on Wednesday?

17 A rectangular packing crate has a height of 4.5 inches and a base with an area of 18 square inches. What is the volume of the crate in cubic inches?

GO ON TO THE NEXT PAGE

18 If $5x - 4 = x - 1$, what is the value of x?

20 If b is a prime integer such that $3b > 10 > \frac{5}{6}b$, what is one possible value of b?

19 A box of donuts contains 3 plain, 5 cream-filled, and 4 chocolate donuts. If one of the donuts is chosen at random from the box, what is the probability that it will NOT be cream-filled?

21 The Tyler Jackson Dance Company plans to perform a piece that requires two dancers. If there are 7 dancers in the company, how many possible combinations of dancers could perform the piece?

GO ON TO THE NEXT PAGE ⟶

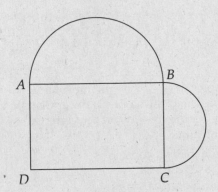

22 In the figure above, if semicircular arc *AB* has length 6π and semicircular arc *BC* has length 4π, what is the area of rectangle *ABCD*?

23 Let $\heartsuit{x}$ be defined for all positive integers x

as the product of the distinct prime factors of

x. What is the value of $\dfrac{\heartsuit{6}}{\heartsuit{81}}$?

SPICE PRICES OF DISTRIBUTOR D

Spice	Price per pound
cinnamon	$8.00
nutmeg	$9.00
ginger	$7.00
cloves	$10.00

24 The owner of a spice store buys 3 pounds each of cinnamon, nutmeg, ginger, and cloves from Distributor D. She then sells all of the spices at $2.00 per ounce. What, in dollars, is her total profit (1 pound = 16 ounces)?

25 Points *E*, *F*, *G*, and *H* lie on a line in that order. If $EG = \dfrac{5}{3}EF$ and $HF = 5FG$, then what is $\dfrac{EF}{HG}$?

IF YOU FINISH BEFORE TIME IS CALLED, YOU MAY CHECK YOUR WORK ON THIS SECTION ONLY. DO NOT TURN TO ANY OTHER SECTION IN THE TEST.   **STOP**

Time—30 Minutes
30 Questions

For each question in this section, select the best answer from among the choices given and fill in the corresponding oval on the answer sheet.

Each sentence below has one or two blanks, each blank indicating that something has been omitted. Beneath the sentence are five words or sets of words labeled A through E. Choose the word or set of words that, when inserted in the sentence, best fits the meaning of the sentence as a whole.

Example:

Medieval kingdoms did not become constitutional republics overnight; on the contrary, the change was ----.

(A) unpopular
(B) unexpected
(C) advantageous
(D) sufficient
(E) gradual

1 Plants that grow in the desert or on high rocky ledges can survive long periods of ---- because they hoard water in their leaves, stems and root systems.

(A) darkness   (B) inactivity   (C) dormancy
   (D) warmth   (E) drought

2 Thanks to his eloquence and logic, Liam spoke ---- and made it difficult for even his bitterest opponents to ---- his opinions.

(A) monotonously. .clash with
(B) charmingly. .yield to
(C) tediously. .contend with
(D) abhorrently. .concede to
(E) persuasively. .disagree with

3 Many myths and legends, however ----, often possess a grain of truth.

(A) delightful   (B) accurate   (C) eternal
   (D) unbelievable   (E) important

4 Ancient Greek playwrights often included the device of divine intervention in their work; just as circumstances became dire, a ---- would descend from Olympus and rescue the hero from almost certain death.

(A) hero   (B) warrior   (C) luminary
   (D) deity   (E) liberator

5 The apparent ---- with which professional skiers descend the slopes is deceptive; this activity requires ---- effort and intense concentration.

(A) trepidation. .conscious
(B) focus. .resolute
(C) nonchalance. .strenuous
(D) consideration. .unpredictable
(E) insouciance. .minimal

6 Miranda, in her desire to foster ----, often felt compelled to ---- readily to others in tense situations.

(A) cooperation. .object
(B) consistency. .defer
(C) dissension. .surrender
(D) discourse. .appeal
(E) harmony. .acquiesce

7 Early psychoanalysts challenged many of the most ---- notions of human behavior and compelled many to alter their dearly held assumptions about human nature.

(A) elusive   (B) derided   (C) volatile
   (D) cherished   (E) contemplative

8 Although detractors labeled Margaret Thatcher's policies ----, she asserted that her ideas moved the United Kingdom forward.

(A) premature   (B) autocratic   (C) regressive
   (D) democratic   (E) radical

9 Some subatomic particles, ---- only through their effects on other bodies, have been compared to outer planets whose ---- was first deduced from eccentricities in other planets' orbits.

(A) feasible. .irregularity
(B) palpable. .creation
(C) imaginable. .falsity
(D) perceptible. .existence
(E) verifiable. .proximity

GO ON TO THE NEXT PAGE

10 Wary of unorthodox treatments, many doctors are reluctant to concede that nutritionists have a ---- argument for the use of dietary regulation as preventive medicine.

(A) cogent   (B) cursory   (C) vacillating
   (D) feckless   (E) vehement

Each question below consists of a related pair of words or phrases, followed by five pairs of words or phrases labeled A through E. Select the pair that best expresses a relationship similar to that expressed in the original pair.

Example:

CRUMB : BREAD ::

(A) ounce : unit
(B) splinter : wood
(C) water : bucket
(D) twine : rope
(E) cream : butter

11 STOCKING : LEG ::

(A) waistband : skirt
(B) ankle : foot
(C) button : lapel
(D) cast : body
(E) glove : hand

12 PARK : RECREATION ::

(A) kitchen : cooking
(B) fence : sitting
(C) tree : climbing
(D) yard : playing
(E) bus : driving

13 OUNCE : WEIGHT ::

(A) acre : area
(B) scale : mass
(C) inch : yard
(D) menu : portion
(E) variety : difference

14 CREST : WAVE ::

(A) climax : action
(B) elegy : memory
(C) example : paradigm
(D) milestone : distance
(E) landmark : territory

15 LOW : COW ::

(A) gosling : goose
(B) swarm : bee
(C) hutch : rabbit
(D) chirp : bird
(E) bed : oyster

16 HAMLET : VILLAGE ::

(A) street : sidewalk
(B) convertible : car
(C) building : skyscraper
(D) photograph : portrait
(E) cottage : house

17 MALLEABLE : SHAPED ::

(A) flexible : bullied
(B) amenable : persuaded
(C) tolerable : handled
(D) pliable : hardened
(E) negotiable : sold

18 ANALGESIC : PAIN ::

(A) anesthetic : surgery
(B) palliative : violence
(C) operation : health
(D) enthusiasm : anger
(E) prosthesis : limb

19 NOVICE : EXPERIENCE ::

(A) questioner : knowledge
(B) invader : bravery
(C) narrator : objectivity
(D) ingenue : talent
(E) rube : sophistication

GO ON TO THE NEXT PAGE

20 GRISLY : DISGUST ::

(A) happy : grief
(B) endearing : affection
(C) redolent : joy
(D) boring : interest
(E) bitter : repulsion

21 DIATRIBE : ABUSIVE ::

(A) rant : condemnatory
(B) doctrine : orthodox
(C) eulogy : laudatory
(D) refrain : musical
(E) judgment : fearful

22 SECRETE : FIND ::

(A) muffle : hear
(B) cover : open
(C) exude : ignore
(D) smile : sadden
(E) explain : comprehend

23 INDELIBLE : PERMANENCE ::

(A) united : individuality
(B) qualified : employment
(C) unavoidable : toleration
(D) inconsistent : compatibility
(E) flimsy : tenuousness

GO ON TO THE NEXT PAGE →

Each passage below is followed by questions based on its content. Answer the questions following each passage on the basis of what is <u>stated</u> or <u>implied</u> in that passage and in any introductory material that may be provided.

Questions 24–35 are based on the following passage.

The role of women has historically been different in different cultures. The following passage presents an analysis of women in Frankish society by Suzanne Fonay Wemple.

Although the laws and customs in lands under Frankish domination emphasized the biological function and sexual nature of women, they did not
Line deprive women of opportunities to find personal
(5) fulfillment in a variety of roles. Frankish women could sublimate their sexual drives and motherly instincts in ways not available to women in ancient societies. Their labor, moreover, was not as exploited as it had been in primitive tribal societies.
(10) Queens had access to power not only through their husbands but also through churchmen and secular officials whom they patronized. As widows, acting as regents for their sons, they could exercise political power directly. The wives of magnates
(15) issued donations jointly with their husbands, founded monasteries, endowed churches, cultivated interfamilial ties, transmitted clan ideology to their children, supervised the household, and administered the family's estates when their
(20) husbands were away. Whether they contracted a formal union or entered into a quasi-marriage, their children could inherit. As widows, they acted as guardians of their minor children, arranged their marriages, and in the absence of sons, wielded
(25) economic power as well. In the dependent classes, women shared their husbands' work, produced textiles and articles of clothing both for their family's and the lords' use, and were instrumental in bringing about the merger of the free and slave
(30) elements in society.

For those who wished to free their bodies, souls, and brains from male domination and devote their lives to the service of God, Christianity provided an alternative way of life. Although, in relation to the
(35) total population, women in religious life remained a small minority even in the seventh and eighth centuries, when many female communities were founded, their roles, social functions, and cultural contributions have an importance for the history of
(40) women that outweighs their numbers. This alternative way of life was available not only to the unmarried but also to widows. Monasteries served as places of refuge for married women as well. The rich and the poor, at least until the late eighth
(45) century, were accepted as members. Women from all walks of life, as well as relatives, friends, and dependents of the foundresses and abbesses, were invited to join the new congregations. Freed from the need to compete for the attention of men,
(50) women in these communities sustained each other in spiritual, intellectual, scholarly, artistic, and charitable pursuits. Writings by early medieval nuns reveal that female ideals and modes of conduct were upheld as the way to salvation and as
(55) models of sanctity in the monasteries led by women. By facilitating the escape of women from the male-dominated society to congregations where they could give expression to their own emotions, ascetic ideals, and spiritual strivings, Christianity
(60) became a liberating force in the lives of women. Historians have often overlooked these positive effects and concentrated instead on the misogynistic sentiments perpetuated by the male hierarchy.

24 The passage suggests that women under Frankish law were

(A) confined to narrow social roles
(B) cut off from religious communities
(C) exploited as slaves and servants
(D) defined in physical or biological terms
(E) valued but essentially powerless

25 According to the passage, which of the following describes a difference between Frankish society and more primitive cultures?

(A) Frankish society did not encourage childbearing.
(B) Women in Frankish society were not taken advantage of for their labor.
(C) Women in Frankish society had more social and political power over their husbands.
(D) Women in Frankish society were less likely to work within their homes.
(E) Frankish society defined gender differences in biological terms.

GO ON TO THE NEXT PAGE →

26 The passage suggests that the "access to power" (line 10) enjoyed by Frankish queens

(A) surpassed the influence wielded by their sons and husbands

(B) was greatly increased by their relationship to the church

(C) did not extend beyond the boundaries of their households

(D) permitted them to exercise power, but only indirectly

(E) was based on their relationships to male figures of power

27 The word "transmitted" as used in line 17 most nearly means

(A) announced
(B) taught
(C) enforced
(D) distributed
(E) broadcast

28 It can be inferred from the passage that marriage in Frankish society

(A) was the only means of exchanging wealth

(B) could be entered formally or informally

(C) raised women to positions of influence

(D) held greater importance than in primitive societies

(E) was generally arranged by the bride's mother

29 The word "instrumental" as used in line 28 most nearly means

(A) helpful
(B) skilled
(C) harmonious
(D) resistant
(E) vital

30 Which of the following best describes the difference between "wives of magnates" (line 14) and wives in the "dependent classes" (lines 25–26)?

(A) Wives in the dependent classes cooperated with their husbands, while the wives of magnates did not.

(B) Wives in the dependent classes were powerless in their own households, while the wives of magnates wielded considerable power in theirs.

(C) Wives in the dependent classes were forced by their husbands to perform strenuous tasks, while wives of magnates were not.

(D) Wives of magnates were less likely than wives in the dependent classes to turn to religious communities for refuge and liberation.

(E) Wives of magnates had greater power to administrate their own households than did wives in the dependent classes.

31 According to the author, female religious communities in Frankish society had "importance for the history of women" (lines 39–40) because

(A) Frankish women entered these religious groups in great numbers

(B) they increased the political influence of all Frankish women

(C) women in these communities received superior education

(D) they introduced women to diverse cultural and social activities

(E) they eliminated the rift between married and unmarried women

GO ON TO THE NEXT PAGE

32 The passage implies that Frankish women outside religious communities

(A) felt obliged to compete for male attention
(B) were not inclined to religious feeling
(C) had greatly diminished economic power
(D) did not contribute to Frankish culture
(E) relied on males for emotional support

33 In line 54, "upheld" most nearly means

(A) delayed
(B) endorsed
(C) suspended
(D) enforced
(E) announced

34 According to the passage, Christianity facilitated the "escape of women from the male-dominated society" (lines 56–57) by doing all of the following EXCEPT

(A) permitting women self-expression
(B) insulating women from physical hardship
(C) diversifying women's social roles
(D) removing male social pressures
(E) putting pressure on women to study

35 The passage is best described as

(A) a study of class conflict in a medieval society
(B) an example of religion's influence on secular life
(C) a discussion of the roles of a social group
(D) a demonstration of the need for religious communities
(E) a refutation of a popular misconception

IF YOU FINISH BEFORE TIME IS CALLED, YOU MAY CHECK YOUR WORK ON THIS SECTION ONLY. DO NOT TURN TO ANY OTHER SECTION IN THE TEST.   **STOP**

<table>
<tr><td>

Time—15 Minutes
10 Questions

</td><td>

In this section solve each problem, using any available space on the page for scratchwork. Then decide which is the best of the choices given and fill in the corresponding oval on the answer sheet.

</td></tr>
</table>

Notes:

1.   The use of a calculator is permitted. All numbers used are real numbers.

2.   Figures that accompany problems in this test are intended to provide information useful in solving the problems. They are drawn as accurately as possible EXCEPT when it is stated in a specific problem that the figure is not drawn to scale. All figures lie in a plane unless otherwise indicated.

Reference Information

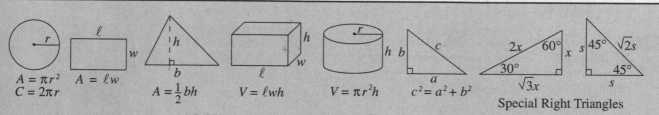

$A = \pi r^2$ $A = \ell w$ $A = \frac{1}{2}bh$ $V = \ell wh$ $V = \pi r^2 h$ $c^2 = a^2 + b^2$ Special Right Triangles
$C = 2\pi r$

The number of degrees of arc in a circle is 360.
The measure in degrees of a straight angle is 180.
The sum of the measures in degrees of the angles of a triangle is 180.

---

1   If $6 - y = 2y - 6$, then $y =$

(A)   0
(B)   2
(C)   4
(D)   6
(E)   12

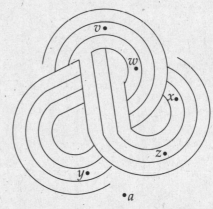

2   Which of the following points can be connected to point a by a continuous path without crossing any line or curve of the figure above?

(A) v
(B) w
(C) x
(D) y
(E) z

GO ON TO THE NEXT PAGE ⟩

Computer Production		
	Morning Shift	**Afternoon Shift**
Monday	200	375
Tuesday	245	330
Wednesday	255	340
Thursday	250	315
Friday	225	360

3   If the above chart shows the number of computers produced at a factory during each shift, on which day is the total number of computers produced greatest?

(A) Monday
(B) Tuesday
(C) Wednesday
(D) Thursday
(E) Friday

4   If a rectangular swimming pool has a volume of 16,500 cubic feet, a depth of 10 feet, and a length of 75 feet, what is the width of the pool, in feet?

(A)   22
(B)   26
(C)   32
(D)   110
(E)   1,650

5   A science class has a ratio of girls to boys of 4 to 3. If the class has a total of 35 students, how many more girls are there than boys?

(A) 20
(B) 15
(C)   7
(D)   5
(E)   1

6   If $\dfrac{n}{8}$ has a remainder of 5, then which of the following has a remainder of 7?

(A) $\dfrac{n+1}{8}$

(B) $\dfrac{n+2}{8}$

(C) $\dfrac{n+3}{8}$

(D) $\dfrac{n+5}{8}$

(E) $\dfrac{n+7}{8}$

7   For positive integer x, 10 percent of x percent of 1,000 equals

(A) x
(B) $10x$
(C) $100x$
(D) $1,000x$
(E) $10,000x$

GO ON TO THE NEXT PAGE ➤

8   Nails are sold in 8-ounce and 20-ounce boxes. If 50 boxes of nails were sold and the total weight of the nails sold was less than 600 ounces, what is the greatest possible number of 20-ounce boxes that could have been sold?

(A) 34
(B) 33
(C) 25
(D) 17
(E) 16

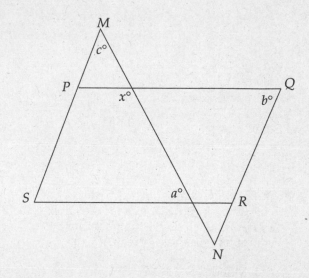

9   If $c = \dfrac{1}{x} + \dfrac{1}{y}$ and $x > y > 0$, then $\dfrac{1}{c} =$

(A) $x + y$

(B) $x - y$

(C) $\dfrac{xy}{x+y}$

(D) $\dfrac{x+y}{xy}$

(E) $\dfrac{1}{x} - \dfrac{1}{y}$

10   If $PQRS$ is a parallelogram and MN is a line segment, then x must equal

(A) $180 - b$
(B) $180 - c$
(C) $a + b$
(D) $a + c$
(E) $b + c$

IF YOU FINISH BEFORE TIME IS CALLED, YOU MAY CHECK YOUR WORK ON THIS SECTION ONLY. DO NOT TURN TO ANY OTHER SECTION IN THE TEST.   **STOP**

NO TEST MATERIAL ON THIS PAGE.

For each question in this section, select the best answer from among the choices given and fill in the corresponding oval on the answer sheet.

The two passages below are followed by questions based on their content and on the relationship between the two passages. Answer the questions on the basis of what is <u>stated</u> or <u>implied</u> in the passage and in any introductory material that may be provided.

Questions 1–13 are based on the following passages.

The discipline of physics has seen a number of changes in the last 100 years. The following passages discuss two of those changes.

Passage 1

It is mandatory to preface any discussion of atoms by paying homage to Democritus, an Ionian philosopher of the fifth century B.C., the earliest
Line known proponent of an atomic theory. Though
(5) Democritus' ideas were in many ways strikingly modern and were promulgated by his more celebrated successor Epicurus, his theory never gained wide acceptance in Greek thought. It had largely been forgotten by the time of the late
(10) Renaissance rebirth of science. While the dramatic rise of the atomic theory over the last century and a half seems to have vindicated Democritus, only the Greek name atom ("indivisible") remains to establish his claim as the father of the theory.
(15) Nonetheless, Democritus' thinking contained the seed of the idea that has dominated twentieth-century physical thought. He was one of the first to perceive that nature on a sufficiently small scale might be qualitatively different in a striking way
(20) from the world of our ordinary experience. And he was the first to voice the hope, today almost an obsession, that underlying all the complex richness, texture, and variety of our everyday life might be a level of reality of stark simplicity, with the turmoil
(25) we perceive representing only the nearly infinite arrangements of a smaller number of constituents.
Today, the notion that simplicity is to be found by searching nature on a smaller level is embedded in physical thought to the point where few physicists
(30) can imagine any other approach.
Democritus' ideas were popular among the philosophically sophisticated founders of modern physics. Galileo, Newton, and most of their contemporaries were atomists, but their beliefs were
(35) based more on intuition than on concrete evidence.

Moreover, the invention of calculus had eliminated the difficulties with continuity that had in part motivated the Greek atomists, so the theory received little attention in the century following
(40) Newton's work. Still, the atomic theory remained a popular speculation among physicists, because it offered the hope that all the properties of matter might ultimately be explained in terms of the motion of the atoms themselves.
(45) It remained for the chemists of the early nineteenth century to find the first solid empirical support for atomism. Without stretching the point too far, it is fair to say that in 1800 the atomic theory was something physicists believed but couldn't
(50) prove, while the chemists were proving it but didn't believe it.

Passage 2

The discovery that the universe is expanding was one of the great intellectual revelations of the twentieth century. With hindsight, it is easy to
(55) wonder why no one had thought of it before. Newton, and others, should have realized that a static universe would soon start to contract under the influence of gravity. But suppose instead the universe is expanding. If it was expanding fairly
(60) slowly, the force of gravity would cause it eventually to stop expanding and then to start contracting. However, if it was expanding at more than a certain critical rate, gravity would never be strong enough to stop it, and the universe would
(65) continue to expand forever. This is a bit like what happens when one fires a rocket upward from the surface of the earth. If it has a fairly low speed, gravity will eventually stop the rocket and it will start falling back. On the other hand, if the rocket
(70) has more than a certain critical speed (about seven

GO ON TO THE NEXT PAGE ⟩

miles per second), gravity will not be strong enough to pull it back, so it will keep going away from the earth forever. This behavior of the universe could have been predicted from Newton's theory of
(75) gravity at any time in the nineteenth, the eighteenth, or even the late seventeenth centuries. Yet so strong was the belief in a static universe that it persisted into the early twentieth century. Even Einstein, when he formulated the general theory of
(80) relativity in 1915, was so sure that the universe had to be static that he modified his theory to make this possible, introducing a so-called cosmological constant into his equations. Einstein introduced a new "antigravity" force, which, unlike other forces,
(85) did not come from any particular source, but was built into the very fabric of space-time. He claimed that space-time had an inbuilt tendency to expand, and this could be made to balance exactly the attraction of all the matter in the universe, so that a
(90) static universe would result.

1 In line 6, the word "promulgated" most nearly means

(A) plagiarized
(B) dismissed
(C) protected
(D) obscured
(E) promoted

2 From the information presented in Passage 1, which of the following can be properly inferred about Democritus?

(A) Although his view was initially met with skepticism, Democritus was among the first to advocate an atomic theory.
(B) Although he was more known for his work in politics, Democritus also made important scientific discoveries.
(C) His ideas were incompatible with those of Galileo and Newton.
(D) Democritus was unduly credited with being the father of Greek atomism.
(E) Democritus was more known for his discovery of calculus than for his theory of atomism.

3 Which of the following does the author of Passage 1 suggest about the physical world?

(A) The composition of everyday things will remain a mystery forever.
(B) Understanding matter is much simpler than scientists once believed.
(C) Despite the diversity of the physical world, all matter may have a single underlying component.
(D) Although physicists use simple models to describe matter, the principles underlying the models point to a more complex reality.
(E) The theories developed by Democritus accurately explain all aspects of everyday matter.

4 The "obsession" which the author describes in line 22 can best be described as

(A) Democritus' desire to see his ideas accepted by the scientific community.
(B) physicists' search for Democritus' original writings on atoms.
(C) the author's own search for the principles underlying matter.
(D) early nineteenth century chemists' search for the first solid evidence of atomism.
(E) modern scientists' quest for a simple unifying property of everyday matter.

5 Which of the following can be inferred from Passage 2 about the expanding universe?

(A) It was incompatible with a theory widely accepted in the nineteenth century.
(B) Newton discovered it during his work with gravity.
(C) Most scientists believe that the idea is no longer tenable.
(D) The existence of gravity makes it impossible for the universe to expand.
(E) The expanding universe theory cannot be proven.

GO ON TO THE NEXT PAGE

6 In line 63 the term "certain critical rate" refers to

(A) the rate at which scientific knowledge is growing
(B) an urgent problem which needs solving
(C) the speed at which a rocket must travel in order to move away from the earth
(D) the speed necessary to equal the force of gravity's pull
(E) the meeting point of gravity and the universe

7 The author of Passage 2 mentions Newton in order to

(A) point out the ignorance of many physicists
(B) give one example of a proponent of the expanding universe theory
(C) illustrate the point that the expanding universe theory might have been discovered earlier
(D) provide evidence that the universe is not expanding
(E) show the consequences of a scientist's disregard for a new theory

8 The author's reference to a rocket ship (lines 66–73) serves to illustrate

(A) the implications of an expanding universe
(B) the forces governing the universe's gradual expansion
(C) the similarity of the energy released by the universe and that released by rockets
(D) the way in which gravity prevents the universe from expanding
(E) the theory of a static universe

9 In Passage 2, the author's description of Einstein's general theory of relativity serves to

(A) bolster the author's theory that the universe is expanding
(B) show that modern scientists were reluctant to abandon the theory of a static universe
(C) indicate the creativity that Einstein brought to his work
(D) question the validity of the theory of the expanding universe
(E) underscore Einstein's reliance on Newtonian physics

10 The term "cosmological constant" (lines 82–83) refers to

(A) a mathematical constant employed by Einstein to bring his theories in line with the idea of a static universe
(B) an equation used by Einstein to debunk Newton's ideas about universal expansion
(C) a theory developed by opponents of Einstein's general theory of relativity
(D) the mathematical model that was used to disprove Newtonian physics
(E) the theory that the mass of all matter in the universe must remain the same

11 In the last line of Passage 2 the word "static" most nearly means

(A) charged
(B) conflicting
(C) particulate
(D) unchanging
(E) dynamic

GO ON TO THE NEXT PAGE

12 The authors of both passages would most probably agree with which of the following statements?

   (A) Democritus and Newton both struggled to see their theories accepted by others.

   (B) Neither Democritus nor Newton received credit for his theories.

   (C) Newton, Einstein and Democritus are all responsible in part for setting back modern physics.

   (D) The atomic model of matter and the theory of the expanding universe are mutually exclusive.

   (E) Scientists may adopt particular theories in spite of weak or contradictory evidence.

13 Based on the information in both passages, a difference between atomism and the expanding universe theory is

   (A) the idea of atomism can be traced to the ancient Greeks, while the model of the expanding universe is a relatively recent theory

   (B) atomism is easier to understand and explore than the static universe theory

   (C) atomism was developed for political reasons, while the static universe theory is purely scientific

   (D) the theory of atomism has been proven, while the static universe theory is now thought to be incorrect

   (E) the static universe theory is more adaptable to modern science than is the atomistic theory

IF YOU FINISH BEFORE TIME IS CALLED, YOU MAY CHECK YOUR WORK ON THIS SECTION ONLY. DO NOT TURN TO ANY OTHER SECTION IN THE TEST. **STOP**

DIAGNOSTIC TEST II ANSWERS

Section 1	Section 2	Section 3	Section 4	Section 5	Section 6	Section 7
1. E	1. E	1. A	1. B	1. E	1. C	1. E
2. B	2. D	2. C	2. D	2. E	2. B	2. A
3. B	3. E	3. A	3. A	3. D	3. C	3. C
4. C	4. E	4. A	4. C	4. D	4. A	4. E
5. A	5. C	5. D	5. B	5. C	5. D	5. A
6. C	6. C	6. B	6. D	6. E	6. B	6. D
7. D	7. A	7. B	7. B	7. D	7. A	7. C
8. E	8. B	8. D	8. D	8. C	8. E	8. B
9. D	9. A	9. A	9. B	9. D	9. C	9. B
10. C	10. C	10. C	10. B	10. A	10. E	10. A
11. D	11. B	11. C	11. A	11. E		11. D
12. B	12. C	12. D	12. B	12. A		12. E
13. C	13. E	13. A	13. D	13. A		13. A
14. A	14. A	14. D	14. C	14. A		
15. B	15. B	15. B	15. A	15. D		
16. D	16. A	16. 2	16. 100	16. E		
17. B	17. D	17. 270	17. 81	17. B		
18. C	18. B	18. 0.4	18. 0.75	18. B		
19. D	19. B	or 2/5	or 3/4	19. E		
20. D	20. D	19. 3	19. 0.583	20. B		
21. A	21. A	20. 24	or	21. C		
22. B	22. B	21. 7	7/12	22. A		
23. C	23. C	22. 50	20. 5,7,	23. E		
24. C	24. E	23. 6	or 11	24. D		
25. C	25. C	24. 286	21. 21	25. B		
	26. D	25. 18	22. 96	26. E		
	27. B		23. 2	27. B		
	28. D		24. 282	28. B		
	29. A		25. 0.375	29. E		
	30. B		or 3/8	30. E		
				31. D		
				32. A		
				33. B		
				34. E		
				35. C		

You will find a detailed explanation for each question beginning on page 543.

HOW TO SCORE YOUR DIAGNOSTIC TEST

Verbal

After you have checked your answers to the diagnostic test against the key, you can calculate your score. For the three verbal sections (sections 2, 5, and 7), tally up the number of correct answers and the number of incorrect answers. Enter these numbers on the worksheet on the next page. Multiply the number of incorrect answers by $\frac{1}{4}$ and subtract the result from the number of correct answers. Put this number in box A. Then round the numbers to the nearest whole number and place it in box B.

Mathematics

Figuring your math score is a little trickier, because some of the questions have five answer choices, some have four, and some have none. In sections 1 and 6, count the number of correct answers and incorrect answers. Enter these numbers on the worksheet. Multiply the number of incorrect answers by $\frac{1}{4}$ and subtract this from the number of correct answers. Put the result in box C.

Count the number of correct and incorrect answers in section 3, questions 1–15. (Choice E counts as a blank.) Enter these on the worksheet. Multiply the number of incorrect answers by $\frac{1}{3}$ and subtract this from the number of correct answers. Put the result in box D.

Count up the number of correct answers in section 3, questions 16–25. Put the result in box E. There is no penalty for incorrect Grid-In questions.

Note: Section 4 is experimental and should not be scored.

Add up the numbers in boxes C, D, and E, and write the result in box F.

Round F to the nearest whole number, and place the result in box G.

WORKSHEET FOR CALCULATING YOUR SCORE

VERBAL

	Correct	Incorrect	
A. Sections 2, 5, and 7	_____ – (1/4	_____) =	[A]
B. Total rounded verbal raw score			[B]

Mathematics

	Correct	Incorrect	
C. Sections 1 and 6	_____ – (1/4	_____) =	[C]
D. Section 3 (Questions 1–15)	_____ – (1/3	_____) =	[D]
E. Section 3 (Questions 16–25)	_____ =		[E]
F. Total unrounded math raw score (C + D + E)			[F]
G. Total rounded math raw score			[G]

Use the table on the next page to convert your raw score to scaled scores. For example, a raw verbal score of 39 corresponds to a verbal scaled score of 530; a math raw score of 24 corresponds to a math scaled score of 470.

Scores on the SAT range from 200 to 800.

Note: Since Section 4 is the experimental section it does not count toward your score.

SCORE CONVERSION TABLE

Raw Score	Verbal Scaled Score	Math Scaled Score	Raw Score	Verbal Scaled Score	Math Scaled Score
78	800		36	510	560
77	800		35	510	550
76	800		34	500	540
75	800		33	490	530
74	780		32	480	520
73	760		31	480	520
72	750		30	470	510
71	740		29	460	500
70	740		28	460	490
69	730		27	450	480
68	720		26	450	480
67	710		25	440	480
66	700		24	430	470
65	690		23	430	460
64	680		22	420	450
63	670		21	410	440
62	670		20	400	430
61	660		19	390	430
60	660	800	18	380	430
59	650	790	17	380	420
58	640	770	16	370	410
57	640	760	15	360	400
56	630	740	14	350	390
55	620	730	13	350	390
54	620	720	12	340	380
53	610	700	11	330	370
52	600	690	10	310	350
51	600	680	9	300	340
50	600	660	8	290	340
49	590	650	7	270	330
48	590	650	6	270	310
47	580	640	5	230	300
46	570	630	4	230	300
45	570	620	3	230	280
44	560	610	2	230	260
43	560	600	1	230	250
42	550	600	0	230	240
41	550	590	−1	230	220
40	540	580	−2	230	220
39	530	570	−3	230	200
38	530	560	−4	230	200
37	520	560	−5 and below	230	200

20

Explanations II

What follows is a detailed explanation for each question on this diagnostic test. Although you will naturally be more curious about the questions you got wrong, don't forget to read the explanations for the questions you left blank. In fact, you should even read the explanations for the questions you got right! Our explanations present the safest, most direct solution to each question. Even though you may have gotten a question right, that does not mean you solved it in the most efficient way.

SECTION 1

QUESTIONS	EXPLANATIONS

1 If $\dfrac{12}{4} = x$, then $4x + 2 =$

(A) 2
(B) 3
(C) 4
(D) 12
(E) 14

1. Jim's answer is E.
    If you divide 12 by 4, you'll see that $x = 3$. When you plug $x = 3$ into the term, you'll see that $4(3) + 2 = 12 + 2 = 14$.

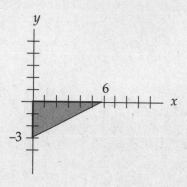

2 In the figure above, which of the following points lies within the shaded region?

(A) $(-1, 1)$
(B) $(1, -2)$
(C) $(4, 3)$
(D) $(5, -4)$
(E) $(7, 0)$

2. Jim's answer is B.
    The shaded region lies in the quadrant where x is positive and y is negative. Given this, you can get rid of answer choices A, C, and E. If you plot answer choices B and D, you'll find that $(1, -2)$ is inside the shaded region, while $(5, -4)$ is not.

3 If n is an even integer, which of the following must be an odd integer?

(A) $3n - 2$

(B) $3(n + 1)$

(C) $n - 2$

(D) $\dfrac{n}{3}$

(E) n^2

3. Jim's answer is B.
    There are variables in the answer choices, so this is a Plug In question. If $n = 2$, then answer choice B is the only answer choice that gives you an odd integer:
    $$3(n + 1) = 3(2 + 1) = 3(3) = 9.$$

4 $x\sqrt{4} - x\sqrt{9} =$

(A) $-5x$
(B) $-x\sqrt{5}$
(C) $-x$
(D) x
(E) $3x$

4. Jim's answer is C.
    This question is much easier if you work out the square roots first. We know that $\sqrt{4} = 2$ and $\sqrt{9} = 3$, so we can rewrite the question like this: $2x - 3x = -x$.

SECTION 1

|

5 Six cups of flour are required to make a batch of cookies. How many cups of flour are needed to make enough cookies to fill 12 cookie jars, if each cookie jar holds 1.5 batches?

(A) 108
(B) 90
(C) 81
(D) 78
(E) 72

5. Jim's answer is A.
You need to take this question one step at a time. First, figure out how many batches there are in 12 jars of cookies. If one jar holds 1.5 batches, then twelve jars will hold 12×1.5, or 18 batches. Now you need to figure out how much flour is needed for 18 batches. If you need six cups of flour for one batch, then for 18 batches you will need 18×6, or 108 cups.

6 If Circle O has a diameter of 9, then what is the area of Circle O?

(A) 81π

(B) $\dfrac{9}{2}\pi$

(C) $\dfrac{81}{4}\pi$

(D) 18π

(E) 9π

6. Jim's answer is C.
The formula for the area of a circle is πr^2, so we need to find the radius of the circle. We know that the diameter is 9, and the radius is half of the diameter, so the radius is $\dfrac{9}{2}$. Since there are fractions in the answer choices, you might as well keep the radius as a fraction. The area of the circle is $\left(\dfrac{9}{2}\right)^2 \pi$, which equals $\dfrac{81}{4}\pi$.

7 Cindy has a collection of 80 records. If 40 percent of her records are jazz records, and the rest are blues records, how many blues records does she have?

(A) 32
(B) 40
(C) 42
(D) 48
(E) 50

7. Jim's answer is D.
The idea of the rest in this question can save you from doing unnecessary arithmetic. If 40 percent of the records are jazz, then the rest, or 60 percent, are blues. Since there are 80 records, just use your calculator to find 60 percent of 80, which is 48.

8 How many even integers are there between 2 and 100, not including 2 and 100?

(A) 98
(B) 97
(C) 50
(D) 49
(E) 48

8. Jim's answer is E.
From 1 to 100, there are 50 even integers. If we don't include 2 and 100, then there are only 48.

QUESTIONS	EXPLANATIONS

9 If b equals 40 percent of a, then, in terms of b, 40 percent of $4a$ is equal to

(A) $\dfrac{b}{40}$

(B) $\dfrac{b}{4}$

(C) b

(D) $4b$

(E) $16b$

9. Jim's answer is D.
If there are variables in the answer choices you should…Plug In! First, cross out that phrase in "terms of b," because we don't need it. Next, let's plug in a number for a. This is a percent question, so let $a = 100$. Since b is 40 percent of a, that means $b = 40$. If $a = 100$, then $4a = 400$. Use your calculator to find 40 percent of 400, which is 160. That's your target answer. Since $b = 40$, answer choice D gives you 160.

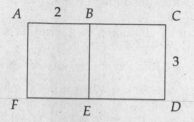

10 In the figure above, the perimeter of square $BCDE$ is how much smaller than the perimeter of rectangle $ACDF$?

(A) 2
(B) 3
(C) 4
(D) 7
(E) 16

10. Jim's answer is C.
Remember that the perimeter is the sum of all the sides. $BCDE$ is a square, so all the sides are equal. Since $CD = 3$, each side of the square is 3. Add up all four sides to find the perimeter, which is 12. $ACDF$ is a rectangle, which means that the opposite sides are equal. $AB = 2$, so $FE = 2$ also. BE is a side of square $BCDE$, so BE equals 3, but it's also the side of the rectangle, and that means the opposite side, AF, also equals 3. Add up all the sides of $ACDF$ to find the perimeter: $2 + 2 + 3 + 3 = 16$. To find out how much smaller the perimeter of $BCDE$ is, just subtract: $16 - 12 = 4$.

SECTION 1

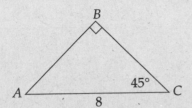

11 In the triangle *ABC* above, if *AC* is equal to 8, then *BC* is equal to

(A) $8\sqrt{2}$

(B) 8

(C) 6

(D) $4\sqrt{2}$

(E) $3\sqrt{2}$

11. Jim's answer is D.

The sides of a 45:45:90 triangle have a special pattern, which you can find in the gray box at the beginning of every math section. Each leg of a 45:45:90 triangle is equal to the hypotenuse divided by $\sqrt{2}$. Since the hypotenuse in triangle *ABC* is 8, *BC* must be equal to $\dfrac{8}{\sqrt{2}}$. You can't have a square root on the bottom of a fraction; multiply the top and the bottom by $\sqrt{2}$. That gives you $\dfrac{8\sqrt{2}}{2}$, which equals $4\sqrt{2}$. Also, you could have used Ballparking to eliminate A and B. Since the hypotenuse of a right triangle is always the longest of the three sides, *BC* must be less than 8.

	Number Sold	Average Weight per Parrot (in pounds)
Red Parrots	5	2
Blue Parrots	4	3

12 The chart above shows the number of red and blue parrots Toby sold in May and the average weight of each type of bird sold. If Toby sold no other parrots, what was the average (arithmetic mean) weight of a parrot in pounds that Toby sold in May?

(A) 2

(B) $2\frac{4}{9}$

(C) $2\frac{1}{2}$

(D) 5

(E) 9

12. Jim's answer is B.

Use Average Pies:

Red: 10 / (5 | 2)   Blue: 12 / (4 | 3)   Total: 22 / (9)

In the first pie you have the number of red parrots sold, which is 5, and the average weight, which is 2. That gives you a total weight of 10 pounds. In the second pie you have the number of blue parrots, which is 4, and the average weight, which is 3. That gives you a total weight of 12. To find the average weight of all the parrots, you need to find the total weight of all the parrots. This is simply the total of the red plus the total of the blue. In the last pie you have the total number of parrots, which is 9, and the total weight of all the parrots, which is 22. This gives you an average weight of $\frac{22}{9}$, or $2\frac{4}{9}$.

13 If $999 \times 111 = 3 \times 3 \times n^2$, then which of the following could equal n ?

(A) 9
(B) 37
(C) 111
(D) 222
(E) 333

13. Jim's answer is C.
This question can be backsolved easily, using your calculator. Just punch in 111×999 and you get 110,889. Then try out the answer choices, starting with C. If $n = 111$, then $3 \times 3 \times (111)^2 = 110,889$.

SECTION 1

14 If $x + 6 > 0$ and $1 - 2x > -1$, then x could equal each of the following EXCEPT

(A) -6

(B) -4

(C) -2

(D) 0

(E) $\dfrac{1}{2}$

14. Jim's answer is A.

The question is essentially asking which of the answer choices cannot be a value of x. So just try each answer choice one at a time by plugging the number into each of the two inequalities in the question, and see which one doesn't fit. If $x = -6$, is $-6 + 6 > 0$? No, because zero is not greater than zero. So -6 is the exception.

15 In 1985, Andrei had a collection of 48 baseball caps. Since then he has given away 13 caps, purchased 17 new caps and traded 6 of his caps to Pierre for 8 of Pierre's caps. Since 1985, what has been the net percent increase in Andrei's collection?

(A) 6%

(B) $12\dfrac{1}{2}\%$

(C) $16\dfrac{2}{3}\%$

(D) 25%

(E) $28\dfrac{1}{2}\%$

15. Jim's answer is B.

This question has several steps, so don't try to do it all at once. Take it one step at a time. Andrei starts out with 48 baseball caps. In the first step, Andrei gives away 13 caps, so he has 35 left. In the next step, he buys 17 new caps, so now he has 52. Then Andrei gives Pierre 6 caps (46 left) and gets 8 caps in return. In the end, Andrei has 54 baseball caps, which is 6 more caps than he had originally. The percent increase is $\dfrac{6}{48}$. You can change this to a percent by converting the fraction to a decimal and then multiplying by 100 on your calculator: $\dfrac{6}{48} \times 100 = 0.125 \times 100 = 12.5\%$.

SECTION 1

| QUESTIONS | EXPLANATIONS |

Questions 16 and 17 refer to the following definition:
For all real numbers x, let $\otimes x$ be defined as $2x^2 + 4$.

16 What is the value of $\otimes 4$?

(A) 16
(B) 18
(C) 20
(D) 36
(E) 72

16. Jim's answer is D.
According to the function, $\otimes x = 2x^2 + 4$. To find the value of $\otimes 4$, just substitute 4 for x:

$$2(4)^2 + 4 = 2(16) + 4 = 32 + 4 = 36.$$

17 What is the value of $\otimes 3 + \otimes 5$?

(A) $\otimes 4$
(B) $\otimes 6$
(C) $\otimes 8$
(D) $\otimes 10$
(E) $\otimes 15$

17. Jim's answer is B.
To find the value of $\otimes 3 + \otimes 5$, find the values of 3 and 5 separately: $\otimes 3 = 2(3)^2 + 4 = 22$; and $\otimes 5 = 2(5)^2 + 4 = 54$. So $\otimes 3 + \otimes 5 = 76$. You already know that $\otimes 4 = 36$ from question 16, so you can cross out A. Answer choice C is the Joe Bloggs answer, because Joe simply adds 3 and 5, and it can't be that easy. If you ballpark answer choices D and E, putting 10 or 15 in the function will give you a number bigger than 100, and you're looking for 76, so D and E are too big. That means the answer is B by Process Of Elimination.

18 What is the greatest number of regions into which an equilateral triangle can be divided using exactly three straight lines?

(A) 4
(B) 6
(C) 7
(D) 8
(E) 9

18. Jim's answer is C.
The Joe Bloggs answer is E, because Joe simply chooses the greatest number. If you draw three straight lines through the center of the triangle, you get six regions, so you know that you can have at least six. Therefore, you can eliminate A. But that was too easy. That means Jim's answer must be 7 or 8. If you don't have time, you can guess between C and D. Here's how you can actually get seven regions:

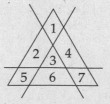

SECTION 1

QUESTIONS	EXPLANATIONS

19 Elsa has a pitcher containing x ounces of root beer. If she pours y ounces of root beer into each of z glasses, how much root beer will remain in the pitcher?

(A) $\dfrac{x}{y} + z$

(B) $xy - z$

(C) $\dfrac{x}{yz}$

(D) $x - yz$

(E) $\dfrac{x}{y} - z$

19. Jim's answer is D.
Whenever there are variables in the answer choices, you should always Plug In. Let's say $x = 20$, which means there are 20 ounces of root beer in the pitcher. Next, let's make $y = 3$ and $z = 4$. That means Elsa pours 3 ounces into each of 4 glasses, so she pours a total of 12 ounces. The question asks how much root beer remains in pitcher, so your target answer is $20 - 12$, or 8. Go to the answer choices and plug in $x = 20$, $y = 3$, and $z = 4$. In answer choice D, $x - yz = 20 - (3)(4) = 20 - 12 = 8$.

20 A bag contains 4 red hammers, 10 blue hammers, and 6 yellow hammers. If three hammers are removed at random and no hammer is returned to the bag after removal, what is the probability that all three hammers will be blue?

(A) $\dfrac{1}{2}$

(B) $\dfrac{1}{8}$

(C) $\dfrac{3}{20}$

(D) $\dfrac{2}{19}$

(E) $\dfrac{3}{8}$

20. Jim's answer is D.
To figure out probability, you need to work with fractions; the total number of possible outcomes goes on the bottom, and the number of desired outcomes goes on the top. To figure out the probability of selecting three blue hammers, you need to figure out the probability of getting a blue hammer each time a hammer is selected. The first time, there are total of 20 hammers and 10 of them are blue, so the probability of getting a blue hammer is $\dfrac{10}{20}$, or $\dfrac{1}{2}$. When the second hammer is selected, there are only 19 hammers left, and only 9 of them are blue. So the probability of getting a blue hammer the second time is $\dfrac{9}{19}$. When the third hammer is selected, there are a total 18 hammers left and 8 are blue, so the probability of getting a blue hammer on the third try is $\dfrac{8}{18}$, or $\dfrac{4}{9}$. To find the probability of selecting three blue hammers, you need to multiply the three separate probabilities: $\dfrac{1}{2} \times \dfrac{9}{19} \times \dfrac{4}{9} = \dfrac{2}{19}$. By the way, A and B are Joe Bloggs answers.

SECTION 1

QUESTIONS	EXPLANATIONS

21 There are k gallons of gasoline available to fill a tank. After d gallons have been pumped, then, in terms of k and d, what percent of the gasoline has been pumped?

(A) $\dfrac{100d}{k}\%$

(B) $\dfrac{k}{100d}\%$

(C) $\dfrac{100k}{d}\%$

(D) $\dfrac{k}{100(k-d)}\%$

(E) $\dfrac{100(k-d)}{k}\%$

21. Jim's answer is A.
Variables in the answer choices? Plug In! This is a percent question, so make $k = 100$ and $d = 40$. If 40 out of the 100 gallons have been pumped, that equals 40%. So 40% is your target answer. When you plug $k = 100$ and $d = 40$ into the answer choices, A gives you 40. Plugging In turns a hard question into a much easier question.

22 If $a = 4b + 26$, and b is a positive integer, then a could be divisible by all of the following EXCEPT

(A) 2
(B) 4
(C) 5
(D) 6
(E) 7

22. Jim's answer is B.
To find out what numbers a could be divisible by, you need to try different values of b. If $b = 1$, then $a = 4(1) + 26 = 30$. In this case, a is divisible by 2, 5, and 6, so you can cross out A, C, and D. If $b = 4$, then $a = 42$, which is divisible by 7, so cross out choice E. That only leaves choice B, which must be the answer.

SECTION 1

QUESTIONS	EXPLANATIONS

23 Ray and Jane live 150 miles apart. They each drive toward the other's house along a straight road connecting the two, Ray at a constant rate of 30 miles per hour and Jane at a constant rate of 50 miles per hour. If Ray and Jane leave their houses at the same time, how many miles are they from Ray's house when they meet?

(A) 40

(B) $51\frac{1}{2}$

(C) $56\frac{1}{4}$

(D) 75

(E) $93\frac{3}{4}$

23. Jim's answer is C.

For this question you need to know the distance formula: distance = rate × time. This is also a perfect question to Backsolve. The question asks how far Ray and Jane will be from Ray's house when they meet. Start with C: if they are $56\frac{1}{4}$ miles away from Ray's house, and Ray traveled from home at 30 miles per hour, then you can figure out the time he traveled using the "rate × time = distance" formula (and your calculator): $56\frac{1}{4} = 30 \times$ time. In this case Ray has traveled for $1\frac{7}{8}$ hours. Jane has been traveling for the same amount of time at a rate of 50 miles an hour, so you can figure out how far Jane has traveled: distance = $50 \times 1\frac{7}{8}$. If Jane has traveled $93\frac{3}{4}$ and Ray has traveled $56\frac{1}{4}$, then they have traveled a total of 150 miles when they meet. Bingo! You're done.

24 If $x = y + 1$ and $y \geq 1$, then which of the following must be equal to $x^2 - y^2$?

(A) $(x - y)^2$
(B) $x^2 - y - 1$
(C) $x + y$
(D) $x^2 - 1$
(E) $y^2 - 1$

24. Jim's answer is C.

Whenever there are variables in the answer choices you must Plug In. Since $x = y + 1$ and $y \geq 1$, we can make $x = 5$ and $y = 4$. In that case $x^2 - y^2 = 25 - 16 = 9$, so 9 is your target answer. When you plug $x = 5$ and $y = 4$ into the answer choices, C gives you 9. Plugging In turns a hard question into a much easier question.

25 If x is an integer, which of the following could be x^3?

(A) 2.7×10^{11}
(B) 2.7×10^{12}
(C) 2.7×10^{13}
(D) 2.7×10^{14}
(E) 2.7×10^{15}

25. Jim's answer is C.

The question asks which of the answer choices could be x^3. If x is an integer, then the cube root of one of the answer choices should be an integer. You should be able to find the cube root on most scientific calculators. Here, the answer is C: $2.7 \times 10^{13} = 27 \times 10^{12}$ and $\sqrt[3]{27 \times 10^{12}} = 3 \times 10^4$, which equals 30,000 (an integer).

SECTION 2

1 Nuclear power plants are some of the largest producers of ---- wastes, with each plant producing barrels of radioactive material that must be stored in special protective containers.

- (A) biodegradable
- (B) artificial
- (C) reasonable
- (D) durable
- (E) hazardous

1. Pam's answer is E.
The blank in this sentence is a word that describes the wastes produced by nuclear power plants. What do we know about the wastes? The wastes are *radioactive materials* that have to be stored in *protective containers*, which means they must be dangerous, so *dangerous* would be a good word for the blank. Answer choice E, *hazardous*, is the best match for *dangerous*.

2 The scientific community was ---- when a living specimen of the coelacanth, long thought to be ----, was discovered by deep-sea fishermen.

- (A) perplexed. .common
- (B) overjoyed. .dangerous
- (C) unconcerned. .local
- (D) astounded. .extinct
- (E) dismayed. .alive

2. Pam's answer is D.
Let's start with the second blank. The doctors for this blank are *living specimen* and *long thought*. If they found a *living* specimen, and the whole scientific community is talking about it, then the creature must have been long thought *dead*. So we can put *dead* in the second blank, and the only second blank word that matches *dead* is *extinct*, in answer choice D. The first blank word, *astounded*, makes sense because you would certainly be surprised if something you thought was dead turned out to be alive.

SECTION 2

QUESTIONS	EXPLANATIONS

3 After the governor's third trip overseas, voters complained that he was paying too little attention to ---- affairs.

   (A) intellectual
   (B) foreign
   (C) professional
   (D) aesthetic
   (E) domestic

3. Pam's answer is E.
The doctors here are *third trip overseas* and *voters complained*. Why would the voters complain about the governor taking a lot of trips abroad? If he's always away in a foreign country, then he probably isn't paying a lot of attention to the affairs of his own country. So we can put *his own country* in the blank. Looking to the answer choices, *domestic* is the best match; it means the opposite of *foreign*.

4 The Roman Emperor Claudius was viewed with ---- by generations of historians until newly discovered evidence showed him to be a ---- administrator.

   (A) suspicion. .clever
   (B) reluctance. .inept
   (C) antagonism. .eager
   (D) indignation. .incompetent
   (E) disdain. .capable

4. Pam's answer is E.
For this question we need to figure out the relationship between the blanks. Claudius was viewed one way by generations of historians, *until newly discovered evidence* changed everyone's mind. So the words in the blanks must be opposites. We can get rid of answer choices B and D, because the words aren't opposites. In choices A, C, and E, the first word is negative and the second is positive, so they are all possibilities. To narrow it down, let's look at the second blank, which describes Claudius' ability as an administrator. Would it make sense to call him an *eager* administrator? Not really, so get rid of C. Between A and E, the best answer is E because it makes more sense to say that they used to think of Claudius with *disdain*, and now they think of him as *capable*. In answer choice A, *suspicion* and *clever* aren't really opposites.

SECTION 2

5 Communities in primitive areas where natural ---- is scarce must be resourceful in order to secure adequate nutrition.

    (A) education
    (B) competition
    (C) sustenance
    (D) agriculture
    (E) assistance

5. Pam's answer is C.
The doctors in this sentence are *scarce* and *nutrition*. In these primitive areas, something is scarce, so they have to be resourceful in order to find nutrition. What is scarce? It must be nutrition, that's why they have to be resourceful in order to find it. So we can recycle the doctor and put *nutrition* in the blank. Looking at the answer choices, *sustenance* is the best match for *nutrition*. Answer choice D, *agriculture*, is close, but *agriculture* doesn't mean *nutrition*.

6 Anthony's ---- expression masked an essentially cheerful nature.

    (A) jubilant
    (B) inevitable
    (C) dour
    (D) pert
    (E) serene

6. Pam's answer is C.
The doctors in this sentence are *masked* and *cheerful nature*. If Anthony's cheerful nature is masked, then he must not be very cheerful at the moment. We can recycle the doctor and put *not cheerful* in the blank. The best match for *not cheerful* in the answer choices is *dour*. If you didn't know what all the words meant, you should at least have been able to eliminate any words you did know that didn't match our word for the blank.

7 Morgan's interest was focused on ---- the division between theory and empiricism; she was convinced that a ---- of philosophy and applied science was possible and necessary.

    (A) eliminating. .synthesis
    (B) maintaining. .restoration
    (C) crossing. .stabilization
    (D) ignoring. .duplicity
    (E) denying. .delineation

7. Pam's answer is A.
Let's start with the first blank. The first doctor in the sentence is *division between*. Morgan wants to do something with the division between *theory* and *empiricism*. In the second part of the sentence we learn that she thinks doing something with philosophy and applied science is *possible and necessary*. If doing something with both things together is possible and necessary, then she must be *against* the division, so the word in the first blank is negative. That means we can get rid of answer choice B. Since Morgan is against the *division*, she must be convinced that a *combination* is possible and necessary, so we can put *combination* in the second blank. Looking at the answer choices, the best match for *combination* in the second blank is *synthesis* in answer choice A.

SECTION 2

8 The professor highlighted the importance of
---- the experiences of many different ethnic
groups when he warned against ---- policies
that fail to consider the wide variety of
cultural standards.

(A) portraying. .discriminatory
(B) considering. .myopic
(C) remembering. .alluring
(D) delineating. .captivating
(E) disparaging. .pedantic

8. Pam's answer is B.
Let's start with the second blank. The
professor is warning against policies that
fail to consider the *wide variety* of cultural
standpoints, so the policies must be *narrow*.
That means we can put *narrow* in our
second blank. We can cross out answer
choices C, D, and E, because none of the
second words in those blanks means
narrow. *Discriminatory* in choice A fits the
topic of the sentence, but *discriminatory*
doesn't mean *narrow*. Also, this is a difficult
question; *myopic*, in B, is definitely a
difficult word. In the first blank, it makes
sense to say that the professor wants to
consider the experiences of different groups,
because he's against policies that *fail to
consider* them. So B is the best answer.

9 Although at times Nikolai could be
disagreeable and even ----, more often than
not he was the most ---- person you could
hope to meet.

(A) contentious. .complaisant
(B) disgruntled. .befuddled
(C) contradictory. .disconcerted
(D) misguided. .solicitous
(E) curmudgeonly. .didactic

9. Pam's answer is A.
Let's start with the second blank. The
doctor in this sentence is *disagreeable*, and
the trigger word for the second blank is
although, which means that the word in the
second blank is the opposite of *disagreeable*.
Therefore we can put *agreeable* in the
second blank. Looking at the answer
choices, the only word that matches
agreeable is *complaisant*.

SECTION 2

QUESTIONS	EXPLANATIONS

SHEPHERD : SHEEP ::

(A) sociologist : statistics
(B) driver : conveyances
(C) gardener : plants
(D) critic : reviews
(E) artist : murals

10. Pam's answer is C.
A SHEPHERD tends SHEEP, and a *gardener* tends *plants*.

11 VANDAL : DAMAGE ::

(A) victim : crime
(B) pest : annoyance
(C) temper : shouting
(D) addiction : weakness
(E) arbitrator : dispute

11. Pam's answer is B.
A VANDAL causes DAMAGE, and a *pest* causes *annoyance*.

12 SNARE : ANIMAL ::

(A) nest : bird
(B) pouch : kangaroo
(C) net : fish
(D) kennel : dog
(E) forest : raccoon

12. Pam's answer is C.
A SNARE is used to trap an ANIMAL, and a *net* is used to trap a *fish*.

SECTION 2

13 CACOPHONOUS : EAR ::

   (A) outrageous : order
   (B) objectionable : commotion
   (C) erroneous : mind
   (D) noisome : mouth
   (E) rank : nose

13. Pam's answer is E.
CACOPHONOUS means unpleasant to the EAR. *Rank* means unpleasant to the *nose*. If you weren't able to make a sentence, you should have eliminated any answer choices that did not have a clear and necessary relationship. For example, *erroneous* means mistaken, and that has nothing to do with *mind*. As it turns out, the only answer choice that has a clear and necessary relationship is E.

14 BELLIGERENCE : AGGRESSOR ::

   (A) insensitivity : boor
   (B) confidence : prelate
   (C) irascibility : pacifist
   (D) truculence : ingrate
   (E) affectation : shrew

14. Pam's answer is A.
We can make a better sentence if we reverse the order of the words. An AGGRESSOR shows BELLIGERENCE. A *boor* shows *insensitivity*. If you weren't able to make a sentence, you should have eliminated any answer choices that did not have a clear and necessary relationship. As it turns out, the only answer choice that has a clear and necessary relationship is A.

15 INCORRIGIBLE : REFORM ::

   (A) immutable : speak
   (B) intractable : manage
   (C) impartial : decide
   (D) intolerable : criticize
   (E) intangible : understand

15. Pam's answer is B.
INCORRIGIBLE means difficult to REFORM and *intractable* means difficult to *manage*. If you weren't able to make a sentence, you should have eliminated any answer choices that did not have a clear and necessary relationship. For example, *impartial* means not taking sides, and that has nothing to do with *decide*. As it turns out, the only answer choice that has a clear and necessary relationship is B.

SECTION 2

Each passage below is followed by questions based on its content. Answer the questions on the basis of what is <u>stated</u> or <u>implied</u> in the passage and in any introductory material that may be provided.

Questions 16–22 are based on the following passage.

A parable is a symbolic story that, like a fable, teaches a moral lesson. The parable below was written by the Czech author Franz Kafka, and was published in 1935.

Poseidon sat at his desk, doing figures. The administration of all the waters gave him endless work. He could have had assistants, as many as he
Line wanted—and he did have very many—but since he
(5) took his job very seriously, he would in the end go over all the figures and calculations himself, and thus his assistants were of little help to him. It cannot be said that he enjoyed his work; he did it only because it had been assigned to him; in fact, he
(10) had already filed petitions for—as he put it—more cheerful work, but every time the offer of something different was made to him it would turn out that nothing suited him quite as well as his present position. And anyhow, it was quite difficult to find
(15) something different for him. After all, it was impossible to assign him to a particular sea; aside from the fact that even then the work with figures would not become less but only pettier, the great Poseidon could in any case only occupy an
(20) executive position. And when a job away from the water was offered to him he would get sick at the very prospect, his divine breathing would become troubled and his brazen chest would begin to tremble. Besides, his complaints were not really
(25) taken seriously; when one of the mighty is vexatious the appearance of an effort must be made to placate him, even when the case is most hopeless. In actuality, a shift of posts was unthinkable for Poseidon—he had been appointed God of the Sea in
(30) the beginning, and that he had to remain.
What irritated him most—and it was this that was chiefly responsible for his dissatisfaction with his job—was to hear of the conceptions formed about him: how he was always riding about through the
(35) tides with his trident. When all the while he sat here in the depths of the world-ocean, doing figures uninterruptedly, with now and then a trip to Jupiter as the only break in the monotony—a trip, moreover, from which he usually returned in a
(40) rage. Thus he had hardly seen the sea—had seen it fleetingly in the course of hurried ascents to Olympus, and he had never actually traveled around it. He was in the habit of saying that what he was waiting for was the fall of the world; then,
(45) probably, a quiet moment would yet be granted in which, just before the end and after having checked the last row of figures, he would be able to make a quick little tour.
Poseidon became bored with the sea. He let fall
(50) his trident. Silently he sat on the rocky coast and a gull, dazed by his presence, described wavering circles around his head.

SECTION 2

QUESTIONS	EXPLANATIONS

16 Lines 9–10 suggest that Poseidon regarded his work with

(A) resignation
(B) enthusiasm
(C) indifference
(D) intimidation
(E) destructiveness

16. Pam's answer is A.
In lines 9–10, the passage says, *It cannot be said that he enjoyed his work; he did it only because it had been assigned to him.* Poseidon is clearly not very happy with his job, but he does it anyway. The word that best describes this attitude is *resignation*.

Answer choice B is wrong because the passage says the Poseidon *filed petitions for… more cheerful work*, so he definitely wasn't enthusiastic about his job.

Answer choice C is wrong because Poseidon certainly had an opinion about his job. He didn't like it.

Answer choice D is way off. Poseidon wasn't happy, but there's nothing in the passage to indicate that he was intimidated by his work. After all, he's a god.

Answer choice E can't be right, because the passage never says that Poseidon was destructive.

17 In line 26, the word "vexatious" most nearly means

(A) pleased
(B) cursed
(C) doomed
(D) troubled
(E) indisposed

17. Pam's answer is D.
Vocabulary-in-context questions should be answered like sentence completions. Go back to the passage, find the word *vexatious*, and cross it out. Then read the sentence and come up with your own word. The sentence says that *his complaints were not really taken seriously.* We're talking about Poseidon's *complaints*, so Pam's word must have a similar meaning. The best match for *complaints* is *troubled*.

Answer choice A is wrong, because *pleased* is a positive word and you can figure out from the context that *vexatious* is negative.

Answer choices B and C are wrong because they're *too* negative. Poseidon complained and he was unhappy, but things weren't *that* bad.

Answer choice E has nothing to do with the meaning of *vexatious*. If you don't know what *indisposed* means, look it up.

SECTION 2

QUESTIONS	EXPLANATIONS

18 The word "conceptions" in line 33 most nearly means

(A) origins
(B) opinions
(C) discussions
(D) plans
(E) explanations

18. Pam's answer is B.
Here's another vocabulary-in-context question. Go back to the passage, find the word *conceptions*, and cross it out. Then read the sentence and come up with your own word. The sentence in the passage tells us that Poseidon was *irritated* when he found out that people thought he *was always riding about through the tides with his trident*. If he's upset about what people think about him, that means he's upset about their *opinions* of him.

Answer choice A is a Joe Bloggs answer. Joe doesn't look at the word in context. He just chooses an answer that reminds him of the word. In this case, *conceptions* makes Joe think of conceiving an idea (or, perhaps, a child). That makes him think of *origins*.

Answer choices C, D, and E don't make sense in context. It wouldn't make sense to say that Poseidon didn't like to hear about the *discussions* formed about him, or the *plans* formed about him, or the *explanations* formed about him.

19 It can be inferred from the author's description of Poseidon's routine (lines 40-43) that

(A) Poseidon prefers performing his duties to visiting Jupiter
(B) Poseidon is too busy to familiarize himself with his kingdom
(C) Poseidon requires silence for the performance of his duties
(D) if the world falls, Poseidon will no longer be able to travel
(E) Poseidon's dissatisfaction with his job detracts from his efficiency

19. Pam's answer is B.
In lines 40–43, the passage says, *Thus he had hardly seen the sea—had seen it only fleetingly . . . and he had never actually traveled around it.* If you read further, you also learn that Poseidon was waiting for the fall of the world so he would have a *quiet moment* to *make a quick little tour* of the sea. From that we can infer that Poseidon is too busy to see his own kingdom, so Pam's answer must be B.

Answer choice A gets it backward. The passage says that Poseidon's trips to visit Jupiter are the *only break in the monotony* of his jobs, so if anything, he *prefers* the trips to his duties, not the other way around.

Answer choice C is wrong because the passage doesn't say anything about Poseidon needing silence.

Answer choice D contradicts the passage. Poseidon is waiting for the fall of the world so that he can finally get out and *make a quick little tour* of his domain, which he has never had a chance to see.

Answer choice E is wrong because the passage doesn't say anything to suggest that Poseidon is inefficient.

SECTION 2

QUESTIONS	EXPLANATIONS

20 According to the passage, Poseidon's dissatisfaction with his job primarily stems from

(A) the constant travel that is required of him

(B) the lack of seriousness with which his complaints are received

(C) the constantly changing nature of his duties

(D) others' mistaken notions of his routine

(E) his assistant's inability to perform simple bookkeeping tasks

20. Pam's answer is D.

The lead word for this question is *dissatisfaction*, so you should go back to the passage and find where it mentions Poseidon's dissatisfaction. Lines 31–35 describe what is *chiefly responsible for his dissatisfaction*. He does not like *to hear of the conceptions formed about him: how he was always riding about through the tides with his trident*. According to the passage, Poseidon doesn't actually get out much at all, so people have the wrong idea about what he actually does. This is exactly what answer choice D says.

Answer choice A contradicts the passage. Poseidon was so irritated by the false idea people had that he was always riding around with his trident.

Answer choice B is a trap. The question asks what is *primarily* responsible for Poseidon's dissatisfaction. Although something similar to choice B is mentioned earlier in the passage, it's not *chiefly responsible for his dissatisfaction* (line 32). Use the lead words to make sure you are reading in the right place.

Answer choice C contradicts the passage. Poseidon does the exact same thing every day. That's why he's so bored and unhappy.

Answer choice E is incorrect because the passage says that Poseidon actually did most of the bookkeeping tasks himself, leaving little for his assistants to do (lines 5–7).

SECTION 2

21 The author of the passage portrays the god Poseidon as

(A) a dissatisfied bureaucrat
(B) a powerful deity
(C) a disgruntled vagabond
(D) a capable accountant
(E) a ruthless tyrant

21. Pam's answer is A.

This is a general question, so you only need to know the main idea of the passage. The passage portrays Poseidon as someone who sits around working out *figures* all day and doesn't go out much. Poseidon is also clearly unhappy (as we learned in questions 19 and 20), so he is best described as a *dissatisfied bureaucrat*.

The other answer choices are wrong because they don't fit the main idea of the passage. Poseidon may be a *deity*, but the passage doesn't characterize him as being *powerful*. Poseidon is definitely not a *vagabond*, and he's definitely not a *tyrant*. Answer choice D is half-wrong, which means that it's all wrong. Although the description of Poseidon's duties make him sound like an *accountant*, the passage focuses on his unhappiness, not his *capabilities* as an accountant.

22 Poseidon is unable to change occupations for all of the following reasons EXCEPT

(A) his appointment as God of the Sea is inherently unchangeable
(B) he has fallen into disfavor with the gods on Mount Olympus
(C) he cannot imagine a life away from the water
(D) nothing else suits him as well as his present position
(E) his job must be appropriate to his elevated status

22. Pam's answer is B.

This is an EXCEPT question, so you should definitely save it for last. We need to know why Poseidon is unable to change his job, so we need to go back to the passage and find where that is discussed. Remember, we're looking for the reason that is *not* mentioned, so we can eliminate answer choices that are mentioned.

The passage mentions answer choice A in lines 29–30: *he had been appointed God of the Sea in the beginning, and that he had to remain.* Answer choice C is in lines 20–22: *when a job away from the water was offered to him he would get sick at the very prospect.* Answer choice D is in lines 13–14 (*nothing suited him quite as well as his present position*), and answer choice E is in lines 19–20 (*Poseidon could in any case only occupy an executive position*). Therefore B must be the answer.

SECTION 2

Each passage below is followed by questions based on its content. Answer the questions on the basis of what is <u>stated</u> or <u>implied</u> in the passage and in any introductory material that may be provided.

Questions 23–30 are based on the following passage.

The following passage was excerpted from a book called *The Extraordinary Origins of Everyday Things*, which was published in 1987.

Because early man viewed illness as divine punishment and healing as purification, medicine and religion were inextricably linked for centuries.
Line This notion is apparent in the origin of our word
(5) "pharmacy," which comes from the Greek *pharmakon*, meaning "purification through purging."

By 3500 B.C., the Sumerians in the Tigris-Euphrates valley had developed virtually all of our
(10) modern methods of administering drugs. They used gargles, inhalations, pills, lotions, ointments, and plasters. The first drug catalog, or pharmacopoeia, was written at that time by an unknown Sumerian physician. Preserved in
(15) cuneiform script on a single clay tablet are the names of dozens of drugs to treat ailments that still afflict us today.

The Egyptians added to the ancient medicine chest. The Ebers Papyrus, a scroll dating from
(20) 1900 B.C. and named after the German Egyptologist George Ebers, reveals the trial-and-error know-how acquired by early Egyptian physicians. To relieve indigestion, a chew of peppermint leaves and carbonates (known today as antacids) was
(25) prescribed, and to numb the pain of tooth extraction, Egyptian doctors temporarily stupefied a patient with ethyl alcohol.

The scroll also provides a rare glimpse into the hierarchy of ancient drug preparation. The "chief of
(30) the preparers of drugs" was the equivalent of a head pharmacist, who supervised the "collectors of drugs," field workers, who gathered essential minerals and herbs. The "preparers' aides" (technicians) dried and pulverized ingredients, which were blended
(35) according to certain formulas by the "preparers." And the "conservator of drugs" oversaw the storehouse where local and imported mineral, herb, and animal-organ ingredients were kept.

By the seventh century B.C., the Greeks had
(40) adopted a sophisticated mind-body view of medicine. They believed that a physician must pursue the diagnosis and treatment of the physical (body) causes of disease within a scientific framework, as well as cure the supernatural (mind)
(45) components involved. Thus, the early Greek physician emphasized something of a holistic approach to health, even if the suspected "mental" causes of disease were not recognized as stress and depression but interpreted as curses from
(50) displeased deities.

The modern era of pharmacology began in the sixteenth century, ushered in by the first major discoveries in chemistry. The understanding of how chemicals interact to produce certain effects
(55) within the body would eventually remove much of the guesswork and magic from medicine.

Drugs had been launched on a scientific course, but centuries would pass before superstition was displaced by scientific fact. One major reason was
(60) that physicians, unaware of the existence of disease-causing pathogens such as bacteria and viruses, continued to dream up imaginary causative evils. And though new chemical compounds emerged, their effectiveness in treating disease was still based
(65) largely on trial and error.

Many standard, common drugs in the medicine chest developed in this trial-and-error environment. Such is the complexity of disease and human biochemistry that even today, despite enormous
(70) strides in medical science, many of the latest sophisticated additions to our medicine chest shelves were accidental finds.

SECTION 2

23 The author cites the literal definition of the Greek word *pharmakon* in line 6 in order to

(A) show that ancient civilizations had an advanced form of medical science

(B) point out that many of the beliefs of ancient civilizations are still held today

(C) illustrate that early man thought recovery from illness was linked to internal cleansing

(D) stress the mental and physical causes of disease

(E) emphasize the primitive nature of Greek medical science

23. Pam's answer is C.

According to the first paragraph, *early man viewed... healing as purification*, and this *notion is apparent in the origin of our word for 'pharmacy.'* The passage then gives the meaning of the Greek word *pharmakon*, which is *purification through purging*. Therefore, the literal definition is cited in order to give an example of how early man thought of healing as *purging*, or *internal cleansing*, as it is paraphrased in answer choice C. Remember, the answer to most specific questions will be an exact *paraphrase* of what the passage says.

Answer choice A doesn't make any sense. Did *ancient* civilization have an *advanced* form of medical science? No way. Don't forget to use your common sense.

Answer choice B doesn't answer the question, and it is irrelevant. We're talking about ancient medicine, not ancient beliefs in general.

Answer choice D is wrong because the passage doesn't say anything in the first paragraph about the mental and physical causes of diseases. This is mentioned much later in the passage. Make sure you're reading in the right place

Answer choice E is too extreme, and it actually contradicts the passage. In lines 40–42, the passage says that *the Greeks had adopted a sophisticated mind-body view of medicine*, so they were certainly not *primitive*.

SECTION 2

24. It was possible to identify a number of early Sumerian drugs because

(A) traces of these drugs were discovered during archaeological excavations

(B) the ancient Egyptians later adopted the same medications

(C) Sumerian religious texts explained many drug-making techniques

(D) a pharmacopoeia in Europe contained detailed recipes for ancient drugs

(E) a list of drugs and preparations was compiled by an ancient Sumerian

24. Pam's answer is E.

The lead words in this question are *early Sumerian drugs*, which should lead you back to the second paragraph. According to lines 12–17, the *first drug catalog, or pharmacopoeia, was written... by an unknown Sumerian physician. Preserved in cuneiform script on a single clay tablet are the names of dozens of drugs to treat ailments that still afflict us today.* So it was possible to identify a number of early Sumerian drugs because somebody back then wrote them all down, which is exactly what answer choice E says.

Answer choice A is wrong because the passage doesn't say anything at all about traces of the drugs being found in archeological excavations. If it's not in the passage, then it's not Pam's answer.

Answer choice B is wrong because the passage says in line 18 that the Egyptians *added* to the ancient knowledge of medicine. The passage doesn't say that they used the *same* medications as the Sumerians.

Answer choice C is wrong because the passage doesn't say anything at all about *Sumerian religious texts.* Go back to the passage and read.

Answer choice D is way off the topic. The passage is about ancient civilizations, *not* about Europe. Modern Europe didn't even exist back then. Read the answer choices carefully.

SECTION 2

25 The passage suggests that which of the following is a similarity between ancient Sumerian drugs and modern drugs?

(A) Ancient Sumerian drugs were made of the same chemicals as modern drugs.

(B) Like modern drugs, ancient Sumerian drugs were used for both mental and physical disorders.

(C) The delivery of ancient Sumerian drugs is similar to that of modern drugs.

(D) Both ancient Sumerian drugs and modern drugs are products of sophisticated laboratory research.

(E) Hierarchically organized groups of laborers are responsible for the preparation of both ancient Sumerian and modern drugs.

25. Pam's answer is C.
This question asks about Sumerian drugs again, so you need to go back to the second paragraph. This time the question is looking for a similarity between Sumerian drugs and modern drugs. According to lines 8–10, *the Sumerians in the Tigris-Euphrates river had developed all of our modern methods of administering drugs.* So the similarity between Sumerian and modern drugs is in the *methods of administering drugs*, which is paraphrased in answer choice C as the *delivery* of drugs. Remember, the answer to most specific questions will be an exact *paraphrase* of what the passage says.

Answer choice A is wrong because the passage says that the Sumerians had the same methods of *administering* drugs, not that they used the same chemicals. Besides, it doesn't make any sense to say that an ancient civilization had the same chemicals that we do now. They didn't have penicillin, or anything like that, did they? Don't forget about common sense.

Answer choice B is wrong because the passage doesn't talk about mental and physical disorders until much later in the passage. Use the lead words to make sure you are reading in the right place.

Answer choice D doesn't make any sense at all. Were ancient Sumerian drugs the products of *sophisticated laboratory research*? No way! Use common sense.

Answer choice E is wrong because a hierarchy of drug producers was part of *Egyptian* society, not *Sumerian* society.

SECTION 2

26 The "hierarchy" referred to in line 29 is an example of

(A) a superstitious practice
(B) the relative severity of ancient diseases
(C) the role of physicians in Egyptian society
(D) a complex division of labor
(E) a recipe for ancient drugs

26. Pam's answer is D.

For this question, you should read before and after the word *hierarchy* to give yourself some context. In the fourth paragraph, the passage talks about the *hierarchy of ancient drug preparation*. In lines 29–36, the passage describes the different people involved in the process of making drugs, including the *chief of the preparers of drugs*, the *collectors of drugs*, the *preparers*, the *preparers' aides*, and the *conservator of drugs*. With all these different jobs, the *hierarchy* must be an example of a *division of labor*.

Answer choice A is wrong because the fourth paragraph doesn't say anything about superstitious practices.

Answer choice B is wrong because the passage doesn't say anything about the severity of ancient diseases.

Answer choice C is close, but the fourth paragraph is about the people who *made drugs* in ancient Egypt, not the doctors who administered the drugs.

Answer choice E is also wrong because the fourth paragraph is about the people who made the drugs, not the recipes for the drugs themselves. Read carefully.

SECTION 2

27 According to the passage, the seventh-century Greeks' view of medicine differed from that of the Sumerians in that the Greeks

(A) discovered more advanced chemical applications of drugs

(B) acknowledged both the mental and physical roots of illness

(C) attributed disease to psychological, rather than physical, causes

(D) established a rigid hierarchy for the preparation of drugs

(E) developed most of the precursors of modern drugs

27. Pam's answer is B.

The lead words in this question are *the seventh-century Greeks*, which should lead you to the fifth paragraph. The question asks how the view of medicine *differed* between the Greeks and the Sumerians. According to lines 40–42, *By the seventh century B.C., the Greeks had adopted a sophisticated mind-body view of medicine.* If this view was newly adopted by the Greeks, it must of have been different from what the Sumerians thought. So the difference is that the Greeks had a *mind-body* view. *Mind-body* is paraphrased in answer choice B as *the mental and physical roots of illness.*

Answer choice A is wrong because the passage doesn't say anything about *advanced chemical applications.* Read carefully.

Answer choice C contradicts the passage. The Greeks believed that it was necessary to treat the mind *and* the body. That is the point of the fifth paragraph. Go back and read it again.

Answer choice E is wrong because the word *most* makes it a *must* answer. The Greeks didn't develop *most* of the precursors of modern drugs. What about the Egyptians and the Sumerians?

SECTION 2

28 In line 46, the word "holistic" most nearly means

(A) psychological
(B) modern
(C) physiological
(D) integrated
(E) religious

28. Pam's answer is D.
Go back to the passage, find the word *holistic*, and cross it out. Then read the sentence and come up with your own word. The paragraph is talking about how the Greeks had a *mind-body* view of medicine, meaning they believed it was important to treat the mind as well as the body. Since they believed in treating the whole person, that means they *emphasized* an *approach to health* that included everything. So we use *included everything* in place of the *holistic*. The best match in the answer choices is *integrated*.

Answer choices A and C are wrong because *holistic* doesn't just describe the psychological perspective or just the physiological perspective, but both together.

Answer choice B gets the time frame wrong. The Greeks were *ancient*, not *modern*.

Answer choice E misinterprets the passage. The Greeks had a holistic perspective *despite* their belief in deities.

29 The passage indicates that advances in medical science during the modern era of pharmacology may have been delayed by

(A) a lack of understanding of the origins of disease
(B) primitive surgical methods
(C) a shortage of chemical treatments for disease
(D) an inaccuracy in pharmaceutical preparation
(E) an over-emphasis on the psychological causes of disease

29. Pam's answer is A.
The lead words in this sentence are *modern era of pharmacology*, which should lead you to the sixth paragraph. This paragraph talks about how the modern era of pharmacology began, but the question asks what delayed *advances in medical science* during the modern era.

So you need to keep reading into the next paragraph to find the answer: *physicians, unaware of the existence of disease-causing pathogens such as bacteria and viruses, continued to dream up imaginary causative evils.* So the problem was that doctors didn't really know what caused diseases, and that is exactly what answer choice A says.

The other answer choices are wrong because none of them is mentioned anywhere in the passage. Go back and read the second to last paragraph carefully.

SECTION 2

30 In the final paragraph, the author makes which of the following observations about scientific discovery?

(A) Human biochemistry is such a complex science that important discoveries are uncommon.

(B) Chance events have led to the discovery of many modern drugs.

(C) Many cures for common diseases have yet to be discovered.

(D) Trial and error is the best avenue to scientific discovery.

(E) Most of the important discoveries made in the scientific community have been inadvertent.

30. Pam's answer is B.

To answer this question, you just need to read the final paragraph and find out what the passage says about *scientific discovery*. According to the last paragraph, *many of the latest sophisticated additions to our medicine chest shelves were accidental finds*. In other words, many modern drugs were discovered by accident. Answer choice B paraphrases the idea of *accidental finds* as *chance events*.

Answer choice A doesn't make any sense. Are discoveries in biochemistry *uncommon*? Most biochemists would probably disagree. Don't forget to use common sense.

Answer choice C may actually be true, but the passage doesn't mention it, so it can't be Pam's answer. Remember, Pam's answers come right out of the passage. You don't need any outside knowledge.

Answer choice D is wrong because the word *best* makes this a *must* answer. How do we know that trial and error is the *best* way to make scientific discoveries? The passage never says that it's the best way.

Answer choice E is wrong because it is also a *must* answer. Is it really true that *most* of the important scientific discoveries have been accidents? Besides, we're only talking about *drugs* here!

SECTION 3

SUMMARY DIRECTIONS FOR QUANTITATIVE COMPARISON QUESTIONS

<u>Answer:</u> A if the quantity in Column A is greater;
B if the quantity in Column B is greater;
C if the two quantities are equal;
D if the relationship cannot be determined from the information given.

AN E RESPONSE WILL NOT BE SCORED.

Column A	Column B

$x = 3$

1

$\dfrac{x}{10}$ $\dfrac{x}{100}$

1. Jim's answer is A.

   You can solve this question easily on your calculator. Just convert both of the fractions to decimals by dividing the top of the fraction by the bottom: $\dfrac{3}{10}$ = .3 and $\dfrac{3}{100}$ = .03. Since .3 is greater than .03, Column A is greater.

2

The average (arithmetic mean) of 1, 199, and 700	The average (arithmetic mean) of 10, 90, and 800

2. Jim's answer is C.
   In Column A, the sum of the number is 900. There are three numbers, so you need to divide 900 by 3, which gives you an average of 300. For Column B, the sum of the numbers is also 900, and there are also three numbers, so the average must be the same.

$-3 < z < 0$

3

$3 - z$ $z - 3$

3. Jim's answer is A.
   Always be sure to plug in twice for quant comp questions. You need to plug in numbers for z that are between -3 and 0. If $z = -2$, then Column A is 5 and Column B is -5. Since Column A is bigger, you can cross out choices B and C. Now plug in a weird number. If $z = -1.5$, then Column A is 4.5 and Column B is negative -4.5. Since Column A is still greater and this is an easy question, you can be sure that A is the answer.

$110° / a°$

$111°$
$b°$

4

a b

4. Jim's answer is A.
   This question tests the rule of 180 (not Fred's Theorem). There are 180 degrees in a straight line. So $a + 110 = 180$, which means $a = 70$, and $b + 111 = 180$, so $b = 69$. Since 70 is greater than 69, Column A is greater than Column B.

SECTION 3

QUESTIONS	EXPLANATIONS

Column A **Column B**

$$3 > p > 1$$

5

$$\frac{p}{2}$$ $$\frac{p+2}{4}$$

5. Jim's answer is D.
Always be sure to plug in twice for quant comp questions. You need to plug in numbers for p that are between 3 and 1. If $p = 2$, then Column A is 1 and Column B is 1. Since the columns can be equal, you can cross out choice A and B. Now plug in a weird number. If $p = 1.5$ (use your calculator) then Column A is .75 and Column B is .875. The columns are no longer equal, so you can get more than one result. That means the answer must be D.

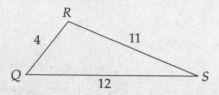

6 | Area of Triangle QRS | Perimeter of Triangle QRS |

6. Jim's answer is B.
First, draw a line segment from point R perpendicular to QS. This is the altitude of triangle QRS, and it must be less than 4. The formula for the area of a triangle is $\frac{1}{2} \times$ base $\times$ height. The base is 12, and if the height were 4, the area would be 24. Since the height is actually less than 4, the area must be less than 24. You don't have to find the actual value of area, though. Whatever the area is, the perimeter (the sum of all the sides) is 27. Column B is bigger regardless of the exact value of Column A.

ABCD is a square

7
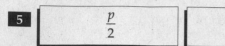
$$\frac{\text{the length of } AC}{\text{the length of } AD}$$ $$2$$

7. Jim's answer is B.
Since we don't know what the side of the square is, we can plug in a value. Let's say the side is 3. The diagonal of the square divides it into two 45:45:90 triangles. If you look in the gray box at the beginning of the section, it tells you that the sides of a 45:45:90 triangle are in a ratio of $1:1:\sqrt{2}$. If the side of the square is 3, the diagonal must be $3\sqrt{2}$.

Therefore $\dfrac{AC}{AD} = \dfrac{3\sqrt{2}}{3}$, or $\sqrt{2}$. Since $\sqrt{2}$ is less than 2, Column B is bigger.

SECTION 3

QUESTIONS	EXPLANATIONS

QUESTIONS

Column A   **Column B**

Line segments FG and JK intersect at point X such that $FX = \dfrac{1}{2}GX$

8

JX	$\dfrac{1}{2}KX$

1,000 milliliters = 1 liter

9

The number of 1.9 milliliter portions that can be poured from a bottle containing 0.8 liters of fluid	400

A is the average (arithmetic mean) of 2 consecutive positive even integers.

10

The remainder when A is divided by 2	1

EXPLANATIONS

8. Jim's answer is D.
   The question tells you how JK divides up FG, since it says $FX = \dfrac{1}{2}GX$. But you have no idea how JK itself gets divided up when the two lines cross. JX might equal $\dfrac{1}{2}KX$, or maybe not. So the answer must be D. Since question 8 is pretty close to the difficult third of quant comp, C would be the Joe Bloggs answer.

9. Jim's answer is A.
   You need to attack this question one step at a time, with the help of your calculator. First you need to figure out how many milliliters are in .8 liters. To do this, you can set up a proportion:

$$\frac{1}{1,000} = \frac{.8}{x}$$

   Solve for x, and you get 800. If there are 800 milliliters of fluid, and you want to divide it into 1.9 milliliter portions, you simply divide 800 by 1.9, which gives you 421.05. So Column A is greater than Column B.

10. Jim's answer is C.
    Since you don't know what the two consecutive positive even integers are, you can plug in values for them. Let's use 2 and 4. A is the average of 2 and 4, so $A = 3$. In Column A, when 3 is divided by 2 the remainder is 1, so the columns are equal. If you plug in different numbers, the results are the same.

SECTION 3

Questions 11-12 refer to the following definition:
For all numbers n, let $\{n\}$ be defined as $n^3 + 2n^2 - n$

Column A	Column B

11 $\{-2\}$ $\{-1\}$

11. Jim's answer is C.
Make sure you start by crossing out B, which is the Joe Bloggs answer because –1 is greater than –2. This function question is just a substitution exercise. We know that $\{n\} = n^3 + 2n^2 - n$, so $\{-2\} = 2$ and $\{-1\} = 2$. Since $\{-2\} = 2$ and $\{-1\} = 2$, the answer must be C.

12 $\{x\}$ $\{x + 1\}$

12. Jim's answer is D.
Joe Bloggs picks B, because $\{x + 1\}$ looks bigger, so you should cross out B immediately. Since this question has variables, you can plug in, but you must be sure to plug in at least twice. Start with an easy number. If $x = 2$, then $\{2\} = 14$ and $\{3\} = 42$. Since Column B is bigger, you can cross out choices A and C. Since you already crossed out B, the answer must be D. But you can prove it by plugging in a weird number. If $x = -2$, then $\{-2\} = 2$ and $\{-1\} = 2$. Now the columns are equal.

13 | The ratio of nickels to dimes in Jar A, where there are 4 more nickels than dimes | The ratio of nickels to dimes in Jar B, where there are 4 more dimes than nickels |

13. Jim's answer is A.
You don't know how many dimes or nickels there are, so you can plug in some numbers. In Jar A, there are 4 more nickels than dimes, so we can say there are 7 nickels and 3 dimes. In that case, the ratio of nickels to dimes in A would be 7 to 3, or $\frac{7}{3}$. In Jar B, there are 4 more dimes than nickels, so we can say that there are 3 nickels and 7 dimes, so the ratio of nickels to dimes would be 3 to 7, or $\frac{3}{7}$. Column A is bigger because $\frac{7}{3}$ is bigger than $\frac{3}{7}$. You can't plug in negative numbers, fractions, or zero, because you're talking about quantities of nickels and dimes, and you can't have half a nickel. If you plug in again, you will get the same result.

SECTION 3

Column A   **Column B**

14 | The area of a parallelogram with base 8 and perimeter 36 | The area of a parallelogram with base 16 and perimeter 36 |

14. Jim's answer is D.
The formula for the area of a parallelogram is base × height. Even though the parallelogram in Column B has a bigger base, you have no idea what the height of either parallelogram is, so you can't say for sure what the area of either one is. Of course, the parallelogram in B could be bigger. But if the parallelogram in Column A had a height of 6, and the parallelogram in B had a tiny height, such as 1, then the one in B would be smaller than the one in A. Since either parallelogram can be bigger, depending on what you make the height, then the answer must be D. Joe Bloggs thinks B is bigger because it has a bigger base. But this is a hard question. Just Say No to Joe.

$$a + b = c$$
$$a - c = 5$$
$$b - c = 3$$

15 | c | 0 |

15. Jim's answer is B.
Joe Bloggs thinks this question is impossible. He picks D because he thinks D means "I don't know." But you know better than Joe. You can use the first two equations as simultaneous equations. In the second equation, add c to both sides so the c's are in the same place. Then line up the equations like this:
$$a + b = c$$
$$a = c + 5$$
When you subtract the equations, you end up with $b = -5$. You need to know the value of c for Column A. Since you know the value of b, just pop it into the third equation: $-5 - c = 3$. So $c = -8$. Column B is greater.

16 If $3x = 12$, then $8 \div x =$

16. Jim's answer is 2.
First, solve for x. Divide both sides of the equation by 3, and you get $x = 4$. Then divide 8 by 4, which gives you 2.

SECTION 3

QUESTIONS	EXPLANATIONS

17 In the figure above, $a + b + c =$

17. Jim's answer is 270.
The trick here is that Jim is not asking for the value of a, b, or c. He just wants to know what they add up to. Jim is only testing the Rule of 360. All the angles in the figure make up a circle, so they all add up to 360. The right angle is 90 degrees, so $90 + a + b + c = 360$. Therefore $a + b + c = 270$.

18 Twenty bottles contain a total of 8 liters of apple juice. If each bottle contains the same amount of apple juice, how much juice (in liters) is in each bottle?

18. Jim's answer is .4 or $\frac{2}{5}$.
You can solve this question by setting up a proportion. There are 8 liters in 20 bottles of juice and you need to find out how many liters are in one bottle. Here's what the proportion looks like:

$$\frac{8}{20} = \frac{x}{1}$$

Solve for x, and your answer is $\frac{2}{5}$ or .4.

19 If $4x + 2y = 24$, and $\frac{7y}{2x} = 7$, then $x =$

19. Jim's answer is 3.
You can solve this question using simultaneous equations, because you have two equations with two variables. First, you need to rearrange the equations a bit:

$4x + 2y = 24$, divided by 2 on both sides

becomes $2x + y = 12$. $\frac{7y}{2x} = 7$, multiplied by $2x$ on both sides, becomes $7y = 14x$. This, divided by 7 on both sides, becomes $y = 2x$, which can be manipulated into $2x - y = 0$.

Now you can add the equations:

$$\begin{aligned} 2x + y &= 12 \\ \underline{2x - y} &= \underline{0} \\ 4x &= 12 \\ x &= 3 \end{aligned}$$

SECTION 3

20 What is the sum of the positive even factors of 12?

20. Jim's answer is 24.
For this question you need your math vocabulary.
First, list all the factors of 12: 1, 2, 3, 4, 6, 12.
Make sure that you don't miss any factors.
Now add up the even factors: $2 + 4 + 6 + 12 = 24$.

21 Y is a point on segment XZ such that $XY = \frac{1}{2}XZ$.
If the length of YZ is $4a + 6$, and the length of XZ is 68, then $a =$

21. Jim's answer is 7.
It would definitely help to draw out this question:

If $XY = \frac{1}{2}XZ$, that means Y is the midpoint of XZ. So $XY = YZ$, and therefore $YZ = \frac{1}{2}XZ$. If $YZ = 4a + 6$ and $XZ = 68$, then $4a + 6 = \frac{1}{2}(68)$.

Now just solve for a:

$$4a + 6 = \frac{1}{2}(68)$$
$$4a + 6 = 34$$
$$4a = 28$$
$$a = 7.$$

SECTION 3

QUESTIONS	EXPLANATIONS

22 One-fifth of the cars in a parking lot are blue and $\frac{1}{2}$ of the blue cars are convertibles. If $\frac{1}{4}$ of the convertibles in the parking lot are blue, then what percent of the cars in the lot are neither blue nor convertibles?

22. Jim's answer is 50.

You don't know how many cars are in the parking lot, so you can plug in a number. Let's say there are 40 cars in the parking lot. Now read through the question; if $\frac{1}{5}$ of the cars are blue, there are eight blue cars. If $\frac{1}{2}$ of the blue cars are convertibles, there are four blue convertibles. If $\frac{1}{4}$ of all the convertibles are blue, and there are 4 blue convertibles, that means there are 16 convertibles all together. The question asks what percent of the cars are neither blue nor convertibles. At this point, the question becomes a group question, and we have a formula for solving such questions: total = group 1 + group 2 − both + neither. In this question, the total is 40 cars, group 1 is the 8 blue cars, and group 2 is the 16 convertibles. You also know that 4 cars are both blue and convertibles. Now just plug those values into the formula: $40 = 16 + 8 - 4 + n$. Then solve for n, which equals 20. So 20 out of the total 40 cars are neither blue nor convertibles: $\frac{20}{40} = \frac{1}{2} = 50\%$.

SECTION 3

QUESTIONS	EXPLANATIONS

23 Three numbers are considered a "prime set" if their sum is a prime number. If 31, −8 and n are a prime set, what is the least possible positive value of n?

23. Jim's answer is 6.

Since 31 and −8 add up to 23, that means $23 + n$ has to be a prime number in order for 31, −8, and n to be a prime set. You're looking for the smallest positive value of n, so start with $n = 1$ and keep trying numbers until you get a prime number as a result:

$n = 1$	$23 + 1 = 24$ (not prime)
$n = 2$	$23 + 2 = 25$ (not prime)
$n = 3$	$23 + 3 = 26$ (not prime)
$n = 4$	$23 + 4 = 27$ (not prime)
$n = 5$	$23 + 5 = 28$ (not prime)
$n = 6$	$23 + 6 = 29$

Since 29 is the first prime number we got as a result, that means 6 is the least possible positive value of n.

24 A ball bounces up $\frac{3}{4}$ of the distance it falls when dropped, and on each bounce thereafter, it bounces $\frac{3}{4}$ of the previous height. If it is dropped from a height of 64 feet, how many feet will it have traveled when it hits the ground the fourth time?

24. Jim's answer is 286.

It would definitely be helpful to draw out this question. If the ball is dropped from a height of 64 feet, it will travel 64 feet before it hits the ground the first time. Then it will bounce up $\frac{3}{4}$ of 64, or 48 feet. It will then travel down 48 feet, hit the ground a second time, and bounce back up $\frac{3}{4}$ of 48, or 36 feet. The ball travels back down 36 feet, hits the ground a third time, and then bounces up $\frac{3}{4}$ of 36, or 27 feet.

Lastly, the ball travels 27 feet to hit the ground a fourth time. Altogether the ball has gone down 64, up 48, down 48, up 36, down 36, up 27, and down 27. So $64 + 48 + 48 + 36 + 36 + 27 + 27 = 286$.

SECTION 3

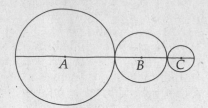

25 In the figure above, the radius of the circle with center A is twice the radius of the circle with center B and four times the radius of the circle with center C. If the sum of the areas of the three circles is 84π, what is the length of AC?

25. Jim's answer is 18.
To answer this question you have to set up an equation. If the radius of C is r, then the radius of B is $2r$ and the radius of A is $4r$. The formula for the area of a circle is πr^2. Since 84π is the sum of the areas of the circles, this is your equation:

$$\pi r^2 + \pi(2r)^2 + \pi(4r)^2 = 84\pi$$
$$r^2 + 4r^2 + 16r^2 = 84$$
$$21r^2 = 84$$
$$r^2 = 4$$
$$r = 2.$$

If $r = 2$, then the radius of C is 2, the radius of B is 4, and the radius of A is 8. Line segment AC is made up of the radius of A, the diameter of B, and the radius of C, so the $AC = 8 + 4 + 4 + 2 = 18$.

SECTION 4

QUESTIONS	EXPLANATIONS

Column A **Column B**

$3x + 5 = 20$

1 $6x$ 40

The average of positive integers p and q is 3.

2 p q

10% of x is 20% of 100

3 x 50

1. Jim's answer is B.
   It is not necessary to solve for x to answer this question. If you subtract 5 from both sides of the question, you get $3x = 15$. Then just multiply both sides by 2, and you get $6x = 30$. So Column A is 30. Therefore, Column B is greater.

2. Jim's answer is D.
   Use an Average Pie. If the average of two numbers, p and q, is 3, then the sum of those numbers is 6. Therefore, $p + q = 6$. But that's all you know. It's possible that $p = 3$ and $q = 3$, in which case the columns are equal. But it's also possible that $p = 4$ and $q = 2$, in which case Column A is greater. Since you can get more than one result, Jim's answer must be D.

3. Jim's answer is A.
   Just translate the expression:
   $\left(\dfrac{10}{100}\right)x = \left(\dfrac{20}{100}\right)100$. Then use your calculator to solve for x, which equals 200. So Column A is greater.

SECTION 4

Column A   **Column B**

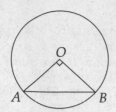

O is the center of a circle

| 4 | The measure of ∠*OAB* | The measure of ∠*OBA* |

On Sunday, 200 customers visited a gas station. Every 20th customer received a free fill-up. Every 30th customer received a discount tune-up.

| 5 | The number of customers who received both a free fill-up and a discount tune-up | 4 |

4. Jim's answer is C.
The trick to this question is making a connection between the circle and the triangle. *OA* and *OB* are the sides of the triangle, but they are *also* radii of the circle, which means they must be equal. If two sides of the triangle are equal, then you have an isosceles triangle. Since angle *OAB* and angle *OBA* are opposite the equal sides of the triangle, they must be equal angles.

5. Jim's answer is B.
Column A asks for the number of customers who received *both* a free fill-up and a discount tune-up. If every 20th customer got the fill-up and every 30th customer got the tune-up, then the first customer to get both was the 60th customer. The next customer to get both was the 120th customer, and the last customer to get both was the 180th customer. Essentially, you are just looking for numbers that are multiples of both 20 and 30. So only three customers got both a tune-up and a fill-up, which means that Column B is greater.

SECTION 4

QUESTIONS	EXPLANATIONS

Column A   **Column B**

$$x^2 > 17$$

6 | $x + 4$ | | 8 |

6. Jim's answer is D.
   You must always plug in *at least twice* for quant comp questions. Since x^2 has to be greater than 17, you can make $x = 5$. In that case, Column A is 9, which is greater than Column B. But is there any way that Column B can be greater? To find out, you need to try one of the special numbers. Can x be negative? Sure. If $x = -5$, then x^2 is still greater than 17. In that case, Column A is -1, which means that Column B is greater. Since you got more than one result, Jim's answer must be D.

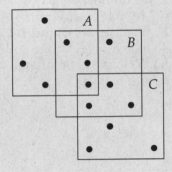

7 | In squares A, B, and C above, the number of points that lie in exactly two squares | | 6 |

7. Jim's answer is B.
   This is not really a math question. We call these visual perception problems. You just need to look at the figure very carefully. There are two points in the area where squares A and B overlap. There are also three points in the area where squares B and C overlap. Now, be careful. Squares A and C actually overlap inside of square B, which means that there are three squares overlapping in that area, so that point doesn't count. There are only five points all together, which means that Column B is greater.

SECTION 4

Column A	Column B

$$x \geq 1$$

8 $x^{(x+2)}$ $(x+2)^x$

8. Jim's answer is D.
You must always plug in *at least twice* for quant comp questions. Since x can be 1, you should start by trying $x = 1$. In that case, Column A equals $1^{(1+2)}$, or 1^3, which is 1. Column B equals $(1+2)^1$, or 3^1, which is 3. So Column B can be greater. What if $x = 2$? In that case, Column A equals $2^{(2+2)}$, or 2^4, which is 16. Column B equals $(2+2)^2$, or 4^2, which is 16. So the columns can be equal. You can get more than one result, so Jim's answer is D.

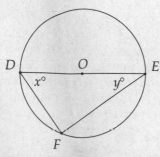

Note: Figure not drawn to scale.

O is the center of a circle with $DF = EF$. Segment DE passes through point O.

9 x 60

9. Jim's answer is B.
The most important thing to notice in this question is that the figure is *not* drawn to scale. That means you can't trust it. You can only trust what the question says. According to the question, $DF = EF$, which means that you have an isosceles triangle, even though it doesn't look that way. Therefore, x and y are equal, because they are opposite the equal sides. DE is the diameter of the circle, so angle DFE must be a right angle. Therefore, x and y both equal 45, which means that Column B is greater.

SECTION 4

Column A **Column B**

10 | The area of a triangle with base $3x$ and height $2x$ | The area of a circle with radius x

On the number line above, the marks are equally spaced

11 | x | $\dfrac{17}{37}$

10. Jim's answer is B.
Start by plugging in a number for x. Let's say $x = 4$. In that case, the base of the triangle is 3×4, or 12, and the height is 2×4, or 8. Now use the formula for the area of a triangle: $\frac{1}{2} \times$ base $\times$ height $= \frac{1}{2}(12)(8) = 48$. So Column A is 48. If $x = 4$, the area of circle with a radius of 4 is 16π. Now, since this is a quant comp question, you need to be careful with approximating the value of π. We need to be a little more precise and say that π is about 3.14. In that case, the area of the circle is 16×3.14, which is 50.24. So Column B is greater.

11. Jim's answer is A.
First, find the distance between $\frac{1}{3}$ and $\frac{1}{2}$, which is $\frac{1}{3} - \frac{1}{2}$, or $\frac{1}{6}$. If you count the intervals on the number line between $\frac{1}{3}$ and $\frac{1}{2}$, you'll find that there are six. So you need to divide $\frac{1}{6}$ by 6, which gives you $\frac{1}{36}$. That means each interval is $\frac{1}{36}$. Since x is one interval less than $\frac{1}{2}$, that means $x = \frac{1}{2} - \frac{1}{36} = \frac{17}{36}$. Now, be careful. The best thing to do is convert both fractions to decimals on your calculator: $\frac{17}{36} = .472$ and $\frac{17}{37} = .459$. Since .472 is greater than .459, that means Column A is greater.

SECTION 4

QUESTIONS	EXPLANATIONS

Column A   **Column B**

12 | The number of distinct 3-player teams that can be drawn from a pool of 5 players | 12

12. Jim's answer is B.
Imagine you have five players: A, B, C, D, and E. How many different ways can you combine them in groups of three? Write it out:

ABC   ACD   BCD   CDE
ABD   ACE   BCE
ABE   ADE   BDE

There are ten different ways to make 3-player teams out of the five players. So Column B is greater.

PN and *OM* are line segments

13 | $g + h$ $i + j$

13. Jim's answer is D.
Remember, the figures in difficult quant comp questions are designed to trick you. You know that $g = j$ because they are vertical angles. But does $h = i$? You have no idea! Joe Bloggs thinks that they are equal because they *look* that way. But this is a hard question, and Joe is always wrong. You can't answer a hard quant comp question by saying, "It looks that way." That's why Jim's answer is D, not C.

Set *A*: {2, –1, 7, –4, 11, 3}
Set *B*: {10, 5, –3, 4, 7, –8}

14 | The median of Set *A* | The average of Set *B*

14. Jim's answer is C.
Remember, the median of a group of numbers is the number that is exactly in the middle of the group when the group is arranged from smallest to largest. To find the median of set *A*, you have to put the numbers is order: –4, –1, 2, 3, 7, 11. Since there are only six numbers, you have to take the average of the two middle numbers, 2 and 3. The average of 2 and 3 is 2.5. To find the average of set *B*, add up all the numbers and divide by six, because there are six numbers. The sum of the numbers in set *B* is 15, and 15 divided by 6 is 2.5. So the columns are equal.

SECTION 4

Column A   **Column B**

$$ax \neq 0$$

15

| $(x - a)^2$ | $-2ax$ |

15. Jim's answer is A.
    Plug in some numbers! If $ax \neq 0$, that means a and x cannot be 0. If $x = 3$ and $a = 2$, then Column A is 1 and Column B is -12. So Column A can be greater. What if $x = -3$ and $a = -2$? In that case, Column A is still 1 and Column B is still -12. How about if $x = 1$ and $a = 1$? In that case, Column A is 0 and Column B is -2. Column A is still greater. As it turns out, no matter what numbers you plug in for a and x, Column A is always greater.

16 A certain clothing store sells only T-shirts, sweatshirts, and turtlenecks. On Wednesday, the store sells T-shirts, sweatshirts, and turtlenecks in a ratio of 2 to 3 to 5. If the store sells 30 sweatshirts on that day, what is the total number of garments that the store sells on Wednesday?

16. Jim's answer is 100.
    Use a Ratio Box:

T-shirts	Sweatshirts	Turtlenecks	Total
2	3	5	10
10	10	10	10
	30		100

You only need to work out the *total* column to figure out the total number of garments that the store sold, which is 100.

SECTION 4

QUESTIONS	EXPLANATIONS

17 A rectangular packing crate has a height of 4.5 inches and a base with an area of 18 square inches. What is the volume of the crate in cubic inches?

17. Jim's answer is 81.
The formula for the volume of a box is length × width × height. But the question gives you the area of the base of the crate, so you already know that length × width = 18. The volume of the crate, then, is simply the area of the base times the height:
18 × 4.5 = 81.

18 If $5x - 4 = x - 1$, what is the value of x?

18. Jim's answer is .75 or $\frac{3}{4}$.
All you have to do is simply solve for x:
$5x - 4 = x - 1$
$5x = x + 3$
$4x = 3$
$x = \frac{3}{4}$ (or .75).

SECTION 4

QUESTIONS	EXPLANATIONS

19 A box of donuts contains 3 plain, 5 cream-filled, and 4 chocolate donuts. If one of the donuts is chosen at random from the box, what is the probability that it will NOT be cream-filled?

19. Jim's answer is .583 or $\frac{7}{12}$.

There are 3 plain, 5 cream-filled, and 4 chocolate donuts, which means there are 12 donuts all together. Of those 12 donuts, 7 of them are NOT cream-filled (3 plain + 4 chocolate = 7). So the probability of randomly selecting a donut that is not cream-filled is simply 7 out of 12, or $\frac{7}{12}$.

20 If b is a prime integer such that $3b > 10 > \frac{5}{6}b$, what is one possible value of b?

20. Jim's answer is 5, 7, or 11.

First, think of a prime number that will make $3b$ greater than 10. How about 5? To see if that fits the other side of the inequality, you need to find the value of $\frac{5}{6}b$. If $b = 5$, then $\frac{5}{6}(5) = \frac{25}{6}$, or 4.166, which is definitely less than 10. Since 5 fits both sides of the inequality, it must be one of Jim's answers. Remember, you only need to find *one* possible value of b.

SECTION 4

QUESTIONS	EXPLANATIONS

21 The Tyler Jackson Dance Company plans to perform a piece that requires two dancers. If there are 7 dancers in the company, how many possible combinations of dancers could perform the piece?

21. Jim's answer is 21.
Let's say you have seven dancers: A, B, C, D, E, F, and G. How many different ways can you pair them up? Write it out:

AB	BC	CD	DE	EF	FG
AC	BD	CE	DF	EG	
AD	BE	CF	DG		
AE	BF	CG			
AF	BG				
AG					

Now count them up: There are 21 different pairs.

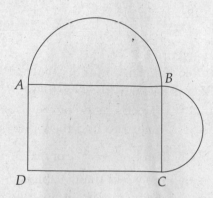

22 In the figure above, if semicircular arc *AB* has length 6π and semicircular arc *BC* has length 4π, what is the area of rectangle *ABCD*?

22. Jim's answer is 96.
You know that *AB* is a semicircle, which means it's half a circle. So the circumference of the entire circle would be $6\pi \times 2$, or 12π. Therefore, the diameter of that circle is 12π. Since *AB* is the diameter, you know that the length of rectangle ABCD is 12. You can also use the same trick to find the width. If the length of semicircle *BC* is 4π, then the circumference of the entire circle would be 8. That means the diameter is 8π, and since *BC* is the diameter, the width of the rectangle is 8. Now you can find the area of the rectangle: length × width = 12 × 8 = 96.

SECTION 4

QUESTIONS	EXPLANATIONS

23 Let $\heartsuit{x}$ be defined for all positive integers x as the product of the distinct prime factors of x. What is the value of $\dfrac{\heartsuit{6}}{\heartsuit{81}}$?

SPICE PRICES OF DISTRIBUTOR D

Spice	Price per pound
cinnamon	$8.00
nutmeg	$9.00
ginger	$7.00
cloves	$10.00

24 The owner of a spice store buys 3 pounds each of cinnamon, nutmeg, ginger, and cloves from Distributor D. She then sells all of the spices at $2.00 per ounce. What, in dollars, is her total profit (1 pound = 16 ounces)?

---

23. Jim's answer is 2.
This is a function question, and the definition of the function is given to you. Whenever you see $\heartsuit{x}$, it means you have to find the product all the distinct prime factors of x. To find the value of $\heartsuit{6}$, you need to find all the distinct prime factors of 6 and then multiply them. First, list the factors of 6: 1, 6, 2, 3. Of those numbers, only 2 and 3 are prime. So $\heartsuit{6} = 2 \times 3 = 6$.

To find the value of $\heartsuit{81}$, list the factors of 81: 1, 81, 9, 3, 27. Of those numbers, only 3 is prime, so the value of $\heartsuit{81}$ is just 3. So value of $\dfrac{\heartsuit{6}}{\heartsuit{81}}$ is $\dfrac{6}{3}$, or 2.

24. Jim's answer is 282.
This is a hard question, so you have stay on your toes. If the owner buys 3 pounds of each spice, that means she pays the following amounts for each spice:

cinnamon: $8 \times 3 = $24
nutmeg: $9 \times 3 = $27
ginger: $7 \times 3 = $21
cloves: $10 \times 3 = $30

So she pays a total of 24 + 27 + 21 + 30, or 102 dollars for 12 pounds of spice. She then sells the spices per *ounce*, so you have to figure out first how many ounces of spices she has. If 1 pound is 16 ounces, then 12 pounds is 12 × 16, or 192 ounces. She sells all the spices at 2 dollars per ounce, so she makes 192 × $2, or $384. To figure out her profit, subtract the amount she paid for the spices from the amount she made selling them: 384 − 102 = 282.

SECTION 4

QUESTIONS	EXPLANATIONS

25 Points E, F, G, and H lie on a line in that order. If $EG = \frac{5}{3}EF$ and $HF = 5FG$, then what is $\frac{EF}{HG}$?

25. Jim's answer is .375 or $\frac{3}{8}$.

Since the question doesn't give you a figure, you should draw one. Then plug in some values.

If $EG = \frac{5}{3}EF$, then you can make $EF = 3$ and $EG = 5$. That means FG must be 2. If $HF = 5FG$, then $HF = 5(2) = 10$. If $HF = 10$ and $FG = 2$, then HG = 8. So $\frac{EF}{HG} = \frac{3}{8}$.

SECTION 5

1   Plants that grow in the desert or on high rocky ledges can survive long periods of ---- because they hoard water in their leaves, stems and root systems.

    (A) darkness
    (B) inactivity
    (C) dormancy
    (D) warmth
    (E) drought

1.   Pam's answer is E.
The doctor in this sentence is *they hoard water in their leaves*. If the plants are hoarding water, they must be doing it to survive long periods without water. So you can put *without water* in the blank, in which case the best match is *drought*.

2   Thanks to his eloquence and logic, Liam spoke ---- and made it difficult for even his bitterest opponents to ---- his opinions.

    (A) monotonously. .clash with
    (B) charmingly. .yield to
    (C) tediously. .contend with
    (D) abhorrently. .concede to
    (E) persuasively. .disagree with

2.   Pam's answer is E.
The doctor for this sentence is *eloquence and logic*. If Liam is eloquent and logical, he must speak very well; therefore, you can eliminate choices A, C, and D because they're negative. Liam's eloquence and logic probably made it difficult for his bitterest opponents to *contradict* his opinions. The best match for *contradict* is *disagree with*, in answer choice E. It also makes sense that Liam's eloquence and logic made him speak *persuasively*.

3   Many myths and legends, however ----, often possess a grain of truth.

    (A) delightful
    (B) accurate
    (C) eternal
    (D) unbelievable
    (E) important

3.   Pam's answer is D.
The doctor is for this sentence is *possess a grain of truth*, and the trigger word is *however*, which means the word that fills the blank will have the opposite meaning of the doctor. The opposite of *possess a grain of truth* is *unbelievable*.

4   Ancient Greek playwrights often included the device of divine intervention in their work; just as circumstances became dire, a ---- would descend from Olympus and rescue the hero from almost certain death.

    (A) hero
    (B) warrior
    (C) luminary
    (D) deity
    (E) liberator

4.   Pam's answer is D.
The doctor in this sentence is *the device of divine intervention*. *Divine* means having to do with a god, so it must be a god that intervened at the last moment in Greek dramas. That means you can put *god* in the blank. Looking at answer choices, *deity* means *god*.

SECTION 5

QUESTIONS	EXPLANATIONS

5 The apparent ---- with which professional skiers descend the slopes is deceptive; this activity requires ---- effort and intense concentration.

(A) trepidation. .conscious
(B) focus. .resolute
(C) nonchalance. .strenuous
(D) consideration. .unpredictable
(E) insouciance. .minimal

5. Pam's answer is C.
The doctors in this sentence are *apparent* and *deceptive*. Professional skiers descend the slopes with apparent *ease*, but this *apparent* ease is *deceptive*. Therefore, it must actually be difficult to ski well. The best way to complete the second part of the sentence is to say that skiing "requires *great* effort and intense concentration." So we can put *great* in the second blank. That gets rid of answer choice E. Then we have *ease* in the first blank, and the best match among the remaining answers is *nonchalance*.

6 Miranda, in her desire to foster ----, often felt compelled to ---- readily to others in tense situations.

(A) cooperation. .object
(B) consistency. .defer
(C) dissension. .surrender
(D) discourse. .appeal
(E) harmony. .acquiesce

6. Pam's answer is E.
The doctors in this sentence are *foster* and *in tense situations*. Since *foster* is a positive word, the word in the first blank must be positive; you can get rid of C and D because they have negative words. If Miranda wants to foster something good, then in tense situations she is probably compelled to give in to others. You can use *give in* for the second blank, which means you can eliminate A. Between B and E, you can eliminate B because *consistency* doesn't make any sense in the first blank. Remember, it's often easier to figure out which answer is wrong than to figure out which one is right.

7 Early psychoanalysts challenged many of the most ---- notions of human behavior and compelled many to alter their dearly held assumptions about human nature.

(A) elusive
(B) derided
(C) volatile
(D) cherished
(E) contemplative

7. Pam's answer is D.
The doctor in this sentence is *compelled many to alter their dearly held assumptions about human nature*, and the trigger word is *and*, which tells you that the blank will agree with the doctor. Here you can simply recycle the doctor: The *notions of human behavior* that psychoanalysis compelled people to change must have been *dearly held* notions. If you put *dearly held* in the blank, the best match is *cherished*.

8 Although detractors labeled Margaret Thatcher's policies ----, she asserted that her ideas moved the United Kingdom forward.

(A) premature
(B) autocratic
(C) regressive
(D) democratic
(E) radical

8. Pam's answer is C.
The doctor in this sentence is *moved the United Kingdom forward*, and the trigger word is *although*, which means the blank must be the opposite of *moved forward*. If you put *moved backwards* in the blank, the best match is *regressive*.

SECTION 5

QUESTIONS	EXPLANATIONS

9 Some subatomic particles, ---- only through their effects on other bodies, have been compared to outer planets whose ---- was first deduced from eccentricities in other planets' orbits.

(A) feasible. .irregularity
(B) palpable. .creation
(C) imaginable. .falsity
(D) perceptible. .existence
(E) verifiable. .proximity

9. Pam's answer is D.
The doctor in this sentence is *first deduced from eccentricities in other plants' orbits*. If subatomic particles are being compared to the outer planets, then these particles must have been *deduced* through their effects on other particles. If you put *deducible* in the first blank, you can get rid of choices A and C. What was deduced about the outer planets and subatomic particles? That they *existed*. So you can put *existence* in the second blank, which means choice D must be the answer. Notice that it would not make sense to talk about the outer planets' *proximity*, or their *creation*, since they are neither close by nor recently created.

10 Wary of unorthodox treatments, many doctors are reluctant to concede that nutritionists have a ---- argument for the use of dietary regulation as preventive medicine.

(A) cogent
(B) cursory
(C) vacillating
(D) feckless
(E) vehement

10. Pam's answer is A.
The doctor in this sentence is *many doctors are reluctant to concede*. If the doctors are reluctant to concede something about the nutritionists' argument, then the nutritionists must have a good argument. So the doctors don't want to concede that the nutritionists' argument is *good*, which means a positive word goes in the blank. If you cross out all the negative words in the answer choices, you're left with A.

SECTION 5

QUESTIONS	EXPLANATIONS

11 STOCKING : LEG ::

    (A) waistband : skirt
    (B) ankle : foot
    (C) button : lapel
    (D) cast : body
    (E) glove : hand

11. Pam's answer is E.
A STOCKING covers your LEG. If you had trouble choosing between D and E, you should have made a more specific sentence. A STOCKING is a *piece of clothing* that covers your LEG. A *glove* is a piece of clothing that *covers* your hand.

12 PARK : RECREATION ::

    (A) kitchen : cooking
    (B) fence : sitting
    (C) tree : climbing
    (D) yard : playing
    (E) bus : driving

12. Pam's answer is A.
A PARK is a place for RECREATION. A *kitchen* is a place for *cooking*. If you had trouble narrowing down the choices, then you were probably missing the idea of *place* in your sentence. Whenever more than one answer fits your sentence, make a more specific sentence.

13 OUNCE : WEIGHT ::

    (A) acre : area
    (B) scale : mass
    (C) inch : yard
    (D) menu : portion
    (E) variety : difference

13. Pam's answer is A.
An OUNCE is a unit of WEIGHT. An *acre* is a unit of *area*. Remember, an ounce doesn't measure weight. A scale measures weight.

14 CREST : WAVE ::

    (A) climax : action
    (B) elegy : memory
    (C) example : paradigm
    (D) milestone : distance
    (E) landmark : territory

14. Pam's answer is A.
The CREST is the peak of the WAVE. The *climax* is the peak in the *action*.

SECTION 5

15 LOW : COW ::

(A) gosling : goose
(B) swarm : bee
(C) hutch : rabbit
(D) chirp : bird
(E) bed : oyster

15. Pam's answer is D.
LOW is the sound of COW. *Chirp* is the sound of a *bird*. If you had trouble making a sentence, you should have eliminated answer choices with unrelated words and then worked backwards. A *gosling* is a baby *goose*. Is a LOW a baby COW? No, eliminate A. A *swarm* is a group of *bees*. Is a LOW a group of COWs? No, eliminate B. A hutch is a home for a rabbit. Is a LOW a home for a COW? No, Eliminate C. A *chirp* is the sound of a *bird*. Is a LOW the sound of a COW? If you don't know the word for the sound a cow makes, then this is a possibility. A *bed* is a place where *oysters* live. Is a LOW a place where COWs live? No, eliminate E.

16 HAMLET : VILLAGE ::

(A) street : sidewalk
(B) convertible : car
(C) building : skyscraper
(D) photograph : portrait
(E) cottage : house

16. Pam's answer is E.
A HAMLET is a small VILLAGE. A *cottage* is a small *house*. If you had trouble making a sentence, you should have eliminated answer choices with unrelated words and then worked backwards. *Street* and *sidewalk* are unrelated, because not all streets have sidewalks next to them; eliminate A. A *convertible* is a *car* with a removable top. Is a HAMLET a VILLAGE with a removable top? Certainly not. Eliminate B. A *skyscraper* is a very tall *building*. Is a VILLAGE a very tall HAMLET? No, eliminate C. You could say that a *photograph* is a type of *portrait*, but VILLAGE and HAMLET have a more specific relationship.

17 MALLEABLE : SHAPED ::

(A) flexible : bullied
(B) amenable : persuaded
(C) tolerable : handled
(D) pliable : hardened
(E) negotiable : sold

17. Pam's answer is B.
MALLEABLE means easily SHAPED. *Amenable* means easily *persuaded*. If you had trouble making a sentence, you should have eliminated answer choices with unrelated words and then worked backward. As it turns out, the only answer choice with a pair of words that have a clear and necessary relationship is B.

SECTION 5

QUESTIONS	EXPLANATIONS

18 ANALGESIC : PAIN ::

(A) anesthetic : surgery
(B) palliative : violence
(C) operation : health
(D) enthusiasm : anger
(E) prosthesis : limb

18. Pam's answer is B.
An ANALGESIC eases PAIN. A *palliative* eases *violence*. If you had trouble making a sentence, you should have eliminated any unrelated answer choices and then worked backward. An *anesthetic* can be used to prevent pain during *surgery*, but does it make sense to say that an ANALGESIC prevents pain during PAIN? No. Eliminate A. An *operation* is not necessarily related to *health*, so you can eliminate C, and *enthusiasm* and *anger* have no relationship, so you can eliminate D. A *prosthesis* is an artificial *limb*. Is an ANALGESIC an artificial PAIN? No, so you can eliminate E.

19 NOVICE : EXPERIENCE ::

(A) questioner : knowledge
(B) invader : bravery
(C) narrator : objectivity
(D) ingenue : talent
(E) rube : sophistication

19. Pam's answer is E.
A NOVICE lacks EXPERIENCE. A *rube* lacks *sophistication*. If you eliminate all the answer choices that contain unrelated words, E is the only answer choice left.

20 GRISLY : DISGUST ::

(A) happy : grief
(B) endearing : affection
(C) redolent : joy
(D) boring : interest
(E) bitter : repulsion

20. Pam's answer is B.
GRISLY means inspiring DISGUST. *Endearing* means inspiring *affection*. If you had trouble making a sentence, you could have used the fact that GRISLY and DISGUST have similar meanings. In other words, they are both negative. *Happy* and *grief* have different meanings (one is positive and one is negative), and so do *boring* and *interest*, so you can eliminate A and D. *Redolent* and *joy* have no relationship, and neither do *bitter* and *repulsion*, which gets rid of C and E. Since this is a difficult question, you could have eliminated E, which is a Joe Bloggs answer, because *repulsion* reminds Joe Bloggs of DISGUST.

21 DIATRIBE : ABUSIVE ::

(A) rant : condemnatory
(B) doctrine : orthodox
(C) eulogy : laudatory
(D) refrain : musical
(E) judgment : fearful

21. Pam's answer is C.
A DIATRIBE is an ABUSIVE speech. A *eulogy* is a laudatory *speech*. If you had trouble making a sentence, you should have eliminated answer choices with unrelated words and then worked backward. The words in answer choice A and E have no relationship, so you can eliminate them.

SECTION 5

22 SECRETE : FIND ::

   (A) muffle : hear
   (B) cover : open
   (C) exude : ignore
   (D) smile : sadden
   (E) explain : comprehend

22. Pam's answer is A.
SECRETE means to make difficult to FIND.
Muffle means to make difficult to *hear*. If you had trouble making a sentence, you should have eliminated answer choices with unrelated words and then worked backward. Answer choices B, C, and D all contain unrelated pairs. *Explain* means to make easier to *comprehend*, but SECRETE does not mean make easier FIND, so you can eliminate E.

23 INDELIBLE : PERMANENCE ::

   (A) united : individuality
   (B) qualified : employment
   (C) unavoidable : toleration
   (D) inconsistent : compatibility
   (E) flimsy : tenuousness

23. Pam's answer is E.
INDELIBLE means having PERMANENCE.
Flimsy means having *tenuousness*. If you eliminate all the answer choices that contain unrelated words, only E is left.

SECTION 5

Questions 24–35 are based on the following passage.

The role of women has historically been different in different cultures. The following passage presents an analysis of women in Frankish society by Suzanne Fonay Wemple.

Although the laws and customs in lands under Frankish domination emphasized the biological function and sexual nature of women, they did not
Line deprive women of opportunities to find personal
(5) fulfillment in a variety of roles. Frankish women could sublimate their sexual drives and motherly instincts in ways not available to women in ancient societies. Their labor, moreover, was not as exploited as it had been in primitive tribal societies.
(10) Queens had access to power not only through their husbands but also through churchmen and secular officials whom they patronized. As widows, acting as regents for their sons, they could exercise political power directly. The wives of magnates
(15) issued donations jointly with their husbands, founded monasteries, endowed churches, cultivated interfamilial ties, transmitted clan ideology to their children, supervised the household, and administered the family's estates when their
(20) husbands were away. Whether they contracted a formal union or entered into a quasi-marriage, their children could inherit. As widows, they acted as guardians of their minor children, arranged their marriages, and in the absence of sons, wielded
(25) economic power as well. In the dependent classes, women shared their husbands' work, produced textiles and articles of clothing both for their family's and the lords' use, and were instrumental in bringing about the merger of the free and slave
(30) elements in society.
For those who wished to free their bodies, souls, and brains from male domination and devote their lives to the service of God, Christianity provided an alternative way of life. Although, in relation to the
(35) total population, women in religious life remained a small minority even in the seventh and eighth centuries, when many female communities were founded, their roles, social functions, and cultural contributions have an importance for the history of
(40) women that outweighs their numbers. This alternative way of life was available not only to the unmarried but also to widows. Monasteries served as places of refuge for married women as well. The rich and the poor, at least until the late eighth
(45) century, were accepted as members. Women from all walks of life, as well as relatives, friends, and dependents of the foundresses and abbesses, were invited to join the new congregations. Freed from the need to compete for the attention of men,
(50) women in these communities sustained each other in spiritual, intellectual, scholarly, artistic, and charitable pursuits. Writings by early medieval nuns reveal that female ideals and modes of conduct were upheld as the way to salvation and as
(55) models of sanctity in the monasteries led by women. By facilitating the escape of women from the male-dominated society to congregations where they could give expression to their own emotions, ascetic ideals, and spiritual strivings, Christianity
(60) became a liberating force in the lives of women. Historians have often overlooked these positive effects and concentrated instead on the misogynistic sentiments perpetuated by the male hierarchy.

SECTION 5

QUESTIONS	EXPLANATIONS

24 The passage suggests that women under Frankish law were

(A) confined to narrow social roles
(B) cut off from religious communities
(C) exploited as slaves and servants
(D) defined in physical or biological terms
(E) valued but essentially powerless

24. Pam's answer is D.
The lead words in this question are *Frankish law*, which should lead you to the beginning of the passage. According to lines 1–3, *the laws and customs in lands under Frankish domination emphasized the biological function and sexual nature of women.* These lines are perfectly paraphrased in answer choice D, which says that women were *defined in physical or biological terms*.

Answer choice A contradicts the passage. Frankish society *did not deprive women of opportunities to find personal fulfillment in a variety of roles* (lines 3–5).

Answer choice B completely contradicts the second half of the passage, which is all about women in religious communities. Always keep in mind the main idea of the passage.

Answer choice C contradicts lines 8–9, which tell us that Frankish society did not exploit women.

Answer choice E is wrong because lines 10–30 say that women had access to power in several different ways.

25 According to the passage, which of the following describes a difference between Frankish society and more primitive cultures?

(A) Frankish society did not encourage childbearing.
(B) Women in Frankish society were not taken advantage of for their labor.
(C) Women in Frankish society had more social and political power over their husbands.
(D) Women in Frankish society were less likely to work within their homes.
(E) Frankish society defined gender differences in biological terms.

25. Pam's answer is B.
The lead words in this question are *ancient societies*, which should lead you back to line 9, where *primitive tribal societies* are mentioned. According to lines 8–9, women's *labor…was not as exploited as it had been in primitive tribal societies*. So the difference between Frankish society and more ancient societies is that women's labor was not exploited. This idea is paraphrased in answer choice B, which says that women were *not taken advantage of for their labor*.

Answer choice A doesn't make any sense. How can it be true that Frankish society did not encourage childbearing? How would they have children? Don't forget to use your common sense.

Answer choice C doesn't make any sense either. Although Frankish women had access to power through their husbands, the passage doesn't say that they had *more* power.

Answer choice D is wrong because the passage never suggests that Frankish women did not work in their homes.

Answer choice E contradicts itself. Gender differences are, by definition, biological differences.

QUESTIONS	EXPLANATIONS

26 The passage suggests that the "access to power" (line 10) enjoyed by Frankish queens

(A) surpassed the influence wielded by their sons and husbands
(B) was greatly increased by their relationship to the church
(C) did not extend beyond the boundaries of their households
(D) permitted them to exercise power, but only indirectly
(E) was based on their relationships to male figures of power

26. Pam's answer is E.
According to lines 10–12, *Queens had access to power not only through their husbands but also through churchmen and secular officials whom they patronized*. Since Frankish queens had *access to power* through their husbands, churchmen, and secular officials, their access to power was *based on their relationships to male figures of power*.

Answer choice A is wrong for the same reason that choice C was wrong in the previous question. Although Frankish women had influence through their sons and husbands, they did not have *more* influence. Also, the word *surpassed* makes this a *must* answer.

Answer choice B is wrong because the phrase *greatly increased* is too extreme, and therefore this is not the kind of answer that Pam would choose.

Answer choice C contradicts the passage. The power of Frankish women *did* extend beyond their households. According to the passage, they had access to power through *churchmen and secular officials whom they patronized*, and this definitely represents power outside the home.

Answer choice D also contradicts the passages. According to lines 12–14, *As widows, acting for their sons, they could exercise political power directly*.

27 The word "transmitted" as used in line 17 most nearly means

(A) announced
(B) taught
(C) enforced
(D) distributed
(E) broadcast

27. Pam's answer is B.
Go back to the passage, find the word *transmitted*, and cross it out. Then read the sentence and come up with your own word. Since the word in context has something to do with *clan ideology* and *children*, a good substitute for the word might be *taught*, since it would make sense that the *wives of magnates* taught clan ideology to their children. If you look in the answers, *taught* is actually a choice.

The other answer choices are wrong because they don't make any sense in context. Choice E is a Joe Bloggs answer, because *transmitted* makes Joe think of *broadcast*.

SECTION 5

28 It can be inferred from the passage that marriage in Frankish society

(A) was the only means of exchanging wealth
(B) could be entered formally or informally
(C) raised women to positions of influence
(D) held greater importance than in primitive societies
(E) was generally arranged by the bride's mother

28. Pam's answer is B.
The lead word in this question is *marriage*, which should lead to lines 20–22. According to these lines, in Frankish society people either *contracted a formal union or entered into a quasi-marriage*. Answer choice B paraphrases this sentence by saying that marriage *could be entered formally or informally*.

Answer choice A is wrong because the word *only* makes this a *must* answer, so it can't be Pam's answer. Besides, does it make sense to say that marriage was the *only* means of exchanging wealth?

Answer choice C implies that marriage always raised women to positions of power, which is definitely not the case.

Answer choice D is wrong because there is no comparison made in the passage between marriage in primitive society and marriage within Frankish society. Read carefully.

Answer choice E is wrong because the passage doesn't say anything about arranged marriages.

29 The word "instrumental" as used in line 28 most nearly means

(A) helpful
(B) skilled
(C) harmonious
(D) resistant
(E) vital

29. Pam's answer is E.
Go back to the passage, find the word *instrumental*, and cross it out. Then read the sentence and come up with your own word. According to the passage, women played a role *in bringing about the merger of free and slave elements in society*. Pam would be much more likely to say that women played a *vital* role than she would to say that they were merely *helpful*.

Joe likes answer choice C because *instruments* make Joe think of *harmony*. The other choices are wrong because they don't make any sense in context.

SECTION 5

QUESTIONS	EXPLANATIONS

30 Which of the following best describes the difference between "wives of magnates" (line 14) and wives in the "dependent classes" (lines 25–26)?

(A) Wives in the dependent classes cooperated with their husbands, while the wives of magnates did not.

(B) Wives in the dependent classes were powerless in their own households, while the wives of magnates wielded considerable power in theirs.

(C) Wives in the dependent classes were forced by their husbands to perform strenuous tasks, while wives of magnates were not.

(D) Wives of magnates were less likely than wives in the dependent classes to turn to religious communities for refuge and liberation.

(E) Wives of magnates had greater power to administrate their own households than did wives in the dependent classes.

30. Pam's answer is E.
According to lines 19–20, the *wives of magnates…administered the family's estates when their husbands were away*. If you read further down you'll find that wives in *dependent classes* did not have this power. That is the difference described in answer choice E. Another way to answer this question is to eliminate wrong answers.

Answer choice A is a very extreme statement. How can it be true that wives of magnates did not cooperate with their husbands? Not even one wife cooperated with her husband? Not ever?

Answer choice B is also a very extreme statement. Were the wives in the dependent classes completely *powerless* in their own homes? That doesn't seem very likely.

Answer choice C is too extreme, and the passage doesn't say anything of the sort.

Answer choice D contradicts what the passage says in lines 45–48.

31 According to the author, female religious communities in Frankish society had "importance for the history of women" (lines 39–40) because

(A) Frankish women entered these religious groups in great numbers

(B) they increased the political influence of all Frankish women

(C) women in these communities received superior education

(D) they introduced women to diverse cultural and social activities

(E) they eliminated the rift between married and unmarried women

31. Pam's answer is D.
The answer to this question does not come until lines 51–53, so if you stopped reading, you wouldn't have found the answer. According to the passage, *women in these communities sustained each other in spiritual, intellectual, scholarly, artistic, and charitable pursuits.* This is paraphrased in answer choice D.

Answer choice A contradicts line 36, which says that women in religious life were still a *small minority*.

Answer choice B is wrong because the passage doesn't say anything about *political influence* in connection with female religious communities.

Answer choice C is too extreme because of the word *superior*.

Answer choice E is wrong because the passage doesn't say anything about a rift between married and unmarried women, and even so, it would be much too extreme to say that this rift was *eliminated*.

SECTION 5

QUESTIONS	EXPLANATIONS

32 The passage implies that Frankish women outside religious communities

(A) felt obliged to compete for male attention
(B) were not inclined to religious feeling
(C) had greatly diminished economic power
(D) did not contribute to Frankish culture
(E) relied on males for emotional support

32. Pam's answer is A.
The only answer choice that comes from something stated in the passage is A. According to lines 48–50, *Freed from the need to compete for the attention of men, women in these communities....* If women in the Frankish religious communities were freed from the need to compete for male attention, that means women outside the communities must have had to compete for the attention of men.

Answer choice B doesn't make any sense. How can it be true that women outside the religious community were not inclined to any religious feeling at all? Just because they weren't nuns doesn't mean they weren't religious.

Answer choice C is wrong because it makes no sense to say that women outside the religious community had *less* economic power. If anything, the opposite would be true.

Answer choice D is too extreme and too offensive. Pam would never say that women outside religious communities did not contribute to Frankish culture at all.

Answer choice E is wrong because Pam would never suggest that women had to rely on men for emotional support. Besides, the passage never says that. Read carefully.

33 In line 55, "upheld" most nearly means

(A) delayed
(B) endorsed
(C) suspended
(D) enforced
(E) announced

33. Pam's answer is B.
Go back to the passage, find the word *upheld*, and cross it out. Then read the sentence and come up with your own word. According to the passage, *female ideals and modes of conduct* had some direct connection with *the way to salvation* and *models of sanctity in the monasteries led by women*. So we could put *were given* or *were taught* in the blank. The best match is *endorsed*.

Answer choice C is a Joe Bloggs answer because *upheld* makes Joe think of *suspended*. The other choices are wrong because they don't make sense in context.

SECTION 5

QUESTIONS	EXPLANATIONS

34 According to the passage, Christianity facilitated the "escape of women from the male-dominated society" (lines 56–57) by doing all of the following EXCEPT

(A) permitting women self-expression
(B) insulating women from physical hardship
(C) diversifying women's social roles
(D) removing male social pressures
(E) putting pressure on women to study

34. Pam's answer is E.
This is an EXCEPT question, so you should definitely save it for last. Pam is asking how Christianity allowed women to escape from male-dominated society, so you have to go back to the passage and find where that is discussed. Remember, you are looking for the answer choice that is *not* mentioned.
   Answer choice A is mentioned in line 59; answer choice B is mentioned in lines 42–43; answer choice C is mentioned in line 38; answer choice D is mentioned in lines 49–50. That leaves choice E.

35 The passage is best described as

(A) a study of class conflict in a medieval society
(B) an example of religion's influence on secular life
(C) a discussion of the roles of a social group
(D) a demonstration of the need for religious communities
(E) a refutation of a popular misconception

35. Pam's answer is C.
This is a general question, so you only need to know the main idea of the passage. The best way to attack this question is to get rid of wrong answers using POE. The passage is not about *class conflict*, so you can get rid of A. It's not about the influence of religion on secular life, so you can get rid of B. It's not strictly about the *need for religious communities*, so you can toss D out. Finally, the passage does not discuss any *misconceptions*, so E is out. The passage is about the roles of women in Frankish society or, in other words, *the roles of a social group*.

SECTION 6

QUESTIONS	EXPLANATIONS

1 If $6 - y = 2y - 6$, then $y =$

- (A) 0
- (B) 2
- (C) 4
- (D) 6
- (E) 12

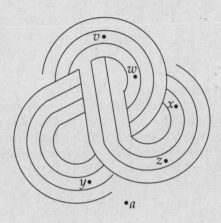

2 Which of the following points can be connected to point a by a continuous path without crossing any line or curve of the figure above?

- (A) v
- (B) w
- (C) x
- (D) y
- (E) z

1. Jim's answer is C.
    To solve for y, begin by adding y to both sides of the equation, which gives you $6 = 3y - 6$. Then add 6 to both sides, which gives you $12 = 3y$. Now divide both sides by 3, and you find that $y = 4$. You can also Backsolve any question that asks you to solve for a variable: $6 - 4 = 2(4) - 6$.

2. Jim's answer is B.
    This is what we call a visual perception problem. It's like a maze. Just put your pencil on a and see which other letter you can connect to a without crossing any lines. The only letter you can reach directly is w, all the way in the middle.

SECTION 6

| | QUESTIONS | EXPLANATIONS |

Computer Production		
	Morning Shift	**Afternoon Shift**
Monday	200	375
Tuesday	245	330
Wednesday	255	340
Thursday	250	315
Friday	225	360

3 If the above chart shows the number of computers produced at a factory during each shift, on which day is the total number of computers produced greatest?

(A) Monday
(B) Tuesday
(C) Wednesday
(D) Thursday
(E) Friday

3. Jim's answer is C.
This is a perfect calculator question. Just add up the morning shift and the afternoon shift for each day and see which total is the greatest. The total for Wednesday (the greatest) is 595.

4 If a rectangular swimming pool has a volume of 16,500 cubic feet, a depth of 10 feet, and a length of 75 feet, what is the width of the pool, in feet?

(A) 22
(B) 26
(C) 32
(D) 110
(E) 1,650

4. Jim's answer is A.
For this question, you need to know that volume equals length × width × height. You know that the volume is 16,500, the depth, or the height, is 10, and the length is 75. Just put those numbers in the formula:
$16,500 = 75 \times w \times 10$.
Use your calculator to solve for w, which equals 22.

5 A science class has a ratio of girls to boys of 4 to 3. If the class has a total of 35 students, how many more girls are there than boys?

(A) 20
(B) 15
(C) 7
(D) 5
(E) 1

5. Jim's answer is D.
Use a Ratio Box:

Girls	Boys	Total
4	3	7
5	5	5
20	15	35

There are 20 girls and 15 boys, so there are 5 more girls than boys.

SECTION 6

6 If $\frac{n}{8}$ has a remainder of 5, then which of the following has a remainder of 7?

(A) $\frac{n+1}{8}$

(B) $\frac{n+2}{8}$

(C) $\frac{n+3}{8}$

(D) $\frac{n+5}{8}$

(E) $\frac{n+7}{8}$

6. Jim's answer is B.
Get ready to Plug In: You need a number for n that gives you a remainder of 5 when you divide it by 8. Let's say $n = 21$. The question asks you which of the answer choices has a remainder of 7. Since $n = 21$, answer choice B equals $\frac{23}{8}$, which gives you a remainder of 7 when you divide.

7 For positive integer x, 10 percent of x percent of 1,000 equals

(A) x
(B) $10x$
(C) $100x$
(D) $1,000x$
(E) $10,000x$

7. Jim's answer is A.
Once again, Plug In: Let's say $x = 50$. Now we can translate the question:

$$\frac{10}{100} \times \frac{50}{100} \times 1000 =$$

If you work this out on your calculator, you should get 50 as your target answer. Since we said $x = 50$, the answer is A.

8 Nails are sold in 8-ounce and 20-ounce boxes. If 50 boxes of nails were sold and the total weight of the nails sold was less than 600 ounces, what is the greatest possible number of 20-ounce boxes that could have been sold?

(A) 34
(B) 33
(C) 25
(D) 17
(E) 16

8. Jim's answer is E.
This is a perfect Backsolve question. The question asks for the greatest possible number of 20-ounce boxes. Start with answer choice C. If there are twenty-five 20-ounce boxes, then there are twenty-five 8-ounce boxes, because a total of 50 boxes were purchased. In this case, the twenty-five 20-ounce boxes weigh 500 ounces, and the twenty-five 8-ounce boxes weigh 200 ounces; the total is 700 ounces. This is too big, because the question says the total weight was less than 600. If C is too big, A and B must also be too big; eliminate all three choices. If you try answer choice D, the total weight is 604 ounces, which is still too big. So the answer must be E.

QUESTIONS	EXPLANATIONS

9 If $c = \dfrac{1}{x} + \dfrac{1}{y}$ and $x > y > 0$, then $\dfrac{1}{c} =$

(A) $x + y$

(B) $x - y$

(C) $\dfrac{xy}{x+y}$

(D) $\dfrac{x+y}{xy}$

(E) $\dfrac{1}{x} - \dfrac{1}{y}$

9. Jim's answer is C.
Here's yet another chance to Plug In because of the variables in the answer choices. In this case, you have several variables. You should start by plugging in values for x and y, and then work out c. Since $x > y > 0$, let's say $x = 6$ and $y = 3$. Therefore, $c = \dfrac{1}{6} + \dfrac{1}{3}$, which equals $\dfrac{1}{2}$. The question asks for the value of $\dfrac{1}{c}$, which is the reciprocal of $\dfrac{1}{2}$, which is 2. This is your target answer. If you plug $x = 6$ and $y = 3$ into all of the answer choices, you'll find that answer choice C equals 2.

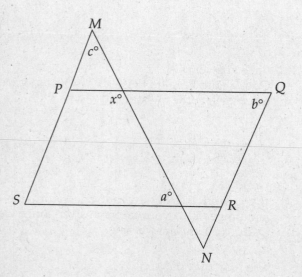

10 If $PQRS$ is a parallelogram and MN is a line segment, then x must equal

(A) $180 - b$

(B) $180 - c$

(C) $a + b$

(D) $a + c$

(E) $b + c$

10. Jim's answer is E.
There are variables in the answer choices again, so Plug In. However, you can't plug in a value for all the variables at once, because you must follow the rules of geometry. (Makes sense, right? It's the last question in the section.) Let's start by saying $a = 70$ and $b = 60$. Since $PQRS$ is a parallelogram, angle Q must equal angle S, so angle S also equals 60. If you look at the big triangle that contains a and c, you already know that two of the angles are 60 and 70, so the third angle, c, must be 50. We know that PQ and SR are parallel and, using Fred's Theorem, we can see that x is a big angle and a is a small angle. So $a + x = 180$. Since $a = 70$, that means $x = 110$. Therefore, your target answer is 110. Plug your values for a, b, and c into the answer choices and you'll find that answer choice E equals 110.

SECTION 7

The two passages below are followed by questions based on their content and on the relationship between the two passages. Answer the questions on the basis of what is stated or implied in the passage and in any introductory material that may be provided.

Questions 1-13 are based on the following passages.

The discipline of physics has seen a number of changes in the last 100 years. The following passages discuss two of those changes.

Passage 1

It is mandatory to preface any discussion of atoms by paying homage to Democritus, an Ionian philosopher of the fifth century B.C., the earliest
Line known proponent of an atomic theory. Though
(5) Democritus' ideas were in many ways strikingly modern and were promulgated by his more celebrated successor Epicurus, his theory never gained wide acceptance in Greek thought. It had largely been forgotten by the time of the late
(10) Renaissance rebirth of science. While the dramatic rise of the atomic theory over the last century and a half seems to have vindicated Democritus, only the Greek name atom ("indivisible") remains to establish his claim as the father of the theory.
(15) Nonetheless, Democritus' thinking contained the seed of the idea that has dominated twentieth-century physical thought. He was one of the first to perceive that nature on a sufficiently small scale might be qualitatively different in a striking way
(20) from the world of our ordinary experience. And he was the first to voice the hope, today almost an obsession, that underlying all the complex richness, texture, and variety of our everyday life might be a level of reality of stark simplicity, with the turmoil
(25) we perceive representing only the nearly infinite arrangements of a smaller number of constituents.
Today, the notion that simplicity is to be found by searching nature on a smaller level is embedded in physical thought to the point where few physicists
(30) can imagine any other approach.
Democritus' ideas were popular among the philosophically sophisticated founders of modern physics. Galileo, Newton, and most of their contemporaries were atomists, but their beliefs were
(35) based more on intuition than on concrete evidence. Moreover, the invention of calculus had eliminated the difficulties with continuity that had in part motivated the Greek atomists, so the theory received little attention in the century following
(40) Newton's work. Still, the atomic theory remained a popular speculation among physicists, because it

offered the hope that all the properties of matter might ultimately be explained in terms of the motion of the atoms themselves.
(45) It remained for the chemists of the early nineteenth century to find the first solid empirical support for atomism. Without stretching the point too far, it is fair to say that in 1800 the atomic theory was something physicists believed but couldn't
(50) prove, while the chemists were proving it but didn't believe it.

Passage 2

The discovery that the universe is expanding was one of the great intellectual revelations of the twentieth century. With hindsight, it is easy to
(55) wonder why no one had thought of it before. Newton, and others, should have realized that a static universe would soon start to contract under the influence of gravity. But suppose instead the universe is expanding. If it was expanding fairly
(60) slowly, the force of gravity would cause it eventually to stop expanding and then to start contracting. However, if it was expanding at more than a certain critical rate, gravity would never be strong enough to stop it, and the universe would
(65) continue to expand forever. This is a bit like what happens when one fires a rocket upward from the surface of the earth. If it has a fairly low speed, gravity will eventually stop the rocket and it will start falling back. On the other hand, if the rocket
(70) has more than a certain critical speed (about seven miles per second), gravity will not be strong enough to pull it back, so it will keep going away from the earth forever. This behavior of the universe could have been predicted from Newton's theory of
(75) gravity at any time in the nineteenth, the eighteenth, or even the late seventeenth centuries. Yet so strong was the belief in a static universe that it persisted into the early twentieth century. Even Einstein, when he formulated the general theory of
(80) relativity in 1915, was so sure that the universe had to be static that he modified his theory to make this possible, introducing a so-called cosmological constant into his equations. Einstein introduced a new "antigravity" force, which, unlike other forces,
(85) did not come from any particular source, but was built into the very fabric of space-time. He claimed that space-time had an inbuilt tendency to expand, and this could be made to balance exactly the attraction of all the matter in the universe, so that a
(90) static universe would result.

SECTION 7

QUESTIONS	EXPLANATIONS

1 In line 6, the word "promulgated" most nearly means

(A) plagiarized
(B) dismissed
(C) protected
(D) obscured
(E) promoted

1. Pam's answer is E.
Go back to the passage, find the word *promulgated*, and cross it out. Then read the sentence and come up with your own word. The first part of the sentence is saying something very positive about Democritus's ideas, so we need a positive word. That means you can eliminate A, B, and D. It doesn't make sense to say that Democritus's ideas were *protected*, so you can cross out C. E is the only choice left.

2 From the information presented in Passage 1, which of the following can be properly inferred about Democritus?

(A) Although his view was initially met with skepticism, Democritus was among the first to advocate an atomic theory.
(B) Although he was more known for his work in politics, Democritus also made important scientific discoveries.
(C) His ideas were incompatible with those of Galileo and Newton.
(D) Democritus was unduly credited with being the father of Greek atomism.
(E) Democritus was more known for his discovery of calculus than for his theory of atomism.

2. Pam's answer is A.
The best way to find the answer to this question is to use POE.
   Answer choice B says that Democritus was known for his work in politics, but this is not mentioned anywhere in the passage.
   Answer choice C says that his ideas were incompatible with those of Galileo and Newton, which contradicts lines 33–34.
   Answer choice D says that Democritus was unduly credited, but the passage is all about giving him proper credit.
   Answer choice E says that Democritus was known for his discovery of calculus, which is not said anywhere in the passage, and it also happens to be completely false.
   That only leaves A.

SECTION 7

3 Which of the following does the author of Passage 1 suggest about the physical world?

(A) The composition of everyday things will remain a mystery forever.

(B) Understanding matter is much simpler than scientists once believed.

(C) Despite the diversity of the physical world, all matter may have a single underlying component.

(D) Although physicists use simple models to describe matter, the principles underlying the models point to a more complex reality.

(E) The theories developed by Democritus accurately explain all aspects of everyday matter.

3. Pam's answer is C.

According to lines 22–26, *underlying all the complex richness, texture, and variety of our everyday life might be a level of reality of stark simplicity, with the turmoil we perceive representing only the nearly infinite arrangements of a smaller number of constituents*. This sentence is paraphrased perfectly in answer choice C.

Another way to answer this question is to use POE:

Answer choice A is much too extreme. Will the composition of everyday things remain a mystery *forever*? Forever is a very long time.

Answer choice B confuses the idea of simplicity in the passage. Even if all matter does have a single underlying component, that doesn't mean that *understanding* it is simple.

Answer choice D contradicts the lines from the passage we quoted above. Scientists hope their models point to an underlying *simplicity*, not an underlying *complexity*.

Answer choice E is also too extreme. Did Democritus's theories explain every single matter? Not likely.

4 The "obsession" which the author describes in line 22 can best be described as

(A) Democritus' desire to see his ideas accepted by the scientific community

(B) physicists' search for Democritus' original writings on atoms

(C) the author's own search for the principles underlying matter

(D) early nineteenth century chemists' search for the first solid evidence of atomism

(E) modern scientists' quest for a simple unifying property of everyday matter

4. Pam's answer is E.

The same lines that we just used for question 3 contain the answer to this question as well. The *obsession* referred to in the passage is the search for *a level of stark simplicity* underlying all *the complex richness* of our everyday life. This idea is paraphrased perfectly in answer choice E, which says that scientists are on a quest for *a simple unifying property of everyday matter*.

The passage is talking about something that is *today almost an obsession*, so choices A and D are wrong because they are not about modern science.

Choices C and D are wrong because they aren't mentioned anywhere in the passage. If it's not in the passage, then it's not Pam's answer.

SECTION 7

QUESTIONS	EXPLANATIONS

5 Which of the following can be inferred from Passage 2 about the expanding universe?

(A) It was incompatible with a theory widely accepted in the nineteenth century.

(B) Newton discovered it during his work with gravity.

(C) Most scientists believe that the idea is no longer tenable.

(D) The existence of gravity makes it impossible for the universe to expand.

(E) The expanding universe theory cannot be proven.

5. Pam's answer is A.

According the passage, *the discovery that the universe is expanding was one of the great intellectual revelations of the twentieth century.*

Answer choice B is wrong because Newton wasn't alive in the twentieth century.

Answer choice C isn't right because the idea was discovered, and is still accepted, by modern physicists.

You can eliminate answer choice D because it's too extreme and contradicts the passage.

Lastly, answer choice E is also too extreme. That only leaves choice A.

6 In line 63 the term "certain critical rate" refers to

(A) the rate at which scientific knowledge is growing

(B) an urgent problem which needs solving

(C) the speed at which a rocket must travel in order to move away from the earth

(D) the speed necessary to equal the force of gravity's pull

(E) the meeting point of gravity and the universe

6. Pam's answer is D.

According to lines 59–65, if the universe *was expanding fairy slowly, the force of gravity would cause it eventually to stop expanding…However, if it was expanding at more than a certain critical rate, gravity would never be strong enough to stop it.*

So the *critical rate* is the rate at which the universe would need to be expanding in order to overcome the force of gravity. This idea is perfectly paraphrased in answer choice D.

Answer choices A and B are wrong because neither is mentioned in the passage.

The passage mentions a critical speed necessary for a rocket to escape earth's gravity, but that's in line 70, not line 63; therefore, choice C doesn't answer the question.

Answer choice E doesn't make sense because it confuses several of the concepts discussed in the passage. Go back and read carefully.

SECTION 7

QUESTIONS	EXPLANATIONS

7 The author of Passage 2 mentions Newton in order to

(A) point out the ignorance of many physicists

(B) give one example of a proponent of the expanding universe theory

(C) illustrate the point that the expanding universe theory might have been discovered earlier

(D) provide evidence that the universe is not expanding

(E) show the consequences of a scientist's disregard for a new theory

7. Pam's answer is C.
Go back to the passage and find where Newton is mentioned. According to lines 54–58, *With hindsight, it is easy to wonder why no one thought of it before. Newton, and others, should have realized that a static universe would soon start to contract under the influence of gravity.*

So the passage uses Newton as an example of a scientist who might have come up with the idea of an expanding universe before it was actually discovered in the twentieth century. This idea is paraphrased in answer choice C.

Answer choice A is wrong because Pam would never suggest that many physicists are *ignorant*. Remember, Pam has great respect for scientists.

Newton wasn't a proponent of the expanding-universe theory, so you can discount answer choice B.

Answer choice D contradicts the main idea of the passage. According to the author, the universe *is* expanding. Go back and read the first sentence of the passage.

Answer choice E is wrong because Newton didn't *disregard* the expanding-universe theory. There was no such theory back then!

8 The author's reference to a rocket ship (lines 66–73) serves to illustrate

(A) the implications of an expanding universe

(B) the forces governing the universe's gradual expansion

(C) the similarity of the energy released by the universe and that released by rockets

(D) the way in which gravity prevents the universe from expanding

(E) the theory of a static universe

8. Pam's answer is B.
According to lines 62–67, if the universe *was expanding at more than a certain critical rate, gravity would never be strong enough to stop it…This is a bit like what happens when one fires a rocket upward from the surface.* So the rocket is being used as an example of how the force of gravity applies to the idea of an expanding universe. Choice B paraphrases this nicely.

Answer choice A is wrong because the rocket ship example is not an *implication* of the expanding universe. The rocket ship is simply an example used to illustrate the implications of *gravity* on the expanding-universe theory.

Answer choice C makes no sense. Is the energy released by a rocket ship similar to the energy released by an entire universe? No way!

Answer choices D and E contradict the main idea of Passage 2. According to the author, the universe *is* expanding.

SECTION 7

QUESTIONS	EXPLANATIONS

9 In Passage 2, the author's description of Einstein's general theory of relativity serves to

(A) bolster the author's theory that the universe is expanding

(B) show that modern scientists were reluctant to abandon the theory of a static universe

(C) indicate the creativity that Einstein brought to his work

(D) question the validity of the theory of the expanding universe

(E) underscore Einstein's reliance on Newtonian physics

9. Pam's answer is B.

The lead words for this question are *Einstein's general theory of relativity*, which should lead you back to lines 78–82. According to these lines, *Even Einstein, when he formulated the general theory of relativity in 1915, was so sure that the universe had to be static that he modified his theory to make this possible.*

So the passage is showing us that, among modern scientists, even Einstein wanted to maintain the idea that the universe is static. He even changed his famous theory of relativity to make this possible. This idea is perfectly paraphrased in answer choice B.

Answer choice A is wrong because the expanding-universe theory is not the *author's* theory.

Answer choice C is incorrect because the passage says nothing about Einstein's creativity. The point is that Einstein disagreed with the expanding-universe theory.

Answer choice D is wrong because the passage never suggests that the expanding-universe theory may not be valid. Just because Einstein didn't agree with the theory doesn't mean it's wrong.

Answer choice E strays too far from the main idea. Remember, the passage is about the expanding-universe theory, not about Einstein's relation to Newton.

SECTION 7

QUESTIONS	EXPLANATIONS

10 The term "cosmological constant" (lines 82–83) refers to

(A) a mathematical constant employed by Einstein to bring his theories in line with the idea of a static universe

(B) an equation used by Einstein to debunk Newton's ideas about universal expansion

(C) a theory developed by opponents of Einstein's general theory of relativity

(D) the mathematical model that was used to disprove Newtonian physics

(E) the theory that the mass of all matter in the universe must remain the same

10. Pam's answer is A.
According to lines 78–82, Einstein wanted so much to maintain the idea of the static universe that he changed his theory of relativity to make this possible. The change he made was to introduce the *so-called cosmological constant*. That is exactly what answer choice A says.

Answer choice B is wrong because Newton didn't have any ideas about the expanding-universe theory. The theory didn't exist back in Newton's time!

Answer choice C is off the mark because the *cosmological constant* is *part* of Einstein's theory of relativity, not an idea developed by his opponents. Read more carefully.

You can't pick answer choice D either, because Newtonian physics has never been disproved, and this is not suggested anywhere in the passage. Remember, the passage is about the expanding-universe theory. Don't forget the main idea.

Answer choice E is incorrect because the passage is not about the *mass* of all matter. Again, everything in the passage relates to the expanding-universe theory.

11 In the last line of Passage 2 the word "static" most nearly means

(A) charged
(B) conflicting
(C) particulate
(D) unchanging
(E) dynamic

11. Pam's answer is D.
Go back to the passage, find the word *static*, and cross it out. Then read the sentence and come up with your own word. According to the passage, Einstein and many other modern scientists were against the idea of an expanding universe. That means they must have believed in a universe that wasn't expanding. So we can put *not expanding* in place of *static*. The best match for *not expanding* in the answer choices is *unchanging*.

The other answer choices are wrong because they don't make any sense in context.

SECTION 7

QUESTIONS	EXPLANATIONS

12 The authors of both passages would most probably agree with which of the following statements?

(A) Democritus and Newton both struggled to see their theories accepted by others.

(B) Neither Democritus nor Newton received credit for his theories.

(C) Newton, Einstein and Democritus are all responsible in part for setting back modern physics.

(D) The atomic model of matter and the theory of the expanding universe are mutually exclusive.

(E) Scientists may adopt particular theories in spite of weak or contradictory evidence.

12. Pam's answer is E.
Since this question involves both passages, you should definitely do it last. The easiest way to answer this question is to use POE.

Answer choice A is only about Passage 1, so you can eliminate it. Newton certainly received credit for his theories, so you can eliminate choice B. Answer choice C is rather insulting to all three scientists mentioned (and Pam never insults scientists), so you can eliminate it. Between choices D and E, choice E is better because it's a *may* answer, and Pam likes wishy-washy answers.

13 Based on the information in both passages, a difference between atomism and the expanding universe theory is

(A) the idea of atomism can be traced to the ancient Greeks, while the model of the expanding universe is a relatively recent theory

(B) atomism is easier to understand and explore than the static universe theory

(C) atomism was developed for political reasons, while the static universe theory is purely scientific

(D) the theory of atomism has been proven, while the static universe theory is now thought to be incorrect

(E) the static universe theory is more adaptable to modern science than is the atomistic theory

13. Pam's answer is A.
According to the passages, Democritus, an ancient Greek scientist, first came up with the theory of atomism, while the expanding-universe theory was first put forth in the twentieth century. That is one clear difference between the two theories, and it also happens to be exactly what answer choice A says.

Choice B is wrong because the passages never suggest that atomism is *easier* to understand than the expanding-universe theory. The comparison is never made.

Choice C is way off base. There is no mention of *politics* anywhere in either passage.

Choice D is too extreme. The passage never says that the theory of atomism had been *proven*. Remember, it's just a theory.

Choice E contradicts the main idea of the passage. Modern science has rejected the static-universe theory in favor of the expanding-universe theory.

The Princeton Review

1

YOUR NAME: _____
(Print)
Last   First   M.I.

SIGNATURE: _____   DATE: __ / __ / __

HOME ADDRESS: _____
(Print)
Number and Street

City   State   Zip Code

PHONE NO.: _____
(Print)

IMPORTANT: Please fill in these boxes exactly as shown on the back cover of your test book.

2. TEST FORM

3. TEST CODE

4. REGISTRATION NUMBER

5. YOUR NAME

First 4 letters of last name				FIRST INIT	MID INIT
A	A	A	A	A	A
B	B	B	B	B	B
C	C	C	C	C	C
D	D	D	D	D	D
E	E	E	E	E	E
F	F	F	F	F	F
G	G	G	G	G	G
H	H	H	H	H	H
I	I	I	I	I	I
J	J	J	J	J	J
K	K	K	K	K	K
L	L	L	L	L	L
M	M	M	M	M	M
N	N	N	N	N	N
O	O	O	O	O	O
P	P	P	P	P	P
Q	Q	Q	Q	Q	Q
R	R	R	R	R	R
S	S	S	S	S	S
T	T	T	T	T	T
U	U	U	U	U	U
V	V	V	V	V	V
W	W	W	W	W	W
X	X	X	X	X	X
Y	Y	Y	Y	Y	Y
Z	Z	Z	Z	Z	Z

6. DATE OF BIRTH

Month		Day		Year	
JAN					
FEB					
MAR	0	0	0	0	
APR	1	1	1	1	
MAY	2	2	2	2	
JUN	3	3	3	3	
JUL		4	4	4	
AUG		5	5	5	
SEP		6	6	6	
OCT		7	7	7	
NOV		8	8	8	
DEC		9	9	9	

Test Code bubbles: 0 A 0 0 0 0 0 0 0 0 0 / 1 B 1 1 1 1 1 1 1 1 1 / 2 C 2 2 2 2 2 2 2 2 2 / 3 D 3 3 3 3 3 3 3 3 3 / 4 E 4 4 4 4 4 4 4 4 4 / 5 F 5 5 5 5 5 5 5 5 5 / 6 G 6 6 6 6 6 6 6 6 6 / 7 7 7 7 7 7 7 7 7 / 8 8 8 8 8 8 8 8 8 / 9 9 9 9 9 9 9 9 9

7. SEX

- MALE
- FEMALE

THE PRINCETON REVIEW

© 1995 The Princeton Review
FORM NO. 00001-PR

Start with number 1 for each new section. If a section has fewer questions than answer spaces, leave the extra answer spaces blank.

SECTION 1

1 A B C D E	11 A B C D E	21 A B C D E	31 A B C D E
2 A B C D E	12 A B C D E	22 A B C D E	32 A B C D E
3 A B C D E	13 A B C D E	23 A B C D E	33 A B C D E
4 A B C D E	14 A B C D E	24 A B C D E	34 A B C D E
5 A B C D E	15 A B C D E	25 A B C D E	35 A B C D E
6 A B C D E	16 A B C D E	26 A B C D E	36 A B C D E
7 A B C D E	17 A B C D E	27 A B C D E	37 A B C D E
8 A B C D E	18 A B C D E	28 A B C D E	38 A B C D E
9 A B C D E	19 A B C D E	29 A B C D E	39 A B C D E
10 A B C D E	20 A B C D E	30 A B C D E	40 A B C D E

SECTION 2

1 A B C D E	11 A B C D E	21 A B C D E	31 A B C D E
2 A B C D E	12 A B C D E	22 A B C D E	32 A B C D E
3 A B C D E	13 A B C D E	23 A B C D E	33 A B C D E
4 A B C D E	14 A B C D E	24 A B C D E	34 A B C D E
5 A B C D E	15 A B C D E	25 A B C D E	35 A B C D E
6 A B C D E	16 A B C D E	26 A B C D E	36 A B C D E
7 A B C D E	17 A B C D E	27 A B C D E	37 A B C D E
8 A B C D E	18 A B C D E	28 A B C D E	38 A B C D E
9 A B C D E	19 A B C D E	29 A B C D E	39 A B C D E
10 A B C D E	20 A B C D E	30 A B C D E	40 A B C D E

DO NOT MARK IN THIS AREA

Start with number 1 for each new section. If a section has fewer questions than answer spaces, leave the extra answer spaces blank.

SECTION 3

1 ⊂A⊃ ⊂B⊃ ⊂C⊃ ⊂D⊃ ⊂E⊃	16 ⊂A⊃ ⊂B⊃ ⊂C⊃ ⊂D⊃ ⊂E⊃	31 ⊂A⊃ ⊂B⊃ ⊂C⊃ ⊂D⊃ ⊂E⊃
2 ⊂A⊃ ⊂B⊃ ⊂C⊃ ⊂D⊃ ⊂E⊃	17 ⊂A⊃ ⊂B⊃ ⊂C⊃ ⊂D⊃ ⊂E⊃	32 ⊂A⊃ ⊂B⊃ ⊂C⊃ ⊂D⊃ ⊂E⊃
3 ⊂A⊃ ⊂B⊃ ⊂C⊃ ⊂D⊃ ⊂E⊃	18 ⊂A⊃ ⊂B⊃ ⊂C⊃ ⊂D⊃ ⊂E⊃	33 ⊂A⊃ ⊂B⊃ ⊂C⊃ ⊂D⊃ ⊂E⊃
4 ⊂A⊃ ⊂B⊃ ⊂C⊃ ⊂D⊃ ⊂E⊃	19 ⊂A⊃ ⊂B⊃ ⊂C⊃ ⊂D⊃ ⊂E⊃	34 ⊂A⊃ ⊂B⊃ ⊂C⊃ ⊂D⊃ ⊂E⊃
5 ⊂A⊃ ⊂B⊃ ⊂C⊃ ⊂D⊃ ⊂E⊃	20 ⊂A⊃ ⊂B⊃ ⊂C⊃ ⊂D⊃ ⊂E⊃	35 ⊂A⊃ ⊂B⊃ ⊂C⊃ ⊂D⊃ ⊂E⊃
6 ⊂A⊃ ⊂B⊃ ⊂C⊃ ⊂D⊃ ⊂E⊃	21 ⊂A⊃ ⊂B⊃ ⊂C⊃ ⊂D⊃ ⊂E⊃	36 ⊂A⊃ ⊂B⊃ ⊂C⊃ ⊂D⊃ ⊂E⊃
7 ⊂A⊃ ⊂B⊃ ⊂C⊃ ⊂D⊃ ⊂E⊃	22 ⊂A⊃ ⊂B⊃ ⊂C⊃ ⊂D⊃ ⊂E⊃	37 ⊂A⊃ ⊂B⊃ ⊂C⊃ ⊂D⊃ ⊂E⊃
8 ⊂A⊃ ⊂B⊃ ⊂C⊃ ⊂D⊃ ⊂E⊃	23 ⊂A⊃ ⊂B⊃ ⊂C⊃ ⊂D⊃ ⊂E⊃	38 ⊂A⊃ ⊂B⊃ ⊂C⊃ ⊂D⊃ ⊂E⊃
9 ⊂A⊃ ⊂B⊃ ⊂C⊃ ⊂D⊃ ⊂E⊃	24 ⊂A⊃ ⊂B⊃ ⊂C⊃ ⊂D⊃ ⊂E⊃	39 ⊂A⊃ ⊂B⊃ ⊂C⊃ ⊂D⊃ ⊂E⊃
10 ⊂A⊃ ⊂B⊃ ⊂C⊃ ⊂D⊃ ⊂E⊃	25 ⊂A⊃ ⊂B⊃ ⊂C⊃ ⊂D⊃ ⊂E⊃	40 ⊂A⊃ ⊂B⊃ ⊂C⊃ ⊂D⊃ ⊂E⊃
11 ⊂A⊃ ⊂B⊃ ⊂C⊃ ⊂D⊃ ⊂E⊃	26 ⊂A⊃ ⊂B⊃ ⊂C⊃ ⊂D⊃ ⊂E⊃	
12 ⊂A⊃ ⊂B⊃ ⊂C⊃ ⊂D⊃ ⊂E⊃	27 ⊂A⊃ ⊂B⊃ ⊂C⊃ ⊂D⊃ ⊂E⊃	
13 ⊂A⊃ ⊂B⊃ ⊂C⊃ ⊂D⊃ ⊂E⊃	28 ⊂A⊃ ⊂B⊃ ⊂C⊃ ⊂D⊃ ⊂E⊃	
14 ⊂A⊃ ⊂B⊃ ⊂C⊃ ⊂D⊃ ⊂E⊃	29 ⊂A⊃ ⊂B⊃ ⊂C⊃ ⊂D⊃ ⊂E⊃	
15 ⊂A⊃ ⊂B⊃ ⊂C⊃ ⊂D⊃ ⊂E⊃	30 ⊂A⊃ ⊂B⊃ ⊂C⊃ ⊂D⊃ ⊂E⊃	

If section 3 of your test booklet has math questions that are not multiple-choice, continue to item 16 below. Otherwise, continue to item 16 above.

ONLY ANSWERS ENTERED IN THE OVALS IN EACH GRID AREA WILL BE SCORED.
YOU WILL NOT RECEIVE CREDIT FOR ANYTHING WRITTEN IN THE BOXES ABOVE THE OVALS.

16 17 18 19 20

Each grid:
⊂/⊃ ⊂/⊃
⊂.⊃ ⊂.⊃ ⊂.⊃ ⊂.⊃
⊂0⊃ ⊂0⊃ ⊂0⊃
⊂1⊃ ⊂1⊃ ⊂1⊃ ⊂1⊃
⊂2⊃ ⊂2⊃ ⊂2⊃ ⊂2⊃
⊂3⊃ ⊂3⊃ ⊂3⊃ ⊂3⊃
⊂4⊃ ⊂4⊃ ⊂4⊃ ⊂4⊃
⊂5⊃ ⊂5⊃ ⊂5⊃ ⊂5⊃
⊂6⊃ ⊂6⊃ ⊂6⊃ ⊂6⊃
⊂7⊃ ⊂7⊃ ⊂7⊃ ⊂7⊃
⊂8⊃ ⊂8⊃ ⊂8⊃ ⊂8⊃
⊂9⊃ ⊂9⊃ ⊂9⊃ ⊂9⊃

21 22 23 24 25

Each grid:
⊂/⊃ ⊂/⊃
⊂.⊃ ⊂.⊃ ⊂.⊃ ⊂.⊃
⊂0⊃ ⊂0⊃ ⊂0⊃
⊂1⊃ ⊂1⊃ ⊂1⊃ ⊂1⊃
⊂2⊃ ⊂2⊃ ⊂2⊃ ⊂2⊃
⊂3⊃ ⊂3⊃ ⊂3⊃ ⊂3⊃
⊂4⊃ ⊂4⊃ ⊂4⊃ ⊂4⊃
⊂5⊃ ⊂5⊃ ⊂5⊃ ⊂5⊃
⊂6⊃ ⊂6⊃ ⊂6⊃ ⊂6⊃
⊂7⊃ ⊂7⊃ ⊂7⊃ ⊂7⊃
⊂8⊃ ⊂8⊃ ⊂8⊃ ⊂8⊃
⊂9⊃ ⊂9⊃ ⊂9⊃ ⊂9⊃

BE SURE TO ERASE ANY ERRORS OR STRAY MARKS COMPLETELY.

PLEASE PRINT
YOUR INITIALS

First	Middle	Last

Start with number 1 for each new section. If a section has fewer questions than answer spaces, leave the extra answer spaces blank.

SECTION 4

1 A B C D E	16 A B C D E	31 A B C D E
2 A B C D E	17 A B C D E	32 A B C D E
3 A B C D E	18 A B C D E	33 A B C D E
4 A B C D E	19 A B C D E	34 A B C D E
5 A B C D E	20 A B C D E	35 A B C D E
6 A B C D E	21 A B C D E	36 A B C D E
7 A B C D E	22 A B C D E	37 A B C D E
8 A B C D E	23 A B C D E	38 A B C D E
9 A B C D E	24 A B C D E	39 A B C D E
10 A B C D E	25 A B C D E	40 A B C D E
11 A B C D E	26 A B C D E	
12 A B C D E	27 A B C D E	
13 A B C D E	28 A B C D E	
14 A B C D E	29 A B C D E	
15 A B C D E	30 A B C D E	

If section 4 of your test booklet has math questions that are not multiple-choice, continue to item 16 below. Otherwise, continue to item 16 above.

ONLY ANSWERS ENTERED IN THE OVALS IN EACH GRID AREA WILL BE SCORED.
YOU WILL NOT RECEIVE CREDIT FOR ANYTHING WRITTEN IN THE BOXES ABOVE THE OVALS.

16 17 18 19 20

(Grid-in response areas with fraction bars and decimal points, digits 0–9)

21 22 23 24 25

(Grid-in response areas with fraction bars and decimal points, digits 0–9)

BE SURE TO ERASE ANY ERRORS OR STRAY MARKS COMPLETELY.

PLEASE PRINT YOUR INITIALS

First Middle Last

Start with number 1 for each new section. If a section has fewer questions than answer spaces, leave the extra answer spaces blank.

SECTION 5

1 A B C D E	11 A B C D E	21 A B C D E	31 A B C D E
2 A B C D E	12 A B C D E	22 A B C D E	32 A B C D E
3 A B C D E	13 A B C D E	23 A B C D E	33 A B C D E
4 A B C D E	14 A B C D E	24 A B C D E	34 A B C D E
5 A B C D E	15 A B C D E	25 A B C D E	35 A B C D E
6 A B C D E	16 A B C D E	26 A B C D E	36 A B C D E
7 A B C D E	17 A B C D E	27 A B C D E	37 A B C D E
8 A B C D E	18 A B C D E	28 A B C D E	38 A B C D E
9 A B C D E	19 A B C D E	29 A B C D E	39 A B C D E
10 A B C D E	20 A B C D E	30 A B C D E	40 A B C D E

SECTION 6

1 A B C D E	11 A B C D E	21 A B C D E	31 A B C D E
2 A B C D E	12 A B C D E	22 A B C D E	32 A B C D E
3 A B C D E	13 A B C D E	23 A B C D E	33 A B C D E
4 A B C D E	14 A B C D E	24 A B C D E	34 A B C D E
5 A B C D E	15 A B C D E	25 A B C D E	35 A B C D E
6 A B C D E	16 A B C D E	26 A B C D E	36 A B C D E
7 A B C D E	17 A B C D E	27 A B C D E	37 A B C D E
8 A B C D E	18 A B C D E	28 A B C D E	38 A B C D E
9 A B C D E	19 A B C D E	29 A B C D E	39 A B C D E
10 A B C D E	20 A B C D E	30 A B C D E	40 A B C D E

SECTION 7

1 A B C D E	11 A B C D E	21 A B C D E	31 A B C D E
2 A B C D E	12 A B C D E	22 A B C D E	32 A B C D E
3 A B C D E	13 A B C D E	23 A B C D E	33 A B C D E
4 A B C D E	14 A B C D E	24 A B C D E	34 A B C D E
5 A B C D E	15 A B C D E	25 A B C D E	35 A B C D E
6 A B C D E	16 A B C D E	26 A B C D E	36 A B C D E
7 A B C D E	17 A B C D E	27 A B C D E	37 A B C D E
8 A B C D E	18 A B C D E	28 A B C D E	38 A B C D E
9 A B C D E	19 A B C D E	29 A B C D E	39 A B C D E
10 A B C D E	20 A B C D E	30 A B C D E	40 A B C D E

CERTIFICATION STATEMENT
   Copy in longhand the statement below and sign your name as you would an official document. DO NOT PRINT.

   I hereby agree with The Princeton Review that the SAT is nothing to fear and certify that I am the person who will conquer it.

_____

_____

_____

SIGNATURE: _____   DATE: _____

The Princeton Review

1

YOUR NAME: _____
(Print)   Last   First   M.I.

SIGNATURE: _____   DATE: __ / __ / __

HOME ADDRESS: _____
(Print)   Number and Street

_____
City   State   Zip Code

PHONE NO.: _____
(Print)

IMPORTANT: Please fill in these boxes exactly as shown on the back cover of your test book.

2. TEST FORM

3. TEST CODE   **4. REGISTRATION NUMBER**

5. YOUR NAME

First 4 letters of last name				FIRST INIT	MID INIT
A	A	A	A	A	A
B	B	B	B	B	B
C	C	C	C	C	C
D	D	D	D	D	D
E	E	E	E	E	E
F	F	F	F	F	F
G	G	G	G	G	G
H	H	H	H	H	H
I	I	I	I	I	I
J	J	J	J	J	J
K	K	K	K	K	K
L	L	L	L	L	L
M	M	M	M	M	M
N	N	N	N	N	N
O	O	O	O	O	O
P	P	P	P	P	P
Q	Q	Q	Q	Q	Q
R	R	R	R	R	R
S	S	S	S	S	S
T	T	T	T	T	T
U	U	U	U	U	U
V	V	V	V	V	V
W	W	W	W	W	W
X	X	X	X	X	X
Y	Y	Y	Y	Y	Y
Z	Z	Z	Z	Z	Z

6. DATE OF BIRTH

Month	Day	Year
JAN		
FEB		
MAR	0 0	0 0
APR	1 1	1 1
MAY	2 2	2 2
JUN	3 3	3 3
JUL	4 4	4
AUG	5 5	5
SEP	6 6	6
OCT	7 7	7
NOV	8 8	8
DEC	9 9	9

Test Code bubbles: 0 A 0 0 0 / 1 B 1 1 1 / 2 C 2 2 2 / 3 D 3 3 3 / 4 E 4 4 4 / 5 F 5 5 5 / 6 G 6 6 6 / 7 7 7 / 8 8 8 / 9 9 9

Registration Number bubbles: 0–9 columns

7. SEX

MALE
FEMALE

THE PRINCETON REVIEW

© 1995 The Princeton Review
FORM NO. 00001-PR

Start with number 1 for each new section. If a section has fewer questions than answer spaces, leave the extra answer spaces blank.

SECTION 1

1 A B C D E	11 A B C D E	21 A B C D E	31 A B C D E
2 A B C D E	12 A B C D E	22 A B C D E	32 A B C D E
3 A B C D E	13 A B C D E	23 A B C D E	33 A B C D E
4 A B C D E	14 A B C D E	24 A B C D E	34 A B C D E
5 A B C D E	15 A B C D E	25 A B C D E	35 A B C D E
6 A B C D E	16 A B C D E	26 A B C D E	36 A B C D E
7 A B C D E	17 A B C D E	27 A B C D E	37 A B C D E
8 A B C D E	18 A B C D E	28 A B C D E	38 A B C D E
9 A B C D E	19 A B C D E	29 A B C D E	39 A B C D E
10 A B C D E	20 A B C D E	30 A B C D E	40 A B C D E

SECTION 2

1 A B C D E	11 A B C D E	21 A B C D E	31 A B C D E
2 A B C D E	12 A B C D E	22 A B C D E	32 A B C D E
3 A B C D E	13 A B C D E	23 A B C D E	33 A B C D E
4 A B C D E	14 A B C D E	24 A B C D E	34 A B C D E
5 A B C D E	15 A B C D E	25 A B C D E	35 A B C D E
6 A B C D E	16 A B C D E	26 A B C D E	36 A B C D E
7 A B C D E	17 A B C D E	27 A B C D E	37 A B C D E
8 A B C D E	18 A B C D E	28 A B C D E	38 A B C D E
9 A B C D E	19 A B C D E	29 A B C D E	39 A B C D E
10 A B C D E	20 A B C D E	30 A B C D E	40 A B C D E

DO NOT MARK IN THIS AREA

Start with number 1 for each new section. If a section has fewer questions than answer spaces, leave the extra answer spaces blank.

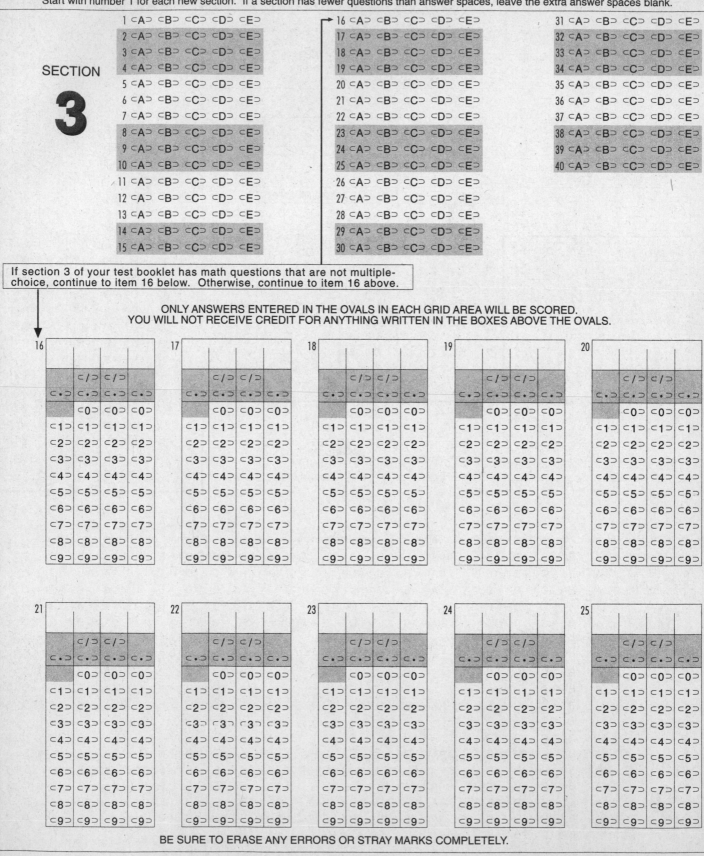

SECTION

3

1 cAɔ cBɔ cCɔ cDɔ cEɔ
2 cAɔ cBɔ cCɔ cDɔ cEɔ
3 cAɔ cBɔ cCɔ cDɔ cEɔ
4 cAɔ cBɔ cCɔ cDɔ cEɔ
5 cAɔ cBɔ cCɔ cDɔ cEɔ
6 cAɔ cBɔ cCɔ cDɔ cEɔ
7 cAɔ cBɔ cCɔ cDɔ cEɔ
8 cAɔ cBɔ cCɔ cDɔ cEɔ
9 cAɔ cBɔ cCɔ cDɔ cEɔ
10 cAɔ cBɔ cCɔ cDɔ cEɔ
11 cAɔ cBɔ cCɔ cDɔ cEɔ
12 cAɔ cBɔ cCɔ cDɔ cEɔ
13 cAɔ cBɔ cCɔ cDɔ cEɔ
14 cAɔ cBɔ cCɔ cDɔ cEɔ
15 cAɔ cBɔ cCɔ cDɔ cEɔ

16 cAɔ cBɔ cCɔ cDɔ cEɔ
17 cAɔ cBɔ cCɔ cDɔ cEɔ
18 cAɔ cBɔ cCɔ cDɔ cEɔ
19 cAɔ cBɔ cCɔ cDɔ cEɔ
20 cAɔ cBɔ cCɔ cDɔ cEɔ
21 cAɔ cBɔ cCɔ cDɔ cEɔ
22 cAɔ cBɔ cCɔ cDɔ cEɔ
23 cAɔ cBɔ cCɔ cDɔ cEɔ
24 cAɔ cBɔ cCɔ cDɔ cEɔ
25 cAɔ cBɔ cCɔ cDɔ cEɔ
26 cAɔ cBɔ cCɔ cDɔ cEɔ
27 cAɔ cBɔ cCɔ cDɔ cEɔ
28 cAɔ cBɔ cCɔ cDɔ cEɔ
29 cAɔ cBɔ cCɔ cDɔ cEɔ
30 cAɔ cBɔ cCɔ cDɔ cEɔ

31 cAɔ cBɔ cCɔ cDɔ cEɔ
32 cAɔ cBɔ cCɔ cDɔ cEɔ
33 cAɔ cBɔ cCɔ cDɔ cEɔ
34 cAɔ cBɔ cCɔ cDɔ cEɔ
35 cAɔ cBɔ cCɔ cDɔ cEɔ
36 cAɔ cBɔ cCɔ cDɔ cEɔ
37 cAɔ cBɔ cCɔ cDɔ cEɔ
38 cAɔ cBɔ cCɔ cDɔ cEɔ
39 cAɔ cBɔ cCɔ cDɔ cEɔ
40 cAɔ cBɔ cCɔ cDɔ cEɔ

If section 3 of your test booklet has math questions that are not multiple-choice, continue to item 16 below. Otherwise, continue to item 16 above.

ONLY ANSWERS ENTERED IN THE OVALS IN EACH GRID AREA WILL BE SCORED.
YOU WILL NOT RECEIVE CREDIT FOR ANYTHING WRITTEN IN THE BOXES ABOVE THE OVALS.

BE SURE TO ERASE ANY ERRORS OR STRAY MARKS COMPLETELY.

PLEASE PRINT
YOUR INITIALS

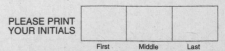

First   Middle   Last

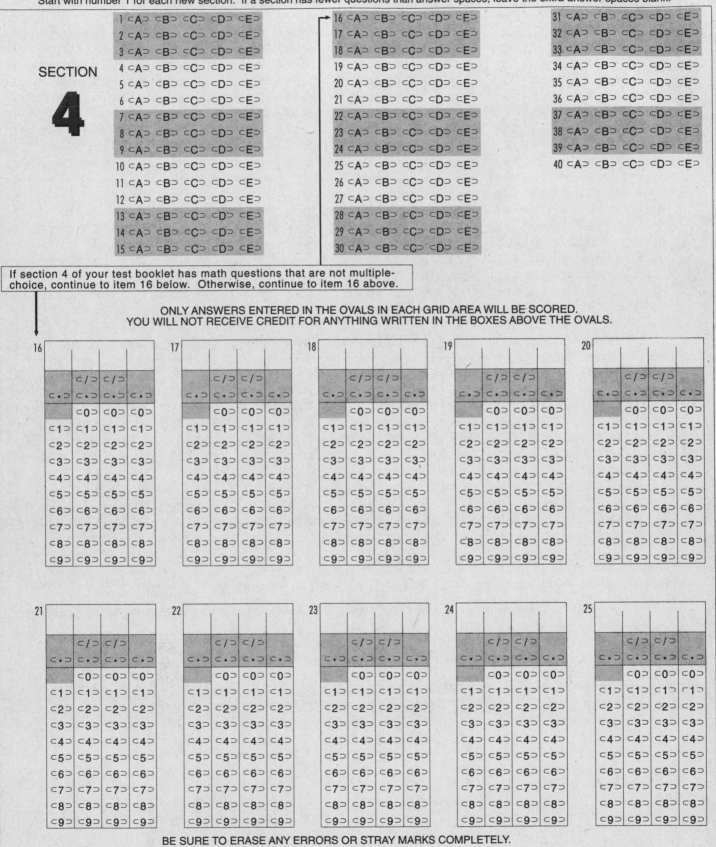

Start with number 1 for each new section. If a section has fewer questions than answer spaces, leave the extra answer spaces blank.

SECTION 4

1 A B C D E
2 A B C D E
3 A B C D E
4 A B C D E
5 A B C D E
6 A B C D E
7 A B C D E
8 A B C D E
9 A B C D E
10 A B C D E
11 A B C D E
12 A B C D E
13 A B C D E
14 A B C D E
15 A B C D E

16 A B C D E
17 A B C D E
18 A B C D E
19 A B C D E
20 A B C D E
21 A B C D E
22 A B C D E
23 A B C D E
24 A B C D E
25 A B C D E
26 A B C D E
27 A B C D E
28 A B C D E
29 A B C D E
30 A B C D E

31 A B C D E
32 A B C D E
33 A B C D E
34 A B C D E
35 A B C D E
36 A B C D E
37 A B C D E
38 A B C D E
39 A B C D E
40 A B C D E

If section 4 of your test booklet has math questions that are not multiple-choice, continue to item 16 below. Otherwise, continue to item 16 above.

ONLY ANSWERS ENTERED IN THE OVALS IN EACH GRID AREA WILL BE SCORED.
YOU WILL NOT RECEIVE CREDIT FOR ANYTHING WRITTEN IN THE BOXES ABOVE THE OVALS.

BE SURE TO ERASE ANY ERRORS OR STRAY MARKS COMPLETELY.

Start with number 1 for each new section. If a section has fewer questions than answer spaces, leave the extra answer spaces blank.

SECTION 5

1 ⊂A⊃ ⊂B⊃ ⊂C⊃ ⊂D⊃ ⊂E⊃	11 ⊂A⊃ ⊂B⊃ ⊂C⊃ ⊂D⊃ ⊂E⊃	21 ⊂A⊃ ⊂B⊃ ⊂C⊃ ⊂D⊃ ⊂E⊃	31 ⊂A⊃ ⊂B⊃ ⊂C⊃ ⊂D⊃ ⊂E⊃
2 ⊂A⊃ ⊂B⊃ ⊂C⊃ ⊂D⊃ ⊂E⊃	12 ⊂A⊃ ⊂B⊃ ⊂C⊃ ⊂D⊃ ⊂E⊃	22 ⊂A⊃ ⊂B⊃ ⊂C⊃ ⊂D⊃ ⊂E⊃	32 ⊂A⊃ ⊂B⊃ ⊂C⊃ ⊂D⊃ ⊂E⊃
3 ⊂A⊃ ⊂B⊃ ⊂C⊃ ⊂D⊃ ⊂E⊃	13 ⊂A⊃ ⊂B⊃ ⊂C⊃ ⊂D⊃ ⊂E⊃	23 ⊂A⊃ ⊂B⊃ ⊂C⊃ ⊂D⊃ ⊂E⊃	33 ⊂A⊃ ⊂B⊃ ⊂C⊃ ⊂D⊃ ⊂E⊃
4 ⊂A⊃ ⊂B⊃ ⊂C⊃ ⊂D⊃ ⊂E⊃	14 ⊂A⊃ ⊂B⊃ ⊂C⊃ ⊂D⊃ ⊂E⊃	24 ⊂A⊃ ⊂B⊃ ⊂C⊃ ⊂D⊃ ⊂E⊃	34 ⊂A⊃ ⊂B⊃ ⊂C⊃ ⊂D⊃ ⊂E⊃
5 ⊂A⊃ ⊂B⊃ ⊂C⊃ ⊂D⊃ ⊂E⊃	15 ⊂A⊃ ⊂B⊃ ⊂C⊃ ⊂D⊃ ⊂E⊃	25 ⊂A⊃ ⊂B⊃ ⊂C⊃ ⊂D⊃ ⊂E⊃	35 ⊂A⊃ ⊂B⊃ ⊂C⊃ ⊂D⊃ ⊂E⊃
6 ⊂A⊃ ⊂B⊃ ⊂C⊃ ⊂D⊃ ⊂E⊃	16 ⊂A⊃ ⊂B⊃ ⊂C⊃ ⊂D⊃ ⊂E⊃	26 ⊂A⊃ ⊂B⊃ ⊂C⊃ ⊂D⊃ ⊂E⊃	36 ⊂A⊃ ⊂B⊃ ⊂C⊃ ⊂D⊃ ⊂E⊃
7 ⊂A⊃ ⊂B⊃ ⊂C⊃ ⊂D⊃ ⊂E⊃	17 ⊂A⊃ ⊂B⊃ ⊂C⊃ ⊂D⊃ ⊂E⊃	27 ⊂A⊃ ⊂B⊃ ⊂C⊃ ⊂D⊃ ⊂E⊃	37 ⊂A⊃ ⊂B⊃ ⊂C⊃ ⊂D⊃ ⊂E⊃
8 ⊂A⊃ ⊂B⊃ ⊂C⊃ ⊂D⊃ ⊂E⊃	18 ⊂A⊃ ⊂B⊃ ⊂C⊃ ⊂D⊃ ⊂E⊃	28 ⊂A⊃ ⊂B⊃ ⊂C⊃ ⊂D⊃ ⊂E⊃	38 ⊂A⊃ ⊂B⊃ ⊂C⊃ ⊂D⊃ ⊂E⊃
9 ⊂A⊃ ⊂B⊃ ⊂C⊃ ⊂D⊃ ⊂E⊃	19 ⊂A⊃ ⊂B⊃ ⊂C⊃ ⊂D⊃ ⊂E⊃	29 ⊂A⊃ ⊂B⊃ ⊂C⊃ ⊂D⊃ ⊂E⊃	39 ⊂A⊃ ⊂B⊃ ⊂C⊃ ⊂D⊃ ⊂E⊃
10 ⊂A⊃ ⊂B⊃ ⊂C⊃ ⊂D⊃ ⊂E⊃	20 ⊂A⊃ ⊂B⊃ ⊂C⊃ ⊂D⊃ ⊂E⊃	30 ⊂A⊃ ⊂B⊃ ⊂C⊃ ⊂D⊃ ⊂E⊃	40 ⊂A⊃ ⊂B⊃ ⊂C⊃ ⊂D⊃ ⊂E⊃

SECTION 6

1 ⊂A⊃ ⊂B⊃ ⊂C⊃ ⊂D⊃ ⊂E⊃	11 ⊂A⊃ ⊂B⊃ ⊂C⊃ ⊂D⊃ ⊂E⊃	21 ⊂A⊃ ⊂B⊃ ⊂C⊃ ⊂D⊃ ⊂E⊃	31 ⊂A⊃ ⊂B⊃ ⊂C⊃ ⊂D⊃ ⊂E⊃
2 ⊂A⊃ ⊂B⊃ ⊂C⊃ ⊂D⊃ ⊂E⊃	12 ⊂A⊃ ⊂B⊃ ⊂C⊃ ⊂D⊃ ⊂E⊃	22 ⊂A⊃ ⊂B⊃ ⊂C⊃ ⊂D⊃ ⊂E⊃	32 ⊂A⊃ ⊂B⊃ ⊂C⊃ ⊂D⊃ ⊂E⊃
3 ⊂A⊃ ⊂B⊃ ⊂C⊃ ⊂D⊃ ⊂E⊃	13 ⊂A⊃ ⊂B⊃ ⊂C⊃ ⊂D⊃ ⊂E⊃	23 ⊂A⊃ ⊂B⊃ ⊂C⊃ ⊂D⊃ ⊂E⊃	33 ⊂A⊃ ⊂B⊃ ⊂C⊃ ⊂D⊃ ⊂E⊃
4 ⊂A⊃ ⊂B⊃ ⊂C⊃ ⊂D⊃ ⊂E⊃	14 ⊂A⊃ ⊂B⊃ ⊂C⊃ ⊂D⊃ ⊂E⊃	24 ⊂A⊃ ⊂B⊃ ⊂C⊃ ⊂D⊃ ⊂E⊃	34 ⊂A⊃ ⊂B⊃ ⊂C⊃ ⊂D⊃ ⊂E⊃
5 ⊂A⊃ ⊂B⊃ ⊂C⊃ ⊂D⊃ ⊂E⊃	15 ⊂A⊃ ⊂B⊃ ⊂C⊃ ⊂D⊃ ⊂E⊃	25 ⊂A⊃ ⊂B⊃ ⊂C⊃ ⊂D⊃ ⊂E⊃	35 ⊂A⊃ ⊂B⊃ ⊂C⊃ ⊂D⊃ ⊂E⊃
6 ⊂A⊃ ⊂B⊃ ⊂C⊃ ⊂D⊃ ⊂E⊃	16 ⊂A⊃ ⊂B⊃ ⊂C⊃ ⊂D⊃ ⊂E⊃	26 ⊂A⊃ ⊂B⊃ ⊂C⊃ ⊂D⊃ ⊂E⊃	36 ⊂A⊃ ⊂B⊃ ⊂C⊃ ⊂D⊃ ⊂E⊃
7 ⊂A⊃ ⊂B⊃ ⊂C⊃ ⊂D⊃ ⊂E⊃	17 ⊂A⊃ ⊂B⊃ ⊂C⊃ ⊂D⊃ ⊂E⊃	27 ⊂A⊃ ⊂B⊃ ⊂C⊃ ⊂D⊃ ⊂E⊃	37 ⊂A⊃ ⊂B⊃ ⊂C⊃ ⊂D⊃ ⊂E⊃
8 ⊂A⊃ ⊂B⊃ ⊂C⊃ ⊂D⊃ ⊂E⊃	18 ⊂A⊃ ⊂B⊃ ⊂C⊃ ⊂D⊃ ⊂E⊃	28 ⊂A⊃ ⊂B⊃ ⊂C⊃ ⊂D⊃ ⊂E⊃	38 ⊂A⊃ ⊂B⊃ ⊂C⊃ ⊂D⊃ ⊂E⊃
9 ⊂A⊃ ⊂B⊃ ⊂C⊃ ⊂D⊃ ⊂E⊃	19 ⊂A⊃ ⊂B⊃ ⊂C⊃ ⊂D⊃ ⊂E⊃	29 ⊂A⊃ ⊂B⊃ ⊂C⊃ ⊂D⊃ ⊂E⊃	39 ⊂A⊃ ⊂B⊃ ⊂C⊃ ⊂D⊃ ⊂E⊃
10 ⊂A⊃ ⊂B⊃ ⊂C⊃ ⊂D⊃ ⊂E⊃	20 ⊂A⊃ ⊂B⊃ ⊂C⊃ ⊂D⊃ ⊂E⊃	30 ⊂A⊃ ⊂B⊃ ⊂C⊃ ⊂D⊃ ⊂E⊃	40 ⊂A⊃ ⊂B⊃ ⊂C⊃ ⊂D⊃ ⊂E⊃

SECTION 7

1 ⊂A⊃ ⊂B⊃ ⊂C⊃ ⊂D⊃ ⊂E⊃	11 ⊂A⊃ ⊂B⊃ ⊂C⊃ ⊂D⊃ ⊂E⊃	21 ⊂A⊃ ⊂B⊃ ⊂C⊃ ⊂D⊃ ⊂E⊃	31 ⊂A⊃ ⊂B⊃ ⊂C⊃ ⊂D⊃ ⊂E⊃
2 ⊂A⊃ ⊂B⊃ ⊂C⊃ ⊂D⊃ ⊂E⊃	12 ⊂A⊃ ⊂B⊃ ⊂C⊃ ⊂D⊃ ⊂E⊃	22 ⊂A⊃ ⊂B⊃ ⊂C⊃ ⊂D⊃ ⊂E⊃	32 ⊂A⊃ ⊂B⊃ ⊂C⊃ ⊂D⊃ ⊂E⊃
3 ⊂A⊃ ⊂B⊃ ⊂C⊃ ⊂D⊃ ⊂E⊃	13 ⊂A⊃ ⊂B⊃ ⊂C⊃ ⊂D⊃ ⊂E⊃	23 ⊂A⊃ ⊂B⊃ ⊂C⊃ ⊂D⊃ ⊂E⊃	33 ⊂A⊃ ⊂B⊃ ⊂C⊃ ⊂D⊃ ⊂E⊃
4 ⊂A⊃ ⊂B⊃ ⊂C⊃ ⊂D⊃ ⊂E⊃	14 ⊂A⊃ ⊂B⊃ ⊂C⊃ ⊂D⊃ ⊂E⊃	24 ⊂A⊃ ⊂B⊃ ⊂C⊃ ⊂D⊃ ⊂E⊃	34 ⊂A⊃ ⊂B⊃ ⊂C⊃ ⊂D⊃ ⊂E⊃
5 ⊂A⊃ ⊂B⊃ ⊂C⊃ ⊂D⊃ ⊂E⊃	15 ⊂A⊃ ⊂B⊃ ⊂C⊃ ⊂D⊃ ⊂E⊃	25 ⊂A⊃ ⊂B⊃ ⊂C⊃ ⊂D⊃ ⊂E⊃	35 ⊂A⊃ ⊂B⊃ ⊂C⊃ ⊂D⊃ ⊂E⊃
6 ⊂A⊃ ⊂B⊃ ⊂C⊃ ⊂D⊃ ⊂E⊃	16 ⊂A⊃ ⊂B⊃ ⊂C⊃ ⊂D⊃ ⊂E⊃	26 ⊂A⊃ ⊂B⊃ ⊂C⊃ ⊂D⊃ ⊂E⊃	36 ⊂A⊃ ⊂B⊃ ⊂C⊃ ⊂D⊃ ⊂E⊃
7 ⊂A⊃ ⊂B⊃ ⊂C⊃ ⊂D⊃ ⊂E⊃	17 ⊂A⊃ ⊂B⊃ ⊂C⊃ ⊂D⊃ ⊂E⊃	27 ⊂A⊃ ⊂B⊃ ⊂C⊃ ⊂D⊃ ⊂E⊃	37 ⊂A⊃ ⊂B⊃ ⊂C⊃ ⊂D⊃ ⊂E⊃
8 ⊂A⊃ ⊂B⊃ ⊂C⊃ ⊂D⊃ ⊂E⊃	18 ⊂A⊃ ⊂B⊃ ⊂C⊃ ⊂D⊃ ⊂E⊃	28 ⊂A⊃ ⊂B⊃ ⊂C⊃ ⊂D⊃ ⊂E⊃	38 ⊂A⊃ ⊂B⊃ ⊂C⊃ ⊂D⊃ ⊂E⊃
9 ⊂A⊃ ⊂B⊃ ⊂C⊃ ⊂D⊃ ⊂E⊃	19 ⊂A⊃ ⊂B⊃ ⊂C⊃ ⊂D⊃ ⊂E⊃	29 ⊂A⊃ ⊂B⊃ ⊂C⊃ ⊂D⊃ ⊂E⊃	39 ⊂A⊃ ⊂B⊃ ⊂C⊃ ⊂D⊃ ⊂E⊃
10 ⊂A⊃ ⊂B⊃ ⊂C⊃ ⊂D⊃ ⊂E⊃	20 ⊂A⊃ ⊂B⊃ ⊂C⊃ ⊂D⊃ ⊂E⊃	30 ⊂A⊃ ⊂B⊃ ⊂C⊃ ⊂D⊃ ⊂E⊃	40 ⊂A⊃ ⊂B⊃ ⊂C⊃ ⊂D⊃ ⊂E⊃

CERTIFICATION STATEMENT

Copy in longhand the statement below and sign your name as you would an official document. DO NOT PRINT.

I hereby agree with The Princeton Review that the SAT is nothing to fear and certify that I am the person who will conquer it.

_____

_____

_____

SIGNATURE: _____   DATE: _____

FOR TPR USE ONLY	VTR	VTFS	CRR	CRFS	ANW	SCR	SCFS	5MTW	MTFS		5AAW	AAFS	5GRW	GFS
	VTW	VTCS	CRW	ANR	ANFS	SCW	MTR	4MTW	MTCS	AAR	4AAW	GRR	4GRW	
								0MTW			0AAW		0GRW	

DO NOT MARK IN THIS AREA

PART IX

Writing Skills Component Sample Section

Time—30 Minutes
39 Questions
(1–39)

For each question in this section, select the best answer
from among the choices given and fill in the corresponding
oval on the answer sheet.

Directions: The following sentences test your knowledge of grammar, usage, word choice, and idiom.

Some sentences are correct.
No sentence contains more than one error.

You will find that the error, if there is one, is underlined and lettered. Elements of the sentence that are not underlined will not be changed. In choosing answers, follow the requirements of standard written English.

If there is an error, select the one underlined part that must be changed to make the sentence correct and fill in the corresponding oval on your answer sheet.

If there is no error, fill in oval Ⓔ.

EXAMPLE:

The other delegates and him immediately
  A   B   C
accepted the resolution drafted by the
                                    D
neutral states. No error
                    E

SAMPLE ANSWER

Ⓐ ● Ⓒ Ⓓ Ⓔ

---

1 Revered as one of the world's most
           A
versatile geniuses, Leonardo da Vinci

excelled in every endeavor he attempted
            B
and serving as a prototype for the
        C   D
Renaissance man. No error
                    E

2 The twins wanted to be a member of the
                                A
team, but the captain had already made
        B   C
her selections. No error
    D   E

3 Of the nominees for the Nobel Prize in
        A   B
literature this year, few are as qualified as
                        C   D
the English novelist Anthony Powell.

No error
  E

4 The recent production of Arthur Miller's *A*
                          A
View From the Bridge exemplifies the

strength of this unsung masterpiece

and demonstrates that the work has been
    B   C
ignored unjust. No error
        D   E

GO ON TO THE NEXT PAGE ⟩

5 Yoga is $\underset{A}{\underline{\text{more than}}}$ simply a $\underset{B}{\underline{\text{series of}}}$ stretches and poses; it is a means of centering oneself spiritually and $\underset{C}{\underline{\text{focus}}}$ in such a way $\underset{D}{\underline{\text{as to}}}$ put one's life in order. $\underset{E}{\underline{\text{No error}}}$

6 $\underset{A}{\underline{\text{Prior to}}}$ the Industrial Revolution, children and parents $\underset{B}{\underline{\text{spend}}}$ a great deal $\underset{C}{\underline{\text{of time}}}$ working together to meet the needs $\underset{D}{\underline{\text{of the family}}}$. $\underset{E}{\underline{\text{No error}}}$

7 The fund-raising campaigns $\underset{A}{\underline{\text{of many}}}$ public radio and television stations $\underset{B}{\underline{\text{are}}}$ often $\underset{C}{\underline{\text{viewed by}}}$ subscribers as a necessary, $\underset{D}{\underline{\text{albeit}}}$ undesirable, evil. $\underset{E}{\underline{\text{No error}}}$

8 Neither the president $\underset{A}{\underline{\text{nor}}}$ the CEO of the three sister companies $\underset{B}{\underline{\text{was}}}$ able to determine why the last quarter's financial reports $\underset{C}{\underline{\text{were}}}$ so inconsistent with previous $\underset{D}{\underline{\text{years}}}$. $\underset{E}{\underline{\text{No error}}}$

9 If one is interested $\underset{A}{\underline{\text{in}}}$ learning more about Jacob Lawrence, $\underset{B}{\underline{\text{you should}}}$ visit the Metropolitan Museum of Art when next $\underset{C}{\underline{\text{his}}}$ work $\underset{D}{\underline{\text{is exhibited}}}$. $\underset{E}{\underline{\text{No error}}}$

10 In many colleges in the Northeast, it is $\underset{A}{\underline{\text{necessarily}}}$ for students $\underset{B}{\underline{\text{to wear}}}$ snowshoes to get from the dormitory to $\underset{C}{\underline{\text{their}}}$ classes $\underset{D}{\underline{\text{during}}}$ the winter months. $\underset{E}{\underline{\text{No error}}}$

11 $\underset{A}{\underline{\text{Just as}}}$ parents vary in their readiness to have their babies learn $\underset{B}{\underline{\text{to}}}$ walk, babies vary in $\underset{C}{\underline{\text{their}}}$ readiness to take $\underset{D}{\underline{\text{his or her}}}$ first step. $\underset{E}{\underline{\text{No error}}}$

12 While in training, each member of the team $\underset{A}{\underline{\text{were}}}$ required to focus exclusively on the tasks associated $\underset{B}{\underline{\text{with}}}$ $\underset{C}{\underline{\text{her}}}$ position, and therefore had little sense of the functioning of the team $\underset{D}{\underline{\text{as a whole}}}$. $\underset{E}{\underline{\text{No error}}}$

GO ON TO THE NEXT PAGE →

13 The gift that Karen and Mary ultimately purchased for her mother was much less
A   B   C
expensive than the gift they originally intended to purchase. No error
D   E

14 Vocalists are often able to sing oratorios
A   B
in flawless Latin, even if none of them have ever studied Latin in school.
C   D
No error
E

15 Thomas Pynchon's novel *The Crying of Lot 49* has been lauded for it's satirical prose
A   B
and favorably described as akin to Joyce's
C   D
Ulysses. No error
E

16 John knew he should've went home on the
A
team's bus when he had the chance
B
instead of waiting for the bus to return to
C   D
bring home the spectators. No error
E

17 Many students find Shakespeare's
A
Richard III impossible to understand; yet,
B
when proper conveyed, students can often
C
learn from the familial turmoil and inner
conflict that occurs in the play. No error
D   E

18 Many scholars agree that there has been
A   B
no greater contributor to the advancement
of architecture in the twentieth century
C
than that of Frank Lloyd Wright. No error
D   E

19 Constructing a fence ought not to be seen
A
as an insurmountable task; rather, it
B
should be viewed as a challenge that can
C
be accomplished by a combination of
D
perseverance and patience. No error
E

GO ON TO THE NEXT PAGE

20 My parents told me that <u>in France they sometimes</u> do not wear bathing suits on the beach.

 (A) in France they sometimes
 (B) in France some people
 (C) some French people
 (D) in France there are some who
 (E) in France, men and women

21 Today's computers <u>are becoming not only more varied and powerful, but also less expensive</u>.

 (A) are becoming not only more varied and powerful but also less expensive
 (B) not only are becoming more varied and powerful, they cost less
 (C) become not only more varied and powerful, they become less expensive
 (D) becoming more varied and powerful, but also less expensive
 (E) become more varied and powerful, not only, but also less expensive

22 <u>Getting off the chairlift, Neil adjusted his boot buckles, polished his goggles, and skied down the slope</u>.

 (A) Getting off the chairlift, Neil adjusted his boot buckles, polished his goggles and skied down the slope.
 (B) He got off the chairlift, Neil adjusted his boot buckles, polished his goggles, and skied down the slope.
 (C) After getting off the chairlift, Neil adjusted his boot buckles, polished his goggles, and then he went skiing down the slope.
 (D) Neil, after getting off the chairlift, adjusted his boot buckles, polished his goggles, and was skiing down the slope.
 (E) After he got off the chairlift, Neil adjusted his boot buckles, polished his goggles, and skied down the slope.

23 Since they have been told not to do so in their school books, students often hesitate to write in their personal books; yet, circling an unknown word or underlining an important phrase <u>is critically when one wishes to truly learn something</u>.

 (A) is critically when one wishes to truly learn something
 (B) is critically being as one might wish to truly learn something
 (C) is critical when one wishes to truly learn something
 (D) is critical when you truly want to learn that something has been
 (E) can only be seen as critical when one wishes to truly learn something

GO ON TO THE NEXT PAGE

24 One of Humphrey Bogart's earlier movies, Samuel Spade is a detective trying to solve the mystery of his partner's death in *The Maltese Falcon.*

(A) One of Humphrey Bogart's earlier movies, Samuel Spade is a detective trying to solve the mystery of his partner's death in *The Maltese Falcon.*

(B) One of Humphrey Bogart's earlier movies, *The Maltese Falcon* is a movie in that Samuel Spade, detective, tries to solve the mystery of his partner's death.

(C) One of Humphrey Bogart's earlier movies, *The Maltese Falcon* is a mystery in which Samuel Spade tries to solve his partner's death.

(D) In *The Maltese Falcon*, one of Humphrey Bogart's earlier movies, Samuel Spade is a detective trying to solve the mystery of his partner's death.

(E) In *The Maltese Falcon*, one of Humphrey Bogart's roles is that of Samuel Spade, a detective trying to solve the mystery of his partner's death, and it was also one of his earlier movies.

25 While Boudin's own paintings have never been held in that high regard, he is seen as having played a critical role in the education of Impressionist painter Monet.

(A) While Boudin's own paintings have never been held in that high regard, he is seen as having played a critical role in the education of Impressionist painter Monet.

(B) While Boudin's own paintings were never regarded highly, Monet is seen as having been one of his most educated students.

(C) It is seen that Boudin's critical role in educating the Impressionist painter Monet was held in higher regard than his paintings.

(D) Since Boudin's own paintings have never been held in that high regard, he has been seen as having played a critical role in the education of Impressionist painter Monet.

(E) Since Boudin's own paintings, which were never held in that high regard, were seen as having played a critical role in the education of Impressionist painter Monet.

26 Although everyone was forewarned about the upcoming exam, yet only three students out of the entire class passed it.

(A) yet only three students out of the entire class

(B) only three students out of the entire class

(C) only three students, which was out of the entire class,

(D) yet only three students that were forewarned out of the entire class

(E) but only three students out of the entire class

27 The committee chairpersons agreed to return to their respective committees and they would discuss the proposals made by the executive board.

(A) to return to their respective committees and they would discuss

(B) upon return to their respective committees, thereby discussing

(C) to return to her respective committees and discuss

(D) to return to their respective committees discussing

(E) to return to their respective committees and discuss

28 The clog has come back into fashion recently, yet few people know that originally it was called the sabot, made by hollowing a single piece of wood, and was worn by peasants in Europe.

(A) it was called the sabot, made by hollowing a single piece of wood, and was worn by peasants in Europe

(B) it was called the sabot, making it by hollowing a single piece of wood, and worn by peasants in Europe

(C) it was called the sabot, made by hollowing a single piece of wood, and worn by peasants in Europe

(D) it was called the sabot, making it by hollowing a single piece of wood, and was worn by peasants in Europe

(E) it was called the sabot, and the peasants made it by hollowing a single piece of wood, and wore it in Europe

GO ON TO THE NEXT PAGE

29 Many say that, <u>after inventing an explosive more powerful than any then known</u>, Alfred Nobel instituted the Nobel Peace Prizes to atone for his "accomplishment" and relieve his conscience.

(A) after inventing an explosive more powerful than any then known
(B) after inventing an explosive that was more powerful than any that were then known
(C) after he invented an explosive more powerful than he or any others had then known
(D) after he invented an explosive, it being more powerful than any then known
(E) after inventing an explosive more powerful then any than known

30 For many a brilliant actor, <u>being free to interpret their character as they wish</u> is more important than being well paid.

(A) being free to interpret their character as they wish
(B) being free to interpret his or her character as they wish
(C) being free to interpret their character as they wishes
(D) being free to interpret his or her character as he or she wishes
(E) being free to interpret his or her character as he or she wish

31 On Sunday afternoons, Omar and his family enjoy playing Monopoly with the neighbors, <u>and they always win.</u>

(A) and they always win
(B) even though they always win
(C) even though the neighbors always win
(D) and the neighbors, they always win
(E) it being that the neighbors always win

32 Although he was not an advocate of psychiatrists, <u>Sigmund Freud was respected by Albert Einstein as a social philosopher, and worked with him to promote peace</u> during the Nazi uprising.

(A) Sigmund Freud was respected by Albert Einstein as a social philosopher, and worked with him to promote peace
(B) Sigmund Freud was respected by Albert Einstein, since he was a social philosopher, and they worked to promote peace
(C) Albert Einstein respected Sigmund Freud as a social philosopher, and they together worked to promote peace
(D) Albert Einstein respected Sigmund Freud as a social philosopher who was working with him to promote peace
(E) Albert Einstein respected Sigmund Freud as a social philosopher, and worked with him to promote peace

33 After getting her driver's license, Jenny used her father's car <u>as often as possible, and her father said to put less miles on it</u> by walking to school and work.

(A) as often as possible, and her father said to put less miles on it
(B) as often as possible; eventually her father told her to put fewer miles on it
(C) as often as possible, but then eventually her father told her to be putting fewer miles on it
(D) as often as possible; eventually her father told her to put less miles on it
(E) as often as possible, and her father said to be putting less miles on it

GO ON TO THE NEXT PAGE

Directions: The following passage is an early draft of an essay. Some parts of the passage need to be rewritten.

Read the passage and answer the questions that follow. Some questions are about particular sentences or parts of the essay or the entire essay and ask you to consider organization and development. In making your decisions, follow the conventions of standard written English. After you have chosen your answer, fill in the corresponding oval on your answer sheet.

(1) Our town needs to make more of an effort to make its museums accessible to children. (2) Raised with frequent exposure to sculpture and paintings, it is much more likely that young people will mature into artists and patrons of the arts.

(3) It is often quite easy to accomplish a great deal simply. (4) Placed slightly lower on the walls, paintings become more visible to children. (5) But extensive programs to encourage children to appreciate art are often not a necessity. (6) Children have a natural enjoyment of art. (7) A museum is an excellent place for a child. (8) We must only understand that these young museum patrons can not help acting like them. (9) Children should not be asked to be silent, or spend long periods of time in front of any one piece. (10) If necessary, museums should set up special "children's times" during which young people may roam through the building, enjoying the artwork in their own way. (11) A wonderful learning experience! (12) Children can have a great time, and at the same time gain an appreciation of art. (13) Precautions could be taken to make sure that no damage was done.

(14) This is necessary because places like museums must be available for everyone. (15) These changes can not happen overnight, but if we volunteered and were helping to make these changes in our town's museums, we can realize the goal of making them accessible to people of all ages.

34 Which of the following could best replace the word *"But"* in sentence 5 (reproduced below)?

But extensive programs to encourage children to appreciate art are often not a necessity.

(A) However,
(B) Rather,
(C) Indeed,
(D) Notwithstanding,
(E) And yet,

35 Which version of the underlined portion of sentence 8 (reproduced below) provides the most clarity?

We must only understand that these young museum patrons can not help acting <u>like them</u>.

(A) (as it is now)
(B) like it
(C) as if they were
(D) like what they are
(E) like children

36 Sentence 13 could be best improved if the author were to

(A) describe possible damage
(B) explain the precautions to be taken
(C) give a historic precedent
(D) extend her argument to include other institutions
(E) explain the mission of a museum

37 Which of the following represents the best revision of sentence 4 (reproduced below)?

Placed slightly lower on the walls, paintings become more visible to children.

(A) (As it is now)
(B) Placing them slightly lower on the walls, the paintings become more visible to the children.
(C) For example, placing paintings slightly lower on the walls makes them more visible to children.
(D) For example, when placed slightly lower on the walls, children can see the paintings better.
(E) Placed paintings that are lower on the walls are more visible to children.

38 Which of the following is the best way to revise sentences 10 and 11 (reproduced below)?

If necessary, museums should set up special "children's times" during which young people may roam through the building, enjoying the artwork in their own way. A wonderful learning experience!

(A) To avoid disrupting everyone else, create "children's times" in the museum, during which children could roam throughout the building, enjoying the artwork in their own way and a wonderful learning experience.

(B) Museums should set up "children's times." This would be a wonderful learning experience. Children could roam through the museum. Children could enjoy the artwork in their own way.

(C) If necessary, museums should set up a wonderful learning experience called "children's times." During it, young people could roam throughout the building, enjoying the artwork in their own way.

(D) To enjoy artwork in their own way, children should be given the freedom to roam throughout the building. This would be a wonderful learning experience, and it could be called "children's times."

(E) To avoid disrupting other museum-goers, museums should set up special "children's times." During these times, children would be allowed to roam throughout the building and enjoy the artwork in their own way. What a wonderful learning experience!

39 In context, sentence 14 could be made more precise by changing the phrase *"This is"* to which of the following?

(A) That is
(B) These changes are
(C) The reasons for these changes is that they are
(D) It is
(E) These changes, as mentioned above, are also

IF YOU FINISH BEFORE TIME IS CALLED, YOU MAY CHECK YOUR WORK ON THIS SECTION ONLY. DO NOT TURN TO ANY OTHER SECTION IN THE TEST. **STOP**

PSAT WRITING SKILLS COMPONENT ANSWER KEY

1. C						
2. A						
3. E						
4. D						
5. C						
6. B						
7. E						
8. D						
9. B						
10. A						
11. D						
12. A						
13. A						
14. C						
15. B						
16. A						
17. C						
18. D						
19. E						
20. B						
21. A						
22. E						
23. C						
24. D						
25. A						
26. B						
27. E						
28. C						
29. A						
30. D						
31. C						
32. E						
33. B						
34. A						
35. E						
36. B						
37. C						
38. E						
39. B						

You will find a detailed explanation for each question beginning on page 647.

TO SCORE YOUR PSAT

First, go back to the end of Chapter 19 to check the answers to sections 1-4. Since you have to do some skipping around, be sure you are looking at the right sections and the right question numbers as you score your test.

Next, check your Writing Skills Component answers. Count up the number of correct and incorrect answers and enter them in the Writing Skills Component scoring worksheet. Tally up the number of correct and incorrect verbal answers and enter them in the appropriate worksheet spaces. Tally up the number of correct and incorrect answers from the *first* math section and enter those numbers on the worksheet. Then, tally up the number of correct and incorrect Quant Comps and enter those numbers on the worksheet. Finally, tally up the number of correct Grid-Ins and enter that number on the worksheet (you do not need to count incorrect answer choices on Grid-Ins since you do not lose anything for wrong answers on Grid-Ins).

Finally, calculate your raw scores using the worksheets provided. To calculate your Verbal raw score, subtract $\frac{1}{4}$ of the number of verbal questions incorrect from the number correct, and round it off. To calculate your Writing Skills raw score, do the same. To calculate your Math raw score, you must treat the different types of problems individually. Calculate the first section as usual (correct minus $\frac{1}{4}$ incorrect). Then subtract $\frac{1}{3}$ of the number of Quant Comps incorrect for the number of correct Quant Comps. Add up these two numbers. Finally, add in the number of Grid-Ins correct, and round this number. Compare your raw scores to the PSAT Score Conversion Table to determine your overall PSAT score.

WORKSHEET FOR CALCULATING YOUR SCORE

VERBAL

	Correct	Incorrect	

A. Verbal Sections   _____ – (1/4 × _____) =   [____] A

B. Total rounded verbal raw score   [____] B

MATHEMATICS

	Correct	Incorrect	

C. First Section   _____ – (1/4 × _____) =   [____] C

D. Quant Comp.   _____ – (1/3 × _____) =   [____] D

E. Grid-Ins   _____ =   [____] E

F. Total unrounded math raw score (C + D + E)   [____] F

G. Total rounded math raw score   [____] G

WRITING SKILLS COMPONENT

	Correct	Incorrect	
A. Writing Skills	_____	$- (1/4 \times$ _____ $) =$	▭ A
B. Total rounded WSC raw score			▭ B

Use the table on the next page to convert your raw score to scaled scores. For example, a raw verbal score of 28 corresponds to verbal scaled score of 53; a math raw score of 24 corresponds to a math scaled score of 56.

Scores on the PSAT range from 20 to 80.

SCORE CONVERSION TABLE

Raw Score	Math Scaled Score	Verbal Scaled Score	Writing Skills Scaled Score	Raw Score	Math Scaled Score	Verbal Scaled Score	Writing Skills Scaled Score
52		80		26	58	51	66
51		79		25	57	50	64
50		78		24	56	49	62
49		76		23	55	48	60
48		75		22	54	47	58
47		74		21	53	47	57
46		73		20	52	46	56
45		72		19	51	45	56
44		71		18	50	44	55
43		69		17	48	43	54
42		67		16	47	42	53
41		66		15	46	41	51
40	80	65		14	45	40	50
39	78	64	80	13	44	39	49
38	76	63	78	12	43	38	48
37	74	62	77	11	42	37	46
36	72	61	76	10	40	36	44
35	69	60	75	9	39	35	43
34	68	59	74	8	38	33	42
33	67	58	73	7	37	32	41
32	65	58	72	6	36	30	40
31	64	56	71	5	35	28	39
30	63	55	70	4	34	27	38
29	62	54	69	3	33	26	36
28	61	53	68	2	31	25	34
27	60	52	67	1	30	24	32
				0	28	22	30

21

Writing Skills Component Explanations

What follows is a detailed explanation for each question in the Writing Skills Component. Although you will naturally be more curious about the questions you got wrong, don't forget to read the explanations for the questions you left blank. In fact, you should even read the explanations for the questions you got right! Our explanations present the safest, most direct solution to each question. Even though you may have gotten a question right, that does not mean you solved it in the most efficient way.

SECTION 1

QUESTIONS	EXPLANATIONS

1 <u>Revered as</u> one of the world's most
     A

versatile geniuses, Leonardo da Vinci

excelled <u>in</u> every endeavor he attempted
     B

and <u>serving as</u> <u>a prototype</u> for the
     C   D

Renaissance man. <u>No error</u>
           E

1. Pam's answer is C.
Revered as is fine, so cross it off. *Leonardo da Vinci excelled <u>in</u>* (that's correct, so cross it off)... *and <u>serving</u> as...* Your verbs are not parallel. It should be *excelled in* and *served as*.

2 The twins wanted to be <u>a member</u> of the
            A

team, <u>but</u> the captain <u>had already made</u>
     B   C

<u>her selections</u>. <u>No error</u>
   D   E

2. Pam's answer is A.
The twins are two people who wanted to be *members*...they cannot be *a member*. Subject-verb agreement.

3 <u>Of</u> the nominees <u>for</u> the Nobel Prize in
   A   B

literature this year, <u>few</u> are <u>as qualified as</u>
           C   D

the English novelist Anthony Powell.

<u>No error</u>
  E

3. Pam's answer is E.
No error.

4 The recent production <u>of</u> Arthur Miller's *A*
           A

View From the Bridge exemplifies the

strength of this unsung masterpiece

<u>and demonstrates</u> that the work <u>has been</u>
      B   C

ignored <u>unjust</u>. <u>No error</u>
      D   E

4. Pam's answer is D.
Production <u>of</u> is fine, so cross it off. *And demonstrates* is also fine. The work *has been* (no problem here) ignored how? *Unjustly*. You need an adverb to modify the verb *ignored*.

SECTION 1

QUESTIONS	EXPLANATIONS

5 Yoga is <u>more than</u> simply a <u>series of</u>
          A   B

stretches and poses; it is a means of

centering oneself spiritually and <u>focus</u> in
                                    C

such a way <u>as to</u> put one's life in order.
           D

<u>No error</u>
   E

6 <u>Prior to</u> the Industrial Revolution, children
   A

and parents <u>spend</u> a great deal <u>of time</u>
            B   C

working together to meet the needs

<u>of the family</u>. <u>No error</u>
   D   E

7 The fund-raising campaigns <u>of many</u>
                                  A

public radio and television stations <u>are</u>
                                      B

often <u>viewed by</u> subscribers as a necessary,
      C

<u>albeit</u> undesirable, evil. <u>No error</u>
   D   E

8 Neither the president <u>nor</u> the CEO of the
                            A

three sister companies <u>was</u> able to
                        B

determine why the last quarter's financial

reports <u>were</u> so inconsistent with previous
        C

<u>years</u>. <u>No error</u>
   D   E

---

5. Pam's answer is C.
Yoga is <u>more than</u> simply a <u>series of</u> stretches and poses—no problems in the first phrase, so cross off A and B. Now pull the verbs out: It is a means of *centering*...and *focus*... they are not parallel. Focus should be *focusing.*

6. Pam's answer is B.
<u>*Prior to*</u> *the Industrial Revolution*...no problem here, so cross off A. *Children and parents* <u>*spend*</u> ...*Spend* is present tense, but we are talking about the past. It should be *spent.*

7. Pam's answer is E.
No error.

8. Pam's answer is D.
Neither ... <u>*nor*</u> is fine, so cross off A. *The CEO...*<u>*was*</u> is also fine. *Financial reports* <u>*were*</u> (no problem) *inconsistent with previous* <u>*years*</u>. Not with previous *years,* with previous years' *financial reports.*

SECTION 1

9 If one is interested <u>in</u> learning more about
                                    A

Jacob Lawrence, <u>you should</u> visit the
                        B

Metropolitan Museum of Art when next

<u>his</u> work <u>is exhibited</u> .
 C   D

9. Pam's answer is B.
If one is interested <u>in</u> learning is fine (cross it off). *You should...*The subject of the first phrase is *one*, so one it should stay. *You* is incorrect.

10 In many colleges in the Northeast, it is

<u>necessarily</u> for students <u>to wear</u> snowshoes
 A   B

to get from the dormitory to <u>their</u> classes
                                    C

<u>during</u> the winter months.   <u>No error</u>
 D   E

10. Pam's answer is A.
It is <u>necessarily</u> for students <u>to wear</u> ...no, it is *necessary* for students to wear something.

11 <u>Just as</u> parents vary in their readiness to
        A

have their babies learn <u>to</u> walk, babies
                            B

vary in <u>their</u> readiness to take <u>his or her</u>
            C   D

first step.   <u>No error</u>
                    E

11. Pam's answer is D.
<u>Just as</u> parents is fine (bag it). *Babies learn <u>to</u> walk*—no problem here. *Babies vary in <u>their</u> readiness* (okay) *to take <u>his or her</u> first step.* Pronoun problem...*babies* and *their* are plural, so they must be taking *their* first step.

12 While in training, each member of the team

<u>were</u> required to focus exclusively on the
 A

tasks associated <u>with</u> <u>her</u> position, and
                    B   C

therefore had little sense of the functioning

of the team <u>as a whole</u> .   <u>No error</u>
                    D   E

12. Pam's answer is A.
Each member...<u>were</u>—don't think so. Each member *was*.

SECTION 1

QUESTIONS	EXPLANATIONS

13 The gift that Karen and Mary ultimately

purchased for <u>her</u> mother <u>was</u> much <u>less</u>
        A   B   C

expensive than the gift they originally

intended <u>to purchase</u>. <u>No error</u>
          D   E

13. Pam's answer is A.
The gift that Karen and Mary purchased for <u>her</u> mother…Whose mother?

14 Vocalists <u>are</u> often able <u>to sing</u> oratorios in
           A   B

flawless Latin, even if none of them <u>have</u>
                                C

ever <u>studied</u> Latin in school. <u>No error</u>
      D   E

14. Pam's answer is C.
*Vocalists <u>are</u> often able <u>to sing</u> oratorios in flawless Latin…*A and B are both fine, so cross them off. *Even if none… <u>have</u> …None* is a singular noun, so it needs a singular verb. It should be *has.*

15 Thomas Pynchon's novel *The Crying of Lot 49*

<u>has been</u> lauded for <u>it's</u> satirical prose and
   A   B

<u>favorably</u> described as <u>akin to</u> Joyce's
     C   D

Ulysses. <u>No error</u>
          E

15. Pam's answer is B.
Thomas Pynchon's novel <u>has been</u> is fine, so cross it off. *Lauded for <u>it's</u> …Lauded for it is?* It should be *its.*

16 John knew he <u>should've went</u> home on the
                A

team's bus when he <u>had</u> the chance
                B

<u>instead of</u> waiting <u>for</u> the bus to return to
   C   D

bring home the spectators. <u>No error</u>
                      E

16. Pam's answer is A.
*John knew he <u>should've went</u> home…*Actually, John *should have gone* home.

SECTION 1

QUESTIONS	EXPLANATIONS

17 Many students find Shakespeare's *Richard*
    A

III impossible to understand; yet, when
            B

proper conveyed, students can often learn
  C

from the familial turmoil and inner conflict

that occurs in the play. No error
  D   E

17. Pam's answer is C.
Many students find…so far, so good.
Impossible to understand… no problem, so
cross off A and B. *When proper
conveyed*…*properly* conveyed. You need
an adverb to modify a verb.

18 Many scholars agree that there has been
          A   B

no greater contributor to the advancement

of architecture in the twentieth century
  C

than that of Frank Lloyd Wright. No error
  D   E

18. Pam's answer is D. .
Pull it apart: *Scholars agree* is fine so cross
off A. *There has been* no greater contributor
is also fine. *Advancement of
architecture*…no problem. *No greater
contributor*… *than that of Frank Lloyd
Wright*. The *that of* is incorrect—it should
say *no greater contributor than Frank…*

19 Constructing a fence ought not to be seen as
          A

an insurmountable task; rather, it should
          B

be viewed as a challenge that can be
          C

accomplished by a combination of
          D

perseverance and patience. No error
          E

19. Pam's answer is E.
No error.

SECTION 1

20 My parents told me that <u>in France they sometimes</u> do not wear bathing suits on the beach.

(A) in France they sometimes
(B) in France some people
(C) some French people
(D) in France there are some who
(E) in France, men and women

20. Pam's answer is B.
Ambiguous pronoun. Who doesn't wear bathing suits on the beach? Eliminate A. E changes the meaning of the sentence. C and D are not as well written as B.

21 Today's computers <u>are becoming not only more varied and powerful, but also less expensive</u>.

(A) are becoming not only more varied and powerful but also less expensive
(B) not only are becoming more varied and powerful, they cost less
(C) become not only more varied and powerful, they become less expensive
(D) becoming more varied and powerful, but also less expensive
(E) become more varied and powerful, not only, but also less expensive

21. Pam's answer is A.
This sentence is correct as written.

22 <u>Getting off the chairlift, Neil adjusted his boot buckles, polished his goggles, and skied down the slope</u>.

(A) Getting off the chairlift, Neil adjusted his boot buckles, polished his goggles and skied down the slope
(B) He got off the chairlift, Neil adjusted his boot buckles, polished his goggles, and skied down the slope
(C) After getting off the chairlift, Neil adjusted his boot buckles, polished his goggles, and then he went skiing down the slope
(D) Neil, after getting off the chairlift, adjusted his boot buckles, polished his goggles, and was skiing down the slope
(E) After he got off the chairlift, Neil adjusted his boot buckles, polished his goggles, and skied down the slope

22. Pam's answer is E.
Neil did not do all this while he was getting off the chairlift. Eliminate A. B and D are poorly written. C is not parallel (*adjusted, polished* and *he went skiing...*)

SECTION 1

QUESTIONS	EXPLANATIONS

23 Since they have been told not to do so in their school books, students often hesitate to write in their personal books; yet, circling an unknown word or underlining an important phrase <u>is critically when one wishes to truly learn something.</u>

(A) is critically when one wishes to truly learn something

(B) is critically being as one might wish to truly learn something

(C) is critical when one wishes to truly learn something

(D) is critical when you truly want to learn that something has been

(E) can only be seen as critical when one wishes to truly learn something

23. Pam's answer is C.
Critically is the error in the sentence. Cross off A and B since they don't fix the error. D and E both add extra stuff that makes the sentence awkward.

24 <u>One of Humphrey Bogart's earlier movies, Samuel Spade is a detective trying to solve the mystery of his partner's death in *The Maltese Falcon*.</u>

(A) One of Humphrey Bogart's earlier movies, Samuel Spade is a detective trying to solve the mystery of his partner's death in *The Maltese Falcon*.

(B) One of Humphrey Bogart's earlier movies, *The Maltese Falcon* is a movie in that Samuel Spade, detective, tries to solve the mystery of his partner's death.

(C) One of Humphrey Bogart's earlier movies, *The Maltese Falcon* is a mystery in which Samuel Spade tries to solve his partner's death.

(D) In *The Maltese Falcon*, one of Humphrey Bogart's earlier movies, Samuel Spade is a detective trying to solve the mystery of his partner's death.

(E) In *The Maltese Falcon*, one of Humphrey Bogart's roles is that of Samuel Spade, a detective trying to solve the mystery of his partner's death, and it was also one of his earlier movies.

24. Pam's answer is D.
The original error is a misplaced modifier. The opening phrase modifies the movie *The Maltese Falcon*, not Samuel Spade. Cross off A. All the other answer choices fix this error but introduce new ones. E is out because it is so poorly written. B is also awkward. Be careful on C—can Sam Spade *solve* his partner's *death*?

QUESTIONS	EXPLANATIONS

25 <u>While Boudin's own paintings have never been held in that high regard, he is seen as having played a critical role in the education of Impressionist painter Monet.</u>

(A) While Boudin's own paintings have never been held in that high regard, he is seen as having played a critical role in the education of Impressionist painter Monet.

(B) While Boudin's own paintings were never regarded highly, Monet is seen as having been one of his most educated students.

(C) It is seen that Boudin's critical role in educating the Impressionist painter Monet was held in higher regard than his paintings.

(D) Since Boudin's own paintings have never been held in that high regard, he has been seen as having played a critical role in the education of Impressionist painter Monet.

(E) Since Boudin's own paintings, which were never held in that high regard, were seen as having played a critical role in the education of Impressionist painter Monet.

25. Pam's answer is A.
The sentence is correct as written.

26 Although everyone was forewarned about the upcoming exam, <u>yet only three students out of the entire class</u> passed it.

(A) yet only three students out of the entire class

(B) only three students out of the entire class

(C) only three students, which was out of the entire class,

(D) yet only three students that were forewarned out of the entire class

(E) but only three students out of the entire class

26. Pam's answer is B.
Because the opening phrase of the sentence begins with the trigger word "although," it is incorrect to begin the second half of the sentence with another trigger word. Eliminate A, D, and E. B and C fix the original problem, but C is poorly worded.

SECTION 1

QUESTIONS	EXPLANATIONS

27 The committee chairpersons agreed <u>to return to their respective committees and they would discuss</u> the proposals made by the executive board.

- (A) to return to their respective committees and they would discuss
- (B) upon return to their respective committees, thereby discussing
- (C) to return to her respective committees and discuss
- (D) to return to their respective committees discussing
- (E) to return to their respective committees and discuss

27. Pam's answer is E.
The *they would* makes the underlined phrase incorrect. *The committee agreed to return...and discuss.* Eliminate A and B. D implies the chairpersons are discussing the proposals as they walk in the door. Be careful on C—it fixes the original error but uses the singular pronoun "her" to describe the plural subject.

28 The clog has come back into fashion recently, yet few people know that originally <u>it was called the sabot, made by hollowing a single piece of wood, and was worn by peasants in Europe.</u>

- (A) it was called the sabot, made by hollowing a single piece of wood, and was worn by peasants in Europe
- (B) it was called the sabot, making it by hollowing a single piece of wood, and worn by peasants in Europe
- (C) it was called the sabot, made by hollowing a single piece of wood, and worn by peasants in Europe
- (D) it was called the sabot, making it by hollowing a single piece of wood, and was worn by peasants in Europe
- (E) it was called the sabot, and the peasants made it by hollowing a single piece of wood, and wore it in Europe

28. Pam's answer is C.
The verbs in the sentence are not parallel (*called*, *made* and *was worn*). Eliminate A and D. B fixes the original error, but makes a new error by changing *made* to *making*. E is a big mess.

SECTION 1

QUESTIONS	EXPLANATIONS

29 Many say that, <u>after inventing an explosive more powerful than any then known</u>, Alfred Nobel instituted the Nobel Peace Prizes to atone for his "accomplishment" and relieve his conscience.

(A) after inventing an explosive more powerful than any then known

(B) after inventing an explosive that was more powerful than any that were then known

(C) after he invented an explosive more powerful than he or any others had then known

(D) after he invented an explosive, it being more powerful than any then known

(E) after inventing an explosive more powerful then any than known

29. Pam's answer is A.
The sentence is correct as written.

30 For many a brilliant actor, <u>being free to interpret their character as they wish</u> is more important than being well paid.

(A) being free to interpret their character as they wish

(B) being free to interpret his or her character as they wish

(C) being free to interpret their character as they wishes

(D) being free to interpret his or her character as he or she wishes

(E) being free to interpret his or her character as he or she wish

30. Pam's answer is D.
The sentence incorrectly uses plural pronouns to represent the singular subject. Eliminate A, B, and C for not fixing the error. E fixes the error, but then makes a subject-verb agreement error at the end.

31 On Sunday afternoons, Omar and his family enjoy playing Monopoly with the neighbors, <u>and they always win.</u>

(A) and they always win

(B) even though they always win

(C) even though the neighbors always win

(D) and the neighbors, they always win

(E) it being that the neighbors always win

31. Pam's answer is C.
Who always wins? Pronoun ambiguity is the first problem here. Eliminate A and B. D and E are awkward and missing the appropriate trigger words.

SECTION 1

QUESTIONS	EXPLANATIONS

32 Although he was not an advocate of psychiatrists, <u>Sigmund Freud was respected by Albert Einstein as a social philosopher, and worked with him to promote peace</u> during the Nazi uprising.

(A) Sigmund Freud was respected by Albert Einstein as a social philosopher, and worked with him to promote peace

(B) Sigmund Freud was respected by Albert Einstein, since he was a social philosopher, and they worked to promote peace

(C) Albert Einstein respected Sigmund Freud as a social philosopher, and they together worked to promote peace

(D) Albert Einstein respected Sigmund Freud as a social philosopher who was working with him to promote peace

(E) Albert Einstein respected Sigmund Freud as a social philosopher, and worked with him to promote peace

32. Pam's answer is E.
Misplaced modifier. *Einstein* was not an advocate of psychiatrists (Freud *was* a psychiatrist). Eliminate A and B. D is poorly worded. C is not consistent with the opening phrase and is therefore not as good a choice as E.

33 After getting her driver's license, Jenny used her father's car <u>as often as possible, and her father said to put less miles on it</u> by walking to school and work.

(A) as often as possible, and her father said to put less miles on it

(B) as often as possible; eventually her father told her to put fewer miles on it

(C) as often as possible, but then eventually her father told her to be putting fewer miles on it

(D) as often as possible; eventually her father told her to put less miles on it

(E) as often as possible, and her father said to be putting less miles on it

33. Pam's answer is B.
Lots of problems here. First, the wrong quantity word is used—it should be *fewer* miles, not *less* miles. Eliminate A, D and E. C is poorly worded.

34 Which of the following could best replace the word "*But*" in sentence 5 (reproduced below)?

But extensive programs to encourage children to appreciate art are often not a necessity.

(A) However,
(B) Rather,
(C) Indeed,
(D) Notwithstanding,
(E) And yet,

34. Pam's answer is A.
All the other choices are weak when compared with *however*.

SECTION 1

QUESTIONS	EXPLANATIONS

35 Which version of the underlined portion of sentence 8 (reproduced below) provides the most clarity?

We must only understand that these young museum patrons can not help acting <u>like them</u>.

(A) as it is now
(B) like it
(C) as if they were
(D) like what they are
(E) like children

35. Pam's answer is E.
You must clarify who *them* is. E is the only choice that says *like children*.

36 Sentence 13 could be best improved if the author were to

(A) describe possible damage
(B) explain the precautions to be taken
(C) give a historic precedent
(D) extend her argument to include other institutions
(E) explain the mission of a museum

36. Pam's answer is B.
All the other answer choices are too far out of the scope of this passage.

37 Which of the following represents the best revision of sentence 4 (reproduced below)?
Placed slightly lower on the walls, paintings become more visible to children.

(A) As it is now
(B) Placing them slightly lower on the walls, the paintings become more visible to the children.
(C) For example, placing paintings slightly lower on the walls makes them more visible to children.
(D) For example, when placed slightly lower on the walls, children can see the paintings better.
(E) Placed paintings that are lower on the walls are more visible to children.

37. Pam's answer is C.
The sentence is not well written, so cross off A. D places the children on the walls. B and E are awkward.

38 Which of the following is the best way to revise sentences 10 and 11 (reproduced below)?

If necessary, museums should set up special "children's times" during which young people may roam through the building, enjoying the artwork in their own way. A wonderful learning experience!

(A) To avoid disrupting everyone else, create "children's times" in the museum, during which children could roam throughout the building, enjoying the artwork in their own way and a wonderful learning experience.

(B) Museums should set up "children's times." This would be a wonderful learning experience. Children could roam through the museum. Children could enjoy the artwork in their own way.

(C) If necessary, museums should set up a wonderful learning experience called "children's times." During it, young people could roam throughout the building, enjoying the artwork in their own way.

(D) To enjoy artwork in their own way, children should be given the freedom to roam throughout the building. This would be a wonderful learning experience, and it could be called "children's times."

(E) To avoid disrupting other museum-goers, museums should set up special "children's times." During these times, children would be allowed to roam throughout the building and enjoy the artwork in their own way. What a wonderful learning experience!

38. Pam's answer is E.
Answer choice A is worse than the original because it is a long, run-on sentence. B is just the opposite—several short, non-cohesive sentences. C and D are awkward and do not convey the exact meaning of the original sentence.

39 In context, sentence 14 could be made more precise by changing the phrase *"This is"* to which of the following?
(A) That is
(B) These changes are
(C) The reasons for these changes is that they are
(D) It is
(E) These changes, as mentioned above, are also

39. Pam's answer is B.
The *this* in the sentence needs to be clarified. Get rid of A and D. C and E are long and awkward.

Afterword

ABOUT THE PRINCETON REVIEW COURSE

The Princeton Review course is a six-week course that prepares students for the SAT.

Students are assigned to small classes (eight to twelve students) grouped by ability. Everyone in your math class is scoring at your math level; everyone in your verbal class is scoring at your verbal level. This enables the teacher to focus each lesson on your problems, because everybody is in the same boat.

Each week you cover one math area and one verbal area. If you don't understand a particular topic, some other courses expect you to listen to audio-cassettes.

Not so with The Princeton Review. If you want more work on a topic, you can come to an extra-help session later in the week. Classes in extra help are optional, so usually they are even smaller than regular classes, allowing still more personal attention. If after coming to an extra-help class you still don't understand a concept, or you simply want more practice, you can request free private tutoring with your instructor.

Four times during the course you will take a diagnostic test that is computer evaluated. Each diagnostic is constructed according to the statistical design of actual SATs. Indeed, some of our questions are actual questions licensed directly from ETS.

The computer evaluation of your diagnostic tests is used to assign you to your class, as well as to measure your progress. The computer evaluation tells you what specific areas you need to concentrate on. We don't ask you to spend time on topics you already know well.

Princeton Review instructors undergo a strict selection process and a rigorous training period. All of them have done exceedingly well on the SAT, and most of them have gone to highly competitive colleges. All Princeton Review instructors are chosen because we believe they can make the course an enjoyable experience as well as a learning one.

Finally, Princeton Review materials are updated each year. Each student is given a manual and workbook. Each person receives materials that are challenging but not overwhelming.

Is This Book Just Like Your Course?

Since the book came out, many students and teachers have asked us, "Is this book just like your course?" The answer is no.

We like to think that this book is fun, informative, and well written, but no book can capture the magic of our instructors and course structure. Each Princeton Review instructor has attended a top college and has excelled on the SAT. Moreover, each of our instructors undergoes several weeks of rigorous training.

It isn't easy to raise SAT scores. Our course is more than fifty hours long and requires class participation, quizzes, homework, four diagnostic examinations, and possibly additional tutoring.

Also, for a number of reasons, this book cannot contain all of the techniques we teach in our course. Some of our techniques are too difficult to include in a book, without a trained and experienced Princeton Review teacher to explain and demonstrate them. Moreover, this book is written for the average student. Classes in our course are grouped by ability so that we can gear our techniques to each student's level. What a 900-level Princeton Review student learns is different from what a 1400- or 1600-level student learns.

We're Flattered, But . . .

Some tutors and schools use this book to run their own "Princeton Review course." While we are flattered, we are also concerned.

It has taken us many years of teaching tens of thousands of students across the country to develop our SAT program, and we're still learning. Many teachers think that our course is simply a collection of techniques that can be taught by anyone. It isn't that easy.

We train each Princeton Review instructor two hours for every hour he or she will teach class. Each of the instructors is monitored, evaluated, and supervised throughout the course.

Another concern is that many of our techniques conflict with traditional math and English techniques as taught in high school. For example, in the math section we tell our students to avoid setting up algebraic equations. Can you imagine your math teacher telling you that? And in the verbal section, we tell our students not to read the passage too carefully. Can you imagine your English teacher telling you that?

While we also teach traditional math and English in our course, some teachers may not completely agree with some of our approaches.

BEWARE OF PRINCETON REVIEW CLONES

We have nothing against people who use our techniques, but we do object to tutors or high schools who claim to "teach The Princeton Review method."

> If you want to find out whether your teacher has been trained by The Princeton Review or whether you're taking an official Princeton Review course, call us toll-free at 1-800-2REVIEW.

IF YOU'D LIKE MORE INFORMATION

Princeton Review sites are in dozens of cities around the country. For the office nearest you, call 1-800-2REVIEW.

A Parting Shot from FairTest

Now that you are well prepped for the SAT, there are a few things you should know to help keep the test in perspective. First, your score on the SAT is not a measure of your intelligence; it is a measure of how well you take these kinds of fill-in-the-bubble exams.

Fortunately, in the real world very few people care a fig about whether you know how "mendicant" relates to "beggar." So even if you aren't great at taking multiple-choice tests, you, too, could still become a corporate CEO, a rock 'n' roll star, or president of the United States.

Second, if you choose to apply to colleges that use SAT scores to make admissions decisions, you don't need scores that are astronomical, just within the requisite range. This book will help you reach that goal.

If you've worked hard but your test scores still don't meet your expectations, do not despair: many good schools still want you. Today, more than 200 enlightened colleges and universities have adopted a test-score optional policy for some or all of their applicants. These schools will consider your scores if you submit them, but they won't hold it against you if you don't. They include some of the nation's best schools, ranging from small private liberal arts colleges to large public systems in Oregon and California. They judge students based on years of high school coursework, not on a three-and-a-half-hour standardized test.

Colleges have made the tests optional to attract students who perform well in other areas, but not on standardized tests. By all reports, they are pleased with the results. For example, both Bowdoin and Bates, two small liberal arts colleges, experienced strong growth in the number of minority applicants. At both colleges, applicants who did not submit test scores were accepted at about the same rate as those who did. Students from both groups had very similar grade point averages in college and graduated at about the same rate.

These results may surprise some who think the SAT is an important predictor of performance. Think again. Despite the hype surrounding the SAT, the test adds very little to the ability of college admissions officers to forecast student success. The sole stated purpose of the SAT is to predict first-year college grades.

It doesn't do a great job of meeting even that modest objective. Despite the enormous range of grading practices, high school records still provide a more accurate picture of how well students will fare in their first year of college. The SAT is even less reliable as a predictor of grades in the second and third years of college and beyond.

So why do so many colleges still rely on the test? Many do so in order to maintain an aura of selectivity—to achieve that coveted spot on the college rankings charts. Another reason is convenience. Some highly selective schools attract such well-qualified pools of applicants that a large percentage of those denied entrance could perform well academically. Rejecting students who have modest test scores gives them a relatively cheap and easy way to thin the ranks of applicants. Of course, that practice also harms otherwise qualified students who don't happen to do well on tests, but that's why you bought this book, isn't it?

At FairTest, the National Center for Fair & Open Testing, we are committed to fighting the abuses and misuses of standardized tests. Princeton Review staff have been helpful allies in this fight. They live and breathe the SAT, so they know just how flawed and limited it really is. And they don't mind saying so publicly. So prepare well and "crack" the SAT, but understand that there are good colleges and universities that want you whether you ace the test or not.

For more information about FairTest, or to obtain a list of the test-score optional four-year colleges and universities, send us an SASE to 342 Broadway, Cambridge, MA, 02139.

ABOUT THE AUTHORS

Adam Robinson was born in 1955. He graduated from Wharton before earning a law degree at Oxford University in England. Robinson, a rated chess master, devised and perfected the Joe Bloggs approach to beating standardized tests in 1980, as well as numerous other core Princeton Review techniques. A freelance author of many books, Robinson has collaborated with The Princeton Review to develop a number of its courses.

John Katzman was born in 1959. He graduated from Princeton University in 1980. After working briefly on Wall Street, he founded The Princeton Review in 1981. Beginning with nineteen high school students in his parents' apartment, Katzman now oversees courses that prepare tens of thousands of high school and college students annually for tests, including the SAT, GRE, GMAT, and LSAT.

Both authors live in New York City.

Important Message
for Students and Parents

Many college graduates are in the wrong career. And you don't want to become one of them.

It's understandable, isn't it? After all, at seventeen, it's difficult to predict what you want to do this weekend, much less what your interests are going to be five years from now when you graduate from college. But pretty soon you're going to have to choose a major and then a career path.

DO WHAT YOU ARE can help you figure out your strengths now, instead of down the road after you've spent four years in college. It's a groundbreaking bestseller that has helped half a million people get on the right career track. Unlike any other career book, it uses Personality Type to give students invaluable insight into their strengths and weaknesses and lists dozens of hot occupations that are appropriate to people of each Personality Type.

DO WHAT YOU ARE is the closest thing to "career success insurance" that you can buy. Parents, protect your investment—your graduate! And, students, start off your college career on the right foot.

Satisfied Readers Have Written to Say:

"This book should be required reading for every high school and college student."

"**DO WHAT YOU ARE** is the best career book on the market today."

"This book changed my life!"

"I would highly recommend this book to anyone wondering, 'What do I want to be when I grow up?'"

"**DO WHAT YOU ARE** has unlocked a door to which I wasn't sure I would ever find the key."

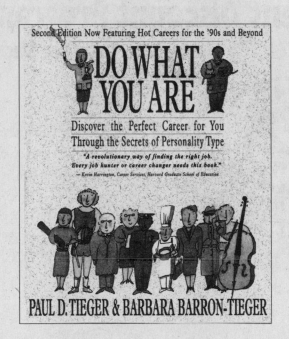

www.review.com

Expert Advice

Pop Surveys

Paying for It

www.review.com

www.review.com

THE
PRINCETON
REVIEW

Getting In

Word du Jour

www.review.com

www.review.com

College Talk

Find-O-Rama College Search

www.review.com

Best Schools

SAT Survival

www.review.com

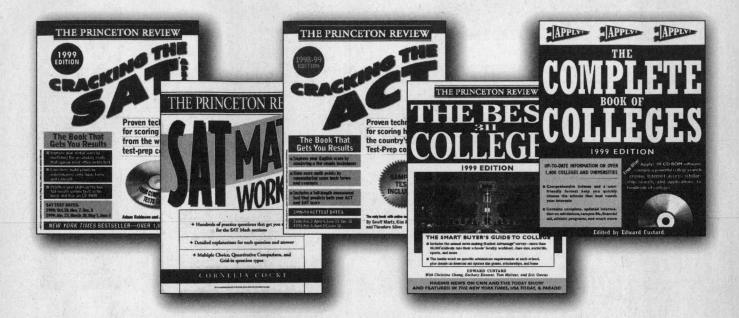

FIND US...

International

Hong Kong
4/F Sun Hung Kai Centre
30 Harbour Road, Wan Chai,
Hong Kong
Tel: (011)85-2-517-3016

Japan
Fuji Building 40, 15-14
Sakuragaokacho, Shibuya Ku,
Tokyo 150, Japan
Tel: (011)81-3-3463-1343

Korea
Tae Young Bldg, 944-24,
Daechi- Dong, Kangnam-Ku
The Princeton Review- ANC
Seoul, Korea 135-280,
South Korea
Tel: (011)82-2-554-7763

Mexico City
PR Mex S De RL De Cv
Guanajuato 228 Col. Roma
06700 Mexico D.F., Mexico
Tel: 525-564-9468

Montreal
666 Sherbrooke St.
West, Suite 202
Montreal, QC H3A 1E7 Canada
Tel: (514) 499-0870

Pakistan
1 Bawa Park - 90 Upper Mall
Lahore, Pakistan
Tel: (011)92-42-571-2315

Spain
Pza. Castilla, 3 - 5° A, 28046
Madrid, Spain
Tel: (011)341-323-4212

Taiwan
155 Chung Hsiao East Road
Section 4 - 4th Floor,
Taipei R.O.C., Taiwan
Tel: (011)886-2-751-1243

Thailand
Building One, 99 Wireless Road
Bangkok, Thailand 10330
Tel: (662) 256-7080

Toronto
1240 Bay Street, Suite 300
Toronto M5R 2A7 Canada
Tel: (800) 495-7737
Tel: (716) 839-4391

Vancouver
4212 University Way NE,
Suite 204
Seattle, WA 98105
Tel: (206) 548-1100

locations

National (U.S.)
We have over 60 offices around the U.S. and
run courses in over 400 sites. For courses and locations
within the U.S. call 1 (800) 2/Review and you will be
routed to the nearest office.